ACCOUNTABILITY
THROUGH
PUBLIC OPINION

FROM INERTIA TO PUBLIC ACTION

ACCOUNTABILITY THROUGH PUBLIC OPINION

FROM INERTIA TO PUBLIC ACTION

SINA ODUGBEMI AND TAEKU LEE

Editors

THE WORLD BANK
Washington, D.C.

ISBN: 978-0-8213-8505-0
eISBN: 978-0-8213-8556-2
DOI: 10.1596/978-0-8213-8505-0

Cover photograph: Joseph Luoman; ©iStockphoto.com / luoman
Cover design: Critical Stages

Library of Congress Cataloging-in-Publication Data
Accountability through public opinion : from inertia to public action / [edited by] Sina Odugbemi, Taeku Lee.
    p. cm.
Includes bibliographical references and index.
ISBN 978-0-8213-8505-0—ISBN 978-0-8213-8556-2 (electronic)
1. Government accountability. 2. Public services—Public opinion. 3. Organizational effectiveness. 4. Performance—Management. I. Odugbemi, Sina. II. Lee, Taeku.
JF1351.A246 2010
320.01—dc22
                                    2010032302

Contents

Figures

Tables

Contributors

Anne-Katrin Arnold is a consultant to the World Bank's Communication for Governance and Accountability Program (CommGAP). She is also a Ph.D. candidate at the University of Pennsylvania's Annenberg School for Communication, where her research focuses on issues of public opinion, the public sphere, and political decision making. Arnold holds an M.Sc. in Communication Research from the Institute for Journalism and Communication Research in Hannover, Germany, and an M.A. in Communication from the University of Pennsylvania, where she started her studies as a Fulbright Scholar. Her publications include articles on public opinion theory, social capital, and ethnic journalism in peer-reviewed journals, as well as a book on social capital and the media.

Harry Blair, Associate Department Chair, Senior Research Scholar and Lecturer in Political Science at Yale University, has focused his research and applied work over the last 15 years on democratization issues, primarily civil society and decentralization. Earlier he had concentrated on South Asian politics and rural development, mainly in India and Bangladesh. On democratization, he has worked in Eastern Europe (principally Balkan countries), Latin America, and Southeast Asia, as well as South Asia. As a consultant, he has served with DFID, FAO, the Ford Foundation, SIDA, UNDESA, UNDP, USAID, and the World Bank. Before coming to Yale, he held academic positions at Bucknell, Colgate, Columbia, Cornell, and Rutgers universities. He holds a Ph.D. from Duke University. His most current publications deal with gauging civil society advocacy, postconflict state building, participatory local governance, and Bangladesh political parties. These publications and other recent writing can be found at http://pantheon.yale.edu/~hb94.

Imraan Buccus is a Research Fellow in the School of Politics at the University of KwaZulu Natal and Research Associate at the Democracy Development Program in Durban, South Africa. He was a Ford Fellowship recipient for his Ph.D. Buccus is also Academic Director of the School for International Training's (SIT) program on Globalisation and Development. SIT is a study-abroad program of world learning in the United States. He is widely published and is the author of numerous papers on public participation, poverty, and civil society and the editor of *Critical Dialogue*, a journal on public participation in governance. Buccus appeared on the *Mail and Guardian* list of South Africa's 300 leading young South Africans in 2008 and is a columnist for Durban's popular morning newspaper *The Mercury*.

Vera Schattan P. Coelho is a social scientist. She is a researcher and coordinates the Citizenship and Development Group at the Brazilian Center of Analysis and Planning in São Paulo, Brazil. Coelho's interests center on new forms of citizen participation, deliberation, and consultation to improve social policies and democracy. She is the author of numerous articles on health policy, pension reform, and participatory governance.

Steven E. Finkel is Daniel H. Wallace Professor of Political Science at the University of Pittsburgh. His areas of expertise include comparative political behavior, public opinion, democratization, and quantitative methods. Since 1997, he has conducted evaluations of the effectiveness of U.S. and other international donors' civic education programs in the Dominican Republic, Kenya, Poland, and South Africa. He is the author of *Causal Analysis with Panel Data* (Sage, 1995) as well as numerous articles on political participation, voting behavior, and civic education in new and established democracies. Between 2004 and 2007, he conducted the first macro-comparative evaluation of the impact of all USAID democracy assistance programs on democratic development in recipient countries (published in *World Politics*, 2007). He holds a Ph.D. in political science from the State University of New York at Stony Brook and has taught at the University of Virginia, Arizona State University, and the Hertie School of Governance in Berlin, Germany.

Archon Fung is Ford Foundation Professor of Democracy and Citizenship at the Harvard Kennedy School. His research examines the impacts of civic participation, public deliberation, and transparency on public and private governance. His *Empowered Participation: Reinventing Urban Democracy* examines two participatory-democratic reform efforts in low-income Chicago neighborhoods. Current projects also examine initiatives in ecosystem management, reduction of toxic substances, endangered species protection, local governance, and international labor standards. His recent books and edited collections include *Deepening Democracy: Institutional Innovations in Empowered Participatory Governance*, *Can We Eliminate Sweatshops?*, *Working Capital: The Power of Labor's Pensions*, and *Beyond Backyard Environmentalism*. His articles on regulation, rights, and participation appear in *Political Theory*, *Journal of Political Philosophy*, *Politics and Society*, *Governance*, *Environmental Management*, *American Behavioral Scientist*, and *Boston Review*. Fung received two S.B.s and a Ph.D. from MIT.

Marshall Ganz is Lecturer in Public Policy at the Harvard Kennedy School. He entered Harvard College in the fall of 1960. In 1964, a year before graduating, he left to volunteer as a civil rights organizer in Mississippi. In 1965, he joined César Chavez and the United Farm Workers; over the next 16 years he gained experience in union, community, issue, and political organizing and became Director of Organizing. During the 1980s, he worked with grassroots groups to develop effective organizing programs, designing innovative voter mobilization strategies for local, state, and national electoral campaigns. In 1991, to deepen his intellectual understanding of his work, he returned to Harvard College and, after a 28-year "leave of absence," completed his undergraduate degree in history and government. He was awarded an M.P.A. by the Kennedy School in 1993 and completed his Ph.D. in sociology in 2000. He teaches, researches, and writes on leadership, organization, and strategy in social movements, civic associations, and politics.

Baogang He is the Chair in International Studies at the School of Politics and International Studies, Deakin University, Australia. He is the author of *The Democratization of China* (Routledge, 1996), *The Democratic Implication of Civil Society in China* (St. Martin's, 1997), *Nationalism, National Identity and Democratization in China* (Ashgate, 2000, with Yingjie Guo), *Balancing Democracy and Authority: An Empirical Study of Village Election in Zhejiang* (Central China Normal University Press, 2002, with Lang Youxing), *Multiculturalism in Asia* (Oxford University Press, 2005, coeditor with Will Kymlicka), *The Search for Deliberative Democracy* (Palgrave, 2006, coeditor with Ethan Leib), *Federalism in Asia* (Edward Elgar, 2007, coeditor with Brian Galigan and Takashi Inoguchi), *Rural Democracy in China* (Palgrave/Macmillan, 2007), and *Deliberative Democracy: Theory, Method and Practice* (China's Social Science Publishers, 2008). He has coauthored and cotranslated several books into Chinese (including John Rawls's *A Theory of Justice*) and has published 43 book chapters and more than 45 international refereed journal articles in English. He has established an international reputation as an authority on Chinese democratization, nongovernmental organizations, and local governance and has gained international recognition in the fields of international relations and Asian studies. Much of his empirical research has been linked to broader theoretical concepts such as civil society and democracy and has attempted to test, modify, and develop theoretical hypotheses.

Janine Hicks is a Commissioner with the Commission for Gender Equality, a statutory, constitutional body tasked with promoting gender equality in South Africa. Her background is in the nonprofit sector, specifically access to justice, democracy and human rights education, and citizen participation in governance sectors. Hicks holds an M.A. from the Institute for Development Studies at the University of Sussex and an LL.B. from the former University of Natal, Durban. She has published extensively on participatory democracy and serves on the boards of local nonprofits the Valley Trust, the Community Law and Rural Development Centre, and Agenda Feminist Media.

Amaney Jamal is an Associate Professor of Politics at Princeton University. Her current research focuses on democratization and the politics of civic engagement in the Arab world. She extends her research to the study of Muslim and Arab Americans, examining the pathways that structure their patterns of civic engagement in the United States. Jamal has written two books. The first, *Barriers to Democracy* (Princeton University Press, 2007), which won the Best Book Award in Comparative Democratization at the American Political Science Association (2008), explores the role of civic associations in promoting democratic effects in the Arab world. Her second book, *Race and Arab Americans before and after 9/11: From Invisible Citizens to Visible Subjects,* an edited volume with Nadine Naber (Syracuse University Press, 2007), looks at the patterns and influences of Arab American racialization processes. She is writing a third book on patterns of citizenship in the Arab world, tentatively entitled *Of Empires and Citizens: Authoritarian Durability in the Arab World.* Jamal is further a coauthor of the book *Citizenship and Crisis: Arab Detroit after 9-11* (Russell Sage Foundation, 2009). She is a principal investigator of the "Arab Barometer Project"; co-PI of the "Detroit Arab American Study," a sister survey to the Detroit Area Study; and Senior Adviser on the Pew Research Center Project on Islam in America, 2006. In 2005 Jamal was named a Carnegie Scholar.

Rob Jenkins is Professor of Political Science at Hunter College and the Graduate Center, City University of New York, where he is also Associate Director of the Ralph Bunche Institute for International Studies. His research in the area of Indian politics and political economy has covered a range of topics—from local-level anticorruption movements to India's engagement with the World Trade Organization. His books include, with Anne Marie Goetz, *Reinventing Accountability: Making Democracy Work for Human Development* (Palgrave Macmillan, 2005), *Democratic Politics and Economic Reform in India* (Cambridge University Press, 2000), and as editor, *Regional Reflections: Comparing Politics across India's States* (Oxford University Press, 2004). He has undertaken advisory work and commissioned research for DFID, UNDP, the United Nations Peacebuilding Support Office, the World Bank, and other agencies. He is currently at work on an edited volume about India's policy on Special Economic Zones and a coauthored book on the politics of India's National Rural Employment Guarantee Act.

William Keith is Professor of Communication at the University of Wisconsin-Milwaukee. He received his Ph.D. from the University of Texas at Austin. His work focuses on the role of argumentation in multiple contexts, including science and public discourse, and the history of the speech field and speech pedagogy. Keith has taught at Oregon State University, Northwestern University, and the University of Oslo. He has also lectured frequently on democracy and speech pedagogy at Duke University, Indiana University, Kansas State University, and the University of Washington. He has published widely on the rhetoric of science, argumentation, and deliberative democracy. He coedited *Rhetorical Hermeneutics* with Alan Gross (SUNY Press, 1998) and most recently *Discussion as Democracy* (Lexington Books, 2007), which won the National Communication Association Diamond

Anniversary Award 2008 and the Daniel Rohrer Award from the American Forensic Association for Best Book of 2007.

Adrian Gurza Lavalle is currently Brazilian Center of Analysis and Planning (CEBRAP) Research Director and since 2000 a fellow researcher at CEBRAP, where he coordinates the Collective Actors and Democracy Research Team. He is an Associate Professor in the Department of Political Science at the University of São Paulo and a member of the management committee of the Development Research Centre for the Future State (2006–10). He is also coeditor of the Brazilian journal *Lua Nova*. His ongoing research focuses on civil society politics and democratic governance. He has published several articles on civil society politics in Brazilian and international journals. His last book (coedited with Ernesto Isunza) is *Democratic Innovation in Latin America: Challenges and Shortcomings of Participation, Civil Society Representation and Social Control* (CIESAS, 2010). He holds a Ph.D. in Political Science from the University of São Paulo and a master's degree in Sociology from the National Autonomous University of Mexico.

Taeku Lee is Professor and Chair of Political Science and Professor of Law at the University of California, Berkeley. He is the author of *Mobilizing Public Opinion* (University of Chicago Press, 2002), which received the J. David Greenstone and the V. O. Key book awards; coauthor of *Why Americans Don't Join the Party* (Princeton University Press, forthcoming); and coauthor of *Asian American Political Participation* (Russell Sage Foundation Press, under contract). He has also coedited *Transforming Politics, Transforming America* (University of Virginia Press, 2006), coedited this volume, and is completing the *Oxford Handbook of Racial and Ethnic Politics in the United States* (Oxford University Press, under contract). Lee has served in administrative and leadership positions at UC-Berkeley and in advisory and consultative capacities for academic presses and journals, research projects, nongovernmental organizations, think tanks, and private corporations. Before coming to Berkeley, he was Assistant Professor of Public Policy at Harvard's Kennedy School of Government. Lee was born in the Republic of Korea, grew up in rural Malaysia, Manhattan, and suburban Detroit, and is a proud graduate of K-12 public schools, the University of Michigan (A.B.), Harvard University (M.P.P.), and the University of Chicago (Ph.D.).

Peter Levine (www.peterlevine.ws) is Director of CIRCLE, the Center for Information and Research on Civic Learning and Engagement, at Tufts University's Jonathan M. Tisch College of Citizenship and Public Service. Levine graduated from Yale in 1989 with a degree in Philosophy. He studied Philosophy at Oxford on a Rhodes Scholarship, receiving his doctorate in 1992. From 1991 until 1993, he was a research associate at Common Cause. In September 1993, he joined the faculty of the University of Maryland. In the late 1990s, he was Deputy Director of the National Commission on Civic Renewal, chaired by Senator Sam Nunn and William Bennett. He is a member of the Deliberative Democracy Consortium's steering committee (www.deliberative-democracy.net), a cofounder of the National Alliance for Civic Education (www.cived.org), and former Chair of the Executive Committee of the Campaign for the Civic Mission of Schools (www.civicmissionofschools.org). Levine is the author of *The Future of Democracy: Developing the Next Generation of American Citizens* (University Press of New England, 2007), three other scholarly books on philosophy and politics, and a novel. He also coedited *The Deliberative Democracy Handbook* (2006) with John Gastil and coorganized the writing of *The Civic Mission of Schools,* a report released by Carnegie Corporation of New York and CIRCLE in 2003 (www.civicmissionofschools.org).

Arthur Lupia is the Hal R. Varian Professor of Political Science at the University of Michigan and Research Professor at its Institute for Social Research. He examines topics relevant to politics and policy, including voting, elections, persuasion, opinion change, civic education, coalition governance, legislative-bureaucratic relationships, and decision making under uncertainty. His writings yield insight about these topics by integrating concepts and tools from cognitive science, economics, political science, and psychology with lessons learned from his work with public and private decision makers around the world.

Devra Moehler is Assistant Professor of Communication at the Annenberg School for Communication, University of Pennsylvania. Her research focuses on political communication, communication and development, African politics, political behavior, democratization, comparative research design, field research methodology, and statistical analysis. Her book *Distrusting Democrats: Outcomes of Participatory Constitution Making* (University of Michigan Press, 2008) examines the effects of participation on the political culture of ordinary citizens. Moehler worked as a Democracy Fellow in USAID's Office of Democracy and Governance, where she helped initiate a pilot impact evaluation program that seeks to conduct a series of multicountry, subsectoral impact evaluations covering the most important kinds of democracy and governance programs. Moehler also provided technical assistance to missions designing experimental and quasi-experimental impact evaluations. Previously, Moehler served for five years as Assistant Professor of Government at Cornell University. She received her Ph.D. from the University of Michigan in Political Science.

Mary Myers is a freelance consultant specializing in radio in Africa. She works from home near Salisbury, in the heart of the English countryside. Myers holds a Ph.D. from Reading University, where her thesis subject was educational radio for rural women in Eritrea. She has worked with the United Kingdom's Department for International Development on many projects, papers, and publications since going freelance in 1996. From 2002 to 2003, she was an adviser on communications and media within DFID's Social Development Division. Currently, Myers has a long-term contract as Media Adviser to DFID and to France's Coopération Internationale in the Democratic Republic of Congo. She has written DFID's guidelines *Monitoring* *and Evaluating Information and Communication for Development Programmes,* and she authored the background paper on communications in development for Tony Blair's Commission for Africa. Myers has traveled and worked in more than 20 countries in Africa, but most recently she has carried out trainings, evaluations, feasibility studies, desk studies, and monitoring missions in Chad, the Democratic Republic of Congo, Madagascar, Malawi, Sierra Leone, and Uganda. Myers works not only for DFID, but also for other NGOs and bilateral and multilateral agencies, including the World Bank. Her current interests include the use of "edutainment," using radio for better governance, media regulation, and evaluating the impact of media interventions in developing countries.

Sina Odugbemi is Program Head of the World Bank's Communication for Governance and Accountability Program (CommGAP). He has over 20 years of experience in journalism, law, and development communication. Before he joined the World Bank in 2006, he spent seven years in the UK's development ministry, DFID. His last position was Program Manager and Adviser, Information and Communication for Development. Odugbemi holds Bachelor's degrees in English (1980) and Law (1986) from the University of Ibadan, a Master's degree in Legal and Political Philosophy (1999) from the University College London, and a Ph.D. in Laws (2009) from the same university with the thesis *Public Opinion and Direct Accountability between Elections: A Study of the Constitutional Theories of Jeremy Bentham and A. V. Dicey.* Odugbemi's publications include a novel, *The Chief's Granddaughter* (Spectrum Books, 1986), and two coedited volumes: *With the Support of Multitudes: Using Strategic Communication to Fight Poverty through PRSPs* (2005) and *Governance Reform under Real-World Conditions: Citizens, Stakeholders, and Voice* (2008).

Samuel Paul is the founder and first chairperson of the Board of Public Affairs Centre (PAC) in Bangalore, which pioneered the use of citizen report cards. He was for many years Professor of Economics and later Director of the Indian Institute of Management in Ahmedabad. He has been a special adviser to the ILO, United Nations Commission on Transnational Corporations, World Bank, and other international agencies. Paul is the author of several books and has taught at the Harvard Business School, Kennedy School of Government, and Princeton's Woodrow Wilson School of Public Affairs. He is a recipient of both national and international awards. Paul's latest book (coauthor) is *Who Benefits from India's Public Services?* (Academic Foundation, New Delhi, 2006). Paul was a member of the Committee on the Indian Prime Minister's Awards for Excellence in Government, Karnataka Government's high-powered Committee on "Greater Bangalore," and the World Bank's Advisory Council for South Asia. He established the Public Affairs Foundation as a sister organization of PAC to provide advisory services within India and abroad.

Enrique Peruzzotti (Ph.D. in Sociology, New School for Social Research) is Associate Professor at the Department of Political Science and International Studies of the Torcuato Di Tella University in Buenos Aires. He coedited the volume *Enforcing the Rule of Law: Social Accountability in the New Latin American Democracies* (Pittsburgh University Press, 2006). Peruzzotti has published articles on social accountability, democratic theory, and democratization in *Global Governance, Citizenship Studies, Journal of Democracy, Constellations, Thesis Eleven, Revista Mexicana de Sociología, Journal of Latin American Studies, Política y Gobierno, Journal of Human Development,* and *Metapolítica,* as well as numerous articles in edited volumes. In 2003–04, he was a Visiting Fellow at the Woodrow Wilson Center for International Studies. He has also been a Visiting Fellow at the Rockefeller Foundation Center in Bellagio, Fulbright Fellow at the University of Columbia, and Visiting Fellow at Cornell University, the University of New Mexico, and the Latin American Institute of the University of London. Peruzzotti is a recurring Visiting Professor for the Doctorate program in Social Science of FLACSO Ecuador. In 2008, he was a Visiting Fellow at the ESRC Non-Governmental Public Action Programme, London School of Economics. Peruzzotti has worked as a consultant for the IDB, UNDP, and the Ford Foundation.

Charles Taber is a Professor of Political Science at Stony Brook University and director of the Laboratory for Experimental Research in Political Behavior. He received his Ph.D. in Political Science in 1991 from University of Illinois at Urbana-Champaign for his dissertation *The Policy Arguer: A Computational Model of U.S. Foreign Policy Belief Systems.*

Gopakumar Thampi heads the Affiliated Network for Social Accountability—South Asia Region and Global, based at the Institute of Governance Studies, BRAC University, Dhaka. Before this position, he headed the Public Affairs Foundation, a nonprofit company, and the Public Affairs Centre, a nonprofit, civil society organization, both based in Bangalore. Thampi holds a doctorate in Entrepreneurial Studies and postgraduate qualifications in Economics, Journalism, and Mass Communication. He is also an alumnus of the European Center for Peace and Conflict Resolution based in Austria, having completed an Advanced Diploma Course on Peace and Conflict Resolution. Developing concepts and approaches to strengthen accountability of institutions in the governance and development sector constitute the core of Thampi's current professional experience. A large part of this work has been carried out through applications of participatory monitoring systems and public advocacy tools in South Asia, Africa, and East and Central Asia. He was a former Head of the Asia Desk at the Transparency International Secretariat in Berlin.

Lily Tsai is an Associate Professor of Political Science at MIT. Her research focuses on issues of accountability, governance, and state-society relations. Her first book, *Accountability without Democracy: Solidary Groups and Public Goods Provision in Rural China* (Cambridge Studies on Comparative Politics, Cambridge University Press, 2007), uses a combination of original survey data and in-depth case studies to examine the ways in which informal institutions provided by social groups can substitute for formal and bureaucratic institutions to hold local officials account-able for governmental performance and public goods provision. Tsai has also pub-lished articles in *American Political Science Review, China Quarterly,* and *China Journal.* Tsai is a graduate of Stanford University. She received an M.A. in Political Science from the University of California, Berkeley, and a Ph.D. in Government from Harvard University in 2004.

Christel Vermeersch is an Economist at the World Bank's Human Development Network, focusing on the Middle East and North Africa, Africa, Latin America, and the Caribbean. She has a Ph.D. in Economics from Harvard University.

Leonard Wantchekon is a Professor of Politics and Economics at New York Univer-sity. He taught at Yale University (1995–2000) and was a Visiting Fellow at the Cen-ter of International Studies at Princeton University (2000–01). He received his Ph.D. in Economics from Northwestern University (1995) and his M.A. in Economics from Laval University and University of British Columbia (1992). Wantchekon is the author of several articles on post–civil war democratization, resource curse, elec-toral clientelism, and experimental methods in the *Quarterly Journal of Econom-ics, American Political Science Review, World Politics, Comparative Political Studies, Journal of Conflict Resolution, Constitutional Political Economy, Political Africaine,* and *Afrique Contemporaine.* He is the editor of the *Journal of African Development,* formally known as the *Journal of African Finance and Economic Development.* Wantchekon is the founding director of the Institute for Empirical Research in Political Economy, which is based in Benin (West Africa) and at New York University.

Everett Young is Visiting Assistant Professor of Political Psychology and Statistical Methods at Washington University in St. Louis. His research focuses on how cogni-tive style affects political opinion formation. He received his Ph.D. in political science from Stony Brook University in 2009.

Laura Zommer graduated in Communications Sciences and as an Attorney-at-Law from Universidad de Buenos Aires (UBA). Currently, she is Communications Director of the Center for the Implementation of Public Policies Promoting Equity and Growth, Professor of Rights to Information at UBA's Social Sciences Faculty, and a contributor to *Enfoques,* the Sunday supplement of *La Nación* newspaper. Previ-ously she was Cabinet Chief at the Secretariat for Interior Security of the Ministry of Justice and Human Rights (2003–04) and a writer specializing in General Informa-tion and Politics at *La Nación* (1997–2003). For her work as a journalist, she obtained a grant to the El País of Madrid and received the "Argentine Attorney Award" from the Asociación de Entidades Periodísticas Argentinas (ADEPA) in 2005, the "Italian Young Journalist Prize" in 2002, the "In Depth Journalist Award" from Inter-American Press Association, Houston, 1999, and the "Public Good" award from ADEPA, 1998.

Acknowledgments

This book contains a compilation of contributions to a workshop in November 2007, "Generating Genuine Demand with Social Accountability Mechanisms," held in Paris, France, as well as specially commissioned articles and case studies from experts from development practice and academia. We would like to thank all contributors to this book and to the workshop, without whose effort this book would not have been possible. The participants in the workshop are listed in the appendixes, and all deserve our gratitude for a fruitful and successful exploration of this topic. We also appreciate the insights shared by the World Bank chairs and discussants at the November 2007 workshop: Lilia Burunciuc, André Herzog, Paolo Mefalopulos, Paul D. Mitchell, Karen Sirker, and Caby Verzosa.

Both the workshop and this publication were commissioned and organized by the Communication for Governance and Accountability Program (CommGAP), operating within the World Bank's Operational Communication Division, External Affairs Vice Presidency. Special thanks go to Helen R. Garcia and Diana Ya-Wai Chung, who conducted the initial needs assessment and preparatory surveys that identified the workshop's major themes. We are grateful to our colleagues from the former Development Communication Division in the External Affairs Vice Presidency of the World Bank and from the Operational Communication Division for providing invaluable guidance and support for CommGAP's continuing work on accountability. Many thanks go to the members of the CommGAP team who organized the workshop as well as to the rapporteurs— Helen R. Garcia, Antonio G. Lambino II, Johanna Martinsson, and Fumiko Nagano—who wrote the report that appears in appendix A. Anne-Katrin Arnold supported the process of assembling and publishing this volume. She has been a brilliant and indispensible help to us as editors. We are in her debt. Taeku Lee is also ever thankful to his faculty assistant, Ayn Lowry, for her expert professional assistance on this project.

We hope that this book will make a contribution to development policy and practice regarding the accountability of governments toward their citizens. We dedicate this book to the citizens of developing countries who stand up to their governments to demand responsiveness and better services, and who will be helped in their efforts, we hope, by the insights that we gather in this volume.

We also wish to acknowledge that we were unable to take in as much of the groundbreaking work in this rich field as we would have liked. In particular, owing to unanticipated administrative hurdles, we were unable to include two projects that were originally planned for in this volume: Jonathan Fox's study of accountability in two antipoverty projects in Mexico and Macartan Humphreys, William A. Masters, and Martin Sandbu's study of an experimental exercise in deliberative democracy in São Tomé and Príncipe.[*] We urge interested readers to go beyond this volume to learn about these projects and discover the many, many others that are in print or in progress.

Sina Odugbemi   Taeku Lee
World Bank   University of California

Note

[*] Humphreys, Macartan, William A. Masters, and Martin E. Sandbu, 2006, "The Role of Leaders in Democratic Deliberations: Results from a Field Experiment in São Tomé and Príncipe," *World Politics* 58 (4): 583–622; Fox, Jonathan, 2007, "Accountability Politics," *Oxford Scholarship Online Monographs*, pp. 243–87.

Abbreviations

ADOPEM	Asociación Dominicana para el Desarrollo de la Mujer
ANC	African National Congress
ATI	access to information
BATF	Bangalore Agenda Task Force
BDA	Bangalore Development Authority
BoA	Board of Approvals
CABA	Ciudad Autónoma de Buenos Aires
CCT	conditional cash transfer
CDCA	Conselho dos Direitos da Criança e do Adolescente
CEBRAP	Centro Brasileiro de Análise e Planejamento
CEM	Centro de Estudos da Metropóle
CI	Consumers International
CLC	Community Law Centre–Durban
CommGAP	Communication for Governance and Accountability Program
CPC	community promotion committees
CPP	Centre for Public Participation
CRC	citizen report card
CSC	Civil Service Commission
CSC	community score card
CSO	civil society organization
CVs	*comités de vigilancia*
DAR	Department of Administrative Reforms
DFID	Department for International Development, U.K.
DPLG	Department of Provincial and Local Government
EU	European Union
FAO	Food and Agriculture Organization (UN)
FSLD	Foundation for Support of Local Democracy
FUNCAD	Fundo do Conselho Municipal dos Direitos da Criança e do Adolescente

GAD	Grupo Acción por la Democracia
G-Watch	Government Watch
HAM	Haute Autorité des Médias
ICT	information and communication technology
IDB	Inter-American Development Bank
ILO	International Labour Organization
IT	information and technology
JMCC	Jerusalem Media and Communications Center
LHC	local health council
LHR	Lawyers for Human Rights
MKSS	Mazdoor Kisan Shakti Sangathan
MP	member of parliament
NAC	National Advisory Council
NCEP	National Civic Education Program
NCT	National Capital Territory
NGO	nongovernmental organization
NIPILAR	National Institute for Public Interest Law and Research
NREGA	National Rural Employment Guarantee Act
OECD	Organisation for Economic Co-operation and Development
OP	Orçamento Particapativo
PAC	Public Affairs Centre
PAF	Public Affairs Foundation
PB	participatory budgeting
PC	Participación Ciudadana
PEN	Poder Ejecutivo Nacional
PETS	public expenditure tracking survey
PNA	Palestinian National Authority
PSU	primary sampling unit
PT	Partido dos Trabalhadores
RSM	Radio Santa María
RTI	right to information
SA	social accountability
SAMs	social accountability mechanisms
SEZ	special economic zone
SIDA	Swedish International Development Cooperation Agency
SIDE	Secretaría de Inteligencia del Estado
SMS	short message service
SSIP	small-scale independent provider
SUS	Sistema Único de Saude
TBA	Trains of Buenos Aires
TIB	Transparency International
UBA	University of Buenos Aires
UMTS	universal mobile telecommunications service

UN	United Nations
UNDESA	United Nations Department of Economic and Social Affairs
UNDP	United Nations Development Programme
USAID	United States Agency for International Development
WOUGNET	Women of Uganda Network
WSP	Water and Sanitation Program
WSP-AF	Water and Sanitation Program–Africa

Section I
Foundations

Taking Direct Accountability Seriously

Sina Odugbemi and Taeku Lee

An Uncertain Turn

International development efforts have recently taken an accountability turn. Between the *Paris Declaration on Aid Effectiveness* (2005)[1] and the *Accra Agenda for Action* (2008),[2] donors active in international development decided to move from making governments in developing countries accountable to the donors to making those governments accountable to their own citizens, plus being responsible for a range of mutual accountability and transparency commitments (High Level Forum on Aid Effectiveness of 2005 and 2008). Since then, "accountability" has come up more and more in the discourse and the programming of international development agencies and private foundations.

The accountability turn is admirable, and it is legitimate to wonder why it took so long to happen. The chief reason appears to be the concentration on the state in international development, not on the full range of institutions that deliver good governance and general welfare. As we shall soon see, those habits die hard. For there is one overarching problem with the accountability turn. It is not yet a serious, meaningful, coherent, and sustained effort. There is far more talk than action. Sadly, "accountability" is becoming the latest in a long line of international development buzzwords. At the time of writing, actors in development appear to delight in announcing their intention to "promote accountability" far more often than they know what it means to do so, and certainly far more than they are committed to doing what it takes: in time, treasure, political fights, and so on.

Let's start with the plethora of approaches and labels. The question is this: What does it mean to make governments accountable to their citizens? In addition, how do you do that? Right now, the answer depends on whom you ask. Here are some of the labels in the current discourse:

- Social accountability
- Multistakeholder engagement
- Multistakeholder initiatives
- Civic empowerment and rights
- Public engagement in policy making and government
- Institutions of accountability
- Demand for good governance/demand-side
- Aid and domestic accountability, and so on.

Many of these labels imply substantive differences. Some initiatives focus on strengthening nonstate institutions of accountability such as civil society. Others focus on processes such as citizen engagement in policy making and service delivery, particularly in health, education, and rural livelihoods. Often observers lump together accountability mechanisms within the state, such as ombudsmen and parliamentary oversight, and accountability mechanisms outside the state, such as citizen scorecards and regular public opinion polling. Some focus on electoral systems and processes. Others concentrate on access to information and ICT (information and communication technology) for Governance or E-Governance. A few worry about strengthening independent media ... too few.

The second major problem, perhaps the really tough one, is the stubborn skepticism of the powerful technocratic professional groups that dominate international development. This persistent skepticism takes at least three forms. The first is: *We should not be doing this; it is too political, too messy, and too much outside our comfort zones. Governments simply don't want to be accountable to their citizens, and there is very little that donors can do about it.* The second is: *Show me that any of these demand-side initiatives work. Show me two or three instances with rigorous evidence where a so-called accountability initiative has worked, and I will pour resources into the work, but I don't believe these examples exist.* The third is the tendency to take an accountability mechanism that has been shown to work and turn it into a technical tool without the engagement with critical publics and public opinion that made it work in the first place. That is what has tended to happen with tools such as public expenditure tracking mechanisms (Reinikka and Svensson 2004).

What is really behind the stubborn skepticism about promoting the accountability of developing country governments to their citizens? At least two fundamental drivers can be identified. The first is the power of mental models acquired through years of technical study. As a recent Center for Future States at the Institute of Development Studies (2010, 2) report points out, many officials working in international development work for organizations that are supply-driven and have short time horizons; and many have hard-won professional knowledge. Such knowledge—about the law, or private investment, or public expenditure management, or delivery of water, health and education services—is entirely valid and indeed essential in certain contexts. But it can get in the way of attempts to understand what is really driving behaviour and development outcomes in poor countries and fragile states.

In such a world, the default position is a technical solution of some kind; whatever is not within the reigning technical frameworks has a hard time being taken seriously, or being incorporated in actual programming. Direct accountability is not yet in favor.

A second driver of the persistent skepticism about making governments accountable to their own citizens is the fact that in almost every development institution working on governance issues, the dominant and dominating tradition is public sector governance, and its paradigm is New Public Management.[3] Rather than seeking to make governments accountable to their own citizens, many efforts have tried to achieve the very opposite. This is what, in a recent and important study, Alasdair Roberts (2010, 135) calls "The Logic of Discipline":

> The logic of discipline is a reform philosophy built on the criticism that standard democratic processes for producing public policies are myopic, unstable, and skewed towards special interests and not the public good. It seeks to make improvements in governance through changes in law that impose constraints on elected officials and citizens, often by shifting power to technocratic-guardians who are shielded from political influence.

Roberts shows how from 1978 to 2008 this tradition of governance reform spread around the globe (and it reached developing countries through the insistence of donor experts), involving many areas of the architecture of government: central banking, fiscal control, tax collection, infrastructure development, the management of main ports, and regulation. The aim in each case was how to insulate decision making from democratic control … and accountability. The question soon became: Who guards these technocrat-guardians? Sadly, this tradition of governance reform remains dominant in the same institutions, which often mouth commitments to the accountability of governments to their citizens.

What it all boils down to at the end of the day is how those working in international development genuinely understand the business of "governance." If they have a state-centric view of governance, then work on promoting the accountability of governments to their own citizens does not have a future in spite of the recent "accountability" turn in the rhetoric. If, however, they truly understand governance to be a textured, embedded, networked process in which citizens and government officials argue, bargain, and, sometimes, come to agreement (Susskind 2008), then the roles of citizens and the capacity of those citizens to hold their governments accountable will be seen as a fundamental part of the governance agenda. The initiatives intent on promoting the accountability of governments to their own citizens will have a secure future in international development ... with potentially exciting development outcomes.

The Proverbial Missing Middle

This is a book about direct accountability, that is, the ability of citizens to directly hold their own governments accountable. We ask frank questions: What does that take? What does that truly involve? We ask these questions because we think there is a missing middle in most of the thinking and work on direct accountability. As figure 1.1 illustrates, program managers in international development are usually clear about the end states they seek, and the status quo they dislike. What is usually not so clear is how to get to those end states, given the status quo. What lies in between is a box of primeval opacity. This work is a contribution to illuminating a modest portion of the darkness ... with a few candles here and there.

Figure 1.1. The Missing Link in Direct Accountability

A. Status quo

- uninformed citizens
- citizen inertia
- lack of political efficacy
- unresponsive governments
- unaccountable governments
- culture of impunity and bad governance

How do we get from A to B?

B. End states sought in accountability work

- informed citizens
- active citizens
- empowered citizens
- responsive government
- accountable government
- citizens able to hold government accountable

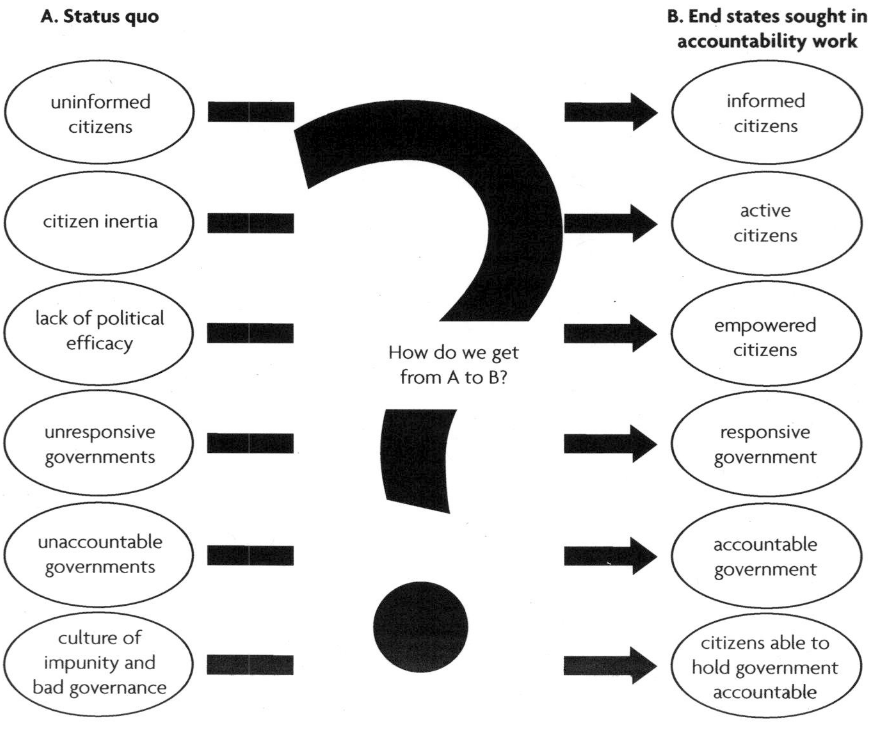

Source: Authors.

We argue that understanding the critical role and potential of regulative public opinion is crucial to how initiative managers get to the end states they seek from the starting points they dislike. For if governance is not simply about force/command but is about arguing, bargaining, and, sometimes, coming to agreement, then two fundamentals of good governance can be identified that are not often mentioned:

1. The public arena/the public sphere, the supreme domain of both politics and governance ... as well as the institutions and processes that determine the character of the public arena in each country; and
2. The majority opinion formed by the citizenry in specific contexts regarding a public issue or controversy at the end of a process of becoming informed, debate, and discussion.

Notice from the above that our conception of public opinion is *discursive* (Herbst 1998). Public opinion is not blind prejudice, nor is it a mere aggregation of attitudes that have not been reflected upon. It is what crystallizes at the end of a process of debate and discussion, with all the relevant information available in the public arena. Public opinion, thus understood, is at the heart of politics; public opinion, thus understood, is at the heart of governance. That is why authoritarian regimes seek to control the flow of information, constrain the size and scope of the public sphere, and muzzle the press. The power they fear is the power of public opinion, because they know that much of their power and legitimacy depends on it (Hume 1987 [1742]). We argue that, by the same token, at the heart of any serious analysis of direct accountability is the nature of regulative public opinion. That is what we seek to demonstrate in this volume.

Coda on the Arab Spring: March 2011

As this volume is going into production, the literal embodiment of "accountability through public opinion" has been spreading like wildfire in the countries of the Middle East and North Africa. On an unprecedented scale in recent history—perhaps the fall of communism in Eastern Europe in 1989 compares—a groundswell of latent public demand for accountability and reform has launched a remaking of longstanding political regimes. Activated mass opinion ranging from minor uprisings to social revolutions has sprung in Algeria, Bahrain, Djibouti, the Arab Republic of Egypt, the Islamic Republic of Iran, Iraq, Jordan, Kuwait, Libya, Lebanon, Mauritania, Morocco, Oman, Saudi Arabia, Sudan, the Syrian Arab Republic, Tunisia, the United Arab Emirates, and the Republic of Yemen. In Tunisia, the 23-year rule of Zine El Abidine Ben Ali tumbled in 28 days; in Egypt, the 30-year rule of Hosni Mubarak was brought down in 18 days; efforts continue to break Muammar Gaddafi's 41-year stranglehold on political power in Libya. As these words are being typed, at least three heads of state (Ali Abdullah Saleh in Yemen, Omar al-Bashir in Sudan, and Nouri al-Maliki in Iraq) have announced that they will not seek reelection in response to popular protests. The deployment of conventional means of controlling power and domesticating disquiet such as state repression, media censorship, and divide-and-conquer tactics have been largely ineffectual against this rising tide of public sentiment. Plainly put, well-tucked prescripts about the stability of autocratic rule, the incompatibility of Islam and democracy, and the irrelevance of public opinion have been made into a hot mess.

How will these events unfold? Will the fever for accountability and reform extend beyond North Africa and the Middle East? Will new, more democratic regimes replace the old, more autocratic ones? These pressing questions (and many, many others) will likely focus the attention of scholars and practitioners alike for quite some time. At the same time, lurking in their shadows is the perhaps deeper question: could any of this have been foreseen? The Danish physicist Niels Bohr is commonly attributed with once having said, "Prediction is very difficult, especially about the future." While this is certainly true at one level, this volume insists that a good deal can be said, concretely, about the importance of public opinion to the aims of good governance and about the conditions necessary for an activated public opinion to emerge. The proof of the relevance of this volume to understanding the transformation of the Arab world in progress, of course, ultimately rests on the content of its pages.

Specifically and succinctly, then, the volume identifies individual-level (e.g., the battle for short-term attention, the discovery of shared values, the deployment of mobilizing narratives), institutional-level (e.g., constructing public spheres and strong civil society organizations), and mediating factors (e.g., communicative networks that enable the transmission of mobilizing frames and the cultivation of civic education) needed to build the capacity for activated public opinion. These building blocks facilitate movement onward and upward along what we term "the stairway to mobilization" from indifferent general publics to voting publics, attentive publics, active publics, and fully mobilized publics. And the mechanisms that move us up this stairway range from information sharing and attitude change to behavior change and the sustainable mobilization of mass publics. Ultimately, the events of the Arab Spring reinforce our firm conviction that good governance is beholden to communicative processes and institutional contexts that enable ordinary individuals to keep a watchful eye and, as the occasion warrants, to stand up, be counted, and demand the responsiveness of their governments.

The Present Volume

The path to the present volume began in 2007. The World Bank's Communication for Governance and Accountability Program (CommGAP) commissioned a survey and a learning needs assessment of practitioners around the world using newfangled social accountability tools such as citizen report cards and public expenditure tracking mechanisms. The idea was to understand the conditions for effectiveness: Under what conditions were these tools effective in actually making public officials accountable to citizens? The survey and assessment reports led to a global learning event, "Generating Genuine Demand with Social Accountability Mechanisms," in Paris in November 2007. Participants in this workshop included practitioners from around the world who have used these tools in their own as well as other countries; leading scholars and researchers in the fields of communication, political science, social development, social marketing, media development, and governance; and representatives from developing country governments and donor organizations.

The workshop explored three broad questions: First, *How can we use social accountability (SA) mechanisms more effectively and selectively to ensure greater impact and generate genuine demand?* Second, *What is needed (at both the policy and the practice levels) to help ensure that SA tools create the behavior change they intend (change the behavior of public authorities or agencies in some positive way)?* And third, *What can the fields of communication and the allied social sciences (including research into social movements and other forms of collective action) teach us?* (For more information on this learning event, refer to the report in appendix A).

The meeting was a robust, effervescent encounter. One of the highlights was the morning of the second day, when participants forced CommGAP to table an unscheduled debate on the problematic concept of "social accountability." They asked: What was that? What did it really mean? Was it helpful at all? One of the consequences of that discussion was the decision of the co-editors of this volume to make it quite clear that we are interested in direct accountability.

The volume itself took a while to gel. We gradually realized that what we really wanted to illuminate is public opinion. So we had to invite authors who were not at the Paris conference to contribute, do our own thinking, meet, write our (hopefully complementary) pieces, and so on. The result is the present volume and the way it is organized. The volume moves from foundations to questions of structural contexts to analyses of how citizens process information, to the role of media systems, and on to deliberation processes and the interaction between power and public opinion. The case studies illustrate the analytical chapters. In the concluding chapter, we try to capture what we have learned about accountability through public opinion and what the policy implications might be.

Notes

1. Paris Declaration on Aid Effectiveness: Ownership, Harmonisation, Alignment, Results and Mutual Accountability, http://www.adb.org/media/articles/2005/7033_international_community_ aid/paris_declaration.pdf.

2. Accra Agenda for Action, http://www.undp.org/mdtf/docs/Accra-Agenda-for-Action
   .pdf.
3. Nick Manning, "The New Public Management and Its Legacy" (2000), http://www.mh
   -lectures.co.uk/npm_2.htm.

References

Herbst, Susan. 1998. *Reading Public Opinion: How Political Actors View the Democratic Process.* Chicago: University of Chicago Press.

Hume, David. 1987 [1742]. "Of the First Principles of Government." In *Essays, Moral, Political, and Literary,* ed. Eugene F. Miller, 32–36. Indianapolis: Liberty Fund.

Institute of Development Studies. 2010. *An Upside Down View of Governance.* Brighton, U.K.: Institute of Development Studies.

Reinikka, Ritva, and Jakob Svensson. 2004. "Local Capture: Evidence from a Central Government Transfer Program in Uganda." *Quarterly Journal of Economics* 119 (2): 679–705.

Roberts, Alasdair. 2010. *The Logic of Discipline: Global Capitalism and the Architecture of Government.* New York: Oxford University Press.

Susskind, Lawrence. 2008. "Arguing, Bargaining, and Getting Agreement." In *The Oxford Handbook of Public Policy,* ed. Michael Moran, Martin Rein, and Robert E. Goodin, 269–395. New York: Oxford University Press.

2

The (Im)Possibility of Mobilizing Public Opinion?

Taeku Lee

The basic charge of this volume is as simple as it is elusive. How can individual incentives and institutional mechanisms be designed and used to generate genuine demands for accountability? The problematic is simple because its underlying logic is transparent. Social accountability mechanisms, properly designed, should improve the ability of state actors and the development community to read accurately the needs of the populations they serve and provide the public goods and public policies that match those needs. I take accountability here to be a benchmark of good governance that finds evidence of its presence in the conjoint occurrence of three outcomes: transparency in the relationship between principals and agents, a sense of obligation among agents to be responsive to their principals, and the power for principals to punish or pink-slip their agents if they do not do so. *Social* accountability is the approach to achieving this accountability through the civic society mechanisms that rely on citizen engagement and participation. Institutional innovations such as participatory budgeting, citizen advisory boards, civic journalism, public expenditure tracking, social audits, and citizen report cards work to the extent that unauthorized, dispossessed, or otherwise quiescent principals make their needs and demands known to their elected and appointed agents. Their agents, as a result, better understand their constituency's preferences and work toward addressing them meaningfully and effectively.

Yet the problematic is also elusive if for no other reason than that such a seamlessly interdependent relationship between citizens and the state is so rarely achieved. The simplicity of the logic behind social accountability is not so easily translatable into mobilized publics and institutionalized mechanisms that work. If the mechanisms here were as obvious and optimal as they appear, their ends should already be achieved, save for the transaction costs of institutionalizing such arrangements. Yet the "haves" remain as they are everywhere, and in stark and sobering contrast to the "have-nots." It is simply not tenable that public will among the have-nots tolerates and gives assent to poverty, child labor, sweatshops, discrimination, environmental degradation, occupational hazards, corruption and waste, and other unwelcome outcomes that remain rife in the world. No one, of course, expects social accountability mechanisms to be a panacea for the inability of states and markets to regulate our political and economic arrangements justly and effectively. Nor should we expect them to be so.

How, then, do we reckon a role for public opinion to generate bottom-up demand for political accountability? Perhaps the proper precept here follows the intuition behind the view, usually attributed to Sir Winston Churchill, that "democracy is the worst form of government except for all those other forms that have been tried from time to time."[1] The ideal should not be the enemy of the possible. Under currently lived conditions that are clearly suboptimal, more is to be gained from figuring out how to design institutional arrangements that can push us to *more* optimal states of affairs than there is to dickering willy-nilly about the *most* optimal state of affairs. In this chapter, I take this precept to heart and examine the limits and opportunities that public opinion—properly conceived and meaningfully motivated—places on the prospects of generating genuine demand for accountability. I start where most such treatments of public opinion end: with a heavy dose of skepticism and dismay about the potential for public opinion as a foundation for responsiveness, accountability, and good governance. Against this view, I argue that a variety of constructions of public opinion and a broad range of political contexts can be identified in which constructed publics are either well adapted or ill-suited to the background aims of political accountability.

The Impossibility of Generating Genuine Demand?

At least two interrelated questions about public opinion ought to begin any conversation about whether "genuine demand" for accountability can be generated. The first is whether public opinion can be coherent and competent enough to be an active, autonomous pressure for political responsiveness and good governance. The second is whether effective mechanisms are in place for the public to voice its will to state actors and be heard. Much of the focus among advocates of social accountability has been on this second question, and rightly so. Absent institutional arrangements such as community scorecards, citizens' report cards, participatory budgeting, and public expenditure tracking, the transaction costs for citizens to become active and for the public's will to become voiced are often simply too high. Absent mechanisms that allow for the public to express their will to political leaders, the elites have no immediate incentives—save for the minimal conditions of regular elections and referenda under democratic regimes—to sway to that will.

The relevance of the second question—which many of the chapters in this book address—is premised on successfully clearing the first question about the very possibility of a public will itself. Institutional arrangements such as social accountability mechanisms can work only if the people know what they want, are mad about not getting it (or not being able to tell their representatives what they want), and are willing to invest a piece of themselves into changing the status quo. Here we find a long tradition of distrust and defeatism. Walter Lippmann (1922), for instance, writes disparagingly about public opinion as a "blooming, buzzing confusion" and nothing more than fictive "pictures in our heads." More recently, Jürgen Habermas (1989), Noam Chomsky (1992), and others decry public opinion as a form of "manufactured publicity" that does little more than uphold political consent and legitimacy for ruling elites, irrespective of their performance in government. Even Winston Churchill, whose conditional defense of democracy we cited earlier, is also alleged to have acerbically avowed, "the argument against democracy is a five minute conversation with the average voter."

The rub here is that the strongest evidence from empirical studies of political behavior tells us that these premises are rarely met, at least not without the sort of care and attention to institutional design and message framing that we are here to talk about. Scholars regularly line up, single file, behind Philip Converse's (1964) conclusion that most data on public opinion represent "non-attitudes." Research abounds to show that ordinary people give inconsistent answers to a question when asked that question at different times and in different contexts; they appear stunningly ignorant of even the basic facts about politics and whom they are being governed by; their views on defining political issues of the day do not cohere in any consistent way with their self-avowed political orientation; they appear to hold views that run directly against their own material well-being; those who stand most to gain from changes in the status quo appear least inclined to do anything about it; and so on.

The most damning versions of this skepticism about public opinion reprise V. O. Key's charge that "the voice of the people is but an echo. The output of an echo chamber bears an inevitable and invariable relation to the input" (1966, 2). Rather than lead the charge for elite policy makers (and agencies that implement their policies) to do better via greater transparency and participatory inputs, it may then be the case that the public follows instead. Elite actors—attuned to a changing political environment that cultivates pressures to achieve accountability—may design mechanisms that generate public demand and mobilize citizen engagement to their advantage. As this view goes, the public comes to equate the building of dams in India's Narmada River Valley, China's Three Gorges, or Zimbabwe's Zambezi River Basin with economic development—and not the displacement of people, the placement of indigenous cultures at risk, and the degradation of the environment—because political elites and media conglomerates control the message (Khagram 2004). To the cynic who sees herself as a realist, perhaps social accountability mechanisms do little more than act as an institutional shill for ruling elites who benefit from the status quo.

In Defense of a Public Will

Is this volume, then, a nonstarter? Are we doomed to fail before we begin? I think clearly not. As many of the chapters in this volume attest, many cases and country contexts demonstrate a meaningful and genuine sense of public will that is mobilized and that nurtures and sustains the kind of mutual interdependence between citizens and the state that is at the heart of political accountability and responsiveness. Several recourses exist here beyond simply giving up on the public (as many, if not most, academic political scientists in the United States have done) or viewing the public as horses being led to water by political elites and made to drink.

The first defense of the regulative ideal of public opinion is to note that most scholarship on the subject is based entirely on the analysis of survey data. The great allure of polls is their ability—when properly sampled to reflect a representative cross section of the population in question—to let the few speak efficiently and accurately for the many. Yet surveys are just one among many possible ways of gauging the public's views on politics and governance. Throughout history a diversity of alternate modes of public political expression has been found, ranging from festivals, strikes, riots, charivaris, study circles, and coffeehouse chats to focus groups, political caucuses, elections, and revolutions. With the relentless march of modern technology, ever newer forms of public expression are emerging, from radio and television talk shows, to televised "town hall meetings" and "deliberative polls," and, most recently, to Internet-based venues such as blogs and social networking sites.

Perhaps more important than the multiplicity of modes of public expression are the various shortcomings of survey data as a sole measure of public opinion. Here Pierre Bourdieu (1979), echoing Herbert Blumer (1948), controversially declares that "l'opinion publique n'existe pas" (public opinion doesn't exist) because surveys make three troublesome assumptions: that everyone's opinion is equal; that, on a given issue, everyone actually holds an opinion; and that a consensus exists about what questions merit asking (and, by corollary, that surveys can know what that consensus is). Beyond this ontological concern, surveys are also limited methodologically. Specifically, survey researchers operate on the premise that their questions can replicate the function of surgical probes into their respondents' minds. Viewed thus, the best way to gauge public opinion is by testing individuals in isolation, anonymously, using a fixed script, and deracinated from the messy, hurly-burly, real-world contexts in which politics happens.

A second defense of public opinion harks back to Churchill's conditional defense of democracy. The public's will may not look coherent and competent enough to be a source of genuine demand for accountability and social change *all the time, under all circumstances, across all contexts.* Yet it does not follow from this logically, that genuine demand cannot be generated from the bottom-up sometimes, under some circumstances, in some contexts. Quantitative social science research—of the sort that uses opinion surveys to condemn the civic competence of ordinary citizens—is built on predicting and explaining average events based on probability theory (note the language of "central tendency," "expected value," and "maximum likelihood").

Collective demands for accountability are not ordinary events. They occur within "windows of opportunity" as a result of the convergence of many factors that the remaining chapters in this book will examine, including (1) properly motivating and adequately informing state and civil society actors, (2) institutionalizing mechanisms for two-way communications between the state and civil society, (3) building citizen capacity through deliberative moments and civic education, (4) training journalists and civil society actors to value and work for accountability, (5) fostering horizontal and lateral relations within the state to work in concert, and so on. The contrast, in shorthand, is between explaining average events—which will prefigure the seeming impossibility of generating meaningful and sustained public demand for accountability—and understanding best practices in the real-world circumstances where that public demand is wrought.

A Framework of Political Contexts for Generating Public Will

Thus far I have noted several flawed and interrelated sources of skepticism about the possibility of a generative, regulative public opinion. Skeptics rely too single-handedly on opinion surveys; these opinion surveys often test for the presence of impractically high standards of civic competence and find most people wanting most of the time; norms of social science scholarship demand attention to the average, most likely, occurrence and presume the irrelevance of exceptional moments of mobilized public will and inspired citizen activism. If standard practices and modes of inquiry fail us, then, how should we proceed?

A variety of ways lead forward, many of them represented well in other chapters of this volume. Here I highlight four critical dimensions of public opinion that present a general framework of the political contexts in which real publics are constructed. The dimensions correspond to the following questions about public opinion:

1. Which public?
2. What mode of expression?
3. What kind of influence?
4. How authorized a public?

These critical dimensions, I argue, must be situated in a proper understanding of power and empowerment. In sum, this framework does not educe a single best optimum of a mobilized public will and activated citizenry. Rather, its chief aim is to map out a terrain of possibly constructed publics, their inputs and their influence, for a given social accountability mechanism.

Defining Publics

The first critical dimension of public opinion is defining which public is the target of mobilization and activation: That is, for a given social accountability mechanism, who can be engaged and whom do we want to engage? In an Aristotelian realm where the ideals of citizenship are indissoluble from the ends of human development, the answer would be "everybody." This, of course, is an impractical ideal. Hewing to a narrow, minimalist conception of citizen participation—the franchise—voter turnout rates are strikingly variable across national contexts, and dismayingly low in countries that purport to have deep participatory roots. In the United States and Switzerland, two countries with proprietary claims on the origins of democracy, voter turnout rates hover just around 50 percent. In India, the most populous democracy in the world today, it inches barely several percentage points higher. Universal participation is also impractical in the specific context of generating genuine inputs into social accountability mechanisms because such ubiquitous levels of citizen activism would almost surely overwhelm institutional capacity and foster bargaining and coordination problems in heterogeneous publics.

At the other polar extreme to universal participation would be a form of oligarchy or clientelism, where only those few and well-connected individuals who stand directly and materially to gain from being politically active will do so. Going to this extreme ensures a very high degree of personal commitment and investment among any participants. It also, however, gives us little hope for a sanguine view of genuine "bottom-up" inputs to social accountability mechanisms. The outcome of any participatory process under these circumstances, much like in a "stacked jury," would be a foregone conclusion. Furthermore, the outcome would likely be at great odds with the desires and interests of the general public.

Between the two extremes, however, is a capacious range of "publics" in which participation is selective yet sufficiently representative of *something* to engender a meaningful sense of accountability. The "public" may be self-selected (anyone wishing to participate doing so), recruited selectively (for example, recruiting usually quiescent groups such as the poor or religious and ethnic minorities), or recruited through a random selection process (such as in citizen juries, deliberative experiments, or opinion polls), or it may even be organized entities (either in civil society—churches, school councils, hometown associations, soccer clubs, and the like—or in the interest groups and lobbying professions, either as direct stakeholders or as agents of un- or underrepresented constituencies).

Thus, one key design element to mobilizing public will is specifying how inclusive or exclusive participation needs to be to serve the ends of accountability versus elite decision makers. As the arrows in figure 2.1 indicate, as a general pattern a trade-off likely also can be found between how representative a public is and how staunch and easily mobilized they are. A critical point here is that we have no *one* ideal standpoint on which public is best suited to mobilize. Rather, a menu is at hand of possible publics to activate, depending on the particular institutional design elements of a given social accountability mechanism and on a given political context—for example, organizational resources, social movement repertoires, strategic communication frames, political opportunity structures, and external audiences.

One additional point to make on properly recognizing which "public" is or ought to be mobilized on a given issue, via a given social accountability mechanism, is that the term "citizen" too has important shades of distinction. At the national level, following T. H. Marshall's (1950) still-useful categorization, a great deal of variance can be found across boundaries in the development of civil, political, and social rights. Even as a legal status, not all citizens are equal and full members of a polity. Numerous examples abound in the U.S. context, for example. Looking back through history, men exclusive of the landed gentry, all women, indigenous peoples, immigrants from Asia, colonized Mexicans, forced migrants from Africa, adults younger than 21 years of age, to name only a few examples, have either been conferred citizenship with limited rights and privileges or been denied citizenship altogether. Looking to the present, citizenship in the United States continues to be incomplete and unequal for convicted felons (who, in many states, can no longer vote), gay and lesbian couples (who, in most states, are not recognized as a legal union), unauthorized migrants (who, in many states, have no access to basic social rights), underage minors (who can sire and mother children, but cannot vote), and so on with the mentally ill, indigenous peoples, homeless, and other marginalized groups.

Above the national level, as Yasemin Soysal (1994), Rainier Bauböck (1994), Aihwa Ong (1999), and others argue, citizenship is also increasingly "denationalized." This is especially so in the European Union (EU) context, where the legal status of citizenship extends into multiple nation-states (so too for immigrants who naturalize in countries that allow for dual-citizenship arrangements). Even beyond the EU and the legal basis of citizenship, the political basis

Figure 2.1. From General Publics to Stakeholders

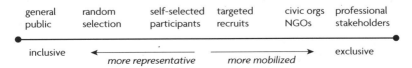

Source: Author.

Note: NGO = nongovernmental organization.

of citizenship activism—where in the civic republican tradition, citizenship "is not just a means to being free; it is the way of being free itself" (Hannah Arendt)—is increasingly local (subnational) and transnational. Moreover, newly inscribed ends of justice such as "capabilities" and "human security" are theorized explicitly across borders.

In this sense, citizenship is an important textured layer to our dimension of participatory inclusion/exclusion. It is important because we must be careful not to rely on prefigured and valorized conceptions of "citizen" in bounding a target population of participants. Many of the most transformative social movements involve the demands for greater inclusion and full citizenship—take the recent examples of the explosive urban uprisings in the Paris *banlieue* and beyond in 2005, the immigrant protest marches across American cities in 2006, or the protests led by monks in Yangon in 2007—and we risk missing such critically transformative moments by sticking to one particular view.

It is further important to keep in mind the varieties of citizenship because varying understandings of what citizenship entails at the individual level also can be identified. Some individuals may view their citizenship purely as a legal status—with accompanying rights (such as access to public services or legal counsel) and attendant privileges and obligations (such as jury duty, military service, or electoral office). Others may find in this thin conception of citizenship a deep psychic release and freedom from fear—fear of political persecution, deportation, or other legally justified sanction. Yet others may view their citizenship as a civic, republican virtue or as an aspiration to an ideal human form.

Modes of Public Expression

Another critical dimension is what counts as evidence of public "will" and citizen "activism." As noted earlier, in contemporary, industrialized societies the technologies of marketing consumption and surveying political preferences have developed to the point where many scholarly and practical responses to the question "What does the public want?" or "What is the public willing to fight for?" start and end with the opinion poll. Good reasons are given for this reliance on a randomly sampled, but putatively representative, public. Myriad reasons also exist to be cautious, if not critical, of this reliance. For the present, I skirt this nettle bush save for returning to the observation that a remarkable diversity of modes of public expression is found beyond the opinion poll. Among the social accountability mechanisms discussed in this volume, public expenditure tracking and citizen report cards rely on surveys, whereas community scorecards allow for focus groups and public meetings, and participatory budgeting allows for direct and deliberative decision making.

Across these multiple modes of public political expression, each counts as evidence of the public's will in varying degrees, conditioned on who the "public" is and how much "will" is in evidence. Here again, I want to emphasize the range of possible participatory inputs. At one end of the spectrum is the ideal-ized Athenian forum or New England town hall meeting that is part of our political mythos in the United States, where we directly do the work of politics. Participatory budgeting and Local Health Councils in Brazil aim, in the main, for this ideal. At the opposite end are very passive forms of input—viewing a political debate on the television, attending a public informational meeting, listening to a petitioner on the street.

As figure 2.2 shows, between passive consumption of political information and active deliberation and collective decision making lie a range of modes of participation that enable individuals to voice their political will and—to the extent that preferences are sometimes endogenous to participation as the "new social movements" literature on identity formation suggests—even allow for the transformation and empowerment of that will. In figure 2.2, the spectrum ranges from cheap to costly modes of participation.

In parallel with the costs of participation is a spectrum that varies in how informative participation is to elite decision makers (watching a televised debate in one's apartment conveys little information beyond aggregate media market share; engaging in civil disobedience or partaking in a participatory budgeting exercise conveys a great deal about what citizens want and how intensely they want it). Also in parallel with the cost dimension is the level of publicity or anonymity for a given mode of participation. In more authoritar-ian states, inspiring people to express their political will publicly may be a very high threshold indeed.

Power and Empowerment

In choosing between modes of mobilizing public inputs to a given social accountability mechanism, such factors are critical to consider and demand careful answers to questions such as "How much information do we need (or, can we handle)?" and "Will we put participants in harm's way by inviting modes of participation that a ruling regime will not tolerate?" They also push us toward a third key dimension that ought to be part of any discussion of institutional design: the kind of influence we seek from citizens. Ruling elites (especially local and national elites) are often interested only in their citizens' viewpoints to the extent that it allows them to manage the potential for

Figure 2.2. From Passive Inputs to Direct Decision Making

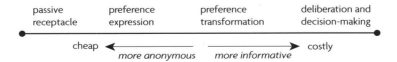

Source: Author.

dissent. Viewed from the participants' standpoint, activism in itself is often no impetus to social change or political accountability.

What, then, is the range of ways that participatory inputs could influence or constitute governance? Here Sherry Arnstein's classic 1969 essay "A Ladder of Citizen Participation" is a useful point of departure (figure 2.3).[2] Arnstein describes an eight-rung ladder ranging from "the empty ritual of participation" to "real power needed to affect the outcome." Thus, at the lowest rungs are participatory inputs staged to either mimic genuine inputs ("manipulation") or appease a public that might be mobilized with breads and circuses ("therapy"). In the middle are what Arnstein sees as forms of "tokenism" that allow the public to voice their demands, but with no guarantee that they will be heard or that those in power will be held accountable for turning a deaf ear. Then at the very top are levels of citizen influence and power that allow for varying degrees of direct decision making.

Figure 2.3. The Ladder of Participatory Inputs

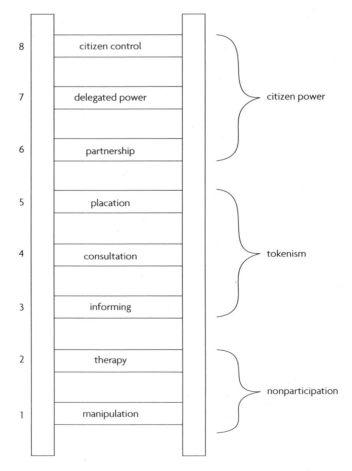

Source: Adapted from Arnstein 1969.

This schematic helps to temper the credulous devotion of some to participation for its own sake. Not all modes of participation are equal. In Arnstein's scheme—adapted and redefined in figure 2.4—modes of participation such as citizen control and negotiated forms of power sharing are more informative to state actors. They are also far more costly to achieve, however: State actors have to concede a great deal of their authority to make it happen, and citizens have to risk the swift and sometimes arbitrary hand of repression. If only citizen-elite partnerships or direct citizen control count as real power, this is too high a barrier to entry for most elite decision makers in most political contexts. A willingness to hear out the public and be held accountable to them is one thing, but sharing power or ceding it altogether is an entirely different matter. Moreover the dichotomy between citizens and elites (the ruled and their rulers) itself blurs into oblivion the higher one moves up this ladder of participation, and, from the perspective of the ruling elite, there is no guarantee that a citizenry with genuine power can be so easily ratcheted down once it is mobilized.

This variation in power sharing brings us to a final critical dimension of public opinion, shown in figure 2.5. Not all individuals in a society feel equally empowered or authorized to speak their minds on political matters; that is, a range of empowerment stretches from anomie or alienation to full authorization. Some individuals might opt out of politics as a result of their psychic estrangement or sense of being controlled and exploited. Others might be unincorporated because they are not socialized into the customs, norms, and civic education that habituate and authorize the sphere of political action. Yet others, whether by trait of personality, familial socialization, social network position, or some other factor, feel fully authorized to speak their mind on political matters.

Figure 2.4. From Ritual to Co-governance

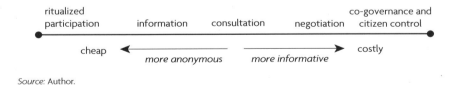

Source: Author.

Figure 2.5. Civil Society and Authorizing Public Opinion

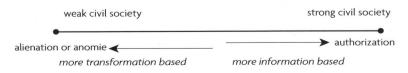

Source: Author.

As John Gaventa (1982) powerfully recounts in his study of an Appalachian mining community in the United States, grievance and exploitation all too often are accompanied by quiescence, not rebellion. Gaventa explains this failure of mobilized public demands by defining three faces of power that are illuminating. In the first face, power is manifest through direct and observable decision making, with powerful winners and powerless losers. In the second face, power is visible through agenda setting, with some issues making their way to a decision and others left off the agenda altogether. In the third face, power is invisible and seen only indirectly in subjective states of mind—for example, in how the underprivileged often choose to understand their own situation by attributing blame to their own individual motivational deficits, rather than structural dynamics that serve to exploit their labor or corrupt their politicians.

This view of power gives insight into the range of subjective understandings that individuals bring to the construction of "public opinion." In cases in which power seeps down to the third face, public opinion cannot be a generative force for accountability without transformation of that consciousness and belief system itself. When power is contested primarily in the first face, among individuals in society who feel equally authorized to be political beings irrespective of their material circumstances, the battle over public opinion is more dependent on having access to information and using that information to foster collective action. The states of alienation and anomie that prevail in the third face are likelier to be sustained in more repressive political regimes and under conditions of weak civil society, whereas publics that feel authorized to demand accountability are likelier to coalesce in more democratic regimes and under conditions of strong civil society.

It is important here to note that many social accountability mechanisms such as citizen scorecards and right-to-information legislation are information based and geared to mobilize already authorized publics to voice their political viewpoints. They are less well designed to transform and activate publics that are, in Paulo Freire's (1970) term, engaged in a "culture of silence." By contrast, more directly participatory mechanisms of social accountability have the potential to break the cycle of quiescence by galvanizing the powerless to engage in self-determinative acts and reflect on them. In this sense, social accountability mechanisms need to consider power not just in the conventional terms of "power-over," as in a state's power over its subjects. Rather, they need also to take seriously more processual and collective conceptions of "power-to" and "power-with," as in citizens' power to work with one another to collectively demand change, responsiveness, and accountability. (See, e.g., Guinier and Torres 2003).

Notes

1. From a House of Commons speech on November 11, 1947.
2. I am indebted to Archon Fung for pointing me to Arnstein's work.

References

Arnstein, Sherry. 1969. "A Ladder of Citizen Participation." *Journal of the American Planning Association* 35 (4): 216–24.

Bauböck, Rainier. 1994. *Transnational Citizenship: Membership and Rights in International Migration.* Aldershot: Edward Elgar.

Blumer, Herbert. 1948. "Public Opinion and Public Opinion Polling." *American Sociological Review* 13: 542–54.

Bourdieu, Pierre. 1979. "Public Opinion Does Not Exist." Translated by M. C. Axtmann. In *Communication and Class Struggle.* Vol. 1: *Capitalism, Imperialism,* ed. Armand Mattelart and Seth Siegelaub. New York: International General.

Chomsky, Noam. 1992. *Manufacturing Consent: The Political Economy of the Mass Media.* New York: Pantheon.

Converse, Philip. 1964. "The Nature of Belief Systems in Mass Publics." In *Ideology and Discontent,* ed. David Apter. New York: Free Press.

Freire, Paulo. 1970. *Pedagogy of the Oppressed.* New York: Herder and Herder.

Gaventa, John. 1982. *Power and Powerlessness.* Urbana: University of Illinois Press.

Guinier, Lani, and Gerald Torres. 2003. *The Miner's Canary: Enlisting Race, Resisting Power, Transforming Democracy.* Cambridge, MA: Harvard University Press.

Habermas, Jürgen. 1989. *Structural Transformation of the Public Sphere.* Cambridge, MA: MIT Press.

Key, V. O. 1966. *The Responsible Electorate.* New York: Vintage Books.

Khagram, Sanjeev. 2004. *Dams and Development: Transnational Struggles for Water and Power.* Ithaca, NY: Cornell University Press.

Lippmann, Walter. 1922. *Public Opinion.* New York: Macmillan.

Marshall, T. H. 1950. *Citizenship and Social Class and Other Essays.* Cambridge, UK: Cambridge University Press.

Ong, Aihwa. 1999. *Flexible Citizenship.* Durham, NC: Duke University Press.

Soysal, Yasemin Nuhoğlu. 1994. *Limits to Citizenship: Migrants and Postnational Membership in Europe.* Chicago: University of Chicago Press.

3

The Public and Its (Alleged)
Handiwork

Sina Odugbemi

Power concedes nothing without a demand. It never did, and it never will.

—Frederick Douglass

Introduction

How do you organize a political community such that citizens are truly able to hold their governments accountable, where that "implies both mechanisms for the active monitoring of public officials and the means of enforcing public expectations" (Bessete 2001, 38–39)? Constitutional theory provides two broad approaches. The first approach says the solution is to have periodic elections, separation of powers, and a system of checks and balances, what Montesquieu calls making sure power checks power by "the arrangement of things" (quoted in Bessete 2001, 155). In the words of James Madison in *Federalist,* No. 47: "The accumulation of all powers, legislative, executive, and judiciary, in the same hands, whether of one, a few, or many, and whether hereditary, self-appointed, or elective, may justly be pronounced the very definition of tyranny" (Madison, Hamilton, and Jay 1987/1788, 249).

We all know the usual devices of liberal constitutional democracy: separation of the powers of law making, law executing, and law adjudicating; special majorities for some decisions; checks and balances; bicameral legislatures; and so on. The insights of that tradition of political thought remain true. Yet a growing consensus holds that although these constitutional devices are all well and good, they are not enough. Everywhere around us are elected representatives of the people in so-called liberal constitutional democracies, and they still contrive not to be truly accountable to the people.

Elections are the main accountability mechanism in representative democracies (Prezeworski, Stokes, and Manin 1999, 3). Yet it is becoming clearer by the day that although elections are hugely important, they are not enough. First, in most representative systems accountability is mediated: Rulers are formally accountable to legislatures, not directly to the people (Laver and Shepsle 1999, 249). Once elected rulers survive an election they can contrive to forget about the body of electors until another election comes around. Second, elections are a fuzzy and unreliable accountability mechanism (Dunn 1999, 335). An election involves a vast, complicated jumble of issues. Yes, it can occasionally allow citizens to "throw the bastards out," but it is certainly not a reliable means of making leaders accountable on *specific issues*. It is certainly not a sure-fire means of getting improved delivery of public services or the government's focus on the needs of the vast majority of citizens (Goetz and Jenkins 2005).

The second broad approach to organizing a political community such that citizens can hold their governments accountable directly is to find ways of making sure that the people themselves can control the government. On this view, the cure is deepening the dependence of government on the people themselves, empowering the people themselves, providing them with mechanisms for sanctioning misrule. In other words, the second broad approach relies on what Jon Elster calls "democratic checks and controls" depending directly on the people themselves (Elster and Slagstad 1984, 7–8). In what follows, I aim to spell out what the second approach really means.

I do not want to suggest, however, that an irreconcilable difference exists between the two approaches. They can and *should* be combined. After all, as James Madison famously said in *Federalist*, No. 51: "In framing a government which is to be administered by men over men, the great difficulty lies in this: you must first enable the government to control the governed; and in the next place oblige it to control itself. A dependence on the people is, no doubt, the primary control on the government; but experience has taught mankind the necessity of auxiliary precautions" (Madison, Hamilton, and Jay 1987 [1788], 269).

The Public as a Political State

Discussions of the role of *the Public* in governance often start from a romantic assumption of the role of the Public in the founding of political systems. As is well known, in political philosophy social contract theories state that governments are the creation of the people, they are invested with certain powers, they are trustees of those powers, and we, the people, are therefore entitled to accountability. Although democratic revolutions have occurred where we have had what Andreas Kalyvas (2008) calls "the politics of the extraordinary" and "popular foundings" of democratic societies, these are exceptions rather than the rule. We have no choice but to think of the problem of accountability in situations of ordinary politics, in political communities of all kinds, even those where democratic revolutions took place. For instance, I belong simultaneously to two political communities (Nigeria and the United Kingdom), and in neither did a "popular founding" occur.

Yet the key idea here is that, whatever the political context, *the Public* is a structural fundament, a political state. The key idea is that accountability—monitoring the government at whatever level, and deploying mechanisms for enforcing public expectations—is the work of the Public. This involves a wider conception of governance than that which we normally deploy: It involves recognizing that governance is not something only the formal institutions of the state do; it involves recognizing that governance is something the Public also has to be engaged in if government is going to be responsive and accountable. This is why the helpful accounts of politics in this regard are those in which the attitudes, opinions, and activities of the Public are a structural fundament. Incomplete and unhelpful are those accounts of politics that concentrate exclusively on what leaders and their officials, legislators, and judges do. Happily, we have a rich and distinguished tradition of political thought of the useful and complete variety, whose leading lights include Jeremy Bentham, John Dewey, and Hannah Arendt. We are going to briefly explore the relevant aspects of the political thought of each of these thinkers for resources to draw on in thinking about the role of the Public. Now, what do they tell us?

We start with Arendt because her political thought is the most complex. One of her key insights is her normative definition of power. She says: "While strength is the natural quality of an individual seen in isolation, power springs up between men when they act together and vanishes the moment they disperse" (Arendt 1958, 200). She illustrates the point in the following way. A small but well-organized group of men can rule a much larger group if the latter do not act together. Yet once people learn to act together, no ruler is too powerful to be overthrown by them. Power, then, arises from people acting in concert, but it is fragile because so many wills have to agree.

Arendt's second key insight is the centrality of the public realm. According to her, the public realm in a republic is "constituted by an exchange of opinion between equals" (Arendt 1963, 93). The public realm is where citizens meet, it is the "space of appearances," where citizens discuss common concerns and make decisions. This is where the role of public opinion comes in. According to her: "Opinions are formed in a process of open discussion and public debate, and where no opportunity for the forming of opinions exists, there may be moods—moods of the masses and moods of individuals, the latter no less fickle and unreliable than the former—but no opinion" (pp. 268–69). She deplores the fact that much of what is called modern representative government "has degenerated into mere administration. ... [T]he people are not admitted to the public realm, once more the business of government is the privilege of the few" (p. 175).

For John Dewey, the essential problem of government is accountability: "The essential problem of government thus reduces itself to this: What arrangements will prevent rulers from advancing their own interests at the expense of the ruled? Or, in positive terms, by what means shall the interests of the governors be identified with those of the governed?" (1927, 98). His answer is that "[o]nly through constant watchfulness and criticism of public officials by citizens can a state be maintained in integrity and usefulness" (p. 69). He teaches us that it is important to create a unified, fraternal public conscious of itself and its role in government. Without creating "a Great Community, the Public will remain in eclipse" (p. 142). The Public will not be effective; it will be easy prey for bad rulers.

For Dewey, what needs to be done is to keep seeking to improve public debate and discussion, and the mechanisms and conditions that facilitate the process. He urges the centrality of free social inquiry, and of publicity, free debate, and discussion. As he says, to create a "democratically effective public" (1927, 157), the only possible solution is "the perfecting of the means and ways of communication of meanings so that genuinely shared interest in the consequences of interdependent activities may inform desire and effort and thereby direct action" (p. 155). Finally, he argues, the constitution of a democratically effective Public is really the same as the proper formation of public opinion: "Communication of the results of social enquiry is the same thing as the formation of public opinion. ... For public opinion is judgment which is formed and entertained by those who constitute the public and it is about public affairs" (p. 177).

According to Dewey, without debate and discussion—informed by the latest facts and knowledge—any opinion formed is mere "opinion" in the derogatory sense, not "public opinion." Mere opinion is based on prejudice, and it is unstable. It is important to note in this regard Arendt's distinction between opinion properly so called and mere moods. I believe they are both making the same point.

Now, let us consider the political thought of Jeremy Bentham. Bentham is uniquely important because he focused to an amazing degree on ways of creating a system of government with accountability as its primary value. In Bentham's language, our central question becomes: How do you organize government such that you prevent misrule and ensure that the focus of the activities of government is the greatest interest of the greatest number of the citizens? Bentham's answer is that *everything* depends on the people. The people themselves must act to prevent misrule. He says public opinion—the Public Opinion Tribunal—is the real check on misrule. As a result, he emphasizes the need for active, vigilant citizens. In *Securities against Misrule,* he writes trenchantly: "Of everything that is thus done or endeavoured at the success depends upon the spirit, the intelligence, the vigilance, the alertness, the intrepidity, the energy, the perseverance, of those of whose opinions Public Opinion is composed" (Bentham 1990, 139).

Note the range of vigorous nouns he deploys: spirit, intelligence, vigilance, alertness, intrepidity, energy, and perseverance. Citizens must take an interest in government, seek to be informed, witness official wrongdoing when it occurs, cry foul, publicize it, insist on redress and punishment, and so on. Without citizen vigilance and activism, he insists, it is impossible to prevent misrule.

Bentham's is not a naive faith in the power of public opinion. He recognizes that the Public Opinion Tribunal needs help to function effectively as a mechanism for holding governments accountable. So in Bentham's constitutional thought he stresses the need for three structural supports. First, he believes you must give all citizens basic education. Citizens must be able to read and write to be able to vote. He thinks all citizens must be able to follow what is going on in public affairs to be truly competent citizens. Second, he insists on open and transparent government to a fanatical degree. Long before Freedom of Information Acts became fashionable, Bentham campaigned for totally open government, including architecture that allows members of the public to observe public officials at work. His model of government is the Panopticon, a system that allows an observer to observe everyone in the system without their knowing whether they are observed. Applied to governance the Panopticon implies complete transparency where the Public can always observe the government without the government knowing whether they are being watched. Bentham says that all evil in government thrives in secret. He wants citizens to know everything that is going on, then they can debate and discuss the activities of government in the Public Opinion Tribunal and, quite literally, hand down judgments (Bentham 1983).

Third, Bentham says the Public Opinion Tribunal cannot do the work of holding governments accountable without a free press. In his view, for the individuals in a political community to form opinions about misrule by public functionaries a number of processes must take place. The facts must be extracted. The members of the public must be notified of these facts. The facts must be transmitted or diffused throughout the political community. The facts must be debated. Opinions and judgments must be formed. A free press is fundamental to this process (Bentham 1989, 292). Bentham goes as far as to say that in a representative government only the principal minister or prime minister is more important than the editor of a newspaper of mass circulation: "By the Prime Minister impulse is given to the machinery of the political sanction: by the Editor of the prime popular Newspaper, to that of the social sanction" (Bentham 1990, 46). Bentham believes that if you have a citizenry with basic education, a vast array of public sources of information about public affairs, and a torrent of clear information on what government is doing, then the Public Opinion Tribunal will do its work as the "grand corrective of all political evil" (p. 223).

Beyond Sentimental Wooliness

The tradition of political thought that we have been discussing is not about sentimental wooliness or naive idealism. It is, in fact, based on a somewhat pessimistic or hardheaded view of human nature. At the basis of the tradition is the belief that human beings are in the main self-regarding creatures, that when they are given public office they will pursue their own interests unless there is credible sanctioning power. Bentham, for instance, argues that although human beings are capable of altruism, anyone designing systems of government is wise to assume self-interest. This is why citizens who want securities against misrule have only themselves to rely on. Citizens must develop a capacity to sanction bad governance, whatever the level. Otherwise, no reliable securities against misrule exist. Those in power, to paraphrase Frederick Douglass's epigraph to this chapter, never concede without a demand.

This tradition of political thought is unsentimental in another way. It accommodates political realities in different contexts but points toward a clear path to securing direct accountability. What are these realities? In many societies, the path to an effective Public is strewn with obstacles. For one thing, divisions are rife. Ethnic and sectarian divisions often stand in the way of common action or a sense of solidarity by those who ought to constitute the Public. For quite another, authoritarian political control still bedevils many societies. The powers of law making, law adjudicating, and law executing are still effectively concentrated in a few hands, even in so-called democracies. As we saw above, that is the very definition of tyranny. In such political communities, organizing an effective Public is a tough row to hoe.

Nonetheless, mobilizing an effective Public remains the task. As we conclude, it is important to make a distinction between (a) processes and (b) structures and institutions.

The Process View

At the heart of the direct accountability effort—or the creation of an effective Public—is somehow unleashing the power of informed public opinion, a critical force in all political communities that all rulers are wary of. Carmen Malena has prepared a good diagram showing the building blocks of social accountability (see fig. 3.1). As you study it, you realize that the force expected to be at work is informed, mobilized public opinion. In each context, the question is: How do you get to mobilized public opinion? This is why the place to start is a realistic assessment of the contextual challenges through a sound political economy analysis, especially answers to the following questions:

Figure 3.1. Social Accountability Building Books

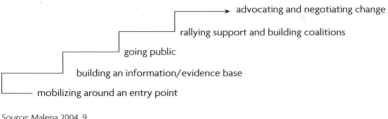

Source: Malena 2004, 9.

- How does governance really work in this context?
- What are the rules of the game?
- What are the strengths and the weaknesses of the Public?
- What structures exist to support the Public?
- What are the viable paths to effectiveness for the Public?

Such a clear-eyed process is crucial to effective strategy.

Structures: The Open, Inclusive Public Sphere

Much, if not most, of the work currently being done on social accountability ignores the structural context. We have ongoing efforts supposedly designed to strengthen social accountability mechanisms in contexts where the media are muzzled, access to official information is close to zero, civil society organizations are hamstrung, and basic political rights hardly exist. Yet, as all the great political thinkers reviewed earlier make clear, an open, inclusive public sphere (as modeled in figure 3.2) is crucial to the effectiveness of the Public. What are the characteristics of an open, inclusive public sphere? They are

- Constitutionally guaranteed civil liberties, especially freedom of expression, opinion, and assembly;
- A media system that is free, plural, and not under state control;
- Access to official information and a culture of open and transparent government;
- A public political culture of free debate and discussion and civic vibrancy; and
- Equal access to the public arena by all citizens. (Odugbemi 2008, 15–37)

The point is this: The public sphere—as in the ancient agora—is where the effective Public happens, comes into being, finds its voice, sanctions official transgressions, earns respect. If you revisit Malena's Social Accountability Building Blocks in figure 3.1 and ask "Where do these activities take place?" the only answer is that they take place in the public arena, and they are facilitated only where the context has an open, inclusive public sphere. This is why it is

Figure 3.2. The Open, Inclusive Public Sphere

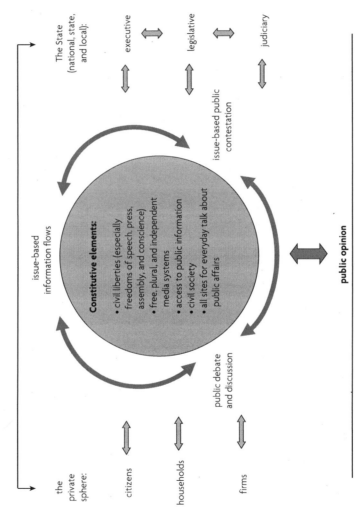

the
private
sphere:

citizens

households

firms

public debate
and discussion

issue-based
information flows

Constitutive elements:
● civil liberties (especially
  freedoms of speech, press,
  assembly, and conscience)
● free, plural, and independent
  media systems
● access to public information
● civil society
● all sites for everyday talk about
  public affairs

issue-based public
contestation

public opinion

The State
(national, state,
and local):

executive

legislative

judiciary

Source: Odugbemi 2008, 30.

very strange that much of the work being done supposedly to strengthen social accountability mechanisms—much of which has been inspired by processes in *democratic* India—ignores the fundamental importance of the nature of the public sphere, and ignores the need to seek every opportunity to work toward the creation of an open and inclusive one.

Conclusion

Citizens can hold governments accountable only if they are organized into an effective Public. This applies whatever the level of government: village, district, national. The Public is a permanent office beyond periodic elections—an additional instrument to hold governments accountable between elections and when traditional means of accountability (elections, separation of powers, checks and balances) are not efficient. The Public is part of any system of government that takes direct accountability seriously. *The Public is a political state.* An organized Public produces informed public opinion on the great questions and issues of the day, and this opinion—once formed at the end of a process of debate and discussion—is a critical force in politics. It has power to change the incentives of public officials. An effective Public, however, needs support structures. It needs an open, inclusive public sphere.

References

Arendt, Hannah. 1958. *The Human Condition.* Chicago: University of Chicago Press.

Arendt, Hannah. 1963. *On Revolution.* London: Penguin Books.

Bentham, Jeremy. 1983. *Constitutional Code.* Volume 1. Edited by F. Rosen and J. H. Burns. *The Collected Works of Jeremy Bentham.* Oxford: Clarendon Press.

Bentham, Jeremy. 1989. *First Principles Preparatory to Constitutional Code.* Edited by Philip Schofield. *The Collected Works of Jeremy Bentham.* Oxford: Clarendon Press.

Bentham, Jeremy. 1990. *Securities against Misrule and Other Constitutional Writings for Tripoli and Greece.* Edited by Philip Schofield. *The Collected Works of Jeremy Bentham.* Oxford: Clarendon Press.

Bessete, J. M. 2001. "Political Accountability." In *International Encyclopedia of the Social & Behavioral Sciences,* vol. 1, ed. Neil J. Smelser and Paul B. Baltes. Oxford: Elsevier.

Dewey, John. 1927. *The Public and Its Problems.* Athens, OH: Ohio University Press.

Dunn, John. 1999. "Situating Democratic Political Accountability." In *Democracy, Accountability and Representation,* ed. Adam Prezeworski, Susan C. Stokes, and Mernard Manin. Cambridge, UK: Cambridge University Press.

Elster, Jon, and Rune Slagstad, eds. 1984. *Constitutionalism and Democracy.* Cambridge, UK: Cambridge University Press.

Goetz, Anne Marie, and Rob Jenkins. 2005. *Reinventing Accountability: Making Democracy Work for Human Development.* Basingstoke, UK: Palgrave Macmillan.

Kalyvas, Andreas. 2008. *Democracy and the Politics of the Extraordinary: Max Weber, Carl Schmitt, and Hannah Arendt.* Cambridge, UK: Cambridge University Press.

Laver, Michale, and Kenneth A. Shepsle. 1999. "Government Accountability in Parliamentary Democracy." In *Democracy, Accountability and Representation,* ed. Adam Prezeworski, Susan C. Stokes, and Mernard Manin. Cambridge, UK: Cambridge University Press.

Madison, James, Alexander Hamilton, and John Jay. 1987 [1788]. *The Federalist Papers.* Edited by I. Kramnick. New York: Penguin Books.

Malena, Carmen. 2004. "Social Accountability: An Introduction to the Concept and Emerging Practice." Social Development Papers No 76, December, World Bank, Washington, DC.

Odugbemi, Sina. 2008. "Public Opinion, the Public Sphere, and Quality of Governance: An Exploration." In *Governance Reform under Real-World Conditions: Citizens, Stakeholders, and Voice,* ed. Sina Odugbemi and Thomas Jacobson, 15–37. Washington, DC: World Bank.

Prezeworski, Adam, Susan C. Stokes, and Mernard Manin, eds. 1999. *Democracy, Accountability and Representation.* Cambridge, UK: Cambridge University Press.

Section II
Structural Context

•
•

4

Gaining State Support for Social Accountability

Harry Blair

If social accountability is to be successful in enabling ordinary citizens and civil society organizations to hold public power holders responsible for their actions,[1] then the state must support—actively or passively—the mechanisms to be used in exacting it.[2] This chapter will explore the sources of that support and what those sources require to underpin the social accountability mechanisms (SAMs) that depend on them. I will argue that the types of state support vary across a whole spectrum from intensely active to extremely reluctant, covering a wide range of mechanisms, all of which foster social accountability in some fashion. Accordingly, international donor agencies and programmers face a great variety of choices in selecting particular mechanisms to assist.

The chapter begins with a brief glance at the entire spectrum of state response to citizen demands for social accountability, which range from enthusiastic support to repressive opposition. I then zero in on the more positive part of that spectrum in detail and look at various degrees of positive support with examples. The following section, focusing on the sources of state support, asks what induces the state to respond to SAMs. The final part offers a brief look at several patterns emerging from the analysis.

The Spectrum of State Response

Citizens asking the state for social accountability can be met with a variety of responses, as indicated in figure 4.1. At the most positive extreme, a city mayor might respond with such enthusiasm to a citizen delegation demanding better sewage and garbage removal that he or she sets up an elected

Figure 4.1. Spectrum of State Response to Social Accountability Initiatives

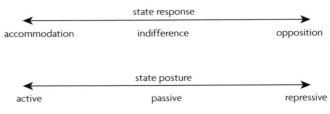

Source: Author.

board to superintend city sanitation services with powers to sanction inadequate performance. At the most negative extreme, a state executive might respond to public demonstrations seeking greater government accountability by bringing in military troops to fire on the demonstrators.[3] Between these two opposites of embracing and suppressing lies a neutral zone of indifference, in which the state neither encourages nor discourages mechanisms through which citizens exercise accountability. For example, a government might allow newspapers to publish whatever they wished, while neither supporting them (such as by subsidizing their delivery by mail) nor opposing them (such as through censorship). Another way to look at these three responses would be to consider them as state postures that are active, passive, and repressive, as shown in figure 4.1.

Figure 4.2 provides a more finely grained depiction of the left two-thirds of the spectrum in figure 4.1, as it turns the axis on its side to give a greater sense of the rank ordering from most to least degree of support. In addition, the state's support for SAMs is divided into active (indicating positive action of some sort on the part of the state) and passive (in which the state essentially takes no action to support or oppose citizen efforts to exercise accountability). The resulting figure with its attempted rank ordering then hopefully matches up with the mechanisms and examples shown in table 4.1.[4]

In table 4.1, I have tried to sort 15 mechanisms for exercising social accountability by placing them in a descending rank order according to the degree of state support they receive. For each mechanism is shown its "source of authority" (how it got introduced to the political system), the essential requirements for its success (what it will take for it to function successfully as a SAM), whether it requires significant state financing, and whether it operates at a national or local level. A capsule discussion of each mechanism follows, progressing by the levels shown in table 4.1, beginning with mechanisms getting the most active state support and proceeding to those receiving the most passive support. The better-known SAMs, such as elections or civil society, will be presented abstractly, and brief examples will be provided for those likely to be less familiar.

Figure 4.2. Spectrum of State Support for Social Accountability Mechanisms

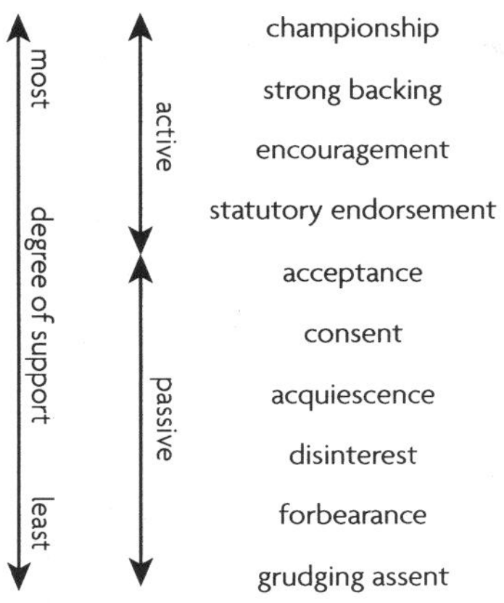

championship

strong backing

encouragement

statutory endorsement

acceptance

consent

acquiescence

disinterest

forbearance

grudging assent

Source: Author.

When the State Takes an Active Posture

State as champion: A justifiably well-documented initiative, *participatory budgeting* (PB), originated during the early 1990s in the southeastern Brazilian city of Porto Alegre, under the leadership of its mayor at the time, Olivio Dutra. In the PB process, annual neighborhood meetings determine municipal investment priorities and elect delegates to district meetings that consolidate the proposals and feed them into a citywide system that through a transparent allocation algorithm translates them into actual investments. District delegates elected to a city-level council consolidate the budget and monitor its implementation, at which point the next year's cycle begins. Widely adopted in Brazil and numerous other countries, PB has transformed a patron-client structure in which upward citizen loyalty was traded for top-down political largesse into one based around citizen priorities as its main input into budgetary decision making.[5] The key to PB's success was the leadership and commitment provided by Mayor Dutra and his successors, without which it would surely have quickly failed.

Decentralization of state authority: Decentralization is a second mechanism in which the state must play an ongoing role as champion for reform to ensure any success. Real devolution of authority can bring decision making and accountability closer to affected citizens and, by directing investments where they are most needed, act as a powerful force for poverty alleviation. Intruding as they do into the basic structure of a country's governance, decentralization initiatives require legislative (perhaps even constitutional) action and executive implementation. Moreover, in many countries, they also require displacing parliamentarians accustomed to deploying central expenditures as patronage tools in their constituencies and bypassing bureaucrats habituated to siphoning off a large portion of central funds passing through their hands on the way

Table 4.1. Social Accountability Mechanisms and Their Origins

State posture	Mode of state support	Mechanism	Source of authority	Requirements for success	State financing?	National or local level
Active (Most ↔ Least)	Championship	Participatory budgeting (Porto Alegre, Brazil)	Executive leadership	Executive commitment	Y	L
		Decentralization program (many examples)	Legislative act + implementation	Political will	Y	L
	Strong backing	Ombudsman (Philippines)	Legislative act + implementation	Ombudsman authority to redress	Y	N
		Statutory oversight board (Vigilance Committees, Bolivia)	Executive leadership + legislative act	Citizen competence, executive commitment	Y	L
		Citizen review board (Rationing Committee, Mumbai)	Executive leadership + citizen activism	Citizen competence, executive cooperation	N	L
	Encouragement	Citizen report cards (Bangalore, India)	Civil society	Citizen competence, executive responsiveness	N	L
	Statutory endorsement	Elections (many examples)	Constitution	Outside monitoring	Y	L
		Legislative oversight (African parliaments)	Constitution	Legislative autonomy + abandoning patronage orientation	Y	N
Passive (Least ↔ Most)	Acceptance	Civil society advocacy and lobbying (many cases)	Openness to civil society	Genuine pluralism and competition	N	N or L
	Consent	Public interest lawsuits (Delhi air pollution case)	Constitution	Independent judiciary	N	N
	Acquiescence	Media (many cases)	Constitution	Executive restraint	N	N
	Disinterest	Privatization (market exercises accountability—many cases)	Executive decision and/or legislative act	Market competition	N	N
	Forbearance	Human rights organizations (Amnesty International; Human Rights Watch)	International pressure	Executive restraint + independent media	N	N
		Corruption report card (Mymensingh, Bangladesh)	Civil society activism	Executive restraint	N	L
	Grudging assent	Demonstrations (Estrada ouster; Orange Revolution)	Citizen movements	Executive restraint	N	N or L

Source: Author

Note: Y = yes, N = no (column 6); L = local, N = national (column 7).

down to lower levels. Thus, it is not surprising that many decentralization initiatives flounder and wither as they run up against these elements. Equally daunting, when authority really does pass downward, local elites may simply seize control of the devolved power and use it to their own advantage. In short, an immense political will is needed to make decentralization succeed.[6]

State providing strong backing: Many countries have *ombudsman* institutions, which can act as powerful mechanisms for social accountability.[7] One particularly impressive example comes from the Philippines, where the ombudsman can investigate and prosecute any public official for malfeasance, whether on a complaint or acting on his or her own accord, and can mandate any official to perform any legal act or prevent any illegal one (TAN 2002). Theoretically, the ombudsman's scope extends even to the president of the country. More typical is the Croatian ombudsman, who can report official misbehavior to the parliament and publicize findings to the media but cannot take any legal action against wrongdoers (Blair and others 2007). Clearly, the ombudsman's scope of authority is key here. Also critical, however, is the support the state provides to his or her office and the integrity shown by the incumbent. Historically, the Philippine ombudsman office has been so starved of resources that it has become enfeebled, and occupants of the office have been tainted with serious charges of corruption and cronyism.[8] The ombudsman can be powerful indeed as an engine of social accountability, but it needs both full authority and strong support from the state to be effective.

As part of its Popular Participation Law reforming local governments in the mid-1990s, Bolivia set up a *statutory oversight board* in each of its 311 municipalities. These *comités de vigilancia* (CVs or vigilance committees), whose members were selected from some 13,000 territorially determined traditional organizations (most often peasant associations), were intended to act as a check on the newly elected municipal governments. The CVs were charged with preparing local investment plans, monitoring the elected council's implementation of investment, and lodging actionable complaints when they observed malfeasance. The law was pushed through by a president determined to enfranchise the country's majority indigenous population, who until then were largely excluded from governance. Although somewhat hobbled by lack of capacity for their new tasks, the councils and CVs did bring a significant measure of accountability to local governance in Bolivia.[9]

Citizen review boards: These can likewise be effective instruments when given strong state backing. All too often, citizen monitoring boards are captured by the institutions supposedly being monitored, but sometimes strong executive leadership and independently minded citizens can impose a degree of accountability. A good example comes from Mumbai, India, where in the early 1990s the nongovernmental organization (NGO) Rationing Kriti Samiti (Rationing Action Committee) set up groups of local consumers to monitor shops in the public distribution system, which were widely reported to gouge on prices, stint on quality, and siphon off public food grain supplies to private channels. Backed by the government bureaucrat then in charge of rationing, these vigilance committees were able to pressure shop owners to post prices publicly and offer samples for consumer inspection, while periodically reporting their findings to the city government.[10]

State encouragement: In 1994, the Public Affairs Centre, an NGO in Bangalore, India, launched a *Citizens Report Card* initiative, which surveyed some 1,140 households to assess their views of public service providers in such sectors as water and energy supply, transport, telephones, and hospitals. Not surprisingly, respondents voiced rather pessimistic opinions. A second survey in 1999 found matters improved, though less so than had been hoped. Municipal officials did take notice, however, and—especially after the second survey—undertook serious reforms to improve transparency and responsiveness in service provision. These efforts appeared to have paid off in a third survey taken in 2003, which showed among other things that citizen satisfaction with electricity provision had increased from 6 percent in 1994 to 94 percent nine years later. Similarly, satisfaction with water supply improved from 4 percent to 73 percent and with government hospitals from 25 percent to 73 percent.[11] The report card effort bears some similarities to the Mumbai ration shop initiative presented in the previous paragraph (for example, both were conceived and implemented by NGOs and involved no direct costs to the state), but in the Bangalore case, the critical factor on the state's part was not executive leadership but rather state responsiveness to the report card findings. Thus, although the state encouraged the experiment by being responsive to the first two reports, it did not actively support the Public Affairs Centre in its work.

Statutory endorsement: The ultimate accountability mechanism in a democracy, of course, is the genuinely contested national *election,* when the leaders and parties in power must receive judgment from the voters as to whether they should continue or be replaced by others.[12] The authority for elections does not emanate from executive leadership, legislative acts, or citizen activism, however, but rather from a country's constitution. Thus, they occur whether the incumbent president or prime minister (who may fear losing at the polls) wants them or not, and whether political parties (which may lose majorities) or civil society groups (which may lose special preferences) are eager or not. The machinery of the state is required constitutionally to furnish all support necessary for elections to take place. In addition, especially in new democracies, outside monitoring is often needed to ensure that an election is truly "free and fair." Elections, however, are at best exceedingly crude mechanisms of accountability. Voters can give only the widest approval or disapproval, at most delivering a mandate on one or two broad issues, such as ending a war or rolling back a welfare state. To exercise accountability on anything more detailed requires other mechanisms.

Legislative oversight: This provides a horizontal check on the executive and offers many opportunities for exercising social accountability. Parliamentary committees have statutory authority in many countries to investigate virtually any executive behavior and legislate corrective action if needed. For this kind of oversight to function, however, legislatures and legislators must move beyond the patronage orientation that presently characterizes so many of them.[13] Politicians who see their main interest as nurturing neopatrimonial linkages rather than pursuing a larger public interest are unlikely to employ this powerful tool.

When the State Takes a Passive Posture

The mechanisms discussed so far all require some degree of positive state action to function, but numerous others rely on citizen activism of one sort or another, with the principal requirement for the state being that it passively permit these engines to work. Another way to look at the active/passive difference is that the active mechanisms count on the state exercising a *supply* function, whereas the passive ones depend on *demands* being made on the state.

State acceptance: Although *civil society advocacy* has been recognized as a fundamental component of democracy at least since de Tocqueville's *Democracy in America,* it cannot by definition be a state-sponsored activity.[14] Civil society organizations do require acceptance by the state, however, which can amount to formal recognition or registration, special privileges (such as tax deduction status for donations), and in some cases even state financial support.[15] But once these steps have been taken (or in the case of informal organizations, even in the absence of such measures), the principal role of the state is to be open to civil society's demands and to respond to its advocacy efforts, which comprise a huge range of activity, from requests for information to lobbying state officials and legislators to large demonstrations.

In the end, it is hard to overestimate the importance of civil society as a social accountability tool, for after elections it constitutes the main mechanism through which citizens hold the state to account for what it does and does not do. Equally important, whereas elections form a very blunt instrument for determining who will manage the state, civil society inputs can be as finely honed as the situation requires (for example, neighborhood citizens demanding that a town council repair the water distribution system in their part of town). But civil society does not form a social accountability tool just by existing, for it is all too easy for a small group of elite voices to dominate inputs to state decision making. To be effective, civil society must be genuinely pluralistic and competitive, so that all can participate.

State consent: Many legal systems, especially those in the common law tradition, allow *public interest lawsuits,* in which a citizen can bring legal action to compel the state to implement what it is statutorily required to do. In allowing such suits, the state has given its consent for citizens to launch efforts to demand accountability but otherwise does not assist them; the burden is on the citizen to make a credible case that the state has not fulfilled what the law requires it to do. A good example comes from Delhi, India, where a small NGO consisting mainly of a very determined lawyer, fortified by an environmental think tank and a media eager to publicize stories of municipal malfeasance, brought suit against the city government to compel it to implement laws long on the books regarding air pollution. The group's efforts took more than five years, but eventually the national Supreme Court ordered the city to phase out leaded gasoline, require two-cycle engines to use premixed (less polluting) fuel, and buy buses using compressed natural gas as their fuel. Collectively, these measures produced a dramatic impact, reducing carbon monoxide by 32 percent within several years and sulfur dioxide by 39 percent. In addition to a tireless environmental lawyer, requirements here were a truly independent judiciary and a free media.

Acquiescence: By publicizing state corruption, wrongdoing, and incompetence and in the process generally spreading embarrassing as well as personally harmful and even untrue stories about those managing state affairs, *independent media* are a constant thorn in the side of any government.[16] But although the press may at times be irresponsible and even licentious in de Tocqueville's analysis,[17] independent media are critically necessary to democracy, for they make public to all what otherwise only a few insiders would know, and the publicity puts pressure on the state to account for its actions and inactions. Without independent media, the entire edifice of democracy would soon crumble; they are its sine qua non. If it wishes, the state may facilitate the media's ability to flourish (for example, by subsidizing postage rates, giving access to television channels, or purchasing advertisements), but its main role is simply to acquiesce in allowing the media to follow its own path, even when the results are harmful to it.[18]

Disinterest: Privatization can be considered a SAM if it is carried out so that assets previously operated monopolistically become competitive in the marketplace. Privatizing a decrepit public telephone system with provision for encouraging new competition such as cell phones, for example, could greatly improve and expand phone service. Competition between landline systems and multiple cell phone networks would maintain accountability through the market. Some kind of executive decision or legislative act would be needed to set the process in motion, and some sort of regulation would probably be necessary to preclude oligopolistic tendencies, but the basic state posture here would be one of disinterest.

State forbearance: With the media, the state must acquiesce in permitting bad news to emerge, but this is counterbalanced by the media's role in giving a platform to state leaders, publicizing government programs, disseminating information of state accomplishments, and alerting citizens to emergencies. *Human rights organizations* constitute another mechanism that the state must endure when they produce bad news, but here there is no counterbalancing good news: Whenever groups such as Amnesty International or Human Rights

Watch issue a report, it is unfavorable (often highly so) to the state. For its part the state in turn can be sorely tempted to respond by suppressing domestic human rights organizations and banning international ones, but both kinds draw their authority not so much from constitutions or domestic statutes but from international pressure on the state to allow them to work. The state, then, is compelled to exercise forbearance in allowing these groups to function, even when it knows the results will be unpleasant. The only real way to evade the bad news is for the state to become more attentive to human rights, that is, more accountable.

Another mechanism requiring state forbearance is the *corruption report card.* In some ways, it resembles the citizen review board discussed above under the rubric of active state support for SAMs. Both are initiated by civil society organizations, involve surveys, need publicity to have an impact, require some cooperation from the state to occur, and entail no direct costs to the state. But whereas the Mumbai bureaucrat in charge of food rationing strongly backed the NGO undertaking the surveys and advocating conformity to state regulations, state officials rarely if ever welcome corruption inquiries, for obvious reasons. The Bangladesh chapter of Transparency International (TIB) sponsored a corruption survey in Mymensingh District during 2000, focusing on the primary education system.[19] Not surprisingly, the survey did indeed find significant levels of corruption. Students reported paying unauthorized fees for admission to school, books, sporting events, promotion to the next class, and the like, all of which are supposed to be free. Many of those eligible for the state's Food for Education Program had to pay a bribe to be admitted to it and were shortchanged in the program's grain distribution. In addition, almost half the teachers surveyed reported having to pay bribes to officials at higher levels.[20] Local advocacy groups founded by TIB then held press conferences and met with education officials to present the findings and urge improvements. Whether the education system will improve remains to be seen, but citizen awareness of its shortcomings has certainly increased.

Grudging assent: In some circumstances the right to protest publicly can mushroom into mammoth *demonstrations* threatening the state itself. There can come a time when the state must decide whether to put down popular antistate protests by force or accede to the demands of the demonstrators. Sometimes the state has elected to repress the demonstrators, as in Myanmar in 1990 and then again in September 2007, but in other instances it has given in, as in the two "EDSA revolutions" in the Philippines (1986 and 2001), when the military deserted the executive office or in Ukraine in 2004, when international pressure restrained the president from crushing the popular movement against him. In the latter cases, the state found itself compelled to give a grudging assent to the demonstrators and their demands.

We have now covered the entire SAM spectrum. In the next section, I will focus on where the mechanisms come from—what induces the state to support them.

Origins of State Support for SAMs

The first three origins of state support discussed below originate in the supply side of the governance equation. Ultimately, of course, they derive from demand originating in the society (for example, constitutions derive their authority from a country's citizenry), but in the present context, they create or enable SAMs to function. In other words, they deal with supply. The next two origins come more directly from the demand side of governance.

Constitution: Theoretically, the firmest source of support for a SAM lies in a country's constitution, which lays out the ultimate "rules of the game" for conducting public business. For constitutional authority to function, however, the government of the day must be committed to enforcing it. Most constitutions guarantee human rights, for instance, but few states are totally scrupulous in upholding such declarations. Constitutional assurances of free speech are also frequently abused, although less consistently than those regarding human rights. And although guarantees on elections are probably more consistently honored than those on either human rights or free speech, even these are often violated through vote rigging and similar schemes. International pressure can be helpful, as with human rights, but in the end political will at the top (in this case the will to resist the temptation to harass minorities and suppress dissent) is needed to make constitutions function properly.

Legislation: Although they are less permanent than constitutional guarantees, legislative acts may carry more strength in the short run, for they reflect the intent of the government in power. In the Philippines, for example, the Local Government Code enacted in 1991 radically reformed the country's governance at the local level and was enthusiastically implemented. Fortunately, succeeding national administrations in Manila continued to support it. In Bolivia, the Popular Participation Law of 1994 establishing an arguably more radical transformation in local governance was also vigorously implemented by the executive branch (which had initiated it in the legislature), but subsequent administrations were much less enamored of the law, and much of it languished.

Executive leadership: Even more so than legislation, executive leadership can be a powerful but temporary source of authority for SAMs. Mumbai's Rationing Kriti Samiti worked very well indeed under the patronage of a critical sympathetic bureaucrat, but eventually disaffected politicians sidelined the effort. In contrast, participatory budgeting in Porto Alegre was continued in place by several mayors succeeding its originator, but it depended on their goodwill and backing to endure. Without it, the program would fold up quickly.

Civil society: Unlike the supply-side sources of authority presented so far, civil society is rooted in the demand side of governance. Advocacy campaigns for women's rights or disabled children will go on as long as civil society organizations continue to back them, for although their success depends in significant measure on the responsiveness of state institutions, their authority comes from their constituencies.

International pressure: Human rights organizations also depend on demand-based, nonstate sources of authority but of a different kind. For here, certainly in the difficult cases, their existence is based on external demand from the international community. The post-election Nigerian government surely knew that the human rights team roaming the country in 2007 would release very embarrassing findings about violations relating to the January voting, but the government also knew it would be even more embarrassing to prevent the team from gathering its data, so the research was allowed to proceed. The report was indeed extremely critical (Polgreen 2007).

Deciphering the Spectrum

In the spectrum I have assembled (as shown in figure 4.2 and table 4.1), four modes of active state support exist for SAMs and six modes of passive support, with eight specific types of mechanisms spread over the active modes and seven over the passive modes.[21] Several observations can be made.

The most important mechanisms are not those where state support is most active: Of all the mechanisms presented in table 4.1, the most fundamental are *elections, civil society,* and the *media.* Without periodic free and fair elections, freedom for civil society advocacy, and an independent media, liberal democracy cannot endure, even in the short run.[22] Of these three SAMs, only elections are included in the active half of the spectrum, and even here, actual state support is minimal, essentially comprising the routine of operating the machinery for voting and counting. With civil society and the media, the state's main task is to refrain from interfering with the mechanisms in play.

A majority of mechanisms exist independent of state financing: Of the 15 mechanisms listed in table 4.1, fully nine essentially function with no state funding. Moreover, this assertion pertains to two (civil society and media) of the three (these two plus elections) specified in the previous paragraph as most critical to the sustainability of democratic governance. Thus although all our mechanisms are dependent on the state in some way or other, financial support is not in most cases one of those ways.

The level of state funding and level of state support are not tautological: At first blush, it might seem that state funding and state support must mean basically the same thing, for funding after all is arguably the strongest form of support: If the state seriously wants something, it will pay for it. A glance down the financing column of table 4.1, however, shows that all the "Yes"es are not at the top of the table, and of the two most expensive mechanisms—local government and elections—the second one is in the middle. For the state does not show its support for SAMs mainly through financing them but through the qualities running from championship through grudging assent that primarily involve commitment to democratic norms. To put it another way, state support for SAMs is not necessarily costly in budgetary terms (though, of course, it will be costly in terms of what the state will have to do in being accountable; after all, that is what accountability means).

All authorities for SAMs are contingent on other actors' support: Constitutions must be enforced, legislation must be implemented, executive officers must lead, civil society actors must advocate (and their constituencies must hold together), and the international community must demand entry for human rights organizations. None of these sources will continue in place on their own; all must be continuously attended to.

National and local levels mainly require different mechanisms: In the last column of table 4.1, it will be noted that two SAMs (civil society advocacy and popular demonstrations) come at both national and local levels, but the others are relevant only at one level or the other. For the most part, macro- and microlevels require differing mechanisms of social accountability.

Notes

1. This formulation sums up the definition in widespread use at the World Bank (Malena et al. 2004, 2–3).
2. The "state" here includes all levels of power holders, from nation to village; "local" refers to any level below the nation.
3. Although the positive extreme is admittedly rare, examples of the latter occur more frequently, as with the response of Myanmar's military junta to public demonstrations in late September 2007 (see Mydans 2007).
4. The attempt at rank ordering on the right-hand side of figure 4.2 and in table 4.1 should be regarded as tentative, reflecting a first trial run. The terms used here were chosen to show an ordinal gradation, but comments are most welcome. The English language provides an enormous range of nouns expressing various levels of support (significantly aiding the present exercise), but the degree of overlap between them is also very large (making the task of distinguishing between them harder).
5. Many accounts of PB have been given. Among the more insightful are Gianpaolo Baiocchi, "Participation, Activism, and Politics: The Porto Alegre Experiment and Deliberative Democratic Theory," http://www.ssc.wisc.edu/~wright/Baiocchi.pdf; Bräutigam (2004); Koonings (2004). For a summary of the Porto Alegre experience, see Blair (2008). The World Bank's Public Expenditure Tracking Surveys (PETSs) are somewhat similar to participatory budgeting, but PETSs deal exclusively with monitoring budgets decided elsewhere, whereas PB makes up the investment budget as well as monitors its implementation. See World Bank (n.d.), "Social Accountability Sourcebook," http://www.worldbank.org/socialaccountability_sourcebook/.
6. The literature on decentralization is vast. For two overviews, see Manor (1999) and Blair (2000).
7. See Pope (1996, esp. 55–59) for an overview of this institution.
8. Aries A. Arugay, "From Protest to Participation? Accountability Reform and Civil Society in the Philippines," http://web.kssp.upd.edu.ph/talastasan/papers/arugay_protest_to_participation.pdf.
9. In a sense, they brought far more accountability than their sponsoring president had intended, for the opportunities they provided to indigenous leadership inspired the formation of a coca growers' party that within a few years grew to become Bolivia's dominant political organization, ousting that same president from office and replacing him

with Evo Morales. For a more expanded account of Bolivian local governance, see Blair (1997).

10. See Goetz and Jenkins (2001); their findings are summarized in Ackerman (2005, 16). Eventually local politicians, frustrated at the disruption of their patronage networks, were able to disable the monitoring system, and matters returned to normal, but for a while the mechanism evidently proved quite successful.

11. Suresh Balakrishnan, "Holding the State to Account: Citizen Voice through Report Cards in Bangalore," http://www.adb.org/Governance/Pro_poor/Civil_society/PDF/Bangalore_Suresh.pdf; Public Affairs Centre 2003; Adikeshavalu Ravindra, "An Assessment of the Impact of Bangalore Citizen Report Cards on the Performance of Public Agencies," http://lnweb18.worldbank.org/oed/oeddoclib.nsf/24cc3bb1f94ae11c85256808006a0046/d241684df81fce2785256ead0062de10/$FILE/ecd_wp_12.pdf.

12. Joseph Schumpeter's (1942) insistence that contestation by election is the central defining characteristic of a democracy has generally been held as sacrosanct by the political science community in subsequent decades—one of the few pieces of conventional wisdom in social science not in serious danger of attack.

13. See, for instance, Barkan et al. (2003).

14. "Civil society" is generally defined at present along the lines suggested by Gordon White as "an intermediate associational realm between state and family populated by organizations which are separate from the state, enjoy autonomy in relation to the state and are formed voluntarily by members of society to protect or extend their interests or values" (White 1994, 379). See also de Tocqueville (2007 [1835, 1840]).

15. For instance, some Eastern European countries earmark a proportion of proceeds from state lotteries to civil society or permit citizens to allocate a small part of their income tax returns to the civil society sector. For a discussion of such funding (including attendant transparency issues), see Blair and others (2005, 21–23).

16. Witness British prime minister Tony Blair's outburst just before his leaving office in June 2007, calling the press a "feral beast, just tearing people and reputations to bits" (Cowell 2007).

17. de Tocqueville (2007 [1835, 1840], 147–54).

18. Modern states generally subject the media to some standard of libel and slander, permitting victims to seek legal redress against malicious and damaging falsehoods spread in the media, but these constraints have not significantly impeded the media's execution of a watchdog role.

19. Data in this paragraph are taken mostly from Shahnaz Karim, "Transparency in Education: Report Card in Bangladesh," http://unesdoc.unesco.org/images/0013/001390/139031e.pdf.

20. These results are scarcely surprising in the Bangladesh milieu, where corruption is common. After all, the country did rank as most corrupt among all the countries included in Transparency International's yearly index from 2001 through 2005. Equally interesting, however, is that the corruption levels reported in the education survey were not all that high. Less than 8 percent of families had to pay unauthorized fees for any particular service, and the fees involved averaged about $0.80 (which can be a significant sum for people living on $1 a day, to be sure).

21. As noted elsewhere, the spectrum presented in table 4.1 is subject to modification. There may be too many categories or (less likely) too few. The rank ordering may also need changing. Comments are most welcome.

22. See Diamond (1999, ch. 2; also 2002) on the difference between "liberal democracy" with its safeguards ensuring accountability and lesser types such as "electoral democracy" that have fewer safeguards. One might add that without the addition of freely functioning *human rights organizations,* liberal democracy cannot endure very far beyond the short run.

References

Ackerman, John M. 2005. "Social Accountability in the Public Sector: A Conceptual Discussion." Social Development Paper 82, Participation and Civic Engagement, World Bank, Washington, DC.

Barkan, Joel D., Ladipo Ademolekun, and Yongmei Zhou. 2003. "Emerging Legislatures in Emerging African Democracies." Paper presented at the annual meeting of the American Political Science Association, Philadelphia, 28 August.

Blair, Harry. 1997. "Democratic Local Governance in Bolivia: A CDIE Assessment." *CDIE Impact Evaluation Series,* No. 6, USAID, Washington, DC.

Blair, Harry. 2000. "Participation and Accountability at the Periphery: Democratic Local Governance in Six Countries." *World Development* 28 (January): 21–39.

Blair, Harry. 2008. "Innovations in Participatory Local Governance." In United Nations, Department of Economic and Social Affairs, Division for Public Administration and Development Management, *Participatory Government and the Millennium Development Goals,* 77–124. New York: United Nations.

Blair, Harry, Richard N. Blue, Andrea Feldman, and Carmen Luca. 2007. "Final Evaluation to USAID Project Support for Croatia's Non-Governmental Organizations (CroNGO) 2001–2007." Academy for Educational Development, Washington, DC.

Blair, Harry, Susan Burgerman, Duaa Elzeney, and Robert Herman. 2005. "Civil Society Financial Viability: Key Factors, Challenges and Prospects in a Changing Strategic Environment." Report for USAID, December. Management Systems International, Washington, DC.

Bräutigam, Deborah. 2004. "The People's Budget? Politics, Participation and Pro-poor Policy." *Development Policy Review* 22 (November): 653–68.

Cowell, Alan. 2007. "Blair Compares News Media to 'Feral Beast' in Angry Parting Shot." *New York Times,* June 13.

de Tocqueville, Alexis. 2007 [1835, 1840]. *Democracy in America.* Ed. Isaac Kramnick. New York: W. W. Norton.

Diamond, Larry. 1999. *Developing Democracy: Moving toward Consolidation.* Baltimore: Johns Hopkins University Press.

Diamond, Larry. 2002. "Thinking about Hybrid Regimes: Elections without Democracy." *Journal of Democracy* 13 (April): 21–35.

Goetz, Anne Marie, and Rob Jenkins. 2001. "Hybrid Forms of Accountability: Citizen Engagement in Institutions of Public-Sector Oversight in India." *Public Management Review* 3 (September): 363–83.

Koonings, Kees. 2004. "Strengthening Citizenship in Brazil's Democracy: Local Participatory Governance in Porto Alegre." *Bulletin of Latin American Research* 23 (January): 79–99.

Malena, Carmen, with Reiner Foster and Janmejay Singh. 2004. "Social Accountability: An introduction to the Concept and Emerging Practice." Social Development Papers 76, Participation and Civic Engagement, World Bank, Washington, DC.

Manor, James. 1999. *The Political Economy of Democratic Decentralization.* Washington, DC: World Bank.

Mydans, Seth. 2007. "More Deaths in Myanmar, and Defiance." *New York Times,* September 28,

Polgreen, Lydia. 2007. "Report Traces Twisting Routes of Power in Nigeria." *New York Times,* October 10.

Pope, Jeremy, ed. 1996. *National Integrity Systems: The TI Source Book.* Berlin: Transparency International.

Public Affairs Centre. 2003. "Third Citizen Report Card on Civic Services in Bangalore."
   Public Affairs Centre, Bangalore, India.

Schumpeter, Joseph. 1942. *Capitalism, Socialism and Democracy.* New York: Harper and
   Brothers.

TAN (Transparency and Accountability Network). 2002. "Walking through the Office of the
   Ombudsman: Defining the Job and the OMB Selection Process 2002." TAN, Makati
   City, the Philippines.

White, Gordon. 1994. "Civil society (I): Clearing the analytical ground, democratization
   and development." *Democratization* 1 (July): 378–89.

5

The Workings of Accountability:
Contexts and Conditions

Enrique Peruzzotti

The goal of this chapter is to analyze the different contexts in which the concept of social accountability in being applied. The first section analyzes the intrinsic links that the concept of accountability in general and the term social accountability in particular have with that of democratic representation. The second section focuses on the contextual prerequisites that must be present for the proper working of initiatives of social accountability under representative democracy. The third section concentrates on the applicability of the term to contexts other than representative. The chapter concludes with a short discussion of how to construct a favorable environment for the exercise of civic control beyond the boundaries of democratic representation.

The Introduction of the Social Dimension into Debates on Accountability

The concept of accountability is intrinsically linked to that of representation. It refers to a particular type of bond that politicians establish with the citizenry in so-called representative democracies as the result of the periodical act of political delegation that the electorate makes on elected representatives. In contrast with authoritarian regimes and populist or "delegative" forms of democracy,[1] representative democracies combine an institutional framework of authorization of political power with one oriented to ensuring the responsiveness and accountability of those authorized agents. Under representative government, the citizenry temporarily delegates its power to a group of representatives that are authorized to act with relative independence of the electorate. The modern idea of *free representation* inevitably creates a gap between represented and representatives that is crucial for the proper working of representative institutions. Mechanisms of accountability are designed to ensure that such separation does not result in unresponsive or illegal governments. The central question addressed by the concept of accountability is precisely how to regulate and reduce the gap between representatives and represented while simultaneously preserving the distance between political authorities and citizenry that characterizes the relations of representation.

A government is accountable when institutional conditions are in place that force public officials to disclose, justify, and perhaps be sanctioned for their decisions. The notion of accountability involves a specific form of exchange between two autonomous actors that can be characterized by three distinctive properties. First, the exercise of accountability is always *external*— that is, it entails an act of control by someone that is not part of the body being held accountable. Second, accountability is an *interaction,* a two-way social exchange between those demanding accountability and those being held accountable (the seeking of answers, response, rectification, and so on). Third, relationships of accountability presuppose *a structural asymmetry of power in favor of those who have the right to demand answers* (Mulgan 2003).[2] Delegation of power occurs only within a hierarchical relation: Accountability means that the principal has the right to withdraw the conditionally delegated authority.

Mechanisms of accountability have been classified as horizontal or vertical to the extent that they respectively correspond to the establishment of an intrastate network of mutual controlling bodies and agencies or to the action of the citizenry. *Horizontal mechanisms* focus on the workings and interactions of the complex machinery of internal controls established by the representative democratic state. *Vertical mechanisms* instead focus on the actions of nonstate actors. Two types of vertical mechanisms can be identified: electoral or social. The first one is usually the vertical mechanism that has traditionally commanded most of the attention of democratic theory: It refers to the controlling role played by the electorate through voting. The concept of social accountability, on the other hand, implies some sort of coordinated or collective action by citizens. The term social accountability thus introduces into the classical debate on accountability—which had focused either on the workings of state mechanisms or on isolated voters—the intermediate dimension of civil society.

Civil society might complement and expand the workings of existing mechanisms of accountability in two ways. First, civil society enhances representative government by adding new voices and concerns to the political agenda and by criticizing existing public policies and legislation. Second, civil society can contribute to improve the quality of representative arrangements by demanding effective legal accountability. By denouncing violations of rights or breaches of law and due process by public officials as well as by developing strategies oriented to improve the workings of the mechanisms and agencies that regulate and frame the behavior of political representatives, civil society complements and many times activates mechanisms of legal accountability.

The first group of initiatives refers to the political dimension of the concept of accountability and has been widely analyzed by the literature on social movements and the public sphere approach. The focus of this literature was fundamentally on the indirect politics of influence that has as its main arena a democratic public sphere. The campaigns of social movements to draw the attention of decision-making authorities to previously ignored issues were described as an informal and external system of sensors that helps the political system to remain responsive to the current concerns of the citizenry. In recent years, however, a new form of institutionalized participation has been developed in new democracies that expand the previous debate to include the creation of formal spaces of encounter of civic actors with decision-making centers. Social councils and participatory budgeting are two of the most successful mechanisms oriented to improve both the legal and the political dimensions of accountability. The role of civil society actors in many of the newly created spaces of institutionalized participation goes beyond the one previously attributed by the public sphere approach to include direct involvement of social organizations in decision-making bodies alongside state officials and representatives (Avritzer 2009; Seele and Peruzzotti 2009). Some of these mechanisms have been incorporated into the debate about social accountability.

The second group of activities revolves around the legal dimension of the concept of accountability and has been conceptualized as the politics of social accountability (Peruzzotti and Smulovitz 2006). The concept of social accountability draws attention to the initiatives of control exercised by actors such as civic associations, nongovernmental organizations (NGOs, both local and transnational), social movements, and the media that were commonly neglected by the literature on accountability. The politics of social accountability involve civic efforts with the following goals: (1) to monitor the behavior of public officials and agencies to make sure they abide by the law, (2) to expose cases of governmental wrongdoing, and (3) to activate, in many instances, the operation of horizontal agencies, such as the judiciary or legislative investigation commissions, that otherwise would not be initiated or would be initiated in a biased way. By exposing cases of governmental wrongdoing or human rights violations, activating reluctant state agencies of control, and monitoring the operation of those agencies, civic actors are making a crucial contribution to the enforcement of the rule of law.

Social Accountability under Representative Democracy

As argued in the previous section, the notion of accountability is intrinsically linked to that of democratic representation. More specifically, it describes a specific subtype of democratic relationship: the one that links public officials and citizens in a representative form of democracy. Thus, accountability relations in general and more specifically the politics of social accountability require for its existence and effectiveness a particular type of cultural and institutional context—one that allows for the proper functioning of a *representative form* of democracy. However, the concept of social accountability has also been exported to other types of relationships and contexts that greatly differ from the original framework in which accountability relations unfolded and developed. The term is frequently applied to relationships between NGOs and their beneficiary groups or to international organizations and local partners and groups. In this section, I will focus on the contextual prerequisites that need to be present to ensure a proper exercise of social accountability initiatives in a democratic domestic context. The next section will analyze how well the concept travels when applied to other areas of social life in which the term is now frequently used. Can social accountability flourish in contexts that greatly differ from the domestic representative environment in which accountability relations originated?

What are the contextual prerequisites for the development of social accountability initiatives? The emergence of a politics of social accountability is usually the result of the combination of a series of social, political, and institutional variables that illustrate processes of change within civil society, the state, and the public sphere that allow for the emergence and consolidation of actors and networks specifically oriented around demands for greater governmental transparency and accountability. Four variables can be distinguished that are important to bear in mind when analyzing the context within which initiatives of social accountability operate.

The first variable is *cultural*: the transformation of political identities in the direction of a culture of democratic accountability. This is a basic prerequisite for social accountability demands to emerge. Without a propitious political culture, there will be no environment for the flourishing of this sort of actors or claims. In Latin America, for example, the irruption of these new forms of civic engagement is related to significant changes in the political culture that helped redefine inherited understandings of democratic representation. The dominant democratic tradition in the region, populism, is foreign to the idea of accountability. Relations of representation under populism are built on a blind process of electoral delegation that shows an excess of trust in the leadership skills of the executive. The most distinctive phenomenon of the current democratizing wave is precisely a shift from such an authorization model of representation to one organized around the idea of accountability. The "accountability" model breaks with the "blank check" attitude of political delegation and introduces a healthy concern for the workings of horizontal mechanisms of "institutionalized distrust."

The politics of accountability is a direct outgrowth of the emergence of a more general culture of rights. Rights discourses, and the adoption of a citizenship model of identity, are the backdrop of any accountability claim. It is this culture that builds into society the moral authority to demand accountability from representatives. Without this process of democratic empowering, it is difficult for a relation of accountability between representatives and represented to develop, for, as argued in the first section, relations of accountability presuppose an asymmetrical relationship in which the rights of superior authority stand on the side of the citizenry, not of state authorities. Only the emergence of a culture of rights can thus empower the represented side of the equation and break with other forms of articulation between citizens and the political system such as clientelism or patrimonialism in which citizens are placed in a relation of submission toward public officials.

The second variable is *social:* It refers to the emergence of a sector of civil society interested in the exercise of social accountability as well as the development of a basic social infrastructure to support those new forms of civic engagement. In general, the politics of social accountability is carried out by two sorts of civic actors: protest movements and NGOs. Protest movements are usually the offspring of the mobilization of affected groups against breaches of law by public officials. The persistence of human rights violations under democracy in the form of police violence or crimes that remain unpunished often forces family and friends of the victims to mobilize to demand the activation of judicial proceedings. These actors, when they attain media visibility, are very successful at drawing the support of the general public, and often that support translates into mass mobilizations on behalf of their demands. Given their grassroots and reactive origin, many of these movements are usually short lived and unspecialized. They are, however, a very effective way to show in a vivid form how the accountability deficit directly affects the livelihoods of ordinary citizens.

A second type of actor is the NGO or citizen association. Unlike protest movements, NGOs represent a permanent and professionalized presence in the domestic landscape of many democracies. A crucial watershed in the agenda of social accountability is the consolidation of a network of specialized social organizations to provide crucial support for nonspecialized social actors that engage in protest and denunciation. The development of a network of social watchdog organizations that are thematically specialized and with significant professional skills is also important in creating monitoring agencies beyond the state that can effectively supervise the behavior of public officials and trigger fire alarms wherever a breach of rights or due process occurs. These might not be the most visible actors in the politics of social accountability, yet they are crucial in providing a professional infrastructure to other types of actors and movements that are frequently successful in drawing media attention and popular support. To be effective, NGOs must undergo a process of professionalization and specialization because they frequently deal with very technical issues and are in permanent contact and negotiation with qualified public officials. Once consolidated, the network serves as a think tank of civic organizations that is crucial not only for leveraging the asymmetries of information that exist between representatives and represented but also for developing autonomous proposals for institutional reform.

In those cases in which the domestic watchdog network is weak or underdeveloped, global institutions or actors can play a crucial leveraging role, providing political and technical support to civic actors that might find it difficult to establish significant domestic partnerships with other sectors of society or that encounter open resistance or social indifference toward their cause. In many areas, such as the environment or human rights, domestic civic actors have developed crucial linkages and coalitions with global actors to strengthen their domestic voice and influence.

The third variable relates to *the quality of the public sphere* of a specific democratic regime. As with the more general politics of influence, initiatives of social accountability require a minimum of constitutional guarantees to allow them to successfully intervene in the process of agenda setting. It is thus crucial that different claims go beyond a local impact to reach the national media. The presence of independent or watchdog journalism is essential for the success of any action of social accountability. Protest movements or advocacy organizations commonly view the mainstream media as a potential "strategic ally": The impact of any movement or NGO is directly proportional to the amount of media visibility it is able to gather. Civic actors aim to influence news coverage through a variety of media strategies that range from organizing demonstrations, sit-ins, street theater, and blockade of roads to more sophisticated orchestration of media events, campaigns, and conferences.

The recent development within the media camp of a niche of "advocacy journalism" sites or organizations represents a valuable addition to the politics of social accountability. Groups such as Periodismo Social, Infocívica, Red de Comunicación Ambiental de América Latina y el Caribe, and Adital are based on a productive partnership between journalists and social organizations to produce and distribute alternative reports of social issues that are regularly either ignored or underreported in the mainstream media. Such partnerships also serve to present an alternative framing of a problem or demand, one that challenges the official framing of an issue. Because public officials and agencies are often the primary definers of news narratives, they are able to draw the discursive boundaries of certain issues. Civic groups provide journalists with alternative narratives to official discourses and expertise.

The fourth variable is *institutional* and draws attention to the formal context in which civil society actors operate. Different dimensions of the institutional variable can be distinguished. *First*, a precondition for the exercise of accountability is access to information: Information is the basic input of any action of control. Several authors have argued that the information gap that exists between citizens and government makes citizen accountability impossible. Yet those authors overlooked the crucial role that the network of NGOs and other civic organizations play in developing alternative and independent sources of information. The information deficit must be challenged on two different fronts: (1) It is important to develop an associational infrastructure that could leverage the informational deficit that exists between government and civil society by developing autonomous sources of information and data gathering, and (2) there must be concerted efforts to generate greater governmental openness and improved public access to information.

A major obstacle preventing an effective civic supervision of state authorities in many areas is the lack of relevant, accurate, and easily understandable information on the behavior and activities of public actors. Although the presence of a social watchdog network of NGOs that generates alternative sources of information on government might help reduce the informational asymmetries between civil society and government, it is imperative to introduce legislative reforms to open up state agencies to public scrutiny and to reduce the costs of the processes of information gathering. Active right-to-know policies are required to generate accessible and comprehensible data on government.

Second, it matters whether civic actors demanding accountability encounter entry points within horizontal agencies. Social accountability requires a minimum of responsiveness on the part of the institutionalized system of horizontal controls. Initiatives of social accountability do not reduce themselves to acts of informal control but also actively push for the activation of formal accountability institutions. Especially in contexts in which some of the established horizontal agencies are reluctant to intervene for fear of political reprisals, the social pressure that civic watchdog organizations or mobilized social movements exert makes it difficult for controllers to ignore an issue or to refuse to take a hand in the matter. Given the complexity of the horizontal system of controls, and sometimes the superposition of roles among agencies, civic actors tend to initially engage in a strategy of "multiple activation" until they find a positive response from one of the controlling agencies. The establishment of meaningful and complementary links between social vertical and horizontal forms of accountability will inevitably invigorate mechanisms and agencies of control.

Third, it is also crucial to evaluate how well the interconnected system of horizontal accountability agencies operates to generate effective sanctions on wrongdoers. In this sense, although it is essential for civic actors to find an entry point into the system of horizontal controls to activate formal proceedings, it is also important that the responsive agency operates, in its turn, within a broader conducive environment of interconnected agencies that can put a formal closure to a demand or claim. Accountability usually relies on a complex institutional machinery and cannot solely be carried out by a lonely actor within the state system. It is fundamental that initiatives of social accountability not only elicit an institutional response but also eventually trigger a potential legal resolution that can put an institutional closure to the issue (by absolving or sanctioning those under question). This last issue is critical for preventing the healthy distrust that social accountability entails from turning into a corrosive form of skepticism and generalized distrust toward representative institutions. An institutional environment that systematically fails to provide an adequate formal response to social accountability demands is likely to generate social frustration and feed destructive antipolitical sentiments.

Fourth, it also matters whether the state has actively promoted the introduction of institutional tools that can help advance the practice of social accountability. Several democracies have introduced innovative mechanisms to promote civic engagement and supervision of various state activities. Public budgeting, public hearings, civic watch groups (*veedurias ciudadanas*), legal injunctions (*derecho de amparo*), and the like are some of the new instruments that have been created to facilitate the workings of social accountability.

Fifth, international regimes are broadening the scope of instruments to which domestic actors can resort to demand more accountable government. The adoption by national states of international conventions has introduced a useful set of tools for domestic advocacy organizations and movements, empowering activists to make claims on the state and force public agencies to meet the international standards adopted by the state. Global regimes thus create new opportunities to bring effective pressure on state officials and might help accelerate domestic institutional and legislative change (Grugel and Peruzzotti 2007).

Social Accountability beyond Representative Democracy

In recent years, significant debates have swirled around the need to extend relations of accountability beyond the classic representative framework within which they emerged. Issues of accountability have been raised in the global arena. On the one hand, international movements and activists have focused on the activities and policies of international organizations such as the International Monetary Fund, the United Nations, and the World Bank, pushing them to establish more transparent and more accountable procedures and behaviors (Clark, Fox, and Treakle 2003; Khagram, Riker and Sikkink 2002). On the other hand, the activities of NGOs have raised skepticism from different actors who question the claims of such actors to represent a global civil society. NGOs have been requested to subject themselves to the same accountability standards that they so vehemently demand of governments, corporations, and international organizations (Edwards and Hulme 1995; Jordan and Van Tuijl 2006). As a result of these parallel processes, a series of initiatives have been launched to introduce accountability mechanisms into organizations and actors that do not operate within the classic parameters of the representative framework.

The debate on the accountability of NGOs and international organizations has particularly focused on what is considered a primary deficit within both types of organizations: the lack of so-called *downward accountability mechanisms.* It is not that international organizations or NGOs do not engage in relations of accountability. In fact, a series of well-established accountability mechanisms and control devices over the decisions or actions of those organizations are in place. The problem, it is argued, is that generally those mechanisms are mechanisms of "upward accountability," that is, they are geared exclusively toward more powerful actors that have delegated either political or economic power in those organizations and that thus have the authority and the means to demand accountable behaviors.

Almost all international institutions are immersed in relations of accountability to those governments that participate as members of the institutions' executive boards and finance the organizations' activities. Multilateral agencies are formally accountable to the member nation-states that integrate the board of executive directors, and frequently the board's vote is based on a weighted system depending on each nation's financial contribution. Similarly, most NGOs have to account to their donors. In those cases a clear act of delegation of power is seen—be it political or economic power, or both—that conditions the exchange. The economic dependency of NGOs on external sources, for example, forces them to compete in an international philanthropic market. Donors thus have the opportunity of exercising ex ante and ex post accountability. In the first case, the establishment of filtering mechanisms on the pool of prospective applicants plays an important screening function. In the second case, the existence of evaluation procedures as well as the possibility of exercising sanctioning power also acts as an important mechanism of accountability. Because the evaluation that the donor makes about the performance of a particular organization will determine whether the donor will continue to support the organization's activities, the organization has an incentive to guide its actions by taking into consideration the eventual reaction of the funding source. As with elections, the "rule of anticipated reaction" applies: Anticipating the likely response of the donor agency at the moment of evaluating the final report, the organization decides to behave in a responsible manner. Similarly, the delegation of political power to an organization's board of directors is usually accompanied by the establishment of accountability mechanisms for the member states that are represented on the board.

Both of the previously described examples fit into what I have defined as the nature of accountability relations: a form of interaction in which one of the actors (1) holds claims to superior authority and (2) has the capability to demand answers and impose sanctions because the actor has temporarily delegated authority to a certain group of representatives. Whether it is political or economic power that is being delegated, such delegation implies an asymmetrical relationship that provides great incentives for organizations to be accountable. What happens, however, with other forms of interactions where the power relationship is tilted toward the organization? What happens in those cases of so-called downward accountability where the actors that are the alleged beneficiaries of institutional reforms to promote organizational openness find themselves in a situation of disempowerment? Can international institutions or NGOs develop *downward forms of accountability* toward those groups that are usually the recipients of their programs or are affected by the policies and programs they implement? Although it is usually assumed that a variety of mechanisms already exist by which members, boards, and donors can hold leaders or certain organizations accountable, a generalized consensus is found about the underdevelopment of mechanisms of *downward accountability.* Consequently, a large part of the debate has revolved around the need to develop and strengthen mechanisms of downward accountability. The use of the concept of social accountability in this context usually refers to attempts at building downward accountability tools from above by powerful actors interested in redefining their relationship to disempowered stakeholders.

Some of the examples that are frequently shown to illustrate cases of downward accountability refer to situations in which certain elements of an accountability relation are missing. This is the case, for example, of many humanitarian NGOs or social organizations that provide specific services to the poor or to populations affected by natural disaster or war. In such situations, no delegation of power is seen from the constituencies that are the subject of the intervention to the organization that is implementing the services or programs. Not only are the basic conditions of an accountability relationship not present (exchange among two actors, one of whom holds rights of superior authority, autonomy of the account holder, and so on), but we are frequently confronted with situations that are the very opposite of ideal accountability relationships: It is the NGOs or multilateral agencies that are clearly in the power positions whereas the targets of their intervention not only lack equal standing, but also too often stand in a relationship of extreme dependency in regard to the material goods or services that the organizations provide. In those cases in which the exchange stops short of being an exchange between equals (or even less an exchange where the targets of the accountability mechanism are autonomously exerting rights of superior authority), the interactions cannot be fully framed as an exercise of accountability. Changes might contribute to develop much-needed feedback from the targeted populations or might help to develop mechanisms of organizational self-evaluation, although these cannot yet be technically considered an accountability relation.

How can one construct a favorable context for the flourishing of *downward accountability?* As with representative relations, NGOs or international organizations can contribute to fostering a more conducive social, cultural, and institutional environment for social accountability actors to emerge. Briefly stated, the building of social accountability mechanisms demands a process that begins with the empowerment of those actors who will have primary responsibility for carrying the controlling roles. Fostering a language and a culture of rights in which accountability discourses and demands can eventually emerge is perhaps the initial step. Social accountability can grow only in a rights-based culture and, thus, presupposes a rights-based approach to developmental policies. Establishing incentives for the emergence of self-sustaining forms of autonomous organizations that can act as external controllers and provide outlets for independent voices is the second step. As I have argued, the exercise of social accountability requires the building of a basic societal infrastructure of watchdog organizations and movements. Finally, it is important to build a facilitating institutional environment that will ease public access to information and provide social actors with sanctioning power that could enable them to exert pressure for social or international organizations to perform.[3] Access to information, the building of institutionalized participatory arenas of interaction between civic actors and organization officials, and the establishment of some form of sanctioning mechanism are crucial for the proper working of social accountability tools.

The building of social accountability mechanisms can thus follow two different roads: It can be the product of autonomous initiatives from below by actors that view themselves as carriers of rights, or it can be promoted by more powerful actors from above that are interested in the building of a social and institutional environment to exercise accountability. Of course, social accountability cannot be exercised if there are no empowered and autonomous social actors. Yet international organizations and NGOs can play an important role in creating the preconditions for the emergence of such actors through education, the building of civic capacities, and the creation of institutional tools to leverage power relations, providing voice and sanctioning power to previously ignored social actors. The building of social accountability mechanisms should be seen as an important tool for the promotion of a rights-based approach to development, for it will not only allow officials to gain important insights into the impact of their decisions and policies on the people directly affected, but, more important, also serve to trigger a process of mutual learning and synergy between developmental actors and the communities in which they operate.

Notes

1. For some of the features of the representative bond in those regimes see De la Torre (2000), De la Torre and Peruzzotti (2008), and O'Donnell (1994).
2. This is an aspect of the notion of accountability that is sometimes overlooked when the concept is "exported" into other areas of social life, such as the current debate about the accountability of NGOs toward their donors, members, and clients. I will return to this issue in the next section.
3. As illustrated, for example, in the creation of the Inspection Panel Board.

References

Avritzer, Leonardo. 2009. *Participatory Institutions in Democratic Brazil.* Washington, DC, and Baltimore: Woodrow Wilson Center Press and John Hopkins University Press.

Clark, Dana, Jonathan Fox, and Kay Treakle, eds. 2003. *Demanding Accountability: Civil-Society Claims and the World Bank Inspection Panel.* Lanham, MD: Rowman & Littlefield.

De la Torre, Carlos. 2000. *The Populist Seduction in Latin America: The Ecuadorian Experience.* Athens, OH: Ohio University Center for International Studies.

De la Torre, Carlos, and Enrique Peruzzotti, eds. 2008. *El retorno del pueblo. Populismo y nuevas democracias en America Latina.* Quito: Flacso Ecuador.

Edwards, Michael, and David Hulme, eds. 1995. *Beyond the Magic Bullet: NGO Performance and Accountability in the Post-Cold World.* New York: Kumarian Press.

Grugel, Jean, and Enrique Peruzzotti. 2007. "Claiming Rights under Global Governance: Children's Rights in Argentina." *Global Governance* 13: 199–217.

Jordan, Lisa, and Peter Van Tuijl, eds. 2006. *NGO Accountability: Politics, Principles & Innovations.* London: Earthscan Publishers.

Khagram, Sanjeev, James V. Riker, and Kathryn Sikkink, eds. 2002. *Restructuring World Politics: Transnational Social Movements, Networks and Norms.* Minneapolis: University of Minnesota Press.

Mulgan, Richard. 2003. *Holding Power to Account: Accountability in Modern Democracies.* New York: Palgrave Macmillan.

O'Donnell, Guillermo. 1994. "Delegative Democracy." *Journal of Democracy* 5 (1): 55–69.

Peruzzotti, Enrique, and Catalina Smulovitz, eds. 2006. *Enforcing the Rule of Law: The Politics of Social Accountability in the New Latin American Democracies.* Pittsburgh: Pittsburgh University Press.

Seele, Andrew, and Enrique Peruzzotti, eds. 2009. *Participatory Innovation and Representative Democracy in Latin America.* Washington, DC, and Baltimore: Woodrow Wilson Center Press and John Hopkins University Press.

6

Associations without Democracy: The West Bank in Comparative Perspective

Amaney Jamal

Across the developing countries, a new discourse on civil society has entered mainstream politics. Scholars evaluating the potential for democracy in these developing states and activists seeking to effect democratic reforms have focused much of their attention on civic associations. They argue that civil societies help to hold states accountable, represent citizen interests, channel and mediate mass concerns, bolster an environment of pluralism and trust, and socialize members to the behavior required for successful democracies.[1]

International organizations have also clearly accepted the premise that strong civic groups will promote democratization and political stability and have enthusiastically funded projects they deem useful for enhancing activities leading to civil society. Such organizations have the tools—money, influence, and the backing of the international community—to affect the growth of civic associations around the world. Of World Bank–financed projects approved in fiscal year 1995, for instance, 41 percent involved nongovernmental organizations (NGOs) compared with an average of 6 percent for projects approved between 1973 and 1988.[2] If participation in civic associations grows, the argument goes, so too will democratic forms of government—and all from grass-roots efforts.

In the West Bank, ruled by the Palestinian National Authority (PNA) since 1993, Palestinian associational leaders are no exception to the worldwide enthusiasts who have applauded the potential democratizing role of civil society. Leaders emphasize their commitment to achieving social improvement through their associations. As a Palestinian associational leader commented in

1999, "These goals [building civic associations] are important so that we can accomplish an overall development and obtain the building of a democratic society that offers all the opportunities in work and education and the availability of all the services and social equality."

These leaders are enthusiastic because associational life in Western democracies reinforces patterns of civic engagement that mediate democratic practices and forms of participation.[3] Several key features of these democratic institutions are directly related to the viability of civic organizations. Democratic governments, for instance, do not normally promote their own interests at the expense of the public, and citizens have avenues of political recourse for holding public officials accountable for misuse of public office for personal gain. Citizens of democratic polities, moreover, can participate in both politics and an associational life that is directly political. Implicit in current examinations of the effectiveness of associational life for the promotion of attitudes, activities, and belief systems favorable to the sustenance of democracies, however, is the understanding that associations and their immediate surroundings are supported by existing democratic structures, laws, and practices.

Yet these same Palestinian leaders also express concern about the ability of civil society to influence democratic change. In their accounts, by 1999 the PNA was creating realities that stifled the progress of democratic change. More broadly, many scholars in the rest of the Arab world in general have begun to question whether an active and vibrant civic polity will induce democratic change (Bellin 2000, 2004; Ismael 2001; Schlumberger 2000). This is a difference of practice and context and begs the question whether civic associations in the service of political reform travel well from the democratic West, where states are not embedded in societies as they are in the rest of the world. In states where government extends its overreaching arms into all facets of civil society, as is characteristic of many nondemocratic and state-centralized nations, governments intervene more directly in associational life: They promote specific agendas, fund certain programs, and monitor associational activities. Particularly in polarized nondemocratic nations, such as the West Bank economy and other Arab countries, ruling governments extend their influence by promoting associational agendas that directly serve their political mandate to the detriment of the general interests of the polity and of basic democratic procedures.

This chapter explores the relationship between associational life and democracy in the West Bank. Despite their role in Western democracies, I argue, civic associations—regardless of whether they are church societies or sports clubs—reproduce elements of the political context in which they exist and structure themselves accordingly. Where associational contexts are dominated by state-centralized, patron-client tendencies, then associations too become sites for the replication of those vertical ties.

By examining associational realities in the context of the West Bank economy during the height of the Oslo Peace Process (1993–99), this chapter offers key insights into the political conditions that promote or depress "democratizing associationalism." In the context of authoritarianism, associational life cannot be expected to yield the types of democratic values and outcomes affiliated with associationalism in Western democracies. This chapter examines in particular the relationship between associational life in the West Bank economy and levels of civic engagement among the Palestinian citizenry. Before we address this issue, however, it is worth examining more closely the argument championing civic associations in the democratic West, especially in the United States.

It is difficult to argue with the proposition that civic associations—the YMCA, the Elks Club, church groups, bowling leagues, trade unions, and so on—form the bedrock of modern Western democracies. The habits of association foster patterns of civility important for successful democracies (de Tocqueville 1956). Civic organizations serve as agents of democratic socialization. In *Democracy in America,* Alexis de Tocqueville attributes the success of American democracy to its rich associational life. Associations serve as "schools for civic virtue." "Nothing," de Tocqueville asserts, "is more deserving of our attention than the intellectual and moral associations of America. ... [In associations,] feelings and opinions are recruited, the heart is enlarged, and the human mind is developed, only by the reciprocal influence of men upon each other" (de Tocqueville 1956, 200–01). Scholars who follow de Tocqueville posit that citizens who participate in civic organizations are more likely to learn the importance of tolerance, pluralism, and respect for the law. Associational members learn not only that they have a right to be represented by their governments, but also that they learn more about their potential political roles in society (Diamond and Plattner 1996, 232–33).

Democracy and Associationalism: Revisited

The argument that higher levels of civic engagement are a product of associational life is the cornerstone of most contemporary literature on civil society. Active civic participation and engagement are necessary to sustain competent, responsive, and effective democratic institutions. Larry Diamond and Marc Plattner argue that "a rich associational life supplements the role of political parties in stimulating participation [and] increasing the political efficacy and skill of democratic citizens" (Diamond and Plattner 1996, 232–33). Hence, in democracies, especially Western ones, associational life helps instill values and practices essential to democratic governance.

Associational life also seems to increase the levels of social capital (networks and interpersonal trust) among members. In *Making Democracy Work,* Robert Putnam argues that trust and norms of reciprocity increase within organizations, thereby augmenting the likelihood of cooperative ventures among members of society as a whole. This increase in social capital in turn encourages people to "stand up to city hall" or engage in other forms of behavior that provide an incentive for better government performance. In Putnam's formulation, the density of horizontal voluntary associations among citizens (in contrast to the vertical associations under the dominion of the state) correlates with strong and effective local government: "strong society, strong state" (Putnam 1993, 176).

Associations also foster democracy by mobilizing ordinary citizens in the political process. They and other civic networks can serve as political catalysts, bringing constituents into mainstream politics. The competition among these organized groups in the public arena results in public policy initiatives. In this view, associations are critical in a representative democracy because they funnel constituency preferences to mainstream policy debates (Huckfeldt, Plutzer, and Sprague 1993; Rosenstone and Hansen 1993; Verba, Nie, and Kim 1978). Civic organizations also reduce the costs of collective action by serving as collectivizing forums that bring citizens together.

Finally, civic organizations with substantial memberships can place the necessary constraints on authoritarian impulses with the government. Civic organizations serve as key sites for political mobilization, recruitment, and expression, serving as counterweights to centralized governing apparatuses and encouraging sectors of society to oppose authoritarian tendencies. Associational life is particularly important in helping to hold states accountable, pressuring them to make more democratic concessions, and checking the powers of authoritarian leaders. In Eastern Europe and the former Soviet Union, for instance, civic organizations contributed to the downfall of communist regimes (Evans 1997; Huntington 1993; Przeworski 1991). This idea has been at the crux of much of the literature on mobilization, opposition-regime relations, social movements, and revolutions.

The relationships between associational life and democratic outcomes reveal an underlying theme: a convergence of changes in attitude among individuals at the associational level and increasing political participation within society as a whole, both of which are supportive of democratic outcomes. Associational members with higher levels of social capital exhibit a "self-interest that is alive to the interests of others" and therefore tend to care more about local community affairs. This in turn drives associational members to express their concerns through appropriate political channels (Putnam 1993, 88). Active associational members with high social capital are also more likely to cooperate with others in ways that support democratic forms. When local concerns arise, members are more likely to take their complaints to local government officials rather than develop clientelistic ties. When attitudes and behaviors converge through active civic participation, democratic institutions become more effective.

Associational life, the argument goes, not only promotes and consolidates democracies, but also makes democratic institutions stronger and more effective. Yet little attention has been paid to the fact that most of the research linking associational life to broader and more effective forms of civic engagement relies on evidence from democratic, mostly Western states, where autonomous interest groups already exist and are able to influence government in bottom-up fashion.[4] These studies conclude that in democracies associational life is important in enhancing the generation of specific qualities important for democratic citizenship, such as political efficacy, interpersonal trust, moderation, and support for democratic institutions and forms of political participation. The assumption that democratic institutions and autonomous interest groups *already exist* is embedded in the causal mechanisms linking individuals, at the associational level, to broader and more collective forms of participation that support institutional democratic outcomes. However, how could higher levels of civic engagement lead to more conscientious voters, for example, if the right to vote freely is not already guaranteed?

The causal mechanisms that link associational members to broader forms of political participation within democracies depend on the availability of democratic participatory institutions. The posited relationship between civic associations and democracy is a circular and self-reinforcing relationship. Democratic socialization, the promotion of social capital that enables broader forms of democratic participation, and the mobilization of interests through democratic channels are all based on an unexamined norm of democracy: Associations will promote the attitudes and behaviors important for members to make use of *existing* democratic political institutions.[5] The relationships between higher levels of civic engagement and more effective democratic governance therefore shape and reinforce one another in an endogenous relationship. Democratic institutions shape the way associations link their members to broader forms of political participation. Associations also instill attitudes and behaviors supportive of the available democratic structures in society.

Putnam has found that interpersonal trust is valuable for enhancing behavior that supports democratic rule. Higher levels of interpersonal trust also work to reinforce democratic rule, but they may be less applicable to nondemocratic settings. In nondemocratic states, indeed, it is not clear how social capital can enhance the democratic governance of a regime. Social capital in democratic settings may create opportunities for citizens to collectively seek the help of democratic institutions and thus legitimate these democratic institutions. This may also be true in nondemocratic regions, where higher levels of social trust can enable citizens to seek out local public officials through any available avenue—whether formal (directly through the state) or informal (through clientelistic channels). Seeking the help of local public officials in this manner similarly legitimizes authoritarian state behaviors and clientelistic channels. Just as associational life in northern Italy promotes civic engagement in ways that are important for the efficiency of northern Italy's local governance, so too does associational life in southern Italy promote civic engagement in ways that sustain the inefficiency of local governance in southern Italy. Does the lack of social capital in southern Italy promote ineffective democratic institutions? Or do ineffective democratic institutions promote levels of civic engagement, including social capital, supportive of nondemocratic procedures and institutions? If the latter is true, I posit, then social capital can be important in the reinforcement of any government in power, regardless of whether it is democratic or nondemocratic.

So Western democracies, where states are not embedded in their societies, differ from nondemocratic states in the Arab world (and elsewhere) in important and marked ways. Most notably, in Western democracies, autonomous interest groups already exist, channels of political participation are already guaranteed, and blatant clientelism, patronage, and corruption play a less important role in everyday political life than they do in the Arab world. What, then, is to be said about the role of associations in enhancing levels of civic engagement in nondemocratic settings, such as the West Bank economy, where existing political institutions do not support the types of civic participation associated with more effective democracy?

Open to question, then, is the premise that civic associations will promote democracy unequivocally across the board. Putnam, for one, argues that "those concerned with democracy and development in the South [Italy] ... should be building a more civic community" (Putnam 1993, 185). In Putnam's argument, such community should result from a higher degree of associational participation. Implicit in this is the correspondence of higher levels of social capital with higher levels of support for democratic procedures and norms. Other scholars make the same point, with similar implications. Larry Diamond and Marc Plattner write that "associational life can ... promot[e] an appreciation of the obligations as well as the rights of democratic citizens" (Diamond and Plattner 1996, 230–31). It is inconceivable, however, that Putnam meant to correlate higher levels of social capital with support for antidemocratic procedures and norms—indeed, with anything other than democratic institutions and procedures, if the goal is more effective democratic institutions.[6] Furthermore, the improvement of democratic governance through civic engagement depends on the existence of associational life within democratic contexts where political institutions are both available and responsive. Otherwise, how would interest in local affairs promote democratic outcomes in areas where the channels of expression or the ability to lobby local representatives is either limited or inaccessible? In these areas, higher levels of interest in community affairs do not necessarily correlate with broader forms of political behavior that advance democracy or shore up democratic norms. The means to do so in each context are simply too different.

The Importance of Political Context

I am arguing that the overall political context in which associations operate shapes the ways in which associations may or may not produce democratic change. Too often, associations that house civil society are credited with heroic accomplishments without paying specific attention to the ways that preexisting state-society relations mediate associational activities and patterns of operation.[7] For example, in institutions where the survivability of associations is linked to regime endorsement, civil society can and in many instances does reinforce existing political regimes and not democracy per se.

Because political institutions shape both civic engagement and civic attitudes, the content and form of civic engagement will differ across varying political contexts. People engage their surroundings, which in turn shape attitudes and beliefs about civic participation. Although higher levels of civic engagement in democratic frameworks may lead to patterns of participation conducive to or supportive of democracy, in nondemocratic settings higher levels of civic engagement may not necessarily lead to similar trajectories of participation. Thus, the absence of accessible channels of political participation will not only hinder some forms of participation, but also shape one's attitudes and beliefs about participation. Individuals will develop opinions, attitudes, norms, and perceptions influenced directly by the political context in which they operate. Because patterns of political participation differ in nondemocratic settings, patterns of civic engagement should differ as well. Even within similar contexts, variation will exist among members' civic engagement according to associational interaction with the political world around them.

Associational Life in the West Bank Economy

The PNA, though ostensibly democratic, in truth mirrors much of the rest of the Arab world and is a classic authoritarian state that reinforces the centrality of the government through a network that includes both formal and informal patron-client relationships. Participatory institutions and strong associations do exist in the West Bank economy, but the PNA rules authoritatively, centralizing its power, and without clear provisions that limit its dominance. During the 1980s, for instance, the strategies of political mobilization employed by local elites dramatically expanded associational life in the West Bank economy. In the 1990s, international donor assistance contributed to the growth of the voluntary sector as well. Although participation in these associations has enlivened civic engagement, the relationships between the main dimensions of civic engagement (political knowledge, civic involvement, and community engagement), interpersonal trust,[8] and support for democratic institutions yield different returns from those anticipated from associational life in democracies. In the absence of viable democratic institutions that separate and decentralize authority, the same patterns of civic engagement that pave the way to more effective democratic institutions in *already* democratic settings may generate attitudes and behaviors in settings like that of the West Bank economy that either reinforce the prevailing political status quo or distance citizens from the regime in power. Furthermore, where centralized governing institutions, clientelistic ties, and local corruption restrict associational life, civic associations—depending on their relationship to their immediate political surroundings—will shape patterns of civic engagement that reflect an association's position within its political context. Thus, in some cases associational life may produce dimensions of democratic citizenship, such as support for democratic institutions; however, in other cases it may produce dimensions of engagement that support authoritarian rule, specifically, the ruling authoritarian government. I argue that the way organizations orchestrate and negotiate relationships with the political institutions around them influences the way organizations affect patterns of civic engagement, interpersonal trust, and support for democratic institutions among their members.

The existence of clientelism today "defies the modern notion of representation, where all citizens should be guaranteed equal political access" by mere virtue of citizenship (Roniger and Gunes-Ataya 1994, 9). Instead, clientalism provides clients with paths to exclusive services and influence in return for their support of their patron. It subverts the democratic process: the client who receives money to vote in a certain way, the individual who is granted political access because he or she supports the party in power, the woman who pays lip service to the state in return for benefits. The list is endless (Fox 1994, 151; Kitschelt 2000; Roniger and Gunes-Ataya 1994, 9). The PNA is rife with such relationships, which take the form of a pyramid-shaped clientelistic network characteristic of strong, one-party states. The major beneficiaries of clientelism in these states are regime affiliates. The second arrangement is what I will call the diffused clientelistic model, and it relies on a less centralized government apparatus. In this latter model, clientelism permeates virtually all social arenas. Electoral clientelism, factional clientelism, and business clientelism are examples of scattered clientelistic networks.[9] Power relations in these settings are distributed among numerous leaders. In the diffused clientelistic network, no one centralized nucleus of authority controls political access. In the pyramid model, the state is the premier patron, and secondary and tertiary patrons are directly linked back to the state.[10]

The impact of state clientelism in state-centralized regimes (those that extend to all domains of civil society) on the democratic effects of associational life is multidimensional. The parameters of this political context constrain associational life at numerous junctures. Primarily, state-sponsored associations receive immediate political access and benefits not accorded to nonstate associations. Clientelistic networks further reinforce vertical linkages between state leaders and citizens, at the expense of horizontal linkages among associations. This dual effect of centralized clientelism structures the ways in which associations interact with their political environment and with one another. Where associations derive resources and benefits from the state, they are more likely to endorse government initiatives—even if those initiatives are nondemocratic. Further, because associations are linked to the state, they rely less on one another.

State-centralized clientelism is characteristic of many states in the Arab world, and not just in the West Bank economy. Many of the regimes encourage "the formation of a limited number of officially recognized, non-competing, state-supervised groups," extending government influence to all facets of society (Anoushiravan and Murphy 1996). Arab countries tend to fit this category of states that exhibit both control and support of civic organizations. "It is textbook knowledge and hardly contested that Arab socio-political systems are characterized by strongly neo-patrimonial political rule and thus by asymmetric relation of superiority and subordination," argues Schlumberger. "This is paralleled in society at large by networks of patronage and clientelism that pervade not only the political realm but societies as a whole." States across the Middle East are so deeply embedded in clientelistic relations that, as Schlumberger goes on to argue, Arab civil societies are "in no position to impose reforms or even exert pressure to an extent beyond the control of the state" (Schlumberger 2000, 114, 117; see also Hamzeh 2001).

Centralization is possible because of the coercive, centralized capacity of the state (Bellin 2004). Kohli argues, "When the polity is organized as a democracy coercion definitely cannot be the main currency that leaders utilize to influence socioeconomic change" (Kohli 1994, 98). In the Arab world, the state is not held accountable because very few mechanisms exist through which non-regime-supporting associations can do so. Opposition is swiftly quelled or defeated. In these formulations, Arab societies are either in government-supporting networks or they are not. Ismael argues, "Throughout the region, states attempted to impose hegemony over civil society through oppressive and coercive measures administered through juridical, administrative, or security channels. In regimes that oppress and persecute political opposition, there is little room for autonomy" (Ismael 2001, 74). Without autonomy, there can be little room for viable and competitive civil organizations outside government networks. Any organizations outside state-centralized relations are economically deprived and cannot depend on formal institutions to represent their interests. Because these associations exist in centralized authoritarian settings, their ability to produce change is next to impossible.

Data and Tests

Does associational life in the West Bank economy promote desirable democratic qualities such as interpersonal trust and support for democratic institutions? What about other civic engagement indicators, such as political knowledge, community engagement, and civic involvement, considered important for democratic citizenship?

During six months of field research in the West Bank, I gathered data from three sources to test the proposition that associational life is related to civic engagement and civic attitudes supportive of democratic outcomes. In these data, I found evidence indicating that any assessment of the effect of associational life on individual attitudes and behaviors needs to take into account the overall political environment in which associations operate.[11] Using survey data and open-ended interviews with associational leaders in the West Bank economy, I examined (1) the difference in attitudes between associational members and nonassociational members, (2) the role associational leaders play in mediating civic engagement, and (3) whether different types of associations promote varying levels and patterns of civic engagement and civic attitudes.[12]

The Jerusalem Media and Communications Center (JMCC) administered the first survey instrument, a random assessment of 1,200 Palestinians. This survey measured the differences in political participation patterns and civic attitudes of both members and nonmembers of civic associations in the West Bank economy. The second survey consisted of 422 associational members in the West Bank economy. A more elaborate and extensive instrument, this second survey builds on the JMCC survey. This survey gathered data on five basic dimensions of civic engagement and civic attitudes: (1) interpersonal, (2) support for democratic institutions, (3) community engagement, (4) degree of involvement in voluntary groups (civic involvement), and (5) political knowledge.[13]

I randomly sampled Palestinian civic associations from a comprehensive list of approximately 1,100 civic associations in the West Bank economy, including women's groups, charitable societies, sports clubs, and youth associations. I obtained this list from the Birzeit Research Center in Ramallah.[14] Visiting more than 100 sites, I carried out more than 60 open-ended ethnographic interviews with associational leaders, observing their organizational functions in Ramallah, Nablus, Hebron, Bethlehem, East Jerusalem, Tulkarem, and the surrounding villages. I asked leaders a series of questions about their associations, the role of the leaders in the association, why leaders are involved, the types of programs within their associations, and the relationship between the different associations and the PNA. Although some leaders were comfortable speaking in English, I administered the majority of interviews in Arabic. Of the more than 60 associational leaders I initially interviewed, only 42 qualified for the data analysis of this study.[15] I randomly sampled 10 to 15 members from each of the 42 associations included in this study. This sample of associational members answered a survey instrument prepared in Arabic to obtain information on civic attitudes, behaviors, and activities. The associations in this study represent areas from across the West Bank economy, and pertinent control variables include source of funding, socioeconomic status, and proximity to the PNA.[16]

Findings

An examination of the impact of associational life on levels of interpersonal trust, based on a random sample of 1,200 Palestinians, corroborates what most of the literature on associational life claims (see table 6.1). The expected relationship between participation in voluntary associations and levels of interpersonal trust emerges clearly in some of the polling data from 1999. We can use a logistic regression model to assess the effects of associational participation on trust, controlling for pertinent demographic variables such as education, gender, age, and reported employment status. The results suggest that associational membership has an independent, positive effect on levels of interpersonal trust.

To understand the real dynamics of associational life, however, one must disaggregate the evidence and look more carefully at the kinds of associations to which people belong. My survey of 422 associational members in West Bank economy civic organizations, which cut across a wide variety of associational and socioeconomic typologies, indicates that higher levels of interpersonal trust are inversely related to support for democratic institutions and other important indicators of civic engagement.[17]

Examining Interpersonal Trust

Although current studies on interpersonal trust—such as Putnam's (1993) *Making Democracy Work*—do capture intrasocietal variations among social capital, they do not underscore the effect that political context has on this variation. Many studies emphasize associational types but do not extend their studies to either the associational terrain or the roles associations play within their immediate political environments. The nondemocratic nature of PNA rule undermines any checks or barriers to clientelism and patronage. That the PNA is not confined or restricted to democratic institutions allows it to

Table 6.1. OLS Regression Analysis of the Relationship between Demographic Variables and Levels of Interpersonal Trust among the General Palestinian Population

	Interpersonal trust
Associational member	0.126***/(0.049)
Work	0.051/(0.047)
Gender	0.036/(0.045)
Education	−0.068***/(0.018)
Age	0.001/(0.002)
Constant	3.25**/(0.160)
R^2	0.0157
N	1,022

Source: Author.
Note: See the appendixes to this book for operationalization.
**significant at the 0.05 level; ***significant at the 0.01 level.

continue to support its clients, granting them special permissions and rights, while denying those basic rights to non-PNA supporters. The current PNA (in 2010) is more restricted by the rule of law but continues to enjoy significant levels of immunity.

The associational terrain in the West Bank economy is highly affected by Fatah mobilization strategies. Fatah has a significant presence on the associational scene, and its associations generate considerable support for the PNA. These associations also access the PNA's clientelistic networks, thus linking their members to the broader institutions of the PNA and reaping rewards, benefits, and political access for their support. Levels of interpersonal trust among these winners are higher than among nonclientelistic members. As supporters of the PNA, they are noticeably less enthusiastic about democratic reform.

The impact that associational life has on trust, therefore, is not equally structured. Levels of trust are shaped by the degree of clientelism (support for PNA) within relationships between associations and the PNA (see table 6.2). Further, levels of trust correspond neither to any of the pertinent indicators of civic engagement nor to support for democratic institutions. This flies in the face of the expectations of the existing literature on civic associations and democracies. Associations that serve as clientelistic gateways themselves provide the context in which individuals trust others, yet these associations do little to promote their patterns of civic engagement or engage support for democratic institutions.

Scholarly works on interpersonal trust link it to active levels of civic engagement; the more one engages in democratic civic life, the more one trusts (and vice versa; see, for example, Almond and Verba 1963; Inglehart 1990; Ulsaner 1999). In the West Bank economy, higher levels of interpersonal trust do not correspond to indicators of civic engagement such as concern for one's community, political knowledge about events and news in one's surroundings, and the degree of civic involvement (see tables 6.3A and 6.3B). Members involved with clientelistic associations achieve political access that

Table 6.2. Degree of Associational Clientelism and Levels of Interpersonal Trust

	Low interpersonal trust	High interpersonal trust	Total
Non-PNA-supporting association	72.46%	27.54%	100.00%
	$N = 121$	$N = 46$	$N = 167$
Semisupporting PNA association	69.57%	30.43%	100.00%
	$N = 80$	$N = 5$	$N = 85$
PNA-supporting association	53.97%	46.03%	100.00%
	$N = 34$	$N = 29$	$N = 63$

Source: Author.
Note: Pearson's χ^2 (2 df) = 7.3652, Pr = 0.025, $N = 345$. Coding for "PNA-supporting associations" category derived from open-ended interviews. See coding in appendix A.

Table 6.3. Measuring Interpersonal Trust, Support for Democratic Institutions, and Civic Engagement

A. Interpersonal Trust and Civic Engagement Indicators

	Community engagement		Political knowledge		Civic involvement	
	Low	High	Low	High	Low	High
Low trust	40.89%	59.91%	33.72%	66.28%	50.00%	50.00%
	$N = 85$	$N = 127$	$N = 58$	$N = 114$	$N = 112$	$N = 112$
High trust	35.35%	64.5%	29.55%	70.45%	41.58%	58.42%
	$N = 35$	$N = 64$	$N = 26$	$N = 62$	$N = 42$	$N = 59$
	Pearson's χ^2 (1 df) = 0.6401, Pr = 0.424		Pearson's χ^2 (1 df) = 0.4641, Pr = 0.496		Pearson's χ^2 (1 df) = 1.9776, Pr = 0.160	

Note: No significant relationship between levels of interpersonal trust and civic engagement.

B. Interpersonal Trust and Support for Democratic Institutions

	Support for democratic institutions		
	Low	High	Total
Low trust	40.61%	59.39%	100.00%
	$N = 93$	$N = 136$	$N = 229$
High trust	51.52%	48.48%	100.00%
	$N = 51$	$N = 48$	$N = 99$
	Pearson's χ^2 (1 df) = 3.3367, Pr = 0.068		$N = 328$

Source: Author.
Note: A significant inverse relationship exists between interpersonal trust and support for democratic institutions.

offers them representation, security, and protection, which increases their levels of interpersonal trust. Associational clients also reproduce hierarchical structures within their associations that mirror the hierarchy outside the association. These structures within the association produce forms of interpersonal trust not compatible with civic engagement. Further, in settings not guided by democratic norms of participation, the incentives remain low for members to collectively seek to engage one another to produce change or derive benefits from the state. Their demands and needs are already met through the patron-client network, so why should they disrupt a satisfying status quo?

For these same reasons, levels of interpersonal trust generated in clientelistic associations do not correspond with levels of support for democratic institutions (table 6.4B). Support for democratic institutions clearly undermines the methods of rule of the PNA, which provides its supporters with access, representation, security, perquisites, and benefits. Democratic reforms could undermine the very regime that supports the clients. If the PNA were to fall, what form of government would emerge is not clear, and Palestinians have had enough of chaos and occupation. Sticking with a satisfactory if not ideal situation is far better than risking becoming "losers" in a new political order.

Table 6.4. Civic Engagement Indicators and Support for Democratic Institutions

A. Associational Clientelism and Support for Democratic Institutions

	Support for democratic institutions		
	Low	High	Total
Non-PNA–supporting association	38.98%	61.02%	100.00%
	$N = 69$	$N = 108$	177
PNA-supporting association	48.17%	51.83%	100.00%
	$N = 79$	$N = 85$	164

Note: Pearson's χ^2 (1 df) = 2.9253, Pr = 0.087.

B. Levels of Support for Democratic Institutions and Levels of Civic Engagement

	Community engagement		Political knowledge		Civic involvement	
	Low	High	Low	High	Low	High
Low support	43.41%	56.59%	40.18%	59.82%	51.80%	48.20%
	$N = 56$	$N = 73$	$N = 45$	$N = 67$	$N = 72$	$N = 67$
High support	33.52%	66.48%	26.62%	73.38%	39.44%	60.56%
	$N = 61$	$N = 121$	$N = 41$	$N = 113$	$N = 71$	$N = 109$
	Pearson's χ^2 (1 df) = 3.1493, Pr = 0.076		Pearson's χ^2 (1 df) = 5.4458, Pr = 0.020		Pearson's χ^2 (1 df) = 4.8401, Pr = 0.028	

Source: Author.

Table 6.4 further explores support for democratic institutions as a function of membership in a clientelistic or nonclienetlistic association. Members in hierarchically structured clientelistic associations are less supportive of democratic institutions than members in nonclientelistic associations. Because nonclientilistic organizations are not linked to the clientelistic networks of the PNA, their participation is based on horizontally dictated exchanges with other members. As such, the face-to-face interactions increase their levels of civic engagement (table 6.4B). Community engagement, civic involvement, and political knowledge are all higher among higher democratic supporters.

Conclusion

Current studies of the role of associational life in promoting social capital and civic engagement useful for democratic outcomes address cases that have been guided by the democratic contexts of the studies. Most studies, that is, have been conducted from a perspective that assumes democratic preconditions. Whether higher levels of civic engagement and interpersonal trust lead to stronger democratic outcomes, I argue, depends on the intervening variable of an inclusively democratic polity. Such a polity not only guarantees citizens' rights but also restricts clientelism and guarantees that corruption and abuses of power are publicly addressed. In these cases, civic engagement reflects the preexisting democratic environment, and civic behavior is predicated upon established participatory conduits.[18]

Associations do not emerge and function within a vacuum. Where vertical patron-client relations are embedded in state-society affairs, and are further exacerbated by preexisting polarization and politicization, there is no reason to believe that the associational terrain will not conform to the environmental dictates. Based on this evidence, one questions the conclusion that civic associations necessarily promote democracy. In the case of the West Bank economy, the quantity of associations does not appear to be a significant factor in shaping civic attitudes. Rather, the nature of associational ties to the ruling government shapes civic attitudes. An increase in the number of associations in the West Bank economy will not increase support for democratic institutions because the existing political environment will segregate these associations into either pro- or anti-PNA camps.

Clearly, context matters. Only after we understand how different contexts affect patterns of interpersonal trust and their relationship to civic engagement will we have a nuanced understanding of the role of civic engagement in democratic reform. Crowning interpersonal trust with benevolent and unequivocal "democratic" residuals may be applicable in democratic settings, but it certainly is not in nondemocratic ones. Although the high levels of cooperation fostered by interpersonal trust are useful for the efficiency of democratic institutions, this form of cooperation is also useful to support authoritarian settings. Authoritarian leaders depend on their supporters and followers to cooperate to protect the interests of the state and its rulers. The forms of social capital praised in current scholarly discourses as useful for democracy are also useful for authoritarianism.

In this chapter, I demonstrate that not all forms of associational life are useful in promoting the type of interpersonal trust and civic engagement useful for democracy. I demonstrate that an overall assessment of the democratic functions of civic life needs to be juxtaposed with an examination of other pertinent qualities important for democratization, such as support for democratic institutions. In other words, interpersonal trust as a dimension of social capital on its own in settings that are nondemocratic reveals very little about the prospects of patterns of behavior important for democratization.

Notes

1. Abu-Amr (1996); Blair (1970); Clark (1995); Hadi (1997); Huntington (1993); Ibrahim (1995); Norton and Ibrahim (1995); World Bank (1994).
2. World Bank, "New Paths to Social Development: Community and Global Networks in Action," Working Paper 22339, 31 May 2000, 8 August 2002, http://lnweb90.worldbank .org/EXT/epic.nsf/ImportDocs/2CD962F09A155D5F852573BD005EE8F6?opendocum ent&query=VN.
3. Clientelism and corruption do exist in democracies; however, according to Piatonni, "[e]xisting democracies strike different compromises between the protection of particular interests and the promotion of the general interest, hence represent different mixes of particularism and universalism" (2001, 3).

4. Seminal works in this vein include Putnam (1993) and Verba, Schlozman, and Brady (1995).

5. The fourth claim, that associations can serve as counterweights to the state, is also applicable only in settings where civic sectors will not face harsh retaliation for advancing agendas that contradict or undermine the rule of regime in power.

6. As Fukuyama says, "[a]n abundant stock of social capital is presumably what produces a dense civil society, which in turn has been almost universally seen as a necessary condition for modern liberal democracy (in Ernest Gellner's phrase, 'no civil society, no democracy')" (2001, 11).

7. Berman (1997, 401) and Fung (2003) present discussions on the ways in which civic associations may operate against democracy.

8. In this study, I employ interpersonal trust to include as well a sense of responsibility toward others in society.

9. See, for example, India (Craig 2002).

10. See Hagopian (1994); Kohli (1994); Powell (1970). Discussion of the importance of centralization for clientelistic linkages between citizens and states. This definition largely incorporates Fox's (1994) definition of authoritarian clientelism. His definition captures clientelistic relations "where imbalanced bargaining relations require the political subordination of clients and are reinforced by the threat of coercion." My definition extends beyond that of Fox to encompass the centralized nature of authoritarian clientelistic regimes characteristic of many Arab states. Similar patterns are found in patterns of India's rule under the Congress Party in the 1950s and in Brazil under Arena until the mid-1970s.

11. I spent three months on this project in 1998 and three months in 1999.

12. The collection of all survey data took place in PNA-controlled territories of the West Bank: areas A and B, but not C. During the interim period, the PNA obtained full control and sovereignty over 17 percent of the West Bank; this Palestinian-controlled area was designated area A. Area B, consisting of roughly 24 percent of the West Bank, is under joint Israeli-Palestinian rule. In area B, Palestinians are responsible for all civilian affairs, and Israel is responsible for security matters. Area C, the remaining 59 percent of the West Bank, remains under full Israeli control and jurisdiction.

13. Questions were drawn from surveys that have already been used to measure levels of civic engagement elsewhere cross-nationally. I use survey questions that have been used by the National Election Survey (NES): Almond and Verba (1963), Verba, Schlozman, and Brady (1995), the Pew Survey on Trust, and the Public Opinion Service surveys on democratic culture. In some cases, I modified questions so that they address the particularities of the Palestinian case.

14. Because the Law of Associations had not been ratified in 1999, civic associations in the West Bank and Gaza economies were not required to register with any government office. As a result, some associations obtained licensing from the Ministry of Social Affairs, others from the Ministry of the Interior, and yet others from the Ministry of Justice. Once the Law of Associations was passed in August 1999, civic associations were to register with the Ministry of the Interior. Because of these circumstances, I was unable to obtain a comprehensive list of licensed associations from any government office. However, the list I did obtain was far more comprehensive than any of the other independent lists I gathered from the ministries, United Nations offices, and various other research NGOs.

15. The remaining associations not included in this study did not have sufficient memberships necessary for this study or did not operate in PNA-controlled areas. Qualifications for membership include frequent attendance requirements, fee payment, and the right to vote within the association.

16. See appendix A to this book for survey questions.

17. Members in civic associations come from all levels of the socioeconomic spectrum.
18. Not all associations in democracies influence members similarly. The content and form of levels of civic engagement in associations in such areas as inner cities and ghettos, where citizens may feel marginalized, oppressed, mistreated, or discriminated against, will be different in content and form than civic engagement in associations that are not constrained in these ways.

References

Abu-Amr, Ziad. 1996. "Pluralism and Palestinians." *Journal of Democracy* 7: 83–93.

Almond, Gabriel, and Sydney Verba. 1963. *Civic Culture.* Princeton, NJ: Princeton University Press.

Anoushiravan, Ehteshami, and Emma Murphy. 1996. "Transformation of the Corporatist State in the Middle East." *Third World Quarterly* 17 (4): 753–72.

Bellin, Eva. 2000. "Contingent Democrats: Industrialists, Labor, and Democratization in Late-Developing Countries." *World Politics* 52 (January): 175–205.

Bellin, Eva. 2004. "The Robustness of Authoritarianism in the Middle East: Exceptionalism in Comparative Perspective." *Comparative Politics* 36 (January): 139–57.

Berman, Sherri. 1997. "Civil Society and the Collapse of the Weimar Republic." *World Politics* 49 (April): 401–29.

Blair, Harry. 1970. "Donors, Democratization, and Civil Society: Relating Theory to Practice." In *NGO State and Donors,* ed. David Hulme and Michael Edwards. New York: St. Martin's Press.

Clark, John. 1995. "The State, Popular Participation, and the Voluntary Sector." *World Development* 32 (4): 593–601.

Craig, Jeffrey. 2002. "Caste, Class, and Clientelism: A Political Economy of Everyday Corruption in Rural North India." *Economic Geography* 78 (1): 21–41.

de Tocqueville, Alexis. 1956. *Democracy in America.* Ed. by Richard D. Heffner. New York: New American Library.

Diamond, Larry, and Marc Plattner. 1996. "Toward Democratic Consolidation." In *The Global Resurgence of Democracy,* ed. Larry Diamond and Marc Plattner. Baltimore: John Hopkins University Press.

Evans, Peter. 1997. "The Eclipse of the State? Reflections on Stateness in an Era of Globalization." *World Politics* 50 (1): 62–87.

Fox, Jonathan. 1994. "The Difficult Transition from Clientelism to Citizenship: Lessons from Mexico." *World Politics* 46 (January): 151–84.

Fukuyama, Francis. 2001. "Social Capital, Civil Society, and Development." *Third World Quarterly* 22 (February): 7–20.

Fung, Archung. 2003. "Associations and Democracy: Between Theories, Hopes, and Realities." *Annual Review of Sociology* 29: 515–39.

Hadi, Mahdi Abdul. 1997. "Decentralized Cooperation: Complement or Substitute to State-State-Cooperation?" Paper presented at the Research Group of European Affairs, February, University of Munich, Munich, Germany.

Hagopian, Frances. 1994. "Traditional Politics against State Transformation in Brazil." In *State Power and Social Forces: Domination and Transformation in the Third World,* ed. Joel Migdal, Atul Kohli, and Vivienne Shue. Cambridge, UK: Cambridge University Press.

Hamzeh, Nizar. 2001. "Clientelism, Lebanon: Roots and Trends." *Middle Eastern Studies* 37 (3): 167–78.

Huckfeldt, Robert, Eric Plutzer, and John Sprague. 1993. "Alternative Contexts of Political Behavior: Churches, Neighborhoods and Individuals." *Journal of Politics* 52 (2): 365–81.

Huntington, Samuel. 1993. *The Third Wave: Democratization in the Late Twentieth Century.* Norman, OK: University of Oklahoma Press.

Ibrahim, Saad Eddin. 1995. "Democratization in the Arab World." In *Toward Civil Society in the Middle East? A Primer,* ed. Jillian Schwedler. Denver: Lynn Rienner.

Inglehart, Ronald. 1990. *Culture Shift in Advanced Industrial Society.* Princeton, NJ: Princeton University Press.

Ismael, Tariq. 2001. *Middle East Politics Today: Government and Civil Society* Gainesville: University Press of Florida.

Kitschelt, Herbert. 2000. "Linkages between Citizens and Politicians in Democratic Polities." *Comparative Political Studies* 33 (August–September): 845–79.

Kohli, Atul. 1994. "Centralization and Powerlessness: India's Democracy in a Comparative Perspective." In *State Power and Social Forces: Domination and Transformation in the Third World,* ed. Joel Migdal, Atul Kohli, and Vivienne Shue. Cambridge, UK: Cambridge University Press.

Norton, Augustus Richard, and Saad Eddin Ibrahim. 1995. "The Future of Civil Society in the Middle East." In *Toward Civil Society in the Middle East? A Primer,* ed. Jillian Schwedler. Denver: Lynne Rienner.

Piatonni, Simona. 2001. *Clientelism, Interests, and Democratic Representation* Cambridge, UK: Cambridge University Press.

Powell, John Duncan. 1970. "Peasant Society and Clientelistic Politics." *American Political Science Review* 64 (June): 411–25.

Przeworski, Adam. 1991. *Democracy and the Market: Political and Economic Reforms in Eastern Europe and Latin America.* Cambridge, UK: Cambridge University Press.

Putnam, Robert. 1993. *Making Democracy Work.* Princeton, NJ: Princeton University Press.

Roniger, Luis, and Ayse Gunes-Ataya. 1994. *Democracy, Clientelism, and Civil Society.* Boulder, CO: Lynne Rienner.

Rosenstone, Steven, and Hansen, John. 1993. *Mobilization, Participation, and Democracy.* New York: Macmillan.

Schlumberger, Oliver. 2000. "The Arab Middle East and the Question of Democratization: Some Critical Remarks." *Democratization* 7 (winter): 104–32.

Ulsaner, Eric. 1999. "Democracy and Social Capital." In *Democracy and Trust,* ed. Mark Warren. Cambridge, UK: Cambridge University Press.

Verba, Sydney, Norman H. Nie, and Jae-On Kim. 1998. *Participation and Political Equality.* Cambridge, UK: Cambridge University Press.

Verba, Sydney, Kay Lehman Schlozman, and Henry Brady. 1995. *Voice and Equality: Civic Voluntarism in American Politics.* Cambridge, MA: Harvard University Press.

World Bank. 1994. *National Endowment.* Washington, DC: World Bank.

Section III
Information and Accountability

7

Necessary Conditions for Increasing Accountability

Arthur Lupia

The purpose of this chapter is to increase the accountability of public decision makers. It proceeds by focusing on conditions under which a target audience can be brought to demand greater accountability from those in power. In other words, if a target population thinks in ways that lead it to demand greater accountability, then decision makers may have a greater incentive to be responsive to that population's needs.

Increasing a target population's demand for accountability is not always easy. This chapter reviews a common challenge inherent in increasing a target population's demand for accountability. It then describes how to use insights from several social scientific disciplines to manage this challenge.

We begin by considering the challenge. Suppose that we want a target population to demand greater accountability at some point in the near future (Time 2) than they do now (Time 1). For the population to increase their demands between Time 1 and Time 2, they must be provided with information that leads them to think about public decision makers in a different way.

Our challenge begins with the fact that biology and chemistry govern important elements of this process. They place severe constraints on a person's ability to pay attention to many kinds of information. They also create important asymmetries in the kinds of things that people are likely to remember. As well-intentioned information providers ranging from teachers to parents have experienced, it is common for target audiences to ignore most of the information that well-intentioned people provide to them and, then, to forget most of the information that does manage to get through. People seeking to increase the demand for accountability cannot change these limits and asymmetries.

The challenge continues with the fact that many well-intentioned people (such as scholars or representatives of international agencies) who seek to help target audiences tend to blame these audiences for their lack of attention to, or memory of, the information that is being provided. My thesis is that in many cases the larger problem lies with the people who are sending the information. Instead of blaming the audience for not paying attention or remembering, people who seek to help the audiences should think about whether and how they can convey their ideas in ways that are more likely to gain attention and be remembered.

Hence, the question for us becomes *Under what conditions can we help a target population increase their demand for accountability?* In this chapter, I draw an answer from a framework that I have developed for the general problem of increasing civic competence. My main premise is that many people who attempt to increase others' competence develop ineffective strategies because they work from false beliefs about how people learn. They tend to rely on folk theories of learning that do not withstand scientific scrutiny. When their efforts fail, they blame target populations for their lack of motivation. In reality, however, the correctable part of the problem is the unrealistic expectations of the people who are providing the information. I find that applying and integrating basic social scientific insights about attention, memory, and strategic communication to problems such as increasing the demand for accountability can improve the effectiveness and efficiency of competence-increasing endeavors.

In what follows, I describe a means for helping organizations and scholars who wish to increase a target population's demand for accountability. After defining a dependent variable that allows us to talk about what such an "increase" constitutes, I then highlight two conditions that are often ignored but absolutely necessary to convert an audience that at Time 1 is not capable of demanding accountability into an audience that has such a competence by Time 2.

The first necessary condition is *the battle for attention and working memory.* If one person wants to increase the competence of others by providing information to them, the target audience must pay attention to that information rather than all of the other stimuli that regularly compete for their attention. The second necessary condition is *the battle for elaboration and long-term memory.* In short, even if a piece of information is attended to, it can increase competence only if it is remembered in a particular way.

Necessary Conditions

To begin this argument, I need to offer a few definitions. *Webster's New Collegiate Dictionary* defines a person as competent if he or she has "requisite or adequate ability or qualities." As synonyms, it lists able and sufficient. Webster's definitions for "able" include "having sufficient power, skill, or resources to accomplish an object" and "marked by intelligence, knowledge, skill, or competence." By civic competence, then, I mean a person's ability to accomplish well-defined tasks in the role of resident, citizen, voter, juror, or legislator. A target population's ability to demand accountability is such a task.

What conditions are necessary to help a target population gain this competence? For an answer to this question, it is helpful to think about the currency of exchange in communicative environments. I refer to this currency as an utterance. An utterance is a cluster of sounds or images that people use to convey ideas.

A layperson's view of human communication treats utterances as if they allow ideas to travel from one mind to another unadulterated—as if the ideas motivating the utterance are absorbed en masse. Yet this view is contradicted by a basic fact about human communication—all but the simplest utterances are parsed. People assign meaning to a word, a sentence, a paragraph, a speech by breaking it down and paying attention to some parts while ignoring many others (see, for example, Kandel, Schwartz, and Jessell 1995, 651–66). For example, when reading a newspaper or watching a television program, people vary in the attention that they pay to certain aspects of it; they do not simply consume all of the content as a whole—they pick the presentation apart.

If we want our utterances to increase an audience's competence at demanding accountability, it is necessary that the target population parse the utterances in a way that allows the information to change the beliefs they initially held. Many people who seek to improve others' competence proceed as if such persuasion is a seamless process for which known aspects of how people parse utterances present no important complications. An expansive scientific literature proves otherwise.

Many researchers examine why, when, and how one person can induce another to change his or her ideas. Psychologists conduct laboratory experiments on persuasion that document correspondences between the attributes of a speaker or his or her utterances and the reactions of the target audience (Hovland, Janis, and Kelley 1953 and McGuire 1985 are classic references). Economists construct models of strategic communication that clarify how factors such as self-interest and competition affect the credibility of utterances (see Banks 1991 for a review). Cognitive scientists develop neural networks that document the kinds of experience patterns or motivations that an organism would need to change its orientation toward performance-relevant objects (see Churchland and Sejnowski 1992). These literatures provide important insights about when and how persuasion can occur. As such, they provide evidence useful for understanding when we can help target audiences increase their demand for accountability.

Collectively, this work implies that if we are to succeed, then our communicative strategy must satisfy two necessary conditions:

1. The key points we want to convey must win *the battle for attention and working memory.*

2. The key points we want to convey must win *the battle for elaboration and long-term memory*.

The Battle for Attention and Working Memory

When one person attempts to convey an idea to others, the utterance is but one of many stimuli to which members of the target population can attend. In the battle for attention, an utterance must fend off competitors such as aspects of prior or future events with which a person may be preoccupied, the simultaneous actions or utterances of others, background noise, the color of the wallpaper, and so on. For the utterance to deliver a specific idea, the target audience must also pay specific attention to the parts of the utterance necessary to convey the idea. For example, if someone says "Colin Powell contends that the Iraqis have not disarmed" and knowing this fact is essential to accomplishing a specific task (such as demanding accountability), then the target audience must parse the utterance in a way that leads to its members adopting this particular view of the relationship between Powell and the Iraqis. If the target audience focuses exclusively on one aspect of the statement—say, it hears "Colin Powell" and thinks about his childhood in Harlem rather than his relationship to the Iraqis—then exposure to the utterance need not result in the target audience's acquiring the information that accomplishing the task requires.

The fact that paying attention to an utterance precludes attention to other stimuli in one's environment implies that attention is associated with opportunity costs. Such costs give people an incentive to direct their attention in ways that rationalize the sacrifices. They are why we are more likely to attend to stimuli that are most likely to cause a large increase in the pleasure one experiences or a large decrease in the pain than to stimuli that are more mundane. For example, people in the path of a fast-moving train have an incentive to direct much of their attention to any stimulus that will help them to avoid the train.

If we can convey our ideas to target audiences in utterances that provide greater decreases in pain or increases in pleasure than other available stimuli, then we will gain an advantage in the battle for attention. If, by contrast, the audience views our utterances less urgently, we should not expect to gain their attention. Even if they appear to be listening to what we are saying, they are likely thinking about other things. At such moments, persuasion is impossible, and our efforts to increase demands for accountability are likely to fail.

This fact about attention contradicts a common belief held by many people who have an interest in increasing a target audience's competence. Many people believe that information that is important to them must also be important to others. Political scientists and people who write about politics for a living, for example, are very interested in the names of certain officeholders or in particular parliamentary rules in the legislatures that they study. Some political scientists and journalists jump to the conclusion that knowledge of such facts is not only essential to professional political scientists, but should be known by everyone. They are frequently surprised to find that most people do not know the answer to these questions and have no interest in learning them. In many cases, target audiences have already figured out that they cannot act upon these pieces of information in a constructive way (Lupia 2006). Therefore, if the goal is to increase a target audience's competence and demand for accountability, it is essential to understand the kinds of information in which target audiences are interested in paying attention and then choosing the subset of that information that will lead them to make effective demands.

Other research provides important clues about how people choose the utterances to which they attend. Studies of the brain and language, for example, reveal that generally an exact correspondence does not exist between ideas stored in the brain and the words that one can use to express these ideas. Ideas are stored as activation potentials in neural networks. They represent associations between a person's body and their environment, but need not correspond directly to particular words. As a result, most ideas can be expressed in multiple ways. For example, we describe death differently to adults than to children, and we explain scientific phenomena differently to experts than to novices. In both cases, what we want to express is the same, but we must use different words to convey our ideas to different types of audiences.

So, if a speaker wants to persuade a target population to attend to a particular set of ideas, he or she has an incentive to condition an utterance on the audience's likely reaction. At the same time, the audience may have an incentive to condition its reaction to the utterance on the speaker's motivation for offering it. This is especially true in political contexts. If, for example, I know that you have the same preferences as I do on trade policy with Mexico, then I may use this information to derive a meaning from your utterance that I might have interpreted differently had I known us to have conflicting interests. Alternatively, my interpretation of your claim about the effectiveness of a particular policy may depend on whether I know you to be a conservative or a liberal.

When people choose how to express their ideas, this decision is properly described as strategic. When people think about how to interpret information provided by others, this too has a strategic component. When speakers who can choose how to express themselves interact with people who can choose how to respond, their interaction is properly characterized as strategic communication.

Game-theoretic analyses clarify important attributes of such interactions. These studies show that if a target audience perceives a speaker to have sufficiently conflicting interests, or no expertise on the issue at hand, then its members will ignore any utterance from that speaker (Crawford and Sobel 1982; Lupia and McCubbins 1998). The findings parallel efforts in psychology that identify speaker attributes that affect persuasiveness (O'Keefe 1990, 130–57).

Because an audience is often uncertain about these attributes, their perceptions of speakers' motives affect how they parse what they hear. Even if a speaker possesses information that can increase a target audience's competence, his or her low credibility with that audience may lead the audience to ignore his or her advice. When attempting to increase civic competence, "source credibility" is essential.

Above and beyond the attributes of attention just mentioned, there are the barriers to increasing competence posed by the physical limitations of short-term, or working, memory. Working memory (henceforth WM) is the activity in the brain where information from the world is kept available for access into long-term memory.

For our purposes, two WM attributes are particularly important: limited capacity and high rates of decay. Many scientists have examined WM's capacity. Although no exact agreement exists on the number of items (a.k.a. chunks) that can be stored simultaneously in WM, there is agreement that the number is less than a dozen (Kandel, Schwartz, and Jessell 1995, 664) and a high concentration of results suggesting that the typical operative limit is five to nine items (Baddeley and Hitch 1974). This means that at any moment, of all the stimuli to which you could attend, you must ignore all but perhaps six or seven. As a consequence, a substantial difference is seen between wanting someone's sustained attention and getting it.

These physical attributes of WM have many implications for how to (and how not to) increase demand for accountability. For present purposes, I will emphasize that the mere presentation of an utterance by someone who wishes to increase another's competence cannot be presumed sufficient for such an increase. In a world where any particular issue is one of many potential concerns, winning the battle for attention will be difficult. For a mechanism to increase competence in practice rather than just in theory, the battle cannot be ignored—it must be waged.

The Battle for Elaboration and Long-Term Memory

Once an utterance earns attention, it must be processed. If it is processed in certain ways, aspects of it can be stored in long-term memory (henceforth LTM) and retrieved for future thinking. If the utterance is ignored or is not processed in these ways, then it is—from a cognitive perspective—gone forever. If it is gone forever, it provides no basis for new beliefs, which is another way of saying that persuasion is impossible and that the utterance will not help us to increase a target audience's demand for accountability.[1] Therefore, a necessary condition for success is that the target audience parse the utterance carrying our key points in a way that produces a unique cognitive legacy in LTM.

The physical foundation of LTM is found in the distribution of specialized cells throughout the brain. Chemical reactions within and across these structures generate activation potentials for particular kinds of mental responses. You can think of activation potentials as corresponding to probabilities of recalling stimuli to which you were once exposed. Learning involves changing these activation potentials. The physical embodiment of learning that smoking is highly correlated with lung cancer, for example, is a change in activation potentials that makes you more likely to associate pain and death with smoking.

If one person's utterance does not change another person's activation potentials, then the utterance cannot increase the target audience's competence. An attempt to increase another's competence requires changed activation potentials. But not any change will do. The change must give the target audience the ability to accomplish a task (such as demand accountability at Time 2) that it was not able to accomplish before (at Time 1).

Several lines of social scientific research reveal how we can make better predictions about when an utterance will leave a unique cognitive legacy in LTM. Examples include the Elaboration Likelihood Model (Petty and Cacioppo 1986) and the Heuristic Systematic Model from Social Psychology (see, for example, Eagly 1993). The basic idea of these models is that if a person is sufficiently engaged with a stimulus (the central/systematic route of information processing), it will leave a stronger and more robust residue in memory.

When people take the time to contemplate what a speaker says (that is, when they generate internal counterarguments for the purpose of comparison or when they elaborate), these aspects of the utterance are more likely to be coded as distinct from prior aspects of memory. As Schacter (2001, 26) argues, "subsequent memory improves when people generate sentences or stories that tie together to-be-learned information with familiar facts and associations." These aspects of the utterance are, as a result, more likely to survive as distinct new memories. The alternative (peripheral/heuristic) route, by contrast, entails processing of details from which inferences are easily drawn (such as noticing that an endorsement comes from the Sierra Club rather than reading its argument). When an audience does not take the time to elaborate on an utterance, the utterance is less likely to generate distinct memories.

These facts imply that it can be hard to get participants in an educational setting to remember the parts of a presentation that teachers or organizers might want them to remember. To see why, think about the most important events in your life: your marriage, the birth of a child, times spent with your best friends, personal accomplishments, and deep disappointments. Chances are that most of these events took place over a series of hours or days. How much do you remember about them? Even if you focus with all your might, you can probably generate only tiny fragments of these critical events. Recall from LTM is not like bringing up an old document on your computer—which comes back exactly the way you saved it. There is significant decay.

People who seek to increase the competence of target populations are often surprised to learn about how little they can control what participants will remember. "The better argument," a construct that deliberative practitioners have used to characterize what participants will recall from a deliberative setting, can easily be crowded out in LTM by something else, such as an outrageous joke whispered between audience members. To scientists who have worked in laboratories, conducted experiments on thinking or learning, or rigorously engaged the evidence and logic of such literatures, the facts about cognition listed above are foundational elements of what is known about learning.

The competition among stimuli for a place in the LTM of any conscious human is fierce and ever present. Utterances that convey novel and immediately relevant information are privileged in such competitions (see, for example, Kandel, Schwartz, and Jessell 1995, ch. 21). For people who wish to increase others' competence, the implications of these attributes of attention and memory is that success requires an understanding of the problem at hand from the target audience's perspective. What matters do its members see as urgent? Regardless of how we, as scholars or representatives of international organizations, perceive our propositions or worldviews to be, our educational presentations will fail to increase competence if we ignore, or discount as irrelevant, the perspectives of target populations. In many cases, when a target audience fails to pay attention to, or remember, what experts have said to them, the fault for failure lies at least as much with the experts as it does with the audience.

Collectively, the research on attention, communication, and memory described above reminds us that different kinds of people pay attention to and remember different kinds of things. Therefore, an attempt to increase demands for accountability is more likely to succeed if it recognizes the challenges of winning the battles for participants' attention and memory. If people claim that they can increase the demand for accountability without thinking about the conditions under which types of people will pay attention to, and be influenced by, certain kinds of presentations—that is, if they claim that the science of learning and persuasion does not apply to the likely success of their presentation—this is a sign that the educational endeavor is likely to have little or no impact. The social science research agendas referenced above can help us speak to target audiences in more effective ways. They can help us increase the likelihood that a target audience can, at Time 2, demand greater accountability than when we first encountered it at Time 1.

Conclusion

Extant social scientific research has clarified important dynamics of attention and memory that can be applied to questions of how to give a target audience new skills. Scholars and practitioners alike can benefit from greater attention to this class of scientifically validated observations.

Note

1. I describe memory as a process in which a stimulus can create a new memory that is not necessarily the stimulus itself. My motivation for this phrasing is work on online processing, which demonstrates that a stimulus can affect beliefs (and attitudes) without the stimulus itself being memorized (Hastie and Pennington 1989).

References

Banks, Jeffrey S. 1991. *Signaling Games in Political Science.* New York: Routledge.

Baddeley, Alan D., and Graham J. Hitch. 1974. "Working Memory." In *Recent Advances in Learning and Motivation,* vol. 8, ed. G. H. Bower, 47–90. New York: Academic Press.

Churchland, Patricia S., and Terrence J. Sejnowski. 1992. *The Computational Brain.* Cambridge, MA: MIT Press.

Crawford, Vincent, and Joel Sobel. 1982. "Strategic Communication Transmission." *Econometrica* 50: 1431–51.

Eagly, Alice H. 1993. *The Psychology of Attitudes.* New York: Harcourt.

Hastie, Reid, and Nancy Pennington. 1989. "Notes on the Distinction between Memory-Based versus On-Line Judgments." In *On-Line Cognition in Person Perception,* ed. John N. Bassili, 1–17. Hillsdale, NJ: Erlbaum.

Hovland, Carl I., Irving L. Janis, and Harold H. Kelley. 1953. *Communications and Persuasion: Psychological Studies in Opinion Change.* New Haven, CT: Yale University Press.

Kandel, Eric R., James H. Schwartz, and Thomas M. Jessell. 1995. *Essentials of Neural Science and Behavior.* Norwalk, CT: Appleton and Lange.

Lupia, Arthur. 2006. "How Elitism Undermines the Study of Voter Competence." *Critical Review* 18: 217–32.

Lupia, Arthur, and Mathew D. McCubbins. 1998. *The Democratic Dilemma: Can Citizens Learn What They Need to Know?* New York: Cambridge University Press.

McGuire, William T. 1985. "Attitudes and Attitude Change." In *Handbook of Social Psychology,* ed. Gardner Lindzey and Eliot Aronson, 233–346. New York: Random House.

O'Keefe, Daniel J. 1990. *Persuasion: Theory and Research.* Newbury Park, CA: Sage.

Petty, Richard E., and John T. Cacioppo. 1986. *Communication and Persuasion: Central and Peripheral Routes to Attitude Change.* New York: Springer.

Schacter, Daniel L. 2001. *The Seven Sins of Memory: How the Mind Forgets and Remembers.* Boston: Houghton-Mifflin.

•
•
•

8

Information Processing, Public Opinion, and Accountability

Charles S. Taber and Everett Young

"Democracy is the art and science of running the circus from the monkey-cage," quipped H.L. Mencken in 1949. It's hard to disagree. While steering the ship of democracy would appear to be a formidable task, requiring the sharpest, best-informed, most focused pilots, both casual observation and a mountain of research results confirm that sharp, knowledgeable, and focused would not describe democracy's ultimate decision makers—the voters. Citizens prove to be politically unsophisticated, uninterested, and ill-informed. They frequently hold undemocratic values. They can endorse a broad principle on one hand and, on the other, a policy that would embody its opposite. Yet American democracy not only survives, but also thrives. And the monkeys still run the circus. Somehow, apparently dysfunctional citizens constitute a functional public. The ship does not run aground.

This chapter reviews public opinion research through the lens of individual-level information processing. We are *less* concerned with what results after the noise of public opinion "cancels out," leaving aggregate public opinion in its wake, and *more* concerned with how the minds of citizens process and respond to political inputs (see also Kinder 1998; Kuklinski and Quirk 2000; Lavine 2002; Lodge and McGraw 1995; McGraw 2000; Sniderman 1993; Sullivan, Rahn, and Rudolph 2002).

Public Opinion and the Democratic Citizen

The "democratic imperative," Donald Kinder (1998) writes, is to translate "opinion into action." By this view, public opinion is the lifeblood of democracy.

So perhaps we had better be certain such a thing exists: Do individual citizens in fact want particular policies, and can they authentically come to know, communicate, and act on what it is they want?

Opinion Formation

In a sense, ours is a discussion of "private opinion." For this chapter assumes opinion is generated by, and within, individual citizens: however insignificant a single opinion in the scheme of mass politics, when an opinion forms, this event is an individual's response to external and internal political discourse. Sometimes the citizen seeks out this discourse; more often it arrives unsolicited, or even unrecognized as political information. This information is interpreted, evaluated, and integrated by individual citizens into private political attitudes and beliefs by multiple processes, both conscious and unconscious—but all residing inside the individual. These attitudes become "public opinion" when the citizen acts on them—by voting, attending a rally, answering a survey, discussing politics, attempting to persuade. We recognize of course that politics may be a "sideshow" for most (Dahl 1961, p. 305). Indeed, many Americans may have little ability to trace the origins of their attitudes, and indeed whether their attitudes exist in stable and retrievable form remains in doubt. But the fact remains that the Enlightenment concept of democracy still regards opinion as something that inheres in individuals, and we intend to treat opinion formation as a process that occurs at that level. Before opinion becomes public, it is formed and held privately.

Sensible though this sounds, objections are possible. There is a respectable approach to public opinion that treats it as a collective, emergent phenomenon, drawing its political meaning (and coherence) only from the aggregate, after the "statistical noise has cancelled" (Blumer 1946; MacKuen, Erikson, and Stimson 1989; Stimson 1991). Some forms of this view argue that this emergent, organic phenomenon is fundamentally untraceable to individual members of the polity. Public opinion is reified into a thing unto itself, not unlike consciousness when viewed as distinct from its microlevel neural correlates. Taking this view is surely valuable where understanding the broad political *effects* of millions of opinions is impeded by the overwhelming complexity of individual-level processes. But we argue that in understanding the *causes* of opinion—not just the tendency of "mean opinion" to drift in response to certain types of social events, but also the reason people hold the attitudes they hold—this aggregate view is of limited use.

Some objections to our methodological individualism may really mean that individuals do not form opinions in a vacuum, that the opinions made public around them have profound influence. Hence, John Ruskin (2001/1864) says of the common man that "he thinks by infection, catching opinion like a cold" (p. 48). "Spokesperson for the herd" is James Stimson's characterization of the individual citizen (1991, p. 2). People are aware of a sort of average opinion that is located in or across the herd, and their own opinions are, both consciously and unconsciously, moved by this awareness—and feed back into creating this societal average. Widespread publication of polling data obviously helps to create people's perception of what the "public's opinion" is. Alternately, some high-profile event may drive opinions systematically in one direction or another. People were, for example, highly unified in their affects in the aftermath of the September 11 terrorist attacks on the United States. Similar conversations were no doubt repeated millions of times between Americans of many different ideological proclivities, both in private and in the media, helping to create a similarity of opinion across America. Moreover, propaganda may seek to manipulate opinions—and may move the "mean opinion" needle noticeably. All of these positions articulate a model by which some external force explains average public opinion without recourse to private processes.

But we think it is clear that such "forces" can act only through individuals. To the extent that the above explanations of average opinion omit individuals from the causal sequence, they eliminate important intermediate processes and break the explanatory chain (Greenstein 1969; Hyman 1955). External factors do not directly cause aggregate opinion; external forces exert their direct effects on individual information processors. Emergent opinion "organisms" have no inherent powers to receive and process information. Furthermore, there are times when the "collective" or average opinion is not of one recognizable voice, and variation among individuals demands explanation. Sometimes, opinions polarize. In these cases, it is hard to imagine satisfactory explanation without accounting for individual processes and individual differences in how political information is processed.

Opinion Aggregation

Once formed, how are opinions combined together to affect public policy in a democracy? The normative individualism of the Enlightenment yields a simple answer: as with votes, they are counted, with all individuals' opinions on a particular issue weighted equally. In keeping with this principle of *majoritarian aggregation*, the early view of survey instruments (Thurstone 1927) thus presented public opinion as discoverable in the marginal frequencies for a sample in meaningful response categories. Normatively, the modal response in those margins might reasonably be viewed as a democratic "mandate" for government. This view is still influential, but is questionable on both political and psychological grounds.

An alternate view, *weighted aggregation*, recognizes that individual opinions, in reality, do not carry equal weight. There are "power elites." There are "opinion elites," at levels ranging from the social circle to Internet bloggers to national television cable networks. A one-person, one-opinion account of public opinion is thus, empirically, a naïve description of the public mandate.

Even 50 years ago, when political cynicism was lower than today's levels, Robert Dahl (1961) deflated the myth of individual equality in a democratic policy with these words: "In a political system where nearly every adult may vote but where knowledge, wealth, social position, access to officials, and other resources are unequally distributed, who actually governs?"(p. 1). The idea that an empirically valid opinion aggregation requires differential weighting should thus receive stronger consideration than it has heretofore, and this weighting may even need to vary from issue to issue (Converse 1964; Lavine and Gschwend 2002).

Another explanation of how "private opinion" gives rise to an articulable public opinion—we will call it *compositional aggregation*—involves a deliberative process inherent to social discourse. In *The Rational Public* (1992) Benjamin Page and Robert Shapiro describe a *collective deliberation* in which myriad "conversations" among citizens—from coffeehouse tête-à-têtes and supper-table family discourse to dispensations from political officials and media elites, and everything in-between—sum to a "national conversation," with each individual contributing only bits and pieces to the whole, sometimes in the form of fully-formed opinions, but just as often in the form of questions, criticisms, or partial ideas. Individuals need not master even a single issue. The most interesting form of compositional aggregation views individuals as embedded in social networks, and dependent on such networks for political information and the frames through which they understand politics (Huckfeldt and Sprague 1987; Page and Shapiro 1992). According to Robert Huckfeldt and John Sprague (1995), "If citizens are seen as individually disconnected information processors, we are unlikely to make significant progress toward relating the study of individual voters to the larger study of politics and electorates. Alternatively, to the extent that the citizens are seen as being interdependent, then electorates become more than the simple summation of individual citizens" (pp. 290–91). While this "embedded citizen" view might seem at first unfriendly to the methodologically individualistic approach taken in this chapter, such a view would be a misinterpretation. The suggestion that opinions are formed within individual minds carries no suggestion that such minds are *autonomous* as information processors; indeed, the brain-centric view and its focus on automaticity can sometimes approach an outright denial of autonomy. Nor does Huckfeldt and Sprague's approach, which merely holds that individual information processors dwell in an information environment of which other individuals are an indispensable part, suggest that individual-level political information processing can be removed from the causal chain and leave an explanation of political opinion formation intact. The Huckfeldt and Sprague approach is theoretically unique in that it models aggregation on the *input* side of individual information processing rather than only on the output side.

Information Processing

It is possible to speak of individual-level opinion formation without taking account of individual citizens' *information processing*. A strictly *behaviorist* model does exactly this. The individual is conceptualized as an unspecified package of responses—a "black box"—and the responses that are "outputted" are seen as products purely of the environmental input stimuli. To account for individual variation, however, we need models that take account of the mental mechanisms that intervene between stimulus and response. A simple *perceptual model* is a first step in this direction. In this model, the individual's *subjective perceptions* of environmental stimuli influence the probabilities that one or another response output will be selected. A still more sophisticated view is a *cognitive architecture model*, which accounts for subjective perceptions and further attempts to delineate the cognitive processes—long- and short-term memory, attention, interpretation and evaluation of stimuli both external and internal, conscious and unconscious deliberation—that act on these perceptions to produce a behavioral output. In more sophisticated cognitive architecture models, mental activity and subsequent behavior might be seen to interact with each other and with the environment. Both of these latter two models are information-processing models, and are the theoretical basis for the work we will discuss henceforth. The "intervening mechanisms" presumably occur entirely by virtue of brain activity. Hence, they cannot be observed directly except perhaps by neurophysiological imaging of various kinds (Morris, Squires, Taber and Lodge 2003; Schreiber and Zaller 2001), and even then the processing of actual semantic meaning cannot be observed, at least with current technology.

We can lay out the basic assumptions inherent in the information-processing perspective as follows:

- Citizens are information processors embedded in an "information environment." Mental processing is interactive (i.e., responds to *and* contributes to) environmental and internally stored information.
- Information is perceived, stored, deliberated upon and updated—in symbolic form, i.e., not as raw data, but as concepts—by the "mind" of the citizen. The mind is viewed as a general symbol processor.
- Mental processes take time and effort. Timing and interference experiments can measure this aspect of mental processes, and offer a window into the workings of the mind.
- The symbol processing of the mind rests on an underlying physical substrate (the nervous system).

The dominant model of cognitive structure and processing today is the associative network model of memory. However, before describing it, let us take a historical detour to provide some context.

Historical Overview

The information-processing approach to human psychology is the intellectual offspring of several different influences. To begin, the Enlightenment concept of man is not to be minimized. Man as a "rational calculator"—a view taken to its apex in Charles Babbage's attempt to design a mechanical analytical engine—asserted the possibility of an intellect capable of transcending human nature. The mechanistic determinism of this machine's form and process is an important part of the story. Freud's mentalism, less acknowledged in cognitive psychology, was nonetheless important in establishing that mental events—even unseen ones—must be accounted for in any understanding of human behavior. In addition, early social psychologists' exploration of the organization of memory (Bartlett 1932; James 1890), higher cognitive learning (Tolman 1932); cognitive motivation (Festinger 1957; Heider 1946, 1958), and attitudes (Allport 1935) were instrumental in giving rise to what would later become known as the cognitive revolution.

By the 1950s, behaviorism and its refusal to account for mental states was proving unsatisfying as a way forward in understanding especially more complex behaviors. Edward Tolman (1932), though himself a behaviorist, showed that "shallow learning" theories (e.g., Hull 1930) failed to explain rats' ability to learn their way through mazes. Additionally, behaviorist theories seemed incapable of explaining language acquisition and the ability to solve complex problems; theories about mental states and processes were not so limited (Broadbent 1958; Bruner, Goodnow, and Austin 1956; Chomsky 1957; Miller 1956; Newell, Shaw, and Simon 1958).

While analogies between human reasoning and computing machines are centuries old, the advent of the digital computer is perhaps the dominant influence on the information-processing perspective. Its parallels to the mind are almost unavoidable, because it is an obvious and ubiquitous information input-processing-output device with which nearly everyone in the world is familiar. Herbert Simon wrote in 1980: "It might have been necessary a decade ago to argue for the commonality of the information processes that are employed by such disparate systems as computers and human nervous systems. The evidence for that commonality is now overwhelming." Humans were well prepared to see the parallels between computer and mind, and the *computational philosophy of mind* has unavoidably been the preeminent "frame" driving the cognitive revolution, even leading to a wholly new cognitive science at the intersection of psychology, computer science, and philosophy (Boden 1988; Feigenbaum and Feldman 1963/1995; Luger 1995).

While the cognitive revolution was raging in psychology, the discipline of economics was experiencing a parallel movement—rational choice—in which individuals' behavioral choices were explained entirely by the maximization of utility. To explain behavior, one posited a *homo economicus* as opposed to *homo psychologicus*. Seminal thinker Herbert Simon is largely to thank for tying the two concepts together by distinguishing bounded from substantive rationality (Simon 1978, 1985). The bounded rationality model of behavior was acceptable to many political psychologists and political economists alike, with the "bounded" part—notions of "satisficing" rather than maximizing, of limited information-processing or observational capacity—bringing, for some political psychologists, *H. psychologicus* into formal mathematical models through a wide-open back door. Some argue that a common acceptance of bounded rationality renders political economy and political psychology natural partners in the broader study of political behavior.

Cognitive Process

The associative network model of memory (Anderson 1983; Collins and Quillian 1969) is the dominant conceptual framework for modeling cognitive architecture, and it has influenced public opinion research even where theory is not explicitly based on it.

The Associative Network Model of Memory

Associative Network theory depends heavily on the architectural distinction between long-term memory (LTM) and working memory (WM) (Anderson 1983; Atkinson and Shiffrin 1968; Broadbent 1958; James 1890; Miller 1956). This distinction drives some of the most remarkable contrasts characteristic of human cognition: we have a seemingly unlimited memory-storage capacity, but retrieval is inefficient and unreliable; we can vividly recall events from early childhood, but have trouble finding the car keys we set down moments ago; we process staggering amounts of data automatically (nonconsciously, that is), but can attend consciously to so few items simultaneously that the complex and lucid thought to which philosophers aspire (and, perhaps, to which rational choice purists necessarily subscribe) seems almost maddeningly out of reach.

LTM provides virtually unlimited storage for recording experience and mental activity, and it is organized associatively. Processing in LTM is very fast and can occur along multiple parallel tracks, though recall may be limited by memory decay over time. WM is a short-term memory store for objects in the focus of current conscious attention, and it is quite limited in capacity. The limited capacity and serial processing of conscious WM are the primary reasons for a host of severe cognitive limitations on normative rationality (Simon 1985) that have motivated the rise of psychological models of public opinion. By contrast with severe limitations on conscious processing in WM, citizens can process a great deal of information unconsciously in LTM, a point of considerable interest in current research.

The bicameral model of memory so far is static and lacks a *process* for memory retrieval—the movement of information from LTM into WM. The primary mechanism is *spreading activation* in LTM. At any moment, all concepts in memory have *some* level of activation or arousal. Any mental processing—conscious or unconscious—causes and entails the raising and lowering of the activation level of a concept node. As a node becomes more active, it raises the activation level of its "neighbors." Finally, and most important, the probability that a concept will "pop" into conscious awareness (i.e., be recalled into WM) is monotonically increasing in that concept's activation level (for a more technical discussion, see Taber and Timpone 1996). Conscious experience increases the activation level of certain memory objects; reading about George W. Bush up-regulates the corresponding concepts in LTM, for example. (This conscious experience need not come from such an external source of course—it could itself come from spreading activation.) Next, activation spreads automatically to linked nodes, and from there to "second-order" nodes, and so on, in a "fan effect" (see Thomsen, Lavine, and Kounios 1996). Finally, activation decays rapidly. As conceptual nodes lose activation, they are less accessible for conscious processing. Some memory objects may, however, be quite chronically accessible (Bargh, Chaiken, Govender and Pratto 1992; Fazio, Sanbonmatsu, Powell and Kardes 1986; Neely 1977).

A Stage Model of Information Processing

The structural foundation of associative network theory has yielded a number of different models of information processing, but one common approach with applications in political psychology divides information processing into broad stages (Lodge 1995; Lodge and Taber 2000; Ottati and Wyer 1990; Steenbergen and Lodge n.d.; Taber 1998; Taber, Lodge, and Glathar 2001; Wyer and Ottati 1993), such as the following four.

- *Exposure and attention.* Information must enter WM—must be attended to—before it can influence downstream processing.
- *Interpretation.* New information cannot remain as raw data and, to have semantic meaning, must be *interpreted* in light of (be "mapped onto") existing knowledge in LTM. Thus given meaning, the information can influence subsequent processing.
- *Evaluation.* Attitudes are formed, like-dislike "ratings" encoded, summary impressions constructed, and updates made to all of the above regarding political objects such as groups, candidates, or issue positions. Thus, the evaluative implications of information give the information motivational power to drive opinion formation and behavior.
- *Storage.* Interpreted and evaluated information becomes knowledge for future "use" in further information processing when it is linked into the associative LMT network.

There are some drawbacks to the enumeration of stages, however organizationally tidy it may be. First, it implies a preordained sequence, with mental processing proceeding as though through lines of unchangeable programming code. Mental processing is not so orderly or so repeatable. Second, there is probably insufficient attention on automaticity—the steps as stated could potentially *all* occur within conscious awareness as controlled processes, surely an inaccurate representation of information processing. Finally, the general stage model is not a fully "working" process model of cognition. Although the various stages have been studied considerably, including empirical work, the actual mechanisms—the so-called elementary information processes (Payne, Bettman, and Johnson 1992; Taber and Steenbergen 1995)—remain underspecified and there is no consensus about their accuracy.

In sum, the information-processing approach is not new. Its view of man as symbol processor is the thrust of modern cognitive science. These symbol processors are embedded in a complex information environment, and mental processing is driven by—is *composed of*—controlled and automatic manipulations of information (which includes attitudes and beliefs), which can arrive from internal or external sources. Memory is of two kinds—LTM and WM—and, in LTM at least, is represented as organized associatively. At least one model represents information processing as occurring in four stages—attention, interpretation, evaluation, and storage. The following discussion of modern public opinion research specifically involves the first three stages.

Information Processing and Public Opinion Research

The attitudinal model of the citizen's psychology in *The American Voter* (Campbell, et al. 1960) was actually quite sophisticated, and perhaps for this reason, the cognitive movement in public opinion research has not been revolutionary, consisting in surprisingly large part of replies, or at least nods, to Campbell and colleagues. Given the longstanding concern with the structure of beliefs and the attitude constraint behind ideological thinking, the study of the cognitive processing behind these phenomena seemed natural.

Informational Inputs

What types of political information enter into the processing machine that outputs political behavior and opinion formation? Donald Kinder (1998; see also Sears and Funk 1991) identifies three types that may be of special importance to citizens as political organisms: "(1) the material interests that citizens see at stake, (2) the sympathies and resentments that citizens feel toward social groupings, and (3) commitment to the political principles that become entangled in public issues" (p. 800). We next consider each of these information categories for how they motivate citizens as political information processors.

Material self-interest. For both casual political observers and political theorists alike, the importance of self-interest in explaining individuals' political attitudes and behavior has seemed so obvious as to barely be worth challenging. No other motive has been as central for models of *homo economicus*, with even psychologists accepting the potency of egoism in explaining thought and behavior. Commonly heard explanations of people's political behavior are flavored with a cynical realism grounded in self-interest: *of course* people vote this or that way—it serves their self-interest! And yet there are reasons to doubt the empirical validity of this view (Citrin and Green 1990; Sears and Funk 1991).

Empirical explorations of the role of self-interest in political behavior confront an enormous up-front challenge in defining what is to count as self-interest, for however the concept is restricted—and definition necessarily entails restriction—it becomes possible to argue that the "essence" of egoism has been lost. The problem is most easily illustrated by the rather trite example of apparent altruistic generosity that nonetheless provides intrapsychic pleasure to the "giver." Does this pleasure render the altruistic act "self-interested"? And if so, what behavior is ruled out of this catch-all explanation of behavior? David Sears and Carolyn Funk, having conducted the most sustained investigation of self-interest in politics, resist such tautological and unmeasurable concepts of self-interest by quite reasonably restricting its definition using three criteria: interests must be tangible or material; the self involved is the individual or the individual's family; and only imminent outcomes, rather than long-term possibilities, are considered (Sears and Funk 1991).

And—in what never fails to surprise students of political psychology (and, we have found, continually does fail to convince them)—such short-term material self-interest, in study after study, demonstrates extremely weak effects, and often no effect whatsoever, on political opinions on a wide range of issues. Kinder (1998, p. 801) cites examples:

> When faced with affirmative action, white and black Americans come to their views without calculating personal harms or benefits (Kinder and Sanders 1996; Kluegel and Smith 1986). The unemployed do not line up behind policies designed to alleviate economic distress (Schlozman and Verba 1979). The medically indigent are no more likely to favor government health insurance than are the fully insured (Sears et al. 1980). Parents of children enrolled in public schools are generally no more supportive of government aid to education than are other citizens (Jennings 1979). Americans who are subject to the draft are not especially opposed to military intervention or to the escalation of conflicts already under way (Lau, Brown, and Sears 1978; Mueller 1973, 1994). Women employed outside the home do not differ from homemakers in their support for policies intended to benefit women at work (Sears and Huddy 1990). (p. 801)

Furthermore, while the fact that poor national economic performance has negative implications for incumbent presidents has been interpreted by some scholars as evidence of self-interested voting, individual-level analyses typically reveal this as an ecological error—general concerns about the economy trump personal finances in determining the vote (Kiewiet 1983). Ultimately, a litany of null and weak findings compels the conclusion that citizens' political opinions depend mainly on considerations *other than* material self-interest. Only when the material effects on a citizen of a public policy are large, unmistakable, and imminent does self-interest determine opinion—and even then, citizens' opinions are influenced very narrowly (e.g., property owners faced with a large and well-publicized proposed property tax increase may oppose the increase, but they would not be expected to be systematically turned against tax increases generally) (Sears and Funk 1991).

We've now labored considerably to establish the failure of self-interest to push people's opinions around. And yet, self-interest is not without effect in political information processing, for it *does* affect individuals' attention to political information. Citizens whose material interests are implicated in an issue do tend to regard that issue with greater importance than others, although evidence is inconclusive as to whether they consequently pay more attention to information relevant to that issue (Krosnick 1988, 1990). The elderly, the unemployed, blacks, and those in line for tax breaks or increases all place a higher priority on issues that concern them personally (Boninger, Krosnick, Barent, and Fabrigar 1995; Iyengar and Kinder 1987; Sears and Citrin 1982; Tomsen, Borgida, and Lavine 1995).

Group orientations. Could people's affinities for, and sense of belonging to, politically relevant groups explain what self-interest does not? For we have long understood the contribution of social identity to the development of social attitudes (Brewer and Brown 1998; Converse 1964; Deaux, Reid, Mizrahi, and Ethier 1995; Fiske 1998; Kinder 1998). Affiliations with religious, cultural, national, and other recognizable groups are powerful forces for shaping political opinion and behavior, as are "negative identifications"—attitudes we hold toward groups to which we do not belong.

And indeed, social group cleavages have been shown to have important effects on public opinion on disparate issues. One of the most salient examples is the often wide separation between blacks and whites in their mean positions on numerous issues. Although debates continue over the extent of the decline of racial prejudice over the past half century (Kinder 1986; Sniderman and Tetlock 1986a, 1986b) and the role of "realistic group conflict" in generating discrimination (Bobo 1988; Coser 1956), in opinion formation it is clear that race still matters to many Americans (Black and Black 1987; Bobo and Kluegel 1993; Dawson 1994; Kinder and Mendelberg 1995; Kinder and Sanders 1996). Other attitudes that are known to turn on evaluations of a policy-relevant "outgroup" are welfare (Gilens 1999); immigration (Pettigrew and Meertens 1995) and AIDS policy (Price and Hsu 1992).

What factors might we expect to maximally enhance the effect of group identifications on public opinion? One factor is individual differences in ethnocentricity. Much research—most famously *The Authoritarian Personality* (Adorno, Frankel-Brunswick, Levinson, and Sanford 1950)—have established that such a difference between individuals surely exists. A second factor is the extent to which stereotypes are salient and widely shared in the culture. To affect issue positions, people must understand how their group orientations relate to the issue, and elites may manipulate the content of stereotypes to connect groups to specific issues in citizens' minds and in desired ways (e.g., Kinder and Sanders 1996). And third, direct and genuine conflicts of interest between groups surely enhance the extent to which individuals rely on social identity for information processing (Bobo 1988; Coser 1956; Sumner 1906).

Political values. The hypothesis that political values—in the American ethos, some of the most important are individualism, equality, and suspicion of power (Kinder 1998)—provide structure for political knowledge and stability for issue positions (Feldman 1988) seems almost too obvious to mention. For many observers, politics is entirely about principles, is contentious precisely *because* it brings values into conflict, both societally (Feldman and Zaller 1992; Kinder and Sanders 1996; Stoker 1992) and within individuals (Feldman and Zaller 1992; Tetlock 1986). One would expect that values would determine political opinion on a wide range of issues—that issue positions, in fact, are merely specific operationalizations of "parent" values. However, the effects of individualism, egalitarianism, tolerance, and opposition to government power on ostensibly related issue positions have proven surprisingly small, or at best conditional or complicated.

The point is illustrated by research on individualism. "Rugged individualism"—the notion that one is entirely responsible for his or her own predicament—does explain attitudes on government assistance (Feldman 1988; Feldman and Zaller 1992; Kinder and Sanders 1996) and ascriptions of blame for the situations in which poor people find themselves (Feldman 1983; Sniderman and Brody 1977). But it's also true that whites' attitudes toward blacks are more complicated than that. On one hand, opposition to government programs that help blacks can be framed as driven by the principle of individualism: blacks struggle economically because they do not work hard enough (Sniderman 1985; Sniderman and Tetlock 1986b, 1986c). On the other hand, we have seen already that group orientations provide an explanation for the same policy positions, and this is especially true when the value egalitarianism is taken into account (Kinder 1986; Kinder and Mendelberg 2000; Kinder and Sanders 1996; Kinder and Winter 2001).

Selective Exposure

It is not difficult to imagine how political values and group identifications might generate a field of motivational forces, distorting the citizen's relationship to the information environment. While public opinion research has traditionally viewed citizens as passively embedded in an information environment that is beyond their control, researchers increasingly recognize that the information-processing citizens are more actively involved in shaping the information environment they inhabit, if not largely constructing it to their specifications (Kuklinski and Quirk 2000; Lavine 2002; Lodge and Taber 2000, 2001; Rahn, Aldrich, and Borgida 1994; Taber and Lodge 2000; Taber, Lodge, and Glathar 2001; Zaller and Feldman 1992). The central idea is that motivated information processors may selectively attend only to certain information—typically that which supports preferred opinions.

Unsurprisingly, a large literature on "selective exposure" was generated within the cognitive dissonance tradition in social psychology. Surprisingly, it failed to yield straightforward support for this hypothesis (Eagly and Chaiken 1993; Frey 1986; Kunda 1990; Sears and Freedman 1967). However, selective exposure in *political* information processing was quite in evidence in a series of experiments conducted by Charles Taber and Milton Lodge (Taber and Lodge 2000). Subjects seated at a computer and searching an "information board" for information on affirmative action and gun control chose more often to view information that they had reason to expect would support their prior beliefs over information expected to undermine those beliefs. Furthermore, selective exposure effects were strongest among the most politically knowledgeable and those whose priors were the strongest—those who were expected to be the most motivated to filter their information environment.

The Structure of Memory and Interpretation Processes

A principle of information-processing theory is that people do not—cannot—respond directly to uninterpreted external stimuli ("raw data" as described earlier). They must first construct internal representations to give stimuli semantic meaning—what Walter Lippmann (1922) called "pictures in the head." Here we discuss how such representations are structured and how that structure affects the interpretation of newly encountered stimuli. We focus on themes of importance for public opinion; there are more comprehensive reviews available (see Eagly and Chaiken 1993; McGraw and Steenbergen 1995).

The issue of whether political knowledge is structured hierarchically—in particular, whether broad "ideologies" "constrain" lower-order opinions—has been an ongoing debate since Converse's seminal "The Nature of Belief Systems in Mass Publics" (1964). Converse declared that ordinary citizens were "remarkably innocent" (p. 255) of "familiar belief systems that, in view of their historical importance, tend most to attract the sophisticated observer" (p. 256), by which he meant left-right ideology. The absence of hierarchy left issue positions within an individual unconnected to one another, unconstrained by higher-order principles, as well as free to change over time randomly. Public opinion research since Converse consists largely of responses to this challenge (Kinder 1998; Sniderman 1993; Sniderman and Tetlock 1986ca). Even Converse, however, allowed the possibility of "folk ideologies" or ways by which unsophisticated citizens might draw on subcultures to structure narrower sets of politically relevant beliefs. So the door was left open for hierarchical structure in terms of values distinct from the liberalism-conservatism of the national dialogue (Feldman 1988; Hurwitz and Peffley 1987; but see Abramowitz and Saunders 1998).

A similar debate concerns the extent to which people organize political knowledge using schemas (see Conover and Feldman 1991; Kuklinski, Luskin, and Bolland 1991; Lodge and McGraw 1991). A schematic knowledge structure would have memory organized not in discrete nodes with individual links, but in tightly knit subgroups of nodes. When people encounter a political object—say, "Barack Obama"—it is not a single node that is activated, but a particular subnetwork of beliefs and attitudes. And the evidence weighs in favor of schemas. As people spend time thinking about President Obama, or gun rights, or Congress, they tend to "grow" schematic structures in memory, and the more important people regard an attitude, the more structured is their "knowledge" about it (Barent and Krosknick 1995). One important implication for schematic organization is that "unitized" schemas may increase the efficiency of working memory: without schemas, "Obama," "Democrat," "advocates Health Reform," and "willing to compromise" are four distinct memory objects with the potential to occupy more than half of the seven or so available slots in working memory, rendering complex thought about President Obama extremely difficult. Schemas may allow working memory to deal with Obama as one, more complex, object. Also, schemas may be the basis for "pictures in the head" that help us fill in details about political objects by drawing on inferential knowledge, at the risk of inference error.

Although understudied, evaluative affect toward political objects does not appear to act as a hierarchical structuring agent (McGraw and Steenbergen 1995). Lodge and Taber (2000) have developed a theory of motivated cognition positing that political objects carry affective tags that activate automatically when the object is activated in LTM. Although the simple like-dislike-based model does not account for more complex emotions (Marcus and MacKuen 1993), it does provide a nonstructuring role for affect within the associative network model.

Evaluation

Citizens in a democracy are expected to evaluate candidates, groups, and issues, later retrieving and reporting these evaluations in the voting booth or the public opinion survey. Converse (1964) suggested that citizens often fail even to *possess* such opinions. This "nonattitudes" thesis has also sparked hot debate.

We offer two key points regarding this claim. First, measurement error—not citizens randomly changing their attitudes from time point to time point—may have accounted for much of the response instability Converse observed in his panel data. Christopher Achen (1975) reanalyzed the data and concluded that, accounting for measurement error, underlying attitudes were nearly perfectly stable. Second, perhaps response instability is not, as Converse assumed, unsystematic. People may less *hold* attitudes than *construct* them, when asked to report an opinion, by drawing from a sample of related "considerations" about an issue or candidate from LTM (Martin and Tesser 1992; Tourangeau, Rips and Rasinski 2000; Zaller and Feldman 1992). That is, there may be a file-drawer aspect to reporting attitudes and opinions—the "considerations" themselves may carry affective tags, but the answer to the *specific question asked* may be constructed on the fly. The determination of which considerations pop into WM is a stochastic process and is influenced by contextual factors, including the subject's mood, interviewer characteristics, question wording, and the nature of preceding questions. Zaller and Feldman (1992) suggest that citizens possess conflicting considerations on any given topic. Hence, response instability is not a reflection of nonattitudes; instead it reveals ambivalence.

The Zaller and Feldman model presents an image of the citizen pausing to consult his or her LTM, considering aspects of an issue or candidate and weighing likes and dislikes that pop into WM, to produce a survey or vote response. By contrast, "online" models of political evaluation (Lodge, McGraw, and Stroh 1989; Lodge, Steenbergen, and Brau 1995) argue that citizens as information processors "spontaneously extract the evaluative implications of political information as soon as they are exposed to it, integrate these implications into an ongoing summary counter or running tally, and then proceed to forget the nongist descriptive details of the information" (Lavine 2002, p. 227). The evaluation of the political object—candidate, issue position—has already been made and, though updated upon each exposure, is retrievable and reportable.

Memory-based and online models are commonly presented as competing, with memory-based processes seen as more applicable to complex, ambivalent attitude objects (issues) and online processes more applicable to simpler, univalent objects, especially when citizens expect to be asked for a judgment (candidates). But an either-or view is theoretically flawed and empirically unfounded, with the confusion stemming from the failure to discriminate encoding from retrieval effects. Online encoding processes link affect directly to objects in memory, and this affect is retrieved automatically whenever the object is encountered. After one or two evaluations the concept is "hot," affective-charged (Lodge and Taber 2005). When asked to report an evaluation, citizens retrieve considerations and construct an attitude, but the retrieval process will be strongly influenced by the affect that was attached to the concept through an earlier online process. That is, the evidence suggests hybrid models that include both online and memory components (Hastie and Pennington 1989; Taber and Lodge 2003).

Motivated models of evaluation, like earlier cognitive consistency theories (Festinger 1957; Heider 1958) suggest the existence of pressure to maintain evaluative consistency across related attitudes (Kunda 1990; Lodge and Taber 2000; Taber and Lodge 2000; Taber, Lodge, and Glathar 2001). Taber and Lodge theorize three principles. First, evaluative affect is unavoidably attached to the objects stored in LTM—what Robert Abelson (1963) called "hot cognition." Second, such evaluations are updated as new information about the objects is encountered—the online tally. Finally, the affective component of the object is invariably activated along with the activation of the object itself. Taber and Lodge used an affective priming task (Bargh, Chaiken, Govender, and Pratto 1992; Fazio, Sanbonmatsu, Powell, and Kardes 1986) to produce clear evidence for hot cognition and automatic affect in processing a variety of political information (Lodge and Taber 2000, 2001). Subjects demonstrated affect for candidates, groups, and issue positions, and evaluations clearly came to mind too quickly to have been constructed in WM. It is easy to imagine how an automatically activated positive or negative affect about political objects would color, even distort, conscious and unconscious deliberations of which those objects are elements. In one example, subjects display a "disconfirmation bias" (Edwards and Smith 1996; Taber and Lodge 2000) in which counterattitudinal information is treated differently by subjects—they privately counterargue it—than is proattitudinal information. The ironic result is that a presentation of arguments balanced to represent both sides of an issue equally can result in polarization rather than moderation of subjects' opinions.

Our discussion has so far involved only information processes internal to the citizen. But citizens interact with the information environment, and if long-term memory functions at all as a kind of map of the external world, then a consideration of the information environment is necessary for a complete story of how citizens confront and store information. A terrific illustration comes from priming and framing research (Gamson 1992; Iyengar 1991; Iyengar and Kinder 1987; Lau, Smith, and Fiske 1991; Nelson, Clawson, and Oxley 1997). This work recognizes the role of knowledge structures as devices that elites can commandeer and perhaps manipulate to achieve preferred evaluative outcomes in individual citizens. Framing, for example, can involve elites' articulating a new frame or analogy by which citizens can understand an existing political object, with the hope that the new "story" will guide patterns of information storage and, ultimately, opinion formation. Alternately, elites may repeat or highlight an existing frame, habituating its use in citizens' minds, as when Nelson, Clawson and Oxley (1997) showed that by highlighting the free-speech considerations versus the public-order considerations of a hypothetical Ku Klux Klan rally, citizen attitudes toward the rally were manipulated in predictable ways.

The Paradox of the Dysfunctional Citizen

It seems incredible that the American system has survived, given that the American citizen so little resembles the democratic ideal of an informed, interested, rational thinker, respectful of diverse views, ever translating principles and values into policy positions and candidate choices. How do we do it?

Democratic theorists' suspicions that citizens might lack interest in public affairs, given their preoccupation with day-to-day private concerns are entirely supported by survey data (Bennett 1986; Bennett and Resnick 1990). Indeed, citizen apathy may be individually rational, an aspect of a utility-maximizing allocation of costly and scarce cognitive resources, whether viewed in economic (Downs 1957) or psychological (Fiske and Taylor 1991) terms. The miniscule payoff of political engagement may render political information processing an essentially wasteful enterprise for most citizens.

This lack of interest results in political ignorance in America (Delli Carpini and Keeter 1996) at "breathtaking" depth (Kinder 1998, p. 795). Citizens misunderstand basic institutional structure in government; they have little idea about their representatives' issue positions, party affiliations, or even their names. They make frequent reference to what is "constitutional" without the first idea what the Constitution contains. A majority report that they think the United States spends less on Medicare than on foreign aid. And they are ideologically unsophisticated: we have seen reason to worry that citizens' issue positions are unconstrained by coherent values or principles, but are idiosyncratic if not random. It is not clear that citizens are prepared to make usable sense of political discourse at all.

Tolerance of diversity (Mill 1861/1951) is, of course, thought indispensable to functioning democracy. Freedom of speech and of the press do not even wait until the Second Amendment to find expression in the Bill of Rights. And yet public opinion research reveals widespread intolerance in the specific attitudes of American citizens (McClosky 1964; Prothro and Grigg 1960) that contrasts distressingly with their avowed support for tolerance in principle. For example, while freedom of expression is uncontroversial, support for denying that very right to communists, socialists, or atheists is easy to find (Stouffer 1955). In fact, 1970s optimism about increases in Americans' tolerance (Davis 1975; Nunn, Crockett, and Williams 1978) proved short-lived when Americans were found to have remained generally intolerant, though focusing on more diffuse targets (Sullivan, Pierson, and Marcus 1982; but see Wilson 1994). There is good reason to believe that group identification remains a potent motivational force for opinion formation in America and that outgroup hostility gains power under threatening conditions. Post-September 11, 2001, attitudes on immigration and civil liberties exemplify the point.

And yet American democracy does not appear at, or even near, a breaking point. The paradox of the dysfunctional citizen has three potential solutions in the public opinion literature, which we now discuss in turn.

Aggregation

There is a suggestion that, perhaps, the mechanisms—both institutional and accidental—that translate private into public opinion "miraculously" produce coherence out of near-chaos (Kinder 1998). We previously discussed majoritarian, weighted, and compositional aggregation processes. Each provides a possible answer to the dysfunctional citizen problem.

Majoritarian aggregation, recall, is the simple tallying of issue positions into response categories, after which public opinion is read directly from the distribution of responses. Even given citizen dysfunction, this could, one supposes, produce collective rationality by the law of large numbers: citizen inadequacies produce randomness and hence, when combined, cancel out (Kinder 1998). Unfortunately, even setting aside that this account is normatively unsatisfying (Converse 1990), it also suffers from the likelihood that "error" in individual political information processing is not random as the statistical account supposes. If this error is systematically distributed, it will accumulate with aggregation (Page and Shapiro 1992; Bartels 1996)—as, say, poorly informed citizens are disproportionately driven to take certain positions because of the manipulations of elites.

Weighted aggregation upweights the opinions of elites (Stimson 1991) and, thus, seeks to account for informational asymmetries in the polity. Normative and empirical objections again raise their heads, however. First, in adopting this approach we abandon the normative appeal of giving individual opinions equal power, a practice whose adoption in public opinion polling may at least partially produce a beneficently self-fulfilling prophecy. On a related note, elites may be as powerfully driven by majoritarian opinion as they drive it. And second, a normative endorsement of this view assumes that elites are wiser than ordinary citizens. While they may make more informed decisions, we have already seen evidence that these decisions may be "informed" by heavily biased information—and the more informed, the more biased.

We find compositional aggregation and especially its social network variant to be the most satisfactory answer to the dysfunctional citizen paradox among the aggregation theories (Huckfeldt and Sprague 1987, 1995; Page and Shapiro 1992). The perspective essentially tells a story in which interactions between citizens embedded in social networks—with each citizen contributing bits and pieces to the conversation without necessarily possessing "whole opinions"— results in a "coherent national conversation" to which the democratic system can respond. Admittedly, this sounds similar to the "emergent" public opinion organism, with its collective consciousness, confronted early in this essay, but importantly this perspective carefully preserves a place for, rather than sweeping aside, individual information processors. The "story" is most intriguing as it produces theoretical accounts of actual mechanisms by which "the system" constructs public opinion (especially Huckfeldt and Sprague 1995). But it remains a story, and empirical investigations have not progressed much beyond general manifestations of public opinion such as "national mood" (Stimson 1991) or "macropartisanship" (MacKuen, Erikson, and Stimson 1989) or appraisals of merely local effects of social networks on individuals' opinions (Huckfeldt 2001; Huckfeldt and Sprague 1987, 1995). For additional theoretical development of the story, methods of nonlinear systems analysis such as adaptive agent modeling (see Kollman, Miller, and Page 1992) may prove useful.

Processing in Individuals

A nonaggregation solution to the paradox may come from the heuristics literature. The idea is that "individuals use heuristics—mental shortcuts that require hardly any information to make fairly reliable political judgments" (Kuklinski and Quirk 2000, p. 153), producing a kind of "low-information rationality" (Popkin 1991). Among the most useful "cues" that simplify and streamline political processing for citizens are party identification (Campbell, et al. 1960), candidate traits (Popkin 1991), trusted elites (Mondak 1993), interest groups (Lupia 1994), public mood (Rahn 2000), and liberals or conservatives (Sniderman, Brody, and Tetlock 1991). At least one hopes that ill-informed citizens will behave (vote, express opinions) approximately as they would were they to expend more resources gathering political information—and that any errors they made due to shortcut-taking would be random and average to zero.

The evidence on heuristics usage is not an unmitigated source of optimism on this count. As useful and ubiquitous as heuristics are, the heuristics literature largely documents their inferential shortcomings (Nisbett and Ross 1980). Heuristic reasoning can lead citizens seriously astray, and we know of numerous systematic biases that render political heuristics unreliable (Kuklinski and Quirk 2000; Lau and Redlawsk 2001). To illustrate, poorly informed citizens' presidential votes are *not* distributed as well-informed citizens' votes are (Bartels 1996; see also Gilens 2001). If the poorly informed make more use of heuristics—or if they are nonetheless reliant on different sets of heuristics, and one of these possibilities seems likely—the heuristics usage would not, even in theory, approximate rationality or even irrational but sophisticated political engagement.

In positing the online model, Lodge and his colleagues have articulated an alternative to heuristics (Lodge, McGraw, and Stroh 1989; Lodge, Steenbergen, and Brau 1995; Lodge and Taber 2000) that may answer the dysfunctional citizen problem. The important notion is that citizens possess more usable knowledge than they can articulate. Their impressions—even ones as simple as an evaluative "like" or "dislike"—contain within them an immense amount of "work done" processing political information, however unrecoverable the original elements that went into the evaluation. If citizens are asked about their impression of, say, their state's governor, they are likely to offer a ready and quite certain up-or-down appraisal. If asked to explain, the citizens will surely offer a reason, but this reason is likely to consist largely of rationalization, for the full gamut of information upon which their simple evaluation was built is not easily recovered in toto—and certainly not in the course of answering a survey question. Nonetheless, the summary evaluation may represent a perfect combination of all the information yet considered about the governor.

In early work, Lodge and colleagues argued that the online model held out hope for answering the dysfunctional citizen problem more powerfully and optimistically than any other. However, there is good reason now to believe the running online tally may itself be systematically biased. Normatively, belief updating requires an independence between priors and incoming information (Green and Shapiro 1994) that doesn't square with Lodge and colleagues' own evidence on selective exposure. Citizens appear to resist persuasion even in the face of overwhelming counterattitudinal evidence (Lazersfeld, Berelson, and Gaudet 1948), and attitudes can become more extreme after such exposure. Ultimately, while there may be some rational basis for protecting hard-won opinions—it's possible that what we are calling bias may carry a component of healthy skepticism—there is insufficient reason to conclude that online processing rescues behavioral rationality from psychological dysfunction.

External Constraints

A final possible response to the paradox holds that political institutions structure individual choices in such a way as to solve the problem (Lupia and McCubbins 1998; Sniderman 2000). The argument holds that institutions simplify the application of heuristics. Citizens can rely on experts and trusted media sources who may be exceptionally well informed. Institutional penalties, such as reputational damage, for inaccuracy help to "regulate" these sources and keep them trustworthy. However, despite some suggestive experimental evidence (Kuklinski, Quirk, Jerit, and Rich 2001), this point awaits empirical corroboration.

Conclusion

We are convinced that information processing is the approach to public opinion most likely to yield useful scientific knowledge in the future. However, there are complaints. One is that emotion and affect are peripheral considerations in information processing theories. The traditional Enlightenment view of emotion as deleterious to glorious reason is now passé: modern researchers now regard affect as central to human cognition (e.g., Damasio 1994), directing attention, motivating deeper, less heuristic processing, and promoting more efficient knowledge structures in memory. Actually, however, this complaint of too little affect is unfounded. Political psychologists have long been interested in affect, and the role of affect is among the hottest topics today (Judd and Krosnick 1989; Lodge and Taber 2000; Marcus and MacKuen 1993; McGraw and Steenbergen 1995; Ottati, Steenbergen, and Riggle 1992; Rahn 2000; Sniderman, Brody, and Tetlock 1991). Perhaps the unrelenting individualism of the work reviewed here represents a better-founded criticism. The information context in the information processing literature is, indeed, insufficiently accounted for.

But the most critical challenge for the political cognition approach to public opinion is to achieve a fuller accounting of automatic processes. The cognitive revolution in psychology can be told as a play in three acts: first, models of the mind; second, accounting for affect; and third, the ongoing act, a focus on uncontrolled processes (and a concomitant tendency of some researchers to treat ever more, or even all, processes as ultimately uncontrolled). Social psychologists now consider the distinction between automatic and controlled processes a central problem for advances in understanding human cognition (e.g., Banaji, Lemm, and Carpenter 2001; Bargh 1997; Bargh and Chartrand 1999; Bargh and Ferguson 2000; Gardner and Cacioppo 1997; Logan 1992). Some of the most successful models of persuasion, for example, distinguish between systematic (controlled) processes and peripheral (automatic) ones (Eagly and Chaiken 1993; Petty and Wegener 1998). The use of stereotypes as elements of political cognition has also long been seen as an automatic categorization process (Banaji and Dasgupta 1998; Bargh, Chen, and Burrows 1996; Devine 1989; Fiske and Taylor 1991). Even power abuse has been characterized in terms of the uncontrolled and chronic accessibility of power goals in LTM (Lee-Chai and Bargh 2001). Most of the progress on automaticity occurs outside of political science, and public opinion research continues to be biased against, or at least blissfully unaware of, this view. Future progress will be made by treating automaticity more seriously.

Methodologies—especially those that are used habitually—will have to adapt. To survey research, mental processing that occurs outside the conscious awareness of subjects is invisible. And there is now growing evidence that much—perhaps most—of the "work" of even mental *deliberation* occurs outside of conscious awareness (Bargh and Chartrand 1999; Neely 1977; Uleman and Bargh 1989). Conscious responses such as answers to survey questions, moreover, do not reliably track measures of "uncontrolled" behaviors (Crosby, Bromley, and Saxe 1980; Devine 1989). Such is the case, for example, when comparing physiological (fMRI) measures of racial attitudes with, on one hand, unconscious measures (the Implicit Association Test and startle responses, with which fMRI results correlated) and, on the other, the survey-based Modern Racism Scale (with which they did not) (Phelps, et al. 2000). Such findings are not merely indicative of social desirability effects: subjects in such studies appear to be genuinely unaware of their "automatic attitudes." In the years to come, researchers will increasingly be forced to come to grips with what Bargh called "the cognitive monster," the unconscious ocean of activity, compared to which our conscious experience is but resulting waves lapping against the shore.

Bibliography

Abelson, R. 1963. "Computer Simulation of 'Hot' Cognition." In *Computer Simulation of Personality,* ed. S. S. Tomkins and S. Messick. New York: Wiley.

Abramowitz, A. I., and K. L. Saunders. 1998. "Ideological Realignment in the U.S. Electorate." *Journal of Politics* 60 (8): 634–52.

Achen, C. H. 1975. "Mass Political Attitudes and the Survey Response." *American Political Science Review* 69: 1218–31.

Adorno, T. W., E. Frankel-Brunswick, D. J. Levinson, and N. Sanford. 1950. *The Authoritarian Personality.* New York: Harper and Row.

Anderson, J. R. 1983. *The Architecture of Cognition.* Cambridge, MA: Harvard University Press.

Atkinson, R. C., and R. M. Shiffrin. 1968. "Human Memory: A Proposed System and Its Control Processes." In *The Psychology of Learning and Motivation: Advances in Research and Theory,* vol. 2, ed. K. W. Spence and J. T. Spence, 90–197. London: Academic Press.

Banaji, M. R., and N. Dasgupta. 1998. "The Consciousness of Social Beliefs: A Program of Research on Stereotyping and Prejudice." In *Metacognition: Cognitive and Social Dimensions,* ed. V. Y. Yzerbyt, G. Lories, and B. Dardenne, 157–70. London: Sage.

Bargh, J. A. 1997. "The Automaticity of Everyday Life." In *The Automaticity of Everyday Life,* ed. R. S. Wyer, Jr., 1–61. Vol. 10 of *Advances in Social Cognition.* Mahwah, NJ: Erlbaum.

Bargh, J. A. 1999. "The Cognitive Monster: The Case against Controllability of Automatic Stereotype Effects." In *Dual Process Theories in Social Psychology,* ed. S. Chaiken and Y. Trope. New York: Guilford.

Bargh, J. A., and T. L. Chartrand. 1999. "The Unbearable Automaticity of Being." *American Psychologist* 54: 462–79.

Bargh, J. A., and M. L. Ferguson. 2000. "Beyond Behaviorism: On the Automaticity of Higher Mental Processes." *Psychological Bulletin* 126 (6): 925–45.

Bargh, J. A., S. Chaiken, R. Govender, and F. Pratto. 1992. "The Generality of the Automatic Attitude Activation Effect." *Journal of Personality and Social Psychology* 62 (6): 893–912.

Bartels, L. M. 1996. "Uninformed Votes: Information Effects in Presidential Elections." *American Journal of Political Science* 40: 194–230.

Bartlett, F. C. 1932. *Remembering: A Study in Experimental and Social Psychology.* Cambridge, U.K.: Cambridge University Press.

Bennett, S. E. 1986. *Apathy in America.* Dobbs Ferry, NY: Transnational.

Bennett, S. E., and D. Resnick. 1990. "The Implications of Non-Voting for Democracy in the United States." *American Journal of Political Science* 34: 771–802.

Black, E., and M. Black. 1987. *Politics and Society in the South.* Cambridge, MA: Harvard University Press.

Blumer, H. 1946. "Collective Behavior." In *New Outline of the Principles of Sociology,* ed. A. M. Lee, 167–222. New York: Barnes and Noble.

Bobo, L. 1988. "Attitudes toward the Black Political Movement: Trends, Meaning, and Effects on Racial Policy Preferences." *Social Psychology Quarterly* 51: 287–302.

Bobo, L., and J. R. Kluegel. 1993. "Opposition to Race-Targeting: Self-interest, Stratification Ideology, or Racial Attitudes?" *American Sociological Review* 58 (4): 443–64.

Boden, M. A. 1988. *Computer Models of Mind: Computational Approaches in Theoretical Psychology.* Cambridge, U.K.: Cambridge University Press.

Boninger, D. S., J. A. Krosnick, M. K. Barent, and L. R. Fabrigar. 1995. "The Causes and Consequences of Attitude Importance." In *Attitude Strength: Antecedents and Consequences,* ed. R. E. Petty and J. A. Krosnick, 159–90. Mahwah, NJ: Erlbaum.

Brewer, M. B., and R. J. Brown. 1998. "Intergroup Relations." In *Handbook of Social Psychology,* ed. D. T. Gilbert, S. T. Fiske, and G. Lindzey. 4th ed. London: Oxford University Press.

Broadbent, D. E. 1958. *Perception and Communication.* Oxford: Pergamon.

Brown, R. 1986. *Social Psychology.* 2nd ed. New York: Free Press.

Bruner, J. S., J. J. Goodnow, and G. A. Austin. 1956. *A Study of Thinking.* New York: Wiley.

Campbell, A., P. Converse, W. Miller, and D. Stokes. 1960. *The American Voter.* New York: John Wiley and Sons.

Chomsky, N. 1957. *Syntactic Structures.* The Hague: Mouton.

Citrin, J., and D. Green. 1990. "The Self-Interest Motive in American Public Opinion." In *Research in Micropolitics: Public Opinion, 1990,* ed. S. Long, 1–27. New York: JAI Press.

Collins, A. M., and M. R. Quillian. 1969. "Retrieval Time from Semantic Memory." *Journal of Verbal Learning and Verbal Behavior* 8: 240–48.

Converse, P. E. 1964. "The Nature of Belief Systems in Mass Publics." In *Ideology and Discontent,* ed. D. E. Apter. New York: Free Press.

Converse, P. E. 1987. "Changing Conceptions of Public Opinion in the Political Process." *Public Opinion Quarterly* 51: 12–24.

Converse, P. E. 1990. "Popular Representation and the Distribution of Information." In *Information and Democratic Processes,* ed. J. A. Ferejohn and J. H. Kuklinski. Urbana: University of Illinois Press.

Coser, L. A. 1956. *The Functions of Social Conflict.* Glencoe, IL: Free Press.

Crosby, F., S. Bromley, and L. Saxe. 1980. "Recent Unobtrusive Studies of Black and White Discrimination and Prejudice: A Literature Review." *Psychological Bulletin* 87 (3): 546–63.

Dahl, R. A. 1961. *Who Governs?* New Haven, CT: Yale University Press.

Damasio, A. R. 1994. Descartes' Error: Emotion, Reason, and the Human Brain. New York: Grosset/Putnam.

Davis, J. A. 1975. "Communism, Conformity, Cohorts, and Categories: American Tolerance in 1954 and 1972–1973." *American Journal of Sociology* 81 (November): 491–513.

Dawson, M. 1994. *Behind the Mule.* Princeton, NJ: Princeton University Press.

de Tocqueville, A. 1848/1945. *Democracy in America.* New York: Vintage.

Deaux, K., A. Reid, K. Mizrahi, and K. A. Ethier. 1995. "Parameters of Social Identity." *Journal of Personality and Social Psychology* 68 (2): 280–91.

Delli Carpini, M. X., and S. Keeter. 1996. *What Americans Know about Politics and Why It Matters.* New Haven, CT: Yale University Press.

Devine, P. G. 1989. "Stereotypes and Prejudice: Their Automatic and Controlled Components." *Journal of Personality and Social Psychology* 56 (1): 5–18.

Downs, A. 1957. *An Economic Theory of Democracy.* New York: Harper and Row.

Eagly, A. H., and S. Chaiken. 1993. *The Psychology of Attitudes.* Fort Worth, TX: Harcourt Brace Jovanovich.

Edwards, K., and E. E. Smith. 1996. "A Disconfirmation Bias in the Evaluation of Arguments." *Journal of Personality and Social Psychology* 71 (1): 5–24.

Fazio, R. H., D. M. Sanbonmatsu, M. C. Powell, and F. R. Kardes. 1986. "On the Automatic Activation of Attitudes." *Journal of Personality and Social Psychology* 50 (2): 229–38.

Feigenbaum, E. A., and J. Feldman, eds. 1963 [1995]. *Computers and Thought.* Menlo Park, CA: AAAI Press.

Feldman, S. 1983. "Economic Individualism and American Public Opinion." *American Politics Quarterly* 11: 3–29.

Feldman, S., and J. Zaller. 1992. "The Political Culture of Ambivalence: Ideological Responses to the Welfare State." *American Journal of Political Science* 36: 268–307.

Festinger, L. 1957. *A Theory of Cognitive Dissonance.* Palo Alto, CA: Stanford University Press.

Fiske, S. T., and S. E. Taylor. 1991. *Social Cognition.* 2nd ed. New York: McGraw-Hill.

Fiske, S. T. 1998. "Stereotyping, Prejudice, and Discrimination." In *Handbook of Social Psychology,* 4th ed., ed. D. T. Gilbert, S. T. Fiske, and G. Lindzey, vol. 2, 357–411. New York: Oxford University Press.

Frey, D. 1986. "Recent Research on Selective Exposure to Information." In *Advances in Experimental Social Psychology*, vol. 19, ed. L. Berkowitz, 41–80. New York: Academic Press.

Gamson, W. A. 1992. *Talking Politics*. New York: Cambridge University Press.

Gardner, W. L., and J. T. Cacioppo. 1997. "Automaticity and Social Behavior: A Model, a Marriage, and a Merger." In *The Automaticity of Everyday Life*, ed. R. S. Wyer, Jr., 133–42. Vol. 10 of *Advances in Social Cognition*. Mahwah, NJ: Erlbaum.

Gilens, M. 1999. *Why Americans Hate Welfare: Race, Media, and the Politics of Anti-Poverty Policy*. Chicago: University of Chicago Press.

———. 2001. "Political Ignorance and Collective Policy Preferences." *American Political Science Review* 95 (2): 379–96.

Green, D. P., and I. Shapiro. 1994. *Pathologies of Rational Choice Theory*. New Haven, CT: Yale University Press.

Greenstein, F. 1969. *Personality and Politics*. Princeton, NJ: Princeton University Press.

Hastie, R., and N. Pennington. 1989. "Notes on the Distinction between Memory-Based versus On-line Judgment." In *On-line Cognition in Person Perception*, ed. J. Bassili, 1–19. Hillsdale, NJ: Lawrence Erlbaum.

Heider, F. 1946. "Attitudes and Cognitive Organization." *Journal of Psychology* 21: 107–12.

———. 1958. *The Psychology of Interpersonal Relations*. New York: Wiley.

Huckfeldt, R. 2001. "The Social Communication of Political Expertise." *American Journal of Political Science* 45: 425–38.

Huckfeldt, R., and J. Sprague. 1987. "Networks in Context: The Social Flow of Political Information." *American Political Science Review* 81: 1197–216.

Huckfeldt, R., and J. Sprague. 1995. *Citizens, Politics, and Social Communication*. New York: Cambridge University Press.

Hull, C. L. 1930. "Knowledge and Purpose as Habit Mechanisms." *Psychological Review* 37 (6): 511–25.

Hurwitz, J., and M. Peffley. 1987. "How Are Foreign Policy Attitudes Structured? A Hierarchical Model." *American Political Science Review* 81 (4): 1099–120.

Hyman, H. H. 1955. *Survey Design and Analysis: Principles, Cases, and Procedures*. Glencoe, IL: Free Press.

Iyengar, S. 1991. *Is Anyone Responsible? How Television Frames Political Issues*. Chicago: University of Chicago Press.

Iyengar, S., and D. R. Kinder. 1987. *News that Matters: Television and American Opinion*. Chicago: University of Chicago Press.

James, W. 1890. *Principles of Psychology*. New York: Holt.

Judd, C., and J. Krosnick. 1989. "The Structural Bases of Consistency among Political Attitudes: Effects of Political Expertise and Attitude Importance." In *Attitude Structure and Function*, ed. A. Pratkanis, S. Becker, and A. Greenwald, 99–128. Hillsdale, NJ: Erlbaum.

Kiewiet, D. R. 1983. *Macroeconomics and Micropolitics: Electoral Effects of Economic Issues*. Chicago: University of Chicago Press.

Kinder, D. R. 1986. "The Continuing American Dilemma: White Resistance to Racial Change 40 Years after Myrdal." *Journal of Social Issues* 42 (2): 151–72.

Kinder, D. R. 1998. "Opinion and Action in the Realm of Politics." In *Handbook of Social Psychology*, ed. D. T. Gilbert, S. T. Fiske, and G. Lindzey. 4th ed. London: Oxford University Press.

Kinder, D. R., and L. M. Sanders. 1996. *Divided by Color: Racial Politics and Democratic Ideals*. Chicago: University of Chicago Press.

Kinder, D. R., and T. Mendelberg. 2000. "Individualism Reconsidered: Principles and Prejudice in Contemporary American Opinion." In *Racialized Politics: The Debate about*

Racism in America, ed. D. O. Sears, J. Sidanius, and L. Bobo, 44–74. Chicago: University of Chicago Press.

Kinder, D. R., and N. Winter. 2001. "Exploring the Racial Divide: Blacks, Whites, and Opinion on National Policy." *American Journal of Political Science* 45 (2): 439–53.

Kollman, K., J. H. Miller, and S. E. Page. 1992. "Adaptive Parties in Spatial Elections." *American Political Science Review* 86: 929–37.

Krosnick, J. A. 1988. "Attitude Importance and Attitude Change." *Journal of Experimental Social Psychology* 24 (3): 240–55.

———. 1990. "Government Policy and Citizen Passion: A Study of Issue Publics in Contemporary America." *Political Behavior* 12 (1): 59–92.

Kuklinski, J. H., and P. J. Quirk. 2000. "Reconsidering the Rational Public: Cognition, Heuristics, and Mass Opinion." In *Elements of Reason: Cognition, Choice, and the Bounds of Rationality*, ed. A. Lupia, M. D. McCubbins, and S. L. Popkin. Cambridge, UK: Cambridge University Press.

Kuklinski, J. H., R. Luskin, and J. Bolland. 1991. "Where is the Schema? Going Beyond the 'S' Word in Political Psychology." *American Political Science Review* 85 (4): 1341–56.

Kuklinski, J. H., P. J. Quirk, J. Jerit, and R. F. Rich. 2001. "The Political Environment and Citizen Competence." *American Journal of Political Science* 45: 410–24.

Kunda, Z. 1990. "The Case for Motivated Reasoning." *Psychological Bulletin* 1083: 480–98.

Lau, R. R., and D. P. Redlawsk. 2001. "Advantages and Disadvantages of Cognitive Heuristics in Political Decision Making." *American Journal of Political Science* 45 (4): 951–71.

Lau, R. R., R. A. Smith, and S. T. Fiske. 1991. "Political Beliefs, Policy Interpretations, and Political Persuasion." *Journal of Politics* 53 (3): 644–75.

Lavine, H. 2002. "On-line vs. Memory-Based Process Models of Political Evaluation." In *Political Psychology*, ed. K. Monroe, 225–47. Mahwah, NJ: Erlbaum.

Lavine, H., and T. Gschwend. 2002. "Ideology and Rationality." Paper presented at the annual meeting of the International Society of Political Psychology, Berlin, July.

Lazersfeld, P.F., B. R. Berelson, and H. Gaudet. 1948. *The People's Choice*. New York: Columbia University.

Lee-Chai, A. Y., and J. A. Bargh, eds. 2001. *The Use and Abuse of Power*. Philadelphia: Psychology Press.

Lippmann, W. 1922. *Public Opinion*. New York: MacMillan.

Lodge, M. 1995. "Toward a Procedural Model of Candidate Evaluation." In *Political Judgment: Structure and Process*, ed. M. Lodge and K. McGraw. Ann Arbor, MI: University of Michigan Press.

Lodge, M., and K. McGraw. 1991. "Where Is the Schema? Critiques." *American Political Science Review* 85 (4): 1357–64.

Lodge, M., and K. McGraw, eds. 1995. *Political Judgment: Structure and Process*. Ann Arbor, MI: University of Michigan Press.

Lodge, M., K. McGraw, and P. Stroh. 1989. "An Impression-Driven Model of Candidate Evaluation." *American Political Science Review* 83 (2): 399–419.

Lodge, M., M. Steenbergen, and S. Brau. 1995. "The Responsive Voter: Campaign Information and the Dynamics of Candidate Evaluation." *American Political Science Review* 89: 309–26.

Lodge, M., and C. S. Taber. 2001. "Automatic Affect: A Test of Hot Cognition for Candidates, Groups, and Issues." Paper presented at the annual meeting of the Midwest Political Science Association, Chicago, April.

———. 2005. "Implicit Affect for Political Candidates, Parties, and Issues: An Experimental Test of the Hot Cognition Hypothesis." *Political Psychology* 26 (6): 455–82.

Lodge, M., and C. Taber. 2000. "Three Steps toward a Theory of Motivated Political Reasoning." In *Elements of Reason: Cognition, Choice, and the Bounds of Rationality*, ed. A. Lupia, M. D. McCubbins, and S. L. Popkin. Cambridge, UK: Cambridge University Press.

Luger, G. F., ed. 1995. *Computation and Intelligence: Collected Readings*. Menlo Park, CA: AAAI Press.

Lupia, A. 1994. "Shortcuts Versus Encyclopedias: Information and Voting Behavior in California Insurance Reform Elections." *American Political Science Review* 88 (1): 63–76.

Lupia, A., and M. D. McCubbins. 1998. *The Democratic Dilemma: Can Citizens Learn What They Need to Know?* Cambridge, UK: Cambridge University Press.

MacKuen, M., R. S. Erikson, and J. A. Stimson. 1989. "Macropartisanship." *American Political Science Review* 83: 1125–42.

Marcus, G. E., and M. B. MacKuen. 1993. "Anxiety, Enthusiasm, and the Vote: The Emotional Underpinnings of Learning and Involvement during Presidential Campaigns." *American Political Science Review* 87 (3): 672–85.

Martin, L. L., and A. Tesser, eds. 1992. *The Construction of Social Judgments*. Hillsdale, NJ: Lawrence Erlbaum.

McClosky, H. 1964. "Consensus and Ideology in American Politics." *American Political Science Review* 58 (2): 316–82.

McGraw, K. 2000. "Contributions of the Cognitive Approach to Political Psychology." *Political Psychology* 21 (4): 805–32.

McGraw, K., and M. Steenbergen. 1995. "Pictures in the Head: Memory Representations of Political Candidates." In *Political Judgment: Structure and Process*, ed. M. Lodge and K. McGraw, 15–42. Ann Arbor, MI: University of Michigan.

Mencken, H. L. 1949. *A Mencken Chrestomathy*. New York: Knopf.

Mill, J. S. 1861 [1951]. *Three Essays*. Oxford: Oxford University Press.

Miller, G. A. 1956. "The Magic Number Seven, Plus or Minus Two: Some Limits on Our Capacity for Processing Information." *Psychological Review* 63: 81–93.

Neely, J. H. 1977. "Semantic Priming and Retrieval from Lexical Memory: Roles of Inhibitionless Spreading Activation and Limited-Capacity Attention." *Journal of Experimental Psychology: General* 106 (3): 226–54.

Nelson, T. E., R. A. Clawson, and Z. M. Oxley. 1997. "Media Framing of a Civil Liberties Conflict and Its Effect on Tolerance." *American Political Science Review* 91: 567–83.

Newell, A., Shaw, J. C., and Simon, H. A. 1958. "Elements of a Theory of Human Problem Solving." *Psychological Review* 65 (3): 151–66.

Nisbett, R. E., and L. Ross. 1980. *Human Inference: Strategies and Shortcomings of Social Judgment*. Englewood Cliffs, NJ: Prentice-Hall.

Orwell, G. 1946. *Animal Farm*. New York: Harcourt Brace.

Ottati, V. C., M. R. Steenbergen, and E. Riggle. 1992. "The Cognitive and Affective Components of Political Attitudes: Measuring the Determinants of Candidate Evaluations." *Political Behavior* 14 (4): 423–42.

Ottati, V. C., and R. S. Wyer. 1990. "The Cognitive Mediators of Political Choice: Toward a Comprehensive Model of Political Information Processing." In *Information and Democratic Processes*, ed. J. A. Ferejohn and J. H. Kuklinski, 186–216. Urbana, IL: University of Illinois Press.

Page, B. I., and R. Y. Shapiro. 1992. The Rational Public: Fifty Years of Trends in Americans' Policy Preferences. Chicago: University of Chicago Press.

Payne, J. W., J. R. Bettman, and E. J. Johnson. 1992. "Behavioral Decision Research: A Constructive Processing Perspective." *Annual Review of Psychology* 43: 87–131.

Pettigrew, T. F., and R. W. Meertens. 1995. "Subtle and Blatant Prejudice in Western Europe." *European Journal of Social Psychology* 25 (1): 57–75.

Petty, R. E., and D. T. Wegener. 1998. "Attitude Change: Multiple Roles for Persuasion Variables." In *Handbook of Social Psychology,* ed. D. T. Gilbert, S. T. Fiske, and G. Lindzey. 4th ed. London: Oxford University Press.

Popkin, S. L. 1991. The Reasoning Voter: Communication and Persuasion in Presidential Campaigns. Chicago: University of Chicago Press.

Prothro, J. W., and C. W. Grigg. 1960. "Fundamental Principles of Democracy: Biases of Agreement and Disagreement." *Journal of Politics* 22: 276–94.

Rahn, W. M. 2000. "Affect as Information: The Role of Public Mood in Political Reasoning." In *Elements of Reason: Cognition, Choice, and the Bounds of Rationality*, ed. A. Lupia, M. D. McCubbins, and S. L. Popkin, 130–51. Cambridge, U.K.: Cambridge University Press.

Rahn, W. M., J. Aldrich, and E. Borgida. 1994. "Individual and Contextual Variations in Political Candidate Appraisal." *American Political Science Review* 88 (1): 193–99.

Ruskin, J. 2001/1864. "Sesame and Lilies. Lecture I." "Sesame: Of Kings' Treasuries." In *Essays: English and American,* vol. XXVIII, ed. C. W. Eliot. *The Harvard Classics.* New York: Bartleby.com.

Schreiber, D., and J. Zaller. 2001. "Thinking about Politics: A Functional Magnetic Resonance Imaging Study." Unpublished paper presented at the American Political Science Association Annual Meeting, San Francisco, August.

Sears, D. O., and J. Citrin. 1982. *Tax Revolt: Something for Nothing in California.* Cambridge, MA: Harvard University Press.

Sears, D. O., and C. L. Funk. 1991. "The Role of Self-Interest in Social and Political Attitudes." *Advances in Experimental Social Psychology* 24: 1–91.

Simon, H. A. 1978. "Rationality as Process and as Product of Thought." *American Economic Review* 68 (2): 1–16.

———. 1985. "Human Nature in Politics: The Dialogue of Psychology and Political Science." *American Political Science Review* 79 (2): 293–304.

Sniderman, P. M. 1985. *Race and Inequality: A Study in American Values.* Chatham, NJ: Chatham House.

———. 1993. "The New Look in Public Opinion Research." In *Political Science: The State of the Discipline II*, ed. A. Finifter. Washington, DC: American Political Science Association.

Sniderman, P. M. 2000. "Taking Sides: A Fixed Choice Theory of Political Reasoning." In *Elements of Reason: Cognition, Choice, and the Bounds of Rationality,* ed. A. Lupia, M. D. McCubbins, and S. L. Popkin. Cambridge, UK: Cambridge University Press.

Sniderman, P. M., and R. A. Brody. 1977. "Coping: The Ethic of Self-Reliance." *American Journal of Political Science* 21 (3): 501–22.

Sniderman, P. M., R. A. Brody, and P. E. Tetlock. 1991. *Reasoning and Choice: Explorations in Political Psychology.* New York: Cambridge University Press.

Sniderman, P. M., and P. E. Tetlock. 1986a. "Interrelationship of Political Ideology and Public Opinion." In *Political Psychology: Contemporary Problems and Issues*, ed. M. G. Hermann, 62–96. San Francisco: Jossey-Bass.

———. 1986b. "Reflections on American Racism." *Journal of Social Issues* 42 (2): 173–87.

———. 1986c. "Symbolic Racism: Problems of Motive Attribution in Political Analysis." *Journal of Social Issues* 42 (2): 129–50.

Steenbergen, M. R., and M. Lodge. (n.d.) "Process Matters: Cognitive Models of Candidate Evaluation." Mimeograph. Department of Political Science, State University of New York at Stony Brook.

Stimson, J. A. 1991. *Public Opinion in America: Moods, Cycles, and Swings.* Boulder: Westview.

Stoker, L. 1992. "Interests and Ethics in Politics." *American Political Science Review* 86 (2): 369–80.

Stouffer, S. 1955. *Communism, Conformity, and Civil Liberties*. New York: Doubleday.

Sullivan, J., J. Pierson, and G. E. Marcus. 1982. Political Tolerance and American Democracy. Chicago: Chicago University Press.

Sullivan, J. L., W. M. Rahn, and T. J. Rudolph. 2002. "The Contours of Political Psychology: Situating Research on Political Information Processing." In *Thinking about Political Psychology*, ed. J. H. Kuklinski, 23–48. Cambridge, U.K.: Cambridge University Press.

Taber, C. S. 1998. "The Interpretation of Foreign Policy Events: A Cognitive Process Theory." In *Problem Representation in Foreign Policy Decision Making*, ed. D. A. Sylvan and J. F. Voss, 8–28. London: Cambridge University Press.

Taber, C. S., and M. Lodge. 2000. "Motivated Skepticism in the Evaluation of Political Beliefs." Paper presented at the annual meeting of the American Political Science Association, Washington, DC.

Taber, C. S., and M. Lodge. 2003. "First Steps toward a Dual-Process Accessibility Model of Political Beliefs, Attitudes, and Behavior." Paper presented at the Shambaugh Conference on Emotion and Politics, University of Iowa, March.

Taber, C. S., and M. R. Steenbergen. 1995. "Computational Experiments in Electoral Behavior." In *Political Judgment: Structure and Process,* ed. M. Lodge and K. McGraw. Ann Arbor, MI: University of Michigan Press.

Taber, C. S., and R. J. Timpone. 1996. *Computational Modeling.* Sage University Paper Series on Quantitative Applications in the Social Sciences. Newbury Park, CA: Sage.

Taber, C. S., M. Lodge, and J. Glathar. 2001. "The Motivated Construction of Political Judgments." In *Citizens and Politics: Perspectives from Political Psychology,* ed. J. H. Kuklinski. Cambridge, UK: Cambridge University Press.

Tetlock, P. E. 1986. "A Value Pluralism Model of Ideological Reasoning." *Journal of Personality and Social Psychology* 50: 819–27.

Thomsen, C. J., E. Borgida, and H. Lavine. 1995. "The Causes and Consequences of Personal Involvement." In *Attitude Strength: Antecedents and Consequences*, ed. R. E. Petty and J. A. Krosnick, 191–214. Mahwah, NJ: Erlbaum.

Thomsen, C. J., H. Lavine, and J. Kounios. 1996. "Social Value and Attitude Concepts in Semantic Memory: Relational Structure, Concept Strength, and the Fan Effect." *Social Cognition* 14: 191–25.

Thurstone, L. 1927. "A Law of Comparative Judgment." *Psychological Review* 34 (4): 273–86.

Tolman, E. C. 1932. *Purposive Behavior in Animals and Men.* New York: Appleton-Century-Crofts.

Tourangeau, R., L. J. Rips, and K. Rasinski. 2000. *The Psychology of the Survey Response.* Cambridge, UK: Cambridge University Press.

Uleman, J. S., and J. A. Bargh, eds. 1989. *Unintended Thought.* New York: Guilford.

Wilson, T. C. 1994. "Trends in Tolerance toward Rightist and Leftist Groups, 1976–1988: Effects of Attitude Change and Cohort Succession." *Public Opinion Quarterly* 58 (4): 539–56.

Wyer, R. S., and V. C. Ottati. 1993. "Political Information Processing." In *Explorations in Political Psychology*, ed. S. Iyengar and W. J. McGuire, 264–95. Durham, NC: Duke University Press.

Zaller, J. R. 1992. *The Nature and Origins of Mass Opinion.* Cambridge, UK: Cambridge University Press.

Zaller, J. R., and S. Feldman. 1992. "A Simple Theory of the Survey Response." *American Journal of Political Science* 36: 579–616.

9

Information, Social Networks, and the Demand for Public Goods: Experimental Evidence from Benin

Leonard Wantchekon and Christel Vermeersch

Introduction

The role of information and civic engagement in economic performance has attracted a great deal of attention in the recent development debate. The empirical political agency literature has identified public access to information as a key determinant of corruption levels and public goods provision in developing countries (see, for example, Besley and Burgess 2002; Reinikka and Svensson 2003). More recently, Keefer and Vlaicu (2008) explain the predominance of clientelism and low levels of public goods provision by the lack of reliable information on policies and candidates. The goal of this chapter is to contribute to this literature by investigating the relationship between membership in information and social networks and the demand for public goods. By membership in information and social networks, we mean use of media outlets as sources of information, participation in associative life and political discussions, and connections with the outside world through traveling, language skills, and long-distance family relationships.

We measure a voter's demand for public goods by assessing how his or her voting changes when he or she is exposed to a purely national public goods electoral platform instead of the regular electoral platforms. A major challenge to the estimation of voters' reactions to different electoral platforms is that electoral platforms are consciously chosen by politicians according to voters' characteristics. Even when they follow a particular electoral program, when targeting particular audiences of voters, politicians choose messages they think will appeal to those voters. Hence, the difference between voting patterns among groups of voters is likely to reflect both the electoral platforms used by the politician and the characteristics of the voters. A solution to this endogeneity problem is to randomly expose voters to particular messages and measure their voting response. The data used here originate from a unique field experiment that took place in the context of the first round of the March 2001 presidential elections in Benin. Randomly selected villages were exposed to purely redistributive or clientelistic or purely national public goods platforms, and the remaining villages were exposed to the default mixed platforms. The experiment is unique in the sense that it involves presidential candidates competing in real elections. This avoids the problems of external validity associated with laboratory experiments.

We confirm the finding in Wantchekon (2003) that voters do not favor public goods electoral platforms, as reflected in their sanctioning candidates who use them. Wantchekon found that women are less negatively oriented to these platforms than are men. A study by Fafchamps and Gabre-Madhin (2001) argued that women are the driving forces behind regional commerce in Benin, so the question arises whether the association between gender and demand for public goods is an artifact of the social networks and trade contacts in which women participate. For example, women who travel more might value development of roads and other infrastructure beyond the locality as an important policy issue. We find that individuals who have access to information have a higher demand for or lesser aversion to public goods. We find that voters who are more involved in political discussions are more averse to the public goods platform whereas those who are members of local associations are less averse. We find that, although information and membership in organizations might explain a significant amount of voter response, they do not drive the differential responses between men and women, with women still more responsive to public goods platforms. Finally, we find that certain voter characteristics reduce the aversion to public goods: Quite surprisingly, ethnic affiliates of a candidate respond more positively to a public goods electoral platform. The result also holds true for more educated voters.

This chapter contributes to the growing literature on the impact of information campaigns on the provision of public goods and accountability in governments. Reinikka and Svensson (2003) provide evidence from a policy experiment suggesting that increased public access to information reduced the level of corruption and capture of public funds in Uganda. In another important contribution to the political agency literature, Besley and Burgess (2002) use data from 16 major Indian states for the period 1958–92 to analyze governments' responses to bad economic conditions such as declines in food production and crop flood damage. They find that responses in the form of public food distribution and calamity relief expenditure are higher wherever newspaper circulation is higher. Strömberg (2004) provides similar results in the U.S. context, using data from the implementation of the New

Deal Program in 1933–35. Controlling for a host of relevant economic and demographic variables, he finds that counties with radio listeners received more relief funds. Although we do not make causal claims regarding the impact of media access, our results suggest that media outlets not only affect the nature of the agency relationships between governments and voters, but also may induce voters to have a stronger preference for national public goods. In fact, one may argue that access to media affects accountability partly because it makes voters more public spirited.

The theoretical background of our empirical results is based on Kitschelt and Wilkinson (2007) and especially Keefer and Vlaicu (2008). The latter present a model in which politicians in new democracies have credibility problems and can overcome these problems through either repeated interactions or targeted transfers. They show that, in equilibrium, politicians prefer targeted transfers, which leads to a high level of corruption and low level of public goods. An implicit assumption behind this result is that voters prefer targeted transfers when electoral promises are not credible. This implies that any individual characteristic that would increase a voter's trust in candidates would also increase his or her responsiveness to public goods platforms. In this chapter, we will focus on access to information, education, membership in organizations, and ethnic affiliation. We test the following hypotheses: More informed, more educated, more politically active voters would be more responsive to public goods platforms (because they would be more trusting of the candidates). The result would also hold for those who are from the same ethnic group as the candidate. The chapter further develops the basic results of the Benin experiment presented in Wantchekon (2003). In contrast to that earlier study, which establishes the positive effect of clientelist platforms and the negative effect of public goods platforms as well as the modifying effect of gender and incumbency, this chapter focuses on factors that mitigate the negative effect of public goods platforms (for example, information, education, and ethnicity).

Experimental Design and Data

This chapter identifies the effect of voting platforms on voting behavior using the 2001 experiment described above, which took place during the first round of presidential elections and which exposed randomly selected villages to purely redistributive clientelistic or purely national public goods platforms, while exposing the remaining villages to the default mixed platforms. The experiment took place during the first round of presidential elections in March 2001 in Benin. For more details about politics in Benin, see Wantchekon (2003). In these elections, 16 candidates, representing or endorsed by 16 parties, took part in the first round. The research team identified the five most important candidates and invited four of them to participate in the experiment through the intermediation of their parties. These four candidates were chosen so that there would be two national and two regional candidates, two northern and two southern candidates, and two incumbent and two opposition candidates. The distribution of the candidates who participated in the experiment is presented in table 9.1.

The main concern in the design of the experiment was to avoid any potential effect of the experiment on the election result. For this purpose, the experiment was conducted by candidates only in their respective stronghold districts. An electoral district was defined as a party's stronghold if the party gained at least 70 percent of the votes in each of the previous presidential elections (1991 and 1996). Using this definition, 21 out of the 24 electoral districts in Benin were classified as strongholds of one party, and the others were classified as competitive. Once the strongholds were identified, two stronghold districts were randomly picked for each of the four parties participating in the experiment. For one candidate, Lafia, the choice of districts was done slightly differently. Lafia did not participate in the previous presidential elections, but he participated in the 1999 legislative election. Based on the results of those elections, it appeared that two electoral districts were highly likely to turn out to be his strongholds, and hence, these districts were selected to take part in the experiment. However, it turned out that in one of those districts, Lafia was not the dominant candidate in the 2001 election and that another candidate dominated. Because the experiment was meant to measure voters' response to changes in platforms by the dominant candidate, ex post this district did not qualify to be part of the sample. Table 9.1 summarizes the distribution of strongholds among the experimental candidates.

In each chosen district, two villages were randomly picked to take part in the experiment. If the two villages were less than 20 kilometers apart, the second village was put back into the pool, and another village was picked. Then a coin was flipped to decide which one of the two villages would be in the public goods treatment group, and which one would be in the clientelistic treatment group. According to the 2001 census, the population consists of 6,633 registered voters in the redistributive/clientelistic treatment group, 6,983 voters in the public goods treatment group, and approximately 220,000 voters in the control group. For the purpose of the survey used in this chapter, one village was randomly picked from the control group to be in the comparison group.

Table 9.1. Presidential Candidates and Parties Participating in the Experiment

Party	Candidate	Candidate characteristics			Experimental strongholds
		Affiliation	Area	Office	
FARD-Alafia	Kerekou	National	North	Incumbent	2 Strongholds out of 4
RB	Soglo	National	South	Opposition	2 Strongholds out of 4
PSD	Amoussou	Regional	South	Incumbent	2 Strongholds out of 3
USD	Lafia	Regional	North	Opposition	1 Strongholds out of 1

Source: Authors.

Estimation Method

We estimate the effects of the public goods and clientelistic treatments on voting behavior using the following probit model:

$$P\,(Y_{ij} = 1/x_{ij},\,T_i) = P\,(x_{ij}a + T_i\beta + x_{ij}T_i\gamma + u_{ij} > 0)$$
$$u_i \overset{id}{\sim} N\,(0,\Omega_i)$$

where ij is a categorical variable that takes value 1 if individual j in village i votes for the experimentalist candidate and 0 otherwise, x_{ij} is the vector of individual characteristics for individual j in village i, and T_i is the categorical variable for treatment in village i. The sampling follows a three-stage cluster sampling design: Seven districts were randomly chosen in a stratified way from the sampling frame, the set of stronghold districts of the four experimental candidates. Within each district, two villages were randomly chosen, and within the villages 35 households were randomly sampled, and all adults within the household were interviewed. In the estimation, standard errors are clustered at the village level. Because this allows for any kind of correlation of the observations within the villages, no further clustering is required to account for intrahousehold correlation.

The dependent variable is a categorical variable that takes value 1 if the respondent voted for the experimentalist candidate and value 0 otherwise. Because in all villages the experimentalist was also the dominant candidate, we will interchangeably use the terms experimentalist candidate and dominant candidate. Because the dominant candidate commands at least 70 percent of the votes, and the remaining 15 candidates share the rest, the strategic behavior of the other candidates is unlikely to have a substantial effect on voting outcomes. In the estimation of the effect of the public goods treatment, the sample always consists of all respondents in the public goods treatment villages and all respondents in the control villages. The sample used for estimating the effect of the clientelistic treatment consists of the respondents in the clientelistic treatment villages and in the control villages. Because a substantial number of regressors are categorical variables, we calculate and report the mean marginal effects of the regressors rather than the marginal effects at the mean of the independent variables.

In the analysis, we investigate the modifying effect of voter characteristics on their response to the experimental platforms. Whereas Wantchekon (2003) analyzes the modifying effect of gender, ethnic affiliation, and incumbency of the dominant candidate, we analyze the modifying effect of voter membership in various social and information networks, education levels, socioeconomic status, marital status, and religion.

Our measure of socioeconomic status stems from a principal components analysis of the respondents' housing characteristics. We do not use any direct measures of income because more than 60 percent of respondents report being farmers, and only 2.6 percent are formally employed. It is a well-known issue that surveys of income in such circumstances do not adequately represent household socioeconomic status, and that consumption surveys are preferable. For a variety of reasons, it was not possible to collect consumption data in the survey. The housing indicator compounds information such as the availability of tap water, brick walls (as opposed to mud walls), tile and cement floors (as opposed to mud floors), and electricity in the homestead. Finally, the data contain a self-reported assessment of respondents' income stability and whether they are involved in commercial activities, which we use to perform some robustness checks.

Results

In table 9.2, we confirm that the dataset we use mimics the results found in Wantchekon (2003). In general, the point estimates are consistent with Wantchekon, although estimations using the present dataset are less precise. We think this is because (1) we are using a different dataset and (2) the one-year lag between the election and the survey introduced recall error regarding voting patterns, which decreases the precision of our estimates. The second difference with Wantchekon is that estimates of the treatment effect for the clientelistic experiment are closer to zero in this chapter. We think this is because this study excludes villages where the experimental candidate was

Table 9.2. Estimation of the Treatment Effect

	Public goods experiment			Clientelistic experiment		
	(1)	(2)	(3)	(4)	(5)	(6)
Treatment = 1	−0.108	−0.075	−0.189	0.004	0.022	−0.075
	(0.111)	(0.113)	(0.084)	(0.092)	(0.078)	(0.075)
Ethnic ties = 1		0.142	0.079		0.145	0.075
		(0.055)	(0.067)		(0.084)	(0.056)
Male = 1		−0.010	0.019		0.030	0.011
		(0.025)	(0.019)		(0.015)	(0.016)
Age		−0.002	−0.002		−0.001	−0.001
		(0.001)	(0.001)		(0.001)	(0.001)
Education level		−0.058	−0.138		−0.092	−0.105
		(0.036)	(0.029)		(0.025)	(0.028)
Housing quality PC		0.012	0.010		−0.008	−0.009
		(0.011)	(0.011)		(0.007)	(0.007)
Ethnic ties × Treatment			0.076			0.069
			(0.079)			(0.082)
Male × Treatment			−0.056			0.038
			(0.044)			(0.020)
Education × Treatment			0.139			0.023
			(0.064)			(0.027)
Observations	1,285	1,249	1,249	1,330	1,302	1,302
Pseudo-R^2	0.02	0.06	0.08	0.00	0.09	0.09
Candidate fixed effects?	No	No	No	No	No	No
Sampling weights?	No	No	No	No	No	No

Source: Authors.
Notes: The dependent variable is a categorical variable that takes value 1 if the respondent voted for the experimentalist candidate and value 0 otherwise. The estimation method is Probit. The reported estimates are mean marginal effects. Standard errors are clustered at the village level and are reported in parentheses. PC stands for principal components. Variables with the "PC" suffix were estimated using principal components analysis.

Table 9.3. Estimation of the Treatment Effect: Interaction with Information and Social Network Measures

	Public goods experiment			Clientelistic experiment		
	(1)	(2)	(3)	(4)	(5)	(6)
Treatment = 1	−0.181	−0.202	−0.152	−0.050	−0.027	−0.030
	(0.092)	(0.080)	(0.095)	(0.069)	(0.061)	(0.070)
Ethnic ties = 1	0.057	0.027	0.017	0.052	0.045	0.030
	(0.058)	(0.048)	(0.045)	(0.046)	(0.044)	(0.037)
Ethnic ties × Treatment	0.101	0.117	0.106	0.053	0.030	0.058
	(0.060)	(0.057)	(0.058)	(0.063)	(0.049)	(0.039)
Male = 1	0.026	0.020	0.016	0.018	0.010	0.007
	(0.019)	(0.019)	(0.019)	(0.015)	(0.015)	(0.016)
Male × Treatment	−0.061	−0.052	−0.040	0.054	0.049	0.032
	(0.031)	(0.026)	(0.026)	(0.036)	(0.034)	(0.035)
Age	−0.001	0.000	0.000	−0.001	−0.001	0.000
	(0.001)	(0.001)	(0.001)	(0.001)	(0.001)	(0.001)
Education level	−0.100	−0.089	−0.080	−0.079	−0.066	−0.061
	(0.019)	(0.021)	(0.022)	(0.019)	(0.022)	(0.025)
Education × Treatment	0.077	0.078	0.057	0.012	0.012	0.005
	(0.033)	(0.025)	(0.025)	(0.017)	(0.020)	(0.027)
Media PC × Treatment	−0.059	−0.053	−0.053	−0.045	−0.033	−0.033
	(0.019)	(0.015)	(0.014)	(0.016)	(0.016)	(0.015)
Media PC × Treatment	0.098	0.072	0.063	0.025	0.020	0.035
	(0.030)	(0.017)	(0.019)	(0.021)	(0.017)	(0.020)
Outside contacts PC	−0.044	−0.030	−0.029	−0.028	−0.021	−0.025
	(0.019)	(0.018)	(0.016)	(0.014)	(0.016)	(0.016)
Outside contacts PC × Treatment	0.000	−0.016	−0.009	0.029	0.029	0.034
	(0.024)	(0.024)	(0.019)	(0.019)	(0.021)	(0.026)
Memberships PC × Treatment	−0.019	−0.015	−0.015	−0.013	−0.007	−0.005
	(0.014)	(0.010)	(0.010)	(0.010)	(0.011)	(0.010)
Memberships PC × Treatment	0.084	0.062	0.057	0.029	0.032	0.024
	(0.021)	(0.017)	(0.019)	(0.019)	(0.016)	(0.017)
Political discussion PC	0.034	0.040	0.040	0.023	0.037	0.039
	(0.021)	(0.014)	(0.013)	(0.016)	(0.016)	(0.015)
Political discussion PC × Treatment	−0.091	−0.065	−0.072	−0.032	−0.043	−0.065
	(0.041)	(0.020)	(0.018)	(0.021)	(0.019)	(0.015)
Housing quality PC	0.000	0.000	0.007	−0.013	−0.011	−0.010
	(0.012)	(0.012)	(0.012)	(0.007)	(0.007)	(0.007)
Observations	1,083	1,083	1,083	1,103	1,103	1,103
Pseudo-R^2	0.18	0.26	0.20	0.17	0.22	0.19
Candidate fixed effects?	No	Yes	Yes	No	Yes	Yes
Sampling weights?	No	No	Yes	No	No	Yes

Source: Authors.
Notes: The dependent variable is a categorical variable that takes value 1 if the respondent voted for the experimentalist candidate and value 0 otherwise. The estimation method is Probit. The reported estimates are mean marginal effects. Standard errors are clustered at the village level and are reported in parentheses. PC stands for principal components. Variables with the "PC" suffix were estimated using principal components analysis (cf. table supra).

Lafia. It turns out that the clientelistic message worked particularly well for this candidate, so that excluding him tends to revert the result to zero.

We then proceed to exploring the interaction between treatment and our various measures of social and information networks (table 9.3). Columns 1 through 3 report the results from the public goods experiment, and columns 4 through 6 report the results from the clientelistic experiment. The regressions reported in columns 2, 3, 5, and 6 contain candidate fixed effects, and those in columns 3 and 6 also use sample weights. The standard errors are clustered at the village level. By and large, the public goods treatment leads to a significant decrease in the probability of voting for the experimentalist, and even more so for men. The effect of the clientelistic treatment is negative but non-significant (column 4). The magnitude of the effect of the public goods treatment is very substantial.

We find that respondents who use media outlets react less negatively to the public goods treatment. The interaction effect between use of media and treatment is sizeable: A one standard deviation increase in use of media (1.15) is associated with 7.3 to 11.3 percentage points higher responsiveness to public goods treatment.

Memberships in organizations and political discussions have opposite interaction effects with the public goods treatment. Respondents who are members of parties, unions, or nongovernmental organizations (NGOs) react more positively to the public goods message: A one standard deviation increase in memberships (1.14) is associated with 6.5 to 9.5 percentage points higher responsiveness to public goods treatment. By contrast, a one standard deviation increase in the discussions measure (1.17) is associated with 7.6 to 10.7 percentage points lower responsiveness to this treatment.

One may wonder whether use of media, outside contacts, membership in organizations, and political discussions are just artifacts of the education level and economic status of a voter. In other words, the more educated a voter is, the more likely he or she is to be broadly connected, or vice versa. For this reason, we control for voters' level of education and interact their education level with the treatment variable, and we also control for voters' housing quality. We find that education has a substantial level effect: For example, a shift from no education to primary education decreases the probability of voting for the dominant candidate between 8.0 and 10.0 percentage points. As for the interaction effect with treatment, we find that voters with a primary school education are 5.7 to 7.8 percentage points more likely to vote for the experimentalist candidate in the public goods experiment than voters with no education. There is no such interaction effect in the clientelistic experiment.

The coefficient estimates on education, ethnic ties, gender, and housing quality and their interactions with the treatment variable are robust to the changes in the categorization of the networking and information variables. In addition, the coefficient estimates are quite robust to the addition of candidate fixed effects. The stability of the estimates to the inclusion of village-level controls alleviates concerns that the small sample size might not appropriately balance unobservable village characteristics.

Discussion and Relation to the Literature

Our first main finding is that voters' preferences for public goods differ when they have different access to media. This could be explained in several ways. It is worthwhile to keep in mind that the messages conveyed on television, on the radio, and in newspapers and magazines are largely national in nature. Therefore, voters who listen to the radio or television and voters who read newspapers and magazines may have a better sense or knowledge of the problems of the country as a whole and might be more receptive to a public goods message. In addition, listening to the radio, watching television, or reading the newspapers might foster a sense of community among listeners and readers, which would make them more attentive to the needs of fellow community members. Alternatively, access to the media strengthens voters' ability to monitor the implementation of platforms. Because the implementation of national platforms is inherently more difficult to monitor than for redistributive platforms, it is clear that media access will strengthen support for national platforms.

Our findings differ from those in Strömberg (2004) and Besley and Burgess (2000), who emphasize the role of radio as an information device that facilitates monitoring given voters' preferences. Strömberg (2004) finds that the expansion of radio in the 1930s in the United States led to a substantial increase in the provision of public goods, presumably because radio listeners were more aware of policies that affected them and had better information with which to monitor their political representatives. Besley and Burgess (2000) find that, given citizens' preferences, the media make governments more responsive to citizens' needs. In contrast to these papers, we document how people's preferences differ when their access to the media varies. In addition, we use disaggregated data at the voter level rather than data that are spatially aggregated.

Our second main finding relates to voters' membership in parties, unions, and NGOs. We find that members of such organizations react less negatively to public goods messages than nonmembers. Again, several possible explanations are available for this. First, organizational membership connects people to a regional or national community, which might lead to more knowledge about the needs of the country as a whole. Thus, in a sense, organizations are broad social networks. Second, membership might be correlated with entrepreneurship, which itself might be correlated with a higher expected spatial mobility, which would lead to higher demand for national public goods. Third, members of a party might trust their political leadership more than other people, and hence, they might be more responsive to their leader's message, regardless of the content of the message, a follow-the-leader interpretation. This is different from Olsen's (1982) story, which argues that membership in organizations leads to higher demand for clientelism, as organizations exploit their power to extract rents through policies that benefit them when their opposition is spread and not organized. This is in line with Putnam, Leonardi, and Nannetti's (1993) story of a relationship between organizational membership and better governance and economic performance.

Narayan and Pritchett (1999) analyze the relationship between membership in associations and income in rural villages in Tanzania. In the ordinary least squares analysis, they find a positive and significant correlation between the two measures. In an attempt to identify the causal effect of memberships on income, they use trust as an instrumental variable for memberships and find a significantly larger coefficient estimate, which suggests measurement error in their variable for memberships. We find no positive association between memberships and assets in our data.

The third main finding of the chapter is a positive correlation between local political discussions and the probability of voting for the dominant candidate. The first explanation for this finding is that discussions are an artifact of political support for the dominant candidate. If people prefer discussing political issues with others who share the same political preferences, then people supporting the dominant candidate have more preferred discussion partners and hence will discuss political issues more often. In addition, if there is a danger of being isolated or ostracized when voicing nondominant political preferences, then people supporting a nondominant candidate will talk politics less often. This result is in line with the findings of Beck and others (2002), indicating that interpersonal discussions had a significant effect on the vote for both Bill Clinton and George H. W. Bush in the 1992 presidential elections in the United States.

Another possible explanation for the link between political discussions and voting for the dominant candidate comes from the concept of distance. The discussion variable might capture the geographic distance between households under the assumption that shorter distances lead to more human interactions, among them political discussions. On the other hand, shorter geographic distance might also lead to voting externalities because it facilitates effective transmission of information about voting behavior. The availability of information about voting behavior would in turn make possible social sanctions against community members for deviant voting. In short, geographic distance can be correlated with both political discussions and voting externalities, leading to a correlation between political discussions and voting behavior in the regressions. Because we do not have measures of geographic distance between households, it is not possible to assess whether this story is a plausible explanation for the findings.

Next, we turn to the negative correlation between political discussions and public goods treatments. Our main explanation for this result is that political discussions create communities that are intrinsically local, with little connection to outside communities. This makes it different from memberships in organizations or media usage. Local discussions without links to the outside world reinforce local bonding and demands for redistribution toward the locality.

The stronger preference of women for public goods platforms confirms the robustness of earlier results presented in Wantchekon (2003). In that paper, two potential explanations were provided. The first points to the fact that women are excluded from the most common forms of redistribution and are more responsive to platforms stressing public health or education reforms.

The second explanation focuses on occupational choice. Fafchamps and Gabre-Madhin (2001) find that although men dominate agricultural production in Benin, 80 percent of interregional agricultural product traders in the country are women. They find that a significant proportion of traders travel weekly to other regions of the country and speak several languages. If women dominate trade in general, one might think that women tend to be better informed about social and economic conditions in the country than men and could, for that reason, value broad-based public policies. In our data, we find no evidence that trade in general, as opposed to agricultural trade, is dominated by women, that women travel more, or that they speak more languages than men. For example, 44 percent of traders in our sample are men, and the average number of languages spoken is 1.35 for women and 1.6 for men. Hence, it appears that the results in Fafchamps and Gabre-Madhin (2001) are largely driven by their sampling frame.

Conclusions

An unusual political experiment carried out during the 2001 presidential elections in Benin provided a unique opportunity to investigate the extent to which information and civic community affect voters' responsiveness to national public goods platforms. We find that access to media and membership in local organizations is associated with lower distaste for the public goods platform, whereas persons more involved in political discussions tend to show higher distaste for it. Our results suggest that public access to information and use of media outlets may not only make governments more responsive, but also shape voters' demand for growth-promoting policies. Paradoxically, ethnic ties between voters and candidates can increase the demand for national public goods. Thus ethnic ties and media access have similar effects, arguably because they both enhance voters' ability to monitor politicians. We confirm the finding in Wantchekon (2003) that women are more favorable to public goods platforms, and we show that this cannot be explained by education levels, occupation, or spatial mobility levels. We find no evidence that religion or assets influence voting patterns after controlling for gender, ethnic ties, education, and memberships in social networks.

One of the questions arising from this study is what the treatment effect would have been had the experiment taken place in competitive districts as opposed to noncompetitive districts. For instance, would ethnic affiliates of the dominant candidate remain as responsive to public goods treatment in more competitive and hence ethnic diverse districts? We intend to address this question in future research. In Benin, approximately 80 percent of the districts are noncompetitive, and this includes almost all rural districts and some urban districts. Hence, our results are externally valid for an important part of the country. Another limitation of the current experiment is the fact that experimental platforms were framed either narrowly or broadly and lacked specific policy content. This method contrasts with most impact evaluation works, which pay no attention to politics and political processes. This latter approach clearly limits the extent to which successful interventions can be brought to scale, in contexts in which politicians are unsure about the electoral consequences of advocating those policies. The next step will be to integrate these two approaches to assess the impact of specific policy proposals on electoral responses. Rather than being technical proposals for government bureaucrats, proven policy reforms could become part of the public domain and become the basis of substantial debate in election times. This would involve evaluating the technical aspect of passing an economically efficient policy through the political process to find policies that pass two tests: economic efficiency and political economy considerations.

Bibliography

Beck, P. A., R. Dalton, S. Green, and R. Huckfeldt. 2002. "The Social Calculus of Voting: Interpersonal, Media, and Organizational Influences on Presidential Choices." *American Political Science Review* 96: 57–73.

Besley, T., and R. Burgess. 2000. "Land Reform, Poverty Reduction, and Growth: Evidence from India." *Quarterly Journal of Economics* 115 (2): 389–430.

Besley, T., and R. Burgess. 2002. "The Political Economy of Government Responsiveness: Theory and Evidence from India." *Quarterly Journal of Economics* 117 (4): 1415–51.

Easterly, W., and R. Levine. 1997. "Africa Growth Tragedy: Policies and Ethnic Divisions." *Quarterly Journal of Economics* 112 (4): 1203–50.

Fafchamps, M., and E. Gabre-Madhin. 2001. "Agricultural Markets in Benin and Malawi: The Operation and Performance of Traders." World Bank Policy Research Working Paper 2734, World Bank, Washington, DC.

Glaeser, E., D. Laibson, and B. Sacerdote. 2002. "An Economic Approach to Social Capital." *Economic Journal* 112 (November): 437–58.

Glaeser E., G. Ponzetto, and A. Shleifer. 2007. "Why Does Democracy Need Education?" *Journal of Economic Growth* 12 (2): 77–99.

Heilbrunn, J. 1993. "Social Origin of National Conferences in Benin and Togo." *Journal of Modern African Studies* 31 (2): 277–99.

Helliwell, J., and R. Putnam. 1995. "Social Capital and Economic Growth in Italy." *Eastern Economic Journal* 21 (3): 295–307.

Hodess, R., ed. 2003. *Global Corruption Report 2003.* Berlin: Transparency International.

Keefer, P., and R. Vlaicu. 2008. "Democracy, Credibility and Clientelism." *Journal of Law, Economics and Organization* 24 (2): 371–406.

Kitschelt, H., and S. Wilkinson, eds. 2007. "Patrons, Clients, and Policies." In *Patrons, Clients, and Policies: Patterns of Democratic Accountability and Political Competition.* Cambridge, UK: Cambridge University Press.

Knack, S., and P. Keefer. 1997. "Does Social Capital Have an Economic Payoff? A Cross Country Investigation." *Quarterly Journal of Economics* 112 (4): 1251–88.

Luttmer, E. 2001. "Group Loyalty and the Taste for Redistribution." *Journal of Political Economy* 109 (3): 500–528.

Mason, A., and E. King. 2002. "Engendering Development through Gender Equality in Rights, Resources and Voice." World Bank Policy Research Report, World Bank, Washington, DC.

Mayo, E. 1933. "The Human Problems of an Industrial Civilization." New York: Macmillan.

Miguel, E. 2004. "Tribe or Nation? Nation-Building and Public Goods in Kenya versus Tanzania." *World Politics* 56 (3): 327–62.

Miguel, E., and M. K. Gugerty. 2005. "Ethnic Diversity, Social Sanctions, and Public Goods in Kenya." *Journal of Public Economics* 89 (11–12): 2325–68.

Ministere de l'Agriculture, de l'Elevage et de la Peche, DANIDA et PNUD, République du Benin. 2001. "Etude sur les conditions de vie des ménages ruraux." Government of Benin, Porto-Novo.

Narayan, D., and L. Pritchett. 1999. "Cents and Sociability: Household Income and Social Capital in Rural Tanzania." *Economic Development and Cultural Change* 47 (4): 871–97.

Nwajiaku, K. 1994. "The National Conferences in Benin and Togo Revisited." *Journal of Modern African Studies* 32 (3): 429–47.

Olsen, M. 1982. "*The Rise and Decline of Nations.*" New Haven, CT: Yale University.

Putnam, R., R. Leonardi, and R. Nannetti. 1993. *Making Democracy Work.* Princeton, NJ: Princeton University Press.

Reinikka, R., and J. Svensson. 2003. "The Power of Information: Evidence from a Newspaper Campaign to Reduce Capture." World Bank Working Paper 3239, World Bank, Washington, DC.

Strömberg, D. 2004. "Radio's Impact on Public Spending. " *Quarterly Journal of Economics* 119 (1): 189–221.

Wantchekon, L. 2003. "Clientelism and Voting Behavior: Evidence from a Field Experiment in Benin." *World Politics* 55 (3): 399–422.

Wantchekon, L. 2004. "Ethnicity, Gender and Demand for Public Goods." BREAD Working Paper 067.

World Bank. 1997. *World Development Report 1997: The State in a Changing World.* Washington, DC: World Bank.

Building Capacity through Media Institutions (Media and Journalism)

10

Training Journalists for Accountability in Argentina

Laura Zommer

With over 800 freedom of information requests since 2004 by University of Buenos Aires (UBA) students to the Executive branch of the National Government of Argentina (Poder Ejecutivo Nacional [PEN]) and the three branches of the Autonomous City of Buenos Aires (Ciudad Autónoma de Buenos Aires [CABA]), the project I created to systematically monitor the fulfillment of the national and city freedom of information laws constitutes a continuous and, probably, the most rigorous exercise of freedom of information rights currently carried out in Argentina. In this struggle, the students, besides familiarizing themselves with a legal tool that has the potential of being invaluable in their studies and professional careers, have discovered a wealth of information, ranging from the fact that their relatives have the right to receive free medication to the knowledge that the Ministry of Defense explains the commercial airline transportation crisis with arguments far different from the explanation offered by its minister to the press.

As part of their study program, hundreds of students of Communication Sciences of the Social Sciences Faculty at UBA face the challenge of dealing with government public servants taking refuge behind Presidential Decree 1172/3 and Law 104 of the CABA. Thus, this activity, which recently acquired institutional recognition as an accredited investigation of the Faculty,[1] is a genuine program for monitoring governmental transparency.

History of the Initiative

Freedom of information is one of the topics included in the required Right to Information course taught as part of the Communication Sciences degree.[2]

Until the last semester of 2004, this topic, like many others, was approached with an overview of national and international norms protecting this right and the completion of exercises or practice work with imaginary examples.

I have long been interested in freedom of information, which led me to propose a change in the teaching methodology of this section of the program—with excellent results. I suppose my passion for the topic speaks to my double role as a journalist and lawyer and that during my time as a public functionary—I was cabinet chief of the Interior Security Secretariat of the Ministry of Justice between June 2003 and August 2004—Decree 1172/3 was passed, regulating freedom of information requests for Executive branch matters.[3] At that time, soon after reading the norm, I understood its importance, but also its complexity, and I identified multiple challenges to be overcome. Several challenges related to the actual functioning of the state and the performance of its public servants, but others had to do with the need for citizens to know and make use of this right for the system of freedom of information to really function.

With these challenges in mind, the students themselves suggested the project of systematic monitoring. The methodological change meant we would no longer work with made-up examples, but each student would request information from PEN authorities and other entities covered by the previously cited decree, or from any of the CABA government bodies covered since 1998 under Law 104,[4] which regulates this right in the context of the Executive, Legislative, and Judicial branches of the city's government. The practical exercise was at first done only in my section of the course, but the following year became a requirement for every student in all eight sections of the course. This decision was made by then-adjunct professor and current head of the course Damián Loreti, who especially valued the public university's potential contributions to improving the implementation of freedom of information norms.[5]

The objective of this exercise is twofold: From the pedagogic perspective, it seeks to familiarize students with a tool that will be of value in their studies and careers. From the institutional point of view, it aims to exercise and strengthen governmental organisms' mechanisms of receiving and answering freedom of information requests. Given that Argentines are unfamiliar with this right and that its use is still limited (aside from our students' requests, requests come mainly from the civil society sector and a few journalists),[6] in the course we consider that the realization of this exercise can contribute to initiating a change in the culture of secrecy held for decades by most national and city public servants. According to official statistics from the Sub-secretariat for Institutional Reform and Strengthening of Democracy[7]—which do not correspond with other monitoring results—between April 2004 and July 2005, 386 requests for information were presented, of which 370 were answered, although some in partial form and others extemporaneously.

Results and Findings

Since we started this activity, UBA students have presented 816 requests for information, of which at least 433 have been responded to (about 53 percent).[8] Several requests turned out to be extremely useful for some students, their families, and friends because access to information permitted the exercise of other rights, such as the right to health care in the case of Mariela Salas and Marina Ligorria, who took the class in 2004 and 2006, respectively.

The ministry that received most of the requests was the Ministry of Health, which had 97, followed by Education with 69, Interior with 54, and Economy and Federal Planning with 51 each. These are followed by Work with 41, Chief of Cabinet with 38, Justice with 34, Foreign Relations with 26, and, with far fewer requests, Social Development with 18 and Defense and the General Secretariat of the Presidency with just five each. In addition, the Broadcasting Federal Commission received 23 requests, and the National Institute of Cinema and Audiovisual Arts received 11, one more than the Faculty of Social Sciences of the UBA, where the students study. Thirty-four requests were presented to the government of CABA, and the Buenos Aires Ministry of Health was the local entity that received most of the requests: The 16 requests it received confirmed the specific interest shown by the students in health policies.

Contrary to what one might assume, the great majority of requests did not have to do with corruption, intelligence, defense, national security, or state secrets.[9] Most focused on matters linked to health and education. In many cases the students asked for information available on official websites. This shows, on the one hand, a certain general lack of knowledge about what information the government places at the disposal of citizens and, on the other, that information published on official websites is not simple for the average citizen to find and that the government lacks a proactive attitude toward publicizing public information (except when it carries out targeted campaigns about specific topics, an infrequent occurrence).

Some examples of the requests for official information sought by young students, typically 17 to 20 years old, placed in 2004 are the following:

- The train lines and branches that have stopped working since 1993
- The public works that were carried out in the past five years
- The number of kidnappings that occurred in the past two years
- The annual budget that the government assigns to promoting swimming
- The criteria used for surveying handicapped people and what subsidies they receive
- The infant mortality rate (with specific percentages, causes, and consequences) in the period between May 2003 and June 2004
- The last changes made to the Buenos Aires Código de Convivencia (which regulates petty infractions)
- The president's agenda for the week of October 26–30, 2003[10]

- The decision whether a project was approved to start refurbishing the former Terrabusi factory on San José (supposed to be the new building for the Faculty of Social Sciences of the UBA)
- The national child delinquency index from January 2001 through the time of request
- The number of paid and unpaid staff at the Hospital J. Fernández of the Autonomous City of Buenos Aires
- The annual budget for rural schools in Buenos Aires in 2004 and for national universities in 2005
- The annual budget for education
- The budget for the Catholic Church in 2003
- The budget assigned to AIDS prevention and free medication for people infected with HIV
- The amount invested in the construction of the Yacretá dam.[11]

Two methodologies were used for the requests. In some sections, students had a class and a subsequent recitation, receiving instruction from the professor to correctly formulate their requests. In the remaining sections, students received no help in crafting their requests, to provide information on how authorities respond to average citizens with no expertise or familiarity with legal wording and the specific law. The right to information, recognized expressly in the National Constitution after the 1994 constitutional reform,[12] states that *each individual* has the right to *seek, investigate, receive, and spread* information and ideas of all kinds. For this reason, we were interested in watching the official reaction to imperfect requests, containing mistakes or omissions that any person might commit. This allows us to evaluate the attitude taken by public servants when they detect the difficulties members of society have when exercising a constitutional right.

A strong disparity is evident regarding the performance of the ministers and entities in question, as are improvements over time by some of them. In 2004, out of a total of 36 requests put together by students, 18 were responded to by authorities, some in a timely manner and others not,[13] another 14 had no response, and four were incorrectly formatted or not delivered for various reasons.

The next year, the results were considerably worse in the first semester: of the 94 freedom of information requests presented, only 31 obtained an answer, which represents less than 33 percent. On the whole, 2005 was not a good year for freedom of information in the country: The proposed national freedom of information law that had been awaiting ratification from both chambers of Congress lost parliamentary status, which, through diverse actions, confirmed that Congress is still reticent to recognize the right to information as a human right and not a power held by legislators.

The PEN, which in December 2003 had given an encouraging sign with Decree 1172/3, evinced worrisome backsliding in terms of freedom of information in the field of national administration: (a) the Secretary of State Intelligence (Secretaría de Inteligencia del Estado [SIDE]) excluded itself from coverage by the decree, (b) the Legal and Technical Secretariat of the presidency maintained in two decisions that in certain cases the decree is not applicable because the Rules of Administrative Procedures (Decree 1759/72) take precedence, and (c) the Ministry of the Interior developed in its judicial area a criterion that violated the principle of informality—which states that no formal requirements are needed to make the request (that is, there is no set form or any specifications on how to make the submission of the request)—of President Kirchner's decree and clearly places obstacles in the path of freedom of public information in organizations critical to the function of democracy, such as the Secretary of Homeland Security, the National Migration Direction, and the National Electoral Direction, to name just a few examples.

Among the answered requests, one response from the Secretariat of Human Rights in the National Ministry of Justice deserves to be singled out: It states that "no state archives were found stating which citizens exercised the option granted by Article 23 of the National Constitution to exit by their own will after the 1976 coup." It clarifies that "no archives created by the military dictatorship fitting this description were found, reason for which there is no register regarding people who left the country between November 1974—the date the state of siege was declared—and December 1983." Another notable response came from the chief of the cabinet of the ministers' office, which sent a photocopy of the chief of the cabinet's pay stub to the student who asked what salary that functionary, Alberto Fernández, earned, neglecting to even cross out the bank account number. This approach is questionable under the habeas data law, Law 25.326, which protects personal information. Yet another notable response came from the Ministry of Justice, this one regarding statistics for kidnapping, express kidnapping,[14] and other crimes: Information for the entire country was provided with the exception of the province of Buenos Aires, with the explanation that that jurisdiction did not provide the national office with data.

Also of note were the answers from the Ministry of Health about Chagas disease; one from Education about the budget and local government situation for UBA and another about Communication scholarships to study abroad; another from the Secretariat for the Prevention of Drug Addiction and Drug Trafficking about addiction prevention for which they gave the student a personal meeting; another from the Secretary of Energy about the Use of Rational Energy Program; and, finally, one from the National Commission of Communication regarding the number of complaints currently received by the telephone users organizations and the way it handles them, to which it responded that the information is available on the Internet. In addition, based on the answers to other requests, we note a certain ease of access to budgetary information in the Ministry of Economy and associated agencies and information linked to disclosing social programs, especially in the Ministry of Work.

Student requests to decentralized organizations encountered special diffi-culties. One petitioner was told by phone that the SIDE had excluded itself from the freedom of information decree. With regard to the Ministry of the Interior, which received the most student requests, this organization was clearly the least willing to give out information: Of a total of 12 requests, only one received a response. The response was a letter from the interior minister, Aníbal Fernández, explaining to the student that they would not respond to the request for information from the federal police because it is not compiled and the decree does not require them to do so, except one law that specifically does (which is correct). Of the other 11 requests, six students received letters to their homes stating that before an answer could be released by the General Directory of Judicial Affairs of the Ministry of the Interior, the students would have to "formally constitute a domiciliary address following the terms of Arti-cle 1 and subsequent articles of the Administrative Procedures Regulations (T.O. Decree 1183/91)." The other five received no answer, which is a negative answer, according to the decree.

After the monitoring results were published in the newspaper *La Nación*, the percentage of answered requests increased, although it is impossible to state that the change was due solely to this. Since this publication, more than half of the requests have received official responses. Surprisingly, some minis-tries, such as the Ministry of Interior and Federal Planning, which generally did not respond, have started to do so.

In the second half of 2005, out of a total of 170 requests, 93 were answered, which means that nearly 55 percent of the students received some kind of answer, although in many cases it was only the notification that the extra 10 days would be used or that the request had been addressed to the wrong organization. In the first semester of 2006, 167 students presented requests, and 96 received some sort of response; in the second semester, 165 students presented requests, and 83 received responses. In 2007, the results were even better: out of 184 requests, 112 had some level of success, which equals more than 60 percent.

Although quantitatively—at least in nonsensitive requests—the national and Buenos Aires governments have noticeably improved in their job of pro-viding information, undesirable practices continue to exist. Among them is the fact that the 10-day period allowed by the law for responding to requests is rarely met, and the petitioner is rarely informed that extra time will be taken. During all the years in which the students have been making these requests, information has never been denied them by the use of some excep-tions actually permitted by law. What has been used, as previously mentioned, is the Law of Protection of Personal Information (Law 25.326). On the other hand, one can say fairly that it is easier now than a few years ago for students to address their requests to organizations, even in handwritten form, and to obtain the confirmation of receipt signature and date from the corresponding functionary.

Among the last requests that deserve emphasis are (a) one from a student who requested the times during which a federal police officer was required to be at the corner by her house and who was summoned to her neighborhood commission to give an affidavit with the question and the answer (which, as is to be expected, frightened the student); (b) another request about the accidents provoked by radar system failures between 1990 and 2006, which obtained a different answer from what the minister of defense, Nilda Garré, had declared publicly some months earlier; (c) another request linked to the corruption case involving a Swedish company, Skanska, which has not yet received a formal answer from the Ministry of Planning but led several Energas public servants to state by phone their fear of giving the requested information; and (d) many requests presented to public service providers, such as Edesur and Trains of Buenos Aires (TBA), which were answered, unlike in previous years, when companies refused to accept the decree's applicability to them. An interesting request, which did receive a response, asked for the number of students who entered the National Library in 2006; another asked about the subsidies received by TBA; and a third requested the details of every request for information received by the chief of the cabinet's office to that date.

Looking Forward

The monitoring work carried out by UBA students is not perceived or valued equally by all public servants working on issues relating to freedom of information.[15] Over the years, although a few public servants thanked us for our collaboration in forcing them to exercise and practice the norms and the system of freedom of information, others questioned students' requests for "random information" that was not used later and was considered to be a waste of resources in a country as poor as Argentina.

We do not doubt that the experience is a valuable one, for the students as well as for the public servants, which is the reason we will continue to do it twice a year. We believe, additionally, that the increase in requests for information, and the increase in interest on the part of society regarding the matter, will increase the chances of Argentina's one day having a national Freedom of Information Act and 24 similar provincial laws.

More than 70 countries, including the Dominican Republic, Ecuador, Jamaica, Mexico, Panama, Peru, and the United States, already have laws allowing access to already compiled public information or obligating the government to produce it. In Argentina, the proposed freedom of information law lost parliamentary status on November 30, 2005, because the lower chamber of Congress had not debated it yet, although the upper chamber had approved it on December 1, 2004, with ominous modifications to the text approved by the Chamber of Deputies on May 8, 2003 (see below).

The proposal approved by the deputies was unique in that it was created through a procedure of consultation with civil society unprecedented in the country. More than 20 meetings were held over eight months, in which business people, academics, journalists, nongovernmental organizations, public servants, consultants, industrial associations, and chambers of commerce, in addition to well-known international figures, were consulted by the Anticorruption Office to create a proposed law with the highest level of participation, technical quality, and legitimation. The initiative accepted the basic principles elaborated and agreed on by various organizations of civil society. It maintained that a freedom of information law must contain certain requisites and elements that guarantee its efficiency: widespread legitimation, allowing every person to access information found in the three branches of the state; a few expressly enumerated exceptions; a system of sanctions for public officials who unjustifiably deny information; and rapid judicial remedies to which citizens can turn if their rights are violated.[16] This text, with minor modifications, obtained partial approval in the lower chamber.

However, the text approved by the Senate with changes introduced by the Commission of Constitutional Affairs, presided over by Cristina Fernández de Kirchner—then first lady and leading presidential candidate—substantially restricts the right to freedom of public information and does not respect international and constitutional standards on the issue.[17] The senators' modifications include the obligation on the part of citizens to specify the reasons for the request; the requirement that affidavits be provided along with the requests; the establishment of fees—which vary depending on the stated reasons—to access information; the broadening of the reasons for which information can be classified; the exceptions that permit denial of access to information, such as the term for which a document can be considered confidential; and the ambiguity of the definition of "public information," which extends the obligation to include all private entities. This last point substantially changed the spirit of the proposed law, which, in addition to covering all subsections of all three national branches, included entities linked to the government or that use information of a public nature, such as concession companies for public services and the entities that receive state subsidies.

Nonetheless, in a federal country such as Argentina, it is fundamental for freedom of information to take place not only at the national level, but also at the provincial level, where the picture varies drastically by district. Half of Argentina's 24 jurisdictions have norms—laws or decrees—that, to a larger or lesser extent, recognize or guarantee this right. Freedom of information laws were approved in two provinces in 2005: Entre Ríos (Decree P.E. Provincial 1169/05) and Santiago del Estero (Law 6.753), although in the second case it meant a clear retreat, because it invalidated Law 6.715, created at the start of the 2005 federal intervention. The new law demands the invocation of interest to solicit information, which means that the petitioner must justify the reason that would enable him or her to have the right to access the information requested. These jurisdictions have joined the 10 that already had a form of protection for this right: Buenos Aires (Law 12.475 of 2000), Autonomous City of Buenos Aires (Law 104 of 1998 and Statutory Decree 1424/99), Córdoba (Law 8.835 [Ley Carta al Ciudadano] and Law 8.803 of 1999), Chubut (Law 3.764 de 1992), Jujuy (Law 4444 of 1989 and Agreed Decree 7930/03), La Pampa (Law 1.654, which grants the right only to journalists, not private individuals), Misiones (Decree 929/00), Río Negro (Law 1.829 of 1984 and Provincial Decree 1.028/04), Salta (Provincial Decree 1574/02), and Tierra del Fuego (Law 653 of 2004).

It would be interesting to see this same exercise carried out in several universities across the country. This approach would permit the extension of knowledge about the right to freedom of information among the population and contribute to good practices in the public sector. Doing so requires only the will and the initiative of a group of students and professors.

It is, however, true that the UBA experience could be much more valuable if all the information obtained to date were put at the disposal of the community, something that does not currently happen because of lack of resources. If the requests and the answers were actually archived, scanned, and put on a website, investigators, journalists, and citizens could consult them and access the information that will otherwise just become old paper as time passes.

Notes

1. Recognized by Board Resolution Number 2109 in 2007.
2. The head professor for the course is Damián Loreti; until July 2007 Henoch Aguiar held the post.
3. Decree 1172/3 was passed by President Néstor Kirchner on December 3, 2003. The full text of the norm is available at http://www.mejordemocracia.gov.ar/TextoDecreto1172–2003.php.
4. Law 104 was sanctioned by the Legislature of the Autonomous City of Buenos Aires on November 19, 1998. The full text of the norm is available at http://www.ciudadyderechos .org.ar/derechosbasicos_l.php?id=15&id2=92&id3=55.
5. The exercise conducted in the course is possible thanks to the support and efforts of Damián Loreti and the other professors of Right to Information—Angel Lanzón, Víctor Pesce, Diego Veljanovich, Esteban Lescano, Ezequiel Klass, and Mariano Román—and would be impossible without the participation and enthusiasm of the students, and the special work of compiling, analyzing, and systematizing carried out by student assistant Alejandro Crespo. Other student assistants and students work on a volunteer basis, including María Fernanda Arenas, Valeria Celis, Romina Colman, Emiliano Delio, Wanda Fairman, Vanesa Fognani, Laura Galiñanes, Natalia Mutuberria, and Inés Selvood.
6. To spread information among citizens, in May 2007, CIPPEC (Centro de Implementación de Políticas Públicas para la Equidad y el Crecimiento, or Center for the Implementation of Public Policies Promoting Equity and Growth) and Grupo Clarín created a Practical

Guide to Freedom of Information that was published as a special four-page supplement in the newspaper with the widest circulation in the country and eight provincial papers. The guide, which we created with Natalia Torres, is available at http://www.cippec.org/Main.php?do=documentsDoDownload&id=196.

7. The Sub-secretariat for Institutional Reform and Strengthening of Democracy is the office in charge of the implementation of Decree 1172/3. Its website is www.mejordemocracia.gov.ar.

8. The "at least" refers to the fact that statistics about the amount of requests presented and answers received are compiled only at the end of each semester, and if an office responds outside the legal term, the fact is not always recorded because not all students report it to the program after the end of the course.

9. These are topics for which most laws in the country and internationally provide some type of exemption.

10. This is a request directly related to the General Rules for the Management of Interests of the Executive Power, covered in Annex III of Decree 1172/3.

11. All the requests, and their corresponding answers, are available on request at the office of the Vice Dean of the Social Sciences Faculty of UBA, M.T. de Alvear 2230, first floor, Buenos Aires.

12. Article 75, subsection 22 of the Carta Magna included various human rights treaties and international pacts recognizing the right to information. Article 19 of the Universal Declaration of Human Rights states: "Every individual has the right to freedom of opinion and expression; this right includes not being bothered because of these opinions, being able to investigate and receive information and opinions and to spread them, without frontiers, by any medium of expression." Article 13, subsection 1 of the American Human Rights Convention states: "Everyone has the right to freedom of thought and expression. This right includes freedom to seek, receive, and impart information and ideas of all kinds, regardless of frontiers, either orally, in writing, in print, in the form of art, or through any other medium of one's choice." And article 19, subsection 2 of the International Pact of Civil and Political Rights says: "Every person has the right to freedom of expression; this right encompasses the freedom to seek, receive and spread information and ideas of all kind, without regard for national borders, be it orally, in written form, or in printed or artistic form or any other procedure of their choice."

13. Decree 1172/3 states that the person receiving the request is obliged to permit access to the information at the time it is solicited or to provide it in no more than 10 days. The term can be extended, exceptionally, for another 10 days, as long as the person communicates as much to the solicitor with adequate justification before the end of the term. Law 104 of the Autonomous City of Buenos Aires gives 10 business days and the possibility of a 10-day extension.

14. Express kidnapping is a crime in which a person is kidnapped for a few hours, usually not more than one day, and a small ransom is demanded for their release.

15. At the end of each semester, the course holds an open class in which results of the monitoring are presented and functionaries and members of civil society working toward freedom of information are invited to attend. The former Subsecretary for Institutional Reform and Strengthening of Democracy Marta Oyhanarte participated in two of these events.

16. The international experience allowed the creation of consensus regarding what a freedom of information law must contain to effectively channel requests for information. Some of the main requirements are

    • Widely recognizing the right for every citizen, without discrimination
    • Not requiring citizens to give reasons for their requests for information

- Clearly determining areas in which there may be exceptions: Exceptions should be presented precisely, remembering that the principle is public information and secrecy an exception
- Contemplation of mechanisms of appeals, in the case that information has not been provided, and creating norms permitting the justice system to resolve such cases.

A document about the minimum requirements is available at http://www.adc.org.ar/download.php?fileId=356.

17. Various organizations that have been pushing the approval of a freedom of information law for years—the Asociación por los Derechos Civiles, Centro de Implementación de Políticas Públicas para la Equidad y el Crecimiento, Centro de Estudios Legales y Sociales, Fundación Ambiente y Recursos Naturales, and Fundación Poder Ciudadano y el Instituto de Estudios Comparados en Ciencias Penales y Sociales—created a document, distributed in the Senate, outlining the main objections to the Constitutional Affairs Committee's decision, later approved by the Senate vote. To access the full document and the chronology of the proposed law's passage through Congress, see http://www.farn.org.ar/prensa/vs041203.html.

11

Well-Informed Journalists Make Well-Informed Citizens: Coverage of Governance Issues in the Democratic Republic of Congo

Mary Myers

Having been asked to write about building an informed citizenry in developing countries, my starting point is to assert that we cannot have an informed citizenry without informed media. For this, we need to build support for journalists and for media professionals.

As Sina Odugbemi has so succinctly stated in *With the Support of Multitudes,* "the mass media are the chief mediators of political reality, the main sources of political and economic intelligence, and significant influencers of public opinion" (Mozammel and Odugbemi 2005, 18). This chapter takes the example of the Democratic Republic of Congo and highlights issues arising from Britain's Department for International Development's (DFID) experience of supporting the media sector in that country.

In this chapter, I aim to show that if we want greater information dissemination on the roles and responsibilities of government, we first must have media professionals who understand what those roles and responsibilities are. We need to educate journalists. We need to tackle the cultural and economic problems of the media sector. We need, again to quote Odugbemi, to support the development of a "free, independent and plural mass media system" and to train journalists to cover the Poverty Reduction Strategy and other development and governance issues in an "intelligent and inclusive way" (Mozammel and Odugbemi 2005, 19).

Setting the Scene

The Democratic Republic of Congo, that vast and fragile state in the center of Africa, has much in common with the rest of the continent when it comes to shortcomings in its media sector. Here we find media that are disorganized, impoverished, and susceptible to corruption. A lamentable lack of trust is present between citizens, the state, and the media. Strikingly low literacy rates exist among the general population according to the World Bank (65.5 percent), and large parts of the country are beyond the reach even of FM radio signals, let alone within reach of newspapers, TV, or the Internet. Media infrastructure (such as power lines, radio antennas, transmitters, and printing presses) has been ruined by years of neglect and war. The majority of journalists have had no formal training, and most media outlets are shoestring operations. Civil society is weak, and, despite 80 percent participation in recent elections, civic participation is still in its infancy. Citizens are unaware of their basic rights and freedoms and completely unused to having a say in the running of their country.

And yet, despite this grim background, extraordinary creativity and vibrancy are also found in the Congolese media sector. Radio is a key source of information for most of the population; the press is relatively free by regional standards (though still far from ideal), and media outlets are many and various—even to the point of chaos. Over the last five years, the number of radio stations in the country has tripled to an estimated 450, and TV stations are growing quickly: a survey in 2008 counted 82 TV channels in the country (51 in the capital alone, with an estimated 5 million viewers) (Frère 2008). The written media are also diverse with at least 228 newspapers appearing on a regular basis nationwide (Frère 2008). Despite all the difficulties of recent years, the media have kept Congolese music and culture alive through the darkest of times.

Challenges

Let us start with the most pressing priorities of the Congolese media sector. Perhaps the biggest challenge is that of economic viability. It is a truism to say that as long as the press is not financially independent it cannot be editorially independent—but nowhere is this truer than in the Democratic Republic of Congo. The problem here is the widespread practice of *coupage*—literally, the practice of journalists taking their cut. *Coupage* is another name for brown-envelope journalism: journalists and editors being paid to run certain stories, paid to turn up at press conferences and to cover events, or simply given money to cover their "transport," "dinner," or "per diems." This practice is perpetuated by politicians, business interests, and even international donors. For instance, at the launch of the Participatory Poverty Assessment in Kinshasa in 2006 the World Bank was expected to pay the local media to cover the event.

Coupage has its roots in a lack of public purchasing power and investment on the one hand, and, on the other hand, a willingness by powerful interest groups—including warlords, charismatic churches, diamond barons, and politicians—to buy themselves positive publicity in the press. Even in the capital, Kinshasa, with its population of approximately 8 million, the market is not sufficiently large to sustain newspapers on their cover price alone. This state of affairs, coupled with low pay and lack of job security, has resulted in corruption among journalists and editors and, of course, bias, sensationalism, and lies.

Some Solutions

Clearly, what is needed to clean up the media sector is to tackle this economic problem at its base, and to help media outlets become viable businesses in their own right, so that they are no longer dependent on—or at the mercy of—vested interests and can pay their staff a living wage.

In the Democratic Republic of Congo, DFID was the first of several international donors to support Radio Okapi, which is a United Nations radio station with an independent editorial line guaranteed by the Swiss nongovernmental organization (NGO) Fondation Hirondelle, committed to national coverage, unbiased reporting, and quality journalism. Radio Okapi is the creation of the international community and is financially independent. As such, its journalists—some of whom are French, Swiss, and Canadian, but most of whom are Congolese—are able to withstand physical and political threats and can raise issues that would be much more difficult for their counterparts in the national media who have no United Nations (UN) protection and who are not paid a respectable wage.

DFID has been promoting financial self-reliance, through, for example, supporting the Paris-based Panos Institute, by running training courses in situ for media managers. The idea is that business know-how is imparted in the workplace and not—as so often happens—in a foreign environment away from the real-life pressures of the newsroom. The other advantage of in situ training is that it removes the temptation of attending training just for the sake of collecting a per diem—a practice that is regrettably widespread.

The fact that media outlets *could* become commercially viable is proven by a study showing that the growing advertising market in the Democratic Republic of Congo would be worth $53.5 million per year by the end of 2010 (IMMAR 2007). Businesses and investors—such as cell phone and cosmetics companies—are keen to sponsor and advertise through the mass media but are finding that the sector is too disorganized and too ill-equipped to measure its audiences in a reliable manner. With marketing training and support for proper audience surveys, this could change the commercial outlook to the advantage of media managers.

Culture of Fear

Another big challenge is the general culture in which journalists find themselves. In common with many other countries, in the Democratic Republic of Congo this is unfortunately a culture of fear and self-censorship. For individual journalists, this can range from a well-founded fear for their lives at the hands of trigger-happy soldiers, to the fear of interrogation and imprisonment at the hands of the authorities, to the danger of being closed down on flimsy pretexts. Six journalists were assassinated between 2005 and 2009, and in 2009, 75 other cases of assault, torture, threats, imprisonment, and other harassment were registered by the human rights group Journaliste en Danger. Many killings of journalists over the past few years have not even come to court, let alone resulted in convictions. This means, of course, that investigative reporting is almost nonexistent and the watchdog function of the media is limited, for fear of reprisals against individuals and against media outlets as a whole. The situation in the Democratic Republic of Congo is not helped by the legal void that presently exists, pending the passing of new press laws, meaning that outdated licensing and libel laws can be and are being invoked by government representatives and other powerful people as a means to silence their critics.

The Need for Regulation

As long as no protected space exists in which the media can hold governments to account, the public will never be properly informed about the authorities that rule them, nor will there be genuine demand from the population for rights and services. The right strategy here is to help sustain an independent media regulatory body to create space between the government and the media, reminding both of their responsibilities toward the other and safeguarding freedom of the press. International donors have been supporting the Haute Autorité des Médias (HAM), the national independent media regulator, which was originally created as a result of the Congo peace talks in 2003. This support has been as basic as funding the HAM simply to hold regular meetings and to have office space and equipment in the provinces with which to monitor the press and the airwaves. Around the 2006 elections, DFID spent nearly $1 million on this authority and, despite setbacks (notably an attack by an angry mob on HAM's headquarters), found that the benefits of this support have justified the cost. Having a structure to act as a buffer against government dominance of the airwaves and its censorial tendencies and having a regulator to rein in hate media during the 2006 elections proved invaluable.

International donors have also been funding human rights groups, notably Journaliste en Danger. Activities have included training around 200 national correspondents around the country to issue alerts in cases of attacks on press freedom and securing legal aid for journalists who are arrested. This is essential work for helping combat the culture of fear that pervades the journalistic profession.

Traditions

Another aspect of the culture within which journalists find themselves is little or no tradition of questioning authority or of probing issues in any depth. This can be attributed in part to the culture of fear and self-censorship just discussed. It can also be attributed to the extra costs involved. It is also partly to do, however, with a more generalized tradition of veneration of age and authority, respect for the "big man," and a sense that experts must not be questioned. Thus, we find the microphone left on and politicians allowed to pontificate at great length with barely a word of interruption. We find the microphone is rarely turned toward ordinary citizens to enable their voices to be heard, as it is not a natural instinct for journalists to value the opinion of "the man or woman in the street." We also find many journalists whose natural instincts are like those in a recent case of an Antonov airplane crash in Kinshasa who, rather than going down to the crash site to investigate the cause for themselves, told their editor they would wait for the "official statement" to be issued.[1]

Positive Examples

One effective option to counteract this culture of inertia, and to promote a spirit of enquiry, is to lead by example. Since it began broadcasting in 2002, one of Radio Okapi's many successes is the way it has raised the bar for other indigenous radio and TV stations in the country. Now we find many other stations copying Radio Okapi's formats, discussion programs, and news-gathering techniques. By comparison, the national broadcaster—the Radio-Télévision Nationale Congolaise, always a mouthpiece of government—looks even more like an old-fashioned, disorganized propaganda tool. Although Radio Okapi can be a thorn in the government's side at times, its stance of promoting peace and democracy and the strong role it plays in civic education have led to its recognition, even by the Minister of Information, as a national asset that the Democratic Republic of Congo could ill afford to lose.

Another civic education instrument funded by the international community is a newspaper called the *Journal du Citoyen* (Citizen's Newspaper). This appears regularly as a free insert in the most widely available newspapers in Kinshasa and is distributed around the country by the UN, churches, NGOs, and other civil society groups. On the day that it appears, the newspaper in which it is inserted regularly sells out. The *Journal du Citoyen* proves that development and good governance *can* sell papers.

Complex Issues

The perennial challenge for serious journalists—the world over—is to engage and inspire a mass audience on governance themes that are often complex, invariably dry, and sometimes very technical. The first step, of course, is for journalists to understand these issues themselves. This is not an easy task, even in countries where education up to degree level is a given. In a country such as the Democratic Republic of Congo where most journalists have little more than a secondary school certificate, the challenge is even greater. For instance, in a recent training course on budgetary issues for journalists in Kinshasa, many could not differentiate between "a million" and "a billion." Added to the need to overcome this basic lack of education, journalists must also cope with the bewildering complexity and sheer scale of the governance context itself. For instance, in the Democratic Republic of Congo, 33 candidates stood in the presidential election in July 2006, and now the governing coalition behind President Kabila is composed of a bewilderingly large group of 30 parties. As many as 9,632 candidates contested the legislative elections; in the upcoming municipal elections, 200,000 candidates are expected to contest local elections in the provinces, which have recently been redrawn, raising the number from 11 to 26.

Not only are governance and budgetary issues complicated in themselves, but in the Democratic Republic of Congo—as in many other African countries—literally no local words exist to describe them. So, for instance, the words for "constitution" and "polling station" simply are not found in Tshiluba, Kikongo, or Lingala. Luckily an enterprising group of editors from Radio Okapi have drawn up a five-language dictionary that guided journalists in these matters during the electoral period and beyond.

Engaging the Audience

Other groups, such as the NGO Search for Common Ground, produce civic education content for rebroadcast via the Democratic Republic of Congo's extensive network of local community radio stations. DFID has been funding this work since 2004, and this project is now reaching an approximate audience of 20 million via 100 local radio stations. Search for Common Ground's approach to governance and democracy issues is to make the formats for their messages engaging and entertaining. They argue, quite rightly, that unless an issue is put across in a compelling way, you lose your audience. Their approach is to use soap opera formats, phone-ins, live debate programs, and other print and theater formats that back up their radio work. For instance, they have a fictional character named Mopila, a taxi driver, who along with his family, friends, and passengers guides listeners through the metaphorical twists, turns, and roadblocks on the road to democracy. The result is a mass audience that is gradually becoming educated about issues such as elections, the constitution, decentralization, civics, and human rights. One might say this education is happening almost by stealth, because it is packaged in such an entertaining way.

Two-Way Dialogue

Funding these sorts of radio programs and these kinds of NGOs and community media is one way to communicate governance issues to a mass audience—and, of course, the key is to include formats such as phone-ins, listeners' letters, radio club inputs, and the like—in short, a two-way dialogue to ensure that the audiences can have their say, ask questions, and clarify issues for themselves.

A concrete example of this two-way dialogue is currently being initiated by NGOs, broadcasters, and civil society groups in provincial towns around the Democratic Republic of Congo. This is done through a series of public meetings on good governance—*tribuneaux populaires*—at which local government representatives answer questions posed by members of the public. These meetings are broadcast simultaneously by several community radio stations at once, thereby reaching a much larger audience than the live event itself. Thus, the power of broadcasting brings the town hall meeting—debates about important issues such as water supplies, corruption, mining and forestry rights, erosion, and electricity supplies—straight into people's homes.

Access to Information

To reiterate a point already made: It is necessary for journalists and media professionals to have access to appropriate information to cover governance issues properly. For this access, they need specialist training on everything from local legislation to universal legal and human rights principles. They need documentation centers, including fast, inexpensive, and reliable access to the Internet to access news and online training opportunities, to exchange information with colleagues, and to research relevant issues. They need better and regular relationships with specialist local and international NGOs. Some of DFID's partners are starting to provide these items. For example, Panos has established four provincial focal centers for community radios (called *poles d'appuie a la radio indépendante*), which provide computer training and Internet access to a whole network of radio stations in the east (Bukavu), center (Mbuji-Mayi and Kisangani), and southeast (Lubumbashi) of the country. (This has involved a British-based charity, Computer-Aid, donating more than 60 refurbished Pentium computers to the country for this program.)

Finally, journalists also need access to government information, which means that government must, in turn, improve the way it disseminates information and must relate to journalists in a more open and transparent way. In the Democratic Republic of Congo, we currently find a rather chaotic mixture of great secrecy on the part of government and, in contrast, a somewhat ludicrous lack of mastery of the facts, as was recently noted by a journalist who asked the Minister of Health whether he welcomed a new Ebola testing center set up with foreign aid, to which the Minister replied that this was good news, but the first he had heard of it.[2] Going forward, DFID, in partnership with other donors such as Sweden and France, is providing wider support to the entire media sector in support of democratization and accountability, including support for relationship building between the Congolese media and government ministries.

Future Challenges

The Congolese context is a very particular one—with huge needs and challenges—but one from which lessons can be drawn and applied to other countries on the subject of governance and media support. I have attempted to show that in the Democratic Republic of Congo, DFID and other donors have started to think and act strategically about media support and have linked these activities explicitly and directly with governance issues. I believe that these media programs will gradually result in a better-informed citizenry.

Meanwhile, much still remains to be done, and much is still unknown. For example, how to reach women and youth and forest dwellers deep in the jungle, who, as far as we know, are largely cut off from the mass media? How to communicate with a 60 million–strong population, most of whom have no access to roads or electricity, cannot read or write, and have never even heard of a Poverty Reduction Strategy Plan? A huge communication challenge still lies ahead, but strengthening the mass media is part of the answer.

Notes

1. Personal communication, Jean-Claude Labrecque, Station Chief, Radio Okapi, Kinshasa, October 5, 2007.
2. Personal communication, Françoise Mukuku, Radio Okapi, Kinshasa, October 9, 2007.

References

Frère, Marie-Soleil. 2008. *Le paysage médiatique congolais.* Paris: France Coopération Internationale.

GRET (Groupe de Recherche et d'Echanges Technologique). 2006. *Cartographie de Medias.* Kinshasa, Democratic Republic of Congo: Groupe de Recherche et d'Echanges Technologique.

IMMAR. 2007. Le potentiel publicitaire de Radio Okapi en RDC. Final summary report. IMMAR, Paris.

Mozammel, M., and S. Odugbemi. 2005. *With the Support of Multitudes: Using Strategic Communication to Fight Poverty through PRSPs.* London: DFID.

12

Communication Technologies for Accountability

Anne-Katrin Arnold

Introduction

Accountability depends on the flow of information. Citizens need information about public services to hold their government accountable for those services—without knowledge of how things are and how things should be, there is not much for which citizens can request accountability. Citizens themselves need to be able to communicate with the government to voice their grievances and articulate their demands to those responsible for providing them with goods and services. To have their voices heard by the government, citizens need communication platforms and channels that amplify their demands and communicate whether or not they award the government with legitimacy. Access to information, voice, and a communication infrastructure therefore seem to be among the main prerequisites for effective accountability.

In the ideal world of a democratic public sphere, mass media are the major players in the space between civil society and government and facilitate communication between both. The media convey information from the government to the citizens and provide a space for deliberation, producing public opinion, which is then channeled back to the government. If this loop is undistorted and uninterrupted, accountability should be a logical outcome.

However, the communication loop between government and civil society is distorted and disrupted. Economic and political pressures shape the public sphere and distort communication flows, limiting citizens' possibilities to form considered public opinion and demand accountability. In this context, information and communication technology (ICT) has been hailed as a means for citizens to reclaim their place in the public sphere. The following discussion will show that ICT is far from being a universal remedy, but does indeed provide potential for rebalancing the communication flows in the public sphere and giving citizens a stronger voice in demanding accountability.

In this chapter, I will describe the role of traditional mass media for accountability and will point out their problems and shortcomings in providing the three communication prerequisites of accountability: access, voice, and infrastructure. I will then discuss the potential of ICT for overcoming these obstacles—or not.

To set up this discussion, I will briefly position the role of the media and communication technologies in the context of the public sphere, discuss the merits and problems of mass media as well as ICT for providing the prerequisites for effective accountability, and then draw on real-world examples to illustrate the potential of ICT to give citizens improved means for holding their government accountable.

A word of caution: A large part of the theoretical discussion in this chapter is based on research on Western countries. This is due to a lack of systematic study of the social, and partly of the economic and political, characteristics of mass media systems in developing countries. However, I will incorporate a developing country focus wherever possible and will highlight the role of ICT in the developing world in the second part of this chapter, which deals with real-world examples of how ICT is used to strengthen accountability in a development context.

ICT, Accountability, and the Public Sphere

The discussion of ICT's functions and potentials for accountability starts with a strongly simplified model of Jürgen Habermas's conceptualization of the public sphere. Habermas (1991) understands the public sphere as space between state and civil society. In this space, government and citizens exchange information and services: Citizens communicate their demands to the government and, if satisfied with how these are met by the government, reward legitimacy to the government in office. The government provides rules, regulations, and public goods and services to the citizens. As has been argued throughout this book, the mere delivery of services without accountability is not sufficient to achieve good governance. Habermas did not consider accountability as part of the public sphere, but here it will be assumed to be a prerequisite for citizens awarding legitimacy to the government. A very simplified model of Habermas's work (1991, 2006), with accountability as an added factor, systematizes the public sphere and its communication flows as shown in figure 12.1.

The public sphere must provide an infrastructure for these exchanges to happen. Apart from the delivery of services and goods, the exchange flows in figure 12.1 are information flows: The government provides rules, regulations, and accountability, and the citizens make demands and provide legitimacy in

Figure 12.1. Exchanges between States and Citizens

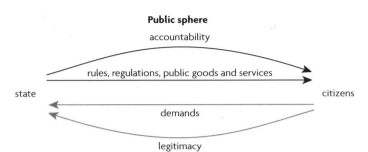

Source: Adapted from Habermas 1991, 2006.

the form of feedback to the government. The mass media have traditionally been one of the most important channels for communication in the public sphere.

From figure 12.1, we can deduce a number of essential requirements for a functional communication between state and citizens through the public sphere. If the public sphere is understood as infrastructure for public discourse, it must provide *communication channels and platforms for citizen demand*. The nature of communication in the public sphere is clearly two-way: The government provides *information* to citizens, and citizens need *voice* to express their demands as well as their loyalty to the state (legitimacy). This is a simple formula: There is two-way communication between the state (information) and civil society (voice) that is transmitted through the infrastructure of the public sphere (channels and platforms for citizen demand).

As Habermas (1991, 2006) posits, today's public sphere is distorted so that not all of these three prerequisites are fulfilled in a way that government and citizens alike have opportunities to make use of information flows. Political and economic interests interrupt communication channels to and from citizens, constraining citizens' roles in the public sphere and their ability to hold governments accountable. In the following section, I will discuss how mass media and ICT can be subject to distortions in the public sphere and will ask whether ICT has the potential to level the playing field for citizens to some degree.

Access to Information

Access to information is a core prerequisite for citizens to exercise their rights in any form of government. Without information they cannot know what their government is doing, which services they are eligible for, what the general state of those services is, what other people's experience with regard to those services is, which political factions work toward citizens' needs, and which do not. In general, citizens cannot make informed political decisions without access to information. ICT plays a fundamental role in this regard, and this role extends beyond the abilities of traditional media.

In democracies, the information-providing function of ICT mainly deals with political decision making: no information, no informed decision that aims at improving an individual's situation or the situation of society. The normative assumption underlying democracy is the idea of active citizens choosing who should govern a country—elections are the ultimate means of holding governments accountable. According to Ramsden (1996), the core of democracy is choice; therefore, voters have to be enabled to make an informed choice. The electorate can make informed decisions only if they are aware of qualifications, characters, issue positions, political philosophies, and the office in question. For Berelson, Lazarsfeld, and McPhee (1954), a rational decision is an issue-based one. The voter should be knowledgeable—aware and informed about issues, their history, the relevant facts, the alternatives, the consequences, and the parties' or candidates' position on them. Democratic theory wants voters to carefully consider the candidates' position and their own, eventually deciding for the candidate closest to them (Kim, Scheufele, and Shanahan 2005). The role of information is evident here. Campaigns are a vital part of the democratic process and should ideally provide information enabling voters to make informed decisions about which party or candidate is closest to their preferred issue policy. Campaigns strongly rely on the media, and as recent examples in the United States have shown, new media technologies have proven to be effective tools in campaigning.[1]

The role of ICT in autocratic states is a different one, but may be even more important for enabling citizens to hold their governments accountable. Because these countries lack the most obvious means of accountability—elections—and often also lack the most simple information mechanisms from the government—public information provision—ICT must bridge a considerable gap that traditional media have not been able to close. Several factors hinder the ability of television, newspapers, and to some extent radio to provide an avenue for accountability, which may to some degree be overcome by ICT.

Technical reach: In developing countries with low technological standards, television and newspapers are unlikely to reach a large audience. Television sets are relatively expensive and need mechanisms such as antennas or cable boxes to receive broadcasts. Newspapers require a distribution infrastructure as well as an advanced degree of literacy to be effective in disseminating information. In remote areas and in poor countries in general, both are unlikely. Radio is the one traditional mass medium that has a wide reach across developing countries. Radio sets are relatively cheap to produce, as is radio content. In terms of technical reach, radio as of now outperforms any new information technology: The Internet, especially broadband Internet, remains a medium for the more affluent classes and has not yet reached a significant degree of penetration in the developing world. Computers and any related connectivity are rare in the global South. Mobile phones may be the only ICT that soon may come to rival radio. In mid-2009, people used

4.06 billion mobile phones.[2] Because mobile phones are increasingly able to combine technologies of both traditional and new media—television, Internet, and newspapers over the Internet—they may be able to reach audiences that have been elusive for most mass and individual communication technologies so far. Mobile phones provide a technical foundation for media convergence: Several different kinds of media come together in one device. This device then provides a single access point to information and participation in communication.

Literacy: In Western democracies, newspapers have been shown to be the most reliable and trusted source of political information, at least as compared to radio and television (for example, Moy and Scheufele 2000). Reading a newspaper, however, does require basic literacy as well as a certain experience with regard to processing written and possibly abstract information. This limits the utility of newspapers for information in the poorest countries considerably. In addition to basic literacy, researchers have pointed to the importance of media literacy for being able to utilize information effectively. Where basic literacy is low, media literacy is unlikely to be in better shape. Radio is a possible exception because it does not require basic literacy and possibly only a lower degree of media literacy to be utilized. Radio messages can be simple or elaborate so that listeners with different levels of education and information-processing capacities can be addressed. Of course, literacy—both basic and with regard to media—is also one of the biggest obstacles for most ICT as means for accountability. Internet users, for instance, require considerable technical abilities in addition to literacy, as well as the ability to find relevant and trustworthy information online. The general openness of the Internet is an opportunity for dialogue on the one hand, but a danger for getting lost in an overwhelming amount of information with varying degrees of usefulness and trustworthiness on the other. If one considers the sheer amount of available information and sources, the Internet may even require the highest literacy rate of all communication technologies potentially available to citizens. Mobile phones as a platform for the convergence of communication technologies may not overcome the literacy requirements for using the Internet, but they can provide services that require less literacy, such as television content. They still require technical and basic literacy, but may reduce the level that is necessary for making effective use of the technology.

Economic and political pressures: In developing countries, traditional media are mostly privately financed, donor financed, or controlled by the government. If a medium is commercially organized, economic pressures may stand in the way of its use as a channel for accountability. Market competition may lead to an overly strong focus on soft news that attracts wider audiences or on communication that benefits, for instance, advertisers (for more discussion on this and related issues see Norris and Odugbemi 2009). In many developing countries, strong political players own large parts of the media and thereby have a convenient alley into the public sphere for their own political convictions.

These dangers seem to be less relevant for new communication technologies. The Internet in particular provides access to information and communication for people with very little political or economic clout. In several countries, recent political developments have shown how citizens circumvent political interests by circumventing national borders—or servers. However, ICT is subject to a mix of economic and political pressures that regard not so much content as infrastructure. Digital frequencies and Universal Mobile Telecommunications Service (UMTS) licenses are often auctioned off by governments, opening up possibilities for economic pressures (such as the highest bidder) and political corruption (such as awarding frequencies and licenses to political or other allies). Again, it seems that mobile phones have a strong potential to overcome these problems. Mobile phones in the hands of an individual can reach a large number of people without the drawback of politically or economically marked content. Even in this case, however, one must be aware of the dangers of interception of communication and locating phone users that are deemed political opponents. Indeed, the advantages of mobile phones provide opportunities not only for citizens asking for accountability, but also for extreme and destructive forces.

Voice

Years ago, the magazine *The New Yorker* printed a now-famous cartoon of a dog sitting in front of a computer with the caption "On the internet, nobody knows you're a dog." This line highlights the unique feature of the Internet that on the Web, anyone can be (almost) anything, including a citizen, a speaker for human rights, and a champion of democracy. This is a matter not only of anonymity, but also of voice, its reach, its magnification, and its echo.

Two-way communication first and foremost means not only that the government that has means for communicating to its citizens, but also that citizens have the possibility of communicating back to the government, that they have the chance to be heard. Traditional media are mostly one-way communication channels, with only a few and limited openings for citizen feedback. Citizens can indeed write letters to the editors, or call in to a radio talk show, but these means allow only a few individual voices into the arena of public discourse. ICT, on the other hand, not only allows for a wide range of communication forms and channels that citizens can use, but also magnifies their voices and thereby increases their chances of making the government responsive.

Bourdieu, who had little sympathy for television, nevertheless saw a chance for social groups and movements to achieve greater visibility through media coverage of their positions and activities.[3] This effect, which can be squashed by economic and political pressures, is potentially much stronger through ICT, especially through the Internet. Politically active citizens can use the Internet to build their own public, to benefit from expertise available on the Internet, to recruit followers and thereby increase the size and reach of their network, and to organize their activities (DiMaggio and others 2001; Rheingold 2000; Wellman and others 2001). Costs for mobilizing on the Internet are relatively low because physical presence is not required, political risks can be minimized through anonymity, and economic cost does not exceed the costs of actually going online. Research on these issues mainly comes from Western countries, but it may be argued that the principle of mobilization through ICT can be applied to the developing world.

When ICT magnifies the voices of citizens, however, it also magnifies the voices of individuals and groups that are not supportive of democracy. When violence broke out after the 2007 general elections in Kenya, several radio stations were accused of inciting or at least supporting aggressive action by calling for violent acts against groups of people. New communication technologies increase the reach of hate speech considerably. Hate speech abounds on the Internet, and because the Internet is—and should be—widely unregulated, access to those sites cannot be restricted. Citizens again need a considerable degree of literacy to correctly interpret extremist information. Citizen demand for accountability is no doubt a vital part of public discourse. The same principles that allow for citizen participation in public discourse also allow for disruptions and violations of the rules of public discourse. Fighting the danger of hate speech on the Internet, however, would open all avenues to fighting citizen communication through the Internet. This we can see in several countries that censor the Internet, publicly citing extremist and disruptive forces as motives, but indirectly closing communication channels for legitimate citizen voices.

Channels and Platforms for Citizen Demand

Just as ICT provides the infrastructure for a two-way flow of information between citizens and government, it also provides the infrastructure for a public forum modeled after the ideal of the ancient agora. An ideal agora brings together diverse and plural viewpoints that serve as the basis for informed public deliberation. According to Norris and Odugbemi (2009, 18), "this process is perhaps most critical in postconflict states and deeply divided societies, as a way of encouraging dialogue, tolerance, and interaction among diverse communities, reducing the underlying causes of conflict, and building the conditions for lasting peace."

Traditional media in the West face realities that hinder the establishment of an agora of equal voices. Political and economic interests inhibit access to communication channels for citizens. Market-based media systems make it difficult for citizens to be heard. Only a few lines of access exist, most of them administered by a profession that is reliant on the economic powers that pay their wages and the political powers that provide their stories. Letters to the

editor—selected by the editor and possibly edited—and a few seconds of opinion in a television or radio street survey can by no means constitute a public
discourse. Radio call-in shows have a stronger resemblance to citizen participation in the public sphere. A somewhat recent television phenomenon—talent
shows that ask viewers to vote over the Internet or mobile phone for their
favorite candidate—have been hailed as truly democratic and may indeed have
a higher turnout than major elections. It is obvious, however, that the subject
of the vote in such cases has very little to do with the subject of democracy. Not
only is the outcome of such votes of little relevance to the lives of the people,
but even the fundamental mechanism of the public sphere—deliberation—is
missing entirely.

The situation may be less bleak in developing countries, at least with regard
to opportunities for citizens to insert their voices into the public dialogue
somehow. Radio has low technical and editorial barriers, allowing citizens to
use it to make their voices heard. Television and newspapers, on the other
hand, tend to be influenced by political and economic factions.

Convergence

Every new technology offers new opportunities—but also new challenges. The
Internet provides an abundance of information that has not been available to
any generation of citizens before ours. As the amount of information grows,
however, the need for information literacy is growing as well. Just because citizens now get their news online does not mean they get their news from someone else. The most trusted and most used online news sources in Western
countries typically are the major news sources offline: BBC, the *New York
Times,* and others. Those trusted news sources acquire wider reach through
ICT—the old content converges with the new technology. Small independent
radio stations can get their news online and broadcast it to even the most
remote areas, and the *New York Times* could be "read" in the poorest communities just as well as on Wall Street. Similarly, BBC breaking news can reach even
the most rural villages through smart phones that allow access to online sources.
Content is available on different platforms, in real time or on demand.

Regulators are challenged with two basic forms of convergence. Technical
convergence concerns the merging of delivery technologies—infrastructures—
such as mobile phones, radio, television, and satellite. Content convergence
refers to the possibility of providing the same content on different platforms.
A third form of convergence might be most challenging to regulators: Content
actually merges with technology. Telecommunication providers produce Internet content, and telephone companies provide Internet services: We may term
this institutional convergence, although there is also a strong economic component. ICT has been regarded as a matter of telecommunication, regulated
quite differently and by different administrative bodies than traditional media

as a matter of information dissemination. Issues of hate speech, pornography, intellectual property, and freedom of information have not been a regular focus of agencies that work on the distribution of frequencies, provider competition, auctioning UMTS licenses, and the like.

Henten, Samarajiva, and Melody (2006) illustrate convergence in a matrix with horizontal convergence at the level of technology as well as at the level of content, and with vertical convergence of technology and content (table 12.1). Different technologies have been regulated differently in the past, but there is now a general shift toward treating technology in a neutral manner. The European Union, for instance, applies technology-neutral regulation.

Content convergence also happens at the horizontal level of this matrix. For example, content on the Internet is currently treated differently than content on television. Because of the digital nature of the content, however, a television show can easily be broadcast online. Regulators here face the issue of extending provisions for television content (for example, the ban on pornography or hate speech) to the Internet, which so far has been unregulated in this regard. Should provisions be extended, issues of freedom of speech would be raised and, most acutely, issues of how to enforce them.

The biggest challenge is convergence on the vertical level of this matrix. Great Britain, for instance, is addressing this challenge by uniting five regulatory bodies into one, the Office of Communications, that has authority both for content and for technology regulation.

The regulatory challenge of conversion cannot be discussed in this chapter. However, we need to address the consequences for considered public opinion as a crucial instrument of accountability. We have already established that ICT provides new and possibly alternative channels of public discourse. The danger, then, is information overload, information chaos, and information anarchy. Public opinion will not be considered—will strictly speaking not even be public—if citizens get very different information from very different sources with undetermined reliability. If, however, ICT is used in a complementary manner to traditional—established—media, it is possible that additional channels will add alternative content that can then be counterchecked against the products of the traditional media.

Table 12.1. Convergence/Integration and Divergence/Disintegration

	ICT	Telecom	Broadcasting	Other media
Content/services	Software-based content	Telecom-based services and content	Broadcast programs	Film, music, newspapers, and so on
Transport/software	Software	Network services	Transmission	Cinema, video rentals, and so on
Equipment/hardware	ICT hardware	Telecom equipment	Broadcast equipment	Reproduction of films, printing, and so on

Source: Henten, Samarajiva, and Melody 2006, 2.

Being a participant in the public sphere not only requires having a voice, but also requires getting information in the first place. Before citizens can demand accountability, they need to know about their right to do so and about the mechanisms available to them. ICT in convergence with traditional media provides new opportunities to establish this direction of the communication flow. Because the same content can be broadcast through different technologies, content can have a wider, but also a more targeted, reach. In a hypothetical exemplary developing country, the majority of people will be reached by shortwave radio with local, national, and international broadcasts. Few will be reached via satellites, a small elite will read the vernacular press, and even fewer will read international press. Many will have mobile phones, but only a few will have computers with access to the Internet, and they will mostly be in cities that have a university. Media audits need to determine which communication channels have the widest reach, and which reach exactly the audience that is supposed to be targeted. If a campaign to promote accountability needs to reach a large part of the population, a mix of the most popular media will be most effective. A campaign that addresses the rights and means of rural populations to hold public officials accountable will be more successful using radio than advertising in the *International Herald Tribune.*

ICT Applications for Accountability

For discussing specific ICT applications for accountability, we return to figure 12.1 on the exchanges between state and citizens in the public sphere. The state delivers public goods and services, rules, regulations, and accountability. Citizens deliver demands and legitimacy, which both can be subsumed under the term *citizen voice.* In countries with restricted media systems or with a strong economic influence on the media, mass media can only insufficiently transmit all of this, or all of this with equal bandwidth. ICT provides opportunities to broaden the reach of citizen voice and to encourage and enable an accountable response from the state. Indeed, many small projects utilize ICT to foster governments' accountability toward citizens and citizens' ability to demand accountability. Scattered attempts have been made to catalog these projects, notable among them the Technology for Transparency Network.[4] The network provides an open source platform that maps and evaluates projects that promote transparency and accountability through the strategic use of ICT. In the spirit of the open Web, everyone can contribute and enter a project into the database. Considering the large number—but limited size—of relevant projects, this approach seems promising to get a grip on a new and not well-documented field.

Earlier in this chapter, I suggested that access to information, voice, and platforms and channels for citizen demand are prerequisites for effective accountability. I have also discussed how ICT could help fulfill these prerequisites. In the following discussion, I will give real-world examples of projects that use the potential of ICT to provide access to information and voice through providing a platform or channel for citizen demand.

A nonsystematic overview of existing initiatives suggests four categories of accountability projects. The groups are distinguished by their focus on different aspects of accountability. *Service accountability* initiatives focus on the quality of service delivery and aim to provide citizens with a feedback channel to the government. Citizen report cards are a classic example of service accountability tools. *Democratic accountability* subsumes projects that work toward improving the political performance of governments, making them more accessible to citizens and providing citizens with a channel to monitor the behavior of governments as political entities. A category that is relevant for the broader international development community is *performance accountability:* tools and projects that assess the overall performance of a state as compared with other states. Relevant tools in this category include indicators such as Freedom House's Freedom of the Press and Transparency International's ranking and other aggregate measures that allow for comparing one country's performance in specific areas of governance with another country's performance. *Transparency,* the fourth category, underlies the other three because accountability rests on information. Transparency projects focus more generally on making information available and accessible, without discriminating for specific government functions. In the following sections, I will briefly describe a few exemplary initiatives for each category.

Service Accountability

Service accountability is about the state taking responsibility for the quality of the public goods and services it delivers to its citizens. For states to be thus accountable, citizens need to have a communication channel through which they can transmit their evaluation of public services. Mass media especially are inhibited from doing this job if they are under political control. Strong economic influence on the mass media also presents a hindrance because local grievances of citizens in particular may not be considered as profitable to sell to a wider audience. Smaller and independent media outfits such as community radio stations should be suitable to pick up issues of service delivery; however, they may not have sufficient political clout to make a difference. ICT can make this difference when the government sanctions them as means of communication, as is the case with the TXT CSC initiative in the Philippines.

TXT CSC is a service provided by the Philippines Civil Service Commission (CSC) that is designed to enable citizens to pressure their government to improve services. Text messaging is the predominant communication channel through which citizens can submit complaints or queries. Corrupt behavior, lack or bad quality of services, or inappropriate behavior by civil servants can be reported in real time and will, so the CSC promises, be followed up with the appropriate action. The CSC must respond to queries within one day and usually replies with personalized text messages. TXT CSC has also been used in a Public Service Delivery Audit, in which citizens rated public services via text message (Hanna 2004).[5]

Two complaint systems in Malaysia and India serve a similar function. The Malaysian Penang Watch is a group of citizen activists that gather complaints about local services through their website, forward them to the appropriate authorities, remind the responsible officials to take action, and shame them publicly if they do not.[6] According to the initiators, half of the complaints are successful, although slow Internet connections and lack of access to the Internet complicate their work. Kiirti is a petitioning platform set up by the Indian nongovernmental organization (NGO) eMoksha, through which citizens can lodge complaints online or via telephone.[7] Similar problems are aggregated and can be tracked by interested parties. The organization believes that this kind of participation (lodging complaints) increases accountability, which in turn improves government services.[8]

Democratic Accountability

Democratic accountability includes efforts by the state to improve government and governance as well as citizen initiatives to monitor democratic functions of government. E-government is a form of government accountability that is designed to improve government services and access to them and that also provides a certain degree of transparency with regard to democratic functions of the state. E-government is prominent in development work (as well as in developed countries) and may well be one of the oldest forms of ICT for accountability applications. Less established but recently highly relevant is the use of ICT for monitoring elections and the behavior of elected officials. In several elections in the last two years, portable communication technologies have been used by citizens to monitor and in some cases protest the validity of elections.

E-Government

Paul (2007, 176) describes the e-government projects of the government of India's national Capital Territory of Delhi, defining e-governance as "delivery of government services and information to the public using electronic means." The administration here has set up numerous websites designed to enable the public to find and access information about public services. For instance, one website lists the number of applications received under the Right to Information Act, the number of applications disposed of, the amount of information given, the applications in process, and similar information for appeals. The Delhi Registrar of Cooperative Societies maintains an online presence that keeps track of new applications by associations and their membership. The government also publishes tender notices that are supposed to show citizens

what types of civil works are being undertaken in their area. Several more websites allow citizens to keep track of what the government is doing in several areas
and in some cases enable them to evaluate the quality of the services. This presents a considerable step toward an open and accountable government. It must
be noted, however, that these e-government projects cater to a mainly urban
audience and can therefore be efficient via the Internet. In rural areas with low
connectivity this may be a less effective way of realizing accountability.

Another form of e-government is practiced by the Brazilian House of Representatives, which launched its e-Democracia Project in 2009.[9] Through social
media and face-to-face meetings, citizens are encouraged to contribute their
ideas and concerns regarding lawmaking. They are encouraged to provide
information about a problem that they think needs to be regulated by law, suggest solutions, and provide input into drafting the bill.[10] Cristiano Faria, one of
the implementers of this project, demonstrates actual impact of this form of
citizen consultation in lawmaking: Several concerns voiced by citizens online
have made it into the language of new legislation.

The government of Kenya uses text messages to provide citizens with
information about their services. For instance, the Ministry of Migration
provides a service through which citizens can request information about the
progress of their identity card and the status of their passport by sending a
text message to a specific number. The Electoral Commission of Kenya
launched a voter registration service for the 2007 election through which
citizens were able to register and receive verification of their registration by
texting their ID number. Parents and students can access the results of the
Kenya Certificate of Secondary Education examination by typing a code and
sending it via text message to a specific number (Hellström 2010).

Election Monitoring

The group Ushahidi runs a website that was developed in Kenya to report
instances of violence after the 2008 elections.[11] Ushahidi—"testimony" in Swahili—developed a mapping program that citizens can use to report any kind of
incident and that is now used by many civil society groups around the world.
Vote Report India, for instance, provides an online platform where citizens can
report violations of the Election Commission's Model Code of Conduct.[12]
Since April 2009, citizens have been able to send their reports through mobile
phone text messages, via e-mail, or by entering them directly through the
Internet portal. The program then accumulates all the reports on an interactive
map to point to irregularities in the election process. The information gathered
on the platform is available to citizens via e-mail, really simple syndication
(RSS) feed, and mobile phone text messages. The same platform was used by
Cuidemos el Voto Mashup to monitor the 2009 federal elections in Mexico.

Examples abound of the use of ICT to demand accountability after elections in authoritarian states, although few have systematically been gathered

and analyzed. From media reports, we know about the use of mobile phones in the demonstrations following the presidential election in Iran in June 2009. Members of the opposition, who claimed that the ruling party of President Mahmoud Ahmadinejad manipulated the vote, used mobile phones to bypass the government's clampdown on information. Foreign journalists were banned from reporting on the rallies, so that only limited information about government action could reach both national and international publics.[13] One memorable moment came in the protests when pictures of the murder of a young girl, a member of the opposition, were sent from a mobile phone and reached a large international audience via the Internet as well as traditional media. Iran's government then attempted to jam satellites to prevent sensitive information from leaving the country. BBC reporter Adel Shaygan emphasized the relevance of mobile phones as one of the few if not the only means of holding the Iranian government accountable by the international community: "Video footage taken by protesters from their mobile phones has become the main source by which information has reached the outside world, through sites like YouTube."[14] About six months later, U.S. Secretary of State Hillary Clinton took up this theme in a speech on Internet freedom and ascribed mobile phones a paramount role for accountability, even raising them to a quasi-legal instrument that could indict a government: "In the demonstrations that followed Iran's presidential elections, grainy cell phone footage of a young woman's bloody murder provided a digital indictment of the government's brutality."[15]

The 2009 Iranian elections and the following protests are one of the most recent and one of the strongest examples of ICT being used by citizens to hold their government accountable and voice their grievances on an international stage. The BBC and other international news media added ICT and social media to their usual information sources. In particular, social media such as Twitter played an important role, possibly for the first time, in this particular conflict because they provided a platform for the quick and effective dissemination of information.[16] BBC editor Steve Herrmann explains the role of social media in this particular context: "Among the various impediments to reporting, there's a huge ongoing, informed and informative discussion in Iran between people who care deeply about what is happening there and who are themselves monitoring everything they can, then circulating the most useful information and links."[17] He also points out, however, that the majority of messages come from sympathizers of the opposition. The vast variety of sources and voices come in online based on merit only, and professional journalists are faced with the challenge of quality checking and editing a cacophony of information for their audiences.

Monitoring Officials

The monitoring of democratic functions is relevant outside elections. The Brazilian project Adote um Vereador (Adopt a Councilor), for instance, provides a wiki-platform to encourage citizens to "adopt" local politicians, follow their work, and blog about their observations. The initiators of this project aim to raise political involvement outside election times and to give the electorate better control and influence over the local politicians they elect. Citizen observers of municipal councils in Colombia as well as local accountability portals in Guatemala, run by the NGO Lagún Artean, provide similar platforms.[18]

Performance Accountability

Performance accountability is mainly about the publication of independent indicators that assess the overall performance of a country with regard to a specific issue. In the context of accountability, indicators of media freedom and transparency are among the most noteworthy. The regular publication of these and other indicators is often widely covered in the press, but hardly in the press that is categorized as not free. In such circumstances, the publication of rankings online is suitable for increasing the reach of the performance assessment so that citizens in countries with restricted reporting will have a better chance of being aware of their country's performance.

Freedom House provides large information resources through their online indicators "Freedom of the World" and "Freedom of the Press."[19] Citizens can use the information provided on the methodological background of those indicators to assess the reliability and viability of the data for their own interests. They can also learn about their government's performance in comparison with other countries. Freedom House is an example where a large amount of information on the performance of a country in a specific area is available centrally and is relatively easy to use. However, this information will not reach those that do not have access to the Internet.

The Committee to Protect Journalists faces a similar problem.[20] The initiative monitors the safety of journalists worldwide and provides statistics on how many reporters are killed while doing their job, how many have been imprisoned or otherwise threatened, and how many cases are actually being investigated by the appropriate authorities. Again, the organization works with an online portal, e-mail lists, and RSS feeds—not even all journalists will be able to access information that is thus presented.

Organizations that publish general indicators on the overall performance of a country in a specific area do not seem to make use of the full spectrum of ICT yet. Possibly because of the complexity and technicality of their data, they mostly work online and rely on the mass media to pick up their stories and present them to a wider audience. Data of this kind may also be considered as being less relevant or interesting for citizens, and more relevant for an expert community, whose members usually have access to the Internet. However, I argue that a large potential exists to improve accountability by making performance indicators available through mobile ICT so that more citizens can be informed about their country's comparative performance in a specific area.

Transparency

Transparency is obviously at the heart of accountability. Citizens can hold governments accountable only if they know what the government is doing, what it is supposed to do, and what their own rights are in demanding responsiveness from officials. Typical transparency applications track budgets, independently investigate background information on political issues in countries with a repressed media system, provide information about political candidates, compare the votes of citizens with those of their elected representatives, advocate for more transparent campaign financing, and provide many more tools for increasing transparency in governments.[21]

As of September 2008, 80 countries have passed Freedom of Information Acts, and 34 more are close to passing relevant legislation. Since 2000, an average of six countries per year have passed Freedom of Information Acts (Vleugels 2008). However, access to information legislation alone is not sufficient for transparency. Citizens must know about and must exercise their rights, and governments must be able to provide information. However, many governments in developing countries do not have the capacity for gathering data that they could then publish for citizens to hold them accountable. ICT provides an infrastructure for gathering and providing information, both for the government and for citizens. ICT can foster a form of "transparency bottom up"— citizens gathering information that their governments do not have available and that can then be used both by the governments to improve services and by citizens to hold them accountable. In East Africa, the project Twaweza ("We can make it happen" in Swahili) is getting citizens involved in gathering information on water, health, and education. The project uses mobile phones because the Internet is not prevalent in the region. The information that is needed to hold governments accountable is gathered bottom-up, by those who eventually use it to hold their governments accountable. This circumvents not only government's inability to provide access to information but also its unwillingness.

Many other obstacles exist to providing transparency where ICT can—and does—provide solutions; a small number will be discussed here.[22]

Information needs organization: Information, online and offline, is often spread out over many sources. Hundreds of sources, for instance, websites, provide snippets of information. It is not feasible for citizens to find their way through the data chaos to get a more or less comprehensive picture of their government's activities. Citizens' ability to hold governments accountable would be increased if they could access, for instance, a central online data gateway that organizes information relevant to a specific issue in one place.

Global Voices is an ambitious project that provides a platform for news from all over the world.[23] Hundreds of bloggers provide this community with reports and translations of reports from blogs and citizen media from countries and sources that are not usually covered by the mainstream media. In this sense Global Voices provides a platform for organizing information from a vast variety of sources, although reports are not limited to a single subject area.

Kubatana.net fulfills a similar function but with a different approach.[24] Established in 2001 in Zimbabwe, the portal aggregates and publishes material on human rights and other civic issues. The portal's aim is to fill information gaps between NGOs and civil society organizations in Zimbabwe and provide them with a one-stop-shop for relevant publications.[25] More than 250 member organizations of the electronic network contribute and access information relevant to their work and thereby provide a central gateway for civil society issues.

Information needs context: Mere access to information is insufficient for accountability if it is of a highly technical nature. For instance, the European Space Agency provides online information on water quality in different regions[26]—but this information alone may not be useful to fishermen who have no experience with interpreting earth observation data. For people to understand technical information, it needs to be put into context. Expert intermediaries need to explain what specific measurements and measurement units mean and provide benchmarks for people to know at what point the quality of the water becomes unacceptable.

The Swedish foundation Gapminder provides a remarkable example for this kind of intermediation and interpretation of technical data.[27] Founded by Hans Rosling, a Professor of International Health, the organization takes development data from a large number of sources and packages them in animated graphs that show complicated economic relations in a relatively simple way. This is also an example of performance accountability because development indicators are part of the vast data pool utilized by Gapminder. For example, one of Rosling's animated graphs shows the relationship between income per person and life expectancy at birth. Each country is represented by a bubble in the chart, and the size of the bubble represents the size of the population in a given country. The bubbles move along the axes of the graph as the years progress, showing how the relationship and the size of the population changes over time. This relatively simple animation puts many variables and relationships into an understandable format.

Accountability needs a Community of Practice: Both the problem of information organization and intermediation could be approached by a Community of Practice in different areas of accountability. For instance, organizations working on water quality throughout the world could provide online gateways where relevant data are organized and put into context by intermediaries. The Women of Uganda Network (WOUGNET) is such a Community of Practice with regard to gender issues.[28] WOUGNET, an NGO based in Kampala, combines online, offline, and mobile tools to share information, network, provide technical support to women, and advocate for gender issues. The project provides a common platform for different efforts concerning women's rights and thereby organizes information and focuses on initiatives working toward similar goals.

Accountability needs multiple platforms: Providing data online, even on a central gateway, will still exclude most of those that need the information. The digital divide is a fact, and it does not seem likely that broadband will pervade Africa any time soon. The problem of technical reach, as discussed in the first part of this chapter, can be solved only by combining technologies that provide suitable amounts of information with those that reach large audiences even in the poorest countries. Convergence is key. Accountability therefore needs a multiplatform approach: Access to information needs to be provided through all relevant communication channels. These can include the Internet and mobile phones but will also include community radio and local multipliers such as teachers or priests.

WOUGNET utilizes online platforms, offline workshops, and cell phone applications to advocate for women's rights. In addition to its extensive online resource, Gapminder provides videos, participates in major conferences and talk shows, and utilizes the academic status of its founder to spread their message as widely as possible.

Conclusion

Unfortunately, democracy is not quite saved just yet. As I have discussed, ICT requires a strong degree of literacy with regard to technical capabilities and information selection. Mobile phones as such provide only a single point-to-point communication channel. This may strengthen everyday talk, one important source of considered public opinion, but it does not constitute a public sphere. The Internet on its own has lower potential than mobile technologies because relatively few people have access. ICT often requires costly hardware, which excludes the people from the public sphere that need it most: the poorest, the least educated, and the most remote citizens in any country.

In this chapter, I have argued that mass media have substantial deficiencies in their ability to fulfill the three main communication prerequisites for effective accountability: access to information, voice, and platforms and channels for citizen demand. Some of those deficiencies—but by no means all—can be addressed by ICT, which may provide better and more widespread access to information, a stronger voice for those outside political and economic power centers, and the infrastructure that is necessary to make this voice be heard widely.

Convergence is crucial for the effectiveness of ICT as accountability tools. The unique ability of ICT is to combine those aspects of the mass media that support accountability—for instance, the provision of large amounts of information—with the potentially wider reach and more democratic access and usability of ICT.

Finally, I have introduced a small number of ICT projects and applications that are being used to hold governments accountable. In these particular cases, ICT is successful in fulfilling the main communication prerequisites for accountability. I identified four groups of projects that focus on different aspects of accountability: service accountability, democratic accountability, performance accountability, and transparency. Obviously, this systematization comes from a very limited study of a small number of projects. Other ICT applications will likely add other categories to this first attempt at systematizing accountability applications. I ended this chapter with a number of challenges and recommendations that may help accountability advocates and practitioners to design effective initiatives.

This chapter suffers from its limited scope and lack of systematic knowledge of the role of the mass media for accountability and the public sphere in developing countries, and from the cursory nature of the overview of actual ICT applications for accountability. However, the discussion has shown that ICT is an important addition to the public sphere that could, in convergence with traditional media, significantly increase citizens' opportunities to hold their government accountable.

On the Internet, no one knows you're a dog. ICT is not the solution to everything that is wrong with participation, governance, and accountability. I suggest, however, that these technologies give us a chance, a channel for democracy that we would otherwise not have. On the Web, it is all about efficacy and voice—in particular if you're a dog.

Notes

1. See Borins (2009); A. Kes-Erkul and R. E. Erkul, "Web 2.0 in the Process of E-Participation: The Case of Organizing for America and the Obama Administration" (2009), NCDG Working Paper no. 09–001. http://www.epractice.eu/files/Web%202.0%20in%20the%20 Process%20of%20eParticipation_the%20Case%20of%20Organizing%20for%20 America%20and%20the%20Obama%20Administration.pdf.
2. ITU World Telecommunication/ICT Indicators Database, as of July 29, 2009.
3. P. Bourdieu, "Aufruf gegen die Politik der Entpolitisierung" (2001), http://www.sozialismus-von-unten.de/archiv/text/bourdieu.htm.
4. http://transparency.globalvoicesonline.org.
5. http://www.egov4dev.org/mgovernment/resources/case/txtcsc.shtml.
6. http://www.penangwatch.net.
7. http://www.kiirti.org.
8. http://transparency.globalvoicesonline.org.
9. http://www.edemocracia.gov.br.
10. C. Faria, "Can People Help Legislators Make Better Laws? Brazil Shows How" (2010), http://techpresident.com/user-blog/can-people-help-legislators-make-better-laws-brazil-shows-how.
11. http://www.ushahidi.com.

12. http://votereport.in/blog/press-room/press-release.
13. Huria Choudhari on bbc.com, September 8, 2009, http://www.bbc.co.uk/worldservice/worldagenda/2009/09/090908_worldagenda_iran_2.shtml.
14. http://news.bbc.co.uk/2/hi/programmes/click_online/8120858.stm.
15. http://www.state.gov/secretary/rm/2010/01/135519.htm.
16. http://www.state.gov/secretary/rm/2010/01/135519.htm.
17. http://www.bbc.co.uk/blogs/theeditors/2009/06/social_media_in_iran.html.
18. http://transparency.globalvoicesonline.org.
19. http://www.freedomhouse.org.
20. http://www.cpj.org.
21. http://opengovernance.info/BTKenya, http://inmediahk.net, http://www.votainteligente.cl, http://www.votenaweb.com.br, and http://kepmutatas.hu/english, respectively. The examples listed in this paragraph come from Technology for Transparency Project (2010).
22. These recommendations are inspired by a lively discussion at the Global Voices Citizen Media Summit 2010 in Santiago, Chile, where I had the honor of moderating a discussion on ICT for accountability. The points listed here are the outcome of this discussion, and I am very grateful for the members of this particular panel for their input and inspiring ideas.
23. http://globalvoicesonline.org.
24. http://www.kubatana.net.
25. http://transparency.globalvoicesonline.org.
26. http://www.esa.int/esaLP/SEMO711YUFF_LPgmes_0.html.
27. http://www.gapminder.org.
28. http://www.wougnet.org.

References

Berelson, B. R., P. F. Lazarsfeld, and W. N. McPhee. 1954. *Voting: A Study of Opinion Formation in a Presidential Campaign.* Chicago: University of Chicago Press.

Borins, S. 2009. "From Online Candidate to Online President." *International Journal of Public Administration* 32 (9): 753–58.

DiMaggio, P., E. Hargittai, R. W. Neumann, and J. P. Robinson. 2001. "Social Implications of the Internet." *Annual Review of Sociology* 27: 307–36.

Habermas, J. 1991. *The Structural Transformation of the Public Sphere: An Inquiry into a Category of Bourgeois Society.* Cambridge, MA: MIT Press.

Habermas, J. 2006. "Political Communication in Media Society—Does Democracy Still Enjoy an Epistemic Dimension? The Impact of Normative Theory on Empirical Research." Paper presented at the Annual Conference of the International Communication Association, June 25, Dresden, Germany.

Hanna, N. 2004. "Why National Strategies Are Needed for ICT-Enabled Development." Information Solution Group Working Paper, World Bank, Washington, DC.

Hellström, J. 2010. "Mobile Phones for Good Governance—Challenges and Way Forward." Discussion paper for the World Bank Demand for Good Governance Anchor, Washington, DC.

Henten, A., R. Samarajiva, and W. Melody. 2006. "The Next Step for Telecom Regulation: ICT Convergence Regulation or Multisector Utilities Regulation?" http://link.wits.ac.za/journal/j0301-anders-fin.pdf.

Kim, S., D. A. Scheufele, and J. Shanahan. 2005. "Who Cares about the Issues? Issue Voting and the Role of News Media during the 2000 US Presidential Election." *Journal of Communication* 55 (1): 103–21.

Moy, P., and D. A. Scheufele 2000. "Media Effects on Political and Social Trust." *Journalism and Mass Communication Quarterly* 77 (4): 744–59.

Norris, P., and S. Odugbemi. 2009. "Evaluating Media Performance." In *Public Sentinel: News Media and Governance Reform,* ed. P. Norris, 3–29. Washington, DC: World Bank.

Paul, S. 2007. "A Case Study of E-Governance Initiatives in India." *International Information and Library Review* 39 (3–4): 176–84.

Ramsden, G. P. 1996. "Media Coverage of Issues and Candidates: What Balance Is Appropriate in a Democracy? *Political Science Quarterly* 111 (1): 65–81.

Rheingold, H. 2000. *The Virtual Community: Homesteading on the Electronic Frontier.* Cambridge, MA: MIT Press.

Vleugels, R. 2008. "Overview of all 86 FOIA Countries." http://www.statewatch.org/news/2006/feb/foia-feb-2006.pdf.

Wellman, B., A. Quan Haase, J. Witte, and K. Hampton. 2001. "Does the Internet Increase, Decrease, or Supplement Social Capital? Social Networks, Participation, and Community Commitment." *American Behavioral Scientist* 45(3): 437–56.

Section V
Deliberation and Accountability

13

Minipublics: Designing Institutions for Effective Deliberation and Accountability

Archon Fung

1. Introduction

Activists, foundations, reformers based at nongovernmental organizations, and even some scholars have pursued an array of modest projects that attempt to improve the quality of deliberation, governance, and accountability by creating more perfect public spheres. They convene citizens, in the dozens or hundreds or thousands, but certainly not in the millions or tens of millions, in self-consciously organized public deliberations. Following Robert Dahl, I will call these efforts *minipublics*[1]. Sometimes they resemble town meetings, and sometimes they function as purposeful associations. They look like, because they are, exercises in "reformist tinkering" rather than "revolutionary reform."[2]

Perhaps for these reasons, or because of their modest scale, these efforts have occurred mostly under the radar of democratic and social theorists. Nevertheless, those interested in improving the public sphere should pay more attention to minipublics. Although small, they are among the most promising constructive efforts for civic engagement and public deliberation in contemporary politics. By improving the depth and quantity of public participation, they can improve public opinion and even harness that opinion to enhance the extent to which governments and public officials are accountable for their policies and actions.

I thank Joshua Cohen, Stephen Elkin, James Fishkin, Joseph Goldman, Robert Goodin, Jennifer Hochschild, Sanjeev Khagram, Jane Mansbridge, Nancy Rosenblum, Charles Sabel, Lars Torres, and the participants of the Democracy Collaborative's "State of Democratic Practice" workshop for illuminating suggestions on previous drafts of this chapter. An earlier version of this chapter appeared in the *Journal of Political Philosophy*.

2. Institutional Design Choices

Suppose that you want to improve the quality of civic engagement and public deliberation and that you are in a position—through your access to a modicum of financing or state power—to carry out a project toward this end. You decide to create a minipublic that will convene citizens and perhaps officials to deliberate on some important public concern. This minipublic will contribute to the democratic project of reinvigorating the broader public sphere not only by modeling the ideal, but also by improving the quality of participation and deliberation in a significant area of public life. As with any project of political construction, you face many critical questions.

2.1. Visions and Types of Minipublics

The first important choice, informing all of the others that follow, concerns your ideal of the public sphere. Beyond simply convening citizens to deliberate with one another and participate in public life, what should a minipublic do?

In one vision, the minipublic is an *educative forum* that aims to create nearly ideal conditions for citizens to form, articulate, and refine opinions about particular public issues through conversations with one another. The conditions of deliberation in this minipublic would differ from those in the actually existing public sphere in at least three ways. First, whereas inclusion in actual public debate reflects many kinds of background inequalities—wealth, gender, education, position, and control over the means of communication and production—the minipublic would attempt to fairly include all of these diverse voices. Second, actual public debate frequently falls short of the ideal of deliberation and public reason. Under more ideal conditions, participants would take each others' claims, explanations, reasons, proposals, and arguments seriously. Third, a minipublic might inform citizens by making briefing materials and expertise easily available ("experts on tap, not experts on top," as one slogan from Participatory Rural Appraisal advocates goes).

A second vision of minipublic might be called a *participatory advisory panel*. It aims not only to improve the quality of opinion, but also to align public policies with considered preferences. Participatory advisory panels do not stop after creating the ideal deliberative conditions of the first vision. They also develop linkages to economic or state decision makers to transmit preferences after they have been appropriately articulated and combined into a social choice.[3]

A third vision of minipublic might be called *participatory problem-solving collaboration*. This type envisions a continuous and symbiotic relationship between the state and public sphere aimed at solving particular collective problems such as environmental degradation, failing schools, or unsafe streets.[4] Two broad justifications support this intimate relationship between public and state. First, some public problems are so troublesome that they defy even the best expert solutions. For some of these problems, citizens may invent novel solutions that leverage resources and ingenuity from both the civic and state spheres; the central contribution of this kind of minipublic is creativity. Second, often the state cannot be trusted. Some democratic skeptics locate the central contribution of an improved public sphere in its ability to tether state action and make it publicly accountable.

A fourth vision, call it *participatory democratic governance,* is more ambitious than the other three. This flavor of minipublic seeks to incorporate direct citizen voices into the determination of policy agendas. Proponents of such minipublics often view structures of representative legislation and insular administration as easily captured, or at least biased, toward wealthy and socially advantaged sections of the polity. Injecting direct, mobilized, deliberative citizen participation into democratic governance might favor the voices of the least-advantaged and so offer a procedural antidote that enhances the equity of legislation and policy making.

2.2. Who? Participant Selection and Recruitment

How should individuals come to participate in a minipublic? The most common mechanism is voluntary self-selection. One difficulty with voluntarism, however, is that those who show up are typically better off—wealthy, educated, and professional—than the population from which they come.[5] One solution is to choose specific participants who demographically mirror the general population. Deliberative polling efforts pursue this tack by selecting participants through opinion polling methods. A second option is affirmative action through recruitment: Organizers can solicit participation from groups who are less likely to show up. A third option is to create structural incentives for low-status and low-income citizens to participate.[6] Participation patterns are determined not only by the resource constraints on citizens (favoring the better off), but also by the goods that participatory institutions deliver.[7] In particular, if a minipublic addresses poor peoples' concerns, and if they expect that participation will yield results, then the poor may participate more than the rich.

2.3. What? Subject and Scope of Deliberation

If one presumes that problems of participant selection and bias can be solved satisfactorily, the next large question concerns the subject of deliberation. What public issue will participants consider? Public deliberation is often general in the sense that its rules, structures, and benefits are not thought to depend upon particular topics. All issues are thought to be fair game for debate in the broad public sphere, not least because excluding some subjects would improperly restrict liberty of expression and political freedom.

At the less abstract level of institutional design, however, the choice of subject importantly shapes the subsequent operation and impact of a minipublic. It determines what, if anything, citizens are likely to contribute in terms of insight, information, or resources in the course of participatory deliberation. To identify them, institutional designers should consider whether citizens possess a comparative advantage over other actors such as politicians, administrators, and organized interests. In some areas, citizens can contribute information about their preferences and values that is unavailable to policy makers. In other areas, they may be better positioned to assess the impacts of policies and deliver this feedback to officials. In still other contexts, citizens enhance public accountability when civic engagement allows them to monitor potentially corrupt or irresponsible officials.

2.4. How? Deliberative Mode

A fourth institutional design choice concerns the organization and style of discussions in a minipublic. In a simple formulation consistent with many of those in recent democratic theory, deliberation is a process of public discussion in which participants offer proposals and justifications to support collective decisions.[8] These proposals are backed by justifications that appeal to other participants and by reasons that others can accept. These reasons, for example, may appeal to some common good (for example, "This is the best way to improve our school because …") or common norms of fairness ("You do something for me this time, and I do something for you next time around."). When each participant decides what the social choice should be, he or she should choose the proposal backed by the most compelling reasons. Deliberation is distinctive because, as Habermas put it, there is no force "except the force of the better argument."[9]

At this level of generality, the theory of deliberation does not offer much guidance to the designer of a minipublic. Any particular deliberative process will have more specific aims and obstacles that it must address through training, facilitation, and the structure of discussion.

One aim of the public sphere, for example, is to provide space in which individuals can reach their own considered views and gain confidence in their own perspectives; it is a space where the weak should be able to find their own voice. Some critics have objected that deliberative processes disadvantage those who speak less well, or who speak in ways that are devalued by the dominant culture.[10] The best response to this important criticism contends that a public sphere should be constructed, first and foremost, to allow those without a voice and will an opportunity to find and form both. Processes of reason giving and taking cannot be fair absent this prior process of will formation and development that moves individuals from silence to self-expression. For example, the most important contribution of the public sphere in a Latin American city may be to allow a favela dweller to realize and effectively assert his or her rational self-interests in basic sanitation, water, and education.

In contrast with this approach, some kinds of deliberation aim to generate consensus or to solve concrete problems. Such deliberations might follow the rules of proposal, justification, and planning outlined above. Deliberative institutions in this mode should offer training and education to create informed participants. A facilitator might level the field to allow participants to engage and guide the conversation toward emergent consensus. Deeply divisive issues and positions are sometimes simply ruled out of order. The premium on reaching a fair and good decision may favor the most articulate or popular (rather than the most needy). Indeed, Mansbridge reports that such "unitary" decision processes work to exclude those who reside on the margins.[11]

2.5. When? Recurrence and Iteration

A fifth design choice is the frequency with which a minipublic convenes. The participatory democratic impulse is that more is better. This intuition is incorrect, however, because the frequency of minipublic meetings should follow from their purpose. If a minipublic is convened to deliberatively form or ascertain public opinion on a nearly static issue, as in some educative forums or participatory advisory panels, then one conclusive round of deliberation may be enough. Minipublics devoted to participatory problem solving, ongoing accountability, or democratic governance should be convened more frequently, perhaps many times per year, because their decisions must be frequently updated and because monitoring officials is an ongoing endeavor.

2.6. Why? Stakes

Because engagement depends on interest, a designer should have a clear account of the stakes that participants have in a minipublic's deliberations. Does the discussion concern some issue that affects participants' welfare or deeply held beliefs? Are participants interested because the issue has become a public controversy? In one view, deliberation should be *cold*. Individuals with low stakes in a discussion will be open-minded, begin without fixed positions, and dispassionate. I tend to the opposite view: *Hot* deliberations with participants who have much at stake make for better deliberation. More participants will be drawn to hot deliberations, and they will be more sustainable over time. Participants will invest more of their psychic energy and resources into the process and so make it more thorough and creative. The results of deliberation are more likely to be forcefully supported and implemented. So far as I know, we have no empirical evidence regarding the relative merits, and appropriate circumstances, of hot versus cold deliberation.

2.7. Empowerment

A minipublic is empowered when its conclusions influence public decisions. Nancy Fraser contrasts *strong* publics—those that exercise authority—with *weak* ones.[12] Many minipublics should not be empowered or strong. If participants lack any claim to exercise voice in a decision, empowerment amounts to private capture or an illegitimate delegation of state power. Even when participants have some legitimate claim, the quality of their deliberations may be so poor, or the issue so important, that empowering them would degrade the wisdom or justice of public decisions.

There are good reasons, on the other hand, to empower some minipublics. When a democratic deficit manifests itself as lack of state accountability or when the minipublic is a component of a governance or problem-solving scheme, then empowerment follows from the purpose of public deliberation. As with hot high-stakes deliberation, an empowered, or strong, minipublic can create powerful incentives by offering influence over a slice of state power in exchange for participation.

2.8. Monitoring

Most minipublics are front-loaded in the sense that they aim, like an opinion poll or election, to generate public discussion and refine opinion about a candidate, issue, or policy choice. The expectation and hope is that politicians and officials will take these public deliberations into account in their subsequent decisions. Some minipublics, however, also incorporate back-loaded participation that reviews the quality of ongoing action and implementation. If a minipublic generates sufficient interest to sustain the ongoing participation necessary for monitoring, important benefits can redound to participants.

Public learning is the first important benefit. In minipublics that convene frequently to observe and consider the consequences of various policy decisions or problem-solving strategies, participants also acquire experientially based knowledge—learning by doing—about which decisions are likely to work and which are not in various contexts. Accountability is a second important benefit. In environments where official actions depart from public interests, an important function of a minipublic might be to pressure officials to serve public ends or plans. The transparency made possible by monitoring can enhance legitimacy and good faith.

3. Functional Consequences of Minipublic Design

A healthy minipublic contributes to the quality of democratic governance in several ways. One cluster of contributions concerns the character of participation in a minipublic: the quantity of participation, its bias, and the quality of deliberation. A second cluster concerns informing officials, informing citizens, and fostering the dispositions and skills of citizenship. A third cluster connects public deliberation to state action: official accountability, the justice of policy, and its efficacy and wisdom. A final function of public deliberation and participation is explicitly political: popular mobilization. Consider several rough working hypotheses about how design choices affect a minipublic's capacity to advance these functions.

3.1. Civic Engagement as Quantity of Participation

By definition, all minipublics aim to increase civic engagement by drawing citizens to deliberate. For many of them, the quantity of participation is an important measure of success.

Obvious design features—the capacity of meetings and their frequency (2.5)—set an upper limit on participants. Typically, however, those who organize minipublics do not approach this ceiling. Public apathy and malaise pose more substantial obstacles. Thus, the quantity of participation also depends heavily on the ability of organizers to mobilize individuals. Successful mobilization in turn depends on the presence of supportive community associations and their own recruitment capacity (2.2). Minipublics can also draw participants by creating the structural incentives that make engagement worthwhile. As discussed earlier, the subject of deliberation (2.3), the stakes that participants have in it (2.6), and the extent to which the minipublic is empowered or strong (2.7) all create incentives for participation.

3.2. Participation Bias

Another important dimension of civic engagement concerns the profile of those who participate. Are they disproportionately wealthy, educated, and professional, as they are in nearly all varieties of political participation? Are they drawn evenly and representatively from all sections of the population? Or are disadvantaged citizens *over*-represented?

The factors governing the quantity of participation also affect the direction and magnitude of participation bias. One way to mitigate the natural tendencies toward over representation of the advantaged is for those who operate minipublics to concentrate their outreach and recruitment (2.2) efforts on disadvantaged communities. A second strategy is to create structural incentives that make a minipublic especially attractive to less well-off citizens because it addresses their particular concerns (2.3, 2.6) and empowers them to act (2.7).

3.3. Quality of Deliberation

Minipublics also aim to foster high-quality deliberation. Good deliberation should be rational in the instrumental sense that individuals advance their own individual and collective ends through discussion, brainstorming, information pooling, planning, and problem solving. It should also be reasonable in the sense that participants respect the claims of others and constrain the pursuit of their own self-interest according to the norms of justification. Reasonableness may require participants to restrain themselves when others offer compelling reasons based on common group interests or commonly held norms such as respect, reciprocity, and fairness. Participants should be roughly equal in their opportunities and capabilities to propose ideas and make claims.[13] When they are highly unequal, discourse aimed mainly toward will formation (2.4) may be a necessary precursor to a fuller deliberation.

Whether the aim of deliberation is will formation or reasoned social choice, several design features are likely to enhance the degree of instrumental rationality in the process. Minipublics will exhibit greater rationality when their topics are ones in which participants have epistemic advantages (2.3). For example, citizens have privileged access to their own preferences and values. They may also possess local knowledge that officials and outsiders lack. Recurrence (2.5) and monitoring (2.8) also increase the rationality of deliberations by making additional information available and by making experiential learning possible. Finally, hot deliberation—discussions in which participants have high stakes (2.6) and affect the exercise of public power (2.7)—tends to increase the rationality of processes: Participants have greater motivations to correctly align their ideas and views with their interests and values. Some of the same factors that increase rationality may inhibit reasonableness. Discussions aimed at fostering and clarifying individual preferences, for example, by airing conflicts and advocating conflicting principles, may advance individual rationality while rendering participants less flexible and more self-interested.[14]

3.4. Informing Officials

Another important contribution of public deliberation, then, is that politicians, administrators, or other officials gain information from the process. When these officials, from internal motivation or external incentive, aim to act as responsible agents for the public, the information they gain may improve the quality of policy and public action.

Educative forums and participatory advisory panels (2.1) apprise officials of the considered interests, values, and preferences of citizens. Beyond the design considerations favoring good deliberation generally, the subject of deliberation (2.3) largely determines whether officials can learn from discussion in a minipublic. Officials are more likely to reap informational benefits when the subject is one in which citizens possess special knowledge, or in which their views are divided, opaque, or especially likely to change in the course of deliberative consideration.

Problem-solving and participatory governance minipublics have more ambitious informational goals.[15] Officials may hope to learn not only about the preferences and values of citizens, but also about their own operations and strategies: about what's working and what's not in their problem-solving and policy-implementation efforts. The institutional design considerations conducive to generating this higher-resolution information are just those necessary for a minipublic to consider the details of public action as it unfolds over time: recurrence (2.5) and monitoring (2.8).

3.5. Informing Citizens

Most of those who champion minipublics see citizens, not officials, as their principal beneficiaries. In one survey of organizations that sponsor citizen dialogues, "45% reported that one of their major goals was simply to provide information."[16] Compared with public professionals, citizens typically have more limited access to information and less time and training, and are asked to spread their attention over a larger range of public issues. Most citizens are likely to clarify their views and preferences and learn about substantive policy issues in any effective minipublic. The factors contributing to good deliberation (3.3) also produce information for citizens. Factors that create participant interest—such as stakes and empowerment—also enhance the incentives for citizens to pay attention and exert the energies necessary to become informed.

3.6. Democratic Skills and Socialization

Beyond learning about policies and public affairs, participatory democrats have long claimed that deliberative arenas function as schools of democracy where individuals acquire the skills of citizenship and come to consider public interests more highly in their own preferences and dispositions.[17] The extent to which participation imbues democratic skills and habits has received far more conceptual attention than empirical scrutiny. Absent the empirical basis from which to formulate firm hypotheses about the institutional design of minipublics, two working hypotheses should be tested.

First, citizens are more likely to gain democratic skills and dispositions where deliberations have tangible consequences for them. In empowered (2.7) minipublics where citizens have high stakes (2.6), they also have incentives to conduct structured and purposeful deliberations. Second, minipublics with recurring deliberation (2.5) are more likely to contribute to the development of democratic skills and dispositions than those that convene once or only infrequently. Repeated interaction increases both incentives and opportunities for cooperation.[18]

3.7. Official Accountability

Increasing the accountability of public officials and organizations is another potential contribution of minipublics. Through organized public deliberation, citizens can collectively examine the actions and policies of officials, assess the alignment of this state behavior with their own wishes and values, and attempt to bring the two into conformity. For example, the public generally has an interest in integrity that departs from the corrupt practices found in the governments of many developing, and some developed, countries. Similarly, officials may be accustomed to shirking their jobs or responsibilities in ways that can be corrected through appropriate participatory-democratic supervision.

This function is especially important, and likely to be exercised, where the gap between public interest and state action is large. So minipublics that focus on issues or problems (2.3) where there is an accountability deficit or where reflective public opinion differs substantially from official practice will be more likely to contribute in this way. Appropriate focus is a necessary, but not sufficient, design condition for advancing accountability. Citizens participating in a minipublic must also be able to identify accountability gaps and develop solutions to them. Those in a minipublic cannot increase accountability unless they can press for changes in policy or action that tighten the tether between public and state. These capacities depend in turn on the quality of deliberation (3.3), whether the minipublic is empowered (2.7), and its ability to monitor (2.8) official activities.

3.8. Justice

Minipublics also contribute to the justice of public policy and action when they allow those who are politically weak or excluded to form, express, and press for their preferences and values. Straightforwardly, minipublics that treat subject areas (2.3) in which there is substantial inequity and that enjoy sufficient scope—for example, authority over allocative decisions—are more likely to advance social justice. Enhancing the voice of the disadvantaged also requires their presence (2.2) and accessible modes of deliberation (2.4). Furthermore, a minipublic cannot advance justice without power (2.7).

3.9. Effectiveness

In addition to accountability and justice, deliberation can contribute to the efficacy of public policy and deliberation in at least three ways. First, public deliberation creates opportunities for those who will be subjected to a policy to criticize it, consider its justifications, and perhaps modify it. This discussion may enhance the legitimacy of a policy or agency, and so may make citizens inside and outside a minipublic more disposed to comply and cooperate. Minipublics that have high-quality deliberation (3.3) and affect official action (2.7) are more likely to boost efficacy by generating legitimacy. Second, some minipublics address policy areas (2.3) in which citizens possess comparative advantages—in terms of relevant resources or information—over officials. Third, minipublics can help to improve the details of implementation—its strategies and methods—over time by incorporating popular deliberation into the ongoing governance or problem-solving efforts of public bodies (2.4). The activities of these minipublics may be more likely to be sustained over time (2.5) and devoted in some measure to monitoring and evaluating official action (2.8).

3.10. Popular Mobilization

Turning from policy to politics, one can see that deliberations inside minipublics can contribute to the mobilization of citizens outside of it, especially when they are related to the more encompassing agendas of secondary associations or political actors. For example, citizens may come to support the substantive policy findings of a minipublic because that position is the product of reasoned discussion and open participation. These policy positions may also receive heightened media attention as a result of having been considered in a minipublic.

Some design factors are likely to contribute to the capacity of a minipublic to mobilize these varieties of popular support. First, a minipublic may mobilize political activity if it addresses a salient problem or need (2.3, 2.6). For example, crime and public safety is such an issue in many inner-city neighborhoods, but less so in safe suburban ones. Second, a minipublic is likely to mobilize only if it makes a difference with respect to some salient problem. This, in turn, requires the minipublic to establish a high quality of deliberation (2.4) and that it be empowered to act upon the results of that deliberation (2.7).

The following discussion ranges over many dimensions of design choices and their potential effects. Table 13.1 summarizes these relationships. The columns list institutional design choices, and their functional consequences appear in the rows. The important design features for each function are marked with an "X", and the crucial choices are indicated with a boldface "X."

Table 13.1. Consequences of Minipublic Design Choices

	2.2. Recruitment and selection	2.3. Subject of deliberation	2.4. Deliberative mode	2.5. Recurrence	2.6. Stakes	2.7. Empowerment	2.8. Monitoring
Character of participation and deliberation							
3.1. Quantity	X	**X**		X	X	X	
3.2. Bias	X	**X**			X	X	
3.3. Deliberative quality		**X**	**X**	X	X	X	X
Information pooling and individual transformation							
3.4. Informing officials		**X**		**X**			X
3.5. Informing citizens		**X**	**X**	X	X	X	X
3.6. Democratic skills and socialization				**X**	X	X	
Popular control and state capacity							
3.7. Official accountability		**X**				X	X
3.8. Justice of policy	X	**X**	**X**			X	
3.9. Efficacy of policy		**X**	**X**	X		X	X
Political effects							
3.10. Popular mobilization		**X**	X		X	X	

Source: Author.
Note: More important factors are in boldface.

4. Three Applications

This discussion of minipublic designs and their consequences has been thus far abstract for the sake of generality. To render these concepts and hypotheses more concrete, and perhaps more believable, this section describes the designs and achievements of three actual minipublics. These examples are in no way a representative sample, much less a comprehensive catalog. Rather, they have been chosen to illustrate the great variation in the institutional designs of projects that aim to improve the public sphere.

4.1. Deliberative Polling

The deliberative poll, invented by James Fishkin and his colleagues, attempts to create educative forums that model citizen deliberation under ideal conditions.[19] As Fishkin puts it,

> The idea is simple. Take a random sample of the electorate and transport those people from all over the country to a single place. Immerse the sample in the issues, with carefully balanced briefing materials, with intensive discussion in small groups, and with the chance to question competing experts and politicians. At the end of several days of working through the issues face to face, poll the participants in detail. The resulting survey offers a representation of the considered judgments of the public—the views the entire country would come to if it had the same experience.[20]

In each event, organizers select several hundred participants through a random process similar to those used in ordinary opinion polling (2.2). This method overcomes the obstacle of participation bias (3.2) and guarantees that the actual participants will mirror the underlying population demographically. Deliberative poll designers have also concentrated on creating highly informed deliberation (2.4) by distributing balanced briefing materials to participants before the event, facilitating small group discussions between participants, and making experts available to answer participants' questions. These efforts seem to have fostered open and searching discussions (3.2) in which participants become more informed about policies and consistently alter their views upon fuller reflection.

In other dimensions, however, the design of deliberative polling seems to yield only moderate impacts. Because participants often have low stakes (2.6) in discussions and because they are one-shot affairs (2.5), deliberative polling is unlikely to substantially foster the skills or dispositions of citizenship (3.6) in participants. As described in two of his books, the subjects of deliberative polls have been general public policy questions such as economic policy, criminal justice, the European Union, and energy policy.[21] Citizens enjoy little comparative advantage compared with experts in answering these complex policy questions. At most, they can apprise politicians and administrators about their values and preferences in general terms, but they are unlikely to provide information that improves policy. We therefore judge that deliberative polls have a relatively low potential to inform officials (3.4). Most deliberative polls are not designed to substantially advance popular control over state action or to improve policy. Because they are usually unempowered, the activities within deliberative polls are unlikely to increase the accountability of public officials (3.7), the justice of policies (3.8), or their efficacy (3.9). In some cases, officials have adopted specific policy recommendations from deliberative polling, but this is not the norm. Deliberative polls thus seem to have weak mobilizing capacities (3.10), and typically they are not highly empowered (2.7).

4.2. Oregon Health Plan

In the first three months of 1990, in the U.S. state of Oregon, a nonprofit organization, Oregon Health Decisions, held a series of 46 community meetings throughout the state in which 1,003 residents gathered to "build consensus on the values to be used to guide health service allocation decisions."[22] This public participation process was one result of the health care reform movement in Oregon that began in the early 1980s. At a time when many other states were retrenching, activists and policy makers sought to expand Medicaid coverage to include all of those in the state whose earnings fell below the poverty line.[23] To achieve this expansion but keep it financially feasible, policy makers foresaw difficult and controversial choices regarding the categories of medical conditions and treatments that would be covered by public health insurance. An 11-member panel of health policy experts called the Health Services Commission was to determine which health conditions would be publicly insured and which excluded. The Oregon Basic Health Care Act required the commission to make these decisions based upon values established in a participatory community process. The commission engaged Oregon Health Decisions to organize that process. Oregon Health Decisions, in turn, created a decentralized participatory advisory panel to solicit public input.

Two institutional design features—selection (2.2) and subject (2.3)—of the subsequent assemblies predictably skewed participation toward a narrow band of professionals and citizens of high socioeconomic status. Because meetings were voluntary and little effort seems to have been expended to recruit from disadvantaged communities, participants were typically wealth and highly educated: 67 percent were college graduates, and 34 percent had household incomes greater than $50,000. This minipublic addressed health care, and 70 percent (!) of participants were health care workers. The medically uninsured composed just 9.4 percent of participants.[24]

Despite these serious defects in the character of participation, actual deliberations were well structured (2.4). The careful attention to organization, facilitation, and the relatively high stakes of the subject for participants formed the foundation for engaging discussions. Deliberations were designed to elicit the values that participants, upon reflection, felt should guide health care priorities. Meetings typically lasted two hours. Participants received informational materials, watched a slide show to orient them, and received individual questionnaires concerning health care priorities. Participants then discussed their individual rankings of health care priorities with one another and attempted to reach group consensus on the relative importance of various health care values. Oregon Health Decisions staff generated a summary ranking of priorities by aggregating the results of these community meetings. All of the community meetings ranked prevention and quality of life very highly. These priorities were followed by cost effectiveness, ability to function, and equity. Somewhat lower in importance were mental health and chemical dependency, personal choice, community compassion, impact on society, length of life, and personal responsibility.[25]

The process was moderately empowered (2.7). Health Services Commissioners attempted to combine their own expertise and judgments with the results of the participatory process. They developed a list of 709 condition-treatment pairs and ranked them into 17 categories that roughly corresponded to values expressed at community meetings. Their eventual rankings reflected the values identified by Oregon Health Decisions as most important—prevention and quality of life.[26] This outcome is consistent with the interpretation that officials learned and respected (3.4, 3.7) what was important to the public as approximated by these highly imperfect community meetings.

According to close observers of Oregon health care reform, however, these details about deliberative quality and technocratic interpretation missed the crucial, and somewhat unanticipated, contribution of the participatory process.[27] By the mid-1990s, Medicaid coverage in Oregon had been successfully extended to cover everyone below the poverty line and give partial coverage—for children and pregnant women—to many above the poverty line. Between 1993 and 1996, the number of uninsured Oregonians fell from 17 percent to 11 percent. However, treatment had not been rationed. The funded portion of the condition-treatment pair list provided a substantially *more* generous coverage than the pre–Oregon Health Plan Medicaid package. Political mobilization (3.10) in favor of this more generous and just (3.8) health care policy distinguished Oregon from the many other states where health care reform collapsed over this same period.[28]

4.3. Participatory Budgeting

Nowhere in the United States is there a political entity that possesses both a deep commitment to participatory deliberative democracy and sufficient power to make good on that commitment institutionally. Not so in Latin America. Therefore, our final minipublic examination considers the participatory budgeting system in Porto Alegre, Brazil, as an example of participatory democratic governance. Porto Alegre is the capital city of the state of Rio Grande do Sul and home to 1.3 million inhabitants. In 1989, a left-wing party called the Worker's Party (the Partido dos Trabalhadores, or PT) won the mayoralty on a platform of advancing social justice through participatory democracy. These vague commitments were institutionalized into arrangements under which control over the capital portion of the municipal budget shifted from the city council to a bottom-up decision-making process called the Participatory Budget (Orçamento Participativo, or OP) that combines direct and representative mechanisms.[29]

It works roughly like this. In March of every year, large assemblies are held in each of the city's 16 districts. The assemblies often draw more than a thousand participants and are attended by city hall staff. Citizens in each assembly review the extent and quality of implementation of the projects in last year's budget (2.4, 2.8). The projects under the OP's scope concern basic urban infrastructure in areas such as sewage, housing, pavement, education, social assistance, health, and transportation (2.3). Participants in these meetings also elect delegates to represent specific neighborhoods in subsequent rounds of the OP process. This formula for representation creates incentives for mobilization; the number of delegates allocated to each district increases as a diminishing marginal function of the total participants in that district's assembly.[30] In subsequent rounds, representatives from each district and neighborhood meet to deliberate about the schedule of priority themes in their areas (for example, 1: street, 2: education, 3: housing) and the priorities within each theme (1: street A, 2: street B). These reflective preferences are aggregated into a single city budget (2.7), detailed with particular works and projects, according to a weighted formula that incorporates the schedule of expressed preferences, the population of each district, and the relative deprivation of each district.

Since its inception, the OP has drawn steadily increasing participation as citizens have gained confidence in the institution (3.1). In the 1999 and 2000 cycles, more than 14,000 residents participated in the first round of plenary assemblies. Observers estimate that some 10 percent of the adult population participates in the process annually, though precise estimates are difficult because much participation occurs in numerous informal neighborhood meetings and committee sessions. The design of open meetings combined with strong structural incentives for participation by disadvantaged participants has inverted the ordinary high-socioeconomic status participation bias observed in most political arenas. Poor people are substantially overrepresented in OP meetings (3.1).[31]

This process generates a wealth of detailed knowledge for officials (3.4). Some of this knowledge concerns the values and priorities of residents, such as the difficult trade-offs between issues such as clean water and schools. Officials also gain very specific knowledge about where particular works and projects should be located, and whether they operate successfully or fail. Conversely, residents also gain substantial knowledge (3.5) about where, and whether, public monies are appropriately spent, and about the detailed operations, successes, and failures of city agencies. Through participation in these discussions, citizens likely gain democratic skills of compromise and cooperation (3.6). However, because deliberations focus on very local goods and needs, the institution has not disposed citizens to think about the greater good of the city, the just trade-offs between jurisdictions, or the good of the city through the long arc of time.

The OP has reduced corruption and eroded traditional patronage relationships between city councilors, legislators, businesses, and local notables by making the financial decisions of city government more transparent. One result of this increase in official accountability (3.7) is that many fiscal leaks have been plugged and the actual revenues available for public investment have grown. Good government (through participatory democracy) has in turn increased the legitimacy of the municipal state and increased tax compliance. Advancing both justice (3.8) and efficacy (3.9), city agencies charged with building and operating public works have become much more productive, and the lion's share of new activity has occurred in poor areas.[32]

The treatment of these complex minipublics discussed previously has been necessarily quite compressed and omits many important details. The following two tables summarize these variations and comparisons. Table 13.2 summarizes the institutional design features of the five exemplary minipublics. Table 13.3 summarizes the practical consequences of these design choices. In each table, the most distinctive design features and those discussed in the text are displayed in boldface.

Table 13.2. Institutional Design Features of Three Minipublics

	4.1. Deliberative polling	4.2. Oregon Health Plan	4.3. Participatory budgeting
2.1. Purpose and vision	Simulate ideal deliberative conditions	Align public policy with considered citizen preferences	Participatory democratic governance
Design features of the public space			
2.2. Who? Recruitment and selection	**Representative sample**	Voluntary	**Voluntary + institutional incentive**
2.3. What? Subject of deliberation	**Large-scale public policy questions**	**Health care rationing**	**Capital infrastructure investments**
2.4. How? Deliberative mode	**Clarify principles and positions**	Assert and clarify priorities	Assert and reconcile priorities
2.5. When? Recurrence	One-shot, centralized	One-shot, decentralized	**Frequent, decentralized**
2.6. Why? Stakes	Low	Low-moderate	**High**
Connections from public space to state			
2.7. Empowerment	Low	**Moderate**	**High**
2.8. Monitoring	None	Low	Moderate

Source: Author.
Note: Distinctive design features are in boldface.

Table 13.3. Outcomes in Three Minipublics

	4.1. Deliberative polling	4.2. Oregon Health Plan	4.3. Participatory budgeting
Shape of participation			
3.1. Quantity	Low	Moderate	**High**
3.2. Bias	**Representative**	Positive SES bias	**Inverse SES bias**
3.3. Deliberative quality	**High**	Moderate	Moderate
Information pooling and individual transformation			
3.4. Informing officials	Low	**Moderate**	High
3.5. Informing citizens	**Moderate**	Moderate	High
3.6. Democratic skills and dispositions	Low	Low	Moderate
Popular control and state capacity			
3.7. Official accountability	None	**Moderate**	**High**
3.8. Justice of policy	No	**Moderate**	**High**
3.9. Efficacy of policy	No	Low	**High**
Political effects			
3.10. Popular mobilization	Low	**Moderate**	**High**

Source: Author.
Note: Strengths of each design are displayed in boldface.

5. Conclusion

Many public leaders and organizations are now engaged in the important work of constructing spaces for civic engagement and public deliberation. They describe their efforts and motivations in strikingly similar terms: enhancing participation, creating deliberative democracy, improving civic engagement, making government more accountable, and increasing social justice. This homogeneity is perhaps unsurprising; public intellectuals and democratic activists have described their own projects and ideals in similarly uniform terms.

In practice, however, initiatives created by proponents of participatory and deliberative democracy—projects that I call minipublics—display rich multidimensional variation. Because practitioners are inclined to invest their limited energies in improving their own projects rather than exploring details of like-minded ones, there is surprisingly little discussion in either the scholarly or practical literature on these variations and their implications. I have tried to describe the most important dimensions of difference from the perspective of institutional design. Bringing this variation to light and imposing conceptual structure on it will, I hope, contribute to understanding minipublics and the construction of minipublics that improve democratic governance by enhancing the quality of public opinion, enabling participatory problem solving, and strengthening channels of official accountability.

Notes

1. This terminology follows Robert Dahl's notion of a minipopulus (1989) and Jack Nagel's (1992) notion of Deliberative Assemblies on a Random Basis. As explained later, my notion of a minipublic is both more inclusive and more connected to both civil society and the state than either Dahl's or Nagel's proposals.

2. Unger (1987).

3. See Gastil (2000) for a discussion of existing participatory advisory panels, including the Citizens Jury, and his proposal for one kind of powerful minipublic of this type: citizen panels.

4. Cohen and Sabel (1997); Fung and Wright (2003); Weber (1999).

5. Nagel (1987); Verba and Nie (1972).

6. This mechanism is similar to the notion of selective incentives that help overcome collective action problems. Structural incentives differ from selective incentives in that benefits from the former inhere in the structure of minipublics and in particular in the subjects they address. Benefits for participants come from their potential collective and social effects rather than in ancillary "positive inducements" (Olson 1971, 133).

7. Cohen and Rogers (1983).

8. Cohen (1989); Gutmann and Thompson (1996).

9. Habermas (1984, 25).

10. Fraser (1992); Mansbridge (1980); Sanders (1997).

11. Mansbridge (1980).

12. Fraser (1992, 132–36).

13. This discussion utilizes Rawls's coordinates of rationality, reasonableness, and equality.

14. Jacobs, Cook, and Carpini (2000).

15. See section 2.1 for a discussion of distinctions between these three varieties of minipublics.

16. Jacobs, Cook, and Carpini (2000, 22).

17. Pateman (1970); Verba, Schlozman, and Brady (1995).

18. This line of reasoning suggests that participation in consequential and ongoing minipublics such as school governance committees will have more salutary consequences for citizenship than participation in the juries (few consequences for the deliberators and the one-shot) that de Tocqueville famously lauded: "Juries are wonderfully effective in shaping a nation's judgment and increasing its natural lights. ... It should be regarded as a free school which is always open. The main reason for the practical intelligence and the political good sense of the Americans is their long experience with juries" (de Tocqueville 1969, 275).

19. Fishkin (1991, 93).

20. Fishkin (1995, 162).

21. Fishkin (1991; 1995).

22. Hasnain and Garland (1990). See also Sirianni and Friedland (2001).

23. Jacobs, Marmor, and Oberlander (1998, 2).

24. Hasnain and Garland (1990); see also Nagel (1992) for criticism and discussion.

25. Hasnain and Garland (1990, 5–6).

26. Nagel (1987, 1992).

27. This account follows Jacobs, Marmor, and Oberlander (1998).

28. Jacobs, Marmor, and Oberlander (1998, 9).

29. This account is drawn from Baiocchi (2001) and Santos (1998).

30. See Baiocchi (2001). The number of delegates for a district is determined as follows: for the first 100 persons, one delegate for every 10 persons; for the next 150 persons, one for 20; for the next 150, one for 30; for each additional 40 persons after that, one delegate. To cite an example, a district that had 520 persons in attendance would have 26 delegates.

31. Baiocchi (2001).

32. Baiocchi (2001).

Bibliography

Baiocchi, Gianpaolo. 2001. "Participation, Activism, and Politics: The Porto Alegre Experiment and Deliberative Democratic Theory." *Politics and Society* 29 (1): 43–72.

Benhabib, Seyla. 1996. "Toward a Deliberative Model of Democratic Legitimacy." In *Democracy and Difference: Contesting the Boundaries of the Political,* ed. Selya Benhabib, 67–94. Princeton, NJ: Princeton University Press.

Button, Mark, and Kevin Mattson. 1999. "Deliberative Democracy in Practice: Challenges and Prospects for Civic Deliberation." *Polity* 31 (4): 609–37.

Chan, Sewell. 2001. "D.C. Residents Dish Out Ideas; 3,500 Citizens Provide Criticism, Suggestions for City Leaders at Summit." *Washington Post* (October 7): C1.

Cohen, Joshua. 1989. "Deliberation and Democratic Legitimacy." In *The Good Polity,* ed. Alan Hamlin and Philip Pettit, 17–34. New York: Basil Blackwell.

Cohen, Joshua, and Joel Rogers. 1983. *On Democracy.* New York: Penguin Books.

———. 1992. "Secondary Associations and Democratic Governance." *Politics and Society* 20 (4): 393–472.

Cohen, Joshua, and Charles Sabel. 1997. "Directly-Deliberative Polyarchy." *European Law Journal.* 3 (4): 313–42.

Cottman, Michael H. 1999. "A View from the Summit: D.C. Residents Turn Out to Hash Out Their City's Future." *Washington Post* (November 21): C1.

Dahl, Robert A. 1989. *Democracy and Its Critics.* New Haven, CT: Yale University Press.

de Tocqueville, Alexis. 1969. *Democracy in America.* Translated by George Lawrence, edited by J. P. Mayer. New York: Harper and Row.

Fearon, James D. 1998. "Deliberation as Discussion." In *Deliberative Democracy,* ed. Jon Elster, 44–68. Cambridge, U.K.: Cambridge University Press.

Fishkin, James. 1991. *Democracy and Deliberation: New Directions for Democratic Reform.* New Haven, CT: Yale University Press.

Fishkin, James. 1995. *The Voice of the People.* New Haven, CT: Yale University Press.

Fraser, Nancy. 1992. "Rethinking the Public Sphere: A Contribution to the Critique of Actually Existing Democracy." In *Habermas and the Public Sphere,* ed. Craig Calhoun, 109–42. Cambridge, MA: MIT Press.

Fung, Archon. 1999. "Street Level Democracy: A Theory of Popular Pragmatic Deliberation and Its Practice in Chicago School Reform and Community Policing, 1988–1997." Ph.D. dissertation, Massachusetts Institute of Technology.

Fung, Archon. 2001. "Accountable Autonomy: Toward Empowered Deliberation in Chicago Schools and Policing." *Politics and Society* 29 (1): 73–104.

Fung, Archon, and Erik Olin Wright. 2003. "Thinking about Empowered Participatory Governance." In *Deepening Democracy: Institutional Innovations in Empowered Participatory Governance,* ed. Archon Fung and Erik Olin Wright, 3–44. London: Verso Press.

Gastil, John. 2000. *By Popular Demand: Revitalizing Representative Democracy through Deliberative Elections.* Berkeley, CA: University of California Press.

Government of the District of Columbia. 2001. *Accomplishments since the First Citizen Summit.* Report on file with author.

Gutmann, Amy, and Dennis Thompson. 1996. *Democracy and Disagreement: Why Moral Conflict Cannot Be Avoided in Politics, and What Can Be Done about It.* Cambridge, MA: Harvard University Press.

Habermas, Jürgen. 1984. Translated by Thomas McCarthy. *Theory of Communicative Action.* Volume 1. Boston: Beacon Press.

———. 1989. *The Structural Transformation of the Public Sphere: An Inquiry into a Category of Bourgeois Society.* Cambridge, MA: MIT Press.

———. 1992. "Further Reflections on the Public Sphere." In *Habermas and the Public Sphere,* ed. Craig Calhoun, 422–61. Cambridge, MA: MIT Press.

———. 1996. *Between Facts and Norms: Contributions to a Discourse Theory of Law and Democracy.* Translated by William Rehg. Cambridge, MA: MIT Press.

Hasnain, Romana, and Michael Garland. 1990. *Health Care in Common: Report of the Oregon Health Decisions Community Meetings Process.* Portland: Oregon Health Decisions.

Hirst, Paul. 1994. *Associative Democracy: New Forms of Economic and Social Governance.* Amherst, MA: University of Amherst Press.

Isaac, Thomas T. M. (with Richard W. Franke). 2000. *Local Democracy and Development: The Kerala People's Campaign for Decentralised Planning.* New Delhi: Leftword.

Jacobs, Lawrence R., Fay Lomax Cook, and Michael Delli Carpini. 2000. "Talking Together: Public Deliberation and Discursive Capital: A Report to the Pew Charitable Trusts." Report on file with author.

Jacobs, Lawrence, Theodor Marmor, and Jonathan Oberlander. 1998. "The Political Paradox of Rationing: The Case of the Oregon Health Plan." Innovations in American Government Program, John F. Kennedy School of Government, Harvard University, Cambridge, MA.

Mansbridge, Jane. 1980. *Beyond Adversary Democracy.* New York: Basic Books.

Matthews, David. 1999. *Politics for People: Finding a Responsible Public Voice.* 2nd ed. Urbana, IL: University of Illinois Press.

Nagel, Jack H. 1987. *Participation.* New York: Prentice Hall.

———. 1992. "Combining Deliberation and Fair Representation in Community Health Decisions." *University of Pennsylvania Law Review* 140 (5): 1965–85.

Olson, Mancur. 1971. *The Logic of Collective Action: Public Goods and the Theory of Groups.* Cambridge, MA: Harvard University Press.

Pateman, Carole. 1970. *Participation and Democratic Theory.* Cambridge, U.K.: Cambridge University Press.

Putnam, Robert. 1993. *Making Democracy Work: Civic Traditions in Modern Italy.* Princeton, NJ: Princeton University Press.

Putnam, Robert. 2000. *Bowling Alone: The Collapse and Revival of American Community.* New York: Simon and Schuster.

Sanders, Lynn M. 1997. "Against Deliberation." *Political Theory* 25 (3): 347–76.

Santos, Boaventura de Sousa. 1998. "Participatory Budgeting in Porto Alegre: Toward a Redistributive Democracy." *Politics and Society* 26 (4): 461–510.

Sirianni, Carmen, and Lewis Friedland. 2001. *Civic Innovation in America: Community Empowerment, Public Policy, and the Movement for Civic Renewal.* Berkeley, CA: University of California Press.

Skocpol, Theda. 1999. "How American Became Civic." In *Civic Engagement in American Democracy,* ed. Theda Skocpol and Morris Fiorina, 27–80. Washington, DC: Brookings Institution Press.

Skogan, Wesley G., and Susan M. Hartnett. 1997. *Community Policing: Chicago Style.* New York: Oxford University Press.

Unger, Roberto. 1987. *False Necessity: Anti-Necessitarian Social Theory in the Service of Radical Democracy.* Cambridge, U.K.: Cambridge University Press.

Verba, Sidney, and Norman Nie. 1972. *Participation in America.* New York: Harper and Row.

Verba, Sidney, Kay Lehman Schlozman, and Henry E. Brady. 1995. *Voice and Equality: Civic Voluntarism in American Politics.* Cambridge, MA: Harvard University Press.

Weber, Edward P. 1999. "The Question of Accountability in Historical Perspective: From Jacksonian to Contemporary Grassroots Ecosystem Management." *Administration and Society* 41 (4): 451–94.

Deliberation and Institutional Mechanisms for Shaping Public Opinion

Baogang He

Over the past decade, China has experimented with numerous controlled forms of political participation. Despite China being an authoritarian, one-party regime, Chinese political leaders have tested a variety of democratic innovations (He and Thøgersen 2010). However, none have been more widely applied than the deliberative model.

Two decades ago, the introduction of village elections acted as an instigator for further political reform in China. The implementation of approval and recall voting at the local level and the establishment of new deliberative venues, deliberative polls, and public hearings were also facets of change. Through this change came the gradual acceptance of selected civil society organizations and the right of citizens to sue the state. It also provided the public with greater access to government information. Although uneven in scope and effectiveness, many of these initiatives appear to have genuinely *deliberative* elements— that is, they are able to identify and shape public opinion and generate considered public judgment through discussion and debate. As an added measure, they generate deliberative influence, from which political leaders take guidance, and on which they rely for the legitimacy of their decisions (Leib and He 2006).

This chapter synthesizes various strands of participatory and deliberative institutions in China with a focus on five deliberative polling experiments that I have helped organize. It examines the efforts of institutionalizing deliberative mechanisms and practices and assesses the efficacy of such mechanisms in changing public opinion, engendering participatory habits, and generating demands for political accountability.

204 Accountability through Public Opinion

The Development of Deliberative Institutions in China

In the 1990s, numerous villages began to conduct meetings that enabled representatives to deliberate village affairs. Many of the new *deliberative* institutions
and experiments have occurred in rural areas and can often be directly linked
to new political empowerments such as elections and approval voting.[1] However, even unelected local urban leaders are increasingly employing methods
such as *consultative meetings* or public hearings as a means of winning public
support for local projects. In the Shangcheng district of Hangzhou, a public
consultation is held once a month. In the district of Luwan of Shanghai, about
100 public hearings were held between 2001 and 2002.

The practice of holding public hearings has also developed at the national
level. In 1996, the first national law on administrative punishment introduced
a provision stipulating that a *public hearing* must be held before any punishment is given.[2] As a result, more than 359 public hearings on administrative
punishment were held in Shanghai alone between October 1996 and June
2000. The now-well-known Article 23 of the Law on Price passed by China's
National Congress in December 1997 specified that the prices of public goods
must be decided through public hearings. At least 11 provinces developed
regulations to implement the national law, with 10 referring to the idea of
transparency and openness, and nine referring to the idea of democracy. Further, more than 1,000 public hearings on pricing were held across China
between 1998 and 2001. The Law on Legislature, passed in 2000, requires public hearings to be an integral part of the decision-making process for all legal
regulations and laws. More than 39 legislative public hearings were held at the
provincial level between 1999 and 2004, and Shanghai took a leading role in
organizing four (Shengyong and He 2006, 445).

Although these reforms are by nature consultative, the features of deliberation have emerged in China through the development of citizen juries, public
hearings, and deliberative polling. The search for persuasive reasons, the
changes in individual preference due to discussion, and the shaping of public
opinion through debate are all features of an emerging deliberative element.
In using the term *deliberative,* this chapter recognizes the difference between
public consultation under Mao and the deliberative forums that have developed in recent years.

Although China has achieved much in the development of deliberative institutions, numerous shortcomings remain to be addressed. To take one example
of a public hearing that I observed in Wenling city in 2004: The discussion was
centered on the economic advantages of a local Buddhist temple. I identified
five shortcomings with this public hearing. First, the 200 participants were
self-selected, rather than randomly selected and therefore far from representative of the town's population (we used a random selection method in our
deliberative polling experiment). Second, the participants were not provided
information before the public hearing (we prepared and provided briefing

materials in our experiment). Third, limited time (only two hours) was allowed for discussion, and only 27 of the 200 participants were able to express their opinions and preferences (we extended our deliberation time to one day and alternated between small group discussions and two plenary sessions). Fourth, public dialogue was largely manipulated by the elite, meaning that participants lacked a truly equal voice (we attempted to achieve political equality through facilitators who were required to ensure that each participant made an equal contribution to the discussion). Finally, fifth, given the vested interest of the agency, ordinary citizens remained generally powerless and had a minimal effect on the outcome (our deliberative polling made a direct link between deliberation and decision; see the Zeguo case that follows).

The Deliberative Polling Experiment in China

The design of deliberative polling (DP), with random sampling and balanced briefing materials, speaks to all of these deficiencies mentioned earlier in a transparent way. We embarked on an initiative to employ DP in China in 2005–10, in a local environment that had a fortunate mixture of enterprising local leadership and substantial deliberative experience. Wenling city, a county-level city with a vibrant private economy, is admittedly atypical, but illustrative of the wide variety of institutional innovations, as well as the degree to which the Chinese Communist Party is stimulating lower-level experimentation. Wenling had, by increments, developed an institution that combined an empowered citizenry with deliberation—a form and degree of deliberative democracy that is very unusual in the developed democracies, let alone in authoritarian contexts.

The first democratic *kentan* forum (or "heart-to-heart discussion") was held in 1996, in an attempt by local leaders to find a replacement for the increasingly ineffective methods of ideological mobilization. From 1996 to 2000, more than 1,190 deliberative and consultative meetings were held at the village level, 190 at the township level, and 150 in governmental organizations, schools, and business sectors.

In 2004, a "democratic discussion forum" attended by the deputies of the local People's Congress catalyzed a new development. Local leaders discovered that deliberating controversial issues opened an avenue not only for support from citizens, but naturally also for opposition, which then increased the political value of open decision making. To diffuse responsibility and gain legitimacy for decisions on any controversial issue, the local party organization decided that deputies of the local People's Congress should vote on certain difficult issues in a deliberative meeting. In 2004, Wenling was awarded the national prize for Innovations and Excellence in Local Chinese Governance.

Still more was to come: In a fourth development in 2005, Wenling city introduced China's first experiment in DP, using the device developed by James

Fishkin to set priorities for the city's budget. Deliberative polling uses random sampling to constitute a deliberative forum that is descriptively representative of the population, thus avoiding the biases of self-selected citizens' bodies. Participants learn and deliberate for a minimum of one day, to simulate what public opinion might be were it informed and deliberative. Unlike in deliberative polls elsewhere, however, officials in Wenling treated the deliberative poll as an empowered representative assembly by announcing in advance that they would abide by the results of the poll.

The deliberative polling project in Zeguo Township, Wenling city, allowed a random sample of average citizens to deliberate about which infrastructure projects would be funded in the coming year. The process of DP is intended to represent what the public would think if it had a chance to become more informed. In Zeguo Township, it was many things at once: a social science investigation, a public policy consultation, and a public discussion in its own right. It built on the local practice of *kentan* but avoided that practice's shortcomings of inequality, a lack of representation, and lack of clear results (Fishkin, He, and Siu 2008; Fishkin and others 2010).

The second DP experiment took place in Zeguo Township on March 20, 2006. It involved 237 randomly selected citizens who participated in a one-day event deliberating the expenditure of the annual budget, the advantages and disadvantages of each project, and the ranking of options for 2006. The experiment made three improvements to the 2005 experiment. First, an electoral list rather than the household register was used; thus each individual participant, rather than household, formed the unit for the random selection process. As a result, 99 women were randomly selected, constituting 41.8 percent of the sample. Moreover, participants not only were provided detailed information about the projects but also were taken to visit each project site. On the day of the deliberation, all experts were available for consultation. Second, Zeguo Township's leadership reserved 5–10 percent of its annual budget for new priorities raised in the DP. Participants expressed a genuine concern with environmental issues. As a result, one officer was delegated responsibility for environmental affairs, and approximately one million yuan was allocated to clean up the whole town. Each village received 8,000 yuan to build a rubbish collection center, and an additional 1,000 to 3,000 yuan was provided for the clean-up of the remaining garbage in the village. The third and final improvement resulted in the formation of a supervising group comprising randomly selected deputies to ensure that the results of the DP were implemented. These deputies were permitted to question the Zeguo Township government about the implementation process through the Zeguo Township People's Congress.

The third DP experiment involved 197 randomly selected citizens and was held on February 20, 2008, in the Zeguo Township of Wenling city. Three improvements emerged from this experiment. First, the content of DP was widened to encompass all of the town's budgetary issues. Budgetary issues are a vital priority for any contemporary government. In China, the reform of participatory budgeting is concerned not only with the transformation of government functions, but also with the establishment of a modern public financial system. Zeguo Township in particular sets an example of the way in which participatory budgeting can be conducted through public deliberation. The government of Zeguo Township prepared a 48-page "2008 Zeguo Township Budget of Expenditures" detailing the Y 248,523 million. The budget allocation list was more detailed than that of previous participatory budgeting projects in Wenling city. During the National People's Congress in 2007, several deputies criticized the Ministry of Finance, stating that the central and local budgets were so nebulous that the deputies were unable to perform an audit. Only budgets with detailed allocations could be useful for auditing purposes. Consequently, the 48-page document provided by the Zeguo Township government set a higher standard for the transparency and openness of participatory budgeting.

The second improvement relates to the way in which the participants interacted with the deputies of the local People's Congress. The interaction was a twofold process. To better understand the formation of public opinion, 63 deputies observed the entire DP process. Similarly, 10 of the 197 participants were randomly selected to observe the way in which the deputies deliberated the budget at the meeting of the local People's Congress on February 29, 2008. This improved level of interaction between citizens and deputies has directly affected the decision-making process.

The third improvement focuses on the outcome of the experiment. The People's Congress of Zeguo Township and the Zeguo Township government endorsed public opinion following the deliberative process. Together with the People's Congress, the township government made a decision to increase the budget from Y 20,000 to Y 100,000 to meet public demand seeking an increase in the pension for rural senior citizens. In responding to the request for additional infrastructure funding, the township government and People's Congress reallocated 400,000 RMB to subsidize construction in these poor and hardship villages. When public opinion was divided on whether two million RMB should be spent on the redevelopment of the Wenchang Pavilion, the local People's Congress and Zeguo Township government cut funding to one million RMB. This decision received public support. Before the deliberation, the mean support for the Wenchang Pavilion was 5.9. However, it dropped to 5.0 in the second survey following deliberation. Similarly, the Zeguo government's decision to increase environmental funding by 8.89 percent was largely a result of the 2005, 2006, and 2008 deliberative polls, which determined that environmental issues were a key priority for citizens.

The 2005 and 2006, Zeguo Township deliberative polls provided the basis for another more specialized experiment. In July 2006, a public official familiar with the Zeguo Township deliberative polls organized a deliberative poll among the workers at Long Biao, a local factory. Rising levels of production resulted in the company's profits increasing from Y 150 million in 2003 to Y 650 million in 2005. However, a shortage of migrant workers meant that the company was lacking a stable workforce. I helped Ren Jianfei from the Zeguo Township government to organize the deliberative forum in Long Biao. Rong Jianrong, the general manager of Long Biao Enterprise (Group), and He Zhongsheng and Chen Gangyi from Long Biao executed the experiment. The deliberative forum addressed enterprise decision making, enterprise management, enterprise innovation, enterprise culture, labor protection, and labor and management relations. A random sample of 89 representatives completed the questionnaires before and after the deliberation. The participants were divided into six small groups, each of which involved a 90-minute deliberation, followed by a 90-minute plenary meeting to discuss the matters with general managers. The group discussion was chaired by trained facilitators who were local school teachers. The aim was to ensure that each participant was given an equal opportunity and amount of time to express his or her views freely. Senior managers were excluded from the group discussion, and each participant was allocated a number to protect his or her identity. This anonymity was to encourage freedom of expression without the fear of punishment from senior managers. The plenary meeting provided all the participants with the opportunity to raise questions with senior managers, who then had an opportunity to offer their explanations.

Although the randomly selected employees were initially suspicious, they ultimately became actively involved in the deliberative process. The enterprise owner was initially anxious about the outcome, but he was pleased following the results of the deliberative forum. The forum not only encouraged information exchange within the enterprise, but also offered migrant workers the chance to meet the general manager of the factory for the first time and enabled them to express their concerns directly to the senior managers. The process has led to concrete improvements in working conditions at the factory. For example, the managers have installed air conditioners for each dormitory, extended the hours the library is open, provided compensation for overtime, and increased employee salaries. Moreover, the most significant improvement occurred at the management level. Before the deliberative forum, family members dominated the management structure. Learning of the strong discontent with the family management expressed by the participants during the deliberative forum, family members gave way to professional managers. The process fundamentally reformed the company structure, creating additional channels for greater interaction between employees and managers. This case demonstrates the way in which deliberative democracy can be used in a private enterprise to manage and address conflicting interests and present a number of opportunities to improve business and organizational management (He and Yuhua 2008).

Deliberative polling was also carried out in Bianyu village, Zeguo Township, by the village party secretary and myself. With a population of 1,400, Bianyu village had held several consultative meetings in the past. However, the deliberative quality of each meeting had been classed as poor, and participants had a limited impact on decision making. Deliberative polling in 2006 overcame many of these deficiencies. Rather than a one-shot deliberative meeting, a series of DP meetings were held over a period of four months (March–June 2006). Five key issues were considered: migrants, a village plan, waste management, tree planting, and management of collective village land. Each issue was significant and needed to be addressed through public consultation. The 84 participants were made up of elected village representatives and approximately 60 randomly selected participants to ensure the representation of a broad range of interests. In addition, 12 randomly chosen migrant workers were invited to participate in the event. Participants were provided with briefing material outlining the five issues as well as a questionnaire on the various solutions. The first deliberative meeting was held on the evening of March 19, and the final meeting was held on June 26, 2006.

Each participant was randomly assigned to one of six groups. Each group met for two hours for a total of four meetings that were chaired by a trained facilitator. In an attempt to test the efficacy of different facilitation strategies, different groups were facilitated in different ways. Three of the groups were facilitated in a way that reflects conventional practice for deliberations of this kind. The other three groups were facilitated in a way that encouraged participants to offer reasons and counterreasons and to consider the best interest of the community as a whole. I trained the facilitators twice over two days and wrote instructions for them.

After the four meetings each participant was asked to complete a questionnaire detailing a number of disputed issues and solutions. The questionnaire included questions on whether the village should build a special home for "new people" (migrants) or whether the village should impose certain fees on the villagers for collecting rubbish. The result of the survey revealed the level of public opinion in the village and represented village policies in relation to the above-mentioned issues. It was interesting to note that despite most participants' being initially opposed to the construction of a new building for migrant workers, they ultimately reached a high degree of consensus in support of the construction. It is also worth noting that participants who originally diverged on issues achieved a greater degree of consensus on many key issues. For instance, before deliberative polling, 46 percent of the participants supported the bagging of garbage; conversely, 54 percent supported each household's taking their garbage to a big garbage bin instead. The two opinions were basically evenly matched. However, after the deliberation the corresponding proportions became 17.8 percent and 82.2 percent, placing the latter proposition in a position of absolute superiority (He and Wang 2007).

Institutionalization

As early as 2002, Wenling city in Zhejiang decided that townships must hold four democratic roundtables each year. The requirements of Document No. 7 were intended to promote the institutionalization of democratic roundtables and to achieve real results. No fewer than four roundtables were to be held each year at the township or street committee level, and two at the village or community level. This would be worth four merit points. Responsibility for carrying out the roundtables would be shared between the Party's Departments of Organization and Propaganda. Chen Yimin, an officer in the Wenling City Propaganda Department, devised an examination and assessment system to actively promote the deliberative democracy system. It was stated that purely ceremonial or futile attempts at conducting roundtables would not score points. In 2005, Taiping Street was docked three merit points for failing to hold a roundtable, whereas Zheguo Township that year gained four points for setting a high standard with its DP system. Although such institutional methods may attempt to prevent the stagnation of democratic deliberative institutions, they also pose a problem of formalism. To pass the city's inspections, each township randomly selects a few minor issues and arranges for some people to attend.

Habituation is an important dimension of the institutionalization of deliberative practice. The promotion and frequent use of deliberation in Wenling received the support of both officials and peasants. As a result, deliberative democracy is widely accepted as a means of resolving social conflicts. Zeguo Township is a case in point. Party Secretary Jiang Zhaohua and Mayor Wang Xiaoyu have adopted DP methods on three separate occasions. They have also used a public opinion poll to reach consensus on construction projects in the town. When they encountered major issues of land and migration, the party secretary and mayor also thought of using democratic deliberation methods to formulate public policy that considered both scientific data and public opinion.

Fujian Province has ruled that one-fifth of its villagers or one-third of village representatives may jointly request a village-level democratic hearing meeting. In some villages in Wenling, democratic discussion has become customary. When village leaders fail to hold a democratic roundtable, the villagers ask the reason why. A failure to hold a democratic roundtable has been met with opposition from peasants. This new culture has placed new pressures on village leaders, and this pressure from the people is the most important impetus for the sustainable development of deliberative institutions.

The citizen forms the fundamental basis for achieving a sustainable deliberative institution. When peasants become modern citizens, they seek to safeguard their rights. They demand that a system of deliberative democracy be put into practice. Sustainable development of democratic institutions is possible only when citizens strive and struggle to achieve this. Reliance on an enlightened leadership, rather than the participation of citizens, places the idea into question. Only when people begin to regard institutions of democratic deliberation as part of their lifestyle, and only when these institutions form a new tradition of Chinese culture, can they truly take root.

Effects of Deliberative and Participatory Institutions

Enhancing Local Governance

Assessment of the effects of these deliberative and consultative institutions is no doubt subject to different criteria. In accordance with the liberal criterion of effective constraint on the state, these deliberative institutions have little impact on a powerful state. Following a more communitarian criterion of the enhancement of collective solidarity and social trust, some deliberative institutions do, in fact, solve thorny problems, help to maintain local stability and security, and enhance collective solidarity. On a participant satisfaction dimension, the Wenling survey found that 137 (53.1 percent) were extremely satisfied with the democratic discussion forum, 34 (13.2 percent) were relatively satisfied, 30 (11.6 percent) neutral, and 10 (3.9 percent) were not satisfied.

Participatory and deliberative institutions contribute to what John Stuart Mill called "government by discussion." Public deliberation has been translated into public authority and power and has formed a collective will to generate pressure on irresponsible behavior such as taking shared public space or littering in public areas. Deliberative institutions enhance community cohesion, empower citizens to participate in political processes, and help them to develop democratic skills and the democratic disposition. Beyond citizen empowerment, public deliberation has also increased state legitimacy and local order. To the extent that deliberative and consultative processes aim to achieve accountability and responsiveness, just and fair policies for the parties concerned, and a deep linkage between the ruled and the rulers, these benefits do tend to accrue.

The Wenling survey, for example, found that 225 respondents (87.2 percent) agreed, whereas 11 (4.3 percent) disagreed, that democratic discussion forums have made local government more responsible and have helped to develop a democratic decision-making process. In this survey, 209 (81 percent) agreed that democratic discussion forums have made policy-making processes transparent and have made policy implementation easier. Nevertheless, 18 respondents (7 percent) agreed with the statement that democratic discussion forums make things worse because they generate different voices that are difficult to unify.

Deliberative institutions increase the capacity of the local community to resolve conflicts by altering preferences, generating recognition and respect among those with different interests and opinions, and enhancing governability. In the deliberative process the nature of a problem is demonstrated, different solutions are compared, and new alternatives crafted. Group deliberation induces individuals to reveal their preferences and views truthfully, forces individuals to consider the perspectives of others, and makes them willing to compromise and reach agreement. Consensus is often achieved for seemingly intractable problems. This result can be found in numerous cases reported in academic studies and journalists' reports.

The Empowerment of Citizens

Measures and strategies are being deployed to empower citizens, ensure authenticity, and reduce manipulation. For example, in 2004 in Wenling, a law was put in place to regularize deliberative institutions. Citizens can use this law to demand that a local official hold a deliberative meeting. Civic groups and workers are encouraged to participate in the deliberative process so that ordinary people have a say, and the powers of citizens are increasing through the voice of civic associations.

Citizen evaluation meetings, in particular, give citizens an opportunity to issue judgments about the quality of deliberation, and they can exert great pressure on local leaders to facilitate genuine deliberation. In the areas in which decisions are made immediately after a public deliberation, efficacy is enhanced by eliminating the "empty talk" critique launched against many deliberative institutions that do not produce a policy impact.

Regularized participatory and deliberative institutions and meetings empower individuals with a set of rights and procedures, such as the right of public consultation, the right to equal standing in public, and the right to initiate a meeting and make motions. These are tremendous rights for citizens to have. National law stipulates that all public policies must go through a consultative and deliberative process before being implemented. These institutions and meeting have generated a special form of deliberative citizenship with distinctive rights, resources, and duties. In particular, deliberative citizens are entitled to the right to ask the government to respond to the result of deliberation. The Wenling survey found that 148 respondents (57.3 percent) agreed that the deliberative and participatory meetings embody the right to gain information, 184 (71.3 percent) agreed that they had a right of participation, and 137 (53.1 percent) agreed that they had a right to monitor government.

A significant development in empowering citizens is that some local leaders even give up some power in the process of developing deliberative institutions. In the Zeguo Township experiment, most officials sat outside a classroom to observe a meeting, and they were not allowed to speak to influence the choice of ordinary citizens. In the end, the final choice of the citizens was endorsed by the Zeguo Township People's Congress as official policy. Citizens were empowered through the process of an open and transparent democratic mechanism, and the experiment contributed to the construction of social capital and a mutual trust between the local government and citizens. Zeguo Township Party Secretary Jiang Zhaohua admitted, "Although I gave up some final decision-making power, we gain more power back because the process has increased the legitimacy for the choice of projects and created public transparency in the public policy decision-making process. Public policy is therefore more easily implemented."

Deliberation is a process by which people make themselves citizens. It is a citizenship-building mechanism through which participants learn about one another, exchange opinions, and raise their moral consciousness. Take the example of one deliberative and consultative meeting that discussed cable TV in 2004 in Hangzhou. It turned out to be a process of citizenship education. Although some residents argued that migrants and local residents should enjoy the same right to education, including the cable system, even without paying their fair share in taxes, others argued that residents should all contribute equally to the development of the cable service—that is, it is unfair for some residents not to pay the fee but have several outlets on the cable system. In another case, the participants discussed the local environment, and some criticized the behavior and values of unemployed persons who refused to do cleaning jobs that they considered to be too menial and suitable only for "second-class citizen peasants." In these examples, although what was said to the migrants and unemployed classes was not especially generous, all citizens were able to learn one another's perspectives and respectfully discuss difficult issues that affected the fate of the broader community.

Group deliberation has also altered individual preference. Through deliberation, individuals develop more general and common perspectives with regard to interest-related issues. Deliberation is a social process in which citizens develop their proficiency and skills in engaging in dialogue, carrying out cooperative projects, and respecting mutual interests. An internal aspect of deliberation involves the process through which participants challenge themselves and look at other viewpoints so that they may develop into reflective citizens. To the extent that some citizens changed their minds in the cable and local environment meetings (and they did), this is evidence of what most Westerners already know about deliberation: that it can help people change their minds on important policy matters.

Notes

1. Approval voting is an institutional innovation whereby citizens will evaluate the performance of cadres through filling out the survey questionnaire, which functions as a sort of voting system when competitive and electoral democracy is absent.
2. This is the law to regulate how governments can punish or impose fines on those who violate administrative rules.

References

Fishkin, James, Baogang He, Bob Ruskin, and Alice Siu. 2010. "Deliberative Democracy in an Unlikely Place: Deliberative Polling in China." *British Journal of Political Science* 40 (2): 435–48.

Fishkin, James, Baogang He, and Alice Siu. 2008. "Public Consultation through Deliberation in China." In *Governance Reform under Real-World Conditions: Citizens, Stakeholders, and Voice,* ed. Sina Odugbemi and Thomas Jacobson, 461–75. Washington, DC: World Bank.

He, Baogang, and Stig Thøgersen. 2010. "Giving the People a Voice? Experiments with Consultative Authoritarian Institutions in China." *Journal of Contemporary China* 19 (66): 675–92.

He, Baogang, and Chunguang Wang. 2007. "Deliberative Democracy in Rural China: A Case Study of Bianyu Experiment." *Sociological Studies* (Beijing) no. 3: 56–73.

He, Baogang, and Xie Yuhua. 2008. "Participation at Workplace: A Case Study of Deliberative Forum in Longbiao Company." *Twentieth-First Century* (Hong Kong, China) no. 4: 102–12.

Leib, Ethan, and Baogang He, eds. 2006. *The Search for Deliberative Democracy in China.* New York: Palgrave.

Shengyong, Chen, and Baogang He, eds. 2006. *Development of Deliberative Democracy.* Beijing: China's Social Sciences Press.

15

Creating Citizens through Communication Education in the United States

William Keith

Introduction

In any democratic or quasi-democratic system, governments should be accountable to their citizens, in the sense not only that government decisions take into account the interests of citizens (this might happen sometimes in an autocracy), but also that citizens decide what their interests are, communicate them to the government, and signal when they feel their interests are served. In this picture, it is too seldom noticed that the first part, deciding their interests, is just as much a matter of communication as the second and third parts, communicating their interests and communicating their satisfaction or dissatisfaction. As others have noted, modern polling techniques tend to presume that most people walk around with well-formed opinions on complex issues, ready at a moment's notice (Fishkin 1995). Even in settings replete with highly educated, well-informed citizens, this may not be true; it is even less true in settings where literacy, education, and impartial media are not readily available.

How, exactly, is the process of opinion formation a communication process? In the most basic sense, people "get their information" from somewhere: the media, their neighbors, the Internet. This, however, is a mainly passive sense of communication (citizen as receiver) and is the notion of communication most likely to provoke anxieties about the manipulation of public opinion. Yet another model is available, the one I want to advocate in this chapter: deliberative democracy, where people's opinions flow, at least in part, from interactions with other citizens. The correct character of these interactions, generally characterized as *discussion*, is hotly debated, as are the potential outcomes from deliberative discussion.

In a classic confrontation in the 1920s, John Dewey and Walter Lippmann played out the contrast between these two views on the formation of citizen thought (Lippmann 1925). Lippmann held in *The Phantom Public* that in a technologically advanced society, only those with sufficient experience could make good decisions, because the average voter was simply unable to muster a rational or cogent opinion on difficult technical policy issues in economics or other areas. Whatever the merits may have been of Jefferson's yeoman farmer as citizen, thought Lippmann, the country in which a farmer's expertise was sufficient was long gone; the public was but a phantom, widely praised but nowhere to be found. Dewey argued, on the other hand, that rational publics could exist; wherever people could come to see a common interest, to perceive themselves as having common cause even with people they did not know personally and never would, a public had come into being. Yet, as Dewey (1927) noted in *The Public and Its Problems,* creating the kind of system in which such publics could have an impact on the state or on governance required addressing the underlying problem: "The essential need is the improvement of the methods and conditions of debate, discussion, and persuasion." The deliberative approach has its advocates and detractors; in particular, those of a harshly *realpolitik* frame of mind often find it too normative and too full of wishful thinking to be taken seriously at the outset. It is worth bearing in mind that if this view were always correct, we would have no functioning democracies at all. Yet it is easy to see the inherent limitations in the "discussion" approach as well, as Harrison Elliot (1928, 11) noted:

> There is no magic in this process [of discussion]. Experience has warned us that not all groups are cooperative and that not all group discussion is creative. Unless the conditions are observed, group discussions may end in a turbulent riot or a hopeless insipidity ... it is easy for a group to talk but difficult for it to do real thinking. In conducting democratic discussion we are attempting a difficult feat. ... Well-meaning friends of group thinking have dealt it the hardest blows. ... Democracy is not secured by throwing questions to a crowd without any preliminary preparation; that is anarchy.

Despite this, discussion and forums continue to inspire and motivate citizen activists. In this chapter, I will try to detail, based on historical evidence and experience, practical outlines of a deliberative approach. My sources are the "discussion movement" and the "forum movement," widespread attempts in the United States during the 1920s through the 1940s to reinvigorate and reinvent face-to-face democracy (Keith 2007).

Speaking like a Citizen

The forum approach can strike some people as unrealistic or just odd when first encountered. Every approach will have its assumptions; even the most rigorous kind of *realpolitik* has its assumptions. I want to outline the ones made here, by noting opposing assumptions and indicating where this discussion will fall between them.

Local versus universal: Clearly, politics is always highly local. Different cultures, societies, religions, economies, and much else contribute to the ineluctably local nature of politics. Yet despite all this diversity, I will assume that characteristics exist that liberal democracies share, or can share, despite all their differences. This does not mean we should not attend to the local or the different, just that we be open to a level of description that transcends them. For example, even if "discussion" is a universal component of deliberation, the exact mechanics of discussion will surely differ from culture to culture, language to language. Making the necessary translations and adjustments to local conditions should not be a barrier to invoking general concepts.

Systemic versus partial approach: By systemic I mean that governance is not a simple matter of governmental procedures and processes (as complex as some of these, such as voting, may be in practice). Rather, governance is a vast and complex system that includes government, people, society, culture, language, religion, and economics. Naturally we will find multiple channels for accountability in such a system, as well as multiple bottlenecks and blockages. There will not be one, or just a few, direct ways to create accountability; I think that many approaches are valid in different situations, and I see myself as offering but one tool among many.

Face-to-face versus mediated communication: As countries grow ever larger, the world grows ever smaller because of the myriad means of mass communication, from television to books and newspapers to the Internet. The promise of such communication—its ubiquity—goes hand-in-hand with its dangers— control by governments or structural or economic bias. I am willing to argue, however, that for all its difficulties something remains to be said for face-to-face citizen communication. It is not a panacea, but as we shall see it can be a powerfully motivating and transformative experience.

Rational versus emotional: Although the meaning of rationality, to an extent, may vary by culture and context, it remains a desideratum of deliberative democracy. At minimum, having reasons and sharing them is a reasonable standard that can be adapted to many conditions. This is not a claim that emotion is invalid or has no place in deliberation, just that deliberation, as a communication practice, foregrounds the rational. I will assume that rationality includes a wide variety of a narrative and rhetorical practices.[1]

Means and ends: Finally, I will assume, along with John Dewey, that no nondemocratic road to democracy exists; in parlous times, this seems to many a dangerous assumption—can we wait for the practices and ethos of democratic life to take hold? In my view, there may be no real choice. Few installed democracies have succeeded. In practice, this means that people should not resort to force, propaganda, counterpropaganda, agitprop, and the like.

Accountability requires, at some level, a feedback loop from citizen participation to government law, policy, or action; this loop can be through government-provided mechanisms, news media, or voting on candidates or issues. Yet sometimes citizens actively form opinions and take positions through interactions with others. How do deliberative moments actually happen? The danger is that deliberative forms, organized with clear goals, may simply reproduce either passivity or unhelpful partisanship. So participants need to learn to communicate in appropriate ways. These ways of speaking should not be coerced and will not be foreign to most participants, but they need to be explicitly called forth and encouraged.

Public Audience

Part of the burden of the democratic context is the burden of speaking reasonably to those we do not agree with. Addressing others as partisans, from a position of partisanship, may not be the most effective way to cope with difference; James Madison long ago pointed out the corrosive potential of faction. It is not that citizens should not have strong points of view; they should be able to muster arguments that could appeal to those who hold different positions. The key here is that a civic discussion is not between private individuals, but between citizens, not between "you" and "I" but "us." If one assumes that people possess enough of a sense of common civic identity, partisan positions should be argued with reference to shared interests and values. Obviously, room exists for reasonable disagreements about the best policies to promote public health or national security or a robust economy. Characterizing others as not just wrong but evil, however, or speaking only to those who already agree is not likely to either be persuasive or advance the understanding of the problems and solutions.

Public Reason

A version of Habermas's conception of public reason is important for deliberative settings (Habermas 1998; see also Bohman 1996). "Public reason" is reason adapted to a democratic polity, in the sense that the reasons given are reasons that all citizen groups or stakeholders could potentially accept. Reasoning based in marginalizing or persecuting a particular group, or based in personal advantage, is not public reason. Citizens should certainly maintain points of view, and argue them, but not by employing arguments that fail to recognize the interests of other citizens or even their status as citizens. Public reason advocates for "us" and tries to make clear how a given policy or choice benefits the public, even if individuals will be unhappy with it. For example, in advocating a public health program, the tax necessary to pay for the program will probably make some participants unhappy. Rather than saying "So what? *I* need health care" (an appeal to personal benefit), however, an advocate for the program could point out that many people will have access to it, that it is humane, and that it may save the state money overall, especially in the long run—reasons that appeal to the public good. An emphasis on public reason counteracts the tendency to use political discourse simply to air personal grievances and attempt to settle scores; grievances should be brought forward, and sometimes redressed, but not using justifications that cannot be applied to the group overall.

Cooperation

Despite the legitimately heated disagreement that often attends political discussion, a focus on conflict, whether in terms of tone or structuring the interaction as a debate rather than discussion, may not produce the best results. Introducing participants to a cooperative approach to problem solving may be useful. Participants ought to be able to understand conflicts and disagreements within a framework of cooperation, in the sense that they are disagreeing to make progress on a problem generally recognized as important. Cooperatively oriented groups do not need to strive for consensus, which may not only be unreasonable, but also be harmful to productive group process. Instead, they need to continually remind themselves that their process and their disagreements are part of a common project of problem solving.

Citizens are constituted as such through modes of communication in settings that enable them speak as citizens, and *not* just processes or procedures such as voting. The trick is to find the right combination of forms (structure of interaction) that enables people to speak in the citizenship frame.

Forms of Interaction

In this section, I will discuss three face-to-face forms of interaction. Many more might be mentioned, and in particular hybrid forms that combine face-to-face with mediated interaction over the course of multiple sessions are very interesting.[2] These examples show both the differences and the similarities of face-to-face forms.

Study Circles

Study circles have been around for quite a while. They are descended from the American "Chautauqua Study Circles" of the 1870s, which grew far beyond their Methodist Bible study roots and made their way to Germany, Sweden, and Denmark, from where the idea was reintroduced to the United States. The basic study circle is similar to the book clubs popular today: A group of people decide to meet on a regular basis to discuss books or reading, based not on their literary interest, but their public interest; in many cases an organizing authority provides book selections as well as study and discussion questions.

Groups are nonpartisan and geographically based; generally discussants are neighbors. To an extent, this can make it harder for people to speak as citizens, because they know one another privately and may share many private interests. Nonetheless, it has the advantage of providing a kind of supported learning environment, where people can have the resources to investigate and sift through new ideas and policies; the group helps ensure that no one will get completely "stuck" in trying to understand or think through the issues. In such a setting, meeting with neighbors in someone's home, discussion is likely to be easy and informal, rather than stiff and debate-like. Study circles have the advantage also of exploiting and developing social capital, as people share information and expertise and deepen their relationships based on discussion of public issues.

Forums

Forums are events organized explicitly for public discussion. Traditionally, the forum has the following basic structure: A speaker, normally an expert on a subject matter, speaks, and afterwards the audience engages him or her with a question-and-answer discussion, which is the "discussion." Many variations on this form exist. A forum might have multiple presenters, each giving a short speech on one side or portion of the issue (the "symposium"); multiple presenters might discuss among themselves on the stage before opening the discussion up to the audience (the "panel discussion"); two presenters might have a more-or-less formal debate, followed by questions from the audience (the "forum debate"). The forum, unlike the study circle, relies on a supply of expert speakers who should be able to communicate complex material clearly to lay audiences. The forum has a more directly educational and indirectly deliberative function, because discussion per se is fairly limited. Forums, as opposed to study circles, can bring in a much larger segment of a community; in the memorable arrangement of forums in Des Moines, Iowa, in the middle 1930s, weekly forums convened at grade schools and monthly forums at high schools, bringing in automatically different segments of the community. Forums at their best can bring new and vital information and arguments to a community that stimulate discussion long after the speaker has gone.

Town Meetings

Town meetings are usually represented as harkening back to the tradition of the Scandinavian *alting* or "all-think (together)"; sometimes they are aligned with the classical Athenian *ekklesia,* the assembly of voting citizens. They are typically intended to mimic as closely as possible local practices of deliberation. Deliberation means, in a sense, choice, or the reasoning and discussion that leads to choice. So deliberation is not a philosophical ramble, but a kind of discourse that ends in a decision. Even bodies without decision-making power can deliberate as if they had it, and this produces a fairly different process than the forum.

Town meetings, as deliberative, typically try to include all relevant stakeholders, to make sure that all positions are heard. Town meetings that are not pro forma (with designated representatives attending) may take in a broader or narrower range of the community depending on the issue and the kinds of stakeholders. The government may well sponsor or participate in town meetings as part of its own decision-making process, although dangers to this approach are present, as noted in the next section. Organizers can structure town meetings in many different ways; *The Deliberative Democracy Handbook* details many case studies and shows the particular creativity of Brazil and Australia.[3] Technology may enhance town meetings by allowing them to combine face-to-face and mediated interactions.

All of these types of civic discussions can be held in various combinations and repetitions; there is no reason they cannot be linked together in useful ways, depending on the setting.

A final consideration about forms is whether they should be *topical* or *formal*. By this I mean that any of the forms might either be convened on a regular basis for its own sake (formal) or convened on a limited basis to learn and deliberate about a specific topic. As much as regular meetings (in the same way the government assemblies and committees meet) seem like a necessary part of a system of accountability, it is unclear whether, without an immediate exigence, the necessary cross section of citizens will want to meet on a regular basis. Experience seems to suggest that bringing people together for a specific topic or purpose will generate more participation, even though it seems like a poor way to hold a government, with all the continuous power of the state, accountable.

Goals

The form of participation, although not the least of an organizer's concerns, is not sufficient by itself. How people participate is just as important as the structures of participation; the quality and meaning of the activity may be equally important to the participants. If people do not fully understand the forum or town meeting, or their place in it, then it will not have the desired outcomes. Participants need to have an investment in the activity. Much depends, therefore, on the possible, practical goals of the activity. Deliberative forms of interaction do not result in direct democracy (as if participants will vote on policy at the conclusion of the meeting), but then again if they bear no connection at all to the formation or selection of policies, citizens will rightly wonder whether there is any point to participating. So a subtle and ongoing problem for any deliberative approach is articulating relevant and achievable goals. In particular, consensus not only is an unrealistic goal for almost all situations, but also is often corrosive, leading participants to feel forced to agree or to prematurely relinquish their positions. If consensus is to take place, it will likely be about a position or policy that will be a result of discussion, not one brought into the discussion, and it may be a partial consensus (everybody likes features of the solution, but no one likes the whole thing). A fixation on consensus reveals more concern with outcome than process. As we will see, a well-functioning process might itself be an important outcome. What are some possible goals?

Government and citizens learning about each other: Mutual understanding is no small goal in many situations. The tendency to see one's political opponents as evil and ignorant, even when they are not, seems universal. Part of crafting policies with broad applicability requires synthesizing diverse stakeholder interests, and this cannot proceed until interests are all out in the open. Sometimes people discover that they are more similar than anyone thought; sometimes they discover the exact nature of their differences. In either case, this is knowledge that proves useful in articulating, defending, and acting on one's view.

In addition, apathy can sometimes be a by-product of feeling that one's views are not represented in the larger public discussion or that no one quite understands them. Having a forum where one can be heard and given the chance to articulate and develop one's point of view can powerfully motivate citizens to continue participating in the process. Of course, sometimes people would like validation, to be told their views are correct, but in many cases the legitimacy of being heard in a neutral setting is sufficient to convince people that they are part of the larger civic conversation.

Education: Interesting questions of public policy are invariably complex and multifaceted, resisting easy summary or superficial treatment. Of course, those who are both literate and motivated can seek out experts or information to improve their understanding of a difficult topic. Study circles, forums, and town meetings can also be occasions for gaining expertise in a subject matter. Not only is interaction with fellow citizens a good way to learn, but also learning a topic in the context of debates or disagreements can be useful in understanding its political aspects, not just a dry digest of information. Forums are especially potent in this regard, because they bring in experts who not only can speak authoritatively on an issue, but also can answer questions about it. Well-constructed study circle materials can also be effective, though there is no one on the spot to answer questions.

Understanding of issues gained through forums can influence voting; because knowledgeable voters are universally agreed to be a prerequisite of a well-functioning democracy, forums' effect on voting indirectly helps to keep the entire system accountable. Knowledge is power, the saying goes, and an informed citizenry can mobilize itself effectively, and, more importantly, can speak with authority to the government. Obviously, if the government, or its agencies, are keeping secrets, that information is harder to get. In many cases, however, an understanding of basic issues in economics or public policy is a powerful tool in the hands of citizens who wish to contest a government policy.

Deliberation: Public forums or town meetings can also be set up to help citizens review and develop policy choices, as well as reasons for and against them. It is important to recognize that even though participants are only going through the motions of deliberating policy (because they have no power to enact or enforce it), the experience is most useful when it is fairly realistic, that is to say, not realistic in format (because parliamentary debate is not an effective or friendly tool for local citizen groups), but realistic in both the diversity of stakeholders and the facts of the issues. A good deliberative experience includes enough variety of positions and viewpoints that participants are forced to engage one another. It should also have sufficient knowledge resources that participants can access relevant facts and hold one another accountable to them.

Lessons from the U.S. Forum Movement

Many different organizations, inside and outside higher education, seek to teach the skills of democratic discussion. What could they learn from the experiments of the 1920s through the 1940s? At each turn, I think, we will see that the devil is in the details. No matter how much theory we bring to the process, the actual details of interaction—who, what, when, where, how?—will determine the success or failure of public deliberation.

Agonism versus Cooperation

In Jane Mansbridge's pioneering work on the practice of public deliberation in the United States, she distinguishes between unitary and adversary democracy. Although the terms would have been unfamiliar, the concepts would have been obvious to the discussionists and the forumites. Adversary democracy is heavily proceduralist, designed to protect the presumably conflicting interests of participants. Unitary democracy assumes that common bonds and social ties allow for the emergence of a consensus point of view. Mansbridge readily admits that her vision of unitary democracy is bound up with the face-to-face tradition of deliberation:

> To people steeped in the adversary tradition, the very notion of unitary democracy usually appears naïve and impractical. They assume that interests are always in conflict, that individuals never respect one another equally, that consensus is always a sham in which some are afraid to make their true feelings known and that face-to-face meetings are too cumbersome to play a significant role in a modern national polity. (Mansbridge 1980, 23)

Mansbridge allows us to see practical problems here, because agonism and cooperation are the communication elements that correspond to adversary and unitary democracy. Obviously, adversary democracy is going to value debate and the clash of ideas (and hence interests), whereas unitary democracy will focus more on discussion and the attempt to find consensus.

Both elements must be present, but it is unclear what the right mix is, or if the right mix depends mostly on the circumstances. The early discussionists probably overemphasized cooperation and consensus (much as Habermas later did). Conflict, however, though entertaining, often does not allow for much progress and may create an atmosphere in which things get so polarized that almost nothing can be accomplished. So there is a problem of finding a balance, both theoretically and practically. Debate, when everyone is being a good sport, can be tremendously productive, and discussion ought in principle to include sharp questioning and well-honed arguments. The practical problems include making sure that, regardless of the specific format of a deliberative group, the members are aware that neither an agonistic nor a cooperative focus is the only one, and that they should maintain a productive tension between the two.

Maintaining the tension is partly a problem of philosophy, how a particular group understands its values and mission. As Francesca Polletta has argued, a group's self-identity may be tied up with rigorous adherence to a particular version of democratic practice, even if that practice is sometimes rather dysfunctional (Poletta 2002, ch. 9). If a group understands deliberation as purely cooperative, then they may deal poorly with the tensions that naturally arise over difficult issues. A group heavily invested in parliamentary procedure, a fairly adversarial system, may find members consistently trying to get around these procedures to introduce some cooperation into the deliberations. In addition, as with other living, breathing social organisms, deliberating groups are individual, and their characteristics will vary. The equilibrium point between struggle and cooperation that produces high functionality will vary from group to group, and so probably no general answer can be found about "ideal" procedures or process that will guarantee quality deliberation.

A related problem concerns the role of consensus. The discussionists and Dewey placed a high value on consensus, and Mansbridge points out that "the central assumption of unitary democracy is that, while its members may initially have conflicting preferences about a given issue, goodwill, mutual understanding and enlightened preferences can lead to the emergence of a common enlightened preference that is good for everyone" (Mansbridge 1980, 25).

Philosophers have tended to focus on whether this is possible (Is such a resolution likely to exist in every case?) or desirable (Habermas long maintained that consensus was the normative ideal in democratic argumentation). The experience of the forums and contemporary deliberative groups suggests that a more pressing concern is whether a preoccupation with consensus enhances the functionality of groups. Very likely, it does not, especially in the short run, but then neither does a speedy recourse to voting and the creation of disenfranchised minorities. Dynamic partial agreements are possible, where everybody agrees (for example) to a description of the problem or on an improvement to the situation, even though it does not constitute a "solution" or a final resolution to the problem.

Scale and Meaningfulness

Scaling up the small-town meeting to accommodate big-city, regional, or national deliberation remains a major problem. Most of what is attractive about the discussion or forum setting does not scale up well; the more people involved, the less actual discussion takes place. We need to reconsider, therefore, the relative desirability of the main features of small groups.

Giving up on face-to-face interaction certainly makes it easier to scale up public deliberation. In Michael Warner's model of circulating texts, deliberating in person barely figures in at all (Warner 2002). To what extent do the goods of deliberation attach to a face-to-face encounter? Mansbridge defends it strongly, even while acknowledging its downside:

> Experience teaches us, however, that in practice face-to-face contact increases the perception of likeness, encourages decision making by consensus, and perhaps even enhances equality of status.... On the positive side, it seems to encourage the actual congruence of interests by encouraging the empathy by which individual members make one another's interests their own. It also encourages the recognition of common interest by allowing subtleties of direct communication. On the negative side, it increases the possibility of conformity through intimidation, resulting in a false or managed consensus. (Mansbridge 1980, 33)

If we agreed completely with Mansbridge on this, however, it would mean that any worthy system of public deliberation would have to be either a very small and possibly representative system (such was the design of the original U.S. republic), or a vast network of small groups of people. Coordinating and consolidating the results of such groups would pose a massive and complex challenge, and it is not at all clear how that challenge would be met.[4] Perhaps technology could step in (Keith 2003). Linked in online systems, large numbers of people could communicate, synchronously or asynchronously, about public issues. Yet the scale problem can reemerge here. Even though the online setting preserves many of the valuable features of face-to-face interaction (more or less, depending on the format: listserv, chat room, bulletin board, and so on), as the numbers of people grow, fewer can interact directly (users can read only so many posts), and the problems of coordinating the results become just as acute as with multiple face-to-face groups.

So probably, like the forums of the 1930s, we are going to be left with deliberation and "discussion" happening in fairly large groups, with from 50 to 500 people. In such a setting, most people would be observers rather than participants. The solution of the 1930s forums was not a bad one. If the goal of the forums is redefined from actual decision making to education, larger groups can be perfectly functional; nonparticipants, even in a large group, can learn a great deal about both the issues and how to think about them.

At this point, however, we need to step back and consider whether we have broken our connection to what was originally attractive about deliberation.

This issue about the loss of connection has two sides, one for organizers and one for participants. For organizers, the problem is: Why go to all this trouble to organize forums? Studebaker and his associates, founders of the Federal Forum Project of 1936–41, had no trouble seeing themselves as part of an evolving adult education movement, one with a liberal, civic purpose. Contemporary organizers seem very concerned with the effectiveness of the format, that they are helping people to directly influence political outcomes. For participants, the issue is similar; they are typically motivated by the sense that their deliberative labors lead to a "real" outcome, that talking has a chance of making a difference with the problem they are considering. If it is "just talk," then why bother? Seen in this way, making forums meaningful and motivating participants amount to figuring out how to get the forums attached to the levers of political power. That turns out to be fairly difficult, especially as the size of the forums is scaled up.[5]

A more powerful way to justify participation in public deliberation approaches politics from a systemic perspective. If we have given up on the "great man" theories of politics, perhaps we need to give up the lingering remains of the "great institutions" accounts of politics. Identifying the "levers of power" solely with the city council, the state legislature, or the U.S. Senate misses the truth that these institutions are deeply and thoroughly bound to a complex set of systems, including public opinion, local constituents or voters, the courts, business interests, the economy, foreign policy, and much else besides. Although it may appear superficially that the legislature can just make things happen, in fact many conditions have to be in place for a law or policy to be passed, let alone enforced. Public opinion—informed and educated opinion, in particular—is very much a part of the political system.[6] As James Fishkin has argued, polls and polling should be derided only when they use uninformed opinions or nonopinions to guide policy. So although the 1930s discussionists and forumites tended to speak of education in terms of preparing better voters, a worthy but limited goal, a revised understanding of the workings of our political system could bring a whole new meaning to the education of citizens through deliberation.

Trust/Suspicion/Neutrality

Deliberative democratic procedures require participants to bracket partisan concerns, at least temporarily, and adopt a somewhat objective standpoint; they need to balance their partisan interests with recognition of other stakeholders' interests. The ability to bracket is clearly a learned skill of civic discourse for most people and cannot be taken for granted. If participants see a deliberative occasion as "partisanship by other means," the discourse may be neither very productive nor educational. Similarly, participants need to have confidence that the forms themselves are not structurally biased toward one group, or one policy, which is a particular problem for events sponsored (even with the best intentions) by government agencies. Unless some effort is expended on declaring and then demonstrating the (reasonable) neutrality of forums or town meetings, perceptions of bias will limit the positive outcomes of the meetings. Obviously, the suspicions that people might have will depend on local history and politics, and just as clearly the means for reassuring them will depend on local conditions. Some thought needs to go into this. Annex 15A reproduces a very interesting statement given to forums in the United States during the 1930s, when people were quite suspicious that they were being used as a propaganda arm of the Roosevelt administration.

Importance of Good Leadership

Whether forums or town meetings, they will need a leader or facilitator, and this person is crucial to the success of the event. Forum speakers have to be interesting and compelling speakers and able to reach audiences no matter what level—or differing levels—of education are present. It is not enough to be an expert on a topic (though some expertise is necessary), and so it is not clear that college professors are always the best choice for forum speakers; as experienced teachers, however, they are often very good at facilitation. Forum leaders and facilitators have a very difficult task; Annex 15B reproduces a list of hints for forum leaders that gives a good sense of the complexity of their job. They not only have to manage the difficult interactions of the event, but also do it in a way that models the best practices of political communication. Leaders and facilitators need to keep things interesting and moving along while convincing their audience they are impartial and that the process is fair to all points of view. Leaders and facilitators should have the tact and skill to quash disruptive elements without appearing heavy-handed or dictatorial. They have to be able to find and hold a thread of argument while challenging participants to articulate clear arguments for their positions.

Good leaders, hidden talent, may well be available in the geographic areas where they are needed, but depending on this is risky. Resources should be devoted to recruiting and training competent leadership, not as an afterthought, but as a central part of any program. Once a forum or a town meeting format is well established and well attended, over a number of years, recruiting leaders from participants will be possible. Until then, however, sponsoring organizations will need to produce sufficient numbers of leaders and facilitators.

The Entertainment Problem

Commentators today regularly complain about "infotainment" and the lack of seriousness applied to political discourse. Yet they speak as if this were a new problem. In the United States, each of the predecessors to the forum disintegrated into a vapor of cheesy entertainment.[7] The plain fact is that keeping people interested is hard. For people accustomed to the fast and visual pace of television and video games, talking heads, even in person, can be less than compelling, which is an argument for a set-up where everybody can talk. We probably have to accept that audiences bring generic expectations to face-to-face deliberation, and those expectations matter. The problem of an entertainment-focused culture is not a new one, but it is possible that movies, television, video games, and the Internet have changed the way people approach live interactions.

One important solution is to fold deliberative practices into activities that are locally compelling and entertaining. As part of a program of music, comedy, or local theater, forums or town meetings might get the attendance they deserve. Giving citizens multiple reasons to show up and interact does not detract from the immediacy and relevance of well-designed programs and allows organizers to tap into local, indigenous types of motivation. When people show up, the possibilities for interaction increase.

The lesson from the lyceum and the Chautauqua is, unfortunately, that some of the things that increase the entertainment value of the civic talk itself, and hence help motivate people to attend, work against high-quality deliberation. The underlying question that remains is whether deliberation and entertainment are intrinsically opposed, or whether the opposition is a practical problem. If it is a practical problem, no one yet seems to have found a good solution. If they are intrinsically opposed, it is not clear why. Video games are also hours of work to learn, yet youths and adults spend the time to learn them. Perhaps the problem is about "fun"; it is fun to listen to someone savage your political opponents, because you can feel smug and secure. As the discussionists pointed out many times, however, real discussion is often uncomfortable. When does discomfort, combined with hard work, become fun? Perhaps this is a problem of education, as Dewey and followers foresaw. If children get the right kind of civic education in their formative years, they might become accustomed to, and even seek out, situations of discomfiting political engagement.

Teaching Communication Skills

In the long run, a strong connection between school curricula and the public forums is an important part of sustaining public involvement in government accountability. Teaching children the skills and meaning of civic discourse may be more effective in the long run than working only with adults.

Teaching public speaking involves both technical and communication skills. Students learn techniques of outlining, organization, research, and argument; however, teaching public speaking (especially for adults) does not have to require a high level of literacy and can easily take place in environments where there is limited access to learning technologies, and it can take place in local or regional dialects. Training in public speaking helps people feel more confident about standing up and speaking, but more importantly, learning to engage audiences as communicators. What I mean is that they do not just "present" information or research, or just tell their personal story, in front of an audience, but they design or adjust their talk to the audience and try to accomplish a goal with them, persuading, motivating, opening new possibilities, and so forth. The most important concept for public speaking is "audience." A group of people listening is not simply a collection of demographic categories (gender, race, class, age, religious affiliation, and so on) but is potentially many different kinds of "publics" depending on how the speaker chooses to address the group. The speaker can address them as citizens, taxpayers, residents of their town or state—or many other identities as well.

The key point is that the speaker addresses the audience in such a way that the audience members can see themselves as more than private individuals—part of a public, with public concerns. This is less training in the performance aspect of speaking (though that is important too) than it is training in the thinking of oneself and others as part of a public that may or may not have interests opposed to the government (which is supposed to serve the public interest). This is a crucial move. If people are going to mobilize themselves for joint action, they must arrive (through mutual persuasion and speaking) at an identity as a public, a position from which they can challenge a government on level rhetorical ground. Most people naturally begin persuasion thinking from their own personal/private interests ("Here's what happened to me ... here's how I have suffered"), but these are easy to dismiss as individual or exceptional problems. As citizens learn to frame their cases *as citizens,* they gain enormous rhetorical power; moving from "this is my problem" to "this is *our* problem" is a precondition to joint action and government accountability. This training can have another effect. As people learn to formulate their problems in terms of a relevant public, they may also be forced to reflect on how their concerns fit into a larger picture; they may come to understand both the connectedness of various problems and the limitations of simple solutions.

Teaching public speaking in the schools, as well as to adults, can be a crucial part of growing a democracy for the future. It is not a panacea, but if democracy is the faith that problems are local, that citizens understand the problems, and that they have a valuable part to play in the solution, training in public speaking may be a precondition to the development of a public sphere in which government accountability becomes a reality.

Annex 15A

Example of Statement for Forum Leaders in the Opening Series

The public forum discussion is one of the oldest and best respected of the traditions of American Democracy. It is a way of adult education by which the people of the community may come to understand the social, economic and political problems of their day and thus exercise their privilege of citizenship with greater responsibility and intelligence.

Public education is promoting its major objective when it conducts an educational program designed to produce a more enlightened public opinion.

In this and other forum meetings, the people may avail themselves of the constitutional rights of free speech and free assemblage in an organized consideration of public affairs.

As the leader of the discussion, it is my purpose to open the subject for discussion; to outline as fairly and impartially as possible the major issues involved in our problem; to interpret briefly the important and opposing points of view on these issues; and to share with you the factual material which is essential to an understanding of the problem.

It is not my purpose to convince you that my opinion on this subject is correct or to urge you to accept my views. Naturally, having studied this problem, I have come to certain conclusions which form the basis of my opinion or action. These conclusions I hold are subject to change in the light of new evidence. If from time to time I express my personal views it will be in the spirit of the phrase "as I see it." But the most important thing in public discussion is not what you or I conclude but how and why we come to a particular conclusion.

Our quest in this discussion is for an understanding of the problem and a clear view of the alternative solutions proposed. We approach this problem in the spirit of give and take, respecting the right of each one of us to hold what opinions he will. We seek by the exchange of opinion, by reminding each other of salient and important facts, and by critically questioning each other's premises, to arrive at a better understanding of the problem before us.

Source: U.S. National Archives and Records Administration, Series 190, Box 2, File, "Memos from the Commissioner," "Exhibit No. 7"; n.d., probably 1936.

Annex 15B

Hints for Forum Leaders

1. Forum leaders should group the audience near the front of the room.
2. Leaders should avoid splitting the audience so that the group is seated on two sides of the aisle.
3. Leaders should give care and thought to lighting. Avoid lights that shine directly in the eyes of the audience.
4. No forum leader should talk longer than forty minutes.
5. If the discussion topic is technical, the leader may vary the set routine of the meeting by interspersing short periods of question and discussions throughout the main presentation.
6. When a question is asked of the forum leader, he should always repeat the question either before he himself answers it, or before he passes the question on for comment to someone in the audience.
7. The leader can and should avoid answering question directly, by turning the question back to the persons asking them or by referring them to other persons in the group. The leader often allows himself to be "put on the spot" by answering too many questions. Hecklers do not enjoy having their question referred to other members of the audience.
8. The leader should avoid sarcasm. Sarcasm on the part of the leader makes people timid and afraid to speak. It kills the possibility of good discussion.

9. In closing the forum a brief summary (two or three minutes) skillfully given is highly desirable. Unless the important points which were brought out by the leader and the audience are summarized, the audience goes home feeling confused.

10. The forum leader should never lose his temper or display irritation over the ignorance or disagreement of any member of the audience.

11. The leader should make members of his audience feel that he values the opinion of each of them.

12. Every leader should know the fundamental principles of public speaking.

13. Whenever possible, a forum leader should tie in local problems with the subject under discussion.

14. Leaders should be adept in changing tactics of discussion. If the discussion drags, a change of tactics or a different approach will often throw new life and spontaneity into a dull meeting.

15. It is just as important and sometimes more important for the leader to conceal, rather than reveal, how much he knows. Audiences are awed and made timid by leaders who display too much knowledge.

16. Leaders, to be successful, must realize that the average individual cannot relate a generalized moral or ethical abstraction to an actual living experience of himself or his neighbors.

17. No forum leader can be successful unless he is truly interested in the workings of the human mind.

18. He should not take sides on the question.

19. He should not talk too much.

20. He should not take it upon himself to answer questions and suggest solutions. Rather, he should refer these questions to the proper discussion leaders and he should leave the formulation of solutions to members of the group.

21. He should not allow anyone to monopolize the talking. ... To stop the talkative individual without hurting his feelings is a matter calling for all the tact that the chairman may possess.

22. He should not allow the group to waste much time giving their guesses about matters of fact. ... The chairman should assign someone to look up the matter and report at the next meeting.

23. He should not be afraid to lead the discussion into points that stir emotions and arouse prejudices if these points are necessary to an understanding of the problem. Steering discussion around such points does not cause the group to forget them.

24. The chairman should, whenever possible, recognize a member who has not spoken in preference to one who has.

25. The chairman should guard the group against the tendency to act first and think afterwards. The whole legislative procedure ... is wise in that it guards against too hasty action.

26. But the chairman should also guard against the opposite extreme, of never taking a position on a question. One of the values in having members of the group vote in some way at the conclusion of the meeting is that it forces them to make a decision.

27. Occasionally, someone may introduce unfortunate personal allusions and attacks into the discussion. This happens but rarely. Usually the best procedure for the chairman is to make no reference to the "hitting below the belt" but to make some remark that will bring the discussion back to the subject. … Only in the case of a continued use of personalities should the chairman make a direct reference to what is happening. Then his position should be clearly and firmly stated: "This discussion is an opportunity to think through an important problem. It is not an occasion for the airing of private differences."

28. Careful study of techniques is essential. … And in a real sense discussion leading can only be learned through experience. It is essentially an art and not a science, to be acquired by watching the performance of the adept and by studying one's own mistakes rather than by learning rules. All art can be learned to some degree, however, and the study of techniques will improve the methods of any leader.

Source: J. V. Garland, *Discussion Methods, Explained and Illustrated* (1951, 1st ed. 1938), 341–43; a footnote reveals that "The first seventeen items are from *Choosing Our Way*, written by John Studebaker and Chester Williams of the Federal Forum Project (1937): while items 18 to 27 are from the booklet *How to Conduct Group Discussion* by A. F. Wilden and H. L. Ewbank, published by the Extension Service at the University of Wisconsin."

Notes

1. For example, see Fisher (1987), Hauser (1999), Rorty (1982), and Young (2000).
2. See Gastil and Levine's *The Deliberative Democracy Handbook* (2005) for examples.
3. Gastil and Levine (2005).
4. Some of the chapters in Gastil and Levine (2005) present creative attempts to deal with this problem, particularly chapters 9 and 10.
5. Again, some of the essays in Gastil and Levine (2005) show creative, though complex, attempts at this; see especially chapters 11–13.
6. In *Who Deliberates?* (1996), Page shows that government actions in response to perceived crises go through complex layers of public deliberation before anything happens, and that even spin by the press does not particularly affect the outcome.
7. Angela Ray (2005, 3) argues that this is exactly what happened to the lyceum movement in the nineteenth-century United States.

References

Bohman, James. 1996. *Public Deliberation: Pluralism, Complexity, and Democracy.* Cambridge, MA: MIT Press.

Dewey, John. 1927. *The Public and Its Problems.* New York: Henry Holt and Company.

Elliott, Harrison S. 1928. *The Process of Group Thinking.* New York: The Inquiry.

Fisher, Walter R. 1987. *Human Communication as Narration: Toward a Philosophy of Reason, Value, and Action.* Columbia: University of South Carolina Press.

Fishkin, James S. 1995. *The Voice of the People: Public Opinion and Democracy*. New Haven, CT: Yale University Press.

Gastil, John, and Peter Levine, eds. 2005. *The Deliberative Democracy Handbook*. San Francisco: Jossey-Bass.

Habermas, Jürgen. 1998. *On the Pragmatics of Communication*. Ed. Maeve Cook. Cambridge, MA: MIT Press.

Hauser, Gerard. 1999. *Vernacular Voices: The Rhetoric of Publics and Public Sphere*. Columbia: University of South Carolina Press.

Keith, William. 2003. "Dewey, Discussion, and Democracy in Speech Pedagogy." In *Rhetorical Democracy: Discursive Practices of Civic Engagement*, ed. Gerard Hauser and Amy Grim, 205–11. Matwah, NJ: Erlbaum.

———. 2007. *Democracy as Discussion*. Lanham, MD: Lexington Books.

Lippmann, Walter. 1925/1993. *The Phantom Public*. Minneapolis: University of Minnesota Press.

Mansbridge, Jane. 1980. *Beyond Adversary Democracy*. Chicago: University of Chicago Press.

Page, Benjamin. 1996. *Who Deliberates?* Chicago: University of Chicago Press.

Polletta, Francesca. 2002. *Freedom Is an Endless Meeting: Democracy in American Social Movements*. Chicago: University of Chicago Press.

Ray, Angela. 2005. *The Lyceum and Public Culture in the Nineteenth-Century United States*. East Lansing, MI: Michigan State University Press.

Rorty, Richard. 1982. *Consequences of Pragmatism: Essays, 1972–1980*. Minneapolis: University of Minnesota Press.

Warner, Michael. 2002. *Publics and Counterpublics*. New York: Zone Books.

Young, Iris Marion. 2000. *Inclusion and Democracy*. Oxford, U.K.: Oxford University Press.

16

Participatory Constitution Making in Uganda

Devra Moehler

In the current wave of democratization, several countries have embarked on innovative constitution-making programs designed to develop democratic norms, in addition to creating formal institutions. The Ugandan process provided for extensive involvement of the general public over an eight-year period. Albania, Eritrea, and South Africa followed with analogous participatory processes. Of late, reformers have advocated for the participatory model of constitutional development in countries as diverse as Iraq and Nigeria.

These and other participatory policies are inspired by a venerable scholarly tradition emphasizing the importance of public involvement in political life. Classical liberal and contemporary participatory theorists optimistically assert that political participation builds democratic attitudes, civic competence, and political legitimacy.[1] In contrast, other scholars are pessimistic about the consequences of extensive citizen involvement in government. They argue that mass participation polarizes the citizenry, frustrates ordinary people, and threatens political stability—particularly during periods of political transition. Although the theoretical literature on the value of participation is extensive, empirical work on its consequences is sparse, especially at the individual level of analysis.[2] How does political participation affect political culture in hybrid polities? Does mass participation invest or disinvest in democracy? This chapter seeks to answer these questions.

Drawing on survey, interview, and archival data, I identify the individual-level consequences of citizen involvement in the Ugandan constitution-making process. The quantitative and qualitative data indicate that participation was significantly related to attitude formation, but not entirely in the manner or direction predicted by either the optimists or the pessimists. My central theoretical argument is that participation affects attitudes in two ways: (1) it increases citizen interest in and exposure to political information, and (2) it changes the standards by which citizens evaluate that information. Importantly, the content of the information imparted through participation determines the direction of attitude change; participation can deliver both positive and negative messages about government. Civic activity does not happen in a vacuum, and people do not mechanically transform information into opinions. Participation must be viewed in context, and participation in hybrid systems that combine elements of democratic and authoritarian rule will have different consequences than participation in well-performing consolidated democracies. If scholars and policy makers want to predict how citizen involvement will affect democratization, they must examine how participants obtain and interpret information about the processes in which they are involved.

Research Design and Methodology

This research project responds to the debates about the democratic implications of participation in general—and participatory constitutional reform in particular—by analyzing the individual-level effects of public participation in the Ugandan constitution-making process. The effects of participation are typically small, gradual, and reciprocal, and thus difficult to detect and substantiate with any degree of certainty.[3] The Ugandan constitution-making process offers a unique opportunity to observe the typically elusive results of participation in a hybrid regime.[4] Ugandan officials and civil-society activists mobilized ordinary people to participate in a variety of activities,[5] over an extended period of time, focused on a highly salient topic—the constitution. Uganda serves as a crucial test case because the effects of participation in the constitution-making process are expected to be more evident than in other instances of public participation.[6]

To examine the effects of citizen participation in constitution making, I employ a multiple methods approach.[7] The bulk of the evidence comes from two sources: (1) a multistage probability sample survey[8] and (2) in-depth unstructured interviews with citizens and local elites in the locations where the survey was conducted.[9] To assess the effects of public participation on civic knowledge and attitudes at the individual level, I rely on statistical analysis of my survey data augmented with qualitative analysis of the in-depth interviews of local elites and citizens from the same locations.[10] The statistical analysis compares individuals with different levels of involvement in the constitution-making process. Although mobilization played a large role in influencing who participated, participation in constitution-making activities was voluntary. Therefore, the initial knowledge, attitudes, and behavior of the citizens who participated are not identical to those of the citizens who did not. I use information on determinants of participation to account for the potential reciprocal effects.

Although I explicitly model reciprocal effects, it is difficult to determine causation from survey data collected at one point in time. Qualitative analysis of in-depth interviews provides additional leverage to untangle the direction of causation and to delineate the causal mechanisms at work.

Participation and Distrusting Democrats

What were the effects of participation on political culture in Uganda? Specifically, did participation increase democratic values, political knowledge, subjective political capabilities, and institutional trust? To answer these questions I use simultaneous equation systems that account for the possibility of reciprocal relationships between participation and attitudes (or knowledge). I first develop a model of the factors that contributed to participation in Uganda;[11] the analysis suggests that citizens participated in the constitution-making process more because mobilizing elites drew them into politics and less because of individually held resources or dispositions.[12] This model then serves as the basis for the subsequent analysis of the consequences of participation. Tables 16.1–16.4 show the results of the second-stage equations predicting democratic attitudes, political knowledge, political capabilities, and institutional trust.[13]

The evidence suggests that that participation in constitution making had a positive estimated effect on democratic attitudes and political knowledge—as the optimists would expect—but had no discernable influence on civic competence. Most notably, the data suggest that participation contributed to the erosion of institutional trust, an effect more in keeping with the predictions of the pessimists. It seems that participation helped to create distrusting democrats[14]— citizens who are democratic in their attitudes but suspicious of their governmental institutions. This strange mixture of support for two rival perspectives presents us with a puzzle. Why were individuals who got involved in the constitution-making process more likely to emerge as distrusting democrats?

Table 16.1. 2SLS Estimates Predicting Democratic Attitudes

	b	Robust SE	Beta
Participation activities index	0.14	(0.05)	0.23**
Demographics and socioeconomic status			
Male	0.15	(0.08)	0.08#
Urban residence	0.10	(0.11)	0.03
Age	−0.01	(0.00)	−0.12***
Primary school	0.23	(0.09)	0.12*
Secondary school	0.22	(0.13)	0.06#
Initial orientation to democracy			
Interest	0.12	(0.05)	0.10*
Baganda ethnicity	−0.19	(0.08)	−0.09**
Basoga ethnicity	−0.24	(0.10)	−0.08*
Mobility	0.06	(0.03)	0.10*
Constant	2.43	(0.20)	

Source: Author.
Note: N = 740; SLS = semiparametric least squares; # $p \leq 0.10$; * $p \leq 0.05$; ** $p \leq 0.01$; ***$p \leq 0.001$.

Table 16.2. 2SLS Estimates Predicting Political Knowledge

	b	Robust SE	Beta
Participation activities index	0.48	(0.28)	0.42#
Demographics and socioeconomic status			
Male	0.27	(0.20)	0.08
Urban residence	−0.02	(0.20)	−0.00
Age	−0.01	(0.00)	−0.10**
Primary school	0.38	(0.18)	0.11*
Secondary school	0.58	(0.23)	0.09*
Access to basic needs	0.07	(0.02)	0.13***
Exposure to information			
Interest	0.13	(0.08)	0.06#
Local council position	0.12	(0.09)	0.07
Closeness to higher official	0.26	(0.13)	0.07#
Associational affiliations	0.01	(0.03)	0.02
Exposure to news on radio	0.03	(0.03)	0.03
Exposure to newspapers	0.05	(0.04)	0.04
Exposure to news in meetings	−0.04	(0.07)	−0.02
Road difficulties	−0.68	(0.30)	−0.07*
Mobility	0.12	(0.04)	0.10**
Constant	1.03	(0.38)	**

Source: Author.
Note: N = 731; # $p \leq 0.10$; * $p \leq 0.05$; ** $p \leq 0.01$; *** $p \leq 0.001$.

Table 16.3. 2SLS Estimates Predicting Political Capabilities

	b	Robust SE	Beta
Participation activities index	0.60	(0.45)	0.29
Demographics and socioeconomic status			
Male	0.93	(0.33)	0.15**
Urban residence	−0.52	(0.32)	0.06#
Age	−0.03	(0.01)	−0.12***
Primary school	0.20	(0.30)	0.03
Access to basic needs	0.04	(0.03)	0.04
Political exposure and experience			
Interest	0.30	(0.14)	0.07*
Local council position	0.40	(0.14)	0.12**
Closeness to higher official	0.54	(0.22)	0.08*
Associational affiliations	0.08	(0.04)	0.09#
Exposure to news on radio	0.19	(0.06)	0.11**
Exposure to newspapers	0.23	(0.07)	0.12**
Exposure to news in meetings	0.18	(0.12)	0.06
Follow public affairs	0.49	(0.12)	0.12***
Support for NRM	0.48	(0.17)	0.08**
Nilotic ethnicity	−0.43	(0.25)	−0.05#
Constant	0.30	(0.74)	

Source: Author.
Note: N = 737; # $p \leq 0.10$; * $p \leq 0.05$; ** $p \leq 0.01$; *** $p \leq 0.001$.

The solution to the puzzle lies in the context in which participation took place: a hybrid regime with serious democratic and institutional shortcomings. Participation in constitution making increased citizen exposure to information about government and altered the criteria they used to evaluate that information by making democratic standards more salient. The joint effect of

Table 16.4. 2SLS Estimates Predicting Institutional Trust

	b	Robust SE	Beta
Participation activities index	−0.22	(0.12)	−0.34[#]
Demographics and socioeconomic status			
Male	−0.01	(0.10)	−0.01
Urban residence	0.10	(0.13)	0.04
Age	0.00	(0.00)	0.04
Primary school	0.12	(0.10)	0.06
Access to basic needs	0.04	(0.01)	0.12**
Influences on opinion of government			
Interest	0.09	(0.05)	0.07[#]
Local council position	0.05	(0.05)	0.05
Closeness to higher official	0.06	(0.09)	0.03
Exposure to news on radio	−0.00	(0.02)	−0.01
Exposure to newspapers	−0.06	(0.03)	−0.10**
Exposure to news in meetings	0.03	(0.04)	0.03
Mobility	−0.04	(0.03)	−0.06
Generalized trust			
Social trust	0.30	(0.09)	0.12***
Exuberant trusting	0.59	(0.07)	0.25***
Support for current leadership			
Support for NRM	0.24	(0.07)	0.12***
Wealth in consumer goods	−0.04	(0.02)	−0.08[#]
Improved living conditions	0.10	(0.03)	0.14***
Constant	2.30	(0.28)	***

Source: Author.

Note: N = 730; [#] $p \leq 0.10$; * $p \leq 0.05$; ** $p \leq 0.01$; *** $p \leq 0.001$.

higher democratic attitudes and knowledge of the undemocratic actions of the government provoked a gradual erosion of institutional trust. Participants are distrustful because they want full democracy and know that the Ugandan government is not delivering it.

Table 16.5 shows the results of an ordinary least squares regression estimating the joint effect of democratic attitudes and political knowledge on trust. The estimated coefficient on the interaction term is negative, indicating that higher democratic attitudes and knowledge are associated with lower institutional trust. Figure 16.1 depicts the predicted values of institutional trust at different levels of political knowledge when democratic attitudes are low, medium, and high. As individuals with democratic ideals learn more about the actual performance of their government, they are predicted to be less trusting, but this is not the case for individuals who reject or are apathetic about democratic ideals.

A selection of quotations from in-depth interviews helps to illustrate the effect of participation on expectations for, knowledge of, and attitudes about the democratic performance of political institutions. One active participant in the constitution-making process said he did not trust the courts because "They don't act like they should—like the law says they should. If you have no money you won't succeed in court" (interview, Sironko District, April 2001). An elderly man (whose signature appeared on his village's constitutional

Table 16.5. Ordinary Least Squares Regression Estimates Predicting Institutional Trust

	b	Robust SE	Beta
Democratic attitudes × political knowledge	−0.04	(0.02)	−0.25[#]
Democratic attitudes	0.03	(0.07)	0.03
Political knowledge	0.08	(0.07)	0.13
Demographics and socioeconomic status			
Male	−0.10	(0.07)	−0.05
Urban residence	0.11	(0.12)	0.04
Age	0.00	(0.00)	0.00
Primary school	0.03	(0.08)	0.02
Access to basic needs	0.03	(0.01)	0.12**
Influence on opinion of government			
Interest	0.06	(0.05)	0.05
Local council position	0.01	(0.05)	0.01
Closeness to higher official	0.03	(0.08)	0.01
Exposure to news on radio	−0.03	(0.02)	−0.05
Exposure to newspapers	−0.07	(0.03)	−0.11*
Exposure to news in meetings	−0.03	(0.04)	−0.03
Mobility	−0.05	(0.03)	−0.07
Generalized trust			
Social trust	0.30	(0.09)	0.12***
Exuberant trusting	0.60	(0.06)	0.25***
Support for current leadership			
Support for NRM	0.21	(0.07)	0.11**
Wealth in consumer goods	−0.04	(0.02)	−0.09*
Improved living conditions	0.11	(0.02)	0.16***
Constant	2.44	(0.30)	***

Source: Author.
Note: N = 736; R^2 = 0.24; [#] $p \leq 0.10$; * $p \leq 0.05$; ** $p \leq 0.01$; *** $p \leq 0.001$.

Figure 16.1. Predicted Values of Institutional Trust

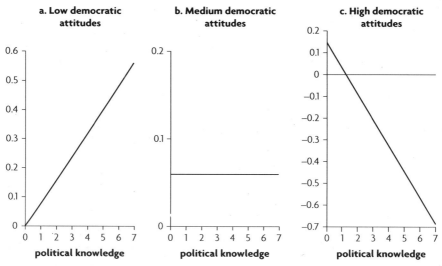

Source: Author.

memoranda) complained that the president was behaving undemocratically: "This isn't a democracy. I can't do anything because I don't have an army. This one [President Museveni] has ruled for 15 years, but he is still going" (interview, Mpigi District, January 2001). Finally, a woman who was active in a women's association during the process also complained that the government was undemocratic: "We are not equal. This one-sided government is not helping us equally with the people from the other side because of other things. But we were told we would be equal once we had democracy" (interview, Lira District, March 2001). In sum, participation in Uganda contributed to the creation of informed distrusting democrats.

If participation in the constitution-making process generated distrust, then reformers elsewhere might be wary of copying the Ugandan experience. However, I argue that the participatory process provided citizens with new tools to critically evaluate the performance of their government institutions. In Uganda, as with most states undergoing transition, infant democratic institutions are imperfectly functioning and incomplete; participation seems to have raised democratic expectations and alerted citizens to existing democratic deficits. I contend that political distrust can facilitate democratization, especially when paired with civic engagement and democratic preferences, as appears to be the case in Uganda. The implications for other constitution-building countries are evident: short-term risks of disillusionment and instability and long-term advantages from a more sophisticated citizenry with the capacity to monitor leaders and promote democratic governance.

Elites and Support for the Constitution

Did participation generate dissatisfaction with the fundamental rules of the game, or just disappointment with the way the game is being played? How did participation in the Ugandan constitution-making process affect public support for the constitution? Again I found that participation furnished Ugandan citizens with additional information and changed the criteria by which citizens evaluate that information. The evidence indicates that participation contributed to the overall support for the constitution by creating a new class of opinionated citizens, most of whom are supportive. In addition, participation seems to have increased the durability of existing support for the constitution by inducing citizens to evaluate the constitution based on procedural fairness rather than on fluctuating personal fortunes (for a discussion of the evidence supporting these claims, see Moehler 2006, 2008). However, among those citizens with opinions, participants were no more likely to support the constitution than were nonparticipants. Table 16.6 shows the effects of participation on four different measures of constitutional support and an index variable. The relationship between participation and support for the constitution is weak, inconsistent, fragile, and often indistinguishable from zero. As the level

Table 16.6. Ordered Probit and Ordinary Least Squares Estimates Predicting Support for the Constitution

	Individual inclusion (Ordered probit)	National aspiration (Ordered probit)	Compliance (Ordered probit)	Attachment (Ordered probit)	Constitutional support Index (OLS regression)
Participation activities index	0.13 (0.04)***	−0.03 (0.04)	0.08 (0.04)*	0.02 (0.04)	0.05 (0.03)#
Demographics and socioeconomic status					
Male	−0.04 (0.11)	0.00 (0.11)	0.04 (0.10)	−0.02 (0.10)	−0.07 (0.08)
Urban residence	0.01 (0.17)	0.21 (0.18)	0.21 (0.17)	0.27 (0.17)	0.18 (0.13)
Age	0.00 (0.00)	−0.00 (0.00)	0.00 (0.00)	0.00 (0.00)	0.00 (0.00)
Primary school completed	0.05 (0.12)	0.01 (0.12)	0.17 (0.12)	−0.17 (0.12)	0.01 (0.09)
Wealth in consumer goods	−0.06 (0.02)*	0.03 (0.03)	0.04 (0.03)	0.04 (0.03)	0.02 (0.02)
Political exposure					
Following of public affairs	0.18 (0.08)*	0.39 (0.07)***	0.17 (0.06)**	0.25 (0.06)***	0.25 (0.05)***
Exposure to news on radio	0.03 (0.04)	−0.01 (0.03)	−0.04 (0.03)	−0.00 (0.03)	−0.01 (0.02)
Exposure to newspapers	0.01 (0.04)	−0.12 (0.04)**	−0.06 (0.04)	−0.07 (0.04)*	−0.06 (0.03)#
Exposure to news meetings	0.02 (0.06)	0.06 (0.06)	−0.03 (0.05)	0.05 (0.05)	0.04 (0.04)
Mobility	−0.04 (0.04)	−0.05 (0.04)	−0.00 (0.04)	−0.11 (0.04)*	−0.06 (0.03)*
Associational affiliations	0.04 (0.02)**	−0.01 (0.02)	−0.04 (0.02)*	0.03 (0.02)	0.01 (0.01)
Local council position	−0.13 (0.05)**	0.06 (0.06)	0.05 (0.05)	0.07 (0.06)	−0.02 (0.04)
Closeness to higher official	0.07 (0.11)	0.28 (0.12)*	0.41 (0.11)***	0.08 (0.12)	0.20 (0.08)**
Support for current leadership					
Support NRM	0.36 (0.10)***	0.20 (0.10)*	0.07 (0.09)	0.43 (0.10)***	0.29 (0.07)***
Improved living conditions	0.02 (0.04)	0.08 (0.04)*	0.07 (0.03)*	0.10 (0.04)**	0.07 (0.02)**
District of residence					
Mpigi	−0.68 (0.15)***	−0.55 (0.13)***	−0.18 (0.13)	−0.33 (0.13)*	−0.38 (0.10)***
Luwero	−0.70 (0.20)***	−0.45 (0.16)**	−0.38 (0.15)*	−0.34 (0.17)*	−0.39 (0.13)**
Nakasongola	−0.61 (0.29)*	−0.42 (0.18)*	−0.12 (0.14)	−0.57 (0.18)***	−0.31 (0.14)*
Lira	−0.34 (0.14)*	−0.18 (0.17)	−0.92 (0.14)***	−0.30 (0.17)#	−0.47 (0.13)***
Intercepts (robust se)	0.13 (0.33)	−0.91 (0.29)	−0.85 (0.27)	−0.19 (0.27)	1.62 (0.23)
	1.37 (0.34)	−0.31 (0.28)	−0.22 (0.26)	0.13 (0.27)	
	1.98 (0.33)	0.15 (0.28)	0.05 (0.27)	0.25 (0.27)	
		1.30 (0.28)	1.00 (0.27)	0.97 (0.28)	
N	526	607	669	667	458
Pseudo R² or R²	0.08	0.07	0.06	0.06	0.25

Source: Author.

Note: OLS = ordinary least squares. Entries are ordered probit or unstandardized OLS coefficients with robust standard errors in parentheses. # $p \leq 0.10$; * $p \leq 0.05$; ** $p \leq 0.01$; *** $p \leq 0.001$.

of participation increases, Ugandans are not significantly more supportive of their constitution.

If participation is not a good predictor of constitutional support at the individual level, what is? The variable measuring the extent to which individuals follow public affairs, the measures of support for the government, and the respondent's location of residence all have consistent and significant effects on attitudes about the constitution. According to qualitative analysis of in-depth interviews, it appears that the views of leaders active in a given area shaped citizen evaluations of both the constitution-making process and the constitution. In Uganda, as elsewhere, the constitution-making process and the constitution itself are difficult for ordinary people to evaluate. Ugandan citizens looked to political elites for cues. Elites also made concerted efforts to influence public opinion on constitutional issues. Both active and inactive citizens seem to have been highly influenced by elite rhetoric. So, although participation may have helped citizens form opinions about the constitution and made those opinions more durable, it appears that the leaders in the area (and not participation) influenced whether citizens came to view the constitution as legitimate or illegitimate.

In Uganda, leaders were polarized in their views of the constitution-making process and the constitution. Most were supportive, but opposition leaders felt deeply alienated by the constitution-making process and excluded from the institutions resulting from the constitution. Elite polarization is reflected in citizen sentiments about the process and the constitution. For instance, my discussion with a 40-year-old man from Mpigi district is representative of citizens in opposition-dominated areas:

Interviewer: Why did you choose statement B: "Our constitution hinders development so we should abandon it completely and design another"?

Respondent: There is a lot left to be desired for it to be a good constitution. It is a biased constitution. It is not a fair constitution. Although we were told we were going to elect people to make the constitution, there was a game behind it. In the elections, some people were put there by the government to run for the Constituent Assembly [CA]. The majority of the people who went through were from the government.

Interviewer: Was your CA delegate put there by the government?

Respondent: It was not here that the government pushed through their candidates, but elsewhere. In this place it was okay for the CA elections. Our CA delegate took our views, but he couldn't win because the government side beat him. It wasn't fair. That is what he told us when he came back. (interview, Mpigi District, January 2001)

This man's perception of the fairness of the elections was based on what he was told by his CA delegate, not on his personal experience. His view contrasts sharply with the views of a school headmaster in Bushenyi district:

> The constitution is based on most of the views we gave. It was the first time for our people to make a constitution for ourselves. We sent there our Constituent Assembly delegates to work on it—not by their own views but by the views of the people. Everyone had a chance to give ideas. (interview, Bushenyi District, April 2001)

In sum, public involvement in the making of a new constitution can have important benefits: It may make citizens more democratic, knowledgeable, discerning, engaged, and attached to the constitution. However, participation has the potential to increase public acceptance of the new constitutional rules only when opposition elites feel included and supportive (or are too weak to influence citizens). Where the process and outcome leave elites feeling polarized and antagonistic, participatory constitution making can exacerbate rather than heal mass divisions and reduce rather than enhance constitutional support. Citizen polarization, rather than distrust, is a serious threat to democratic development.

Theoretical and Policy Implications

The research described in this chapter has theoretical implications for four key fields of inquiry: comparative democratization, political participation, institutional trust, and constitution making. It also offers lessons on "best practices" for policy makers involved in these spheres of activity.

For scholars of democratization, this work demonstrates that political attitudes are subject to short-term influences and are not solely the product of long-term socialization.[15] However, it also warns that political culture is not easily crafted. Democracy promoters seek to simultaneously raise democratic norms and institutional trust—making new democracies both more democratic and more stable. Scholars of democratization similarly assume that advances in one attitude will spill over into the other: Higher trust in government will build support for system norms and greater attachment to democratic attitudes will foster trust in the new institutions.[16] My research indicates that, initially, these goals may be incompatible. During transitions, when institutional performance is low, increases in democratic attitudes are likely to create expectations that undermine institutional trust. Only when institutional performance improves will increases in democratic attitudes and knowledge be accompanied by higher trust.

Moreover, elevating political trust may be not only difficult to achieve in new democracies, but also undesirable. This research calls into question previous assumptions about the constellation of attitudes that are conducive to democratic development. Although most scholars presume that distrust threatens the democratic project, I argue that the development of critical capacity is advantageous for democratization, especially in the medium and long term. In the current wave of transitions from authoritarian rule, regimes are less likely to experience dramatic breakdowns that reinstate dictatorships and more likely to stabilize under hybrid systems that fall short of liberal democracy (Bratton, Mattes, and Gyimah-Boadi 2005; Bratton and van de Walle 1997; Diamond 2002; Levitsky and Way 2002). Transitioning polities are not well served by naive publics who overestimate the quality of democratic governance.[17] In Uganda, active citizens are seemingly more attached to democratic principles and constitutional rules, and simultaneously more attentive to the flawed democratic performance of their political institutions. Uganda's informed distrusting democrats are thus more inclined to hold their leaders accountable to constitutional standards and to push for democratic improvements. Institutional distrust, combined with civic engagement, democratic attitudes, and support for fundamental rules, seems to offer the best recipe for furthering democratization, although individual-level attitudes alone are not sufficient to guarantee progress.

This work also has implications for the study of political participation in both hybrid systems and consolidated democracies. It revises our understanding of political participation by highlighting the critical role that context plays in conditioning the influence of participation on citizen attitudes.[18] By comparing the results in Uganda with the existing studies of developed democracies, I highlight the importance of institutional performance and information environments.[19] In addition, the Ugandan case holds lessons for practitioners seeking to use participation to foster democratic culture. First, much of the participation in the Ugandan process was organized by appointed officials and civic groups rather than by politicians seeking votes. These officials had an interest in mobilizing a broad section of the population to become involved, and the evidence shows that they were successful. In contrast, politicians typically aim to mobilize only those supporters who are already likely to vote. Second, the architects of the Ugandan constitution-making process designed their participatory activities with the goals of educating the public and building democratic attitudes. Programs are more likely to alter political culture when those goals are explicit and programs are designed accordingly. Third, the Ugandan process failed to increase feelings of political efficacy because of lack of sufficient follow-up. It is crucial to continue constitutional education and dissemination of constitutional materials following the promulgation of the constitution. Citizens are likely to conclude that their involvement was efficacious only if they receive detailed feedback about the results of their efforts.

The research contributes to the growing new institutionalist literature on political trust. The influence of participation on trust is undertheorized and inadequately tested. This chapter outlines a comprehensive theory linking participation, institutional performance, and trust that is relevant beyond the specific case.[20] In addition, most of the literature on trust focuses on what makes institutions trustworthy. This research focuses on the two understudied components in the new institutionalist perspective: (1) access to information on institutional trustworthiness and (2) evaluation of that information (Hardin 1998; Levi 1998; Norris 1999; Putnam, Pharr, and Dalton 2000). It provides empirical evidence that participation is associated with those two components. Moreover, the evidence indicates that both citizens' knowledge of institutional performance and their criteria for evaluating performance predict institutional trust.

Finally, this research effort engages the debate between proponents of the traditional elite model of constitution making and advocates of the new participatory approach.[21] The participatory model has the potential to advance a culture of democratic constitutionalism that will support the new system. Citizens who are involved in constitution making are more likely to know and care about the constitution. Importantly, however, participation does not automatically confer constitutional legitimacy as advocates have assumed. Most citizens lack the information and skills to evaluate the fairness of the constitution-making process on their own, and they turn to local leaders for guidance. As a result, elites mediate between participation and constitutional legitimacy, especially in places where citizens lack independent sources of information about the constitution. If the elites are divided and debates are antagonistic, as they were in Uganda, then citizens are likely to develop polarized views of the process and the constitution. In a polity with a robust opposition and no consensus, participatory constitution making can reduce constitutional legitimacy among key sectors of society.

It would be a mistake to assume that any constitution-making process (participatory or otherwise) would be free from the influences of societal cleavages and political differences. However, when the outcome of the process depends on political participation, leaders have a greater interest in mobilizing the public to share their views on the constitution and to support certain provisions. Political wrangles and accusations that might otherwise remain at the elite level are more likely to be passed on to the general public. Furthermore, leaders will find it more difficult to make concessions and build a consensus when negotiations occur under the watch of a mobilized and passionate public. As a result, public participation in constitution making has the potential to make the resolution of societal and political conflicts more difficult by expanding the number of interests that must be considered and by intensifying citizens' preferences.

The analysis of Uganda suggests a number of steps that can be taken to minimize the politicization of the process and the corresponding polarization of public views of the constitution, while still allowing for public involvement. First, leaders should strive to reach some degree of consensus on the constitution-making process and on the final constitutional arrangement before involving the public.[22] Such preparation will prevent a group of elites from rejecting outright the process and the constitution and from convincing the public to do likewise. Reaching a consensus also allows leaders to make necessary concessions before going public with their platforms. Furthermore, a fundamental consensus and commitment to the process must be maintained throughout the time needed to create the constitution.

Second, attempts should be made to insulate the constitution-making process and the constitution makers from the ongoing political process and political leaders. Constitution makers should be prevented from holding political positions at the same time or in the immediate aftermath of the constitution-making process, and government leaders should face sanctions for interfering in the process.

Third, the time allowed for public input should be well defined and limited. In Uganda, the period allotted for constitution making was extended several times. After nearly a decade of organizing to secure constitutional issues, organizations found it very difficult to reorient their programs to deal with non-constitutional issues after promulgation. Furthermore, leaders who began with magnanimous goals became more concerned with maintaining power as time went on. In addition, citizens found it hard to distinguish the constitutional issues about which they had for so long been hearing from broader political issues. Participation takes time to organize, but a year or two of formal public input should be sufficient.

Finally, constitutional education and dissemination of constitutional materials after the promulgation will dampen elites' influence on citizen attitudes. My research shows that having been denied access to neutral information on the constitution, citizens depended on elites' political agendas for information. Continuing civic education will not only raise knowledge and efficacy (as suggested previously), but also counteract the polarization of citizen opinions of the constitution.

In sum, my research warns policy makers against completely abandoning the traditional approach to constitution making, with its emphasis on elite negotiations and inclusive institutions. Mass citizen participation during the constitution-writing process cannot substitute for agreement among leaders about the institutional outcomes. It is not possible to bypass opposing elites and build constitutional support from the ground up, as some might hope.

Notes

1. This article employs the commonly used definition of political participation: "those legal activities by private citizens that are more or less directly aimed at influencing the selection of government personnel and/or the actions they take" (Verba, Nie, and Kim 1978).

2. For theoretical accounts of the consequences of participation, see Almond and Verba (1963); Barber (1984); Berman (1997); de Tocqueville (1945); Finkel (1987, 2003); Hirschman (1970); Huntington (1991); Kasfir (1976); Jane Mansbridge, "Does Participation Make Better Citizens?" http://www.cpn.org/crm/contemporary/participation. html; Mill (1948); Mutz (2002); Pateman (1970); Radcliff and Wingenbach (2000);

Rosenstone and Hansen (1993); Rousseau (1968); Salisbury (1975); Scaff (1975); and Verba, Schlozman, and Brady (1995). For reviews of literature on participation, see Nelson (1987); Salisbury (1975); and Thompson (1970).

3. Jane Mansbridge, "Does Participation Make Better Citizens?" http://www.cpn.org/crm/contemporary/participation.html.

4. Uganda is not a democracy. It is a hybrid system that combines considerable amounts of democratic political competition (between individuals not parties) and public participation with elements of authoritarian rule. Ultimately, citizens who participated in the constitution-making process seem to be especially sensitive to their government's democratic shortcomings.

5. Ugandans engaged in standard activities that are part of the democratic repertoire. As part of the constitution-making process, they attended local government meetings, contacted government officials, wrote editorials, called in to radio-talk-show programs, planned activities with their local associations, campaigned for their favorite candidates, attended rallies, voted, and lobbied government officials.

6. The difference between participation in the Ugandan process and participation in other programs is a difference in magnitude, not a difference in kind. Although the consequences of participation are magnified in the Ugandan case, I expect my analysis to be relevant to other participatory programs.

7. The research data were collected during two visits to Uganda—the first in June and July 1999, and the second from October 2000 through September 2001. In addition to the survey and citizen interviews, data were collected from in-depth interviews with elites, focus groups with ordinary citizens, primary materials from public and private archives, case studies of local nongovernmental organizations, and an analysis of media content.

8. The survey, which I designed and managed, is based on a national probability sample whereby each eligible Ugandan had an equal chance of being included in the sample. The resulting sample comprises 820 adult Ugandans aged twenty-six and older (individuals of voting age during the constitution-making period). Nine districts in the north and west (Bundibugyo, Gulu, Hoima, Kabalore, Kasese, Kibaale, Kitgum, Kotido, and Moroto) were excluded from the sampling frame because of instability and rebel attacks. Therefore, the resulting data are not representative of these troubled areas. I employed a clustered, stratified, multistage, area probability sampling design. After stratifying by urban or rural localities and region (north, east, center, and west), a probability proportionate to population size method was used to randomly select districts, subcounties, and parishes in successive stages. A single primary sampling unit (PSU) was randomly selected from each parish (population data did not exist at the PSU level). The randomly selected PSUs included six urban and 62 rural sites within 13 districts: Apac, Bushenyi, Iganga, Jinja, Kampala, Lira, Luwero, Mayuge, Mbale, Mbarara, Mpigi, Nakasongola, and Sironko. Working with the local council officials, our research teams compiled lists of all the households in each selected PSU. We randomly selected a sample of 16 households from each PSU list. After the households were identified, an interviewer visited each household and listed, by first name, all the citizens aged 26 and older who lived in each household, including those away from home at that time. A single individual was randomly selected from the list of household members through blind selection from a pack of numbered cards. The interview was conducted only with the selected individual. When return calls were unsuccessful, then another randomly selected household (not another individual from the same household) was substituted, and the process of listing and randomly selecting household members was repeated. The survey instrument was a questionnaire containing 92 items based on other surveys, in-depth interviews, and focus-group discussions with a variety of Ugandans. We pretested the instrument in rural and urban locations. The questionnaire was translated into the five languages of

the sampled regions (Luganda, Lugisu, Luo, Lusoga, and Runyankole) using the tech-nique of translation/back-translation. The survey was administered face to face by five teams of trained native-speaking interviewers.

9. I conducted open-ended interviews with three types of Ugandan citizens. First, I selected local elites based on their positions and the likelihood that they would know about the constitution-making activities that took place in their area. Second, at the Electoral Commission Archive in Kampala, I copied the attendance and signature lists from the memoranda, meeting notes, and seminar transcripts that were available from each of the sites. Where possible, I conducted in-depth interviews with citizens identified on these lists to obtain a higher proportion of known participants. Third, I conducted in-depth interviews with randomly sampled individuals.

10. I used the Nvivo qualitative data-analysis program to code and retrieve sections of the interview transcripts. I read through the full transcripts several times and assigned codes to key themes. I then reviewed all passages coded on a given theme, or at the intersection of two themes. This was done in a reiterative process with the quantitative analysis.

11. The measures of participation rely on the respondent's self-report of his or her partici-pation in constitution-making activities before the promulgation of the constitution. I use two different measures to check that the findings are robust to question wording. The primary measure of participation, *the participation activities index,* is an index vari-able created from the sum of six separate survey questions that ask whether the respon-dent participated in a specific constitution-making activity. The alternative measure of participation, *respondent-identified participation,* comes from an open-ended question that was asked earlier in the survey: "Between 1988 and 1995, how did you participate in the constitution-making process?" Up to three activities mentioned by the respondent were recorded as open-ended answers and then post-coded. The findings discussed here are robust to both measures of participation. The tables and figures record the results using the participation activities index.

12. For detailed analysis of the relative influences on participation, see Moehler (2007) .

13. *Democratic attitudes* is a multi-item index constructed from five questions designed to measure the respondent's valuation of the attitude dimensions: tolerance, equality, indi-vidual rights, public involvement in government, and freedom of speech. *Political knowledge* was measured with an index of general knowledge of government (results shown here) as well as with an index of constitutional knowledge. The results are gener-ally similar for both measures of knowledge. *Political capabilities* is an index variable constructed from five questions asking respondents to give self-assessments of their ability to perform a range of political activities: public speaking, leading groups, influ-encing others, understanding government, and serving on a local council. *Institutional trust* is a measure of citizen faith in four government institutions; citizens were asked how much they trusted (1) the police, (2) the courts of law, (3) the local council (at the village or neighborhood level), and (4) the Electoral Commission. For additional infor-mation about variables, the first-stage equations, and the second-stage equations pre-dicting participation, see Moehler (2008).

14. The term "distrusting democrats" is similar to Pippa Norris's (1999) use of "critical citi-zens" and "disenchanted democrats." It is also similar to Pharr and Putnam's (2000) term "disaffected democracies."

15. This research compliments several recent works on democratization, including Bermeo (2003); Bratton, Mattes, and Gyimah-Boadi (2005); Bratton and van de Walle (1997); Carothers (1999); Diamond (1999); Gibson and Gouws (2003); Howard (2003); Reyn-olds (1999); Rose, Mishler, and Haerpfer (1998); and Schaffer (1998).

16. Scholars often conflate different types of political support, but it is important to recog-nize that democratic attitudes and institutional trust have different referents and they

need not co-vary. Democratic attitudes refer to support for the political regime or rules of the game, whereas institutional trust refers to support for the existing structures of the state.

17. Bratton, Mattes, and Gyimah-Boadi (2005) also suggest that lowered trust might benefit Africa. After noting that the average level of institutional trust in 12 African countries is similar to that of Organisation for Economic Co-operation and Development countries, they write: "But, given that the institutions in question often perform abysmally in Africa, one is forced to consider whether Africans are perhaps *too* trusting, or whether they lack the experience or information necessary to arrive at more critical judgments" (229; emphasis in original).

18. Numerous theoretical accounts address the individual-level consequences of participation. For examples, see Almond and Verba (1963); Barber (1984); de Tocqueville (1945); Huntington (1968); Huntington and Nelson (1976); Mill (1948); Pateman (1970); Radcliff and Wingenbach (2000); Rousseau (1968); Scaff (1975); and Verba, Schlozman, and Brady (1995). For reviews of literature on participation, see Jane Mansbridge, "Does Participation Make Better Citizens?" http://www.cpn.org/crm/contemporary/participation.html; Nelson (1987); Salisbury (1975); and Thompson (1970).

19. For empirical research on participatory consequences in developed democracies, see Almond and Verba (1963); Brehm and Rahn (1997); Clarke and Acock (1989); Finkel (1985, 1987); Jackman (1972); Muller, Seligson, and Turan (1987); Pateman (1970); Rahn, Brehm, and Carlson (1999); Sullivan, Piereson, and Marcus (1982); and Verba, Schlozman, and Brady (1995).

20. For example, to explain the decline in institutional trust in the United States, scholars often argue that an expansion of government in the post–World War II period raised citizen expectations (Norris 1999, 22). My theory suggests that participation could also have been responsible for raising expectations. It is possible that new forms of participation that emerged in the 1960s altered participants' ideas about how government should be performing (Tarrow 2000). Furthermore, new information technologies expanded the information on government performance that was available to active citizens. In short, changes in citizen engagement with government might have contributed to the decline in political trust in the United States.

21. Some of the more comprehensive and up-to-date examinations of comparative constitution making include Elster, Offe, and Preuss (1998); Greenberg and others (1993); Hart (2003); Howard (1993); Hyden and Venter (2001); United States Institute of Peace (2005); and Widner (2005a, 2005b).

22. For example, the formal multiparty negotiations of the Convention for a Democratic South Africa established the formula for the constitution-making process and for the basic constitutional principles that had to be respected.

References

Almond, Gabriel A., and Sidney Verba. 1963. *The Civic Culture: Political Attitudes and Democracy in Five Nations*. Princeton, NJ: Princeton University Press.

Barber, Benjamin. 1984. *Strong Democracy: Participatory Politics for a New Age*. Berkeley, CA: University of California Press.

Berman, Sheri. 1997. "Civil Society and the Collapse of the Weimar Republic." *World Politics* 49 (3): 401–29.

Bermeo, Nancy. 2003. *Ordinary People in Extraordinary Times: The Citizenry and the Breakdown of Democracy*. Princeton, NJ: Princeton University Press.

Bratton, Michael, Robert B. Mattes, and Emmanuel Gyimah-Boadi. 2005. *Public Opinion, Democracy, and Market Reform in Africa*. Cambridge, U.K.: Cambridge University Press.

Bratton, Michael, and Nicolas van de Walle. 1997. *Democratic Experiments in Africa: Regime Transitions in Comparative Perspective.* Cambridge, U.K.: Cambridge University Press.

Brehm, John, and Wendy Rahn. 1997. "Individual-Level Evidence for the Causes and Consequences of Social Capital." *American Journal of Political Science* 41 (3): 999–1023.

Carothers, Thomas. 1999. *Aiding Democracy Abroad: The Learning Curve.* Washington, DC: Carnegie Endowment for International Peace.

Clarke, Harold D., and Alan C. Acock. 1989. "National Elections and Political Attitudes: The Case of Political Efficacy." *British Journal of Political Science* 19 (4): 551–62.

de Tocqueville, Alexis. 1945. *Democracy in America.* New York: Knopf.

Diamond, Larry Jay. 1999. *Developing Democracy: Toward Consolidation.* Baltimore: Johns Hopkins University Press.

———. 2002. "Thinking about Hybrid Regimes." *Journal of Democracy* 13 (2): 21–35.

Elster, Jon, Claus Offe, and Ulrich Klaus Preuss. 1998. *Institutional Design in Post-Communist Societies: Rebuilding the Ship at Sea, Theories of Institutional Design.* Cambridge, U.K.: Cambridge University Press.

Finkel, Steven E. 1985. "Reciprocal Effects of Participation and Political Efficacy: A Panel Analysis." *American Journal of Political Science* 29 (4): 891–913.

———. 1987. "The Effects of Participation on Political Efficacy and Political Support: Evidence from a West German Panel." *Journal of Politics* 49 (2): 441–64.

———. 2003. "Can Democracy Be Taught?" *Journal of Democracy* 14 (4): 137–51.

Gibson, James L., and Amanda Gouws. 2003. *Overcoming Intolerance in South Africa: Experiments in Democratic Persuasion.* Cambridge, U.K.: Cambridge University Press.

Greenberg, Douglas, Stanley N. Katz, Melanie B. Oliver, Steven C. Wheatley, and American Council of Learned Societies, eds. 1993. *Constitutionalism and Democracy: Transitions in the Contemporary World.* American Council of Learned Societies Comparative Constitutionalism Papers. Oxford: Oxford University Press.

Hardin, Russell. 1998. "Trust in Government." In *Trust and Governance,* ed. V. A. Braithwaite and M. Levi, 9–27. New York: Russell Sage Foundation.

Hart, Vivien. 2003. *Democratic Constitution Making.* U.S. Institute of Peace Special Report 107. Washington, DC: U.S. Institute of Peace. http://www.usip.org/pubs/specialreports/sr107.html.

Hirschman, Albert O. 1970. *Exit, Voice, and Loyalty: Responses to Decline in Firms, Organizations, and States.* Cambridge, MA: Harvard University Press.

Howard, A. E. Dick, ed. 1993. *Constitution Making in Eastern Europe.* Washington, DC: Woodrow Wilson Center Press.

Howard, Marc. 2003. *The Weakness of Civil Society in Post-Communist Europe.* Cambridge, U.K.: Cambridge University Press.

Huntington, Samuel P. 1968. *Political Order in Changing Societies.* New Haven, CT: Yale University Press.

———. 1991. *The Third Wave: Democratization in the Late Twentieth Century.* Norman, OK: University of Oklahoma Press.

Huntington, Samuel P., and Joan M. Nelson. 1976. *No Easy Choice: Political Participation in Developing Countries.* Cambridge, MA: Harvard University Press.

Hyden, Goran, and Denis Venter. 2001. *Constitution-Making and Democratization in Africa.* Pretoria, South Africa: Africa Institute of South Africa.

Jackman, Robert W. 1972. "Political Elites, Mass Publics, and Support for Democratic Principles." *Journal of Politics* 34 (3): 753–73.

Kasfir, Nelson. 1976. *The Shrinking Political Arena: Participation and Ethnicity in African Politics with a Case Study of Uganda.* Berkeley, CA: University of California Press.

Levi, Margaret. 1998. "A State of Trust." In *Trust and Governance,* ed. V. A. Braithwaite and M. Levi, 77–101. New York: Russell Sage Foundation.

Levitsky, Steven, and Lucan Way. 2002. "The Rise of Competitive Authoritarianism." *Journal of Democracy* 13 (2): 51–65.

Mill, John Stuart. 1948. *Representative Government.* London: Oxford University Press.

Moehler, Devra C. 2006. "Public Participation and Support for the Constitution in Uganda." *Journal of Modern African Studies* 44 (2): 275–308.

———. 2007. "Participation in Transition: Mobilizing Ugandans in Constitution Making." *Studies in Comparative International Development* 42 (1/2): 164–90.

———. 2008. *Distrusting Democrats: Outcomes of Participatory Constitution-Making.* Ann Arbor: University of Michigan Press.

Muller, Edward N., Mitchell A. Seligson, and Ilter Turan. 1987. "Education, Participation, and Support for Democratic Norms." *Comparative Politics* 20 (1): 19–33.

Mutz, Diana C. 2002. "Cross-Cutting Social Networks: Testing Democratic Theory in Practice." *American Political Science Review* 96 (1): 111–26.

Nelson, Joan M. 1987. "Political Participation." In *Understanding Political Development: An Analytic Study,* ed. M. Weiner, S. P. Huntington, and G. A. Almond, 103–59. Boston: Little, Brown.

Norris, Pippa. 1999. *Critical Citizens: Global Support for Democratic Government.* Oxford: Oxford University Press.

Pateman, Carole. 1970. *Participation and Democratic Theory.* Cambridge: Cambridge University Press.

Pharr, Susan J., and Robert D. Putnam, eds. 2000. *Disaffected Democracies: What's Troubling the Trilateral Countries?* Princeton, NJ: Princeton University Press.

Putnam, Robert D., Susan J. Pharr, and Russell J. Dalton. 2000. "Introduction: What's Troubling the Trilateral Countries?" In *Disaffected Democracies: What's Troubling the Trilateral Countries?* ed. S. J. Pharr and R. D. Putnam, 3–30. Princeton, NJ: Princeton University Press.

Radcliff, Benjamin, and Ed Wingenbach. 2000. "Preference Aggregation, Functional Pathologies, and Democracy: A Social Choice Defense of Participatory Democracy." *Journal of Politics* 62 (4): 977–98.

Rahn, Wendy M., John Brehm, and Neil Carlson. 1999. "National Elections as Institutions for Generating Social Capital." In *Civic Engagement in American Democracy,* ed. T. Skocpol and M. P. Fiorina, 111–62. Washington, DC: Brookings Institution Press.

Reynolds, Andrew. 1999. *Electoral Systems and Democratization in Southern Africa.* Oxford: Oxford University Press.

Rose, Richard, William Mishler, and Christian W. Haerpfer. 1998. *Democracy and Its Alternatives: Understanding Post-Communist Societies.* Baltimore: Johns Hopkins University Press.

Rosenstone, Steven J., and John Mark Hansen. 1993. *Mobilization, Participation, and Democracy in America.* New York: Macmillan.

Rousseau, Jean-Jacques. 1968. *The Social Contract.* Harmondsworth: Penguin.

Salisbury, Robert H. 1975. "Research on Political Participation." *American Journal of Political Science* 19 (2): 323–41.

Scaff, Lawrence A. 1975. "Two Concepts of Political Participation." *Western Political Quarterly* 28 (3): 447–62.

Schaffer, Frederic C. 1998. *Democracy in Translation: Understanding Politics in an Unfamiliar Culture.* Ithaca, NY: Cornell University Press.

Sullivan, John Lawrence, James Piereson, and George E. Marcus. 1982. *Political Tolerance and American Democracy.* Chicago: University of Chicago Press.

Tarrow, Sidney. 2000. "Mad Cows and Social Activists: Contentious Mechanisms in the Trilateral Democracies." In *Disaffected Democracies: What's Troubling the Trilateral Countries?* ed. S. J. Pharr and R. D. Putnam, 270–90. Princeton, NJ: Princeton University Press.

Thompson, Dennis F. 1970. *The Democratic Citizen: Social Science and Democratic Theory in the Twentieth Century.* Cambridge, U.K.: Cambridge University Press.

United States Institute of Peace. 2005. *Iraq's Constitutional Process: Shaping a Vision for the Country's Future.* Special Report 132. Washington, DC: United States Institute of Peace.

Verba, Sidney, Norman H. Nie, and Jae-on Kim. 1978. *Participation and Political Equality: A Seven-Nation Comparison.* Cambridge, U.K.: Cambridge University Press.

Verba, Sidney, Kay Schlozman, and Henry E. Brady. 1995. *Voice and Equality: Civic Voluntarism in American Politics.* Cambridge, MA: Harvard University Press.

Widner, Jennifer A. 2005a. "Africa's Democratization: A Work in Progress." *Current History* 104 (682): 216–21.

———. 2005b. "Constitution Writing and Conflict Resolution." *Round Table* 94 (381): 503–18.

Section VI

Power and Public Opinion (Mobilizing Public Opinion)

Collective Movements, Activated Opinion, and the Politics of the Extraordinary

Taeku Lee

The central political fact in a free society is the tremendous contagiousness of conflict ... there is usually nothing to keep the audience from getting into the game.

E. E. Schattschneider

Introduction

On December 1, 1955, an African American seamstress defies a bus driver's demand to give up her seat to a white passenger in Montgomery, Alabama, touching off a year-long boycott of the National City Lines buses in Montgomery and nearly a decade of nonviolent direct action throughout the American South. On April 30, 1977, 14 women wearing white head scarves with names embroidered on them gather at the Plaza de Mayo in Buenos Aires seeking answers about their "disappeared" children, sparking three decades of demonstrations against the military government in Argentina. On June 5, 1989, a lone, anonymous man stands steadfast in the path of a column of four Chinese Type 59 battle tanks, in the culminating moment of seven weeks of protests in Tiananmen Square in Beijing. On August 18, 2006, a Cape Malay Muslim and veteran antiapartheid activist leads 44 others and occupies the provincial offices in Cape Town, South Africa, to protest the government's failure to treat its HIV-positive prisoners with antiretrovirals. On the same day, the XVI International AIDS Society Conference in Toronto declares a Global Day of Action for the following week.

Such moments and movements represent key instances in which a collectivity of ordinary individuals demanded change. In each of these cases, dates of focal events and names of ordinary individuals—Rosa Parks, Azucena Villaflor, the "Tank Man," Zackie Achmat—are etched in memory as signature bearers of collective protest movements—the Civil Rights Movement, the Madres de la Plaza de Mayo movement, the Tiananmen Square massacre, and Treatment Action Campaign. These moments of uprising, etched as they are in our historical consciousness, are improperly understood if simply in terms of names and dates. Behind each date is a longer, diachronic context. Behind each person (even if Mahatma Gandhi, Nelson Mandela, Aung San Suu Kyi) is a greater collective and institutional context. It is simply not that useful to future campaigns for change and accountability to simply know our history or recite key dates and names.

To deploy what we know about how collective demands arise in the service of generating a toolkit for activating public opinion, we need to dig deeper into structural conditions and underlying mechanisms. When do everyday grievances erupt into collective demands for accountability? What are the wellsprings of activated public opinion? What impact do these demands have on political accountability and responsiveness? In scholarly research, these are questions that are usually asked and answered as questions about social movements. In this chapter, I briefly review the current state of research on social movements. Along the way, I note several key limitations and emerging trends in this literature. From this discussion, I then hone in on what our understanding of social movements contributes to our understanding of the circumstances under which the public's will is activated into collective demands for accountability.

Movements as Collective Pathology

We find essentially four kinds of explanations that social scientists have produced to explain how collective demands for change and accountability rise, fall, or are sustained:

- People are swept up into collective frenzy and outrage.
- People cultivate and harness the necessary resources to convert their grievances into collective demands.
- Political conditions sometimes shift just enough to open the stage to voices from below.
- Ideas and identities are activated through frames and narratives.

This sequence of explanations mirrors their chronology in time. Perhaps the earliest scholarly renditions of collective behavior are found in accounts of the behavior of crowds. The earliest influences on this initial set of works are Gustave Le Bon's (1925/1895) view of crowds as an organic entity with a distinct psychosocial dynamic and Emile Durkheim's (1964/1893) view of collective behavior as anomic and irrational. Factors such as anonymity, contagion, and conformity were seen as root causes of collective "disturbances" such as mobs, riots, and revolts. This view of group behavior was compelling to a generation of social scientists in the mid-twentieth century still recoiling from the rise of fascism and other demagogically driven totalitarian and nationalist movements. For these scholars, mass behavior was viewed with suspicion and skepticism, and collectivities acting together were imbued with animated, often disparaging, psychological attributes such as irrationality, hysteria, primal urges, and exaggerated impulses.

Not all renditions of "classical" collective behavior theories took a derogative view of mass behavior. Stripped of value judgments, these works at their core presumed that collective action resulted from underlying stresses and ruptures in the existing social and economic order—whether described in terms of symbolic interactionism (Blumer 1951; Turner and Killian 1972), structural functionalism (Smelser 1963), or relative deprivation (Davies 1962; Gurr 1970). Smelser's (1963) "value-added schema" model, for instance, posited four key factors: (1) underlying structural conditions that bolstered the legitimacy of collective behavior; (2) structural strains, such as economic deprivation; (3) psychological precipitants, such as mass hysteria, collective delusions, or "folk devils"; and (4) a weak or strong apparatus of social control, which ultimately defined whether movements would be short lived or deep rooted.

Such "breakdown" theories often fared quite well in characterizing common elements found in collective action. They more often failed, however, as an explanation of why such action happened at certain moments, places, and with certain groups and not at other moments, places, and with other groups. Appeals to structural breakdowns, importantly, fail to tell us why individuals often vary so markedly in their response to common underlying conditions— for the same objective circumstances, why do some people demand that their governments do better while others remain quiescent? Pointing to underlying structural breakdowns, furthermore, is not helpful in specifying the contexts and conditions under which groundswells for change can be championed. Political regimes, macroeconomic conditions, and social demographics are often unbending constraints, at least over the short-term contexts in which much progress might be achieved by demanding that our governments be more responsive to the will of their people.

Movements as Mobilizing Resources

These breakdown theories eventually fell out of favor in large part as a result of seeming indiscriminate as a predictive theory of when, where, and among whom collective action would transpire. In their place has arisen resource mobilization theory. This evolution from structural breakdowns to organizational resources roughly paralleled the shift in scholarly attention from a general focus on "collective behavior" to a more specific focus on "social movements." This transference mirrored the outbreak of bottom–up demands for change and empowerment—from the Civil Rights Movement, the antiwar movement, and the women's rights movement in the United States, to the May 1968 student revolts in Paris and the "Prague Spring" uprisings in Czechoslovakia, to anticolonialist demands for political autonomy in Africa, Asia, and Latin America.

The basic tenets of resource mobilization theory are straightforward. Collective demands are no longer thought of as bootless cries for responsiveness and restitution, stirred by the maddening moment of the crowd and set in bold relief against the "normal" politics of institutionalized actors. Rather, resource mobilization theorists (for example, McCarthy and Zald 1973, 1977; Piven and Cloward 1977; Tilly 1978) stressed the rationally adaptive behavior of individuals embedded in organizations. People act together and make demands on governments to do their bidding when they have the requisite resources of time, money, and organizational infrastructure to think that their collective behavior might make a difference and effect change. Thus movements and moments of collective action do not arise spontaneously and de novo out of a primordial soup of grievances and social strains. Rather, in terms of keys to activating public opinion, resource mobilization theory implies that the decision to protest strongly is conditioned by a calculus of costs and benefits that are ratcheted up or down as resources, group organizations, and opportunities for strategic action change.

Over time, however, resources alone grew insufficient to explain some of the transformative politics of the day. The midcentury movements for freedom and self-determination in South Africa, India, and the American South, for example, could not easily be explained in terms of monetary or organizational resources alone. As real-world circumstances began to change and as criticisms of the limits of a focus on resources alone began to mount, advocates of resource mobilization theory began to redefine "resources" more capaciously to include a broad range of definitions of resources: moral (such as legitimacy, solidarity), cultural (such as Bourdieu's (1984) concept of "habitus" as a source of structural constraints and contestation of those constraints), social-organizational (such as infrastructure, social networks, and organizations, both social movement organizations and those indirectly related to social movements), human (people, and their labor, experience, expertise), and material (money and capital outlays).

Movements as Political Process

Perhaps more important was the evolution of resource mobilization theory into a more contextualized "political process" model of social movements.

Most closely identified with Doug McAdam's (1982) account of African American protest in the Civil Rights Movement, the political process model specified three key factors necessary to potentiate collective protest:

- Organizational resources
- Structure of political opportunities
- Cognitive liberation.

The political process model is by most accounts the dominant framework for thinking about social movements today. Thus, it is worth unpacking each of these components before revisiting the role of public opinion in generating movements for change.

The requisite resources here cover a broad range of material and nonmaterial goods. The range starts with organizations but extends to have strong local norms of solidarity and incentive structures that motivate participation (see Tsai in chapter 20), well-developed communication networks (see Wantchekon and Vermeersch in chapter 9), and leaders and organizers willing to shoulder the often heavy start-up costs of bringing an issue to the public's attention or raise the call to action. Organizations, more specifically, are both formal (such as movement advocacy organizations and issue-based nongovernmental organizations) and informal (such as churches, clubs, labor unions, and other voluntary associations). The organizational resources that matter start with organizations indigenous to an aggrieved, marginalized group, but often also require the contributory roles of other organizations that have overlapping interests or general sympathies. Of the latter type, one key resource is "movement halfway houses," Aldon Morris's term for organizations such as the Highlander School in the United States whose primary purpose is to build capacity and train a cadre of future activist leaders (Morris 1984).

The opportunity structures identified in the political process model refer to shifting balances of power that generate felicitous moments for contestation. The idea of "political opportunity structures" dates back to explanations of why some U.S. cities experienced race riots and urban uprisings in the 1960s while others did not (Eisinger 1973). Opportunity structures open up whenever there are changes in underlying conditions or relations that disrupt and undermine the legitimacy of an existing status quo. Examples of such changes are wars, prolonged periods of joblessness, large-scale inter- and intranational migration of peoples, elite fragmentation and disunity, industrialization (or deindustrialization), and the like. The key intuition is that these relatively longer-term processes sometimes create short-term moments when a political status quo is vulnerable to challenge and existing power relations are open to potential restructuring.

Public opinion is thus not equally docile or receptive to activation across all contexts. The spring 2006 immigration protest marches in the United States—which seemingly spontaneously brought millions of immigrants and their allies out to the streets across the nation—is a recent example of a potent (unexpected) groundswell made possible by demographic changes (large-scale in-migration to the United States), war (U.S. campaigns in Iraq and Afghanistan), and elite disunity (party polarization and fragmentation). At the same time, activating collective demands requires more than resources and open opportunity structures. It requires the third leg of the political process model, what McAdam (1982) calls "cognitive liberation."

This is a shift in consciousness that relinquishes the belief that the existing status quo is legitimate or unavoidable. Cognitive liberation, in short, is the belief that change is possible and necessary. It is captured in the rallying cry of social movements, from Fanny Lou Hamer's "I am sick and tired of being sick and tired" in the U.S. Civil Rights Movement, to "Amandla" of the African National Congress, to "Sí se puede" of the United Farm Workers movement in California and its updated variant in the 2008 U.S. presidential elections, "Yes, we can!" McAdam's "cognitive liberation," in short, describes the core dynamic of generating bottom-up demands for accountability that is at the heart of *Accountability through Public Opinion.*

We give our sustained attention to what can be gleaned from efforts of social movement scholars to come to grips with cognitive liberation in short order. To better situate the concept, one should note that the political process model can be read as an account that specifies the role of three factors: *resources* (as defined by resource mobilization scholars), *schemas* (that is, cognitive liberation), and the *contexts* (that is, opportunity structures) in which the three interact to sometimes enable collective action and sometimes inhibit it. This specification of resources, schemas, and contexts offers a more complete and satisfying rendering of how collective demands are generated. It also parallels, to an extent, the moveable parts involved in making governments accountable to their people more broadly. In the terms of our volume here, social accountability mechanisms are potentially key resources, the varying vulnerabilities and openness of states (across different levels of governments) represent shifting structural contexts of opportunity, and the activation or quiescence of public opinion is the key schema motivating collective action.

Although this link of resources and schemas to contexts of choice and action is powerful, much also remains to mull over and complain about with the political process model. The most critical attention has probably been in the commonly nonspecific and post hoc conceptualization and operationalization of "opportunity structures." It sounds right that collective demands happen when the structural circumstances are ripe, but it turns out to be really tricky business to define an opportunity structure in a rigorous and testable way that allows us to anticipate why movements happen and why they do not. Instead, it is much too tempting to operate post hoc by observing the presence of contentious politics and reasoning backwards to a conclusion that political opportunity structures must have been present to have enabled that collective behavior. A similar objection might also be thrown the way of resource mobilization theories, where resources were sometimes defined so broadly as to cover both the mundane realm of time, money, and organizations as well as the more abstract realm of culture, consciousness, and morality.

A version of the same general lack of "discriminant validity" carries over to various attempts to describe and study the contributing effects of "cognitive liberation" on the activation of collective demands. Social movement theorists deploy cognate terms that cover roughly similar conceptual terrain as cognitive liberation—among them, oppositional consciousness, collective action frames, and narratives. Important differences exist between these terms of art that will surely continue to keep scholars under gainful employ. For the purposes of this volume, I use "activated public opinion" as a general covering term to describe the process by which individuals move from a state of passively tolerating their objective conditions to a state of actively demanding change and accountability. This idea of an activated opinion is a key focus of this edited volume, so we now sharpen our focus on activating frames and narratives.

Movements and Activating Frames

Terms such as oppositional consciousness, cognitive liberation, collective action frames, and movement narratives represent a pivotal shift back to agency in the social sciences. People are no longer depersonalized entities in accounts of mad crowds or pathological, overcompensating masses pushed to the brink by socioeconomic ruptures. Rather, embodying the spirit of our times, people as actors are now viewed as reasonable, thinking beings with an emancipatory and empowering potential to author their own history. It is in this context that there is a turn to the mobilizing power of schemas, stories, and subjective interpretations of objective circumstances. Opportunity structures, no matter how wide open, and organizational resources, no matter how infinite, fail to generate collective action without a corresponding awakening of spirits of resistance.

What then are the factors that awaken these spirits? In the last two decades, a profusion of work has occurred along two fronts: frames and narratives. We take each in turn. The basic idea of framing is that the range of possible realities out there for us to experience, interpret, and draw meaning from far exceed our reasonable cognitive grasp. To make sense of it all, we often require what Goffman describes as "schemata of interpretation" to "locate, perceive, identify, and label" (1974, 21). A wide range of applications of this idea can be identified, most falling into one of two modes of analysis.

One mode—found most commonly in public opinion research—builds on Amos Tversky and Daniel Kahneman's (1981) theories of decision making under uncertainty, where the phenomenon of interest is the widespread failure of people to conform to economic precepts of rational choice, such as making decisions based on expectation value calculations. Typically, the method of inference is quasi-experimental: respondents in an opinion survey are randomly assigned to treatment or control groups, with "treatments" being exposure to "framed" interpretations of an issue or outcome of interest (see, for instance, Chong and Druckman 2007). Much of the debate here is about the forcefulness of framing effects given the ubiquity of political "messaging." Careful studies are able to show, on a case-by-case basis, that how an issue is framed can have significant, sometimes eye-popping, effects on public opinion. Describing redistributive policies as "helping the poor," rather than as "welfare spending," increases public support for such policies by a magnitude of order. Similarly powerful effects are seen in the choice between "death tax" and "estate tax," between "global warming" and "climate change," and more generally, by cueing the public to think in terms of "episodic frames" or "thematic frames" (specific events, persons, cases as opposed to broader sociopolitical, economic, and historic contexts; see Iyengar 1991).

One limitation of this line of inquiry is that framing effects are easy to demonstrate in the controlled environment of a survey lab, where messages can be tested with the technical precision of a surgical probe. In many hurly-burly political contexts, however, politicians and their parties often compete constantly to issue forth a barrage of countervailing strategic communications intended to persuade, to deceive, to divert attention from one issue to another, or quite simply to drown out the other side. In other political contexts, a dominant regime in power holds command over whether and which messages are communicated to the public. In yet other political contexts, even absent a controlling elite, the public is kept at bay through widespread apathy, ignorance, and quiescence. Under these varying real-world circumstances, how can frames rouse people to action, and which frames prevail?

This brings us to a second mode of analysis on frames with a more specific and specialized focus on their role in collective action and social movements. Frames give meaning to our experiences, and collective action frames render meanings in ways that are "intended to mobilize adherents and constituents, to garner bystander support, and to demobilize antagonists" (Snow and Benford 1988, 198). Here much of the effort has been focused on categorizing types of frames and demonstrating their importance during periods of collective protest. For most scholars in this crowd, the core interpretive tasks accomplished by frames are *diagnostic, prognostic,* and *motivational.*

Diagnostic frames identify collective experiences and name them as problems or grievances. These frames, as a result, center on the perception of an injustice and involve a locus of blame. Quite often for movement leaders and activists, trade-offs are seen between the "objective" root causes of a problem and how that problem should strategically be named and blamed to generate the requisite level of consensus and mobilization. Elected officials and heads of states may not be responsive or accountable on a given issue for reasons beyond their control, yet they may still be the best strategic locus of blame and target for collective demands. In this respect, diagnosis is intimately linked to prognosis.

Prognostic frames are interpretive lenses that propose solutions to a collective problem. They get right to Vladimir Lenin's question, "What is to be done?" Effective prognostic frames are able to toe the balance between the realm of the ideal with the realm of the feasible. Typically, this balancing act includes strategic anticipation of "counterframing"—how opponents (including the state apparatus) will aim to demobilize action through their own acts of framing. Prognostic frames often capture core differences between different (sometimes competing) movement organizations and NGOs in their approach to mobilizing collective action. Organizations with the purpose of radical, direct political action will likely adopt different prognostic frames than organizations aiming to work in concert with state actors or organizations aiming to grow their base among more mainstream publics.

This brings us to motivational frames. This third kind of collective action frame principally interprets an issue in terms of the need for individuals to act, to take hold of one's own (collective) fate. Much like Peter Finch's electric delivery of his rant, "I'm mad as hell and I'm not going to take this anymore," in Paddy Chayefsky's *Network*, "agency" frames often underscore the urgency of now. Some keys unlock successful motivational frames. People are roused to act when frames are able to stress that something must be done, that a situation is severe and intolerable, that change is possible, and that it is one's duty to do something.

Myriad additional finely cut distinctions show how frames can be mobilizing. Given our purpose of distilling useable knowledge and actionable insights from the body of work on social movements, however, these nuances are better suited for other audiences. We simply note here that frames do not motivate action in situ, absent a dizzying number of contextual factors. As we noted earlier, attempts to frame events and problems in ways that can mobilize public opinion often run up against all kinds of mitigating circumstances: a clash of cross-cutting frames between competing factions, an environment of censorship or carefully controlled information flows, a demos that is, for whatever reasons, uninformed and cannot be reached out to.

Movements and Empowering Narratives

Beyond these circumstances, three kinds of contexts enable frames to work more effectively:

- First, political opportunity structures that make collective protests more likely to succeed also make collective action frames more likely to succeed.

- Second, some frames will align and resonate well with the prevailing values and beliefs of some cultures, but not others.
- Third, the audiences to whom a frame or message is targeted can sway its form and content.

The first of these contexts has the ring of a truism, but an important one nonetheless. Contexts that shift power relations—military conflict, long-term joblessness, large-scale demographic shifts, intra-elite feuds, and so on—are just the conditions that prick otherwise passive ears to reconsider the costs of standing deaf in the face of unjust and unaccountable governments. At the same time, these are macrolevel phenomena that are resistant to change through grassroots mobilization. It is, almost by definition, not within the power of the masses to open or close opportunity structures. Rather, it is within the power of the masses to recognize structures as open and act on that opportunity.

The second and third contexts are, however, decision nodes that are more directly within the power of movements and collectivities to shape. Thus they are worth some greater attention. On the alignment and resonance of frames within cultural contexts, it is not enough simply to register the recognition that cultures differ. Some societies (and groups within societies) are more individualistic, others more communitarian; some are more traditional, others more modern; some are more patriarchal, others more matriarchal; and so on. The relative potency of framing collective action in terms of religious motifs, individual valor, intergenerational duties, masculine honor, magical realism, and so on often varies markedly across political contexts of action and accountability.

On this point, the work of Marshall Ganz (in chapter 18), Francesca Polletta (1998; 2006), and others on the motivating power of narratives is very illuminating. Narratives and stories are not merely more literary or artful terms for describing essentially the same thing as "frames." Although frames organize complex inputs into useable units of meaning, narratives weave bundles of meaning into a textured arc of a story.

In stories, underlying realities are documented and interpreted; things happen; protagonists act; there is an ending. The material conditions that people endure daily often need to be documented, if only to combat myths of denial or institutional efforts to render those everyday realities invisible. Once established as facts on the ground, stories often carry moral, normative aspects that allow the reality to be communicated as "unjust," or "intolerable," or simply as a "problem." The fact that things happen and situations change in a narrative necessarily implies that things need not remain as they are. The fact that individuals act—in mobilizing narratives, often in fabled, heroic fashion that changes history itself—can embolden ordinary individuals to author their own destinies. Endings vividly remind audiences that poor material conditions need not persist indeterminately—narratives that mobilize often do so by transporting the collective imagination to a better place.

Each of these aspects of a story has a potentially generative force. Thus, during moments of disruption and disequilibrium—of the sort that open up political opportunity structures—narratives can transform uncertainty and fear into familiar stories that, when well chosen, bring people together, forge common identities, and rouse them to collectively act. Narratives have this quality in part because they give some perspective and situate the experiences of discrete individuals within broader temporal and spatial contexts. Sometimes stories do this by referencing a collective past, as in the nationalist movements that rekindle narratives of oppression, resistance, martyrdom, territory, and identity. Sometimes stories do this by imagining a common future, as in Dr. Martin Luther King, Jr.'s oft-recited dream of a "promised land."

Narratives also function through affective channels. Some of the most powerful and promising new lines of research into public opinion document the intimate link between our emotions and our actions (Brader 2006; Marcus, Neuman, and MacKuen 2000). Stories carry an emotional resonance that frames, understood as cognitive heuristics, do not. Narratives entail empathetic identification with characters and an affective investment in how a story ends. Stories that stay with us do so not out of the cognitive satisfaction of seeing how disparate plotlines are brought together through logic and reason, but because of the affective heights and depths we experience—joy, grief, anger, frisson, and so forth.

Another distinct aspect of narratives is what literary theorists refer to as "narrativity." Stories are not like engineering manuals, cookbooks, or logical proofs, where each step in a chain is ineluctably linked to the next. Stories are successful when there is enough dramatic contingency to require active audience participation and sense making. We flip with eager anticipation from one page to the next wondering if an impossible predicament will be resolved through epiphany, irony, divine intervention, or, in magical realism, momentary flight into fantasy. People can passively receive and reflexively respond to frames, but they cannot fully absorb a story without active engagement.

A related point is that stories do not all carry an arc from "once upon a time" to a tidy "happily ever after." The narratives that stay with us often carry plots with exasperating indeterminacies of meaning or end in whimpers of ambiguity. This characteristic of narrative form invites social processes of sense making. We sit in cafés, join book clubs, convene klatsches, organize symposia to engage, debate, or struggle together in this social process of sense making. Narratives are thus interpretive, experiential, and processual; they are sustained by (and in turn sustain) social spaces and invite individuals and collectivities to become directly invested in the meanings they attach to the narratives.

The final point to note is that narratives should be viewed as a key resource to any grassroots campaign. Myths of common belonging, sacred spaces, lionhearted struggles, corrupting power, and so on do not mobilize action on their own. Rather, it takes leadership, vision, and craft to strategically deploy narratives apposite to particular moments and audiences. At the onset of collective movements, for instance, a narrative of spontaneity is often reproduced—the protagonist of the Montgomery bus boycotts, Rosa Parks, was an ordinary seamstress and not a longtime activist trained in the arts of nonviolent direct action at the Highlander Folk School; the spring 2006 immigration protests in the United States were impromptu rallies that numbered in the millions and not the result of organizational recruitment through ethnic media, churches, soccer clubs, and public schools; the 2009 postelection demonstrations in the streets of Baghdad were an unrehearsed tsunami of public outcry and not the product of backroom negotiations and feverish Internet-based social networking.

Movements and Audiences

This brings us to our last segment. We noted earlier that the effectiveness of framing depends on whether political opportunity structures are favorable, whether the message aligns and resonates well with prevailing cultural mores and belief systems, and finally, whether they are matched to a multiplicity of possible audiences. In any groundswell, one finds bystanders and active participants. Social movement scholars focus preponderantly on the active participants, but bystanders are often the key to the outcome. Bystanders matter because they might be drawn into the fray as sympathizers and activists. Or they might also take up the fight as opponents and counteractivists.

This turn to what audiences see and how they are activated is especially key to thinking about how a collective protest movement can build momentum and mobilize others to join in. Collective movements rarely start fully staffed with an army of the rough and ready. Activating frames and mobilizing narratives are thus important not just to the immediate task of stirring up an already defined core group of activists. Rather, they are also important to the longer-term work of building a groundswell from among otherwise passive observers. E. E. Schattschneider (1960, 2) describes this central dynamic very well:

> Every fight consists of two parts: (1) the few individuals who are actively engaged at the center and (2) the audience that is irresistibly attracted to the scene. ... [T]he spectators are an integral part of the situation for, as likely as not, the audience determines the outcome of the fight. ... To understand any conflict it is necessary therefore to keep constantly in mind the relations between the combatants and the audience. ... This is the basic pattern of all politics.

In the strategic deployment of activating frames and mobilizing narratives, a fundamental relationship exists between the content of the messages and stories and the likely reception of diverse audiences. How this matching is achieved will depend in part on the audiences themselves. Some bystanders differ by types of ascriptive group membership (for instance, race, gender, or age), others by types of acquired group membership (for instance, religion or language), yet others by political characteristics (for instance, attentiveness, efficacy, trust, or ideological views), and so forth. The match to audiences will also depend on why public opinion needs to be activated. In many cases, publics need to be activated to initiate collective protest. In other cases, the purpose is to stem the tide of countermobilization and state repression. In yet other cases, activated publics are necessary to institutionalize and memorialize a collective moment by constructing a shared meaning of that moment and its significance. Each of these scenarios is distinct and requires framing and storytelling tailored to its goals.

What is interesting to note is that the lion's share of what we know about public opinion is of little help in specifying how audiences can be brought into a collective movement. Walter Lippmann (1922), an early critic of the idea that public opinion should guide the actions of politicians, famously declared that the world of politics is "out of reach, out of sight, out of mind" of the general public. More than 80 years later, the apparently unstable, ill-formed, and ill-informed judgment of ordinary citizens is one of the most thoroughly documented findings about public opinion. It is also a deplored finding, for if the public is insufficiently informed about the background facts, specific terms, and likely consequences of policy proposals and electoral alternatives, then citizens' judgments present a shaky foundation for political accountability.

Notable efforts have been made to rescue the idea of a responsible and regulative public. One powerful defense is that individuals are inattentive not as a result of incompetence or ignorance, but rather as a rational response to the complexities and competing demands of modern life. By this line of reasoning, citizens' thoroughness of information or constancy of attention ought not to be the criteria by which political competence is judged. Rather, the proper criteria ought to be whether individuals can draw reasonable inferences and fair judgments about their political affairs *given their level of information and attention*. If one builds on this insight, recent works in opinion research have claimed a central role for political elites and institutions in simplifying complex information and paring down unwieldy choice sets so that democratic citizens might draw reasonable political judgments (Popkin 1991). This elite-driven view of mass opinion presumes a division of labor between elites and masses, in which the work of ordinary citizens is limited to consuming cognitive shortcuts generated by elite signals that reduce uncertainty about what is at stake on a given political issue (Zaller 1992).

Although elegant and parsimonious, this view of opinion dynamics nonetheless does not help us understand how audiences become activated. In particular, if we presume that public opinion changes only in response to what elite actors do and say, no reason exists to expect groundswells for social change and political accountability unless it is in the strategic interests of elites to generate this kind of bottom-up pressure (Lee 2002). If public opinion can guide good governance only through cognitive shortcuts, the ideals of participatory and deliberative citizenship required for political accountability are simply unrealistic expectations: That is, the goal is to discover the conditions under which citizens of *demoi* are able to monitor the performance of their representatives, seek transparency and know how to interpret the information that results, deliberate with reason and on an equal footing, and possess the civic skills to organize and make demands, among other things.

We need to look elsewhere. This elsewhere is found by shifting our understanding of public opinion away from its most commonly practiced mode of inquiry. This orthodoxy is one of predicting most likely scenarios—represented in terms of art like "relative expectations," "median voters," "maximum likelihood," "central limits," and "equilibria." Under this practice, public opinion is rendered by aggregating the responses of individuals, randomly selected out of the contexts in which they live, to a fixed set of questions administered under conditions of anonymity. The seeming incoherence and inconsistency of the voices of public opinion result from sampling responses under these circumstances.

The alternative, then, is not to radically divest the potential power of public opinion from the actual contexts in which people live, injustices are experienced, and resistance is mobilized. Elsewhere (Lee 2002), I have argued for a focus on "activated mass opinion," especially when our aim is to specify the continuum from passive bystanders to active participants making demands. The orthodoxy is well suited to explaining the ordinary conditions of public opinion. Moments when ordinary individuals who are downtrodden, disenfranchised, or otherwise disadvantaged take the helm and collectively protest their circumstances are extraordinary, and we need to recognize them as such.

Activated mass opinion, then, cannot be generated easily by looking to anonymous, private expressions of individuals viewed through regular channels of political participation. We need to look, rather, to understand the key roles of resources (whether organizational, as in civil society organizations, or institutionalized, as in social accountability mechanisms), of schemas (whether frames, more narrowly conceived, or narratives), and of contexts (shifting opportunity structures that disrupt existing power relations and make possible the amplification of voices from below). The shift here is from a public opinion for ordinary times, understood to be scientific and representative of all publics, to an activated public opinion for extraordinary moments, when civil society is strong, public spheres are vitalized, and latent opinions are crystallized.

Only by understanding the movement from the ordinary to the extraordinary can we discover how "latent publics" become activated. Extraordinary moments in which ordinary people rise up to demand accountability require resources and the right contexts. They also require a recognition that a political system is no longer legitimate, just, or accountable; a shift from fatalism and quiescence to an active recognition and assertion of one's rights, and an accompanying emergent sense of power to effect change. As V. O. Key, a faithful defender of the possibility of a regulative ideal of the public, notes, politicians are generally not so concerned with visible and ordinary indicia of public opinion found in polls. Rather, it is "latent opinion" that is "about the only type of opinion that generates much anxiety for political elites" (Key 1961, 262).

Bibliography

Blumer, Herbert. 1951. "Collective Behavior." In *Principles of Sociology,* ed. A. M. Lee, 67–121. New York: Barnes and Noble.

Bourdieu, Pierre. 1984. *Distinction: A Social Critique of the Judgement of Taste.* London: Routledge.

Brader, Ted. 2006. *Campaigning for Hearts and Minds: How Emotional Appeals in Political Ads Work.* Chicago: University of Chicago Press.

Chong, Dennis, and James N. Druckman. 2007. "Framing Theory." *Annual Review of Political Science* 10: 103–26.

Davies, James. 1962. "Toward a Theory of Revolution." *American Sociological Review* 27: 5–19.

Durkheim, Emile. 1964/1893. *The Division of Labor in Society.* Glencoe, IL: Free Press.

Eisinger, Peter K. 1973. "The Conditions of Protest Behavior in American Cities." *American Political Science Review* 67: 11–28.

Gamson, William. 1992. *Talking Politics.* New York: Cambridge University Press.

Goffman, Erving. 1974. *Frame Analysis.* New York: Harper and Row.

Gurr, Ted. 1970. *Why Men Rebel.* Princeton, NJ: Princeton University Press.

Iyengar, Shanto. 1991. *Is Anyone Responsible? How Television Frames Political Issues.* Chicago: University of Chicago Press.

Key, V. O. 1961. *Public Opinion and American Democracy.* New York: Alfred Knopf.

Le Bon, Gustave. 1925/1895. *The Crowd: A Study of the Popular Mind.* New York: Macmillan.

Lee, Taeku. 2002. *Mobilizing Public Opinion.* Chicago: University of Chicago Press.

Lippmann, Walter. 1922. *Public Opinion.* New York: Macmillan.

Marcus, George E., W. Russell Neuman, and Michael MacKuen. 2000. *Affective Intelligence and Political Judgment.* Chicago: University of Chicago Press.

McAdam, Doug. 1982. *Political Process and the Development of Black Insurgency, 1930–1970.* Chicago: University of Chicago Press.

McCarthy, John, and Mayer Zald. 1973. "Resource Mobilization and Social Movements." *American Journal of Sociology* 82: 1212–41.

———. 1977. "Resource Mobilization in Social Movements: A Partial Theory." *American Journal of Sociology* 82: 1212–41.

Morris, Aldon. 1984. *The Origins of the Civil Rights Movement.* New York: Free Press.

Piven, Frances Fox, and Richard A. Cloward. 1977. *Poor People's Movements.* New York: Pantheon.

Polletta, Francesca. 1998. "Contending Stories: Narrative in Social Movements." *Qualitative Sociology* 21: 419–46.

———. 2006. *It Was like a Fever: Storytelling in Protest and Politics.* Chicago: University of Chicago Press.

Popkin, Samuel. 1991. *The Reasoning Voter.* Chicago: University of Chicago Press.

Schattschneider, E. E. 1960. *The Semi-Sovereign People: A Realist's View of Democracy in America.* New York: Holt, Rinehart, and Winston.

Smelser, Neil. 1963. *Theory of Collective Behavior.* Glencoe, IL: Free Press.

Snow, David A., and Robert D. Benford. 1988. "Ideology, Frame Resonance, and Participant Mobilization." *International Social Movement Research* 1: 197–217.

Tilly, Charles. 1978. *From Mobilization to Revolution.* Reading, MA: Addison-Wesley.

Turner, Ralph, and Lewis M. Killian. 1972. *Collective Behavior.* Englewood Cliffs, NJ: Prentice-Hall.

Tversky, Amos, and Daniel Kahneman. 1981. "The Framing of Decisions and the Psychology of Choice." *Science* 211: 453–58.

Zaller, John 1992. *Nature and Origins of Mass Opinion.* New York: Cambridge University Press.

•
•
•
•
•
•

Public Narrative, Collective Action, and Power

Marshall Ganz

The authors of this volume ask how discontented, but compliant, publics can mobilize to demand political change. It is not obvious. Organized collective action to challenge the status quo, as opposed to the occasional outburst of resentment, does not "just happen." Nor does it occur as an automatic response to the availability of tools described elsewhere in this book—citizen report cards, public expenditure tracking, participatory budgeting, social audits, right-to-information acts, and so on. Nor does it arise as a result of a providential convergence of resources and opportunities, as often described by social movement theorists.

Organized collective action challenging the status quo—a social movement—requires leadership that goes far beyond a stereotypical charismatic public persona with whom it is often identified. Unable to rely on established bureaucratic structures for coordination, evaluation, and action, such action depends on voluntary participation, shared commitments, and ongoing motivation. Movements must mobilize under risky conditions not only because well-resourced oppositions often resist their efforts, but also because the undertaking itself is fraught with uncertainty about how—and whether—it can happen in the first place. The capacity of a social movement for effective action depends largely on the depth, breadth, and quality of leadership able to turn opportunity to purpose.

Mobilizing others to achieve purpose under conditions of uncertainty—what leaders do—challenges the hands, the head, and the heart. As shown in figure 18.1, the challenge of the "hands" is one of action, of learning, of adapting, and of mastering novel skills. The challenge of the head is one of strategy,

Figure 18.1. Mobilization of Others

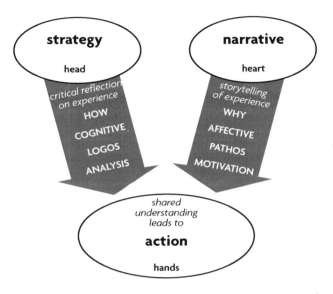

Source: Zac Willette and the author.

imagining how to transform one's resources into the power needed to achieve one's purpose. The challenge of the heart is one of motivation, of urgent need to act, and of hope for success, and the courage to risk it. This is the work of public narrative, the focus of this chapter.

Public narrative is a leadership practice of translating values into action. It is based on the fact that values are experienced emotionally. As such, they are sources of ends worthy of action and the capacity for action. Narrative is the discursive means we use to access values that equip us with the courage to make choices under conditions of uncertainty, to exercise agency. A story is constructed of a plot, character, and moral. A plot is initiated by a challenge that confronts a character with a choice, which, in turn, yields an outcome. Because we identify empathetically with the character, we experience the emotional content of the moment—the values in play, not simply the ideas. Narratives thus become sources of learning, not only for the head, but also for the heart. Public narrative links the three elements of self, us, and now: why I am called, why we are called, and why we are called to act now. Far from new, this framework was articulated by the 1st-century Jerusalem sage, Rabbi Hillel, who, in the *Wisdom of the Fathers*, asks: If I am not for myself, who will be for me? If I am for myself alone, what am I? If not now, when?[1]

Two Ways of Knowing: Why and How

Psychologist Jerome Bruner argues that we interpret the world in two ways— the analytic and the narrative (Bruner 1986). When we cognitively map the world, we identify patterns, discern connections, and hypothesize claims and test them—the domain of analysis. But we also map the world affectively by coding experiences, objects, and symbols as good or bad for us, fearful or safe, hopeful or depressing, and so on.

When we consider action in the face of uncertainty, we have to ask ourselves three questions: *why* must we act, *how* can we act, and *what* must we learn to do. Creative analytic thinking can help us answer the *how* question—how do we use resources efficiently to detect opportunities, compare costs, and so on. We may need to learn new skills to answer the *what* question.

But to answer the *why* question—why does it matter, why do we care, why must we risk action—we turn to narrative. The why question is not simply why we think we *ought* to act, but rather why we *must* act, what moves us, our motivation, our values. Or, as St. Augustine put it, we find ways of going beyond "knowing" the good as an ought to "loving the good" as a source of motivation. (St. Augustine 1991).

Knowing Why: Emotion, Motivation, and Action

Because emotions are the medium through which we experience value, they provide us with vital information about the way we ought to live our lives as well as the motivation to live them in that way. To understand *motivation*— that which inspires action—consider the word *emotion* and their shared root word *motor*: to move. Psychologists argue that the information provided by our emotions is partly physiological, as when our respiration changes or our body temperature alters; partly cognitive because we can describe what we feel as fear, love, desire, or joy; and partly behavioral, as when we are moved to advance or to flee, to stand up or to sit down. So, as figure 18.2 shows, our values are sources of the emotional information that can produce action.

Moral philosopher Martha Nussbaum argues that, because we experience values through our emotions, making moral choices in the absence of emotional information is futile (Nussbaum 2001). She is supported by data about the experience of people afflicted with lesions on the amygdale, that part of the brain central to our emotions. When faced with decisions, people with this disability come up with one option after another, but they can never decide because decisions ultimately are based on values. If we cannot experience emotion, we cannot experience the values that orient us to our world. Thus, our readiness to deliberate, our capacity to deliberate successfully, and our ability to act on our decisions rest on how we feel.

Mobilizing Action

Leadership requires understanding that while some emotions can inhibit mindful action, others can facilitate it. Explaining this relationship, political scientist George Marcus points to two neurophysiologic systems—surveillance

Figure 18.2. From Values to Action

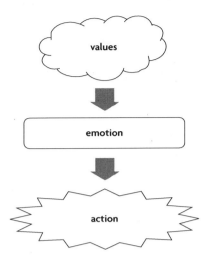

Source: Zac Willette and the author.

and disposition (Marcus 2002). Our *surveillance system* compares what we *expect* to see with what we *do* see, tracking anomalies that, when observed, spark anxiety. Without this emotional cue, we operate out of habit, on autopilot. Anxiety is a way of saying to ourselves, "Hey! Pay attention! There's a bear in the doorway!"

The big question is what we do about that anxiety (so we can figure out what to do about the bear). Our *dispositional system* operates along a continuum from depression to enthusiasm, or from despair to hope. If we experience anxiety in a despairing mode, our fear will kick in, producing withdrawal, rage, or freezing. However, hope inspires curiosity, leading to exploration that can yield learning and creative problem solving. So our readiness to consider action, our capacity to consider it well, and our ability to act on our consideration rest on how we feel.

Leaders engage others in purposeful action by mobilizing those feelings that facilitate action to trump feelings that inhibit action. We often hold conflicting feelings, some of which are more salient at one time than at another. At times, these feelings may have little to do with the present, but rather are a legacy of emotional lessons we learned long ago. Suppose that, as a four-year-old child, you are playing on a swing set at a park when a bigger child tries to kick you off. You run to your parent for help, but your parent laughs it off. In that moment, you are angry and embarrassed, convinced that your parent does not care. You learned counting on others is a bad idea. Now, as an adult, evaluating what to do about a pay cut, this emotional lesson makes it unlikely that you will join other workers to protest. You fear counting on others; you may even tell yourself you deserved that pay cut. And if you are still in the grips of that fear when an organizer comes along and tells you that, with a union, you could keep the employer from cutting your pay, you may see that organizer as a threat. Similarly, the value some people place on not upsetting the boss (teacher, parent, or employer) because of their dependency on that boss may conflict with the value they place on self-respect when the boss does something that violates their sense of self-respect. One person may become angry enough to challenge his or her boss; another may decide to "swallow their pride" or will resist the organizer who points out the conflict. Any resolution can be costly, but one may serve an individual's interests better than another.

Action Inhibitors and Action Facilitators

So the exercise of leadership often requires engaging people in an *emotional dialogue*, drawing on one set of emotions (or values) that are grounded in one set of experiences to counter another set of emotions (or values) that are grounded in different experiences—a *dialogue of the heart*. This dialogue of the heart, far from being irrational, can restore choices that have been abandoned in despair.

As shown in figure 18.3, the major "action inhibitor" is *inertia*—operating by habit and not paying attention. We process most of the information that comes our way on "autopilot," and we respond as programmed. For much of what we do, this is efficient. If something new is going on, however—something

Figure 18.3. Motivating Action

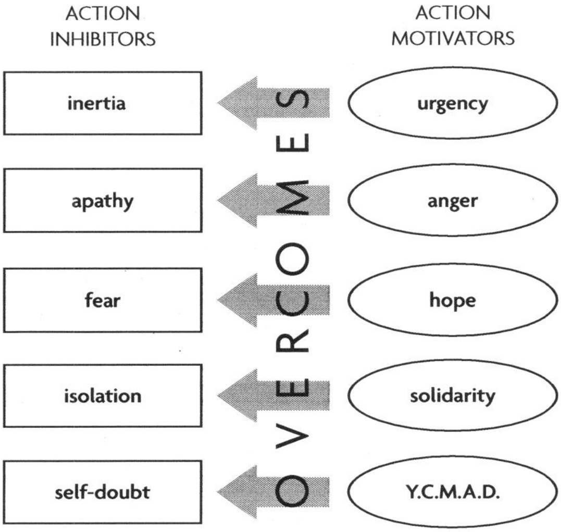

ACTION INHIBITORS		ACTION MOTIVATORS
inertia		urgency
apathy	OVERCOMES	anger
fear		hope
isolation		solidarity
self-doubt		Y.C.M.A.D.

Source: Zac Willette and the author.
Note: Y.C.M.A.D. = You Can Make A Difference.

that might pose a threat or hold out promise—and we stay on autopilot, we may not only miss an opportunity, but also wind up in real trouble.

We can counter *inertia* with *urgency*. Urgency can capture our attention, creating the space for new action. But it is less about time than about priority. My need to complete a problem set due tomorrow supplants a more important need to figure out what to do with the rest of life. An urgent need to attend to a critically ill family member supplants an important need to attend the next business meeting.

Commitment and concentration of energy are required to launch anything new, and creating a sense of urgency often is a critical way to get the commitment that is required. Imagine that someone calls you and says that he is recruiting for a 100-year plan to change the world. This is the beginning, and he will call a meeting sometime over the next six months. Would you be interested in going to that meeting, whenever it happens? However, what if someone calls about an election you care about, with news that the campaign has to contact 3,000 targeted voters before Election Day, just one week away? This person tells you that if 220 volunteers contact 20 voters each, they can reach all the voters and bring this election home— that if you come to the headquarters at 6:00 tonight, you will meet the other volunteers and learn how to reach 20 key voters in your neighborhood. Are you interested? Urgency recognizes that "time is like an arrow." Because launching anything new requires commitment and intense effort, urgency is often the way to make it happen.

What about inertia's first cousin, *apathy*? One way to counter apathy is with *anger*—not rage, but outrage or indignation with injustice. Anger often grows out of experience of a contrast between *the world as it is* and *the world as it ought to be,* how we feel when our moral order has been violated (Alinsky 1971). Sociologist Bill Gamson describes this as using an "injustice frame" to counter a "legitimacy frame" (Gamson 1992). As scholars of "moral economy" have taught us, people rarely mobilize to protest inequality as such, but they do mobilize to protest "unjust" inequality (Scott 1976). In other words, our values, moral traditions, and sense of personal dignity function as critical sources of the motivation to act. This is one reason that organizing is so deeply rooted in moral traditions.

Where can we find the *courage* to act in spite of our *fear*? Trying to eliminate that to which we react fearfully is a fool's errand because it locates the source of our fear outside ourselves, rather than within our hearts. However, trying to make ourselves "fearless" is counterproductive if we wind up acting more out of "nerve than brain." Leaders sometimes prepare others for fear by warning them that the opposition will threaten them with this and woo them with that. The fact that these behaviors are expected reveals the opposition as more predictable and, thus, less to be feared.

What can we do about fear? A choice to act in spite of fear is the meaning of courage. Of all the emotions that help us find courage, perhaps most important is *hope*. So where do you go to get some hope? One source of hope is experience of a "credible solution," not only reports of success elsewhere, but also direct experience of small successes and small victories. A source of hope for many people is in their faith tradition, grounded in spiritual beliefs, cultural traditions, and moral understandings. Many of the great social movements—Gandhi, civil rights, and Solidarity—drew strength from religious traditions, and much of today's organizing is grounded in faith communities.

Relationships offer another source of hope. We all know people who inspire hopefulness just by being around them. "Charisma" can be seen as the capacity to inspire hope in others, inspiring others to believe in themselves. Many people have charisma, but some of us need to be encouraged to use it. Just as religious belief requires a "leap of faith," Cornel West argues that politics requires a "leap of hope" (West 1994). More philosophically, Moses Maimonides, the Jewish scholar of the 15th century, argued that hope is belief in the "plausibility of the possible" as opposed to the "necessity of the probable." And psychologists who explore the role of "positive emotions" give particular attention to the "psychology of hope" (Seligman and Csikszentmihali 2000). In concert with *confidence* and *solidarity*, hope can move us to act.

We can counter feelings of *isolation* with the experience of *belovedness* or *solidarity*. This is the role of mass meetings, singing, common dress, and shared language. This is why developing relationships with the people whom we hope to mobilize is important. Because of the snowball effect, it is much easier to get people to join others who are already active.

Finally, one of the biggest inhibitors is *self-doubt:* I cannot do it. People like me cannot do it. We are not qualified, and so on. When we feel *isolated*, we fail to appreciate the interests we share with others, we are unable to access our common resources, we have no sense of a shared identity, and we feel powerless. We can counter self-doubt with *YCMAD: You Can Make A Difference.* The best way to inspire this belief is to frame what you do around *what people can do*, not what they cannot do. If you design a plan calling for each new volunteer to recruit 100 people, and you provide no leads, training, or coaching, you will only create deeper feelings of self-doubt. It is also important to recognize specific people for specific contributions at specific times and in specific ways. Recognition must be based on real accomplishment, however, not empty flattery. The idea is to spread accomplishment around and then recognize people for those accomplishments. There is no recognition without personal *accountability*. Requiring accountability does not show lack of trust, but is evidence that what one is doing really matters. Have you ever volunteered to walk a precinct in a campaign? You are given a packet with a voter list and told to mark the responses on the list and to bring it back when you are done. What happens if you go out for four hours, do a conscientious job, and return to headquarters ready to report, only to hear, "Oh, thanks a lot. Just throw it over there in the corner. See you next week." What about all your work? Did it not matter enough for anyone to debrief you about it, let alone mark it on a wall chart and try to learn from it? Do you think you will go back "next week?"

Telling Your Public Story

Storytelling is the discursive form through which we translate our values into the motivation to act. As shown in figure 18.4, a story is crafted of just three elements: *plot*, *character*, and *moral*. The effect depends on the *setting*: who tells the story, who listens, where they are, why they are there, and when.

Plot

A plot engages us, captures our interest, and makes us pay attention. "I got up this morning, had breakfast, and came to school." Is that a plot? Why? Why not?

How about the following: "I was having breakfast this morning when I heard a loud screeching coming from the roof. At that very moment, I looked outside to where my car was parked, but it was gone!" Now what is going on? What is the difference?

A story begins. An actor is moving toward a desired goal. Then some kind of challenge appears. The plan is suddenly up in the air. The actor must figure out what to do. This is when we get interested. We want to find out what happens.

Why do we care?

Figure 18.4. Elements of a Story

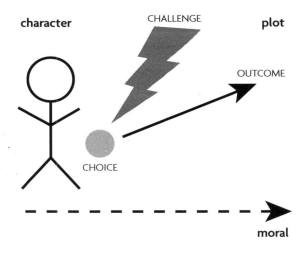

Narrative Structure

Source: Zac Willette and the author.

Dealing with the unexpected—small and large—defines the texture of our lives. No more tickets at the movie theater. You are about to lose your job. Our marriage is on the verge of break-up. We are constantly faced with the unexpected, and what we are going to do. What is the source of the greatest uncertainty around us? Other people. The subject of most stories is about how to interact with other people.

As human beings, we make choices in the present, based on remembering the past and imagining the future. This is what it means to be an *agent*. When we act out of habit, however, we do not choose; we just follow the routine. It is only when the routines break down, when the guidelines are unclear, when no one can tell us what to do, that we make real choices and become the creators of our own lives, communities, and futures. Then we become the agents of our own fate. These moments can be as frightening as they are exhilarating.

A plot consists of just three elements: a *challenge*, a *choice*, and an *outcome*. Attending to a plot is how we learn to deal with the unpredictable. Researchers report that most of the time that parents spend with their children is in storytelling—stories of the family, the child's stories, stories of the neighbors. Bruner (1986) describes this as *agency training*: the way we learn how to process choices in the face of uncertainty. Because our curiosity about the unexpected is infinite, we invest billions of dollars and countless hours in films, literature, and sports events, not to mention religious practices, cultural activities, and national celebrations.

Character

Although a story requires a plot, it works only if we can identify with a character. Through our empathetic identification with a protagonist, we experience the emotional content of the story. That is how we learn what the story has to teach our hearts, not only our heads. As Aristotle wrote of Greek tragedy in *The Poetics*, this is how the protagonist's experience can touch us and, perhaps, open our eyes. Arguments persuade with evidence, logic, and data. Stories persuade by this empathetic identification. Have you ever been to a movie where you could not identify with any of the characters? You found it boring. Sometimes we identify with protagonists who are only vaguely "like us"—like the road runner (if not the coyote) in the cartoons. Other times, we identify with protagonists who are very much like us—as in stories about friends, relatives, neighbors. Sometimes the protagonists of a story are *us,* as when we find ourselves in the midst of an unfolding story in which we are the authors of the outcome.

Moral

Stories teach. We have all heard the ending "and that is the moral of the story." Have you ever been at a party where someone starts telling a story and goes on … and on … and on … ? Someone may say (or want to say), "Get to the point!" We deploy stories to *make a point*, and to evoke a response.

The moral of a successful story is felt understanding, not simply conceptual understanding. When stated only conceptually, many a moral becomes a banality. We do not retell the story of David and Goliath because it teaches us how to vanquish giants. What the story teaches is that a "little guy"—with courage, resourcefulness, and imagination—can beat a "big guy," especially one with Goliath's arrogance. A fearful character, out of anger, acts courageously and emerges victorious. We feel David's fear, anger, and courage, and we feel *hopeful* for our own lives because he is victorious. Stories thus teach how to manage our emotions when challenged—how to be courageous, keep our cool, and trust our imagination— rather than the specific tactics to use in any one case.

Stories teach us how to act in the "right" way. They are not simply examples and illustrations. When stories are well told, we experience *the point*, and we feel hope. It is that experience, not the words as such, that can move us to action, because sometimes that is the point—we have to act.

Setting

Stories are told. They are not a disembodied string of words, images, and phrases. They are not messages, sound bites, or brands, although these rhetorical fragments may reference a story. Storytelling is fundamentally relational.

As we listen, we evaluate the story, and we find it more or less easy to enter, depending on the storyteller. Is it his or her story? We hear it one way. Is it the story of a friend, a colleague, or a family member? We hear it another way. Is it a story without time, place, or specificity? We step back. Is it a story we share, perhaps a Bible story? Perhaps we draw closer to one another. Storytelling is how we interact with each other about values—how we share experiences with each other, counsel each other, comfort each other, and inspire each other to action.

Public Narrative: Story of Self—Story of Us—Story of Now

Leadership, especially leadership on behalf of social change, often requires telling a new public story, or adapting an old one: a story of self, a story of us, and a story of now. As shown in figure 18.5, story of self communicates the values that move us to lead. A story of us communicates values shared by those whom you hope to motivate to join us. And a story of now communicates the urgent challenge to those values that demands action now. Participating in a social action not only often involves a rearticulating of one's story of self, us, and now, but also marks an entry into a world of uncertainty so daunting that access to sources of hope is essential. To illustrate, I'll draw examples from the first seven minutes of then Senator Barack Obama's speech to the Democratic National Convention in July 2004.

Figure 18.5. Self, Us, Now

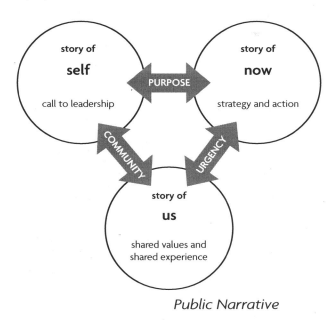

Public Narrative

Source: Zac Willette and the author.

Story of Self

Telling one's Story of Self is a way to share the values that define who you are—not as abstract principles, but as lived experience. We construct stories of self around *choice points*—moments when we faced a challenge, made a choice, experienced an outcome, and learned a moral. We communicate values that motivate us by selecting from among those choice points, and recounting what happened. Because storytelling is a social transaction, we engage our listener's memories as well as our own as we learn to adapt our story of self in response to feedback so the communication is successful. Similarly, like the response to the Yiddish riddle that asks who discovered water—"I don't know, but it wasn't a fish"—the other person often can "connect the dots" that we may not have connected because we are so within our own story that we have not learned to articulate them.

We construct our identity, in other words, as our story. What is utterly unique about each of is not a combination of the categories (race, gender, class, profession, and marital status) that include us, but rather, our journey, our way through life, our personal text from which each of us can teach (Hammack 2008).

A story is like a poem. A poem moves not by how long it is, nor by how eloquent or complicated. A story or poem moves by evoking an experience or moment through which we grasp the feeling or insight the poet communicates. Because we are gifted with episodic memory, based on our ability to visualize past experience, we can imagine ourselves in the scene described (Tulving 2002). The more specific the details we choose to recount, the more we can move our listeners, the more powerfully we can articulate our values, what moral philosopher Charles Taylor calls our "moral sources." (Taylor 1989, p. 91). Like a poem, a story can open a portal to the transcendent. Telling *about* a story is different from telling a story. When we tell a story, we enable the listener to enter its time and place with us, see what we see, hear what we hear, feel what we feel. An actor friend once told me the key was to speak entirely in the present tense and avoid using the word "and": I step into the room. It is dark. I hear a sound. Etc.

Some of us may think our personal stories don't matter, that others won't care or that we should not talk about ourselves so much. On the contrary, if we do public work we have a responsibility to give a public account of ourselves: where we came from, why we do what we do, and where we think we're going. In a role of public leadership, we really don't have a choice about telling our story of self. If we don't author our story, others will. And they may tell our story in ways that we may not like, not because they are malevolent, but because others try to make sense of who by drawing on their experience of people whom they consider to be like us. Aristotle argued that rhetoric has three components—*logos*, pathos, and *ethos*—and this is ethos. The logos is the logic of the argument. The pathos is the feeling the argument evokes. The ethos is the credibility of the person who makes the argument—his or her story of self.

Social movements are often the "crucibles" within which participants learn to tell new stories of self as we interact with other participants. Stories of self can be challenging because participation in social change is often prompted by a "prophetic" combination of criticality and hope. In personal terms, this means that most participants have stories of both the world's pain and the world's hope. And if we haven't talked about our stories of pain very much, it can take a while to learn to manage it. But if others try to make sense of why we are doing what we are doing and we leave this piece out, our account will lack authenticity, raising questions about the rest of the story.

In the early days of the women's movement, people participated in "consciousness raising" group conversations that mediated changes in their stories of self, who they were, as a woman. Stories of pain could be shared, but so could stories of hope (Polletta 2006). In the civil rights movement, blacks living in the Deep South who feared claiming the right to vote had to encourage one another to find the courage to make the claim, which, once made, began to alter how they thought of themselves and how they could interact with their children, as well as with white people, and each other. (Cuoto 1993).

In Senator Obama's "story of self," he recounts three key choice points: his grandfather's decision to send his son to America to study; his parents' "improbable" decision to marry; and his parents' decision to name him Barack ("blessing"), an expression of faith in a tolerant and generous America. He also references his grandfather's choice to enlist and serve in "Patton's army" and his grandmother's choice to "work on a bomber assembly line AND raise a family." Each choice communicates courage, hope, and caring. He tells us nothing of his resumé, preferring to introduce himself by telling us where he came from, and who made him the person that he is, so that we might have an idea of where he is going.

Story of Us

A public story is not only an account of the speaker's personal experience. All self stories are "nested," including fragments of other stories drawn from our culture, our faith, our parents, our friends, the movies we have seen, and the books we have read. Although individuals have their own stories, communities, movements, organizations, and nations weave collective stories out of distinct threads. Our individual threads intersected on the day that John F. Kennedy was assassinated or the day we saw the planes hit the Twin Towers. We shared a crisis, and we learned the morals about how we are to act and how life is to be lived. Points of intersection become the focus of a shared story—the way we link individual threads into a common weave. A Story of Us brings forward the values that move us as a community.

How does the storyteller become part of this larger story? Learning to tell a story of us requires deciding who the "us" is—which values shape that identity and which are most relevant to the situation at hand. Stories then not only teach us how to live, but also teach us how to distinguish who "we" are from "others," reducing uncertainty about what to expect from our community. In the midst of treacherous weather, earthquakes, disease, and other environmental sources of great unpredictability, the behavior, actions, and reactions of the people among whom we live, and our shared stock of stories, give us greater safety.

Our cultures are repositories of stories. Community stories about challenges we have faced, why we stood up to them—our values and our shared goals—and how we overcame them are woven throughout our political beliefs and religious traditions. We tell community stories again and again as folk sayings, popular songs, religious rituals, and community celebrations (for example, Easter, Passover, and the 4th of July). Just like individual stories, collective stories can inspire hope or generate despair. We also weave new stories from old ones. The Exodus story, for example, served the Puritans when they colonized North America, but it also served Southern blacks claiming their civil rights in the freedom movement (MacIntyre 2001).

Organizations that lack a "story" lack an identity, a culture, core values that can be articulated and drawn on to motivate. Leaders learn to tell the story of us—the story of their organization—by identifying the "choice points" of the organization's journey, recounting experiences that communicate the values embedded in the work of the organization.

As figure 18.5 shows, our stories of self overlap with our stories of us. We participate in many us's: family, community, faith, organization, profession, nation, or movement. A story of us expresses the values, the experiences, shared by the us we hope to evoke at the time. A story of "us" not only articulates the values of our community, but also can distinguish our community from another, thus reducing uncertainty about what to expect from those with whom we interact. Social scientists often describe a "story of us" as a collective identity (Somers 1992, 1994).

For a collection of people to become an "us" requires a storyteller, an interpreter of shared experience. In a workplace, for example, people who work beside one another but interact little, don't linger after work, don't arrive early, and don't eat together never develop a story of us. In a social movement, the interpretation of the movement's new experience is a critical leadership function. And, like the story of self, it is built from the choice points—the founding, the choices made, the challenges faced, the outcomes, and the lessons it learned.

In Senator Obama's speech, he moves into his "story of us" when he declares, "My story is part of the American story," and proceeds to list values he shares with his listeners—the people in the room, the people watching on television, the people who will read about it the next day. And he begins by going back to the beginning, to choices made by the founders to begin this nation, a beginning that he locates in the Declaration of Independence—a repository of the value of equality.

Story of Now

Stories of Now articulate the challenges we face now, the choices we are called upon to make, and the meaning of making the right choice. Stories of Now are set in the past, present, and future. The challenge is now; we are called on to act because of our legacy and who we have become, and the action that we take now can shape our desired future.

These are stories in which we are the protagonists. We face a crisis, a challenge. It is our choice to make. We have a story of hope, if we make the right choice. The storyteller among us whom we have authorized to "narrativize" this moment finds a way to articulate our crisis and challenge as a choice, reminds us of our moral resources (our stories—stories of our family, our community, our culture, and our faith), and offers a hopeful vision we can share as we take our first steps on the journey.

A story of now articulates an urgent challenge—or threat—to the values that we share that demands action now. What choice must we make? What is at risk? And where's the hope? In a story of now, we are the protagonists and it is our choices that shape the outcome. We draw on our "moral sources" to find the courage, hope, empathy perhaps to respond. A most powerful articulation of a story of now was Dr. Martin Luther King's speech delivered in Washington, D.C., on August 23, 1963, often recalled as the "I Have a Dream" speech. People often forget that what preceded the dream was a nightmare: the consequence of white America's failure to make good on its promissory note to African Americans. King argued the moment was possessed of the "fierce urgency of now" because this debt could no longer be postponed (King 1963). If we did not act, the nightmare would only grow worse—for all of us—never to become the dream.

In a story of now, story and strategy overlap because a key element in hope is a strategy—a credible vision of *how to get from here to there*. The "choice" offered cannot be something such as "we must all choose to be better people" or "we must all choose to do any one of this list of 53 things" (which makes each of them trivial). A meaningful choice is more like "we all must all choose: Do we commit to boycotting the busses until they desegregate or not?" Hope is specific, not abstract. What's the vision? When God inspires the Israelites in Exodus, he doesn't offer a vague hope of "better days," but describes a land "flowing with milk and honey" (Exodus 3:9) and what must be done to get there. A vision of hope can unfold a chapter at a time. It can begin by getting that number of people to show up at a meeting that you committed to do. You can win a "small" victory that shows change is possible. A small victory can become a source of hope if it is *interpreted* as part of a greater vision. In churches, when people have a "new story" to tell about themselves, it is often in the form of "testimony"—a person sharing an account of moving from despair to hope, the significance of the experience strengthened by the telling of it. Hope is not to be found in lying about the facts, but in the *meaning* we give to the facts. Shakespeare's "King Henry V" stirs hope in his men's hearts by offering them a different view of themselves. No longer are they a few bedraggled soldiers led by a young and inexperienced king in an obscure corner of France who is about to be wiped out by an overwhelming force. Now they are a "happy few," united with their king in solidarity, holding an opportunity to grasp immortality in their hands, to become legends in their own time—a legacy for their children and grand children (Shakespeare, Henry V, Act IV, Scene 3). This is their time! The story of now is that moment in which story (why) and strategy (how) overlap and in which, as poet Seamus Heaney (1991) writes, "Justice can rise up, and hope and history rhyme." And for the claim to be credible, the action must begin right here, right now, in this room, with action each one of us can take. It's the story of a credible strategy, with an account of how, starting with who and where we are, and how we can, step-by-step, get to where we want to go. Our action can call forth the actions of others, and their actions can call others, and together these actions can carry the day. It's like Pete Seeger's old protest song, "One Man's Hands," which reminds us that the targets of social change— from prison walls to unaccountable governments—cannot fall at the hands of any one person, but rather require the concerted hands of a collectivity.

Senator Obama moves to his "story of now" with the phrase, "There is more work left to do." After we have shared in the experience of values we identify with America at its best, he confronts us with the fact that they are not realized in practice. He then tells stories of specific people in specific places with specific problems. As we identify with each of them, our empathy reminds us of pain we have felt in our own lives. But, he also reminds us, all this could change. And we know it could change. And it could change because we have a way to make the change, if we choose to take it. And that way is to support the election of Senator John Kerry. Although that last part didn't work out, the point is that he concluded his story of now with a very specific choice he calls upon us to make.

Through public narrative, leaders—and participants—can move to action by mobilizing sources of motivation, constructing new shared individual and collective identities, and finding the courage to act.

Celebrations

We do much of our storytelling in celebrations. A celebration is not a party. It is a way that members of a community come together to honor who they are, what they have done, and where they are going—often symbolically. Celebrations may occur at times of sadness, as well as times of great joy. Celebrations provide rituals that allow us to join in enacting a vision of our community—at least in our hearts. Institutions that retain their vitality are rich in celebrations. In the Church, for example, Mass is "celebrated." Harvard's annual celebration is called Graduation and lasts an entire week.

Storytelling is at its most powerful at beginnings—for individuals, their childhood; for groups, their formation; for movements, their launching; and for nations, their founding. Celebrations are a way we interpret important events, recognize important contributions, acknowledge a common identity, and deepen our sense of community. The way that we interpret these moments begins to establish norms, create expectations, and shape patterns of behavior, which then influence all subsequent development. We draw on them again and again. Nations institutionalize their founding story as a renewable source of guidance and inspiration. Most faith traditions enact a weekly retelling of their story of redemption, usually rooted in their founding. Well-told stories help turn moments of great crises into moments of "new beginnings."

Conclusion

Narrative allows us to communicate the emotional content of our values. Narrative is not talking "about" values; rather, narrative embodies and communicates those values. It is through the shared experience of our values that we can engage with others; motivate one another to act; and find the courage to take risks, explore possibility, and face the challenges we must face. Public narrative, understood as a leadership art, is thus an invaluable resource to stem the tides of apathy, alienation, cynicism, and defeatism. Stories, strategically told, can powerfully rouse a sense of urgency; hope; anger; solidarity; and the belief that individuals, acting in concert, can make a difference.

Note

1. As noted by Pirkei Avot in *Sayings of the Jewish Fathers* (also translated as "Ethics of the Fathers"). See http://www.sacred-texts.com/jud/sjf/, which is a translation from 1897 by Charles Taylor.

References

Alinsky, Saul. 1971. *Rules for Radicals*. New York: Random House.

Bruner, Jerome. 1986. "Two Modes of Thought." In *Actual Minds, Possible Worlds*, 11–25. Cambridge, MA: Harvard University Press.

Cuoto, Richard A. 1993. "Narrative, Free Space, and Political Leadership in Social Movements." *Journal of Politics* 55 (1): 57–79.

Gamson, William A. 1992. *Talking Politics*. New York: Cambridge University Press.

Hammack, Phillip L. 2008. "Narrative and the Cultural Psychology of Identity." *Personality and Social Psychology Review* 12 (3): 222–47.

Heaney, Seamus. 1991. *The Cure at Troy: A Version of Sophocles' Philoctetes*. New York: Farrar, Straus, and Giroux.

Hebrew Bible. 1 Samuel 17:4–49 (King James Version).

King, Martin Luther, Jr. "I Have a Dream" (speech, Washington, DC, August 28, 1963).

MacIntyre, Alasdair. 2001. "The Virtues, the Unity of a Human Life, and the Concept of a Tradition." In *Memory, Identity, Community: The Idea of Narrative in the Human Sciences*, ed. Lewis P. Hinchman and Sandra K. Hinchman, 241–63. Albany, NY: State University of New York Press.

Marcus, George E. 2002. *The Sentimental Citizen: Emotion in Democratic Politics*. University Park, PA: Penn State University Press.

Nussbaum, Martha. 2001. *Upheavals of Thought: The Intelligence of Emotions*. New York: Cambridge University Press.

Polletta, Francesca. 2006. "Ways of Knowing and Stories Worth Telling." In *It Was Like a Fever: Storytelling in Protest and Politics*, 109–140. Chicago: University of Chicago Press.

Scott, James C. 1976. *The Moral Economy of the Peasant*. New Haven, CT: Yale University Press.

Seligman, Martin E. P., and Mihaly Csikszentmihali. 2000. "Positive Psychology: An Introduction." *American Psychologist* 55 (1): 5–14.

Shakespeare, William. *Henry V*, Act IV, Scene 3.

Somers, Margaret. 1992. "Narrativity, Narrative Identity, and Social Action: Rethinking English Working-Class Formation." *Social Science History* 16 (4): 591–629.

———. 1994. "The Narrative Constitution of Identity: A Relational and Network Approach." *Theory and Society* 23 (5): 605–49.

St. Augustine. 1991. *Confessions*. Book 8. Translated by Henry Chadwick. New York: Oxford University Press.

Taylor, Charles. 1989. *Sources of the Self: The Making of the Modern Identity*. Cambridge, MA: Harvard University Press.

Tulving, Endel. 2002. "Episodic Memory: From Mind to Brain." *Annual Review of Psychology* 53 (2002): 1–25.

West, Cornel. 1994. *Race Matters*. New York: Vintage Books.

"Social Accountability" as Public Work

Peter Levine

"Social accountability" means a set of concrete experiments in which ordinary people—including very poor people in developing countries—assess their own governments' performance. These experiments are part of a broader effort to enhance economic and social development by strengthening civil society and civic engagement. Here I argue that civic engagement should be an integral part of development. Ordinary people have a right to participate in deliberations about development goals and to contribute their own energies and talents. It is less clear that social accountability processes will enhance governments' efficiency, which is their stated purpose. Often the argument for social accountability seems to be that the state ought to deliver services fairly and efficiently, and civil society has a useful role in monitoring the state's performance. I propose an alternative argument. Citizens (members of a community) should work in various ways to define and address common problems and create public goods. Some citizens happen to work for the state, some belong to voluntary associations, and some are unaffiliated. They all owe a measure of accountability to one another. The moment at which the state is held accountable to a voluntary civic association is most useful if it takes place within a much richer context of collaboration and public work that blurs the lines between state and society and develops the civic skills of everyone, including the youngest generation.

Background

Since the 1980s, scholars have paid renewed attention to civil society: that is, voluntary associations and the norms of cooperation and trust that accompany them. It was civil society in the form of dissident groups, churches, and unions that defeated Leninist states in Russia and Eastern Europe. It was also within civil society that the Women's Movement and other powerful social forces arose in the West and achieved major victories. Meanwhile, the *quality* of civil society in a nation or a neighborhood seems correlated with its economic well-being, political resiliency, and even the quality of its schools.[1] A large body of literature, including influential works by James Coleman in sociology, Robert Putnam in political science, James C. Scott in anthropology, and Jean Cohen, Andrew Arato, and Joshua Cohen in political theory, has drawn attention to the importance of civil society and the public's role in a democracy. Some of this research is empirical, finding links between civic engagement and various social outcomes, such as peace and prosperity. Some of the research is normative or philosophical, arguing that people have the right to participate or that political legitimacy depends on participation (regardless of the outcomes).

The members of the World Bank are "countries," which really means governments. Governments provide the Bank's funds and receive its direct loans. However, the World Bank has recognized the importance of civil society since the 1990s. Its publications acknowledge the value of organized and serious efforts to include citizens in the planning, implementation, monitoring, and evaluation of development work. "Citizenship" is defined in the *2007 World Development Report* as membership in a community, which brings obligations of active participation (World Bank 2007, 160). In this and other Bank documents, active citizenship is described as a path to greater equity, less inefficiency and corruption, less conflict, and therefore more effective and durable policies. The idea is that citizens who participate will be more diverse and representative than government officials are, and their interests will be better aligned with the stated goals of development (because they need good services and they cannot profit en masse from corruption). Also, citizens who have been consulted about policies and programs may be more likely to support them and less likely to undermine them. These are basically instrumental reasons for civic engagement: Engagement is seen as a means to other goods.

The Bank's Participation and Civic Engagement group categorizes its work under four headings. The phrase "Enabling Environment for Civic Engagement" means the conditions that will allow nongovernmental organizations (NGOs) and associations to help with development. "Participatory Monitoring and Evaluation" means helping the recipients of development projects to participate in assessing them. The Bank states that this means treating recipients not only as sources of information (such as by interviewing or surveying them), but also as active participants who can advocate their own values and interests. "Participation at Project, Program & Policy Level" means involving "stakeholders" in setting priorities for development, which may not only make the priorities fairer, but also increase the odds that policies will be sustainable because they have durable public support.

The category that I address in this chapter is "social accountability," which John M. Ackerman defines as follows. In general, he writes, "accountability" means a "pro-active process by which public officials inform about and justify their plans of action, their behavior and results and are sanctioned accordingly" (Ackerman 2005, 1). In other words, when there is accountability, true and important information about the performance of the government is disclosed in ways that have consequences (rewards or punishments) for government officials. Social accountability is a particular way to achieve accountability. It relies not on bureaucratic or legal checks, nor on market mechanisms, but "on civic engagement." "It is ordinary citizens and/or civil society organizations who participate directly or indirectly in exacting accountability" (Ackerman 2005, 9, quoting World Bank).

Mechanisms for social accountability vary widely, but the Bank cites several illustrative cases. In Uganda, the government provides detailed information about how it actually spends its education funds, disseminating the data by radio and newspaper. At the same time, control over education has been somewhat decentralized. Armed with detailed information, citizens are able to demand efficient performance from their local schools. In more than 100 Brazilian cities, the municipal government empowers large, basically voluntary citizens' councils to allocate a proportion of the municipal budget through a process called participatory budgeting (PB). And in Rajasthan (India), an NGO began demanding public records and holding informal public hearings to uncover waste and corruption (World Bank 2004).

The Link between Civic Engagement and Human Development

In emphasizing civil society and social capital, the Bank and other development agencies have recognized that countries and communities with high levels of membership in voluntary, not-for-profit associations are also highly developed; they have long life expectancies, high literacy, high wealth per capita, and effective institutions. However, this correlation does not provide a causal theory, let alone a justification for social accountability. In fact, several causal hypotheses have been advanced, including the following (which are not mutually exclusive):

- Economic and social development enhances civic engagement because people who have wealth and education can join groups.
- Civic engagement engenders social capital (trust and networks of cooperation), which enhances economic and social development.

- Civic engagement directly enhances human development (especially health and longevity), because socializing is psychologically rewarding and satisfying.
- Civic engagement improves the performance of government, which leads to economic and social development. This theory seems implicit in the Bank's embrace of social accountability.

This is not the place to weigh those hypotheses. It is, however, useful to disaggregate "civil society" into separate institutions and human behaviors or attitudes. Various aspects of civil society bear different statistical relationships to human development, which is itself a complex amalgam of goods, including wealth, health, literacy, equality, security, freedom, and longevity.

Thus, for example, there is a rather clear and positive correlation between voter turnout by country and the United Nations Development Programme's Human Development Index (figure 19.1).

Although this correlation does not reveal a causal mechanism, we can see that the more developed societies are also democracies in which many people participate by means of a simple but important mechanism: the franchise. Graphs for frequency of signing petitions, participating in boycotts, and participating in demonstrations (using data from the World Values Survey) look basically similar to figure 19.1 of voting and human development.

Figure 19.1. Human Development and Voting

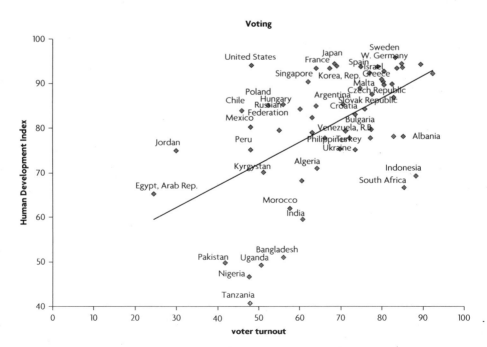

Source: Voter turnout from International Institute for Democracy and Electoral Assistance, averaging over all elections since 1945.

On the other hand, the relationship between the Human Development Index and taking "local community action on issues like poverty, employment, housing, racial equality" is weak but negative (figure 19.2).

The graph for doing "unpaid work for a political party or group" looks similar to figure 19.2. It may be that poor people resort to direct, voluntary action at the local level to compensate for the failure of larger institutions. Note that being involved in one of the social accountability programs cited by the World Bank would be an example of "local community action on issues like poverty, employment, housing, racial equality." Such work is more likely in less developed countries, although that certainly does not mean that local participation *lowers* economic development.

Finally, socializing in organized groups does not seem to have any statistical relationship to human development. Clusters of highly developed and rather poor countries can be identified that show intense participation in social groups. The countries with weak participation in such groups range from poor to rich (figure 19.3).

Taken together, these graphs suggest that expressions of political voice are most closely associated with human development. Membership in voluntary associations is uncorrelated with development. Local political participation has a negative statistical relationship with development, probably because poor people and people who live with ineffective governments must rely on direct action.

Figure 19.2. Local Community Action on Issues Such as Poverty and Employment Housing

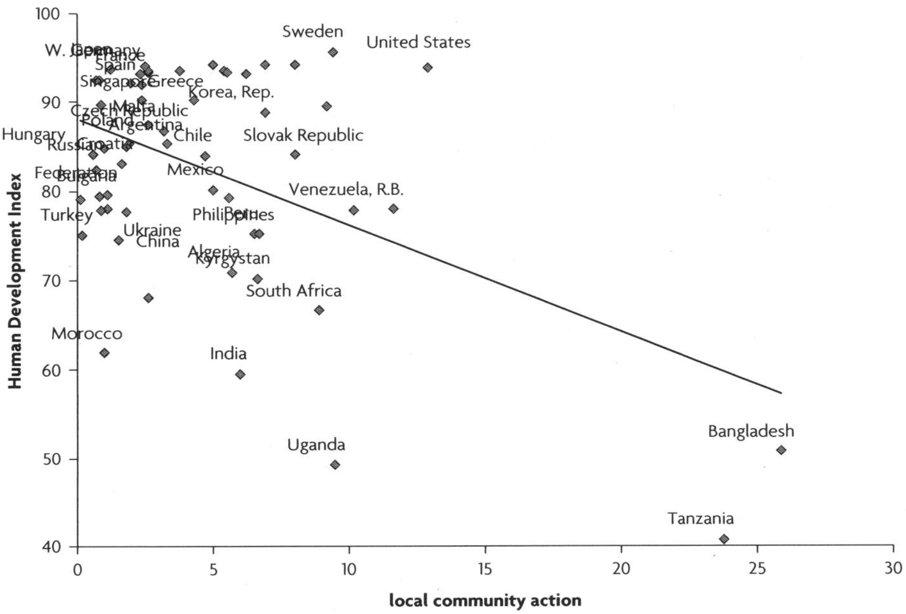

Source: World Values Survey, 1999–2004 wave.

Figure 19.3. Spending Time Every Week with People at Sporting, Cultural, or Communal Events

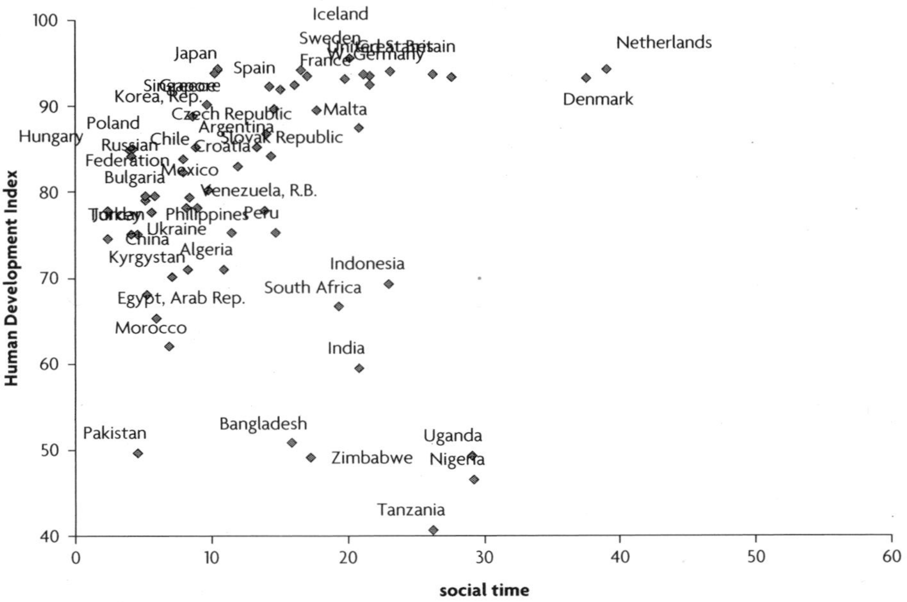

Source: World Values Survey.

Figures 19.1 through 19.3 presume that we have an objective measure of social development (that is, a social welfare function). If this is the case, then we may assess the efficiency or effectiveness of various institutions—specific governments, civil society associations, and markets—by measuring how they affect development. It is an empirical question whether citizens have a useful role to play in governance, either as individuals or through various kinds of organized processes.

However, many philosophers doubt that a social welfare function can be derived from abstract and general principles. Life presents us with numerous values that conflict. Some of these values (such as freedom) cannot be monetized or otherwise compared to other values on a common metric. Therefore, it is necessary to deliberate about what a society should value most.

Deliberation *could* involve only a small number of people, such as a legislature. Indeed, legislatures are sites of intensive discussion and bargaining among especially informed participants. However, the broader public should also discuss issues and express its views. Otherwise, the range of opinions will inevitably be too narrow, and the interests of the parliament and the population will diverge. Besides, voters cannot select representatives unless they already hold explicit, self-conscious preferences for policies. They are unlikely to hold such preferences until they engage in some measure of discussion. Finally, a formal deliberative body such as a parliament must make binding decisions that reflect only the values of the majority, and it can permit only a narrow range of participatory styles from its members. Even a unanimous vote in a legislature often obscures compromises and exclusions. In contrast, civil society is pluralist: It encompasses many separate communities and associations that can reach different conclusions about values and that can allow people to engage in various ways. In some associations, members deliberate and vote; in others, they sew quietly—but both types of groups shape public goods and values.

If this pluralist/deliberative account is right, then it is not ultimately satisfactory to ask whether people need to participate to make governments efficient at generating social welfare, as measured by something such as gross national product per capita or the Human Development Index. Instead, people have a right to determine the outcomes that governments must then pursue. As Amartya Sen writes, the connections between democratic participation and social development "are not only instrumental … but also constructive. Our conceptualization of economic needs depends crucially on open public debates and discussions" (Sen 1999, 147–48).

This argument supports what the World Bank calls "Participation at Project, Program & Policy Level." Members of a community ought to decide on its goals. All the figures presented earlier are irrelevant, because human development (shown on the y axis) cannot even be *defined* legitimately without public participation.

Often citizens are at their most impressive when they deliberate about values. Their perspectives and diverse values are assets in that kind of conversation. Citizens are sometimes less impressive when they try to assess implementation, which can be a highly complex business. Heidi Gantwerk, who designs and runs processes for public participation in the United States and Canada, says that officials and experts can easily "poke holes" in citizens' reports when the topics are technical, but they are impressed by citizens' deliberations about values and goals.[2]

Perhaps it makes the most sense to involve citizens in the evaluation and assessment of governments' performance when the same citizens have already helped to set public priorities, values, and goals. It means little to select goals if administrators then waste or steal money or distort the purpose of state programs through subtle decisions at the implementation phase. At a meeting in Porto Alegre in 2004, Jose Benedito de Oliveira said:

> At the current time, there is no monitoring and control by the citizens [after Participatory Budgeting establishes budgets]. Even if monitoring processes were enhanced, the people are still not part of the implementation processes of the projects that they have demanded to be prioritized. Moreover, PB councils have not yet received any financial statements on the budgets for the implementation of the projects prioritized through the PB. The only information they as citizens get is the official newspaper that lists down all the projects prioritized from the PB processes for the fiscal year of the government, with estimated

amounts of the costs of each project are. But the order in which these projects are implemented, if at all, is a decision for the city government to make, independently of the citizens themselves. Therefore it is important to ask what decisions are really deliberated on by the citizens at different points in the PB process, and at different points in carrying out and implementing these citizen decisions.[3]

De Oliveira has observed that decisions about values and goals arise in the course of administration, not only at the planning phase. Therefore, citizens must continue to participate in the setting of values while policies are implemented.

Tying Accountability to "Public Work"

At this point, I would suggest two ways to think about social accountability. One way begins with the state, which governs by making and implementing authoritative decisions. If the society is democratic, the public

a. Learns what the government is doing
b. Discusses
c. Makes its own authoritative decisions, mainly by voting.

Social accountability enhances all three of the above, by

a. Providing more and better information, through new channels
b. Creating forums for discussion
c. Giving people new authoritative decisions to make.

The World Bank is most comfortable with this model. The Bank has traditionally distinguished politics from administration and has understood its role as primarily administrative or technical. Governments have more legitimacy to make political decisions. "Accountability" means forcing governments to keep their promises. "Social accountability" means using public participation to do this.

At the heart of the social accountability experiments endorsed by the Bank is the flow of information from governments to citizens. Participants in these experiments are like jurors: They learn what is actually going on inside the state and make judgments that have consequences. In the case of PB in Brazil, the best analogy may be legislatures rather than juries, for participants in PB (acting rather like legislators) allocate resources after deliberating.

A different way to think about social accountability is to start with the public. In a democratic society, the public defines problems and works to address them. "Work" means creating public goods: facilities, services, and culture. The "public" means individuals, NGOs, networks, the press, and people who happen to work for the state. In this model, "social accountability" is not from the state to the citizen, but ideally by everyone to everyone.

We can illustrate this distinction by considering two examples that exemplify, respectively, social accountability as a governance process and social accountability as "public work" (Boyte and Kari 1996). First, Samuel Paul (chapter 23 of this volume) describes how NGOs in Bangalore—deeply dissatisfied with the quality of government services—surveyed representative samples of citizens to develop "report cards" for municipal agencies. When the press publicized the results, and some government officials chose to cooperate, the NGOs were able to press the agencies to improve the quality of services. This example started in the nongovernmental sector, but it is possible for a state agency to take the initiative and create a participatory process to reduce public-sector waste and corruption or enhance public satisfaction. As Archon Fung writes, "Through organized public deliberation, citizens can collectively examine the actions and policies of officials, assess the alignment of this state behavior with their own wishes and values, and attempt to bring the two into conformity" (Fung 2003, 350).

In contrast, Lily Tsai (chapter 20 of this volume) describes Chinese village temple community councils that organize religious and communal activities: "Villagers have clear obligations to contribute to and participate in these activities because these collective activities represent group tributes to the village's guardian deities." In short, these groups directly produce public goods through their own hands-on work. Local governmental officials are discouraged from leading the councils, which are religious bodies, "but as ordinary members of the temple group, they diligently fulfill their obligations to contribute to the good of the group." In such associations, members are expected to help in whatever ways they can, and government officials (as members) may assist by leveraging state resources or appealing in their professional capacities to higher agencies. Tsai describes government officials involved in a lineage group (not a temple society) who "used their personal connections with higher-level officials to secure a bank loan" for the group.

Table 19.1 elaborates some differences between these examples. There are valid arguments for both approaches, under appropriate circumstances. As Tsai notes, the "embedded" and "encompassing" forms of participation may be hard to expand to large scale, may be biased toward members of homogeneous groups, and may fail to address systematic failures by the government. Nevertheless, I am generally more optimistic about the public work approach. I believe it has a more plausible account of how to motivate citizens, how to share power, and how to recruit and prepare the next generation.

Motivating Citizens

It seems unlikely that large and representative groups of citizens will consistently volunteer to act like jurors or legislators. Accountability creates a public good (efficient government), but time and effort are private goods. Usually, when people must give up private goods to generate public goods, there is weak participation. Voting presents the same dilemma—in countries where it is voluntary—but voting is quick and easy compared to conducting a social

Table 19.1. Two Models of Social Accountability

	Social accountability as a governance process	Social accountability as part of "public work"
Example	Citizen Report Cards in Bangalore (Paul)	Chinese temple Community Council (Tsai)
Major analogy	Citizens as legislators, jurors, or auditors	Citizens as voluntary workers
Nature of power	Zero-sum: more for citizens means less for the state, thus power must be granted by, or seized from, the state.	Potentially expandable: by working together, citizens create greater capacity.
Intended outcomes	Better policy (more fair and efficient, less corrupt)	Creating public goods
State and civil society	Two sectors that exchange information and negotiate	Lines are blurred: government employees are seen as citizens
Options when problems are uncovered	Legal remedies (lawsuits, calling the police), public disclosure, and shaming	Legal remedies and public disclosure, private suasion and shaming, direct voluntary action to remedy the problem
Accountability	By government, to citizens	In principle, by everyone to everyone
Recruitment	Representative sample of citizens recruited by a government or NGO for the task of monitoring government	Members of an association take on a voluntary task and develop the next generation of active members
Preconditions	Legal rights of assembly and expression, formal system for accountability	Legal rights of assembly and expression, active voluntary associations
Who chooses/frames/defines the problems to be discussed?	Whoever creates the process (usually the problem is inefficiency or corruption in the state sector)	Members of the community

Source: Author.

audit or producing a citizen report card, which require not only time and effort, but also learning and experience. Most real juries are compulsory; most real legislators are paid for their services. These incentives address collective-action problems and produce *reasonably* representative bodies. If social accountability processes are voluntary and unpaid, there is a serious risk that the few who participate will seek private goods for themselves: corrupt or clientalistic benefits from the state. One solution would be to pay or otherwise reward a broad sample of the population to participate. It is not clear, however, that such policies would be sustainable or could avoid their own forms of corruption.

Yet we know that people will work on problems. Even when very poor, they voluntarily contribute immense amounts of time, energy, and money to civil society.[4] They choose to build institutions and associations, maintain facilities, teach and coach the young, serve the needy, and create free performances and works of art. These activities are not analogous to jury service, which is all about information and judgment. They are much closer to *work,* albeit work that is voluntary, unpaid, and relatively satisfying.

Perhaps creative, collaborative, voluntary work attracts some people because of its intrinsic, expressive, and social benefits. We could interpret people's willingness to participate in certain forms of social accountability in the same way. For example, Community Scorecards in Malawi allow villagers to "judge the performance of their local health center" and offer "suggestions for improvement" (World Bank 2004, 13). This does not sound like a mere matter of assessing the performance of a state institution. It sounds more like an effort to improve health in the community in partnership with a local institution. I can easily imagine that devising and implementing the Scorecard also led residents to change their personal behavior and support the clinic with time or goods.

Likewise, Brazilians involved in PB can be seen not merely as holding the government accountable, but as working to build schools, paved roads, clinics, and other facilities in their communities. Assessment of state action is just a moment in a bigger process. Gianpaolo Baiocchi observes that the meetings officially devoted to Orçamento Particapativo (OP)—the name for PB in Porto Alegre—are also opportunities for "broad discussion of community affairs, and much of the agenda is usually filled with discussion of mundane items such as broken pipes, rude bus drivers, and problems at the public health clinic" (Baiocchi 2005, 2). It would be surprising if those discussions never led to direct action such as fixing pipes, chiding bus drivers, and creating associations to work with the clinic. Baiocchi (2005, 56) finds: "The greatest impact of [PB] in Nordeste [a district in Porto Alegre] has been the explosion of new neighborhood associations. Most community activists in the district today trace their history in community involvement to the OP" (56). Even participants, such as Ana, who participate only in the OP forums and not in any other civic associations, gain a "sense of the 'public' … from having worked collectively to make decisions throughout the year and from developing a sense of belonging to a community of others with similar needs or problems" (Baiocchi 2005, 103).

Social accountability processes should not be separated from other opportunities for "public work." States should encourage citizens to teach and serve others and build and maintain public facilities. Social accountability processes should not be seen (or advertised) simply as opportunities to review the performance of the state, but also as chances to build things, solve problems, and improve services.

Locus of Power

I have argued that social accountability is more motivating when understood as a form of public work, not as a technique for governance. A second reason to favor the former theory is its more realistic understanding of how state and civil society are related.

Implicit in some of the literature on social accountability is a clear distinction between the government and citizens. The government administers; citizens review or evaluate. The government employs officials and experts; citizens give time as volunteers or amateurs. This distinction can be overdrawn. Government officials are also citizens and should be encouraged to see themselves as such. Citizens may have expertise; in fact, all human beings are experts at least about the condition of their own lives. Most issues are addressed simultaneously by the state and other institutions. The discussions that occur within political bodies and bureaucracies are influenced by broader conversations; private associations often receive state funds. Baiocchi (2005, 57) notes (and celebrates) "the blurring of lines between the OP and civil society."

Thus, it may be better to say that communities work on issues, and roles exist for the state, private associations, and citizens (some of whom happen to work for the government). Everyone owes some measure of accountability to everyone else, and everyone's work is welcome and potentially important. Mechanisms for social accountability, such as citizens' report cards and public expenditure tracking surveys, are just part of the community's overall work.

Even when the lines between state and civil society are "blurred," power is concentrated somewhere. Some social accountability processes are launched by a law or by a state policy. Others bubble up from grassroots organizations. Some processes have substantial, formal powers. Some have limited official powers, such as the right to allocate a small proportion of the municipal budget (as in PB). Some have only the power of persuasion and publicity.

These differences surely matter. When a process originates from a state decision (as in Porto Alegre, where the Workers' Party municipal government launched PB), decision makers can design it to serve their interests and can choose to end it. On the other hand, because a tangible link to the government is present, citizens' discussions are likely to have some impact on policy. When a process is created by grassroots organizations, the process is independent and is more difficult for the state to manipulate. However, grassroots organizations may or may not be representative of various sectors of the community, and they may or may not be able to sustain their efforts or influence policy.

When a process lacks formal authority, it is not as important that the participants represent the broader community. Even if they are completely self-selected, their discussions of issues and policies can be powerful means to build social capital.[5] However, once a citizen body begins to act like a jury or legislature, the balance of votes has a tangible effect on budgets and policies. Then the state and interest groups have incentives to pack the body with their own followers (Coehlo, Pozzoni, and Montoya 2005, 179–80). Under these conditions, a voluntary system for drawing participants may not generate representative samples, and one should consider such mechanisms as random selection. To select participants randomly, however, requires money. It may even be necessary to *compel* service to ensure high response rates (as with juries). Then the process becomes dependent on governments or other major institutions, which can manipulate it or cancel it when it generates results they dislike.

No recipe may be found for a process that is independent, representative, influential, sustainable, and immune to external influence. It is still important to think clearly about these goals and how they trade off. I suspect that any process will work better if it occurs in a community where diverse members have constructive opportunities to participate in other ways too: exchanging ideas about problems and goals and contributing their own energy and resources (see Biaocchi 2005, 147).

Youth Civic Development

Any effort to encourage broad and constructive civic engagement requires deliberate attention to young people, for several reasons.

First, how we treat youth has a lifelong effect on their attitudes and behaviors, thereby affecting governance and civil society for decades to come.[6] In the words of the *World Development Report,* "Patterns of behavior endure: political participation in adulthood is largely determined by participation in youth" (Word Bank 2007, 164). Sears and Levy (2003, 82) define "the impressionable years" as the "period up to one's late twenties, roughly." During these years, some people develop lifelong identities as active, responsible, ethical participants. Others become lastingly alienated or apathetic. Many factors have been identified that can change these outcomes in adolescence: for instance, the availability of youth clubs and associations, youth voice in schools, and recruitment by political parties. On the other hand, hardly any experiences have been found to change the civic identities of adults over 30.[7]

The most likely explanation is cognitive dissonance. When you are a child, you need not have any stance toward the world of politics, government, current events, and activism. Once you enter adolescence and become aware of this world, you must form opinions about it—and about your place in it. These opinions depend in part on what opportunities you have to engage in politics and civic life as an adolescent. If you are encouraged to participate and you find it satisfying, you may develop an identity as an active, engaged, confident, responsible citizen. If you are excluded from political and civic life or treated badly therein, you may develop an identity as alienated, hostile, or passive. Once you have formed your identity as a citizen, it would require energy and effort—and cause psychological discomfort—to reevaluate. Thus, people tend to remain "dyed in the wool" as citizens, except when massive political changes occur and force them to reconsider.

This means that we should be very careful to provide positive experiences of civic participation to our adolescents. Young people also have somewhat different interests than older people. They are directly affected by education policy, for example, whereas retirement is much farther off. Fair social accountability processes thus require active participation by youth. This is especially important given the age distribution in many developed countries.

Including young people in civic activities requires skill and care. Merely opening the doors to youth may not draw many of them and may not allow them to participate effectively in complex processes such as PB or public expenditure tracking. Deliberations tend to be dominated by the most articulate, experienced, and informed participants and the ones with highest status (Sanders 1997). Youth often have the lowest status and least knowledge and experience. Just as it requires deliberate efforts to include agricultural laborers, indigenous people, racial minorities, and women in grassroots democracy, so incorporating youth voices may require deliberate steps such as holding separate discussions for youth only, creating logical pathways for young people that begin with voluntary service and end with leadership roles, reserving seats for youth, or teaching about civic participation in schools and other formal educational settings.[8] People between the ages of 9 and 15 play a structured role in PB in Barra Mansa, Rio de Janeiro (World Bank 2007, 170).

Developmental psychologists now argue that allowing young people to engage constructively in social and civil affairs is not only good for civil society, but also good for adolescents. Those who have constructive civic roles are more motivated, learn more, and conform better to healthy social norms than their peers who have no such opportunities. This thesis—sometimes called "positive youth development"—has been vindicated in numerous longitudinal studies and some controlled experiments (Eccles and Gootman 2002; Lerner 2004; Levine 2007). It suggests that including young people in social accountability might be an effective way to improve their health, welfare, and human capital, while also making governance more democratic and efficient. Everything would depend, however, on how well young people were incorporated.

Notes

1. For example, Robert D. Putnam shows that the level of adult participation in communities correlates powerfully with high school graduation rates, test scores, and other indicators of educational success at the state level: "States where citizens meet, join, vote, and trust in unusual measure boast consistently higher educational performance than states where citizens are less engaged with civic and community life" (Putnam 2001, 69). Putnam finds that such engagement is "by far" a bigger correlate of educational outcomes than is spending on education, teachers' salaries, class size, or demographics. Also, Gregory B. Markus and colleagues (2002) surveyed 5,626 residents in a diverse set of 14 American cities. Overall, they found powerful correlations between the amount of civic participation, on the one hand, and residents' approval of local government, education, crime, and community, on the other.
2. Interview by the author, October 5, 2007.
3. Notes taken and translated by Rose Marie Nierras as part of a set of interviews conducted by Nierras and the author.
4. In the United States, which happens to be the case I know best, people give about 2 percent of after-tax income to charity, and about one-quarter of the population volunteers regularly.
5. Study Circles in Sweden, the United States, and South Africa are examples. See, for example, Scully and McCoy (2005).
6. For a good summary of recent literature, see Flanagan and Sherrod (1998). The period between ages 14 and 25 is identified as crucial in Niemi and Hepburn (1995).
7. Finkel (2003) reports positive results from adult civic education programs in the Dominican Republic, Poland, and South Africa, but all three were countries in rapid political transition in which adults might be expected to have fluid attitudes toward politics.
8. Carmen Sirianni, "Youth Civic Engagement: Systems Changes and Culture Change in Hampton, Virginia," CIRCLE Working Paper 31 (April 2005), available from www .civicyouth.org.

References

Ackerman, John M. 2005. "Social Accountability in the Public Sector: A Conceptual Discussion." World Bank Social Development Paper 82, Participation and Civic Engagement, World Bank, Washington, DC.

Baiocchi, Gianpaolo. 2005. *Militants and Citizens: The Politics of Participatory Democracy in Porto Alegre.* Palo Alto, CA: Stanford University Press.

Boyte, Harry C., and Nancy N. Kari. 1996. *Building America: The Democratic Promise of Public Work.* Philadelphia: Temple University Press.

Coehlo, Vera Schattan P., Barbara Pozzoni, and Mariana Cifuentes Montoya. 2005. "Participation and Public Policies in Brazil." In *The Deliberative Democracy Handbook: Strategies for Effective Civic Engagement in the 21st Century,* ed. John Gastil and Peter Levine, 174–84. San Francisco: Jossey-Bass.

Eccles, Jacquelynne, and Jennifer Appleton Gootman, eds. 2002. *Community Programs to Promote Youth Development.* Report of the National Research Council and Institute of Medicine, Board on Children, Youth, and Families, Committee on Community-Level Programs for Youth. Washington, DC: National Academies Press.

Finkel, Steven E. 2003. "Can Democracy Be Taught?" *Journal of Democracy* 14 (4): 137–51.

Flanagan, Constance, and Lonnie R. Sherrod. 1998. "Youth Political Development: An Introduction." *Journal of Social Issues* 54 (3): 447–56.

Fung, Archon. 2003. "Survey Article: Recipes for Public Spheres: Eight Institutional Design Choices and Their Consequences." *Journal of Political Philosophy* 11 (3): 338–67.

Lerner, Richard M. 2004. *Liberty: Thriving and Civic Engagement Among America's Youth.* Thousand Oaks, CA: Sage.

Levine, Peter. 2007. *The Future of Democracy: Developing the Next Generation of American Citizens.* Medford, MA: Tufts University Press.

Markus, Gregory B. 2002. "Civic Participation in American Cities." Draft, February.

Niemi, R. G., and M. A. Hepburn. 1995. "The Rebirth of Political Socialization." *Perspectives on Political Science* 24: 7–16.

Putnam, Robert D. 2001. "Community-Based Social Capital and Educational Performance." In *Making Good Citizens: Education and Civil Society,* ed. Diane Ravitch and Joseph P. Viteritti, 58–95. New Haven, CT: Yale University Press.

Sanders, Lynn M. 1997. "Against Deliberation." *Political Theory* 25 (3): 347–76.

Scully, Patrick L., and Martha L. McCoy. 2005. "Study Circles: Local Deliberation as the Cornerstone of Deliberative Democracy." In *The Deliberative Democracy Handbook: Strategies for Effective Civic Engagement in the 21st Century,* ed. John Gastil and Peter Levine, 199–212. San Francisco: Jossey-Bass.

Sears, David O., and Sheri Levy. 2003. "Childhood and Adult Political Development." In *The Oxford Handbook of Political Psychology,* ed. Leonie Huddy Sears and Robert Jervis. Oxford: Oxford University Press.

Sen, Amartya. 1999. *Development as Freedom.* New York: Alfred A. Knopf.

World Bank. 2004. "From Shouting to Counting: A New Frontier in Social Development." World Bank, Washington, DC.

World Bank. 2007. *World Development Report 2007: Development and the Next Generation.* Washington, DC: World Bank.

Holding Government Accountable through Informal Institutions: Solidary Groups and Public Goods Provision in Rural China

Lily Tsai

Formal institutions of accountability are often weak in developing countries (Bardhan 2002). These countries often lack strong bureaucratic institutions for controlling corruption and making sure that lower-level officials are doing their jobs. Democratic institutions such as elections that allow citizens to hold local officials accountable may be unreliable or even nonexistent. Yet even in these countries, some local officials perform better than others. Under these conditions, how do citizens make government officials provide the public services that they want and need?[1]

Existing explanations of governmental performance and public goods provision have focused primarily on the role of strong democratic and bureaucratic institutions. Theories of institutional design argue that the key to good government is providing formal democratic institutions and devolving power to local levels so that citizens can monitor and sanction officials effectively (for example, Dahl 1971; O'Donnell 1996; Rose-Ackerman 2005; Seabright 1996). Theories of civil society and social capital argue that voluntary associations, interest groups, and associational activity can improve governmental performance in democratic systems (Boix and Posner 1998; Edwards and Foley 1998; Ehrenberg 1999; Putnam 1993). In consolidated democracies where formal institutions ensure the incorporation of citizen demands into the policy-making process, autonomous associations and interest groups can help citizens voice their demands more effectively.

What, however, about governmental public goods provision in countries that lack strong democratic and bureaucratic institutions of accountability? Public goods provision is often much more of a problem in developing countries with transitional systems. How do we account for variation in local governmental performance and public goods provision in these systems?

A Model of Informal Governmental Accountability

Public goods provision is always associated with a collective action problem. Everyone has an incentive to take a free ride on the efforts of everyone else. Most models of public goods provision focus on the collective action problem. Alberto Alesina and his associates (1999) argue that public goods provision is poorer in ethnically diverse areas because different ethnic groups have different preferences or tastes for particular public services, thus making any collective decision difficult. Elinor Ostrom (1990) finds that well-designed community social institutions can help overcome obstacles to collective action. Robert Putnam (1993, 2000) argues that dense social networks and norms of trust can make people more likely to cooperate with one another.

These models, however, do not explicitly address the additional problem associated with *governmental* public goods provision—the provision of public goods and services by the government—in systems with weak formal democratic and bureaucratic institutions: the problem of *accountability.* In these systems, overcoming the collective action problem among citizens is not sufficient to guarantee that the government will provide public goods responsibly. Once public funds are in the hands of government officials, how can citizens make sure that officials use these funds to pave roads, build schools, and invest in local public projects? How can citizens have leverage over government officials in the absence of strong formal institutions?

I propose a model of informal governmental accountability. Even when formal governmental accountability is weak, local officials may still have a strong incentive to provide public goods when citizens award them moral standing for doing so. Like other types of prestige, moral standing is "the esteem, respect, or approval that is granted by an individual or a collectivity for performances or qualities they consider above the average" (Goode 1979, 7). In the case of moral standing, esteem or respect is granted for above-average performance of actions considered morally good. Those specific standards and actions vary. Moral standing can be a powerful incentive. It not only makes people feel good about themselves, but also can translate into economic and social advancement. Local officials with higher moral standing may also find it easier to elicit citizen compliance with state policies. Moral standing can be an invaluable resource for accomplishing a variety of political, social, and economic objectives.

When are people more likely to reward officials with moral standing for providing public goods and services? First, citizens and officials must share a set of criteria for moral behavior. At a minimum, these criteria include the principle that contributing to the good of the group deserves moral approval. Without this criterion, the group would not last very long. Second, opportunities must exist for publicizing behavior that meets these shared standards. The more citizens believe that officials really share the group's standards and the more citizens know about whether officials actually behave according to these standards, the more likely they are to award officials moral standing. Like all forms of prestige, moral standing is dependent on the "verbal information disseminated in the community relating news and approval of an individual's activities" (Riches 1984, 235).

I argue that people are more likely to use moral standing to reward local officials for good public goods provision when there are local *solidary groups*— groups based on shared moral obligations as well as shared interests. To provide informal institutions that enable citizens to hold local officials accountable for public goods provision, solidary groups must have two particular structural characteristics. First, they must be *encompassing*, or open to everyone under the local government's jurisdiction. In localities with encompassing solidary groups, social boundaries overlap with political boundaries. Examples of encompassing solidary groups include citizens' groups that monitor town planning decisions in the United States, parish churches in nineteenth-century England (Morris 2001), and village *harambees* or self-help organizations in Kenya (Miguel 1999). Second, solidary groups must be *embedding* in that they incorporate local officials into the group as members. Not all encompassing solidary groups are embedding. English parish churches are often embedding because local officials are likely to attend church services and identify as members of the congregation. In contrast, citizen watchdog organizations in the United States, which are designed to monitor and challenge government, may encompass a particular town or municipality but are unlikely to embed officials into the group as members.

In localities with encompassing and embedding solidary groups, citizens and officials are more likely to share a common set of ethical standards and moral obligations. Members of clans, churches, fraternal organizations, and other solidary groups have strong obligations to the collective. In solidary groups, members are judged according to the group's standards of what constitutes a good person and a good member. Members of church congregations thus feel compelled to contribute something when the donation basket is passed around. Members of clans are expected to and are commended for siding with fellow members in disputes with outsiders. Group activities and dense social networks also provide ample opportunities for individual members to publicize their exemplary behavior. For moral standing to be conferred on an individual, both the individual's actions and the acceptance of shared standards must be "common knowledge" (Chwe 2003). Churches ask for volunteers to help with church activities immediately after services when the congregation is still assembled. In rural China, lineage members are expected to attend group rituals of respect for shared ancestors. These collective gatherings help publicize who is deserving of moral standing in the community.

When the boundaries of a solidary group overlap with the administrative boundaries of the local government, embedded officials have a strong *social* obligation to contribute to the good of the group. Because in this case the group and the public are the same, officials in localities with encompassing and embedding solidary groups can earn moral standing for providing public goods (and suffer severe social sanctions for not doing so). Officials in localities with encompassing and embedding solidary groups thus have an extra incentive to provide public goods and services to their jurisdiction.

Research and Data

To study this issue, I conducted 10 months of in-depth case study research in seven Chinese provinces and surveyed 316 villages randomly sampled from eight counties in four provinces—Shanxi, Hebei, Jiangxi, and Fujian. These provinces were chosen to reflect differences in levels of economic development as well as regional differences between north and south China in terrain, institutional history, and social organization.

Contemporary rural China provides an ideal setting to examine the factors that affect the quality of local governance because of the tremendous variation in the performance of village governments.[2] As in many countries, the Chinese state has decentralized primary responsibility for the provision of basic public goods and services to local governments. During the period of this study (1999–2002), village government officials in China were expected to fund and organize the construction of all public projects *within* the village primarily through resources available within the village (Wong 1997), although this has changed in recent years.

The Importance of Solidary Groups

To illustrate how encompassing and embedding solidary groups can give local officials incentives to provide public goods and services, this section draws on data from in-depth case studies.[3] When solidary groups are both encompassing and embedding, officials who provide public services to the local administrative unit (such as a ward, a town, or a village) are also fulfilling collective obligations to the solidary group. Complying with group norms of collective responsibility enables them to acquire moral standing among all their constituents because, in this case, local administrative boundaries coincide with social boundaries.

Solidary Groups in Rural China

Village temples: The first type of encompassing and embedding solidary group in the Chinese context is the village temple. For example, in West Gate, a village of about 3,900 people in the coastal province of Fujian, the village's temple community council organizes a multitude of religious and community activities for the village. Villagers have clear obligations to contribute to and participate in these activities because these collective activities represent group tributes to the village's guardian deities. Village residents are expected to make donations to help fund these activities. The names of donors and the amount they donated are posted publicly on the temple wall. Village temples are an important symbol of the village community. They provide strong institutions enforcing each member's responsibility to contribute to the collective good and numerous opportunities for publicizing whether members have fulfilled their responsibilities.

West Gate's 12 village officials—who, as with most village officials in China, come from within the village—try hard to be upstanding members of the village temple group. Party Secretary Sun was one of the two top donors to a recent temple reconstruction project, having donated 2000 yuan or about the same as the national annual per capita rural income. Because the Communist Party discourages "superstitious" activities, village officials refrain from taking leadership positions in the temple. But as ordinary members of the temple group, they diligently fulfill their obligations to contribute to the good of the group.

These obligations make West Gate's officials very responsive to citizen demands for public goods and services. In exchange, the temple gives the village officials a good name or, as the temple council head says, "half of the spotlight." Council members also help officials mobilize villagers to attend meetings convened by the village government, convince villagers to give rights-of-way for the construction of a public drainage channel, and monitor the state ban on firecrackers during festivals.

The temple community council in West Gate has a positive effect on local governmental public goods provision because it is both encompassing and embedding. If it were not encompassing, officials would be able only to gain moral standing among some of the villagers. If it were not embedding, officials would be unable to gain any moral standing at all. The moral standing conferred by the temple community council gives an incentive for officials to provide public services, which formal state institutions do not provide.

The importance of having both structural characteristics becomes even clearer when we compare village temples to the other types of solidary groups most common in rural China—village churches and lineage groups.

Village churches: The necessity of embedding local officials is clear if we compare temple groups such as the one in West Gate to village churches, the second type of solidary group. Village temple groups typically embed village officials in their activities, but village churches do not. The state permits Catholic and Protestant churches. But in contrast to its tolerance of village folk temples, the state considers Christianity with its foreign origins to have high subversive potential. Party members are thus prohibited from participating in church activities.

The example of South Bend, a village located in the northern province of Hebei, illustrates how village churches fail to have the same positive impact on village governmental public goods provision as village temples. Almost everyone in South Bend identifies himself or herself as Christian, and at any given service, about one-third of the village is in attendance. A church committee of four male villagers appointed by the priest oversees the maintenance of the church building, materials for church activities and services, and donations from the congregation, which total about 3,000 yuan per year (about US$375), an amount that exceeds the tax revenue the village government is able to extract.

The village Party Secretary of South Bend complains bitterly about his lack of authority among villagers, who, he says, do not trust him because he never goes to church. Instead, he says, the church committee makes all the important decisions in the village. South Bend's village Party Secretary is unable to benefit from the moral standing that the church can confer because the state does not allow him to participate as a member. Relative to the village officials in West Gate, South Bend's Party Secretary has far less incentive to organize public projects. Village government funds are spent instead on the wages of village officials, and the village government does not fund or organize public services. Villagers do not listen to the village Party Secretary, and a high level of tax evasion is found.

As we can see, South Bend's church does not have a positive impact on village governmental performance. It sets clear standards for exemplary behavior and the conferral of moral standing and offers opportunities for members to show that they follow these standards, but village officials cannot take advantage of these opportunities or participate in these institutions. Relative to officials in localities where encompassing and embedding solidary groups exist, officials in South Bend have less incentive to provide public goods because they have little moral standing to gain by doing so. Because South Bend's Party Secretary is not a member of the church, villagers hold him in low regard no matter what he does.

In democratic systems, low regard for government officials can be healthy and can motivate citizens to monitor officials more closely. In these systems, closer monitoring can improve governmental performance because democratic institutions such as elections enable them to sanction officials who perform poorly. Thus, encompassing groups that are not embedding may have a positive impact on local governance in democratic systems. In places that lack democratic institutions, however, autonomous civil society groups or solidary groups that are not embedding have much less direct impact on governmental performance.

Lineage groups: The third type of solidary group commonly found in rural China is based on lineage solidarity. As with temples, village officials almost always take part in their lineage group's activities. Unlike temples and churches, however, which typically have boundaries coextensive with local administrative boundaries, lineage groups vary widely in their scale and overlap with administrative boundaries. When a lineage group encompasses everyone in the village, and membership in the lineage means the same as membership in the village, lineages function in a way similar to temple groups. When the social boundaries of lineage groups do not map onto the administrative boundaries of the village, however, villagers may be fragmented into subvillage groups. The members of a subvillage lineage also feel obligations to their group, but in this case, group obligations are narrower than public obligations to the village community. Subvillage lineage groups can confer moral standing on their group members, but this standing may carry weight only with the group members and not with the rest of the village. Village officials who are embedded in subvillage lineage groups may still try to organize projects, but these projects are likely to favor their group rather than benefit the village as a whole.

We can see how important it is for solidary groups to be encompassing by comparing the two cases of Li Settlement and Pan Settlement. Li Settlement, a village in the southern province of Jiangxi, has an active villagewide lineage group that exerts moral authority over the entire village. Officials in Li Settlement demonstrate their commitment to the lineage and the village by participating in lineage rituals and organizing public projects. They choose to work out of their homes rather than use public funds to construct a government office building. To pave the main village road, officials used their personal connections with higher-level officials to secure a bank loan of 90,000 yuan (about US$11,000). Village officials in Li Settlement feel proud of the work they have done for the village and genuinely seem to feel an obligation to work for the good of the community.

Pan Settlement, on the other hand, is a village in the northern province of Hebei that has three distinct subvillage lineage groups. For decades, two of the subvillage lineage groups have been bitter rivals, accusing each other of favoritism and corruption. Tensions between the subvillage groups have had a negative impact on village governance. Village officials cannot organize public projects on the same scale as neighboring villages. Villagers from one group publicly berate village officials from the other group for the birth control program even though they know the central government actually sets the policy.

When officials are embedded in solidary groups that are not encompassing, such as Pan Settlement's West Gate subvillage lineage group, they may still have strong incentives to contribute to the good of the group. In this case, however, the good of the group will not be synonymous with the public good, and any services provided by officials are likely to favor the particular group to which they belong.

These case studies illustrate how encompassing and embedding solidary groups, such as village temples and villagewide lineages, can provide incentives for local officials to provide public goods and services. Solidary groups that are neither encompassing nor embedding, such as village churches and subvillage lineages, cannot provide the same incentives for governmental public goods provision, although they may use their solidarity and group norms to organize collective projects that do not involve the local government or benefit the village community as a whole.

Findings from Survey Data Analysis

Data from the survey of all 316 villages randomly sampled from eight counties in four provinces suggest that these patterns are generalizable beyond specific cases.[4] The analysis uses six measures of village governmental public goods provision: the per capita village government expenditure on public projects in 2000; the existence of paved village roads; the existence of paved village paths; the proportion of village classrooms usable in rainy weather; the newness of the village school building (this measure was converted from the age of the building, so a higher number indicates a newer building); and the existence of running water. Data analysis suggested that temples—solidary groups that are both encompassing and embedding—are positively associated with village governmental public goods provision. For example, the mean per capita investment in an average village with a temple manager was 99 yuan (about US$12), which was substantially higher than that of an average village without a temple manager, 61 yuan. The probability that the average village with a temple manager had a paved road was 59 percent, whereas the probability that the average village without a temple manager had a paved road drops to 49 percent. Similar patterns were found with the other provision outcomes.

As we might expect from the case studies, village churches, which are encompassing but not embedding, were not associated with better village governmental public goods provision in the survey data analysis. Models of public goods provision that focus on overcoming collective action problems through community norms, social capital, or ethnic homogeneity cannot account for this finding because, as we see in the village case studies, community norms and identity are strong in both villages with encompassing churches and villages with encompassing temples.

Similarly, village-wide lineage groups, which are both encompassing and embedding, were positively associated with village public goods provision, whereas subvillage lineage groups were not. The mean per capita investment for an average village with a single functioning ancestral hall was 132 yuan (about US$17), double that of an average village without any ancestral halls. The probability of paved roads in an average village with a single functioning ancestral hall is 75 percent, whereas the probability in an average village without a single functioning ancestral hall is only 49 percent.

Other Explanatory Factors

Contrary to what we might hope, local governments do not necessarily improve public goods and services substantially as economic development and government resources increase. Resources matter, but so do how they are used. No evidence was found in the survey data analysis that income per capita, size of government assets, and tax revenue per capita had significant positive effects on village governmental public goods provision. Some indication exists that more industrialization and a larger nonagricultural sector were associated with better roads, paths, and running water infrastructure, but perhaps only through private funding channels because greater industrialization was not associated with more village government investment in public projects.

Nor did bureaucratic institutions of top-down control and democratic institutions seem to have sizable positive effects on village governmental public goods provision. Measures of top-down control such as whether village officials were members of the Communist Party or whether bureaucratic performance contracts were implemented did not have a consistently positive effect on governmental public goods provision. Contrary to what theories of democracy might predict, the estimated effects of the implementation of democratic institutions on village governmental public goods provision were very small and in general statistically insignificant. Results remained similar when the implementation of democratic institutions was measured in different ways.

Findings in the previous section suggested that solidary groups with certain structural characteristics could encourage local officials to provide public goods and services even without democracy. These findings suggest that the implementation of elections does not guarantee good governmental performance, especially when other democratic institutions are weak.[5] One problem is that the implementation of village elections has done little to inform citizens about what officials are doing on a day-to-day basis. By the time villagers discover that a corrupt or inept official has drained the public coffers, they may be able to vote him out of office, but they cannot necessarily get the money back. Another problem is that in many places, the rewards of village office have diminished. In more developed localities, people may do better by becoming private entrepreneurs. In poorer localities, the salaries and pensions offered to officials may be important incentives, but it is often in these places that local governments lack sufficient funds to pay salaries on time.

Conclusion

This chapter suggests that when formal institutions of accountability are weak, citizens can make government officials organize and fund needed and desired public goods when they have the right kind of social groups. Solidary groups that are structured to overlap and mesh with government structures can give local government officials important incentives to provide public goods and services that citizens demand even when democratic or bureaucratic institutions do not work effectively. By participating in encompassing solidary groups and fulfilling obligations to work for the good of the group, local officials can earn access to the moral authority conferred by these groups, which can be invaluable for pursuing their personal interests and for carrying out state tasks. Solidary groups that are not both encompassing and embedding may still be able to mobilize their members and provide some public goods and services themselves—but they are less able to hold the government responsible for providing these goods and services.

The experience of rural China suggests several lessons for developing countries more generally. First, economic development is not necessarily correlated with political or institutional development. Good governance may foster economic growth and industrialization, but it is not clear that the converse is true. The evolution of state institutions in different places (even in the same country) does not simply vary in the speed of change; they do not all follow the same trajectory of institutional development.

Second, we need to differentiate between different types of social groups and social capital and to theorize about how they are correlated with particular political and economic outcomes. What the "right" kind of social group is depends on what result we are interested in. This study shows that distinguishing between different types of social groups can reveal that groups with different structural characteristics have very different effects on governmental performance.

Third, the right kinds of social group for governmental performance and public goods provision in transitional systems are not necessarily the ones that increase trust or are autonomous from the state. Without formal institutions that incorporate citizen participation in the policy-making process, the impact of civil society organizations that help citizens voice their opinions and develop organizational skills is not clear. Under these conditions, solidary groups that incorporate agents of the state and offer moral standing as an incentive to contribute to the public good can provide informal institutions of accountability that substitute for formal ones.

In sum, solidary groups and informal institutions can be very beneficial to local governmental performance in transitional systems where formal institutions are weak. In democratic systems, explicit rules about how to change the rules give the system flexibility. In transitional systems, informality and informal institutions can provide this flexibility, sometimes at a lower cost to the state than the building of formal institutions to carry out the same functions. It may be that informal institutions can help stabilize states indefinitely, and what we think of as "transitional" systems are not really transitional at all.

There may also be serious drawbacks, however, to relying on solidary groups to provide informal institutions of accountability. This kind of informal system may also be difficult to "scale up" and may work only at local levels for towns and villages. In cities or at the national level, encompassing and embedding solidary groups may be both less relevant and less likely to exist. More important, this kind of informal system helps citizens obtain more public goods and services than they would otherwise get without this kind of infor-mal system—but perhaps not as much as they would get if there was a system of formal accountability to make sure that higher levels of government also contributed resources and took responsibility for providing local public goods. By relieving pressure on the state in the short term, this kind of informal sys-tem may help to forestall reforms to the formal institutional system that would be more beneficial to both citizens and the state in the long term.

Notes

1. This chapter has been adapted from Tsai (2007b).
2. Although the central government officially refers to village governments as "self-governing organizations," village governments are widely considered part of the state apparatus by higher-level officials, village officials, and citizens themselves. Village governments collect state taxes, enforce state directives such as the birth control policy, and provide village public goods and services.
3. Tsai (2007a) describes these villages in greater depth in a controlled case study comparison.
4. For a more detailed account of measurement and analysis, see Tsai (2007b).
5. Others have also discussed the differences between democracy and accountability (see, for example, Przeworski, Stokes, and Manin 1999).

Bibliography

Alesina, Alberto, Reza Baqir, and William Easterly. 1999. "Public Goods and Ethnic Divi-sions." *Quarterly Journal of Economics* 114 (4): 1243–84.

Bardhan, Pranab. 2002. "Decentralization of Governance and Development." *Journal of Economic Perspectives* 16 (4): 185–205.

Benziger, Vincent. 1993. "China's Rural Road System during the Reform Period." *China Economic Review* 4 (1): 1–17.

Bernstein, Thomas P., and Xiaobo Lu. 2003. *Taxation without Representation in Contempo-rary Rural China.* Cambridge, U.K.: Cambridge University Press.

Boix, Carles, and Daniel Posner. 1998. "Social Capital: Explaining Its Origins and Effects on Governmental Performance." *British Journal of Political Science* 28 (4): 686–93.

Chwe, Michael. 2003. *Rational Ritual: Culture, Coordination, and Common Knowledge.* Princeton, NJ: Princeton University Press.

Dahl, Robert. 1971. Polyarchy: *Participation and Opposition.* New Haven, CT: Yale Univer-sity Press.

Edin, Maria. 2003. "Remaking the Communist Party-State: The Cadre Responsibility Sys-tem at the Local Level in China." *China: An International Journal* 1 (1): 1–15.

Edwards, Bob, and Michael W. Foley. 1998. "Social Capital and Civil Society beyond Put-nam." *American Behavioral Scientist* 42 (1): 124–40.

Ehrenberg, John. 1999. *Civil Society: The Critical History of an Idea.* New York: New York University Press.

Esherick, Joseph. 1987. *The Origins of the Boxer Uprising.* Berkeley: University of California Press.

Evans, Peter. 1995. *Embedded Autonomy: States and Industrial Transformation.* Princeton, NJ: Princeton University Press.

Goode, William J. 1979. *The Celebration of Heroes: Prestige as a Control System.* Berkeley, CA: University of California Press.

King, Gary, James Honaker, Anne Joseph, and Kenneth Scheve. 2001. "Analyzing Incomplete Political Science Data: An Alternative Algorithm for Multiple Imputation." *American Political Science Review* 95 (1): 49–69.

Lam, Wai Fung. 1996. "Institutional Design of Public Agencies and Co-production." In *State-Society Synergy: Government and Social Capital in Development,* 11–47. Berkeley, CA: University of California Press.

Latourette, Kenneth Scott. 1929. *A History of Christian Missions in China.* New York: Macmillan.

Madsen, Richard. 1984. *Morality and Power in a Chinese Village.* Berkeley, CA: University of California Press.

———. 1998. *China's Catholics: Tragedy and Hope in an Emerging Civil Society.* Berkeley, CA: University of California Press.

Miguel, Edward. 1999. "Ethnic Diversity, Mobility, and School Funding: Theory and Evidence from Kenya." Development Economics Discussion Paper Series 14, World Bank, Washington, DC.

———. 2004. "Tribe or Nation? Nation Building and Public Goods in Kenya versus Tanzania." *World Politics* 56: 327–62.

Morris, Robert. 2001. "Structure, Culture, and Society in British Towns." In *The Cambridge Urban History of Britain,* vol. 3, ed. Martin Daunton, 395–426. Cambridge, U.K.: Cambridge University Press.

O'Donnell, Guillermo. 1996. "Illusions about Consolidation." *Journal of Democracy* 7 (2): 55–69.

Ostrom, Elinor. 1990. *Governing the Commons: The Evolution of Institutions for Collective Action.* Cambridge, U.K.: Cambridge University Press.

Przeworski, Adam, Susan C. Stokes, and Bernard Manin. 1999. *Democracy, Accountability, and Representation.* New York: Cambridge University Press.

Putnam, Robert. 1993. *Making Democracy Work: Civic Traditions in Modern Italy.* Princeton, NJ: Princeton University Press.

———. 2000. *Bowling Alone: The Collapse and Revival of American Community.* New York: Simon and Schuster.

Riches, David. 1984. "Hunting, Herding, and Potlatching: Towards a Sociological Account of Prestige." *Man* 19 (2): 234–51.

Rose-Ackerman, Susan. 2005. *From Elections to Democracy: Building Accountable Government in Hungary and Poland.* Cambridge, U.K.: Cambridge University Press.

Seabright, Paul. 1996. "Accountability and Decentralization in Government: An Incomplete Contracts Model." *European Economic Review* 40 (1): 61–89.

Solinger, Dorothy. 1999. *Contesting Citizenship in Urban China: Peasant Migrants, the State, and the Logic of the Market.* Berkeley, CA: University of California Press.

Spence, Jonathan. 1996. *God's Chinese Son: The Taiping Heavenly Kingdom of Hong Xiuquan.* London: Harper Collins.

Tsai, Lily L. 2007a. *Accountability without Democracy: Solidary Groups and Public Goods Provision in Rural China.* Cambridge, U.K.: Cambridge University Press.

———. 2007b. "Solidary Groups, Informal Accountability, and Public Goods Provision in Rural China." *American Political Science Review* 101 (2): 355–72.

Wong, Christine. 1997. "Rural Public Finance." In *Financing Local Government in the People's Republic of China,* ed. Christine Wong, 167–212. Hong Kong SAR, China: Oxford University Press.

Wooldridge, Jeffrey M. 2002. *Econometric Analysis of Cross-Section and Panel Data.* Cambridge, MA: MIT Press.

Yang, Dali, and Subing Fu. 2001. "Elections, Governance, and Accountability in Rural China." Paper presented at the International Symposium on Villager Self-Government and Rural Social Development in China, Beijing, September.

Adult Civic Education and the Development of Democratic Culture: Evidence from Emerging Democracies

Steven E. Finkel

Political scientists have long suggested that the stability and effectiveness of democratic regimes largely depend on the existence of a democratic "political culture": a configuration of attitudes, beliefs, values, and participatory orientations among ordinary citizens that reflects support for democratic principles and institutions, and that facilitates the informed participation of all individuals in the political process (for example, Almond and Verba 1960; Inglehart 1990; Putnam 1993). Although these cultural values have flourished for decades or centuries in established democracies such as the United States and some European countries, many countries in the so-called third wave of democratization face the need to make more rapid changes in the political attitudes and behavioral tendencies of their citizenry. Mass political orientations in many developing democracies are characterized by extremely low levels of social and political participation, lack of tolerance for members of opposing political or ethnic groups, widespread political ignorance, and alienation from institutions and processes. Building supportive democratic political culture in these contexts is thus an especially urgent task.

One promising means of promoting democratic orientations in new democracies is through civic education programs that teach democratic citizenship to young people in classroom settings or to adults in community workshops, lectures, or public forums (Finkel 2003a; Torney-Purta and others 2001). Over the past several decades, an explosion of such programs has taken place in the emerging democracies of Eastern Europe, Africa, and Latin America, with the vast majority funded by the United States, other Organisation for Economic Co-operation and Development donors, or philanthropic organizations seeking to stimulate more democratic political cultures in transition societies (Carothers 1999; Diamond 1999; Niemi and Finkel 2007; Torney-Purta 2002). These programs range from new primary and secondary school curricula on democracy, to local nongovernmental organization (NGO) programs about women's social and political rights, to voter education, to neighborhood problem-solving programs bringing individuals and local authorities together. The United States Agency for International Development (USAID) data suggest that the United States alone spent between thirty and fifty million dollars per year on civic education between 1990 and 2005.[1]

Until recently, however, little effort has been made to assess the impact of civic education programs on their target populations in developing democracies. A growing literature exists on the effectiveness of school-based civics education among children and young adults (for example, Morduchowicz and others, 1996; Slomcyznski and Shabad 1998; Torney-Purta and others 2001). Aside from the work I will describe here, though, few previous studies have attempted to evaluate whether adult civic education programs affected the democratic orientations or behaviors of ordinary individuals (Bratton and others 1999).

Understanding whether and under what conditions adult civic education "works" can help international donors design and implement more effective programs, and the research summarized here contains several specific implications for changing the way that democracy and political participation are "taught" in emerging democracies. The results can also shed light on more general issues related to the role of civil society in promoting democratic stability and effectiveness in developing contexts (Diamond 1999; Gibson 2001; Putnam 1993). Civic education in these contexts is conducted overwhelmingly through secondary groups and associations, sometimes by labor, church, or trade associations, but more frequently by what Carothers (1999) refers to as "advocacy NGOs." These groups are public interest or reformist groups that U.S. and European donors fund in the hopes that they can become part of a "diverse, active, and independent civil society that articulates the interests of citizens and holds government accountable" (Carothers 1999, 87). Examining the effectiveness of adult civic education is thus a means for assessing how civil society groups in general, and advocacy NGOs in particular, affect processes of democratic change in development contexts.

This chapter summarizes two major efforts undertaken on behalf of USAID in the last decade to evaluate the impact of adult civic education programs in emerging democracies.[2] The first study, conducted between 1997 and 1999, assessed the effects of several different adult civic education programs in the Dominican Republic, Poland, and South Africa on individual participation in politics, and on orientations such as political tolerance, efficacy, and trust, which are considered essential components of democratic political culture (see also Finkel 2002, 2003a, 2006; Finkel, Sabatini, and Bevis 2000). Professional survey companies in each country administered questionnaires to a randomly selected sample of individuals trained in each program, as well as to comparable individuals who had not been trained. A total of 4,238 interviews were conducted: 1,924 in the Dominican Republic, 1,375 in Poland, and 939 in South Africa.

The second study, conducted between 2001 and 2003, assessed the effects of the National Civic Education Program (NCEP) in Kenya, an ambitious, countrywide effort of coordinated civic education that aimed to promote democratic values, awareness, and engagement in politics among ordinary Kenyan citizens during constitutional reform and preparation for national elections in December 2002 (see also Finkel 2003b; Finkel and Smith 2011). One important feature of the Kenya study was the addition of a pretest, as interviews were conducted with 1,169 individuals *before and after* they attended NCEP workshops, as well as with 1,139 comparable individuals who did not attend those workshops.[3] The Kenya study thus provides an especially rigorous test of the effectiveness of civic education training programs, because the analysis can account for orientations and behavioral dispositions that individuals bring to the civic education experience. In addition, the Kenya study included questions related to individuals' post–civic education political discussions so that, for the first time, we could assess the possible "secondary" effects of civic education that result from discussions about the training sessions with others who may or may not have attended the sessions themselves.

The programs studied are the following:

Dominican Republic:

- *Participación Ciudadana (PC)* is a national NGO that trained youth and adults to serve as election observers in 1996.
- *Grupo Acción por la Democracia (GAD)* is a civil society mobilization program from the mid-1990s that first educated people on basic rights and obligations in a democracy and then brought them together to discuss national and local issues.
- *Asociación Dominicana para el Desarrollo de la Mujer (ADOPEM)* is a local NGO that trained women community leaders between January 1996 and January 1997 in women's rights, democratic values, democracy in the family, and self-esteem.
- *Radio Santa María (RSM)* is a mid-1990s project that trained intermediaries (typically leaders of rural towns), who then conducted civic education programs in their local communities.

Kenya:

- *National Civic Education Program (NCEP)* is a nationwide, coordinated effort consisting of some 50,000 discrete workshops, lectures, drama presentations, and community meetings conducted by nearly 80 Kenyan NGOs between late 2001 and December 2002. These activities aimed to promote awareness and engagement with the ongoing constitutional reforms and the democratic regime among ordinary citizens in the run-up to national elections in 2002.

Poland:

- *Foundation for Support of Local Democracy (FSLD)* promotes local self-governance, primarily through training for local government officials. Between 1994 and 1995, FSLD chose project leaders, who then brought together citizens in their communities to work on solving local problems.
- *DIALOG Project* (also run by FSLD centers) is a community or group problem-solving project that began in 1991 and conducted information campaigns on key local problems, and then invited citizens and government officials to workshops dealing with the issues.

South Africa:

- *National Institute for Public Interest Law and Research (NIPILAR)* is the lead organization of an NGO consortium operating in the fields of rights education and public interest law. One of the main civic education programs conducted by NIPILAR during the period under study was its women's rights program.
- *Community Law Centre–Durban (CLC)* coordinates approximately 30 legal advice offices in KwaZulu Natal province, which conducted democracy and civic education workshops in the province during the period under study.
- *Lawyers for Human Rights (LHR)* is a national rights awareness and public interest law organization that, during the period under study, conducted workshops emphasizing the Constitution and the Bill of Rights as well as political participation.

Measures of Democratic Orientations

In each country, we asked respondents questions relating to numerous democratic orientations and behaviors. One set of orientations encompasses the individual's "civic competence," following the long-standing presumption that political knowledge, civic skills, and perceptions of political influence or efficacy constitute important resources for meaningful democratic participation. Another set encompasses the individual's adherence to democratic values and norms such as political tolerance, or the extent to which citizens are willing to extend procedural democratic liberties to individuals and groups with whom they may disagree; institutional trust, where citizens should support basic social and political institutions, though not without some willingness to hold elites and the system as a whole to account; and support for democracy as a form of government against alternative political systems. Participation is included as an additional outcome, because civic education also attempts to encourage individuals to take part in democratic politics, especially at the local level. The specific questions used for each of these dependent variables are described at length in previous reports from these studies (Finkel 2002, 2003b, 2006).

Statistical Methodology

Estimating the impact of the civic education "treatment" in these studies, as in much quasi-experimental or observational research, is hampered by the fact that exposure to the programs is entirely voluntary. Hence, participants in the programs are likely to differ from nonparticipants on a host of socioeconomic, demographic, and political factors, many of which may also relate to the democratic attitudes and behaviors that make up our dependent variables. The statistical procedures that we used to overcome (as best as possible) these selection biases depended on the nature of the data collected in the various county contexts. In the first set of studies from the Dominican Republic, Poland, and South Africa, we used what is known as "propensity score matching," a procedure that compares the dependent variables (for example, the score on participation, knowledge, or efficacy) for each individual in the treatment group with the score for individuals in the control group who are *most similar* to the treatment individual on other potentially confounding variables (Morgan and Winship 2007; Rosenbaum and Rubin 1983).

More specifically, an overall logistic regression model was constructed that predicts whether an individual received the civic education treatment from the following variables: education, income, age, gender, community size, time lived in the community, household size, number of children, employment status, student status, church attendance, involvement in church activities, number of voluntary organizations to which the individual belongs, political interest, and attention to the mass media. Each individual is then estimated to have a predicted probability of receiving the treatment from those observed covariates, and the analyses proceed by matching each individual in the treatment group with the individual in the control group with the most similar predicted probability. Then the dependent variables are compared between the treatment and matched control group to determine the net difference between the civic education group and the control group on the variable in question, over and above the effects of the control variables.

The statistical method for the Kenya study differed somewhat because individuals in the treatment and control groups were interviewed *before* and *after* the civic education training sessions were conducted. This allowed us to use the individual's *change* in democratic attitudes and behaviors as our dependent variables, thus overcoming to a significant degree the potential problem that individuals in the treatment group were *already* more democratic than their control group counterparts before the treatment was administered. The change in each democratic orientation or behavior is predicted from variables that represent the individual's exposure to NCEP civic education, as well as potentially confounding factors such as educational attainment, household income, gender, previous exposure to civic education, group memberships, age, gender, church attendance, and urban-rural residence.

Basic Findings[4]

The most important finding from the study is the consistent and relatively large effect of civic education training on local-level political participation. In all four countries, individuals who were exposed to civic education were significantly more active in local politics than were individuals in the control groups, with these differences being the largest of any of the democratic orientations that were analyzed in all countries aside from Kenya. Among the three other countries, the largest effect is seen in Poland, where civic education training by itself led to an increase of one additional instance of local-level political behavior on the part of trained individuals, with average increases of one-third to one-half of an additional behavior for those trained in the other countries. The findings confirm that conducting civic education through secondary associations or "advocacy NGOs" has substantial mobilization effects, as *exposure to democracy training programs translates directly into increased involvement in the political system.*

Further analysis (Finkel 2002) suggests that an important distinction can be made between different types of programs: Those that focus directly on local-level problem solving and community action, and that provide opportunities for individuals to interact with local officials, demonstrate far greater impact on participation than programs characterized by general information-based workshops. These differences can be attributed to the fact that the programs themselves comprise an explicit form of political mobilization: Individuals are brought together for problem-solving activities and put into contact with local leaders, and thus learn how and through what channels to participate at the local level. Individuals' subsequent heightened participation reflects the participatory skills that they developed through the programs, as well as the specific opportunities and channels for participation that the program provided. Civic education, then, can have quite powerful behavioral effects when it is conducted through secondary associations that are actively engaged in local problem solving, community organizing, and collective political action.

Analysis also shows that civic education training had more varied, and more modest, effects on "civic competence" and democratic values such as tolerance and trust. In all contexts aside from South Africa, civic education had generally significant effects on the individual's knowledge about politics and, in all four countries, significant effects on their sense of political efficacy, or belief in their abilities to influence the political system. Thus, civic education is seen to have a positive influence not only on local-level participation, but also on several of the most important cognitive and attitudinal precursors of participation.

At the same time, these programs had more limited impacts on individuals' adherence to democratic values and on support for political institutions. One highly important democratic value, political tolerance, did show modest overall changes in all four country contexts (see also Finkel 2006). On the other values, however, few consistent differences were seen in the changes over time between individuals who were exposed to civic education training and those who were not. Civic education had little impact on individuals' overall support for democracy, to some extent because levels of this value were relatively high in all settings before the programs were implemented. On institutional trust, the effects were insignificant in two settings: mildly positive in South Africa and negative in the Dominican Republic. We interpret these differences as reflecting the political stance of the implementing NGOs versus their respective governments. The results overall, however, show that civic education had generally less success in changing democratic values than civic competence, engagement, and political participation.

Conditions Producing Greater Civic Education Impact

We found evidence in all four country contexts that factors related to the duration and pedagogical nature of individuals' civic education experiences significantly impacted the magnitude of attitudinal and behavioral change. In fact, these findings' consistency and robustness paint a definitive picture of the conditions under which adult civic education is most effective:

- The frequency of attendance at civic education activities is the most important determinant of individual change. Individuals who attended only one or two workshops often showed little change in democratic orientations compared with control group individuals, although there were relatively large gains—even on "difficult" values such as political tolerance—from multiple workshop exposures. In some of the countries, we observed "threshold" effects, such that exposure to "one-off" civic education workshops had no impact on political participation and other democratic orientations, with all change being concentrated among those individuals who attended at least three civic education activities.

- Civic education activities that were conducted with more active, participatory teaching methods were significantly more effective in stimulating democratic change. Respondents who reported that their workshops included methods such as breaking into small groups, staging plays or dramatizations, playing games, problem solving, simulations, or role playing consistently showed greater impact across the entire range of democratic orientations than did individuals who were exposed to more lecture-based instruction. In many instances, moreover, threshold effects were found, such that positive effects occurred *only* when workshops were conducted with many participatory methodologies.

- Civic education activities with instructors that were perceived to be of higher quality also led to greater impact among those trained. Workshops conducted in all four country contexts were most effective when the leaders or trainers were perceived to be "knowledgeable," "inspiring," and "interested." Trainers who did not engage or were not well regarded by the participants had little success in transmitting democratic knowledge, values, or participatory inclinations. Such ratings of instructor quality are necessarily subjective and, like teaching evaluations in other contexts, are difficult to link definitively to student outcomes. However, a large variation is seen in the amount of "training of trainers" that takes place before civic education programs are implemented, and the results suggest that programs that devote more resources to teacher recruitment and training will likely see larger effects on program participants.

These findings provide clear evidence that civic education, under the right conditions, can have substantial impact on democratic participation, values, and attitudes. Unless the "right conditions" are met in practice, however, the overall effects of civic education programs will be much weaker than desired. Here the evidence is not altogether positive: Only minorities of trainees in all four country contexts were trained frequently, with participatory methodologies, and by instructors who were perceived to be of high quality. Much room for improvement remains in future implementation of civic education programs, because the *potential* impacts of civic education shown thus far are often not fully realized.

The "Secondary" Effects of Civic Education

As opposed to focusing solely on the individuals trained in the programs per se, evaluations of civic education also need to examine its potential *indirect* effects, whereby treated individuals may go on to discuss the lessons and ideas from the classes or workshops with untreated members of their social networks. To the extent that civic education stimulates these kinds of posttreatment discussions, democracy education may exert an even greater impact on democratic political culture than previously recognized.

Despite widespread belief within the international donor community that such secondary effects of civic education exist, no evidence has been adduced one way or the other in previous evaluations.[5] In the Kenya study, we tested for these effects with several questions in our posttest survey instrument. First, we asked individuals who attended workshops whether, after the workshop was over, they had discussed the "issues in the workshop" with (1) members of their family, (2) friends, (3) people where they work, and (4) people in groups to which they belong. We then asked them to estimate altogether the number of people with whom they had discussed the workshop issues. We also asked all respondents, those who attended NCEP workshops and those who did not, the following question: "Setting aside any events or workshops that you attended personally, has anyone you know talked to you about events or workshops about democracy and the Constitution that they attended this past year?" Respondents who answered yes were then asked to estimate the number of individuals who discussed their workshop experiences with the respondent.

The Kenya study showed that post–civic education discussions within social networks frequently took place. Among individuals who attended at least one NCEP workshop, nearly 70 percent went on to discuss their workshop experiences with more than five other people. Another 25 percent of the treated population discussed their experiences with five or fewer other individuals. The program's reach was also great among individuals who did not attend any of the program's workshops. Among individuals with no direct exposure to civic education workshops—that is, the "pure" control group—approximately half had some discussion with others in their networks who *did* attend NCEP activities. In fact, about one-quarter of these ostensibly "control" individuals discussed the workshop experiences of three or more other "treated" individuals. This indicates that civic education programs have the potential to reach many more individuals via subsequent political discussions than via formal training.

We then estimated the effect of the two discussion variables by including them in a model of change in each democratic orientation. The results showed significant effects of both factors, but more powerful and consistent effects from discussing the workshop experiences of others. Analysis showed, for example, that respondents who attended three workshops and spoke with five or more other individuals about their workshop experiences had nearly a two in three chance of increasing their political knowledge, compared to a one in three chance of increasing it if the individuals neither attended workshops nor spoke about others' workshop experiences. These effects, moreover, were seen even for individuals in the control group, that is, *even for individuals who did not themselves attend any NCEP workshops.* In fact, the chances of increasing knowledge for respondents in the control group who spoke to many other individuals about their workshop experiences were greater than for many respondents who attended workshops of their own. Thus, individuals may learn substantial amounts about politics through secondary exposure to civic education—even when they themselves do not attend civic education activities.

Conclusions

The studies reported here provide a qualified "yes" to the question of whether democratic political culture can be fostered through adult civic education in new democracies. The findings, from evaluations of 10 civic education programs in four emerging democratic contexts, suggest that civic education can be effective in stimulating local-level political participation, in teaching individuals basic knowledge about the political system, and in developing such important norms and values as political efficacy and tolerance. The findings were consistent across programs and across political contexts, and were shown with varying kinds of data and statistical methodologies. Little doubt exists that adult civic education has the potential to "work" in developing democracies.

At the same time, the pattern of results suggests that effects are influenced strongly by the amount and the duration of the individual's exposure to civic education activities, on the kinds of teaching methods used, and on the perceived quality of the instructors. Substantial numbers of individuals in all four country contexts were *not* trained in the ways that were most conducive to program impact, and to this extent, the impact of all of these programs was more limited than it could—and perhaps should—have been.

Finally, the Kenya study suggests that civic education can have both positive "primary" effects on those who were trained as well as "secondary" effects from posttraining discussion of civic education messages among individuals in the trainees' social networks. Individuals exposed directly to civic education democratic messages often become opinion leaders, communicating new knowledge and attitudes to people within their social networks, many of whom have no direct exposure to the programs themselves. This finding is especially intriguing, because it indicates that the reach and impact of civic education beyond the individuals directly trained may be substantial and may provide further justification among international donors for supporting these kinds of programs.

Theoretically, the results of the studies provide strong support for the role that civil society groups can play in the democratization process, in particular the politically oriented "advocacy NGOs" that international donors widely use as agents of democratic behavioral and value change in developing contexts. Contrary to the view that such groups may be ineffectual because they are insufficiently rooted in a country's indigenous civil society (Carothers 1999; Ottaway and Chung 1999), the findings here indicate that such groups can be relatively effective agents for democratic change *precisely* because they are directly focused on that task, as opposed to more traditional civil society groups that provide more muted cues for political participation and democratic attitude change. It is also the case that advocacy NGOs draw many of the participants for civic education training from other civil society associations such as youth, church, and hobby groups, thus ensuring a wide network of individuals who may be influenced through post–civic education discussion with those who were directly trained. To this extent, the strategy of funding explicitly political civil society organizations to mobilize and integrate individuals into emerging democratic systems, and to diffuse democratic messages throughout the population at large, makes a good deal of sense.

On a more practical level, the findings raise important issues for the implementation of civic education programs in the future. "One-off" civic education workshops, conducted hastily and without proper training of instructors in appropriate pedagogical methods, simply will not work. Programs *must* be implemented in ways that ensure sustained, multiple exposures to democracy messages. They must be taught by qualified and well-trained facilitators using active, participatory instructional methods. Finally, the fact that much of the overall impact of civic education may stem from posttraining discussions implies that programs should provide trainees with pamphlets, books, or other materials that they can share with family, friends, or others in their social networks. The more that individuals are encouraged to speak to others after the fact, the more likely it is that programs will extend their overall reach and exert secondary effects on individuals who themselves did not participate in any training.

Notes

1. These figures were obtained from official USAID activity data, available at http://www.pitt.edu/~politics/democracy/democracy.html as part of the project "Deepening our Understanding of the Effects of US Foreign Assistance on Democracy Building, 1990–2004," principal investigators Steven E. Finkel, Aníbal Pérez-Liñán, Mitchell A. Seligson, and C. Neal Tate.
2. The studies in the Dominican Republic, Poland, and South Africa were commissioned by USAID's Center for Democracy and Governance, Bureau for Global Programs, and implemented by the Washington-based consulting company Management Systems International. The Kenya study was commissioned by USAID/Nairobi and also implemented by Management Systems International.
3. See Finkel (2003b, ch. 2) for more details on the study's sampling procedures and Finkel and Smith (2011) for more on the study's methods and findings, including analyses of the study's three-wave panel component.
4. Detailed presentation of the studies' methodologies and results can be found in Finkel (2002, 2003a) and Finkel and Smith (2011).
5. In fact, the Kenya evaluation reported here was delayed for several months in 2001–03 because of donor insistence that such secondary effects be taken more strongly into consideration in the research design.

References

Almond, G. A., and S. Verba. 1960. *The Civic Culture: Political Attitudes and Democracy in Five Nations.* Newbury Park, CA: Sage Publications.
Bratton, M., P. Alderfer, G. Bowser, and J. Temba. 1999. "The Effects of Civic Education on Political Culture: Evidence from Zambia." *World Development* 27 (5): 807–24.
Carothers, T. 1999. *Aiding Democracy Abroad: The Learning Curve.* Washington, DC: Carnegie Endowment for International Peace.
Diamond, L. 1999. *Developing Democracy: Towards Consolidation.* Baltimore: Johns Hopkins University Press.
Finkel, S. E. 2002. "Civic Education and the Mobilization of Political Participation in Developing Democracies." *Journal of Politics* 64 (4): 994–1020.
———. 2003a. "Can Democracy Be Taught?" *Journal of Democracy* 14 (4): 137–51.
———. 2003b. *The Impact of the Kenya National Civic Education Programme on Democratic Attitudes, Knowledge, Values, and Behavior.* Washington, DC: U.S. Agency for International Development.

————. 2006. "Political Tolerance and Civic Education in Developing Democracies." In *Tolerance in the 21st Century: Prospects and Challenges,* ed. G. Moreno-Riano, 153–88. Lanham, MD: Lexington Press.

Finkel, S. E., C. A. Sabatini, and G. G. Bevis. 2000. "Civic Education, Civil Society, and Political Mistrust in a Developing Democracy: The Case of the Dominican Republic." *World Development* 28 (11): 1851–74.

Finkel, S. E., and A. E. Smith. 2011. "Civic Education, Political Discussion and the Social Transmission of Democratic Knowledge and Values in a New Democracy: Kenya 2002." *American Journal of Political Science.* Forthcoming.

Gibson, J. L. 2001. "Social Networks, Civil Society, and the Prospects for Consolidating Russia's Democratic Transition." *American Journal of Political Science* 45 (1): 51–68.

Inglehart, R. 1990. *Culture Shift in Advanced Industrial Society.* Princeton, NJ: Princeton University Press.

Morduchowicz, R., E. Catterberg, R. G. Niemi, and F. Bell. 1996. "Teaching Political Information and Democratic Values in a New Democracy: An Argentine Experiment." *Comparative Politics* 28 (4): 465–76.

Morgan, S. L., and C. Winship. 2007. *Counterfactuals and Causal Inference: Methods and Principles for Social Research.* New York: Cambridge University Press.

Niemi, R. G., and S. E. Finkel. 2007. "Civic Education and the Development of Civic Knowledge and Attitudes." In *Essays on Cultural Change,* ed. L. E. Harrison and J. Kagen, 77–93. New York: Routledge.

Ottaway, M., and T. Chung. 1999. "Toward a New Paradigm." *Journal of Democracy* 10: 99–113.

Putnam, R. D. 1993. *Making Democracy Work: Civic Traditions in Modern Italy.* Princeton, NJ: Princeton University Press.

Rosenbaum, P. R., and D. B. Rubin. 1983. "The Central Role of the Propensity Score in Observational Studies for Causal Effects." *Biometrika* 70: 41–55.

Slomcyznski, K. M., and G. Shabad. 1998. "Can Support for Democracy and the Market Be Learned in School? A Natural Experiment in Post-Communist Poland." *Political Psychology* 19 (4): 749–79.

Torney-Purta, J. 2002. "The School's Role in Developing Civic Engagement: A Study of Adolescents in Twenty-eight Countries." *Applied Developmental Science* 6 (4): 203–12.

Torney-Purta, J., R. Lehmann, H. Oswald, and W. Schulz. 2001. *Citizenship and Education in Twenty-eight Countries: Civic Knowledge and Engagement at Age Fourteen.* Amsterdam: International Association for the Evaluation of Educational Achievement.

Section VII
Case Studies

22

Is Social Participation Democratizing Politics?

Vera Schattan P. Coelho

Participatory governance, it is argued, makes for better citizens, better governments, and better decisions. According to the accepted wisdom, the inclusion of a broader spectrum of citizens in public life leads to improved circulation of information, greater oversight over the political process, and a more robust public debate, all presumably resulting in more effective and equitable policies.

This may all be true in theory, but it remains difficult to demonstrate in practice. So how can democratic and effective participatory mechanisms be promoted? How can these new forms of democracy be assessed?

This chapter seeks to answer these questions by drawing on lessons from research, conducted by the São Paulo–based think tank Centro Brasileiro de Análise e Planejamento (Brazilian Center of Analysis and Planning, or CEBRAP), on the various mechanisms of social participation related to public policies in Brazil.[1] The sum of these inquiries points to two main conclusions relevant for anyone attempting a similar undertaking.

I would like to thank Andrea Cornwall, with whom I coconvened the Citizenship Development Research Centre (CDRC) Spaces for Change working group and coauthored the introduction of the book with the same name. This chapter returns to various issues that we tackled together in the group's work. I would like to thank John Gaventa, the director, and my CDRC and Centro de Estudos da Metrópole (Center of Metropolitan Studies, or CEM) colleagues for their valuable support, contributions, and suggestions. I would also like to thank Miriam W. and Alexandre Ferraz, with whom I extensively discussed the model presented here, which was developed as part of the project "Defining Indicators for Evaluation of Participatory Experiences" coordinated by Miriam Wyman and Vera Coelho and supported by the Deliberative Democracy Consortium/Hewlett Foundation.

First, the success of participatory mechanisms depends on the combination of several elements: committed public officials, mobilized citizens, and innovative design features. Each of these elements alone will be insufficient to overcome the enormous difficulties of bringing marginalized groups into the policy process. Indeed, success almost invariably requires the simultaneous presence of state actors interested in building alliances with civil society, of citizens and civil organizations that display interest in participating in public policies, and of design features that reduce the asymmetric distribution of resources among participants. Those who are interested in participatory governance therefore need to approach the endeavor in an integrated manner (Coelho 2006).

Second, participatory governance brings to the fore issues related to the distribution of power. Consequently, it is vitally important to ensure that a broad range of actors is represented in these new spaces, including marginalized or disorganized social groups. It is also crucial to recognize that through these forums new forms of representation are emerging as "civil society" comes to be represented in a variety of ways: by individuals, by nominated representatives from nongovernmental organizations, by elected representatives from neighborhood associations, and by members of collective actors such as unions or movements. From this perspective, those who are interested in participatory governance should be prepared to tackle questions related to both inclusion and representation (Cornwall and Coelho 2007). According to these two key findings, it is possible then to devise a model for evaluating and comparing participatory experiments, as CEBRAP has done in Brazil.

The information produced through these evaluations provides a clearer understanding of how these dimensions interact and affect one another and, hence, elucidates *whose* interests participatory experiments are actually serving. To illustrate these points, I will refer to research conducted on the sectoral policy councils that, at least in terms of scale, are the most important participatory mechanism in Brazil. Over 28,000 of these councils have been established for health policy, education, and the environment, among other issues, during the last 20 years. They are found at all levels of government, from local to federal, providing forums in which citizens join service providers and the government in defining public policies and overseeing their implementation.

In the next section, I explain how social, institutional, and political variables determined the different patterns of inclusion that we found in the sectoral policy councils. In the subsequent section, I discuss the complexities and importance of defining criteria to distinguish and track three aspects of such forums. The first aspect, which is most often monitored, is who is being included in these councils. Yet it is also essential to collect more information about the other two aspects: the dynamics of participation and the content of the debates taking place in these forums, as well as the connections being established between them and other branches of the political system. The research in Brazil has helped to develop a model for how to gather and compare all this information.

The final section presents a reflection on the kind of research that is still needed to better understand how social participation and participatory governance links to the democratization of politics and policies.

Unbiased Participation?

The 1988 constitution, which established the formal transition to democracy, defined health as a right of all citizens and a responsibility of the state. It also established the Sistema Único de Saude (Unified Health System, or SUS)—the Brazilian public health system—based on the principles of universality and equity of health care provision. The SUS introduced the notion of accountability (social control) and popular participation. Health councils emerged within the legal framework as the institutions responsible for enabling citizen participation in health governance. They were set up at local, state, and federal levels to be responsible for presenting government projects to the population, as well as for conveying suggestions from the population to the various levels of government.

Health councils are permanent collective bodies that consist of citizens, health professionals, governmental institutions, and health service providers. Currently more than 5,500 health councils are in existence, involving almost 100,000 citizens and a vast number of associations. Health councils are political forums in which participants discuss issues and may make alliances to help the Health Secretariat plan and define priorities and policies. The basic operational norms regulating the SUS stipulate that the number of representatives of civil society must be equal to that of service providers, health professionals, and government institutions taken together. The strength of the municipal health councils largely derives from the law granting them veto power over the plans and accounts of the Health Secretariat. If the council rejects the plan and budget that the Health Secretariat is required to present annually, the Health Ministry, which manages 55 percent of the public health budget, does not transfer funds. Local health councils (LHCs) have similar functions and were created in various Brazilian cities at the intramunicipal level (Coelho, Pozzoni, and Cifuentes 2005).

To better understand the nature of the participation being fostered in these forums, we conducted two rounds of research with LHCs in the city of São Paulo. In the first round, we surveyed all 31 LHCs that exist in the city. In the second round, we researched six LHCs located in the poorest areas of the city.[2] During the first research round, held from 2001 to 2005, we were particularly concerned with the risks that the local councils would be co-opted by the Partido dos Trabalhadores (Workers Party, or PT), which at the time was in control of the city administration and convening a huge process of decentralization, as well as opening up hundreds of participatory forums throughout the municipality.

The research asked two main questions. The first question was concerned with the inclusion of traditionally marginalized groups: How can you check, given the informality that characterizes this type of participation, if groups that do not belong to the relationship networks of public officials actually have the opportunity to participate? Second, if one assumes that it is possible to recognize distinct patterns—that is, a larger and more plural or a narrower range of associations included—can you relate these, as suggested by the literature, to certain characteristics of public officials, design features, or associational life?[3]

The data gathered on the composition of the 31 LHCs showed that some included only one or two kinds of associations, whereas others included up to seven kinds, including councilors with no institutional affiliation of any kind. Councilors reported themselves as representatives of popular health movements, health units, religious associations, neighborhood associations, unions, civil rights groups, participatory forums, homelessness movements, landless peasants movements, community or philanthropic groups, disabled persons associations, or as nonaffiliated representatives. In 16 of the 31 LHCs, more than three kinds of associations were represented, and at least three of them— community groups, disabled associations, and nonaffiliated representatives— had no traditional association with the PT. Of the 15 LHCs with three or fewer kinds of associations, 11 were largely made up of councilors from associations with ties to the PT.[4]

These findings suggest that the LHCs are providing spaces for representation of a range of associations that make up civil society in the city. The first of the conditions needed to guarantee a democratic basis for social participation—the inclusion of a diverse spectrum of actors—was met in 16 out of 31 LHCs.

The research then tried to explain the variation in the number of sectors represented at the LHCs by examining three factors: (1) the way the selection of councilors was conducted, (2) the level of commitment of public officials to the participatory project, and (3) the degree of civil society organization in the different regions of the city.

To identify differences between selection processes that occurred in the various submunicipal authorities, we determined whether a database of associations and movements in the region had been organized, what means were used to publicize the elections (newspapers, radio, Internet, or mail campaigns), whether nominations were granted both to individuals and to organizations, and whether documentation of the entire election process was available.

The commitment of public officials was inferred from the existence of a budget provision, the type of information submitted and the way in which it was made available to councils, the regularity of submission of such information, the presence of the health coordinator within the health council, and councilors' ease of access to the authorities and the information they requested.

The degree of civil society organization was evaluated on the basis of the statistical data gathered by the survey of "Collective Action in São Paulo" and refers to the number of individuals from a sample who declared they had taken part in activities linked to popular organizations (Avritzer, Recamán, and Venturi 2004).

Our initial findings suggested that the inclusion of a wider spectrum of participants could not be explained only by design (publicizing of the selection process), political variables (commitment of public officials), or associative variables (percentage of participants in civil associations). So the question remained: How could the differences in the range of associations represented on different councils be explained?

Next we tried to assess the significance of the simultaneous presence of all the variables and, based on that analysis, discovered a strong pattern.[5] Our analysis suggests that none of the three variables could by itself explain the breadth of segments represented in the councils, but the simultaneous presence of these variables in a given submunicipal authority did favor diversity.[6]

For public officials concerned with ensuring that participatory forums are not merely dominated by more organized and influential groups, these findings suggest the need for working on at least four fronts. Officials need to actively publicize the selection process and the forums' activities, search for ways to involve the less organized groups as well as to facilitate processes of citizen organization, and ensure that resources, information, and personnel are available to support the forums' activities. Finally, officials must document these measures in ways that facilitate learning about how they contribute to the quality of the participatory process. I will turn to the last point in the next section.

Unpacking Participation

I have argued here that multiple factors were needed to guarantee the inclusion of a diverse spectrum of actors in the sectoral policy councils. What happened, however, in the councils once these actors entered it? How did actors connect with broader networks? What about the internal dynamics of the councils? Did they ultimately generate policy inputs?

The authors who analyzed these councils have reached ambivalent conclusions about their characteristics and capacity to impact policy. Whereas various cases presented poor features and relatively little achievement, there were also numerous successful cases. Nevertheless, these conclusions came through a collection of case studies, although, in fact, methodological instruments were not available to move toward a systematic comparison of these experiences. To fill this gap, we began to work on a model of analysis that would allow for evaluation and systematic comparison.

This effort is in line with the work of a growing group of researchers who highlight the need to construct models that enable the analysis, evaluation, and comparison of both procedures and outcomes of participatory mechanisms.[7] To proceed in this direction, we developed a model that differentiates between three dimensions of the institutionalized experiences of social participation:

(1) *Inclusion:* To describe who is being included and the degree of heterogeneity of the participants in relation to sociodemographic, political, and associative characteristics

(2) *Participation:* To describe how the agenda is set and how the organization of the discussions and the practice of deliberation, persuasion, bargaining, and confrontation happen in the meetings, and to map the information flows and the propositions that emerge through this process

(3) *Connections:* To describe the links with the executive and legislative branches at the municipal, state, and national levels, as well as to describe the connections with other participatory forums, other institutions in the health system, and other public and private organizations.

Inquiring about these features helps to describe the forums and produce data that can be used to test hypotheses related to the role of design, as well as the role of social and state actors in defining the performance of the forums. Next, I will unpack these dimensions and describe how this model provides a basis for further empirical testing and theoretical elaboration.

What Is Desirable?

In this section, in the light of a brief literature review, I briefly present the normative debates concerning what is desirable in terms of each of the three dimensions that form our assumptions about LHCs. I then list the variables that make up each of these dimensions. It is worth remembering that the next step involves defining the indicators and criteria that allow the attribution of values (for example, 0 or 1) to each of these variables (and when necessary subvariables).

Inclusion

A heated debate is taking place about the type of inclusion that should be reached through a participatory process. The regulations of the Brazilian health councils mention guaranteeing adequate representation of organized civil society (Cornwall and Shankland 2008). Some authors, however, highlight the need to promote the inclusion of groups traditionally marginalized from the political processes (Cornwall 2008; Gaventa 2006), specifically needy, poorly mobilized, and disorganized groups. Other authors call for the use of random selection as a way to guarantee that the sociodemographic profile of the councilors mirrors that of the population (Fishkin and Luskin 1999). This last method, it is hoped, would avoid favoring not only those with more resources, but also the monopolization of debates by politicized

Table 22.1. Indicators of Inclusion

Variable	Instrument
1. Variation in the socioeconomic and demographic profile of the participants	Questionnaire Information about the socioeconomic profile of the population
2. Party political variation	Questionnaire Information about the party ideological spectrum
3. "Associationalist" profile of the participants	Questionnaire

Source: Author.

collective actors with strongly polarized positions. Table 22.1 presents the variables and instruments related to this dimension.

Each of these perspectives derives from a different understanding of what inclusion is. From a legal perspective, defined in the Brazilian regulations of the health councils, greater inclusion occurs when more civil society organizations are represented. Those that argue for random selection suggest that the sociodemographic profile of the councilors should ideally mirror that of the population. Finally, for those who argue for the need to include the most marginalized groups, greater inclusion will take place once a socioeducational profile that has a significant presence of the poor and less well educated is in place.

Participation

Various studies that analyzed participative experiences highlighted the fact that the relationships between the actors are marked by huge asymmetries, that state agents have excessive power, and that the forums are often captured by party political groups. Numerous authors also highlighted the fact that stakeholders have a strong adversarial and co-optive relationship to one another and that nontransparent mechanisms are used for structuring and displaying the decision-making process.[8]

All of these researchers, however, struggle with the challenges of organizing public debate that guarantees analytic rigor concerning the problem and potential solutions, careful and respectful consideration of information with diverse points of view being provided, provision of sufficient opportunities for participants to speak, and recognition of—though not necessarily agreement with—participants' different approaches to speaking and understanding (Dryzek 2001).

Various authors argue that design features can help to bring highly asymmetrical and conflictive environments closer to the ideal conditions of public debate (Ansell and Gash 2007; Coelho and Favareto 2008; Lieres and Kahane 2006; Rowe and Frewer 2004). It is suggested that facilitative leadership is important for empowering weaker participants. Information, it is argued, should be derived from both expert witnesses and participants' own knowledge of the issues and values, guaranteeing a two-way flow of communication.

Table 22.2. Indicators of Participation

Variable	Instrument
1. Selection procedures	Field observation, minutes
2. Facilitation	Field observation
3. Agenda (who sets; issues in discussion)	Minutes, discussion analysis, field observation
4. Information provided	Minutes, discussion analysis
5. Right to speak	Minutes, discussion analysis
6. Environment (deliberations, persuasion, and confrontation)	Minutes, discussion analysis, field observation
7. Decision-making method	Minutes, field observation
8. Accountability to constituencies	Questionnaire, field observation
9. Satisfaction	Questionnaire

Source: Author.

Other features highlighted are related to the transparency and structure of the meetings. In this sense, it is necessary to verify who sets the agenda, how the process unfolds, and who speaks and is listened to. Furthermore, with reference to the quality of the debate, it is necessary to observe if the discussions are deliberative, if much negotiation takes place, and if the environment is one of dialogue or confrontation. How are decisions made, through quantitative procedures or consensus agreements?

Finally, it is necessary to analyze what new information is added and what kinds of decisions are made. Many authors justify participatory processes based on their potential to bring to light information about the demands and the quality of services that the population receives, as well as inform the population as to what is being debated in terms of health policies. The argument is that by broadening the available information, the possibilities for innovation and adjusting the terms of supply and demand increase (Coelho and others 2010).

In short, to what degree do different methods of selecting representatives, facilitators, well-structured meetings, the availability of information, and mechanisms for publicizing the decisions contribute to the establishment of a democratic process?

From this starting point, we defined nine variables, as listed in table 22.2.

Connections

What enables us to describe, compare, and evaluate the participatory process in terms of its links with the policy process? Here again, there is no simple answer, because considerable debate surrounds what type of connection and what level of coordination are important. We evaluate the existing connections between the LHCs and the policy processes that take place in the executive and legislative branches at the municipal, state, and national levels. We also refer to the connections with other participatory forums, with other institutions in the health system, and with other public and private organizations.

From this starting point, we defined five variables set out in table 22.3.

Table 22.3. Indicators of Connections between the Participatory Forum and Other Spaces and Institutions

Variable	Instrument
1. Hierarchy: legal structures connecting with other arenas, vertical and horizontal delegation	Legislation, in-depth interviews
2. Variation in the range of the network: connections with managers	Minutes, questionnaires
3. Variation in the range of the network: connections with politicians	Minutes, questionnaires
4. Variation in the range of the network: connections with participatory forums	Minutes, questionnaires
5. Variation in the range of the network: connections with other organizations, health units, and government bodies	Minutes, questionnaires

Source: Author.

Comparing Features

The model was worked out in two stages. First, we chose one version, among the various presented earlier, of what should be understood as fostering "more inclusion," "more participation," and "more connections" and detailed the indicators associated with each variable. Second, we defined the criteria that allow the attribution of values (0 or 1) to each indicator.

As an example: The second variable of the "participation" dimension is "facilitation." This variable provides information about strategies used for counteracting asymmetries between participants. The indicator shows the presence or absence of a skilled facilitator conducting the work of the forum. The presence of a skilled facilitator is expected to increase the opportunities for debate and is valued as 1, whereas its absence is valued as 0. Nevertheless, because several variables described in the previous session are continuous, we will provide a brief explanation of the two procedures that can be used in most cases to allow their conversion to dichotomous variables (0 or 1):[9]

- For population characteristics such as gender, age, or skin color, once the profile of the population in the area covered by each council is identified, it is possible to measure the extent to which the distribution observed in the councils and the "normal" distribution observed in the population converge ("normal" ranged from 10 percent above or below this distribution). If a council's profile is in line with the population profile, a value of 0 or 1 is assigned depending on the criteria adopted. For example, in our study we valued as 1 the councils where the gender distribution was in line with the population profile, and as 0 the ones where the educational profile showed a significant presence of less educated participants. Our normative assumption behind these decisions was that we believe in the importance of ensuring a balanced presence of male and female and a significant presence of less educated participants.[10]
- To assess the councils with more connections between the forums and, for example, the health managers, we list all the managers cited in interviews

and minutes related to the councils under study and assign a value of 1 to those councils in which more than the average number of managers, that have been calculated, were cited.

This model was applied to six LHCs located in poor areas of the city that have similar human development indexes. Three methods have been used to gather information: (1) analysis of the legal structure, (2) analysis of the minutes of the council's meetings and decisions, and (3) carrying out of interviews with and administering of questionnaires to the councilors, participants, and managers of the health system. The material collected together with the questionnaires and the minutes has been systematized in two databases, one for the interviews and the other for the minutes. The data were organized in tables referring to each dimension.

This work allowed empirical testing concerning how the variables under study affect one another and highlighted some interesting relationships. For example, in analysis of the results that refer to the dimension of inclusion, the significant presence of the poor and less well educated did not correlate positively with the presence of more types of organizations or more political plurality. These findings reinforce the need to consider the distinction between the variables discussed and the implications of using, as is done in the SUS, selection procedures based on associational representation.

The subsequent analysis of the minutes allowed the systematization of the debates, decisions, and recommendations made by the councils. The interviews with public managers helped in the identification of which of these recommendations have been included in the policy decision-making process. It is important to highlight that the councils where a significant presence of the poor and less well educated was reported were the ones that better performed in terms of articulating alliances with public managers as well as the ones that showed better outcomes in monitoring health care services and raising funds. To better understand these results, we inquired about the history of civil society involvement with health issues in the different areas under study and found that longer histories of involvement helped to explain the successful involvement of the poor and less educated in the councils.

Final Remarks

I began by asking how to promote and assess democratic and effective participatory mechanisms. To deal with these questions, I presented the work in progress of a research program on participatory governance in Brazil that is part of a larger program, the Citizenship Development Research Centre, concerned with understanding the conditions under which citizen engagement and institutional building actively contributes to participatory governance.[11]

As we saw, even in a single city, enormous differences can be found in the process of implementing the local health councils. Nevertheless, patterns could be recognized, and we were able to judge some of them as more "democratic" than others. To make this judgment, we relied on the literature that discusses the dangers and the possibilities associated with social participation and on empirical research that allowed describing and analyzing different procedural dimensions of the councils.

Despite the complexities of dealing with different understandings of what participatory governance is, as well as the dangers of relying too much on normative assumptions regarding democratic governance, I believe that the findings presented in this chapter open a clear path for those interested in empirically recognizing the actors and design features that contribute to bringing a plurality of groups into a productive debate about public issues. This path follows two principles. One is the need to carefully unpack the process and the procedures through which participatory mechanisms are being built concerning the dimensions discussed previously: inclusion, dynamics, connections, and debate content. The other is the permanent need to examine the appropriateness of these processes and procedures against normative statements clearly presented.

As a final and very practical comment, one of the main difficulties we found over these years to advance the comparative dimension of our international work is the lack of documentation concerning participatory experiences. In general they are very poorly documented. In the case of the LHCs described in this article, it was up to us to describe all the characteristics of the councilors— including, for example, age, gender, education—as well as the characteristics of the council itself. The minutes were also uneven; some were very detailed, whereas others presented very poor information about what was discussed in the meetings.

In this sense, from a research perspective, a systematic effort on the part of those involved in organizing participatory forums to better document the profile of participants and to report what was discussed and decided in the meetings and which methodologies were used in the near future can make an enormous contribution to advancing the research about how social participation and participatory governance links to the democratization of politics and policies. From a policy perspective, more investment in synthesizing and communicating the debates and recommendations made by the councils would go some distance in helping to rescue the richness of involving citizens, managers, researchers, and service providers in policy debates as well as in preparing these materials to be used more effectively during other stages of the policy process.

Notes

1. This program is coordinated in Brazil by CEBRAP as part of the Development Research Centre on Citizenship, Participation and Accountability/Institute of Development Studies/University of Sussex, and supported by DFID (Department for International

Development) and CEM with support from FAPESP (Fundação de Amparo à Pesquisa do Estado de São, or Sao Paulo Research Foundation).

2. A detailed description of the research process can be found in Coelho (2006) and Coelho and others (2010).

3. See Abers (2001); Baiocchi (2001); Fung (2004); Heller (2001); Melo and Baiocchi (2007); Wampler and Avritzer (2004).

4. The survey also found that 29 of the 31 LHCs concentrated recruitment in health facilities. Six LHCs included only these. In eastern and southern regions of the city this way of organizing representation is strongly associated with the Popular Health Movement, which has been highly active in those regions since the 1970s and has strong ties with the PT (Bógus 1998). Other categories often historically related to left-wing parties, such as religious associations, participatory forums, and the homeless movement, were also more frequently represented (in 15, 7, and 10 LHCs, respectively).

5. Pearson correlation = 0.531. A correlation of 0.431 also appears for the simultaneous presence of committed managers and inclusive procedures.

6. We found no association between the simultaneous presence of those variables and the Human Development Index that was calculated for each of the 31 submunicipal authorities that host the LHCs.

7. Abelson and Gauvin (2005); Ansell and Gash (2007); Rowe and Frewer (2004); Wyman and Dale (2008). See also E. House and K. Howe, "Deliberative Democratic Evaluation Checklist," evaluation checklist project (2000), http://www.wmich.edu.edu/evalctr/checklist

8. See Avritzer and Navarro (2003); Barnes (2007); Coelho and Nobre (2004); Dagnino and Tatagiba (2007); Mahmud (2004); Mohanty (2007); Ziccardi (2004).

9. A more detailed presentation of how each variable was calculated in the empirical study we held can be found at http://www.centrodametropole.org.br/v1/dados/saude/Anexos_Artigo_Saude_CDRCCEM.pdf

10. For democratic characteristics, we attributed 1 to councils that followed the population profile. For socioeconomic variables, we adopted different criteria: 1 was assigned to councils that had a socio-educational profile with a significant presence of the poor and less well educated.

11. Kabeer (2005); Leach, Scoones, and Wynne (2005); Newell and Wheeler (2007).

References

Abelson, J., and F. Gauvin. 2005. "Assessing the Impact of Public Participation: Concepts, Evidence, and Policy Implications." Centre for Health Economics and Policy Analysis, McMaster University, Ontario.

Abers, R. 2001. *Inventing Local Democracy: Grassroots Politics in Brazil*. Boulder: Westview.

Ansell, C., and A. Gash. 2007. "Collaborative Governance in Theory and Practice." *Journal of Public Administration Research and Theory Advance Access* 18 (4): 543–71.

Avritzer, L., and Z. Navarro, eds. 2003. *A Inovação Democrática no Brasil*. São Paulo: Cortez Editora.

Avritzer, L., M. Recamán, and G. Venturi. 2004. "Associativismo em São Paulo." In *Participação em São Paulo*, ed. L. Avritzer, 11–58. São Paulo: Unesp.

Baiocchi, G. 2001. "Participation, Activism, and Politics: The Porto Alegre Experiment and Deliberative Democratic Theory." *Politics and Society* 29 (1): 43–72.

Barnes, M. 2007. "Whose Spaces? Constestations and Negotiations in Health and Community Regeneration Forums in England." In *Spaces for Change? The Politics of Participation in New Democratic Arenas*, ed. A. Cornwall and V. S. Coelho, 240–59. London: Zed Books.

Bógus, C. M. 1998. *Participação popular em saúde.* São Paulo: Anna Blume.

Coelho, V. S. 2006. "Democratization of Brazilian Health Councils: The Paradox of Bringing the Other Side into the Tent." *International Journal of Urban and Regional Development* 30 (3): 656–71.

Coelho, V. S., and A. Favareto 2008. "Questioning the Relationship between Participation and Development: A Case Study of the Vale do Ribeira, Brazil." *World Development* 36: 2937–52.

Coelho, V. S., A. Ferraz, F. Fanti, and M. Ribeiro. 2010. "Mobilization and Participation: A Zero Sum Game?" In *Mobilising for Democracy: Citizen Engagement and the Politics of Public Participation,* ed. V. Coelho and B. von Lieres. London: Zed Books.

Coelho, V. S., and M. Nobre. 2004. *Participação e Deliberação: Teoria democrática e experiências institucionais no Brasil contemporâneo.* São Paulo: 34 Letras.

Coelho, V., B. Pozzoni, and M. Cifuentes. 2005. "Participation and Public Policies in Brazil." In *The Deliberative Democracy Handbook: Strategies for Effective Civic Engagement in the 21st Century,* ed. J. Gastil and P. Levine, 174–84. San Francisco: Jossey-Bass.

Coelho, V. S., and N. Silva. 2007. "Has the Distribution of Public Health Services Become More Equitable? Reflecting on the Case of São Paulo." In *The Politics of Service Delivery in Democracies: Better Services for the Poor,* ed. S. Shantayanan and I. Widlund, 136–49. Stockholm: Ministry for Foreign Affairs.

Cornwall, A. 2008. *Democratising Engagement: What the UK Can Learn from International Experience.* London: Demos.

Cornwall, A., and V. S. Coelho. 2007. *Spaces for Change? The Politics of Participation in New Democratic Arenas.* London: Zed Books.

Cornwall, A., and A. Shankland. 2008. "Engaging Citizens: Lessons from Building Brazil's National Health System." *Social Science & Medicine* 66: 2173–84.

Dagnino, E., and L. Tatagiba. 2007. *Democracia, Sociedade Civil e Participação.* Chapecó: Argos.

Dryzek, J. S. 2001. "Legitimacy and Economy in Deliberative Democracy." *Political Theory* 29 (October): 651–69.

Fishkin, J., and R. Luskin. 1999. "The Quest for Deliberative Democracy." *The Good Society* 9 (1): 1–9.

Fung, A. 2004. "Survey Article: Recipes for Public Spheres: Eight Institutional Design Choices and Their Consequences." *Journal of Political Philosophy* 11: 338–67.

Fung, A., and O. E. Wright. 2003. *Deepening Democracy: Institutional Innovation in Empowered Participatory Governance.* London: Verso.

Gaventa, J. 2006. "Triumph, Deficit or Contestation? Deepening the 'Deepening Democracy' Debate." IDS Working Paper 264, Institute of Development Studies, London.

Heller, P. 2001. "Moving the State: The Politics of Democratic Decentralization in Kerala, South Africa, and Porto Alegre." *Politics & Society* 29 (1): 131–63.

Kabeer, N., ed. 2005. *Inclusive Citizenship: Meanings and Expressions.* London: Zed Books.

Leach, M., I. Scoones, and B. Wynne. 2005. *Science and Citizens: Globalization and the Challenges of Engagement.* London: Zed Books.

Lieres, B., and D. Kahane. 2006. "Inclusion and Representation in Democratic Deliberations: Lessons from Canada's Romanow Commission." In *Spaces for Change? The Politics of Participation in New Democratic Arenas,* ed. A. Cornwall and V. S. Coelho, 131–51. London: Zed Books.

Mahmud, S. 2004. "Citizen Participation in the Health Sector in Rural Bangladesh: Perceptions and Reality." *IDS Bulletin* 35 (2): 11–18.

Melo, M. A., and G. Baiocchi. 2007. "Symposium on Deliberative Democracy and Local Governance: Towards a New Agenda." *International Journal of Urban and Regional Research* 30 (3): 587–671.

Mohanty, R. 2007. "Gendered Subjects, the State and Participatory Spaces: The Politics of Domesticating Participation in Rural India." In *Spaces for Change? The Politics of Participation in New Democratic Arenas,* ed. A. Cornwall and V. S. Coelho, 76–94. London: Zed Books.

Newell, P., and J. Wheeler. 2007. *Rights, Resources and the Politics of Accountability.* London: Zed Books.

Rowe, G., and L. Frewer. 2004. "Evaluating Public-Participation Exercises." *Science, Technology & Human Values* 29 (4): 512–56.

Wampler, B., and L. Avritzer. 2004. "Públicos Participativos: sociedade civil e novas instituições no Brasil democrático." In *Participação e Deliberação: teoria democrática e experiências institucionais no Brasil contemporâneo,* ed. V. Coelho, and M. Nobre, 210–38. São Paulo: 34 Letras.

Wyman, M., and J. Dale. 2008. "Evaluation Report on Preparing for an Influenza Pandemic: Public Consultation on Publicly-Funded Antivirals for Prevention." Paper prepared for the Public Health Agency of Canada, Toronto.

Ziccardi, A., 2004. *Participación ciudadana y políticas sociales en el ámbito local.* Ciudad de México: UNAM.

23

Stimulating Activism through Champions of Change

Samuel Paul

Organizing collective action by ordinary citizens is not an easy task. This explains why such interventions occur so infrequently and are difficult to sustain. "People Power" in the Philippines or the recent large-scale protests led by monks in Myanmar are rare examples of collective citizen action. Ordinary people are busy with earning a livelihood and supporting their families. It is costly for them to give their time and energies to public issues when they have more important priorities and are unsure that they will benefit from such public participation. It is when a public crisis occurs or a cause affects their survival or deeply held values that they will join together to tackle the problem. A second reason why some people may not engage in collective action is because they believe that they will benefit anyway from what others try to achieve through collective action. This is the "free rider" phenomenon often observed in the public arena in many societies. The benefits of "public goods" cannot be restricted to those who may have led the campaigns to create them. A small group may have worked hard to get a new road in their village, but others will also be able to use the road. The incentive to engage in collective action then tends to be weak because of this spillover effect. A third reason that applies especially to developing countries is the wide prevalence of ignorance among large segments of the population and the difficulties in reaching and communicating with them. For those who organize collective action, this can act as a disincentive. If the costs are prohibitive, large-scale citizen action may not emerge at all.

The examples of citizen action discussed in this chapter do not pertain to major political or national crises. Our focus is on cities and other local areas where it is a bit easier to organize collective action. Even in these smaller spatial units, however, collective action will not emerge unless several conditions are met. The most important condition is severity of the problem faced by the people. It is when an initiative addresses issues of great concern to the people that they can be stimulated to come together for joint action. The "citizen report cards" of Bangalore, India, presented here meet this criterion. The compactness of a spatial unit such as a town or a city makes communication and organization also more manageable. In the following pages, a short account of how civic activism was generated in Bangalore will be presented. The lessons of this experience and their implications are also summarized.

In most developing countries, the provision of essential public services to the people is the responsibility of government. Monopoly in services often results in inefficiency and nonresponsiveness, which in turn causes much public dissatisfaction. In this context, consumers of the services have no recourse to market alternatives. As citizens, however, they can demand better performance from government agencies if they are strongly motivated and organized. However, a person or a group must lead this initiative. This is what happened in Bangalore, where an innovative tool for making such demands was created and later named the "citizen report card." A civil society initiative undertaken over the past decade in Bangalore shows the potential of this tool for collective civic action and increased public accountability.

A report card grades a service provider based on feedback from the users of its services. Services can be rated on different dimensions, and the ratings compared across agencies. This is made possible by the participation of large numbers of citizens who are users of various public services through the survey methodology. The dissemination of the ratings through the media and public meetings can be used to stimulate agency leaders to improve their services, thus substituting for pressures from a competitive market. Report cards, reinforced by advocacy campaigns carried out by civil society groups and the media, provide a tool for increasing and targeting pressures for reform.

The Bangalore experience, with three successive report card initiatives in 1994, 1999, and 2003, shows that success can take time. The first report card, in 1994, gave very low ratings to all the major service providers of the city, creating a sense of shame through public exposure of the problems. It did not make an immediate impact on service improvement, however, as only a few of the providers acknowledged their problems and took corrective action. The second report card, in 1999, showed that limited improvement had occurred in some services. The third report card, in 2003, revealed substantial improvement in almost all the service providers. There was not only a significant increase in citizen satisfaction with the services, but also some decline in corruption.

This success was the result of multiple factors. On the demand side, the report cards and attendant media publicity led to public "glare," or heightened public attention to service problems. This triggered a response on the supply side, as the state government set up a new public-private partnership forum to help the service providers upgrade their services and improve responsiveness. The political support and commitment of the chief minister of Karnataka state, of which Bangalore is the capital, was an important factor. The innovative practices introduced by the partnership forum, the proactive role of external catalysts such as the media and civil society groups, and the learning resulting from the experiments initiated by the different players all contributed to better performance by the city's service providers.

A History of the Initiative, 1993–2003

During 1993–94, a small group of citizens in Bangalore prepared a report card on the public services in their city, based on feedback from the users of these services. The reason for this unusual initiative was the dismal state of essential services in the city and the public perception that government was mostly indifferent to this problem. The report card initiators hoped that their effort would stimulate citizens to demand greater public accountability from the service providers or, at a minimum, give wider publicity to the problem.

Bangalore in 1993 was a growing industrial city with a population of more than 4 million, already becoming a hub of information technology. Yet a quarter of its population was poor, living mainly in slums spread throughout the city. As in other Indian cities, residents depended on several public agencies established by the state government for their essential services. Thus, the city's municipal corporation provided roads, street lights, and garbage removal, while another agency supplied electricity. Water, transport, telecommunications, health care, and urban land and housing were the responsibility of other large public service providers.

In this context, the small citizens' group in Bangalore, which I led, decided to launch a survey to gather feedback on public services. The methodology was to tap into the knowledge and experience of the users of services in a neutral and professional manner. It was the pooling and analysis of this information that formed the basis for the collective civic action. What we generated was a form of "collective feedback" of citizens on a set of essential services. The survey was carried out by a supportive market research firm, with survey costs met through local donations.

Survey development began with an assessment of service-related problems through focus group discussions. Structured questionnaires were then designed and pretested to ensure their relevance and suitability for field-level interviews. The survey covered nearly 1,200 households, with one questionnaire for general households (mainly middle class) and another for slum households (mainly low income). In both cases the objectives were to find out (a) how satisfactory the public services were from the users' perspective, (b) which aspects of the services were satisfactory and which were not, and (c) the direct and indirect costs incurred by users for these services. Satisfaction was measured on a scale of 1 to 7, and ratings for the different dimensions of services were aggregated to yield averages. Trained investigators conducted the field interviews. The results obtained from analysis of the data were used to rate the different service providers in terms of quality of service, corruption, and overall user satisfaction. A structured summary of these ratings for all agencies involved was called the "citizen report card on public services."

A report card can help to improve public services in three ways, all of which came into play in the Bangalore experience. First, when the government's own monitoring is weak or incomplete, efforts to track service delivery from a user perspective can help compensate for this deficiency. A report card can thus serve as a benchmarking exercise. When it is repeated after a year or two, both the government and the citizens can see whether things are improving and take action accordingly. Second, a report card can create a "glare effect." When the results are publicized, the performance of service providers becomes widely known to one and all, bringing shame to an agency whose ratings are bad and, ideally, motivating that agency to perform better. This effect, of course, will work only in settings where there is freedom of the press and a relatively open society. Third, report cards can motivate organized civic groups to be proactive in demanding greater accountability from service providers. They may, for example, engage in dialogue with the agencies on ways to improve services, propose reform options, and promote public awareness about the needed remedies.

Bangalore's first report card in 1994 revealed several interesting patterns (Paul 1995). In the set of middle-income households, satisfaction levels did not exceed 25 percent for any of the seven service providers covered. Dissatisfaction levels were very high among these respondents, reaching 65 percent in the case of the Bangalore Development Authority. Satisfaction with staff behavior in the seven agencies averaged only 25 percent.

Thus, the 1994 report card results from both middle- and low-income households presented a picture of highly unsatisfactory and nonresponsive service providers in the city. The findings were widely publicized in the Bangalore press. Newspapers played a particularly important role in creating public awareness of the findings; a leading paper, the *Times of India,* published weekly features highlighting the findings about individual agencies over several months. The full report card was provided to the state government and to the service providers themselves. Citizen groups were invited to debate the findings and propose ways to deal with the problems highlighted by the report card.

The group of citizens responsible for the initiative did not initially plan for follow-up beyond publication of the report card itself. However, inquiries began to reach us about how this work, along with advocacy for reform, could be scaled up. This growing public interest persuaded us to establish a new nonprofit organization, the Public Affairs Centre (PAC), in Bangalore in 1994. Early activities included responding to requests for advice from three of the seven service providers covered by the report. In particular, the worst-rated agency asked PAC to assist in further investigating its problems and finding remedies (Paul 2002).

Although the providers did not take immediate action to improve their services, a process of reform had begun. In addition to the dialogue of three agencies with PAC, the municipal commissioner also decided to create a joint forum for service providers and civil society. This served not only as an opportunity for dialogue on services, but also as an instrument to generate new reform ideas and experiments.

In 1999, PAC prepared a second report card on Bangalore's public services. The survey methodology used was essentially the same as in 1994, but the sample size was increased to 2,000 households. Two additional agencies were covered, raising the total to nine. The results showed some improvement in public satisfaction with most of the seven agencies that had also been rated in 1994 (Paul and Sekhar 2000). The average satisfaction level, however, was still below 50 percent, even for the better-performing agencies. One disturbing finding was that corruption levels had increased in several agencies. The report card also indicated a clear link between petty corruption and inefficient service provision. Low-income people continued to need more visits to agencies to solve their problems than did their middle-income counterparts. Despite the limited progress demonstrated and the backsliding on corruption, the sequence of two report cards demonstrated how such phenomena could be tracked and highlighted through credible methods, bringing the agencies under a "public scanner."

The follow-up actions in 1999 differed significantly from those in 1994. Well before public dissemination of the results, PAC presented mini–report cards individually to each of the major service providers in the city. This was followed by a seminar for management teams from selected agencies to discuss their experiences with reforms since the first report card. These deliberations, including agencies that had sought PAC's help as well as those that had not, showed that all the agencies were engaged in efforts to improve their services in different ways. Finally, a public meeting was held in which the second report card's findings were presented to both leaders and staff of all the service providers, with citizen groups and media also present. Leaders of the agencies addressed the gathering and explained to the public their plans to deal with the problems highlighted in the report card. This event and the report card findings were widely covered by the news media.

Although the 1999 report card showed only limited improvements in the city's services, it was clear that several of the service providers had taken action to improve service quality and to respond to specific issues raised by the first report card. Several agencies, for example, had improved their billing procedures. In addition, most agencies had started joint forums with users in order to improve responsiveness by staff.

Within a few months of the second report card, the potential for greater impact increased dramatically when the new chief minister of Karnataka state announced the creation of a Bangalore Agenda Task Force (BATF) to improve the city's services and infrastructure, with greater public participation. BATF was established as a public-private partnership involving several nonofficial and eminent citizens (including the author) along with the heads of all service providers. In contrast to the more limited agency responses, this move by the chief minister ensured systemic responses across agencies. It was the first time that a chief minister in India had launched an initiative to improve services for a large city in response to citizen feedback.

In 2003, PAC launched the third citizen report card in Bangalore. The findings were presented at a BATF summit meeting attended by the chief minister, other ministers, and a large number of citizens. For the first time, the report card gave high marks to most agencies, a big improvement from the ratings of 1994 and 1999. Public satisfaction with the services, staff conduct, and problem incidence showed a significant increase. Even corruption levels had come down somewhat. Many factors seem to have contributed to this positive outcome. It is useful to examine them in some detail.

The drivers of change in Bangalore can be divided into two categories. On the one hand, demand-side factors such as citizen and media pressure sparked and sustained the change. This required the context of an open democratic society with institutionalized tolerance of dissent and debate. On the other hand, supply-side factors, in the form of government action to implement reforms, were also indispensable. The government response made possible the interaction between citizens and agencies that led to positive outcomes in improvement of services.

Factors Contributing to Success

In the decade-long report card experience in Bangalore, it is possible to identify three factors on the demand side that worked together to sustain pressure for change. Most important were the report cards themselves and advocacy by a diverse network of civil society groups. These were reinforced by media attention and by public meetings. These factors operated both in sequence and interactively. Thus, the first report card stimulated media publicity as well as civil society activism. By the time of the second report card, civic groups and the PAC were working together to maximize their joint impact.

The Glare Effect of Citizen Report Cards

The Bangalore report cards exerted pressure on the city's service providers in three ways. First, by providing focused information on performance from the perspective of citizens, the reports put the agencies under a public scanner. Such information was new to them, and because much of it was negative, it had the effect of shaming the poor performers. Evidence from the corporate world shows that measuring and quantifying work and outputs tend to make organizations pay more attention to what is being measured. Something similar seems to have happened in the Bangalore service agencies. The chairman of the Bangalore Development Authority (BDA) recalled his reaction after the first report card gave his agency a low rating: "For the first time, there was a feedback from the public on the performance of agencies. My curiosity was triggered by the fact that in the rankings the report card assigned to the various agencies, I found the BDA had got the first rank from the bottom. I thought I should do something about this."[1] A similar motivation is evident in the initiative some agencies took after the first report card to contact PAC for its advice and assistance in improving services. Public agencies tend to be sensitive to adverse publicity, especially in a democracy.

Second, interagency comparisons seem to have worked as a surrogate for market competition.[2] Although each service provider is a monopoly within its distinctive area of activity, the report card sets up a competitive arena by permitting interagency comparison of common attributes. Users, the media, and civil society groups see delays, bribery, and nonresponsiveness as negative features in any service provider. The fact that the chairmen of some of the agencies called PAC to find out where they stood in the second report card before its findings were released shows that organizations do pay attention to how the public views them. Third, it appears that some agency chairmen, at least, saw the report card as an aid in their efforts to reform their agencies. Although the feedback on their agencies was initially negative, these leaders took a positive view of the exercise. They used the findings to goad their colleagues into taking action to improve services. It is important to note that the report card was not a one-time initiative ending with the dissemination of findings. Rather, the first report card was followed up by two more within 10 years and by ongoing advocacy for more responsive and efficient agencies.

Demand Pressure through Civil Society Groups

The report cards helped stimulate complementary public advocacy work, with the two factors having a combined impact on the government and citizens of Bangalore. This advocacy, spearheaded by PAC, was carried out through a network of civic groups and nongovernmental organizations (NGOs) in the city. The number of such groups increased significantly in the period following the first report card. Only about 20 groups were active in 1994; by 2000, their number exceeded 200. Not all of them were dynamic groups. Even so, many did participate in the campaigns and meetings organized by PAC, adding to the public pressure on service providers.

The network included two types of organizations. Neighborhood groups called residents' associations focused on one part of the city but had a direct interest in the performance of all the service providers. Citywide NGOs focused on specific civic or service-related issues. Both kinds of organizations participated in public meetings and seminars where report cards or other civic issues were discussed. These meetings engaged the service providers in active public dialogues, in contrast to the closed personal meetings with officials that previously were customary in all agencies. Some service providers, such as the electricity board, the water and sanitation board, and even the police, subsequently organized their own forums, inviting civil society groups for dialogue. As a result, interactions between organized civic groups and the service providers grew significantly.

Civic advocacy increased the stimulus for reform and responsiveness on the part of the service providers. This was already evident in 1999. After a public meeting held in Bangalore in connection with the second report card, the *Times of India* said in an editorial: "PAC, in creating this forum, has opened doors, even windows, for a healthy tête-à-tête with our service providers. The honesty on display was remarkable . . . this is the spirit of democracy in action. Civil society working in tandem with government for the greater good of all" (November 8, 1999).

In addition to such meetings, several NGOs have made distinctive contributions by carrying out citywide campaigns on specific issues. These campaigns, which mostly assisted in partnership with PAC, have served to strengthen the city's "social capital." One NGO undertook advocacy work linked to property tax reform. Another examined the municipal budget and engaged the city corporation in a debate on service efficiency and public expenditure. A third worked on the improvement of solid waste management.[3]

Reinforcement of Pressure by the Media

The print media in Bangalore played an unusual role by adding their weight to the pressure for better services. In 1994, the newspapers did little more than publicize the negative findings of the report card or other similar critical assessments. Investigative reports on civic issues were few and far between. Subsequently, however, the newspapers began to take a much more proactive role.

After deciding to devote more space to public service problems and related civic issues, several newspapers sought PAC's advice and technical support for special features. One newspaper began a series of reports on the different wards of the city, highlighting their problems and focusing on their elected council members. Another leading newspaper even took the initiative to organize meetings in different parts of the city at which citizens were invited to voice their local problems in the presence of senior officials from a selected group of public agencies. A large number of public officials thus were exposed to the issues of the localities and pressed to respond with answers. These meetings received much publicity in the newspaper, as did the remedial actions taken subsequently. This public process clearly put increased pressure on the agencies to be more transparent and accountable and to deliver on their promises.

The Bangalore report cards were the first to be initiated by PAC. Many other applications of this tool have been seen in Bangalore, however, as well as in other parts of India and in other countries (Paul 2002). One case of special relevance to the poor was PAC's report card on the maternity hospitals for poor women in Bangalore. Its findings led to systematic advocacy work by several NGOs and ultimately to the adoption of important reforms in the management of these hospitals that have benefited low-income mothers and children (Gopakumar 2005; Paul 2002). More recently, PAC has launched new forums for citizen action such as the Coalition against Corruption and Right to Information Group that function in Bangalore in partnership with several other NGOs.

Lessons Learned

When a government and its service providers are nonresponsive or perform poorly, civil society has the responsibility to demand greater accountability. Report cards in conjunction with advocacy can then become a tool to stimulate government and its service agencies to respond to the systemic problems being experienced by the people. Although there is no guarantee of effective responses, because that also depends on agency responsiveness and on the political commitment of government authorities, the Bangalore report cards show the potential for dramatic improvements. The diagnostic value of this tool for agency leaders, combined with the glare effect of public attention, can create strong pressures for greater responsiveness:

(1) *Involve civic groups early in the process:* The dissemination of findings and the follow-up advocacy work are likely to be more effective when concerned civil society institutions are involved from the start. In Bangalore, PAC itself emerged as a civil society initiative. Early consultations with NGOs working with the poor helped sharpen the focus of PAC's later surveys on the problems of poor households. This is important because many NGOs are not familiar with survey methods and analysis. They need to be convinced that this new knowledge will help their cause. This is not to say that they need to become experts in technical matters. Typically, citizens and civic groups are invited to share their understanding of the problems and the kinds of issues for which they would like feedback. They are also given an understanding of the findings and their implications. Their participation and support tend to become stronger when their understanding of the process and potential outcomes is enhanced.

(2) *Choose the problem for collective action with utmost care:* In Bangalore, the crisis in public service delivery was the focus. Dissatisfaction was widespread about public services among the people, and they were sufficiently concerned about it to devote their time and energies to demand change. If the issue had been about public procurement or recruitment of staff in the agencies, it is doubtful that the same interest and commitment to action could have been generated. Disasters and major political crises and scandals may also energize the public to engage in collective action. After a while, however, their interest may peter out, and hence the sustainability of public action will be in doubt. In many issues of public governance, sustained interest and continued action are essential. The causes involved and the modes of action thus become extremely important.

(3) *Strategic use of the media can strengthen collective action:* Communicating with citizens at large is an essential part for the success of civic activism. Not everyone attends all events and discussions. The media can take the message to the wider public. Without proper communication with the media, however, this cannot be accomplished. Media publicity has a direct impact on the policy makers and political leaders too. In Bangalore, the media played a key role in all these respects. The press, for example, saw the issue of public services as a high priority, and they helped disseminate the report card findings and strongly pitched for change. At a later stage, some newspapers started their own campaign and held public meetings in different parts of the city.

(4) *Credible champions are essential to sustain citizen activism:* Spontaneous collective action may occur when people face major crises or disasters. In the governance arena, however, where issues need to be studied and coalitions created, a leadership role must be played by a person or a small group. This is especially true of cases where the generation of knowledge must support action. The report card, for example, provided the kind of information that energized the public and the media to come together to demand change, and for the public agencies to respond. An important prerequisite for effective citizen action initiatives is the credibility of those who lead such campaigns. In the Bangalore case, the report card exercise was seen as impartial and independent. The conduct of the survey and the interpretation of its findings were done with utmost integrity. In general, competent and professionally managed organizations need to act as initiators and catalysts. These conditions apply whether the initiative comes from civil society or from the government.

(5) *A democratic society that permits dissent is a prerequisite:* Collective action by citizens to solve their problems with public agencies may not be feasible in all societies. Nondemocratic cultures and countries may tolerate dissent up to a point but clamp down on such movements when they feel threatened. An essential condition for the success of civic action is a society that

is relatively open and democratic, with some respect for dissent and public debate. In nondemocratic settings such interventions can still be used to expose shortcomings, but mobilizing the citizenry on a large scale may be difficult when the media, for example, is not free. Sustainable campaigns resulting in real improvement in public governance are unlikely without commitment by political leaders to listen to the people and engage in dialogues with them even when they demand change that may threaten the status quo.

Notes

1. The BDA chairman was interviewed in *State of India's Public Services: Benchmarks for the Millennium,* video documentary (Bangalore: Public Affairs Centre, 2003).
2. Market competition has so far affected only one service provider, the Bangalore telecommunications agency, Bharat Sanchar Nigam Ltd. Cell phones had begun to make inroads by the late 1990s.
3. These and similar initiatives are discussed in Paul (2002).

References

Gopakumar, K. 2005. "Can Public Feedback Enhance Public Accountability?" Mimeo, First International Forum on Citizen-Driven Evaluation of Public Services, Beijing.

Paul, S. 1995. *A Report Card on Public Services in Indian Cities: A View from Below.* Bangalore: Public Affairs Centre.

———. 2002. *Holding the State to Account: Citizen Monitoring in Action.* Bangalore: Books for Change.

Paul, S., and Sita Sekhar. 2000. *Benchmarking Urban Services: The Second Report Card on Bangalore.* Bangalore: Public Affairs Centre.

Informed Public Opinion and Official Behavior Change

Gopakumar Thampi

First they ignore you
then they ridicule you
then they fight you
then you win.

—Mohandas Karamchand Gandhi (1869–1948)

The Context

Modern democracies with their concern for nation building and welfare have made use of a centralized public policy as the key mode to design and deliver public services. Although the basic premise underlying the use of public policy as a means of intervention has often gone unchallenged, the modalities of state actions in operationalizing public policy have increasingly come under critical scrutiny. Various reasons account for this. First, the state, in seeking to dominate the social and economic space of a large mass of humanity, has been extremely reductionist in its approach to public policy. Many would argue that this is because of the compulsions of complexity. In the practical terrains where public policies impact on the lives of citizens, however, this approach has come to represent insensitivity, narrow vision, opaqueness, and nonresponsiveness. Perhaps this reductionist approach is sustained by the continuing obsession with normative models of public policy that prescribe and seek maximization. The state in its obligation to impose and validate its own rationality in the exercise of power inevitably tends toward one-sidedness, absence of feedback, and a dominant bureaucracy that co-opts the political system into its role of designing and implementing equitable, efficient deterministic solutions to problems of development.

The reductionist approach often brings in its wake serious problems in the interface with society. Leaving aside geographical variations, significant social, cultural, and economic variations have a significant bearing on the capacity of the polity to respond to competing demands from society. These variations also must be understood in the context of existing historical niches of pluralism that have been achieved through collective protest and organized movements (such as in India and Kenya). Despite all the shortcomings, a major advantage in most democracies is the availability of a state committed to political transaction as the central ordering mechanism.

The second theme in the debate is the use of public policy in designing a governance system for modern societies. Each time a welfare scheme, decentralization model, or development project is designed for a nation, assumptions about existing social conditions and processes do not seem to get serious attention. Be it developing physical infrastructure or policing of groundwater use, public policy often overlooks traditional institutions that have operated (perhaps suboptimally) in many areas with a good deal of success. Notwithstanding the specific benefits that the intervention seeks and achieves, unanticipated consequences abound, which act as "terminators" of traditional institutions upsetting a wide range of local processes.

The third issue is the limited manner in which public policy initiatives look at implementation methodologies. An essential weakness is the assumption that successful "end-game" positions achieved elsewhere can be organized as a single-step operation. For example, improved service delivery by writing up Citizen Charters is a typical limited public initiative, which does not integrate performance appraisal within service providers or citizen awareness and capacity to make use of the provisions envisaged.

The Case Studies

Can informed public opinion bridge some of these divides and create a stimulus for public officials to be responsive to organized public feedback? The rest of this chapter will attempt to answer this question by exploring some recent work of the Public Affairs Foundation in Delhi, India, and in Kenya. The Delhi case study reflects a unique instance of an elected political leader openly seeking public feedback on the delivery of critical public services and using this information to bring about operational changes within organizations and behavioral shifts among public officials. The Kenyan experience, on the other hand, is largely a civil society–led initiative, located within an environment of reforms, to make citizens' voice resonate effectively in an existing reform agenda to make it more inclusive, responsive, and transparent. Although the contexts and triggers vary between the two cases, the common thread uniting these experiences is the potency of an informed public voice to influence public service delivery and facilitate internal reforms within the utilities.

Monitoring of Public Service Outcomes in Delhi: A People's Audit

Emergent narratives in the domain of public accountability increasingly point to the role of user feedback in demanding and catalyzing responsiveness and accountability from providers of public utilities. Faced with very few exit options, users of public utilities are finding creative use of voice mechanisms to effectively highlight critical issues and bring about reforms. Though initially emerging as a "demand side" pressure strategy, public feedback is today perceived by many political leaders as direct feedback from the constituencies on what happens "between elections." The following case study profiles one such enabling instance.

Background

In September 2005, the Chief Minister (Head of the Provincial Government) of Delhi, Sheila Dikshit, invited the Public Affairs Foundation (PAF) to monitor the outcomes of key public services in Delhi, using citizen feedback on the service providers involved. The project was completed in September 2006, and the findings were presented to the media and officials on September 4, 2006. What made this case stand out was that the Chief Minister publicly announced the launch of this audit and openly committed to disclose the findings to the public, irrespective of the nature of the results. The audit was modeled after the well-known Citizen Report Cards, pioneered by the Public Affairs Centre (PAC).

The National Capital Territory (NCT) of Delhi is a unique administrative entity with administrative controls spread across three sets of actors—the central government, an elected state (provincial) government, and the local (municipal) government. The reformist government headed by Sheila Dikshit has been in power since 1998. During the past five or six years, huge investments have been committed to improving public infrastructure, followed by a wide range of reforms in public administration. Two major strands that stand out in the reform agenda are (1) significant investments in public infrastructure (especially in improving mass transport and provision of water) and (2) a wide range of governance applications (such as computerization of land registration and online grievance redress) that have been implemented across the board to make public services more accessible, responsive, and accountable.

The People's Audit covered 14,165 respondents in Delhi and elicited focused feedback on users' experiences across nine public services:

- Provision of drinking water to the urban poor through water tankers operated by the Delhi Jal (Water) Board
- Inpatient services provided by public hospitals run by the municipality and the state government
- Outpatient services provided by public hospitals run by the municipality and the state government
- Public bus transport services provided by the Delhi Transport Corporation

- School education provided by municipality-run primary schools, state government–run primary schools, and state government–run secondary schools
- Services provided by Fair Price Shops and kerosene depots
- Services provided by the motor licensing offices
- Services provided by the subdivisional magistrate's offices
- Services provided by the subregistrar's offices.

Organizational Anchor

The Department of Administrative Reforms (DAR), government of the National Capital Territory Delhi, was the anchor for this exercise. The organizational mandate of DAR—(a) to act as a facilitator, in consultation with the government of India, departments of the Delhi government, its autonomous bodies and undertakings, and other groups; and (b) to improve government functioning through administrative reforms in the spheres of restructuring the government, process improvement, improvement of organization and methods, grievance handling, modernization, citizens' charters, awards programs, and best practices—gave a strong legitimacy to this exercise and brought in clear ownership within the government. The fact that the initiative came from the highest public office also made the heads of the utilities participate in all discussions in the run-up to the project (which, as discussed in a later section, had a major impact on the exercise).

DAR contracted out the study to PAF to design the audit, ensure the quality of the field survey, carry out the analysis and interpretation of the findings, and identify key indicators for reforms and improvements. The field survey was outsourced separately to Nielsen, a leading market and social research agency.

Finding Institutional Champions

For PAF, the key challenge in implementing the audit was manifold. First, hitherto institutional experiences of PAF and its sister concern, PAC, hinged on using the power of public feedback as a civil society–led accountability mechanism. This was the first time that the "instigator" happened to be from the other side (the state)! Second, there was a huge political risk. To what extent will a technical exercise like this insulate itself from unexpected political undercurrents? Also, will the chief minister renege on her promise to come clean with the findings publicly? An early strategy adopted by PAF was to create a common understanding among the utility managers on the intent of this "audit." It is interesting to note here that the chief minister was not too comfortable with the phrase "Citizen Report Card" and instead suggested the term "Social Audit"; the reasoning was that report cards conveyed a notion of evaluation and assessment from outside, whereas a Social Audit would reflect a more transparent and open initiative by the state. However, during the initial interactions with the utility managers, it was clear that a majority of them were not comfortable with the term "audit." PAF had to make repeated presentations to assuage all misplaced concerns about this; ironically, it was the illustration from the Bangalore Report Card that convinced many utility managers of the neutrality and diagnostic power of this approach.

The Big Headlines from the People's Audit

A major finding of the audit was that government has extended access to most services, but has not been able to fully deliver on the quality and reliability of services. A disconcerting finding of this study was the wide variations across geographical locations in Delhi in different aspects of service delivery. This means that in addition to service quality issues, equity in service delivery is a matter of major concern. Spatial variability was observed to be high for most pro-poor services such as provision of water to poor localities through water tankers, provision of food and civil supplies, and land registration. User feedback on interfaces with agencies also pointed to the limitations of reforms that aim to tackle front-end changes. Although increasing adaptations of technology in operations have clearly streamlined processes, the continuing existence of intermediaries and weak monitoring of actual delivery show that more systemic changes are needed to make service delivery more transparent, reliable, and responsive to people. Though Citizen Charters have been created for most services, knowledge about them is quite limited. However, on the positive side, wherever users were aware of Citizen Charters, they recognized their value and found the content useful. The Social Audit also highlighted the fact that very few instances could be found of effective grievance redress whenever users complained about a problem. In addition, the study underscored the fact that very few users who faced a problem actually lodged formal complaints, perhaps indicating little faith in formal grievance redress mechanisms.

From Symptoms to Reforms: Institutional Responses to the Audit

The preliminary findings from the study were presented to the chief minister, her senior officers, and the utility managers on May 25, 2006. The findings were reviewed and discussed in detail. The openness exhibited by the chief minister to acknowledge shortcomings was remarkable; interestingly, the Delhi Jal Board (water utility) of which she is the chairperson was rated the worst in terms of overall satisfaction. Whenever a utility manager came up with a positive secondary statistic (such as the overall pass percentage for schools), she would immediately point to the overall messages indicated by the end users and ask them to pay attention to that. Her message was very clear: "I appreciate all the financial and physical data put out by all of you, but at the end of the day, as a political leader and as the Chief Executive of this government, my interest is in what people on the ground say about the services." It was quite clear that this informed public feedback gave her a new and powerful perspective from which to address issues of public service delivery that are far removed from the gibberish of official statistics.

The draft findings were then circulated to each service and department head to review thoroughly and pose any queries or clarifications to PAF. The final report was drafted by the end of August, and on September 4, 2007, the chief minister released the findings to the public at a press conference. Acknowledging the findings as a clear indicator to the government to focus more on the pro-poor sectors, the chief minister also announced that a high-level committee would be set up to address the concerns coming out of this audit and to assist individual departments and utilities to draft actionable measures. Following this, the chief minister unexpectedly requested PAF to assist the departments in preparing focused reform measures to address some of the emergent concerns. To make this initiative more embedded within the government, a small task force was created under the leadership of the former chief secretary of the Delhi government, who was a major champion of the social audit during the initial phase; PAF provided technical support to this task force.

The task force then designed a series of highly interactive and focused brainstorming sessions with a small team of staff from each department; it was made clear that the team should be representative and cut across different levels within the organization. The first round of meetings focused on creating consensus on the diagnosis of the problems (symptoms) identified in the audit. Subsequent rounds focused on generating specific reform measures. The draft reform measures suggested were then discussed widely within the departments to create broader ownership and consensus:

Round 1: From Symptoms to Diagnosis	
Key finding (symptoms)	Possible reasons (diagnosis)

Round 2: From Diagnosis to Reforms				
Key finding (symptoms)	Possible reasons (diagnosis)	Suggested measures	Expected risks/ barriers	Timeline

Round 3: Generating Consensus on the Reforms				
Key finding	Suggested measures	Comments on the suggested measures	Other workable ideas	Required resources

These intradepartmental discussions created an unprecedented ambience of dialogue and consultations. As one senior staff member remarked, "This is the first time in my entire 27 years in government that we are actually sitting down and talking about how to solve people's problems." A remarkable feature was that many junior-level staff were giving suggestions and creative options. In the food and civil supplies department, a key point of discussion was how to tackle the widely reported cases of underweighing of kerosene (used as a cooking fuel by poor families). One junior official came up with a suggestion to deploy automated vending machines that would give kerosene in sachets. The suggestion was immediately accepted, and today there are many vending machines in operation. Similarly, during discussions to solve the overcrowding of inpatients in government hospitals (the audit had revealed that on an average two to three patients share a bed), a female health official from the municipal health department came up with the suggestion of converting the underutilized medical staff quarters into health facilities. The point to note here is that the reform ideas and initiatives came entirely from within the departments and utilities. The huge reservoir of organizational knowledge and experience was creatively harnessed to bring in a collective effort to examine the informed public voice that was articulated through the social audit and to use the pointers emerging from that audit to carry out internal diagnosis and design effective response mechanisms.

Once the key reform measures were identified, the departmental teams (with help from the task force) unbundled the suggestions into four specific domains: infrastructure improvements, systems/process reengineering, and personnel and community empowerment/engagement. This was also a significant development because the usual trend is to ask for more resources. A comprehensive matrix evolved out of this exercise that detailed the response mechanisms following the audit. A sample is depicted in table 24.1.

Appropriate government orders were then issued to facilitate the implementation of these reforms. The entire process—from the release of the audit findings to the implementation and roll-out of reforms—took just four months. In the meantime, the chief minister asked PAF to prepare for a repeat audit. The findings from the first round are also being published as a book (with a preface by the chief minister); the Delhi government has given PAF the go-ahead to print 1,000 copies, and the chief minister plans to send copies to all other chief ministers in the different Indian states and encourage them to carry out similar social audits.

Strengthening Consumer Voice in the Water and Sanitation Sector in Africa: Citizen Report Cards in Kenya

Reform programs in water and sanitation sectors often target service delivery primarily through capacity building of the "supply" side of service provisioning, such as institutional strengthening, strategic planning, training, and increased budgetary allocations. This bias is premised on pressure to institute

Table 24.1. Strategizing Reforms Based on Citizens' Feedback

Services	Infrastructure improvements	Systems/process reengineering	Personnel related	Community empowerment/engagement
		Reform type		
Education	Creative options such as mobile and chemical toilets Discourage practice of locking toilets from outside Additional toilets for principals and teachers, Pota cabins	Separate engineering wing for school infrastructure Mandatory competency testing of children Teaching through cable TV slots	Improve teacher selection procedures	Set up Vidhyarthi Kalyan Samitis (Student Welfare Committees) for monitoring and raising resources
Health	Upgrade existing centers, explore options for vertical expansion Explore innovative options such as bunker-type beds All encroachments near the entrance of hospitals to be removed Empty doctors' quarters to be utilized, waiting room for bystanders Contract out ambulance services	Audiovideo information at hospitals Centralized information systems at the front desk Installing color-coded signage Redesigning the physical layout, especially the information counters Scientific staff requirement audits and studies	Presence of grievance redress officer to be made mandatory at the hospitals	Adopt Rogi Kalyan Samitis—successful patient welfare forum pioneered in many states Set up help desks with assistance from NGOs; study existing good practices for scale-up Enlist community volunteers
Food and civil supplies	Use automatic dispensers for kerosene	Toll-free help lines to be set up Setting up complaint boxes in each Circle Office, which will be opened by respective area officers once a week	Circle inspectors to visit each retail outlet every month	Citizen Watch Committees to be set up for each outlet and trained through Bhagidhari workshops Encourage independent audits by NGOs on issues of transparency Citizen Charters to be reviewed and published in other local languages such as Punjabi and Urdu Enhance awareness through media advertisements and street theater

Source: Author.
Note: NGO = nongovernmental organization.

reforms and disburse funds and the "expert-driven" generation of the data that are informing the implementation of the reforms. For Kenya, lessons learned in the sector during the 1970s and 1980s demonstrate clearly that it is not sufficient to concentrate on supply-driven mechanisms in the efforts to improve service delivery. There is also a need to capacitate the "demand" side by ensuring that the users of water and sanitation services not only are informed of the stated direction of policy, but also are enabled to exercise their voice through participating, contributing, and even holding the government and service providers accountable for the impact of the policy on citizens' livelihoods. The following narrative discusses a pioneering Citizen Report Card initiative on urban water and sanitation services in Kenya.

Context

In the past two years, the Water and Sanitation Program (WSP) has implemented a project that aims to build the capacity of civil society organizations (CSOs) to engage proactively in the process of water and sanitation sector reform. A specific problem in reform is that many local organizations that represent the interests of the poor may have little knowledge of the issues surrounding urban sector reform, including institutional restructuring, tariff reform, private sector participation, and the current status of legal and regulatory frameworks. This gap exists at the same time that many projects are being formulated in the expectation that CSOs will play a role as partners, usually as intermediaries or service providers for the poor. This gap in understanding is sometimes used as a reason to exclude CSOs from the debate on reform altogether. Where they are brought into the debate, or into project planning, it may be without an adequate grasp of the issues, or even the vocabulary of reform. This is unfair and counterproductive and does not lead to healthy partnerships or well-designed transactions.

The aim of the ongoing WSP project is to facilitate creation of a constructive environment with respect to reform, one that will allow consumer associations and other CSOs to advocate their interests (the poor, the environment) and contribute their skills and capacity.

The first phase of the project established a partnership between Water and Sanitation Program–Africa (WSP-AF), Consumers International (CI), and four consumers associations (in Chad, Kenya, Senegal, and Zambia). During the project, these partners worked to determine what capacity-building needs consumer organizations had and to develop methods and strategies to engage consumer associations and consumers themselves. This led to the publication of the joint WSP-CI report *Moving from Protest to Proposal: Building the Capacity of Consumer Organizations to Engage in Urban Water Supply and Sanitation Sector Reform in Africa.* A key lesson learned from the first phase was that most consumer and civil society organizations lack objective and credible strategies and tools to engage the service providers and policy makers.

Over March 16–17, 2005, WSP-AF, in association with WaterAid, hosted a "practicioners" meeting for partners in Africa to explore potential tools for advocacy and consumer engagement in reforms. Five tools (applied globally) were presented and discussed at the meeting: Community Score Cards, Slum Mapping, Equity Distribution Indicators, Enumeration, and Citizen Report Cards. Each of these tools was presented by a practitioner, and after clarifications, participants discussed the utility, replicability, and contextual fit of these tools. At the end of the deliberations, the Citizen Report Card (CRC) model pioneered and promoted by PAC/PAF was selected (another CRC model was presented by the Social Weather Station, a polling and research agency in the Philippines) as the most viable approach to strengthening consumer voice in the water sector in Africa. WSP-AF subsequently contracted PAF to support an 18-month capacity-building intervention in selected countries in Africa.

Context Setting and Consensus Framing

Given the untested terrain of CRC applications in Africa and the deeply divided and polemical terrain of water rights, PAF and WSP decided that the technical part of the exercise needed to be preceded by an awareness-building and consensus-creating phase. An innovative approach designed in this regard was the "Report Card Roadshows," five-day events at each proposed project site that included individual consultations with key stakeholders—utility managers, regulators, CSOs, media, community-based organizations, survey agencies, and academia—and a highly participatory and transparent one-day workshop. The individual consultations focused on creating awareness of what a CRC is—concept, methodology, outcomes, and applications. The multistakeholder workshop created a space to understand, discuss, and critique the CRC and then collectively evaluate the merit and the contextual fit of the tool.

A key highlight of the CRC-evaluation workshop was a stakeholder evaluation of "8" criteria against which the merit and contextual fit of the tool were discussed and evaluated. The "critical 8" are as follows:

- *Political Context*—How would the political institutions in the country support or hinder methodologies such as the CRC?
- *Decentralization*—Do local bodies have a reasonably high degree of financial and policy-making power?
- *Ability to Seek Feedback from Citizens*—Would organizations feel safe conducting public feedback exercises such as the CRC?
- *Citizens' Ability to Voice Experience*—Do citizens feel free to give honest feedback about government services?
- *Presence and Activism of Civil Society Organizations*—Are there active CSOs in the country? Are they independent and nonpartisan?
- *Survey and Analysis Competency*—Are there demonstrated local skills for survey and analysis?

- *Quality of Media*—Are the media independent? Do they cover issues related to public services? Will they cover CRC findings and present them in an unbiased manner?
- *Responsiveness of Service Providers*—Do service providers seek consumer/user feedback? How open would they be to independent assessments of their performance?

Each stakeholder then proceeded to discuss each of the criterion and score it along a scale of 0 to 10 (0 indicating highly disabling environment and 10 highly enabling). An actual example from Kisumu in Kenya is given in table 24.2.

As is evident from the above scores, a few themes demonstrate much divergence. One is the entire process of decentralization, and the other is the civil society sector. Although most participants agreed that progress on decentralization has occurred, the lack of a clear policy on this seems to be the bone of contention. Though enabling cases of effective interventions by local government institutions can be identified, these seem to be more ad hoc and driven by internal champions. The Kisumu civil society scene, on the other hand, is seen as a highly competitive space with organizations jostling for visibility and resources. Interestingly, at the end of the workshop strong consensus was found among the CSO participants that the CRC may indeed provide a neutral platform to bring together different CSOs and, in that sense, provides a good opportunity for networking and solidarity building.

These scores were then discussed, debated, and analyzed by all participants. Following this, each stakeholder group then proceeded to identify specific opportunities and challenges and gave the final decision. Each group then openly committed to a specific role or input they would bring on board (see figure 24.1).

What the "Roadshow" does is bring in a process of openly examining the tools and approaches from the vantage point of each critical stakeholder. The process also facilitates a forum to voice apprehensions and concerns about the tools and approaches and the likely impacts. Based on this participatory assessment, three cities in Kenya were identified for the project: Nairobi, Kisumu, and Mombasa.

Table 24.2. Assessing the Fit of CRCs: Stakeholder Feedback

Criterion	Government	SSIP	Media	CSO	Average
Political setting	7	5	5	6	5.8
Decentralization	6	6	3	3	4.5
Ability to seek feedback	8	8	8	8	8.0
Ability to voice experience	5	8	9	8	7.5
Activism of CSOs	8	6	2	6	5.5
Survey/analysis competency	7	7	7	8	7.3
Quality of media	5	5	6	8	6.0
Responsiveness of providers	4	6	1	6	4.3

Source: Author.

Note: CSO = civil society organizations; SSIP = small-scale independent provider.

Figure 24.1. Group: Kisumu Government and Utilities

Opportunities and resources	Challenges and obstacles
• existing human resources • engoing local and central government reforms, such as water sector reforms, local authority service delivery action plan, and performance contracts • existing institutional structures • high level of literacy (compared with other parts/regions) • democratic space • intensified public-private partnership agenda	• unprofessional media—often relay wrong information • public apathy and tolerance with status quo • poverty • impact of HIV • political euphoria—fast rise in expectations then very quick decline

Issues still needing examination	The verdict
• representation of sample size and distribution in terms of gender, income, location, and the like • training and education • awareness generation	yes timing: now

Specific role
• institutional anchorage • political direction • legal mandate

Source: Author.

Selecting Local "Drivers"

Two major pointers emerged from the CRC Roadshows: (1) the civil society field was extremely competitive, and the selection of a "lead agency" to drive the CRC in each city must be managed in an open and transparent fashion; and (2) the field survey must be managed by a nonpartisan and technically competent organization. Accordingly, bids were invited from both CSOs and research firms. Two separate panels consisting of representatives from WSP-AF and PAF shortlisted candidates and made the final selections. These processes reinforced the neutrality of the project.

Institutional Arrangements

The CRC process was implemented by stakeholder alliances on two levels: the national level and the city level. The process involved broad participation of diverse partners to facilitate open dialogue at local and national levels and ensure ownership of the outcomes (figure 24.2).

At the national level, a stakeholder alliance was formed to facilitate top-level dialogue on issues around the CRC process. The National Consortium comprised key policy and decision makers from national institutions, including directors from the departments of water and health and local government; chief executives of the regulatory board, water service boards, and utilities; and key officials from NGOs and national civil society institutions.

Figure 24.2. Institutional Setting for Implementing CRCs

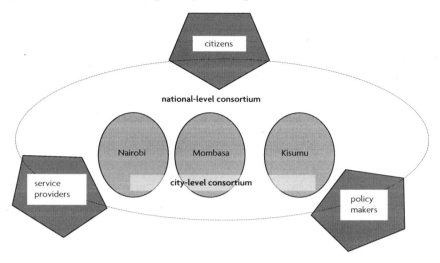

Source: Author.

The city-level consortia were established to jointly own and implement the CRC process in each of the three cities. They comprised representatives from local-based institutions that focus on or are concerned with issues affecting delivery of water and sanitation services in their respective locales.

These tiers helped to attract a broad range of actors into the fold of the initiative. Although bridges were created horizontally across similar stakeholders such as CSOs, critical links were also created vertically between these groups and utilities as well as across different levels of government.

Institutionalizing the Findings and Designing Postsurvey Responses

As a lead-up to the public release of the findings, city-level workshops were organized by the consortia in the three cities to discuss the draft findings and facilitate the utilities' preparing a response to the findings; the process was modeled after PAF's experience in Delhi (as described earlier). The consortia also held preparatory sessions for the press conference so that the key messages were articulated in a positive and proactive manner.

The findings from the CRCs in the three cities were released at a public function on May 29, 2007, in Nairobi. The guest of honor was the Assistant Minister of Water and Irrigation, the Honorable Raphael Wanjala. He officially received the city-level reports from the lead agencies, and the overall report was presented to him by citizen representatives from the informal settlements. The event attracted about 500 participants, including senior utility managers, civil society representatives, mayors, and the media. A slogan in Kiswahili was adopted during this event to unify citizens, service providers, and policy makers in the spirit of dialogue, not confrontation: "Maji na Usafi? Njooni Tujadiliane" (Water and sanitation? Come all, let's discuss and agree).

This slogan was repeated throughout the launch, displayed on T-shirts and banners, and repeated by various presenters. The service providers were comfortable with the mood, which was conciliatory, and called for dialogue over service improvements. Breakaway sessions were held to discuss in depth the city-level findings and to review the responses from the utilities. An unmistakable willingness was seen to present commitments to citizens by service providers and policy makers—not only from the water sector, but also from others such as health, environment, and local government. The minister in his speech encouraged the consortiums to continue meeting to monitor improvements and jointly explore solutions to the issues raised in the CRC. The water boards welcomed continued participation, and the Coast Water Services Board in Mombasa committed to sharing their work plans with the stakeholders to enable them to monitor the outcomes.

Insights and Pointers

Though the contexts differed and the triggers varied, the two case studies discussed earlier reveal a set of indicators that may have implications for the growing repertoire of social accountability tools and approaches. To go over a few pertinent ones:

(a) *Power of empirical data:* Undoubtedly a clear advantage is seen in "counting" the facts and experiences. To a large extent, institutional apathy can be traced to a lack of informed demand from citizens. Civic engagement quite often tends to be anecdotal and emotive and in the process narrows down confrontation and contestation. When accountability tools such as CRCs, community score cards, and social audits raise the level of discourse from the anecdotal to the factual, less defensiveness from public officials is seen in receiving the findings. This was openly articulated in the Kenyan case, where many previous civil society initiatives have failed to create an effective engagement because the issues remained mostly in the anecdotal domain. As one official remarked quite poignantly during one of the CRC Roadshows: "This clearly separates the '*noise*' from the '*voice*'!" The credibility, objectivity, and neutrality of the tool certainly helps in opening doors and windows for a more effective engagement between the citizen and the state.

(b) *Context setting and consensus creation:* Capturing and articulating citizens' voices without adequately preparing the response side will at best result in some quick fixes. It is critical that the process be inclusive, transparent, and participatory in nature. The CRC Roadshows were clearly instrumental in changing the way public officials view demand-led interventions. Much negativity, skepticism, and apprehension centered on the intent and focus of the CRCs; the phrase "report card" itself carried with it a tone of criticism and evaluation. The Roadshows created a forum in which the entire process was subject to collective scrutiny and evaluation. The initial roundtables held in

Delhi with the utility managers and agency heads also helped to create a balanced view of the tool and its implications. These initial sets of activities created a win-win ambience at the beginning of the intervention.

(c) *Public opinion as a trigger for institutional responses:* As shown in the earlier examples, public officials played a key role in using the issues arising from the citizen feedback as diagnostic indicators to design appropriate institutional responses. Usually consultants and external resource persons act as the facilitators/designers of internal reforms; although, technically, they often bring in cutting-edge practices and ideas, very seldom do these find ownership within the department. However, here the series of diagnostic exercises and brainstorming sessions created a sense of internal ownership and commitment to change. The scientific nature of the information collected, the transparency in reviewing the findings before public release, and the fact that the findings reflected both the good and the bad all combined to provide a highly enabling momentum within the departments to identify areas and processes for reforms. The fact that in Delhi all the intradepartment reform strategies incorporated themes and ideas for empowering citizens is a testimony to the acceptance of the demand-side actors within the traditional institutional mind-sets of the bureaucracy.

(d) *Role of strategic communication:* Dissemination of the findings from initiatives such as the CRC is extremely critical for deriving the maximum benefit from the effort. The usefulness of the approach will be quite limited if findings are not shared and used to bring about improvements and reforms. The design of an effective and focused strategy depends on a series of important steps:

- Identifying the target audience and stakeholders
- Deciding the channels and networks and specific activities to reach the audience
- Focusing on project management considerations
- Considering strategic issues.

Specific cases in which communication played a key role in enhancing the impact of a CRC are discussed in table 24.3.

The way in which communication and advocacy multiplied the effect of CRC findings is shown in table 24.4.

Communication Tips That Were Learned

Throughout the dissemination process, attention should be given to present the findings in an unbiased manner. Based on past experience with CRCs, listed below are a few pointers that were learned:

- *Preparing the media in advance:* A successful strategy adopted in the Kenya case and followed in other recent CRC initiatives is to hold media roundtables

Table 24.3. Communication Strategy for CRCs: A Template

Stage of CRC	Communication activity	Objectives	Target audience/ stakeholders
Planning a CRC	Workshops	Sensitizing stakeholders who are part of the CRC implementing team to create a shared understanding of the CRC concepts and applications	Peer CSOs, utility managers, media, academia, and higher government officials
Prelaunch phase	Workshops	Sharing and vetting the findings	Peer CSOs, utility managers, and sector experts
Dissemination	Press conferences, press releases	Disseminating the findings from the CRC	General public
Postlaunch presentations	Targeted presentations	Exploring policy advocacy and wider implications of the findings with specialized groups	CSO networks, professional bodies, and the like

Source: Author.

Table 24.4. Impact of Strategic Communication on the CRC Processes

CRC stage	Impact of sharing of information
Planning	Created a shared understanding of the rationale, objectives, and potency of CRCs. Underscored the transparency of the entire effort. Assisted stakeholders in understanding and unbundling the tasks involved.
Prelaunch phase	Ensured quality checks and endorsed the veracity of findings. Enabled stakeholders to plan in advance media strategies.
Dissemination	Raised awareness on critical issues in public services. Credible and objective findings created a shift in public information from the anecdotal to the evidential. Issues such as corruption that hitherto existed in the realm of the abstract became an objective benchmark.
Postlaunch	Customized information packages enabled focused advocacy efforts with critical and influential groups.

Source: Author.

to sensitize the print and visual media about the CRC and how the media could act as a proactive partner in this endeavor. These interactive sessions held with journalists were to ensure that they understand how the data were collected and analyzed and to give them pointers on how to report these data. In Kenya, special attention was also made to sensitize columnists and TV talk-show hosts to ensure sustained coverage of the key findings in the media, long after the initial "big bang" headlines faded out. These events covered both the "voice" and the "response" sides of the story—alongside the depiction of the major findings, institutional responses were also covered.

- *Presenting information in a holistic manner:* It is important to highlight both the good and the bad areas of performance. A complete picture—both the successes and failures—-must be shared. Effective communication in a CRC is both a "pat" and a "slap."

- *Allowing for shades of gray:* Descriptions, such as waiting time and proportion of users who are completely satisfied, make it possible to present feedback in different shades of gray—instead of a simple good/bad or yes/no. Remember that the CRC captures the subjective experience of users in an objective manner.
- *Conveying findings in a value-neutral manner:* Let the findings speak for themselves instead of using descriptive adjectives or value-laden or biased language.
- *Selectively comparing across services:* Although major differences exist between services, a comparison across providers on comparable criteria puts pressure on poor performers. This comparison creates peer pressure and develops into a substitute for the market.
- *Using a question-and-answer format to present findings:* Past experience has shown that using a question-and-answer format during presentations is an easy way for the audience to digest information. For example, during a presentation, instead of listing statistics about various aspects of drinking water services, ask the question: "In what areas do drinking water services need to improve?" A set of bulleted comments for service aspects where citizens gave poor ratings could follow. In addition, if the questionnaire contained direct questions about areas for improvement, these findings could be included.

References

Consumers International and Water and Sanitation Program. 2004. "Moving from Protest to Proposal: Building the Capacity of Consumer Organizations to Engage in Urban Water Supply and Sanitation Sector Reform in Africa." http://www.consumersinternational .org/media/315524/moving%20from%20protest%20to%20proposal-%20building% 20the%20capacity%20of%20consumer%20organisations%20to%20engage%20in% 20urban%20water%20supply%20and%20sanitation%20sector%20reform%20in% 20africa.pdf.

Public Affairs Foundation. 2007. "Social Audit of Public Services in Delhi." Bangalore.

Water and Sanitation Program–Africa. 2007. "Citizen Report Card on Urban Water, Sanitation and Solid Waste Services in Kenya." http://www.wsp.org/wsp/sites/wsp.org/files/ publications/712200745708_Citizens_Report_Card_-_Summary_Kenya.pdf.

Overcoming Inertia and Generating Participation: Insights from Participatory Processes in South Africa

Imraan Buccus and Janine Hicks

Introduction

The past few decades have witnessed processes of decentralization and democratization that have prompted new governance arrangements in a range of contexts around the world. Some experiences, such as participatory budgeting or decentralized participatory planning, have become models that are currently being rolled out throughout the globe with the expectation that they will help address a series of challenges related to democratic deficit as well as to policy efficiency.

Deepening democracy goes beyond formal processes of democratic building to address questions related to the quality and the inclusive/exclusive nature of modern democracies, especially in the south. The liberal assertion that democratic regimes and values are good in and of themselves is increasingly being challenged by those who are left out of the benefits of development. In many countries in the south, democratic regimes have not fulfilled promises of improving people's lives. In this sense, poverty reduction and social justice have become crucial dimensions of political legitimacy. Clearly, there is a need to rethink the respective roles and relations between social and political actors that have the potential to have an impact on poverty and inequalities.

In this context, we have worked in the arena of participatory governance, forging relationships with civil society organizations and movements, state institutions, and participatory processes in an attempt to deepen levels of public participation in South Africa.

Brief Description of Our Work on Participation

We have worked with a range of civil society organizations that have, as their mission, the strengthening of public participation in governance.

These civil society organizations interact intensely with a diverse range of actors on both sides of the equation, providing research, information, facilitation, and capacity-building services to strengthen both participatory mechanisms of the state as well as advocacy interventions of civil society seeking to influence these mechanisms. Over the years we have worked with citizens and government officials to put into action a diverse range of initiatives to ensure meaningful public participation in government development planning, policy making, and program implementation.

The organizations we work with operate in a national and international climate that is supportive of public participation. The language and practice of public participation have been incorporated into mainstream developmental theory and practice and are applied by most developmental and government stakeholders. However, the effective linkages between participatory mechanisms and core policy and decision-making processes and outcomes, as well as real citizen empowerment and the fostering of state accountability, need frank scrutiny.

Legal and Constitutional Provisions for Public Participation in South Africa

South Africa is a multiparty, representative democracy, under a constitution that is sovereign and that entrenches human rights. In addition, state power is mostly centralized in the national sphere, with only limited power devolved to provinces and local authorities. Despite South Africa's adoption of a representative democratic system, the constitution and some legislation complement the power of elected politicians with forms of participatory governance. In the national and provincial spheres, this takes the form of public consultation by legislatures. In the local authority sphere are found specific legal requirements and structural mechanisms for public participation.

In addition, the public service has committed itself to being more responsive, accountable, and transparent in implementing government policy. On the whole, though, public participation is limited to forms of consultation, usually concerning needs, rather than any real empowerment in political decision making or implementation. Despite this and the history of unresponsive bureaucracy, forms of participation could work as a check on all levels of the state's implementation of housing and other services. Given a political system that is strongly dominated by a single party, the African National Congress (ANC), such participation could operate to achieve greater accountability than that of formal political processes.

The requirement that national and provincial legislatures consult is reflected in Section 59(1) of the 2006 constitution, which states "The National Assembly must (a) facilitate public involvement in the legislative and other processes of the Assembly and its committees." Section 118 makes similar requirements for the provinces. Notably, the constitution makes it clear that decision-making power in this sphere resides with parliament alone, reflecting the reality that public participation is limited to informing the deliberations of parliament.

Significantly, the obligations on the local sphere to consult are more developed. Hence, Section 152(1) of the constitution states that "local government must encourage the involvement of communities and community organizations in the matters of local government." This implies going beyond merely consulting communities as an aid to deliberation. In this regard, the Municipal Systems Act (2000), section 16, obliges municipalities to

> develop a culture of municipal governance that complements formal representative government with a system of participatory governance, and must for this purpose (a) encourage, and create conditions for, the local community to participate in the affairs of the municipality, including in—(i) integrated development planning; (ii) the performance management system; (iii) performance; (iv) the budget; (v) and strategic decisions relating to services.

If these words were vigorously employed, they could lead to highly engaged communities, such as evident in Porto Allegre and other situations where democracy and planning are closely linked.

In addition to requiring that local councils consult communities on key municipal processes, the Municipal Structures Act of 1998 establishes ward committees. Consisting of 10 people and chaired by the ward councilor, ward committees are intended to act as the main means of communication between the council and local communities. Notably, however, as with the national and provincial spheres, legislation makes it clear that decision-making powers rest with the council alone and that public participation around key council processes or through ward committees really means community consultation to aid the deliberations of municipal councils.

Finally, the civil service is bound by the 2001 policy of *Batho Pele* (People First) to "get public servants to be service orientated, to strive for excellence in service delivery and to commit to continuous service delivery improvement." In the words of the policy, "it is a simple and transparent mechanism, which allows citizens to hold public servants accountable for the level of services they deliver." This provides another, less structured but nevertheless important normative resource for civil society and local communities to press for more responsive policy implementation.

Nevertheless, to the extent that government has created "invited spaces" for public consultation, to date these spaces have been largely ceremonial, on the periphery of core decision-making processes, and without bearing on the urgent issues of the moment. This raises the question of whether participation leads to incorporation without redress as some argue, or whether there is a lag in the official policy of "deepening democracy."

Is There Value in Public Participation?

South Africa indeed has adequate legislative, constitutional, and policy provisions for public participation, but the questions that follow quite logically are whether the public participation that takes place is meaningful and whether there really is value in public participation, in the sense of impact on policy and service delivery, as well as strengthening state accountability. Although general consensus holds about the benefits of engaging citizens in governance and development, rationales and approaches have varied widely.

For some scholars, such as Dreze and Sen (1995), participation constitutes an end in itself; for others, it is a means to increase efficiency and cut costs by mobilizing communities to contribute through time, effort, and often money. Some approaches have taken the form of public consultations around specific policy issues or poverty reduction strategies. Others are geared toward co-production and co-responsibility of local communities in the delivery of goods and services.

The extent to which citizens participate and the nature of their participation vary widely. These can range from punctual and instrumental consultations to more meaningful citizen participation in institutionalized spaces. Chambers (2005) argues, though, that by mainstreaming participation into development approaches, participation has lost much of its political and empowering content.

Participation is valued for its contribution to building democratic, empowered, articulated, and informed civil societies. It offers potential for increased accountability and government responsiveness as well as for political socialization of poor and marginalized categories. Especially for the poor, participation and the development of new forms of participatory democracy are seen as new channels to political inclusion and to voice demands and concerns from previously excluded groups.

Nonetheless, in a context such as South Africa, the question of who participates should not be underestimated. Evidence has shown that communities are not harmonious entities, but rather are riddled by complexity and conflicting interests. Local power systems and patronage reinforce inequalities in the social structure and prevent certain groups, often women, ethnic and religious minorities, and the poorest of the poor, from participating on equal grounds and voicing their concerns.

However, significant examples can be identified of successful engagement with state processes, resulting in policy impacts. When the state first introduced the Anti-Terrorism Bill in 2002, a rigorous response was heard from civil society, as well as intensive engagement with public hearings initiated by parliament. This resulted in the bill's being revised several times and eventually being adopted in a radically different version from the original. It can thus be argued that the broader South African civil society's response to the bill has illustrated that it has indeed matured as a collective force in participatory national politics. The fact that it took on this issue with a modicum of success reflects well on the project of democratic consolidation and the fact that the constitution ultimately served to advance the interests of the nation's citizens and not those of the political elite (Buccus and Nadvi 2006).

As a further example, in the local municipality of Mbizana in the Eastern Cape province, an attempt was made by the Human Sciences Research Council to research ways in which the sustainability of water services to the poor could be improved by getting the poor to participate. A set of tools was developed to assess key objectives in water services and to explore their potential use by ordinary people. The purpose was to conduct assessments necessary for regulation and to develop an interface between citizens and local authorities to improve the operations and maintenance of services.

The project succeeded in providing a set of tools for community appraisal and engagement and in developing plans for substantial upgrading of water services throughout the municipality. This, quite clearly, has had a distinct advantage in giving substance to citizen voice. In terms of policy implications, the project has opened up opportunities for ordinary people to engage more effectively in the complex processes of water service regulation.

Conversely, South African academics and activists have questioned the significance of public participation mechanisms, noting that these are disconnected from significant policy decisions and designed to benefit the elite who dominate such processes. Clearly, the legitimacy of outcomes derived from such processes is questionable. Cynical questions have been raised about public participation mechanisms being convened by the state, in full knowledge that key decisions have already been made and participatory processes used purely to observe the letter of the law and prevent any legal challenge.

This would appear to be the case in processes related to provincial border disputes in places such as Matatiele and Khutsong, where communities were invited to comment on proposed incorporation of their districts in neighboring provinces. This incorporation went ahead despite rigorous community opposition to the proposal. Likewise, the public was told in no uncertain terms by leading politicians within the ANC that vehement public reaction against the closure of an elite and highly effective corruption-busting unit, the Scorpions, will have no impact on the party's decision to shut it down. This is a result, it is alleged, of several investigations against senior party officials. Parliament's consultative processes in this light are viewed as a fob to an already formulated decision.

Further, attempts to shoehorn increasing community discontent in response to state economic policy and priorities resulting in increasing poverty, poor state accountability, and slow service delivery into formal participatory processes such as public hearings and local authority planning processes are rejected with contempt by some social actors. This sector views such processes as insignificant in regard to the decisions shaping South Africa's economic and development trajectory, and serving only to domesticate the power of mass action—drawing people from streets into boardrooms, replacing protest placards with PowerPoint presentations, curtailing the scope of engagement, and silencing countless voices along the way. The burgeoning so-called service delivery protests—violent expressions of community discontent at first glance taken as evidence of dissatisfaction with the pace of transformation—are increasingly being viewed by political analysts, such as Steven Friedman (2004), as an expression of the dislocation of communities from elected representatives and government structures and process: a crisis of accountability.

Generating Meaningful Participation

Clearly, the challenge to generate effective, credible, and meaningful spaces and processes for public participation is one of the most significant at this juncture. Although we have not discounted protest as an effective and legitimate means of public participation, we have always argued the need to take advantage of the available spaces to engage in meaningful participation. Clearly for us, a critically important aspect of ensuring participation would be to ensure that new legislative and policy provisions are created and existing means enhanced. In addition to the various training and capacity-building projects we have engaged in, we have also carefully constructed policy paths around participation.

For example, we were invited by the Legislatures Support Programme, a program of the European Union in partnership with the South African government, to develop a public participation strategy for South Africa's provincial legislatures. Another recent development in the area of facilitating participatory habits by enhancing the policy paradigm was when we were contracted by the national Department of Provincial and Local Government (DPLG) to transform the existing national policy framework on public participation into a fully fledged national policy.

We put together a research and drafting team, drawing on research findings and engaging with our colleagues in the Good Governance Learning

Network, a network of South African nongovernmental organizations working toward strengthening participatory local governance, to identify and respond to policy gaps in relation to participation. The final policy draft appears, however, to have been marooned in a policy review process and, with the original instigating official moved to another department, to lack an internal "champion" to drive the process forward.

Nonetheless, during the research process, the interest and response from local authorities and the legislature were encouraging—we were constantly being called on to make presentations on public participation and develop training and planning interventions for individual local authorities in response to conversations arising from the research process. We also were involved in an initiative to look at how democratic spaces can be crafted to enable marginalized groups to engage with policy processes from an empowered position. In this context, we looked at opportunities created for civil society stakeholders to engage in the policy-making process, in ways that sought to overcome obstacles to participation by marginalized groups.

This exploration was grounded in the belief that ordinary people have the right to participate in the decision-making processes that affect their lives, and that informed policy making leads to better policy that is more responsive to communities' needs. Subsequently, we piloted an emerging participatory model—a provincial policy forum—acknowledging some of the inherent challenges and tensions (Buccus and Hicks 2007). This was an innovative attempt to involve citizens in creating new spaces for policy deliberation—a meeting point of government's "invited" and civil society's "claimed" spaces (Cornwall 2004; McGee 2002). This innovative, participatory policy-making space was a serious attempt to generate effective participation.

Making Public Participation More Effective

No doubt a need exists to make participation more effective to further its potential to increase state legitimacy, foster political stability, and prevent violent conflict. These all—potentially—constitute major dimensions to deepening democratic governance for combating poverty and exclusion.

Critical to ensuring that participation does indeed enhance development paradigms is the need to consolidate and enhance current policy and legislative provisions for public participation, including building political will among state stakeholders. What has been lagging has been the ability to ensure that all policy and legislative provisions result in meaningful participation.

A great deal of the work done by civil society organizations with which we have worked has resulted in numerous key lessons and recommendations about making public participation more effective. For example, in the early 2000s, when we crafted a strategy document on public participation for South

Africa's provincial legislatures, the following lessons and recommendations emerged regarding the various spaces provided for public participation:

Scope and timing of public participation

- Legislatures should seek to ensure that community groups are enabled to make input into legislative processes on a timely basis—that is, not after decisions have been made and the scope for influence is minimal. Related to this, legislatures should explore broadening the scope for public participation in the public policy management process—from the framing of issues for policy and legislative consideration, to the drafting of policy or legislation, to its implementation and evaluation.

Public hearings

- With regard to public hearings, a clear system is needed for processing submissions and providing feedback to members of the public on issues raised as well as follow-up on these issues. A serious attempt must be made to engage in prehearing work, whereby particularly marginal communities are enabled to understand the content of proposed legislation and its implications and to develop their responses.
- Related to this, legislatures need to pay careful attention to the dissemination of information to communities to enable them to engage meaningfully with legislation. Creative use of formal and community media, and community and municipality structures, is required. Such initiatives should also be supported by an intensified process of building the capacity of community groups to understand and engage with legislative processes and structures. Ensuring that rural communities are afforded meaningful opportunities to participate cannot be emphasized enough.
- Careful attention needs to be paid to identifying stakeholder groups to invite to public hearings, by categorizing stakeholders through a database. In addressing issues relating to representation and voice within civil society, legislatures should be mindful in planning for hearings about issues of which groups are invited to make presentations or submissions and who speaks on behalf of groups or communities.
- Hearings can be used as a tool to measure the progress and impact of legislatures in implementing their public education and participation programs. Clearly, public hearings must take place in the local language, using plain and simple language. Public hearings themselves could be better facilitated, in a more interactive, participatory manner, making use of discussion groups, to enable greater deliberative dialogue on policy options.

Constituency offices

- Constituency offices should be used to channel information on legislative processes to communities and to facilitate community input into these processes.
- Members should adequately serve their constituency offices, and provincial legislatures should set guidelines on what this entails.

- A need exists for public participation training for constituency office staff. Members should also receive this training and be part of the training process to strengthen networking.
- Constituency officers and members need training on how to make use of the media.
- Constituency offices should be an extension of the legislature, not party offices.

Monitoring and evaluation
- Legislatures need to constantly monitor and evaluate their programs to assess how effective they are in strengthening public participation in legislative processes, and the outcomes of this process need to be fed into program planning. Such a monitoring process ideally should engage civil society stakeholders for their assessment, feedback, and recommendations.

Media and information dissemination
- For assurance of an effective dissemination strategy, a need exists to go beyond mainstream media and make use of community print and electronic (especially radio) productions, because this has the potential of reaching a significantly greater population. Legislatures need to supplement media strategies by making use of local networks—such as schools, church groups, municipalities, and traditional leadership structures—to ensure that diverse and marginalized communities gain access to information in a timely manner.

Language
- Consistent application of plain language principles to all documents, including legislation, is necessary. We recognize that this may take time and additional resources, yet the lack of summarized, plain language versions of policies and legislation under scrutiny further prevents marginalized groups from participating effectively in these processes.

Resources
- In light of the fact that most legislatures are not able to provide concrete figures allocated for public participation activities, more careful attention should be paid to this area, with adequate funding made available. Moreover, sufficient staff are necessary to address issues about participation.

As indicated earlier, having the legislative provision for public participation on its own is not sufficient. It is critical to examine each mechanism to ensure that it functions in a way that makes public participation meaningful.

We were to learn more practical lessons about effective public participation, particularly about building political will for engineering a policy process that would assist in advancing an effective public participation agenda, when we were afforded the opportunity to craft the DPLG's draft national policy on public participation. Some of the insights gleaned about political will for public participation include lessons learned in working with "champions" within state departments.

On reflection, the DPLG policy experience would have been far more successful had we worked to anchor the policy process with a dedicated team of officials within the DPLG, so that there was something of substance within the department that the project could have been anchored to, beyond the inspired individual within the department. Had such a team been developed, and ownership of the policy process encouraged through drawing members into the policy-crafting process, or deliberating recommendations in a better facilitated manner than a formal presentation, we might have secured for ourselves a team with which to work in pushing for the policy document to be taken up and finalized.

Lessons can also be learned about the impact of donors on a policy process. Although donors bring financial muscle to bear on departmental policy prioritizing, and may help civil society bring public participation to the policy agenda, thereby unlocking necessary financial resources, limitations constrain their influence. Such donor interventions assist in opening up the space for policy advocacy, but this does not eliminate the need to secure the political impetus required for actual implementation.

Conclusion

Current public participation mechanisms instigated by the state should continue to be examined critically for their ability to connect citizens with real decision making. The manner in which they are facilitated should constantly be refined to ensure they are accessible to a broader range of stakeholders and enable their participation in more meaningful ways. The experiences in South Africa have shown that current institutions and mechanisms to ensure citizen input into, as well as engagement with, both local planning and national policy processes do provide a space that people and groups have successfully made use of to ensure adequately designed service delivery mechanisms, as well as influence individual policy processes.

It is clear, however, that this influence is at the grace of the state, and despite legislative provisions for participation, with which the state readily complies, this influence is brought to bear only on those policy and planning processes made available by the state for citizen engagement. A set of core and fundamental policy decisions remains behind an iron curtain of political party control, as well as key policy directives that have not and will not be opened up for public debate and input. The latitude for public participation impact on the *formulation of the policy agenda* remains an arena for critical engagement.

In addition, public participation mechanisms cannot on their own channel citizen interaction with and create pressure points on the state, particularly to demand accountability. Such mechanisms are of limited format and relevance to the broader, messier set of developmental challenges that go beyond linear, narrow policy processes. For the foreseeable future, South African citizens will need to continue to draw on a broader, diverse range of advocacy engagement, ranging from protest action to partnerships and even litigation to hold the state to account and ensure delivery of particularly basic socioeconomic rights.

References

Buccus, I., and J. Hicks. 2007. "Crafting New Democratic Spaces: Participatory Policy-Making in Kwazulu-Natal, South Africa." *Transformation* 65: 94–119.

Buccus, I., and L. Nadvi. 2006. "The ATB: The Role of Civil Society in Policy and Legislative Reform." *Critical Dialogue* 2 (1): 28–35.

Chambers, R. 2005. *Ideas for Development.* London: Earthscan.

Cornwall, A. 2004. "Whose Voices, Whose Choices? Reflections on Gender and Participatory Development." *World Development* 31 (8): 1325–42.

Dreze, J., and A. Sen. 1995. *India: Economic Development and Social Opportunity.* Delhi: Oxford University Press.

Friedman, S. 2004. "A Voice for All: Democracy and Public Participation." *Critical Dialogue* 1 (1): 22–26.

McGee, R. 2002. "Legal Frameworks for Citizen Participation." Logolink, University of Sussex.

Civil Society Representation in São Paulo

Adrian Gurza Lavalle

Understanding the dynamics of political representation by civil organizations is at the cutting edge of debate on contemporary democracies. Considerable evidence now is at hand that civil organizations have become de facto and de jure representatives of particular segments of the population and interests in the design, implementation, and monitoring of public policy. Governments are, for a variety of reasons, drawing this new set of collective actors into their policy processes.[1] Conversely, many civil organizations are themselves knocking on government policy doors with increasing insistency. Over the past 20 years different institutional arrangements have emerged to bring these actors directly into executive-branch decision making, for example, through arrangements such as the tripartite policy councils in Brazil, which bring together public officials, private sector service providers, and civil organizations. Often these institutions are part of larger democratic decentralization reforms that, at least formally, seek to redistribute power within the state and between state and society (Grindle 1999; Heller 2001).

As civil organizations acquire a new and active role in political representation, processes of the reconfiguration of representation around the executive may converge to produce a new expansion of democracy—making its institutions more accountable—just as the emergence of mass political parties contributed to the expansion of institutions of political representation and of democracy itself in the early decades of the twentieth century. The current shifts in the form of political representation involve changes in and rearrangements of the workings of the traditional institutions of representative government and an expansion of the locus and the functions of political representation.

Two sets of questions in particular are becoming increasingly important to this debate. First, how do the new roles played by civil organizations interact with the institutions of representative government and policy institutions, and how does this interaction affect policy decision making? Second, whom do civil organizations represent when they act as representatives in the polity, and in what terms is this representation constructed? These two sets of questions are crucial because the contribution of these new roles to democratization hinges in part on both the effects of political representation by civil organizations and how the dilemmas regarding their representativeness are resolved. Civil organizations should be able to engage in making government and bureaucracies more accountable but simultaneously should be, in principle, accountable to their own publics. However, on the one hand, there are no well-established theoretical models that set out how civil organizations could fit as representatives within representative government institutions and within policy processes as well. On the other hand, in Brazil and seemingly in Latin America the large majority of organizations engaged in representational activities do not have electoral mechanisms through which to establish their representativeness, and most are not membership based (Gurza Lavalle, Acharya, and Houtzager 2005; Gurza Lavalle, Houtzager, and Castello 2006a).

This chapter deals with the first set of questions by exploring the main factors that lead civil organizations in São Paulo, Brazil, to explicitly assume the political representations of their publics or beneficiaries (hereafter publics) and some of the possible consequences of this for democracy.[2] The evidence examined here allows us to claim that in São Paulo, and conceivably in Brazil, civil organizations play an active role—although not inherently a positive one—in the reconfiguration of representation both in traditional politics and in the arenas opened up by innovative participative institutions. It also raises the possibility that the political role of civil organizations may counter the gap between political parties and the general population identified in the literature, playing a role in reconnecting the general population to political parties by acting as mediating institutions between candidates and different sectors of the population.

This chapter uses statistical analysis, in the form of a principal model (a logistic regression), to identify the combination of factors with the greatest capacity to predict the propensity of civil organizations to assume the representation of their publics. No intention is made here to generalize empirical accounts as if they were valid propositions for every context. However, the findings do suggest important empirical trends. The data on civil organizations in São Paulo were produced using sampling criteria, explained briefly below, that favored organizations that were more actively working with (or on the behalf of) disadvantaged sectors of the population. In total, leaders of 229 organizations were interviewed in 2002. Because this universe of organizations works with or for social groups that are said to be marginalized in classic representative institutions and from centers of political power, their role as representatives is especially relevant to the debates on the direction of contemporary democracy. However, this chapter's approach, outlined bellow, lays out the clear limit of the research findings, notably the inability to explore all problems related to the effective representation of interests.

The next section sheds lights on the political representation carried out by civil organizations and the lack of systematic studies about such practices. The following section presents briefly the dependent variable, survey, and sample technique. The empirical findings follow. The chapter closes with an interpretation of how political representation by civil organizations seems to be related to electoral representation.

Political Representation by Civil Organizations

The processes of the reconfiguration of political representation have begun to spill over the borders of the electoral arena into areas of social control and representation in executive branches of government, and specifically in processes of public policy making by civil organizations. With this shift, civil organizations de facto carry out legally sanctioned roles as political representatives, even though an unknown factor remains regarding the possible conflicts and rearrangements in regard to traditional electoral institutions.

Let me begin with an example of the changing Brazilian scenario of political representation, which shows, as Dagnino (2002, 290–93) has said, how much traditional understanding of political representation systematically appears to be out of place in contemporary Brazil. It is an instance of conflicts between competing legitimacies of political representation.

The Municipal Council for the Rights of Children and Adolescents (Conselho dos Direitos da Criança e do Adolescente [CDCA]) in São Paulo is one example of many in Brazil's institutional rainbow of policy councils. As part of a federal system of policy councils, it is legally allocated a Municipal Fund (Fundo do Conselho Municipal dos Direitos da Criança e do Adolescente [FUNCAD]), over which councilors have spending authority. Thus, when the city council met in plenary session to approve the budget for 2002, representatives of civil organizations in the CDCA organized a public event where children and teenagers dressed as clowns and dancers came together with a broad array of civil organizations that are either financed by the fund or that mobilize to protect the rights of children and adolescents. The pressure exerted on the city council was aimed at preventing its councilors from blocking amendments that would cut the CDCA's budget. It was undoubtedly a logical response from this group of civil organizations following the discouraging experience of the previous year, when the R$73 million (reais) approved by the CDCA to finance its projects was reduced to the modest sum of R$5 million in the budget approved by the City Council.[3]

The mobilization organized by the CDCA councilors has unusual characteristics: The pressure exerted by the "people" and their "representatives" (councilors) on the "representatives of the people" (legislators) to influence their own vote demonstrates competition between conflicting principles of political representation, as determining budgetary priorities is one of the legal powers of both kinds of representatives. The protest by actors focused on defending the rights of children and adolescents, therefore, is part of a contest between forms of representation and hence much more than just a simple exercise in pressure group tactics.

The new roles of civil organizations carrying out political representation have not been taken up in the *reconfiguration of representation* and the *democratizing democracy* literatures. Studies that explore the reconfiguration of political representation offer interpretations of a transformation in progress at the level of the party system, where the relationship between elected representative and represented citizen is believed to be in flux.[4] In these studies, representation fundamentally resides in the electoral process, and for this reason no need is seen to even explore whether civil organizations are acquiring any role in political representation in contemporary democracies. Political parties are detaching themselves from their social niches, and political and candidates are becoming plebiscitary leaderships thanks to mass media (Manin 1997; Novaro 2000). The possible role of civil organizations in a reconfiguration of representation is defined a priori as irrelevant and nondemocratic (Chandhoke 2003; Przeworski 2002).

Studies of the *democratization of democracy* have, in turn, focused their attention on institutional innovations that embrace various forms of participation in institutional structures for the design and implementation of public policies (Fung 2004; Fung and Wright 2003; Santos 2002). Yet they have recently identified the issue of political representation by civil organizations as an important one, because in these studies it is masked by the emphasis put on "citizen participation." Hence, institutions such as the councils in Brazil are often referred to as spaces for "citizen participation," even though more often than not they bring collective actors (rather than individual citizens) and public officials into contact. That is, the principal protagonist in the new participatory spaces for the design and monitoring of public policies is not the ordinary citizen, but rather the civil organizations legally invested as representatives of the social sectors envisaged by these policies (Gurza Lavalle, Acharya, and Houtzager 2005; Wampler 2004).

In both cases, political representation by civil organizations is avoided rather than confronted. However, the actors themselves are not waiting for the theorists to discover or come to terms with their new political role.

Dependent Variable and Survey in Brief

In the absence of historical or theoretical models for examining the political representation by civil organizations, we decided on an analytic strategy that is inductive and relies on exploring the representation assumed by civil organizations. It entails taking seriously civil organizations' self-definition as representative, that is, actors' public acceptance or rejection of the idea of being representatives. The choice of actors' self-definition as an analytic point of departure is defensible as long as this self-definition is not conflated with *actual* representation. The assumed representation by the actors studied here is far from being mere rhetoric—the findings that are examined here and elsewhere are sufficiently consistent to put to rest any doubts in this respect.[5]

The collection of variables this chapter explores has been generated by a survey of 229 civil organizations in the municipality of São Paulo, undertaken in 2002. During one-hour interviews, organizations responded to a questionnaire that was designed to elicit information about their foundation, mission, degree of formalization, areas of work, publics, and linkages with other societal actors and with other government institutions. The questions that explored relations of the organization to its respective publics (a community, members, target population, and the like) included both closed and open questions. In the latter, interviewees were asked to specify for or with which group of people their organization worked and whether the organization considered itself to be a representative of this group of people. Only afterwards, if the answer was positive, did the interviewer inquire about why the organization considered that it represented the interests of its public. By carefully examining and coding the final question it was possible to lay out the different congruency arguments.

The survey produced a data set that contained a broad range of characteristics of the interviewed organizations. The sample of 229 organizations was selected using a snowball technique. We relied on interviews with 16 local civil organizations, distributed across four quite different districts, to start the snowball sample.[6] This technique is recommended for "drawing out" hidden populations or those in the general population with unusual (hence rare) characteristics, or both (Atkinson and Flint 2003; Goodman 1961). The snowball methodology used for the research was extremely efficient compared with the most common other alternatives used to study civil organizations such as case studies or drawing samples from available lists of organizations.[7] At the same time, the control criteria were designed so as to favor identifying and interviewing the most active civil organizations.

Finally, *assumed representation* was examined as a dependent variable in the field of inferential statistics, specifically by means of probability estimations—relative risk ratios and logistic regressions. (A detailed description of the procedures carried out using these techniques can be found in Houtzager, Gurza Lavalle, and Acharya 2003, annexes 3 and 4; and Gurza Lavalle, Houtzager, and Castello 2005, annex 1.)

Propensity for Assuming Representation

A total of 166 organizations (72.8 percent) defined themselves as representatives of the publics with (or for) which they work. If one takes care not to project assumed representation onto the plane of actual representation, it is possible to show that a clear relationship exists between defining oneself as a representative and exercising activities of political representation. We examined four types of activities in which political representation tends to occur. The four types refer to different dimensions of exercising political representation: (1) new forms of representation within the executive, measured by participation in public policy councils, the participatory budget, or both; (2) direct mediation of demands in regard to specific public agencies, captured here by representation of community or group interests to government institutions; (3) political advocacy by means of aggregation of interests through traditional electoral channels, empirically identified as support to political candidates; and (4) political advocacy by means of the legislature, measured as claim making on the Municipal Council. Using simple addition and starting with the definition of activities as dichotomous variables, we used a value for eventual exercise of political representation to make a comparison between civil organizations that claim and those that deny representation of their publics.

Table 26.1 shows that assumed representation is clearly associated with the exercise of activities of political representation. Although 66 percent of civil organizations that do not claim to be representatives carry out one or none of the four activities described earlier, 52 percent of those that define themselves as representatives carry out three or four of those activities.

More than 90 independent variables were examined for both organizations that considered themselves representatives and those that did not, covering different dimensions of their activities, characteristics, and institutional linkages. These included the organization's publics, involvement of the publics in the activities of the organization, the projection of demands on different levels of public authority, legal institutionalization, and involvement in new participatory spaces in the management of public policies, among other dimensions contemplated in the analysis.

The propensity for civil organizations to define themselves as representatives was sensitive to the effects of 35 variables. The following step was the

Table 26.1. Assumed Representation and Representation Activities
percent

Assumed representation	Representation activities					
	0	1	2	3	4	Total
Yes	9	14	25	41	11	100
No	37	29	20	15	—	100
Total	17	18	23	34	8	100

Source: Author.

Table 26.2. Principal Model

Variable	General frequency	Classify themselves as representatives		
		Percent	Logistic regression	Significance coefficient
Organization supports political candidate	34	0.97	12.80	**
Registered with public utility title	64	0.81	2.86	**
Demand making/ mobilization	130	0.86	5.53	**
Performance of model		Yes	No	Total
(percentage of correct predictions)		85.00	58.06	77.48

Source: Author.
Note: In accordance with conventional statistics, the two asterisks denote highly reliable findings at a 5 percent confidence level.

completion of numerous logistic regressions to eliminate covariation and identify the factors with the greatest predictive capacity. The final result of these series of tests was the creation of a Principal Model comprising three variables: (1) organizations' support for political candidates, (2) their registration as a public utility, and (3) their engagement in mobilization activities and demand making on government programs or institutions. Table 26.2 shows that the model can predict 77 percent of the values in the sample. It performs even better when determining the factors with positive effects on assumed representation, predicting 85 percent of cases.[8]

The fourth column of the table shows the results of the logistic regressions for assumed representation.[9] The support for political candidates by a civil organization is by far the best predictor of assumed representation. This increases by more than 10 times the likelihood that an organization will assume the role of representative of its public. Furthermore, civil organizations that use mobilizations to make claims and demands on different government institutions have a five times greater propensity to do so. The variable "being registered with a public utility title" doubles the likelihood of assumed representation. Although this variable has a markedly lesser effect, it was consistent in all the tests carried out.

Interpreting Connections between Civil Organizations and Traditional Politics

The processes of state reform that have unfolded in recent years, and in particular the wave of institutional innovations that have created new opportunities for citizen participation in policy processes, have intensified the political protagonism of civil organizations. In the case of São Paulo, almost two-thirds of civil organizations in the sample of associations working with or for the popular sectors participate in at least one of the new participatory institutional arrangements, namely, the participatory budget or the policy councils (Houtzager,

Gurza Lavalle, and Acharya 2004).[10] Were this not sufficient to encourage a careful study of these organizations, the case of São Paulo further highlights the broad representative roles assumed by these actors. Almost three-quarters of civil organizations explicitly assert that they represent the social groups that take part in or benefit from their activities. When we take into account the different forms of political representation that lie within reach of civil organizations, we find that these assertions of assumed representation are clearly associated with actual political practices during which representation is likely to occur. The inverse relationship is as consistent: Civil organizations that carry out few or no practices of representation tend *not* to define themselves as representatives of their publics.

This ability of some civil organizations to enter and potentially represent interests of poorer sectors in different policy arenas and in the polity more generally, where these interests are often absent, is also an important reason to pay careful attention to the nexus of societal and political spheres and their institutional sedimentation.

Whether a civil organization claims to be a representative of its public is, in São Paulo, closely linked to its relationship with traditional political structures. More precisely, whether or not an actor supports political candidates is by far the best predictor of assumed representation, followed at some distance by two characteristics—registration as a public interest organization (*utilidade publica*) or mobilization and demand making on public authorities. Supporting political candidates is defined as the engagement of civil organizations over the last five years in supporting particular politicians in their electoral campaigns, possibly in exchange for a commitment from the candidate to work on behalf of the organization's interests or causes. Mobilization and demand making on public authorities—that is, government bodies or programs—speak for themselves and do not require clarification. This characteristic refers to the well-known strategy of putting external pressure on the public authority responsible for decision making. Public registration of an organization as functioning in the public interest, in Brazil, indicates its intention to engage in a sustained relation with the state to help achieve that organization's objectives. The public interest registration is more closely related to policy processes and provides access to public benefits such as fiscal exemptions, subsidies, and budgetary support, as well as contracts for provision of local decentralized public services and licenses for lotteries (Landim 1998, 79–83; Szazi 2001, 89–110). It can also be a requirement for participation in the design and implementation or management of public policies.

The strong relationship between assumed representation and the dynamics of traditional political structures calls to mind at least three considerations that directly question the contemporary debates about the reconfiguration of representation and the democratization of democracy. First, the debate about the democratization of democracy and its emphasis on the potential of citizen participation and civil society has curiously not been accompanied by systematic studies that examine the practices of representation that are actually taking place within so-called participatory institutions, such as policy councils and participatory budgeting in Brazil. The inattention to an issue so crucial to the democratization of democracy agenda may reflect at least in part the fact that representation has been part of the historical and intellectual field of democratic political institutions. However, as shown in this chapter, no exclusionary divide is seen between political representation and civil society. Furthermore, the findings suggest that the "sense of representation" of the organizations in São Paulo has emerged fundamentally out of the interface with policy institutions and, mainly, electoral campaigns and their candidates. This reveals both a wealth of interactions to be examined and the analytical costs of maintaining a rigid distinction between societal actors and political institutions.

Second, if civil organizations can effectively translate assumed representation into actual political representation, this would not seem to occur at the margins of or in opposition to traditional forms of political representation—namely, elections—but above all as a result of and in close connection to these traditional forms. Being engaged in policy councils, and participatory budgeting, as well as having contracts for delivering public services seems to enhance civil organizations' awareness about their emerging role as representatives of their publics. As the representative role of civil organizations could be highly institutionalized, room exists for conflicts with traditional actors about overlapping legitimacies and faculties. Of course, traditional repertoires as mass mobilization are, as would be expected, related to assumed representation.

Contrary to alarmist warnings about the risks that historically crystallized institutions of political representation will be usurped by nonrepresentative actors, the evidence from São Paulo suggests that the reconfiguration of representation runs through the emergence of new societal mediators that interact in a complementary, although not necessarily harmonious, manner—as shown in the example at the beginning of the chapter—with the accepted institutions of representative government. The significance of these mediators points to a peculiar disconnect between parties and political candidates in the dynamics of political representation that filter through civil organizations. While maintaining linkages with the former makes no difference to organizations' propensity to assume representation, providing support to the latter is the most influential positive factor. In other words, the complementary interaction with electoral processes occurs through the political candidates and not the parties, which not only coincides with the consensus in the reconfiguration of representation literature about the personalization of politics but also suggests that important amendments need to be made to the verdict of a growing disconnect between political actors in electoral processes and their base or social niche.[11] Civil organizations appear to function as channels through which citizens are reconnected to politicians.

Third, the interrelationship between societal and political actors would not be surprising were it not for the rigid divisionary lines drawn between "civil society" and "state" or "autonomous civil society" and "traditional politics" by conventional wisdom and several scholars and practitioners in the 1990s and first years of this century (let alone the opposition between "participation" and "representation") (Avritzer 1994, 1997, 2003; Barber 1984; Costa 2002; Keane 1992 [1984]; Nascimento 1999). Parties and candidates invest in specific social fields as part of their political strategy, and civil organizations cultivate preferred political support and alliances to carry out their objectives. It is precisely the civil organizations involved in this reconnection with parties and candidates that present a higher propensity to assume the representation of their publics.

Confirmation that civil organizations are playing a substantial role in the reconfiguration of representation in São Paulo does not say anything about the positive or negative consequences for the quality of democracy. There is no a priori guarantee that the potential political representation provided by civil organizations will in fact be representative, simply because this form of representation is constructed within a "societal," rather than "political," sphere. Clientelism and patrimonialism of various kinds, for example, also tend to occur within "society." This, clearly, brings into play the second set of crucial questions not addressed here: the difficult question of the representativeness of civil organizations and the challenges of evaluating this representativeness with a notion of political representation based on democratic requirements. If civil organizations function as effective new channels of mediation between the population and electoral processes or, as occurs in Brazil, between the population and public administration in the design and implementation of policies, they can contribute to the democratization of democracy *only* if they themselves are representative and accountable to their publics. Political representation by civil organizations is a fact, but its potential to broaden representation and its consequences for democratic reform are in play and uncertain.

Notes

1. Among other very well-known cases are Constitutional Amendments 73 and 74 in India and especially the world-famous People's Planning Campaign in the southern state of Kerala (Chaudhuri and Heller 2002; Heller 2001); Policy Councils and Participatory Budgeting in Brazil (Lüchmann 2007, 2008; Tatagiba 2002); Local Government Code in the Philippines; the Law of Popular Participation in Bolivia; the New Localism in England (Gaventa 2004); the citizen management of the Mexican electoral system (Alonso and Aziz 2005; Aziz and Isunza 2007; Isunza 2006); community-level police experiences such as those implemented in Chicago; as well as participatory spaces all over Latin America (Albuquerque 2008; Grindle 1999), some of which are constitutionally mandated (Hevia de la Jara 2006).

2. A preliminary and much longer version of this chapter was published as an IDS Working Paper 249 (Gurza Lavalle, Houtzager, and Castello 2005). Elsewhere we have explored theoretically the reconfiguration of representation debate and legitimacy challenges faced by civil society (Gurza Lavalle, Houtzager, and Castello 2006b). Empirically, we have surveyed emerging notions of representation among São Paulo's civil organizations (Gurza Lavalle, Houtzager, and Castello 2006a) and shown its main features using a comparative approach with Mexico City civil organizations as a second analytical unit (Gurza Lavalle and Castello 2008). This chapter is part of a larger cross-national study that was undertaken in two cities of Latin America—São Paulo and Mexico City—and two cities in India—Delhi and Bangalore. Other papers and documents related to this project can be found in "Rights, Representation and the Poor: Comparing Large Developing Country Democracies—Brazil, India and Mexico," http://www2.ids.ac.uk/gdr/cfs/research/Phase1/Collective%20Actors.html.

3. For an analysis of the different CDCA administrations that looks precisely at budget issues and specifically the relationship between the CDCA and its fund (FUNCAD), see Gomes da Silva (2003, and for the example used above, 90–98).

4. See Manin (1997), Miguel (2003a, 2003b), Novaro (2000), and Roberts (2002), among others. The relationship between representatives and those represented has been intensely studied in the United States, with the attention focused on the eventual connections between decision making in the legislature by elected politicians and the interests or preferences of the electorate (congruence model). A far smaller and more recent collection of work addresses the debate about the reconfiguration of political representation.

5. See references in note 2.

6. The four local organizations interviewed in each district to start the sample were selected according to distinct criteria, to ensure that the networks of referrals that each would produce would differ, or if these networks converged, it would not be a result of sampling bias.

7. A detailed description of the research design, in terms of both the entry points and the criteria for determining the boundaries of the sample, on the one hand, and of its advantages in regard to other methodological alternatives, can be consulted in Houtzager, Gurza Lavalle, and Acharya (2003), also available at http://www.ids.ac.uk/go/idspublication/who-participates-civil-society-and-the-new-democratic-politics-in-s-o-paulo-brazil. One of the most ambitious case study projects was the Ford Foundation's "Civil Society and Governance Project." Its findings for Latin America can be consulted in the works edited by Dagnino (2002), Olvera (2003), and Panfichi (2003).

8. The performance of the model is the relationship between the predictions carried out by the model and the correctly classified cases in the values observed. Although the models created from the logistics regressions are more consistent when they manage to correctly classify the factors that positively or negatively alter the probability of a determined phenomenon occurring—illness usually being the common example—not all phenomena are equally sensitive to the absence of factors that increase their likelihood of occurring (and vice versa). So, for example, low education levels increase the probability of an individual's being unemployed, but higher levels of education do not improve in equal proportions their likelihood of employment. There are plausible reasons for thinking that assumed representation behaves in a way more similar to "education levels" than to "illness."

9. The fifth column in table 26.2 indicates the reliability or significance of the logistic regression findings for the three Principal Mode variables.

10. Elsewhere we analyze the factors that increase the representation of these groups in the new participatory institutional arrangements. See Gurza Lavalle, Acharya, and Houtzager (2005) and Houtzager, Gurza Lavalle, and Acharya (2003).

11. It is worth remembering that the absence of effects from linkages of civil organizations with traditional political actors is not restricted to parties. It also contemplates churches, trade unions, and professional associations. This clarification is relevant in the São Paulo case because the Church and the so-called new trade unionism played starring roles in the historical period culminating in the transition (see Sader 1988; Singer and Brant 1980).

References

Albuquerque, Maria do Carmo. 2008. "A participação da sociedade na redefinição de políticas de direitos. Os direitos da infância e o direito a moradia em países do Cone Sul na virada para o século XXI." Ph.D. thesis, PROLAM-Universidad de São Paulo, São Paulo.

Alonso, Jorge, and Nassif Alberto Aziz. 2005. "Campo electoral, espacios autónomos y redes. El Consejo General del IFE (1996–2005)." Cuadernos para la democratización no. 1. Programa Interinstitucional de Investigación–Acción sobre Democracia, Sociedad Civil y Derechos Humanos, CIESAS–Universidad Veracruzana, Mexico.

Atkinson, Rowland, and John Flint. 2003. "Accessing Hidden and Hard-to-Reach Populations: Snowball Research Strategies." In *The A–Z of Social Research,* ed. R. L. Miller and J. D. Brewer, 274–80. London: Sage.

Avritzer, Leonardo. 1994. "Modelos de sociedade civil: uma análise específica do Caso Brasileiro." In *Sociedade civil e democratização,* ed. Leonardo Avritzer, 271–308. Belo Horizonte: Del Rey.

Avritzer, Leonardo. 1997. "Um desenho institucional para o novo associativismo." *Lua Nova* no. 39: 149–74.

———. 2003. *Democracy and the Public Space in Latin America.* Princeton, NJ: Princeton University Press.

Aziz, Nassif, Alberto Isunza, and Ernesto Vera. 2007. "La crisis del modelo electoral mexicano: financiamiento, medios, instituciones y política social." *Foro Internacional* 47 (4): 740–84.

Barber, Benjamin R. 1984. *Strong Democracy: Participatory Politics for a New Age.* Berkeley: University of California Press.

Chandhoke, Neera. 2003. "Governance and the Pluralisation of the State: Implications for Democratic Practices in Asia." *Economic and Political Weekly* 38 (28): 2957–68.

Chaudhuri, S., and P. Heller. 2002. "The Plasticity of Participation: Evidence from a Participatory Governance Experiment." Mimeo, Department of Economics, Columbia University.

Costa, Sergio. 2002. *As cores de ercília: esfera pública, democracia, configurações pós-nacionais.* Belo Horizonte: UFMG.

Dagnino, Evelina, ed. 2002. *Sociedade Civil e Espaços Públicos no Brasil.* São Paulo: Paz e Terra.

Fung, Archon. 2004. *Empowered Participation: Reinventing Urban Democracy.* Princeton, NJ: Princeton University Press.

Fung, Archon, and Eric Olin Wright. 2003. "Thinking about Empowered Participatory Governance." In *Deepening Democracy: Institutional Innovation in Empowered Participatory Governance,* ed. Archon Fung and Eric Olin Wright, 3–41. London: Verso.

Gaventa, John. 2004. "Representation, Community Leadership and Participation: Citizen Involvement in Neighbourhood Renewal and Local Governance." Paper prepared for the Neighbourhood Renewal Unit Office of the Deputy Prime Minister, February, London.

Gomes Da Silva, Tatiana de Amorim. 2003. "O enigma da esfinge. Indefinição entre o público e o privado: a relação dos conselheiros de direitos (2000–2002) com o fundo municipal dos direitos da criança e do adolescente de São Paulo." Ph.D. diss., Mestrado em Ciências Sociais, Pontifícia Universidade Católica de São Paulo.

Goodman, Leo. 1961. "Snowball Sampling." *Annals of Mathematical Statistics* 32 (1): 148–70.

Grindle, Merilee S. 1999. *Audacious Reforms: Institutional Reform and Democracy in Latin America.* Baltimore: Johns Hopkins University Press.

Gurza Lavalle, Adrian, Arnab Acharya, and Peter Houtzager. 2005. "Beyond Comparative Anecdotalism: Lesson on Civil Society and Participation from São Paulo, Brazil." *World Development* 33 (6): 951–64.

Gurza Lavalle, Adrian, and Graziela Castello. 2008. "Ssociedade civil, representação e a dupla face da accountability: cidade do México e São Paulo." *Caderno CRH, Salvador* 21 (52): 67–86.

Gurza Lavalle, Adrian, P. Peter Houtzager, and Graziela Castello. 2005. "In Whose Name? Political Representation and Civil Organizations in Brazil." Working Paper 249, Institute of Development Studies–University of Sussex.

———. 2006a. "Representação política e organizações civis: novas instâncias de mediação e os desafios da legitimidade." *Revista Brasileira de Ciências Sociais* 21 (60): 43–66.

———. 2006b. "Representação política e organizações civis: novas instâncias de mediação e os desafi 'democracia, pluralização da representação e sociedade civil.'" *Lua Nova* no. 67: 49–103.

Heller, Patrick. 2001. "Moving the State: The Politics of Democratic Decentralization in Kerala, South Africa, and Porto Alegre." *Politics & Society* 29 (1): 131–63.

Hevia de la Jara, Felipe. 2006. "Participación ciudadana institucionalizada: análisis de los marcos legales de la participación en América Latina." In *La disputa por la construcción de la democracia en América Latina,* ed. Evelina Dagnino, Alberto J. Olvera, and Aldo Panfichi, 367–95. CIESAS/Universidad Veracruzana/Fondo de Cultura Económica, Mexico.

Houtzager, P. Peter, Adrian Gurza Lavalle, and Arnab Acharya. 2003. "Who Participates? Civil Society and the New Democratic Politics in São Paulo, Brazil." IDS Working Paper no. 210, Institute of Development Studies–University of Sussex.

———. 2004. "Atores da sociedade civil e atores políticos—participação nas novas políticas democráticas em São Paulo." In *Participação política em São Paulo,* ed. Leonardo Avritzer, 256–322. São Paulo: UNESP.

Isunza, Vera Ernesto. 2006. "Árbitros ciudadanos de las disputas partidarias. Una mirada sobre los consejos electorales federales en la contienda de 2000 en México." In *Democratización, rendición de cuentas y sociedad civil: participación ciudadana y control social,* org. Ernesto Isunza Vera and Alberto J. Olvera, 545–69. CIESAS/Universidad Veracruzana/Miguel Ángel Porrúa, Mexico.

Keane, John. 1992. *La vida pública y el capitalismo tardío. Hacia una teoría socialista de la democracia.* Mexico City: Alianza.

Landim, Leilah. 1998. "The Nonprofit Sector in Brazil." In *The Nonprofit Sector in the Developing World,* ed. H. K. Anheier and S. Lester, 53–121. Manchester, U.K.: Manchester University Press.

Lüchmann, Ligia. 2007. "A representação no interior das experiências de participação." *Lua Nova* no. 70: 139–70.

———. 2008. "Participação e representação nos conselhos gestores e no orçamento participativo." *Caderno CRH* 21 (52): 87–98.

Manin, Bernard. 1997. *The Principles of Representative Government.* Cambridge, U.K.: Cambridge University Press.

Miguel, Luis Felipe. 2003a. "Representação política em 3-D: elementos para uma teoria ampliada da representação política." *Revista Brasileira de Ciências Sociais* 18 (51): 123–40.

———. 2003b. "Impasses da accountability: dilemas e alternativas da representação política." Paper presented at the XXVII Annual Congress of ANPOCS, Caxambu, October.

Nascimento, Mariângela. 1999. "Democracia e espaço público no Brasil." *Cadernos o CEAS* no. 183: 37–45.

Novaro, Marcos. 2000. *Representación y liderazgo en las democracias contemporáneas.* Rosario: Homo Sapiens Ediciones.

Olvera, Alberto J. 2003. "Sociedad civil, esfera pública y democratización en América Latina: México." Fondo de Cultura Económica, Universidad Veracruzana.

Panfichi, Aldo. 2003. "Sociedad civil, esfera pública y democratización en América Latina: Andes y Cono Sur." Fondo de Cultura Económica, Universidad Veracruzana.

Przeworski, Adam. 2002. "Social Accountability in Latin America and Beyond." *In Enforcing the Rule of Law: Social Accountability in the New Latin American Democracies*, ed. Enrique Peruzzotti and Catalina Smulovitz, 323–33. Buenos Aires: Temas.

Roberts, Kenneth M. 2002. "Party-Society Linkages and Democratic Representation in Latin America." *Canadian Journal of Latin American and Caribbean Studies* 27 (53): 9–34.

Sader, Eder. 1988. *Quando novos personagens entram em cena.* São Paulo: Paz e Terra.

Santos, Boaventura de Sousa, ed. 2002. *Democratizar a democracia: os caminhos da democracia participativa.* Rio de Janeiro: Civilização Brasileira.

Singer, Paul, and Vinicius Calderia Brant, eds. 1980. *São Paulo: o povo em movimento.* São Paulo: Vozes/CEBRAP.

Szazi, Eduardo. 2001. *Terceiro setor. Regulação no Brasil.* São Paulo: IGIFEI/Peirópolis.

Tatagiba, Luciana. 2002. "Os conselhos gestores e a democratização das políticas públicas no Brasil." In *Sociedade civil e espaços públicos no Brasil,* ed. Evelina Dagnino, 47–103. São Paulo: Paz e Terra.

Wampler, Brian. 2004. "Delegation, Authority, and Co-optation: Brazil's Participatory Democracy." Paper prepared for presentation at the American Political Science Association Conference, Chicago.

Embedding the Right to Information: The Uses of Sector-Specific Transparency Regimes

Rob Jenkins

Advocates of enhanced citizen access to publicly held information often overstate the potentially positive impacts of legislative and regulatory reforms designed to enhance government transparency. Claims that access to information will drive home a revolution in governance border on zealotry. This is not to deny that, under the right circumstances, official information regimes, accessible by right, can transform certain dimensions of governance. There are, for instance, the many Indians who have in recent years been able to obtain full and clear title to their land—and therefore the ability to exploit its financial power—because of property records being placed in a central electronic repository. In terms of accountability, this is vastly preferable to the dispersed land registers maintained by village record keepers. These moldering books, still found throughout rural India, are notoriously open to fraud perpetrated by officials in league with influential local leaders. Transparency, however, has not transformed the essential nature of India's land bureaucracy, which still controls a vast collection of veto points relating to property transfer, sale, inheritance, usage, or taxation.

The eternally optimistic are balanced, however, by the equally inflated ranks of right-to-information skeptics, who argue that the costs of making information accessible frequently outweigh the benefits. These costs include the time and energy required to establish a regime of information access (passing legislation, framing administrative procedures, and establishing oversight mechanisms). This is in addition to the costs of operating such a system effectively. More worrying, potentially, is the tendency of accountability extremists to micromanage transparency to the point where it stifles initiative among midranking public-sector employees. This is predictable when officials fear minute scrutiny of their every action, in close to real time as well as ex post, by external assessors with little understanding of the context in which policy options were debated, consensus was generated, or complex deals (involving numerous tradeoffs) were concluded. This critique is exaggerated, especially by those with an interest in maintaining high barriers to information access—but it contains a substantial degree of truth. Several things fuel suspicion of access to information (ATI) as a tool of improved pro-poor governance. First, it is difficult, if not impossible, to obtain convincing statistical evidence to demonstrate that the right to information (RTI) has improved developmental outcomes for poor and marginalized people. Second, too many other factors influence governance institutions to attribute either positive *or* negative outcomes to increased ATI. Third, moreover, many countries have experienced rapid poverty reduction amid highly opaque public-sector bureaucracies. China and Vietnam are the most striking examples.

Even if such criticisms have a degree of validity, they do not constitute sufficient grounds for halting progress toward enhanced access to publicly held information—whether in India or anywhere else. Indeed, the burden of proof must fall to opponents of greater openness. In other words, where is the evidence that China or Vietnam would not have reduced poverty as quickly had their governments improved the regime governing the public's access to government-held information?

The benefits of ATI for social and economic rights can be portrayed in various ways, but it is perhaps best to think of ATI as an element in the strengthening of accountability institutions so that they better support human development (understood as the progressive acquisition of freedoms and the capacities to exercise them). A *lack* of accountability—the failure of oversight and enforcement institutions of various kinds—is a crucial reason why people fail to experience as a concrete reality the national and international rights protections that their governments ostensibly provide them.

Examining transparency in the context of accountability institutions makes sense because accountability, by definition, contains an information-access component. Accountability exists where one party possesses the right to require answers of another, who potentially faces sanction if unforthcoming or unconvincing. The entire process, both the asking for and the rendering of "accounts," involves actors acquiring, shaping, and strategically revealing and concealing information. To exercise surveillance over someone you are holding accountable requires the party under scrutiny to part with information relevant to his or her performance. When in possession of sufficient data (whether qualitative or quantitative), oversight agencies can engage in informed deliberation with officials to whom power has been delegated. The mere possession of a robust ATI regime is useless on its own. Without such a system, however, accountability institutions are rendered meaningless. In the absence of functioning accountability institutions, social and economic rights tend not to be realized.

With information central to all accountability mechanisms, and accountability a crucial element of democratic governance, a strong associative link connects the roots of democracy with efforts to improve transparency.

This chapter examines two case studies from India that indicate the great variety in terms of transparency that can exist even under a national legislative framework guaranteeing the public's right to information. Each of the two case studies represents a type of government initiative—one related to the productive economy, the other to issues of redistribution. Significantly, both promise to create jobs—a key challenge for India as it attempts to achieve "inclusive growth."

On the redistributive side, India's National Rural Employment Guarantee Act of 2005 (NREGA), the flagship antipoverty initiative of Prime Minister Manmohan Singh, contains an interlocking set of transparency provisions. These allow, for instance, laborers who take part in this job-creation program to access official records indicating the hours of work, the payment of wages, the fulfilling of supply orders, and the sanctioning of works projects.

The second case study concerns India's policy on special economic zones (SEZs), an effort to stimulate the productive economy. India's SEZ policy is characterized by opacity. The idea of creating enclaves of intensive productive activity in which firms reap the benefits of sectoral clustering has yielded significant successes in several countries. The means of pursuing such a strategy, however, can vary enormously, and India's methods have been markedly lacking in transparency, which has contributed to weak accountability. The government of India, as well as some of the state governments involved in attracting these private-sector SEZs to their jurisdictions, furnish some basic SEZ data—for instance, concerning the location, size, and prospective uses of an SEZ. Beyond this, however, lie huge obstacles to discovering further details about the qualitative nature of the land parcels concerned, how decisions were made to develop a given SEZ site, who in the bureaucracy was involved in making them, why specific SEZ norms have been changed since the introduction of the act, and how fulfillment of the conditions attached to land-use permissions is monitored.

These two policy domains—the productive and the redistributive—provide a window onto questions about the utility of sector-specific transparency provisions. They suggest that even where generic information-access legislation is in place, there are significant advantages to establishing suitable transparency mechanisms within sector-specific legislation.

The National Rural Employment Guarantee Act

Let us begin with the redistributive case. In India, successive governments have proclaimed that the losers from economic liberalization are to be cushioned, to the degree possible, from dislocations created by the globalization of the Indian economy. Yet, for nearly 15 years following the opening up of the Indian economy in 1991, few concrete measures were taken on a national scale. That changed in 2005, less than a year after the swearing in of Prime Minister Manmohan Singh (of the Congress Party) at the head of the United Progressive Alliance coalition government.

The NREGA is a New Deal–style program that creates unskilled labor opportunities for rural people suffering unemployment and chronic underemployment. The NREGA extends this concept radically by "guaranteeing" employment for each rural household that demands it. The "right" to employment is of limited proportions, providing a maximum of 100 days of labor per rural household. Anyone can ask for employment; one need not be poor to apply. In practice, the work is hard enough that the scheme is self-targeting: Only those seriously in need would endure the work conditions. However, the mere existence of an untargeted benefit creates a risk that corrupt officials will use the names of nonparticipating people to inflate employment lists. The wages of these "ghost workers" can be divided among colluding officials and, in some cases, the "worker" in question. In addition, local officials skim off part of the wages of the genuine workers—those who actually do perform labor. Underpayment of wages is rife in rural India. The abundant avenues for fraud and abuse by the elites who administer government schemes are reason enough for some people to dislike the NREGA, regardless of its impacts. Others consider corruption something people—individually and collectively—should struggle against, not capitulate to.

With precisely this in mind, the framers of the NREGA included specific provisions to enable workers—who might otherwise lose part of their wages—to monitor the actions of project administrators. The legislation guarantees ATI about project work sites, number of workers employed, hours billed, quantities (and price) of building material delivered, and so forth. All this information must, under the statute and the regulations framed to operationalize it, be provided without hindrance and under threat of penalty to officials who fail to produce such information.

Direct citizen engagement in the accountability process—using an information regime designed into a welfare program—represents a new channel, or axis, of accountability, which combines features of the two standard channels: vertical and horizontal accountability. In *vertical* accountability institutions, states are held to account by citizens, jointly and severally, whether through elections and other *formal* processes, or through lobbying or mass mobilization, both of which rely on the existence of a set of *informal* institutions (such as the press and social networks). This is the most direct form of accountability but faces huge challenges (such as clientelism). *Horizontal* accountability institutions are those in which state entities demand answers from (and sometimes possess the power to sanction) other state entities. Auditors-general, anticorruption commissions, bureaucratic oversight boards, parliamentary committees and commissions—these and other bodies stand in for citizens who generally lack the time, expertise, and collective-action resources to monitor the detailed work of their public representatives.

More recently, a third category has emerged, thanks to increased efforts by citizens to engage directly in government processes once reserved for state agencies (Goetz and Jenkins 2005). This category concerns the direct engagement of ordinary people with service providers and state budgeting, auditing, and other oversight processes that have traditionally been the arena of state actors alone. Combining elements of vertical and horizontal accountability, experiments in direct citizen engagement amount to hybrid forms of accountability, located somewhere in between (Goetz and Jenkins 2001). In this sense, they can be thought of as representing a "diagonal" channel of accountability.

Efforts to reinvent accountability systems to increase popular participation in expenditure tracking, public-hearing–style group audits of written accounts, and so forth are sometimes referred to as "direct," "social," or "demand-side" accountability processes. They possess three main characteristics: They bypass the formal institutional intermediaries that delay or subvert accountability systems, they focus on obtaining answers ex ante from policy makers as opposed to the conventional—solely ex post—approach (such as participatory budgeting), and they prioritize the fairness of outcomes, not just procedural correctness.

An important aspect of the NREGA's ATI provisions is how they promote precisely this type of direct accountability seeking. The transparency measures stretch from the beginning to the end of the project cycle: the issuing of job cards to workers, the identification of a work project and site, the payment of wages—all the way to the auditing of physical assets created under the scheme and the accounts submitted in connection with their completion. Because of the thoroughness of its designers, the NREGA has, in effect, created a full-fledged "information regime," in which specific actions trigger the release and (in some cases) dissemination of financial records, employment registers, and project-completion reports.

All of this is underwritten by a purpose-built information technology platform devised for the NREGA's implementation. The NREGA's information technology (IT) system tracks each work project (the laying of a road foundation, the repair of minor irrigation works) and each individual worker/applicant in ways that severely reduce the scope for officials (and their accomplices in local politics) to falsify records and thereby illegally obtain a share of the worker's wages. The full implementation of the IT system has been delayed by, among other factors, the incomplete reach of the government's national data network. According to officials in India's Planning Commission, the problem is being addressed, and by 2012, more than 90 percent of village councils (*gram panchayats*) should—if all goes to plan—be connected.

The IT system allows various levels of access, permitting both individuals and local activists working with them to obtain financial records, which can then be cross-checked against information provided by local workers/citizens. This process of collective verification is itself built into the NREGA, which stipulates that works projects must be subjected to "social audit" in the relevant local government forum (in this case, the village assembly). The rules for conducting such an audit are set forth in detail. Such regulations are not alien to states such as Rajasthan, which in 2000 passed progressive amendments to the state's local government legislation requiring local councils to meet as full village assemblies (*gram sabhas*) to certify the accounts rendered by the village secretary. This requirement is circumvented for the most part in rural Rajasthan, happening "only on paper."

Over the past 15 years, one of the most inspirational examples of using information to advance socioeconomic rights involved precisely the verification of information provided in government-employment programs. The Indian social-activist group the Mazdoor Kisan Shakti Sangathan (MKSS), or Worker and Farmer Power Organization, pioneered these social audit procedures in nonofficial hearings in various parts of Rajasthan throughout the late 1990s. After successfully lobbying the Rajasthan government to pass a state-level RTI Act, MKSS found itself, in the early years of the current decade, in the midst of a campaign demanding that the Rajasthan government adopt an employment guarantee act along the lines of what had existed in the western state of Maharashtra since the early 1970s. The MKSS activists and like-minded advocates in civil society ended up, by late 2004, convincing the lame-duck chief minister of Rajasthan as well as the leader of the national Congress Party, Sonia Gandhi. Mrs. Gandhi became a strong believer that a nationwide Employment Guarantee Scheme would help to demonstrate that the incoming (Congress-led) United Progressive Alliance government was, unlike its Bharatiya Janata Party–led predecessor, concerned about those left behind in India's rush toward prosperity. MKSS-linked activists joined the National Advisory Council (NAC), which Mrs. Gandhi led as a kind of semiofficial think tank. It was via the NAC that RTI campaigners fashioned the NREGA into the progressive piece of legislation it became.

The NREGA's transparency provisions were put in place, it must be noted, despite the fact that India already had RTI legislation on the books and was passing a new and better RTI law at precisely the moment that the NREGA was being formulated and debated. The transparency provisions in the NREGA go beyond mere information provision or the compilation of data on program inputs and outputs. The NREGA provides disaggregated information, which allows engaged citizens to audit in detail the lower- and mid-level bureaucrats whose actions most directly affect their development prospects. These are, for instance, the "junior engineers" dispatched by subdistrict administrations everywhere in rural India to provide "technical sanction" for works projects. In addition, many layers of elected leaders are involved—at the village, block, district, and state levels—thanks to India's multitiered system of democratic local government known as *panchayati raj.* These and other actors have a pecuniary or political incentive to influence implementation of the NREGA, but their interests are often at odds with one another. Members of the state Legislative Assembly are elected from constituencies that overlap those of the elected block-level councils, leading to intense struggles for de facto control over the flow of federal funds, regardless of what is indicated de jure.

India's Special Economic Zones

The second case study comes from India's productive economy, involving both the private sector and an attempt by the Indian state to engage in what, in a different context, Wade (1990) called "governing the market." The Special Economic Zone Act 2005 was passed by India's parliament to allow the creation of Chinese-style export-processing zones, enclaves whose tax breaks and relaxed regulatory requirements are intended to attract foreign investment, spur the creation of world-class infrastructure, and create jobs. Since February 2006, when the SEZ Act came into force, India's usually slow-moving bureaucracy has acted with unprecedented vigor, clearing proposals for more than 500 SEZs.

Although the SEZ Act was passed in the same year as both the NREGA and the RTI Act, its relationship to transparency is far more problematic than in the case of the NREGA. Significantly, the SEZ bill was introduced with little advanced consultation or even warning. It received almost no debate in parliament (at either the committee stage or on the floor of the house), let alone in the wider public arena. The bill was passed with few members of parliament in the chamber and a large proportion of the nation's lawmakers (whether present or absent on that day) severely underinformed about its contents.

India's adoption of the SEZ concept was, according to a former commerce minister, "inspired" by the success of China's SEZs, which turned sleepy provincial backwaters such as Shenzhen into global manufacturing hubs in less than two decades. Even so, India's approach to promoting SEZs is strikingly different from the Chinese policy. Tailoring foreign ideas to fit domestic circumstances is not necessarily a bad impulse. The design of India's SEZ policy, however, and the manner in which it has been implemented, raises suspicions that the Chinese model was indigenized not so much to suit India's national interest as to benefit elite interest groups. These include prominent industrial houses, real estate developers, and (last but by no means least) the politicians and bureaucrats who stand to gain (politically and personally) by acting as midwives at the birth of SEZs. By approving hundreds of small SEZs throughout India, the government has adapted the policy concept to India's federal democratic context, where placating powerful interests at the provincial level cultivates broad-based support among India's diverse elite. Allowing SEZs to be developed by the private sector—in China they were state-owned and operated—was the crucial innovation, as was the involvement of India's state governments.

To implement the SEZ policy, the central government must rely on India's state governments to assist SEZ developers to acquire land, to obtain the necessary clearances from state-level agencies, and to shepherd SEZ applications through the approval process in New Delhi. States are pleased with the investment-promotion opportunities the new policy makes possible and have acted with remarkable alacrity to facilitate the process. State governments have thus demonstrated a high level of "buy-in" to the SEZ policy. Because state governments are ruled by a wide array of political parties, many of whom sit in opposition in the national parliament, their participation as enthusiastic implementers of the SEZ policy should, in theory, weaken the association of the policy with only the parties that make up the United Progressive Alliance coalition government in Delhi. This should, in theory, make the SEZ policy a much less partisan issue.

However, none of the state or nonstate actors involved in the SEZ policy have operated with anything like a sufficient degree of transparency. Where the NREGA made ATI a central pillar of its design, building transparency provisions and procedures for collective citizen auditing into the legislation itself, the SEZ Act 2005 tends toward the opaque.

This is true at almost every point of the SEZ cycle. There is, for instance, a great deal of ambiguity surrounding the minimum requirements for the establishment of a privately operated SEZ in various sectors—and such rules as exist have been subjected to almost constant revision. More problematic is the lack of documentary information on how state governments intend to monitor compliance with various provisions of their agreements with SEZ developers. SEZ developers often obtain state land in addition to buying private land, but state land frequently comes with various sorts of conditions attached, whether environmental or in terms of permitted usage.

Although India's RTI legislation makes it theoretically possible for citizens and their associations to obtain copies of SEZ applications submitted to the interministerial Board of Approvals (BoA), which (as the name implies) authorizes the creation of SEZs, the application documents received are not always complete. Even where it is possible for ordinary citizens to obtain all the documentation submitted by the SEZ's developer, the untransparent nature of the BoA deliberative process means that little or no information is provided about the legal basis on which decisions were taken. This has a close bearing on the nature of the information provided by private-sector applicants seeking approval for their SEZs, because the applications often make dubious (or in some cases outrageously inflated) claims about the benefits likely to result from the establishment of the project in question. The lack of a clear rationale justifying extreme claims in SEZ applications—and the failure of the BoA subsequently to explain its rationale for approving specific projects—was the subject of a close analysis conducted by the Delhi-based Centre for Policy Research (Mukhopadhyay 2008).

Additional ATI considerations are involved in the process by which approved projects establish themselves on the ground. The acquisition of land for SEZs—which up until April 2007, when abuses became too obvious to ignore, was undertaken primarily by state governments on behalf of private promoters—is a very untransparent business. This has fueled suspicions of underhanded tactics, even in cases where transactions appear to have been handled in a relatively straightforward fashion. The lack of publicly available "socioeconomic impact assessment" studies (because these are not mandated by the SEZ Act) is the kind of information deficit that makes accountability institutions unable to perform the essential function of preventing abuses by the state in the process of industrialization.

The applicability of national laws *within* SEZs—which in this sense are perhaps best thought of as special *governance* zones—is also a matter of concern. At many of the larger sites, people will live as well as work in SEZs, and rely on hospitals, schools, and other facilities that emerge within a particular zone's master plan. SEZs are mandated to operate under a special set of governance institutions, in which a government-appointed Development Commissioner wields considerable authority.

Whether it will be possible to make effective use of the RTI under the conditions that will prevail in future SEZs is open to question. Some worry that the ostensibly private-sector nature of SEZs will permit developers to shield many activities behind a cloak of "commercial confidentiality." There is certainly anxiety among activists about the absence of dedicated ATI provisions within the SEZ Act. Without statutorily mandated procedures, requests for documentation on the running of an SEZ may prove ineffective. Whether the rights of SEZ inhabitants (as workers, residents, consumers of services, or just plain citizens) can be protected effectively under such circumstances—especially where the lines separating public authority and private business are blurred—remains to be seen.

Conclusion

These two concurrent policy experiments—one designed to harness the economic benefits of globalization, the other to mitigate its less salutary effects—demonstrate the paramount importance of designing legislation with transparency in mind. In many countries with severely overburdened civil services, national RTI legislation will be insufficient to improve government accountability.

Transparency provisions can be designed into sectoral legislation such that they stimulate collective action. The NREGA is built on a model of participatory planning, execution, and auditing. The reality does not always live up to the ideal, but the efforts that have been unleashed in trying to achieve accountability to local people can significantly improve the governance environment if allowed time to mature.

By contrast, neither the SEZ Act nor the mandarin culture of India's economic bureaucracy invites much direct oversight. The very lack of transparency, however, has generated increased controversy surrounding what was already a highly conflict-ridden implementation process, with many SEZs running into surprisingly energetic resistance among partisan enemies, local landholders, and ideological opponents. During 2007–08, several approved SEZ projects in the state of Goa were halted thanks to a campaign that *did* manage to use RTI at certain points. Had greater transparency been incorporated into the SEZ Act itself, some of the more egregious SEZ projects might never have reached the point where opposition erupted. In cases where there genuinely is nothing to hide, enhanced ATI would nip unfounded rumors in the bud. Cultures of excessive official secrecy usually provide fertile ground for fear-mongering.

Clearly, transparency provisions designed for an antipoverty program would be ill-suited to the process of establishing an industrial township. The nature of the stakeholders is different as well, with the well-defined roles played by officials and beneficiaries under the NREGA far less in evidence in the less-clear-cut world of state-facilitated industrialization, where private-sector participation is voluntary, jurisdictions compete for inward investment, and an entirely new spatially delineated model of development is slowly emerging. If anything, these conditions argue for greater popular scrutiny and more direct public engagement in decisions that will affect not only those living and working in SEZs, but also people from neighboring areas whose natural resources will be affected, and who will suffer, in some cases literally, the downstream effects of poorly regulated economic activity.

References

Goetz, Anne Marie, and Rob Jenkins. 2001. "Hybrid Forms of Accountability: Citizen Engagement in Institutions of Public-Sector Oversight in India." *Public Management Review* 3 (3): 363–84.

———. 2005. *Reinventing Accountability: Making Democracy Work for Human Development.* London: Palgrave Macmillan.

Mukhopadhyay, Partha. 2008. "Ghosts in the Machine." *Hindustan Times,* January 22.

Wade, Robert. 1990. *Governing the Market: Economic Theory and the Role of Government in East Asian Industrialization.* Princeton, NJ: Princeton University Press.

Section VIII
Conclusion

How Can Citizens Be Helped to Hold Their Governments Accountable?

Taeku Lee and Sina Odugbemi

Gradually they're beginning to recognize the fact that there's nothing more secure than a democratic, accountable, and participatory form of government. But it's sunk in only theoretically, it has not yet sunk in completely in practical terms.

—Wole Soyinka[1]

The more strictly we are watched, the better we behave.

—Jeremy Bentham[2]

International development has, as we said in the Introduction, taken an accountability turn. But the turn remains uncertain, and a sense of unreality still lingers regarding how to help citizens hold their governments accountable. Now, although we do not and cannot claim to have all the answers, many useful lessons can be drawn from the contributions to this volume. Our intention, in this concluding chapter, is to draw out the insights without repeating what our learned contributors have already said.

The Macrolevel Governance Context Is Critical and Often Needs Attention

As Peruzzotti argues, a government is accountable when institutional conditions act together to compel public officials to justify their actions and, where necessary, be sanctioned for wrongdoing. In addition, both Blair and Thampi list the set of institutions that need to be working in a certain way for direct accountability mechanisms to work. See in particular Thampi's "The Critical 8."

So it matters whether a country is a functioning democracy, an authoritarian state, or, as is often the case, something else in between.

In the debates around the good governance agenda, this is the "Big G Governance" problem. Does good governance mean liberal constitutional democracy? Or should the agenda be about a more modest ambition, that is, working toward states that are effective and accountable? Sometimes the distinction is overdrawn. For how do you make a state both effective and accountable? Is it not the case that if you think this through properly you will get to democratic governance? This debate matters because it has serious policy consequences. One consequence is already happening. Initiative managers in international development are funding so-called social accountability tools as bolt-ons to projects irrespective of context. Accountability mechanisms invented in democratic India or Brazil are being turned into technocratic tools and used by authoritarian states. Suddenly, context does not matter?

One of the major lessons of this study is that the institutions that strengthen accountability need attention in many countries. Yes, it is difficult long-term work and there are no quick fixes, but it needs to be done if citizens are going to be able to more easily hold their governments accountable.

The Public Sphere/The Agora Matters

The public sphere of a country and how it is constituted matters if you want the citizens to be able to hold their governments accountable. Two recent accountability stories from the United Kingdom and Brazil make the point powerfully.

The expenses scandal that engulfed the British Parliament in 2009 is well known, and at the time of writing the consequences are still being felt. The structural elements of the story remain crucial. First, civil society activists sought to take advantage of the Freedom of Information Act in February 2008 to find out how members of Parliament (MPs) were accounting for their expenses. Parliament tried to block the move. Then someone leaked the information to a major newspaper, *The Daily Telegraph*. Starting on May 8, 2009, the newspaper ran daily stories of the scandalous misuse of public funds by several MPs. The rest of the media ran with the story, which quickly acquired gale-force proportions. Public outrage ensued. The public demanded action. The consequences were dramatic: public apologies by members (MPs), sackings, resignations, de-selections, and criminal prosecutions. An Independent Parliamentary Standards Authority was created and took up work in May 2010, thus depriving MPs of the age-old right to police their own affairs.

The other story is from Brazil, and it concerns abuse of the Federal Payment Card. The federal government of Brazil used spending cards so that officials could pay for expenses and make cash withdrawals. Between 2003 and 2007 the use of this card increased significantly as a way of avoiding lengthy procurement procedures. Expenses charged to the card occurred on weekends and during holidays and included spending in supermarkets, restaurants, coffeehouses, and hotels. Information about Payment Card spending was made available online on the Brazilian Comptroller General's Portal da Transparencia in 2008. Immediately, the media in Brazil picked up the story and published more than 3,000 stories between January and May 2008 on alleged irregularities in the use of the Payment Card. The public was outraged. Subsequently, the use of the Payment Card decreased by 60 percent compared to 2007 (Hage 2008). In other words, the federal officials modified their behavior.

Consider, if you will, the structural essentials of the two stories with regard to bad behavior by public officials:

> Access to official information + civic activism + exposé by independent media + inflamed/activated public opinion = sanctions or behavior change by public officials (direct accountability).

Absent any of these structural elements, it becomes much more difficult for citizens to hold public officials accountable. In other words, if policy makers in international development really want to help citizens hold their governments accountable, they will support these structural elements of a vibrant, inclusive public sphere. First, they will be supporting the transparency agenda through efforts and laws that give citizens access to public information, for at the heart of accountability is the flow of information from government to citizens. Good starting points are the proposals contained in the Carter Center's Atlanta Declaration (2008). Second, they will be supporting the building of free, plural, and independent media systems (for a full treatment of the subject see Norris 2010). Third, they will support the institutional strengthening of civil society, not through mere consultation.

Several of the authors in this volume make all these points eloquently. See in particular the contributions by Jenkins, Wantchekon and Vermeersch, Myers, and Arnold.

Activate Public Opinion: The Surest Security against Misrule

In *Federalist*, No. 51, James Madison makes the key point that a "dependence on the people is, no doubt, the primary control on the government" (Hamilton, Madison, and Jay 1961, 207). Ultimately, holding governments accountable is the responsibility of the citizenry. As Jeremy Bentham rightly points out in his *Securities against Misrule* (1990, 139): "Of everything that is thus done or endeavoured at, the success depends upon the spirit, the intelligence, the vigilance, the alertness, the intrepidity, the energy, the perseverance, of those of whose opinions Public Opinion is composed." Read that again, and it is impossible not to be struck by the range of vigorous nouns Bentham deploys.

In figure 28.1, we show how public opinion fits into the accountability story. The process starts with an official transgression of some kind. It must come

Figure 28.1. The Process of Public Opinion Formation

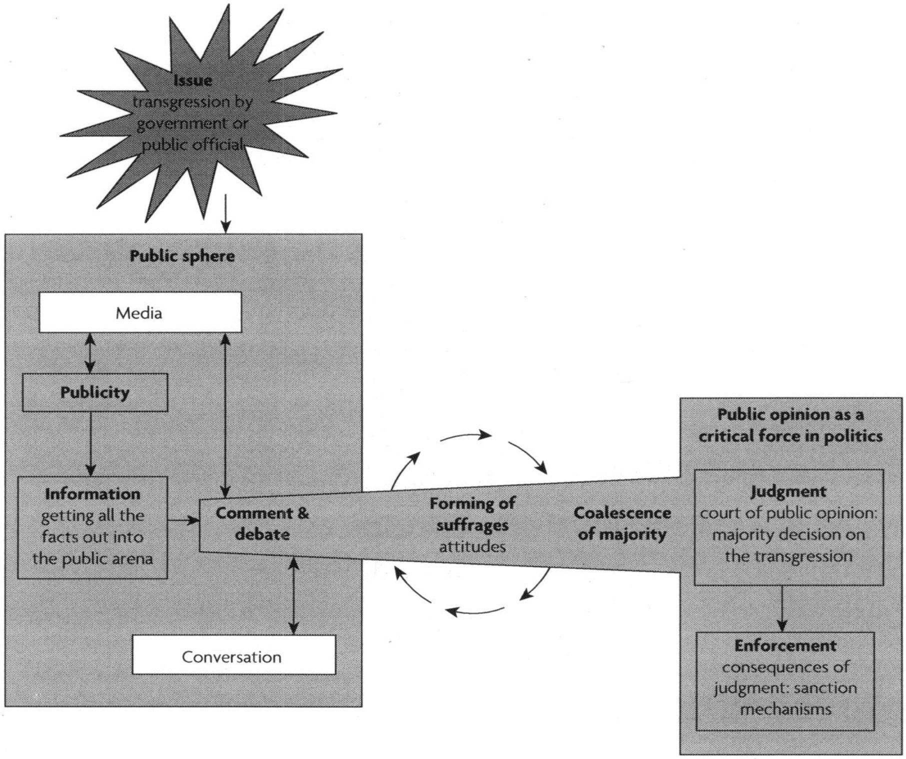

Source: Authors.

out into the open. Officials cannot be held accountable by citizens if the latter do not know what has happened. Once the matter is in the public sphere, various processes take place simultaneously. The media run with the story. More details come out. Debate and discussion ensue not only in the media but also in conversations that citizens have with other citizens at home, at work, in churches, in clubs, and so on. A majority view coalesces: That is public opinion. The point is that once it crystallizes, it is a critical force in politics, and it tends to demand accountability. Finally, public opinion has enforcement mechanisms, as even authoritarian regimes know only too well. These include petitions, sit-ins, demonstrations, protests, and, if pushed, the withdrawal of obedience and open rebellion.

As we have pointed out in our own contributions to this volume, however, whether activated regulative public opinion can work well depends very much on the political context. The point is to understand the power and potential of public opinion and to make its facilitation the object of policy. For it remains the real, always-present force for direct accountability in any political community. Direct accountability mechanisms—sometimes called social accountability mechanisms—are potentially key resources, the varying vulnerabilities and openness of states (across different levels of governments) represent shifting structural contexts of opportunity, and the activation or quiescence of public opinion is the key schema motivating collective action. Note that we use "activated public opinion" to describe the process by which individuals move from a state of passively tolerating misrule to a state of actively demanding change and accountability. Ultimately, this is about agency.

Finally, it is important to note with V. O. Key (1961) that latent opinion makes elites nervous; corrupt elites do not want public opinion activated, and that is the very reason those who care about accountability need to find ways to activate public opinion. Fear is good. This is true whether it is fear of losing one's stranglehold over power and resources, fear of dissipating one's authority and legitimacy to rule, fear of being run out of political office and losing the material and status accoutrements that accompany that office, or fear simply of squandering one's legacy and personal reputation. If you are not afraid you are not accountable.

Several of the contributions to this volume discuss public opinion in relation to accountability. Thampi and Paul give practitioner perspectives. Taber discusses opinion formation. Tsai provides a powerful example of public opinion as social control from rural China and how it regulates the conduct of local officials.

Accountability through Public Opinion

This book has convened the collective expertise of 31 scholars and practitioners, shared 30 chapters, and spanned more than a dozen country contexts. The crux of its contents is this: Accountability, as a goal, cannot be separated from public opinion as a defining input. The considered judgments and mobilized will of the public are not a garnish, a role player, or an otherwise residual aspect of good governance. Rather, when roused to public action, the opinions of ordinary individuals—whose bidding governments presume or are explicitly charged to pursue—can serve as a regular, requisite resource for politicians and public officials who aim to achieve the ends of equity, efficiency, responsiveness, and representation.

As we noted in the introductory chapter, good governance is not simply a matter of finding the best technocratic solutions to social problems, then taking it as an article of faith that the sheer force of the better argument or analysis will carry the day. Nor is good governance achieved by serial logrolls between politically insulated elites or by selectively pandering to privileged constituencies through patronage and pork-barrel politics. *Pace* these accounts, we insist that good governance results from institutionalizing mechanisms for directly monitoring whether rulers say what they do and do what they say, and then holding their feet to the fire if they fail to do these things. Acts have consequences. Government should be no different. The public, properly motivated, can and should be enlisted in the service of keeping those in seats of political power honest.

As a philosophical matter, the public work of *demoi* throughout the developed and developing worlds is centrally involved in any meaningful understanding of accountability and its proper standing in desirable, or at least defensible, systems of governance. Accountability in the realm of governance is fundamentally about institutionalizing Bentham's optic—a relationship of watchfulness and responsiveness between rulers and their subjects. This relationship between those in government and those whom they govern is needed, to paraphrase James Madison, because men are not angels and angels do not govern men. Thus, Madison notes in *The Federalist Papers* (No. 51), "In framing a government which is to be administered by men over men, the great difficulty lies in this: you must first enable the government to control the governed; and in the next place oblige it to control itself. *A dependence on the people is, no doubt, the primary control on the government*" (emphasis added). Philippe Schmitter and Terry Karl (1991, 76) extend this intuition to the very definition of democracy itself as "a system of governance in which rulers are held accountable for their actions in the public realm by citizens, acting indirectly through the competition and cooperation of their elected representatives."

The relevance of public action—the successful activation and mobilization of bottom–up demands for accountability—is not simply a matter for philosopher tracts. Genuine, sustained efforts to build accountable systems of governance require more than technical solutions and the right kinds of economic, statistical analyses of benefits and costs. They require more than "war room" strategies and public relations tactics to smooth over the rough edges of a disgruntled public. They even require more than legitimate constitutional frameworks that aim to bind politicians and bureaucrats from the corrupt excesses of power and authority, elections that punish or reward those in political offices, and social accountability mechanisms that aim to regularize opportunities for public review, deliberation, and response.

Rather, as a practical matter, no constitutional framework, electoral system, or set of deliberative and participatory institutions will achieve accountability without public inputs into that framework, system, and set of institutions. To turn Bugsy Siegel's dictum on its head, it does not matter if you build something if no one comes. The *World Development Report 2004*, for instance, identifies two elements to accountability: "*answerability* (the right to receive relevant information and explanation for actions), and *enforceability* (the right to impose sanctions if the information or rationale is deemed inappropriate)." It then notes, "In principle, elections provide citizens with both answerability (the right to assess a candidate's record) and enforceability (vote the candidate in or out). In practice, democracies vary greatly on both dimensions, as do most attempts to exercise accountability" (World Bank 2003, 79).

The reasons for this great variation in the exercise of accountability are manifold. One source of variation is the heterogeneity of constituencies to whom client services are delivered and government policies and goals are communicated. Another source of variation is the heterogeneity of the services, policies, and goals themselves. Furthermore, the circumstances that necessitate these services, policies, and goals vary, and the contexts in which they must be implemented also vary across geography, time, social, political, and economic conditions. As the *World Development Report 2004* noted, there is no "one size fits all" approach to achieving accountability. At the same time, achieving accountability is not a matter of luck, faith, or the magic of situational circumstances. Rather, identifiable factors facilitate accountability.

Our focus in this volume has been on specifying the factors that engender public action. Governments and service providers may communicate information and explanations fully and transparently, but it is still incumbent on those whose interests are affected to see the relevance of such information and explanations. Likewise, clients and citizens may hold a "right" (real or figurative) to sanction governments and service providers, but that right is meaningless if not acted upon.

Achieving accountability requires more than possessing the proper normative aims or designing the most rational, economically efficient, technologically advanced means of keeping the hands of politicians out of the cookie jar. Accountability requires activation and mobilization of public demands, a constant monitoring and sanctioning function from the bottom up. It requires a public that is willing to take notice, stand up, be counted, and demand government responsiveness. Clients of service provision and citizens of representative governments must be aware and informed about whether their needs and interests are being served or thwarted. They then need the requisite resources and schemas to develop the sense of ownership, agency, and collective efficacy needed to rise to action when the work of agencies and governments fails to address their needs and interests responsively and effectively. How, then, is this regularized public input to be achieved?

As a practical matter, however, the presence of public demands for good governance is typically assumed rather than explicitly examined. The activation and mobilization of public demands, more often than not, is put in a proverbial "black box" as an intangible (albeit key) element of accountability that is inaccessible to systematic analysis and explanation. The *World Development Report 2004,* for instance, contains a clear specification of a three-way relationship between clients, providers, and policy makers and a resulting "long route" and "short route" to accountability (see figure 28.2). The report correctly identifies a link between citizens and politicians (with a goal of "voice") and a link between clients and service providers (with a goal of "client power"), but the underlying levers of public opinion—the mechanisms that move people from inertia to mobilized opinion—are left unexamined.

Our goal in this volume has been to open up this black box of public opinion (see figure 1.1). Inside this black box we have found three key kinds of ingredients for accountability through activated and mobilized public opinion.

At the individual level, building capacity requires winning both the short-term battle for public attention that Lupia and Taber note in their chapters and

Figure 28.2. Long and Short Routes to Accountability

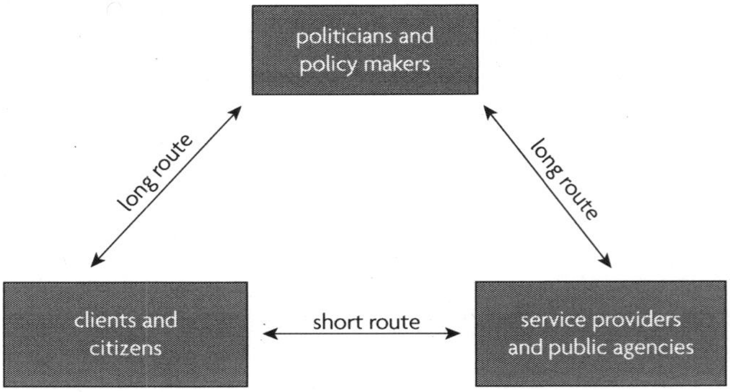

Source: World Bank (2003, 65).

securing a longer-term victory for public action that is properly motivated from a sustained and sustainable sense of ownership. This entails a transformation from being passive recipients of service provision and policy implementation to being active voices for accountability. As the chapters by Ganz, Lee, Tsai, Levine, and Finkel powerfully illustrate, this transformation is achieved not through the transmission of information alone, but rather though the discovery of shared values, the development of civic norms, and the deployment of mobilizing frames and narratives—the cement of society—that link access to information to attitude and behavior change.

At the institutional level, building capacity requires tethering inter- and intraorganizational ties within civil society and interorganizational ties between civil society organizations (CSOs) and government service–providing agencies. As the chapters by Peruzzotti, Jamal, Fung, He, and Humphreys and his colleagues (among others) demonstrate, this entails constructing public spheres—physical and virtual spaces where information and interpretive frameworks are shared, social norms and mobilizing identities are sustained, repertoires and knowledge products of collective action are exchanged, and participatory and deliberative mechanisms are implemented.

A third, mediating level is that of communicative networks—the currency through which publics are kept well versed on what government agencies are (or are not) doing (top-down information flows) and through which they can inform agencies about gaps in service provision and more generally relay their sanctions and demands on state actors (bottom-up information flows). This bridging level—described in various aspects by Taber, Wantchekon and Vermeersch, Zommer, Myers, Arnold, Keith, Finkel, and others—entails the deployment of activating message frames and mobilizing narratives, as well as the cultivation of civic education and the socialization of watchfulness and responsiveness at the public, mass media, CSO, and government levels. It also entails vigilance against the exploitation or expropriation of these two-way information flows, by either manufacturing consent and manipulating opinion (top-down) or selectively extracting clientelistic benefits from government (bottom-up).

These ingredients for accountability through public opinion coalesce into a stairway to mobilization. Mobilization here is explicitly conceived of as a process of moving individuals into collectivities and transforming indifference into motivation and membership. As figure 28.3 shows, four steps in this process move uninvolved individuals in the general public into engaged groups in a mobilized public.

This "Stairway to Mobilization" represents the mobilization process from the perspective of civil society. In addition to the obstacles that CSOs must overcome to mobilize public opinion, we find institutional constraints that will have to be battled. These constraints include, among many others, a weak organizational environment, legal restrictions for engagement, and a repressive political culture that curbs participation through fear.

The "Stairway to Mobilization" begins with the general public (see figure 28.4). Among this group you will always find people who are sympathetic to your specific cause, but you will also always find people who really do not care. As one of us noted in an earlier chapter, moments when public opinion is crystallized and mobilized are extraordinary, and it is unlikely in most cases that the general public can be won over to support you. To move the sympathetic members of the general public one step ahead to the voting public, CSOs need to design information campaigns. Information campaigns put issues on the media and public agenda and inform about the goals, motivation, and strategies of your project or organization. With information

Figure 28.3. The Stairway to Mobilization Process

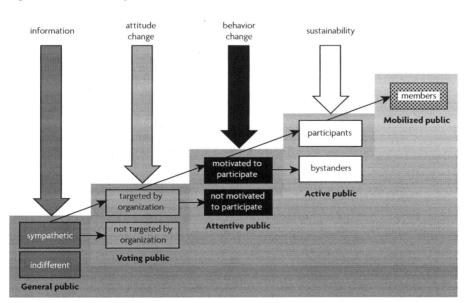

Source: Arnold and Garcia 2009.

campaigns, CSOs can put the problem on the agenda by providing information (through personal communication or the mass media).

It will probably be impossible to reach every sympathetic member of the general public with your information campaign. Some will not hear from you; we call this group "not targeted." The people who were reached by the information campaign now know about your goals, but this does not mean that they agree with your evaluations and suggestions. The next step in the communication will be a campaign that is aimed at attitude change—changing people's attitudes so that they believe that you are right. Through this step you move the members of the voting public into the attentive public because people who care (are sympathetic) and believe that you are doing the right thing will be more likely to be motivated to participate. Attitude change campaigns aim at changing values, beliefs, and worldviews. They explain the "why" through pointing people's attention to specific problems and moral evaluations. Framing and persuasion are among the communication techniques that should be used here.

A communication campaign will probably not change the mind of every person that you target. Where it works, however, you will now have the chance to move people from the attentive public to the active public. Many people are motivated to do something but do nothing in the end, for a variety of reasons.

Figure 28.4. Types of Public

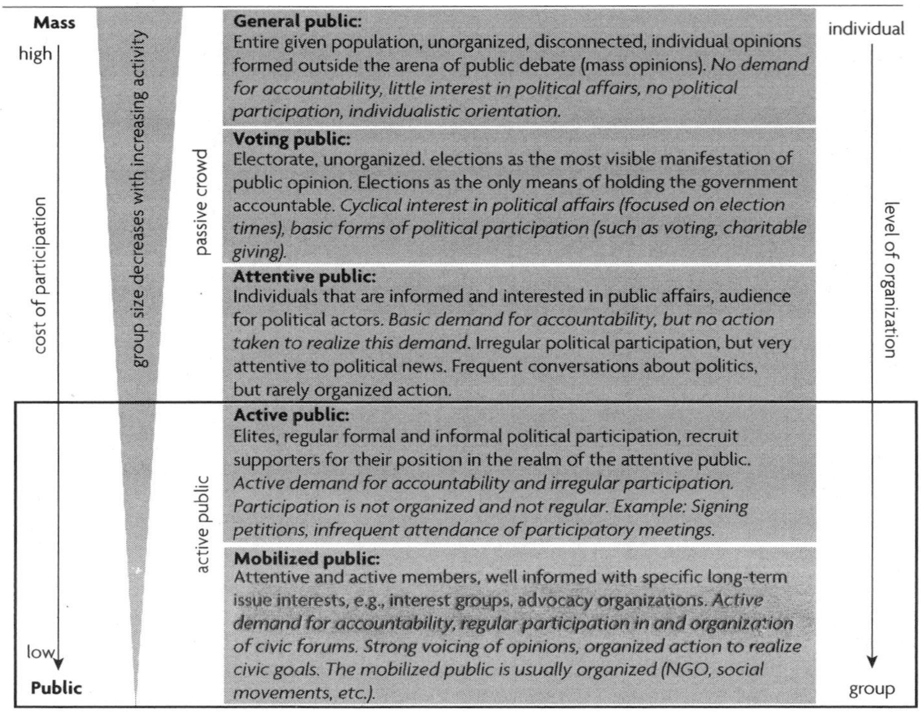

Source: Arnold (2007, 21).

A communication campaign that aims at behavior change will help you to convince the motivated members of the attentive public to actually participate in your cause. It is very difficult to achieve behavior change, to engage hearts, heads, and hands. To do so, you must translate values into action, you must explain the "why" as well as the "how" by embedding your message in a comprehensive story. Public narrative is a communication technique that makes this possible.

The ideal public is the mobilized public, whose members regularly participate and stand up for their cause in an organized manner. Those people that you moved to action will not always stick to it; some may become bystanders. The participants, however, can be won for long-term engagement. For this to happen, a communication campaign must change the incentive structure for public officials and change norms by cultivating new behaviors. This is only possible through long-term and multichannel communication. Membership in organizations can be strengthened through incentives, rituals, social relations, and leadership experience.

With regard to the public sphere, at least five groups in the population need to be considered separately when thinking about accountability. For us, it is important to move people from being passive to active engagement. We need people to move through the stages of the general public, the voting public, and the attentive public, to becoming members of the active and finally of the mobilized public. In these last two groups, we find active and engaged citizens who are involved in both formal and informal political participation (see figure 28.5).

Figure 28.5. Climbing the Stairway to Mobilization

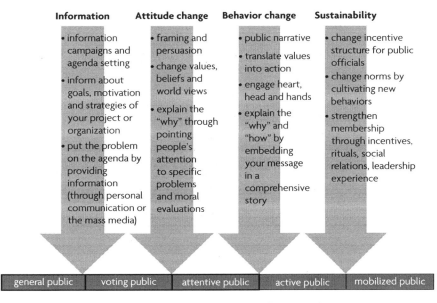

public opinion is crucial to mobilizing people

Source: Arnold and Garcia (2009).

The route from general to mobilized public is difficult to navigate. The public needs to be contacted and informed about an issue; the people need to be motivated to believe in the cause and then to act on it. The most difficult task is to keep citizens motivated, active, and part of a cascading process that ultimately forms a mobilized public.

The path to building a mobilized public involves a series of strategic approaches and techniques in four key areas of communication influence: information, attitude change, behavior change, and sustainability. Bringing about change in values, beliefs, norms, and incentives requires communication processes aimed at information sharing, engagement, discussion, and deliberation. Without these efforts in communication influence, accountability and reform initiatives are not likely to succeed or be sustainable.

Notes

1. From a Feb. 1, 2010 appearance at the University of California, Berkeley. http://conversations.berkeley.edu/content/wole-soyinka.
2. From the unpublished manuscripts of Jeremy Bentham, the Library of University College London.

References

Arnold, Anne-Katrin. 2007. "Tönnies' Concept of Public Opinion and Its Utility for the Academic Field." *Javnost—The Public* 14 (2): 7–30.

Arnold, Anne-Katrin, and Helen R. Garcia. 2009. "Generating Genuine Demand for Accountability: Public Opinion, Persuasion, and the Public Sphere." Learning Module presented on behalf of the World Bank in Johannesburg, South Africa, May 28–June 10.

Bentham, Jeremy. 1990. *Securities against Misrule and Other Constitutional Writings for Tripoli and Greece.* Ed. P. Schofield. New York: Oxford University Press.

Carter Center. 2008. "Atlanta Declaration and Plan of Action for the Advancement of the Right of Access to Information." http://www.cartercenter.org/resources/pdfs/peace/americas/ati_atlanta_declaration_en.pdf.

Hage, Jorge Sobrinho. 2008. "The Role and Work of the Comptroller General of Brazil." Presentation at the workshop "Using Communication Approaches and Techniques to Support Anti-Corruption Efforts: A Learning Event for Anti-Corruption Agencies," Vienna, November 17–19.

Hamilton, Alexander, James Madison, and John Jay. 1961. *The Federalist Papers.* Ed. Jacob E. Cooke. Middletown, CT: Wesleyan University Press.

Key, V. O. 1961. *Public Opinion and American Democracy.* New York: Alfred Knopf.

Norris, Pippa. 2010. *Public Sentinel: News Media and Governance Reform.* Washington, DC: World Bank.

Schmitter, Philippe, and Terry Karl. 1991. "What Democracy Is . . . and Is Not." *Journal of Democracy* 2 (3): 75–88.

World Bank. 2003. *World Development Report 2004: Making Services Work for Poor People.* Washington, DC: World Bank.

Appendix A

> Power concedes nothing without a demand.
> It never did and it never will.
>
> —Frederick Douglass[1]
> Nineteenth-century abolitionist

Generating Genuine Demand with Social Accountability Mechanisms
November 1–2, 2007

Summary Report

The World Bank's Communication for Governance and Accountability Program (CommGAP) held a workshop titled "Generating Genuine Demand with Social Accountability Mechanisms" in Paris, in November 2007. Workshop participants included practitioners from around the world who have used these tools in their own as well as other countries; leading scholars and researchers in the fields of communication, political science, social development, social marketing, media development, and governance; and representatives from developing country governments and donor organizations.[2]

The workshop explored the following broad questions:

- How can we use social accountability (SA) mechanisms more effectively and selectively to ensure greater impact and generate genuine demand?
- What is needed (at both the policy and practice levels) to help ensure that SA tools create the behavior change they intend (change the behavior of public authorities or agencies in some positive way)?

- What can the fields of communication and the allied social sciences (including research into social movements and other forms of collective action) teach us?

The workshop was organized around the following five process stages of SA mechanisms:

PROCESS STAGES		
	1. Analyzing the public sphere/ political context	Features of political context that affect the feasibility and efficiency of SA mechanisms, such as the degree of media freedom and freedom of speech, information, and assembly.
	2. Gaining official support in using SA tools	Approaches and techniques that have proven successful in gaining permission of public officials to allow the SA mechanism to be introduced.
	3. Building citizen competence (informed citizenry)	How to meet citizens' information needs (including those who are marginalized, remote, and illiterate) so that SA tools can work effectively.
	4. Mobilizing public will and inspiring citizen activism (engaged citizenry)	Approaches and techniques for overcoming obstacles to engagement, such as cynicism, despair, and lack of perceived self-efficacy.
	5. Achieving behavior change in public officials through mobilized public opinion	Approaches and techniques used to mobilize public opinion to ensure the preceding stages result in behavior change of public officials and thereby lead to more accountable government.

During the workshop, competing and converging conceptions of SA were discussed, ranging from instances when nongovernmental actors hold governments accountable when internal systems of accountability fail in specific areas of service delivery and with specific SA tools, to the idea that governments should be compelled to be responsive to the public's needs and preferences and that the potency of civic engagement is often neutered through technocratic initiatives. Within this wide definitional spectrum, participants were tasked to present evidence of good practice and applied research, and to deliberate on key topics that contribute to the success or failure of SA initiatives.

The workshop concluded with a final session that addressed the following questions: What next steps will move the work forward? What constitutes good practice? How can we use SA tools better to bridge supply- and demand-side accountability interventions?

This report is organized in five sections corresponding to the five process stages around which the workshop was organized. Each section of this report has the following components: a summary of panel presentations and plenary discussion, a digest of each presentation, and descriptions of approaches and techniques pertaining to each session.

Approaches and techniques were drawn from panelist papers, presentations, and discussions. For the purpose of this report, approaches and techniques are defined as follows:

Approach	A general way of addressing an issue or problem
Technique	A particular method of accomplishing a desired objective

The final section of this report includes recommendations and action steps based on main ideas distilled from each discussion topic.

Session I: Analyzing the Public Sphere/Political Context

This session explored the features of the political context that affect the feasibility and efficiency of SA mechanisms, such as the degree of media freedom and freedom of speech, information, and assembly. The session also provided a broad overview incorporating an inclusive conceptualization of the democratic public sphere, as well as the need to interrogate various dimensions and differential levels of political context as related to the democratic public sphere.

The first speaker urged participants to consider the public sphere as an organizing frame for the various issues related to SA. The speaker defined the democratic public sphere as the space between state and society, with the core components of legally guaranteed civil liberties; freedom of information; access to official information; a public culture of transparency; a free, plural, and independent media system; and a vibrant civil society. Given these features, the democratic public sphere is the rightful site for the deployment of SA mechanisms.

The second speaker asserted that democracy is best served when all citizens have the capability to question authority, seek accountability from the state, and participate in the process of government. Relating the Indian experience in adopting the Right to Information Act of 2005, the speaker argued that an access to information regime is the prerequisite for these conditions. It is also essential to consider the intrinsic role of media in these processes. Genuine demand requires an enabling environment where accountability relationships can flourish.

The third speaker discussed a Mexican nongovernmental organization's (NGO) experience in navigating legal processes to enhance accountability relationships. He argued that three conditions help bring about an SA regime: access to information, communities of practice around these issues, and the existence of a political opposition.

Following the three speakers, the following comments and ideas were elicited during the open forum:

- A place should exist for the willingness of government to give information, not just the ability of citizens to ask for information.
- Civil society's relationship with government can be as either negotiating partner or enemy.
- Is it really possible to navigate any political context? What about contexts in which there is no protection of human rights? Not all SA mechanisms are applicable everywhere, but ways can be found in which to call political authority into account.
- Donors should take a longer-term perspective.
- Search for solutions from within the local context.
- Giving feedback to service providers is essential, as illustrated by the experience of citizen report cards (CRCs) in India and Kenya. If a service provider is a monopoly, citizens do not have the opportunity for exit.
- In the technical work of development, the focus is on finding solutions that are universal, what one participant called "getting to Denmark!" Specialists are supposed to know how to bring about outcomes in any context. Often, however, context and expertise clash.
- We need to help local stakeholders learn how to ask the relevant SA questions—they already know their own context.
- Government is not monolithic. It is possible to engage with certain parts of government to leverage change in others.
- SA mechanisms provide criticism to public officials without political filters.
- The public sphere is a fragmented space, more mosaic than monolith.
- We have been thinking of the citizen as a rational individual, interacting with the public sphere. Yet we have a limited rationality; sometimes what triggers SA are public campaigns that use heuristics, such as celebrity endorsements.
- A need exists to clarify definitions. The public sphere and SA are contested concepts.

Summary of Presentations

Sina Odugbemi, head of the World Bank's Communication for Governance & Accountability Program, urged participants to take a look at the public sphere as an organizing frame for the various issues related to SA. Taking a public sphere perspective requires a keen understanding of political context. Are SA mechanisms effective means of generating genuine demand regardless of context or depending on context? If agreement can be reached on a hospitable set of conditions for the application of these mechanisms, is it sensible for reformers to engage inhospitable environments in similar fashion, or should they deploy a different set of analytical tools?

The democratic public sphere is that space between state and society and is the rightful site for the deployment of SA mechanisms. As such, its constitutive components must be safeguarded and carefully scrutinized. These components include civil liberties; freedom of information; access to official information; public culture of transparency; free, plural, and independent media systems; and a robust civil society and associational life.

George Cheriyan, Associate Director of the Consumer Unity and Trust Society in India, asserted that democracy works best when all citizens have the capability to ask questions from authority, seek accountability from the state, and participate in the processes of government. An access to information regime has the potential to enhance quality to deploy SA mechanisms. Envisaged as a "magic wand against corruption," the Right to Information (RTI) movement in India was a civil society–led initiative, which started in the mid-1990s. The enactment of the RTI in 2005 was a landmark development and provided citizens the right to information, in stark contrast to the official secrets act operating at that time.

It is also essential to take stock of the role of the media in enhancing an RTI regime. Evidence of success includes the finding that in the last two years, India's corruption perception index improved without any other major changes in related areas of law or governance.

Generating genuine demand requires creating an enabling environment. The RTI law is part of this enabling environment and serves as basis for the deployment of SA tools by triggering more transparent and accountable administrative actions and increasing the capacity of civil society organizations (CSOs) to demand better services from government actors. Giving citizens the capacity to access information is only the precondition; people should understand the information received and be able to ask relevant questions.

Relating his organization's experience in engaging in legal action toward enhancing SA, *Jorge Romero León,* Executive Director of Fundar, emphasized the idea that while political context matters, any political environment can be navigated successfully. Although contextual conditions facilitate this navigation, actors can engage in any context in terms of promoting and attaining SA. Nonetheless, context matters in several ways. For example, more political plurality makes available more space for participation. In this way, opposition matters and frames conditions where SA operates.

Part of Fundar's success story can be attributed to the rise of Mexico's congressional opposition in 1997. Contingent with the rise of the opposition was an enhancement of receptiveness toward SA on the part of legislators. It should be noted that political opposition is an important indicator of a plurality of political forces.

Legal resources can be brought to bear on SA initiatives. Fundar does its best to bring legal recourse and resources to bear toward this objective. For example, Fundar challenged the legality of a secret fund kept by the Mexican government.

According to León, three conditions help bring about a social accountable regime. Access to information is the first and most important enabling condition. Citizens and civil society need a law that provides and protects access. Second, communities of practice should be cultivated. The trend toward specialization among organizations requires that good practices be shared. Third, a political opposition should exist, as well as good auditing institutions within government.

From a public sphere perspective, opening up spaces for SA allows for the creation of publics through civil society action. In addition, within this space, the art of political navigation must be shared among organizations.

Relating Indian and Kenyan experiences in implementing CRCs,[3] *Gopakumar Thampi* opined that the semantic of the phrase "citizen report card" itself is important to consider, in that it connotes in simple yet powerful language that the target of the report is subject to evaluation and criticism. This evaluative dimension has implications in terms of gaining support from government officials, as well as mobilizing public opinion. Realizing that you need to break through the barrier of the semantic, on one hand, and harness its power, on the other, is an important insight.

Fine-tuning the technical aspects of the tool should be preceded by an open, transparent, and inclusive awareness- and consensus-building phase. The overarching objective of this awareness-building phase invites stakeholders to ask the question: Is this tool applicable in a particular context? The "Critical 8" framework can help in making this judgment.[4] Stakeholders are asked to rate the local context based on the "Critical 8" and explain how they determined scores. Based on "Critical 8" analyses, for example, the tool was found to be inapplicable in Brunei and Rwanda. Also, a demand assessment is required to find out whether the tool can be effectively applied to a context.

Considering the role of the media is also essential. How will journalists spin/report results? Whether the CRC results show a good and/or bad evaluation, journalists are more likely to focus on the negative. To enhance the integrity of the reporting of the results, extensive media briefings on how to use and interpret findings are required.

The CRC deromanticizes civil society. The perennial search for reform champions is challenged by the realization that civil society is a contested context populated by players with what are often competing agendas.

Approaches and Techniques

Following is a list of approaches and techniques for analyzing the public sphere/political context.

APPROACHES

Assess the macrolevel context through a public sphere analysis	This approach provides a systematic framework for delineating the features of the public sphere, including its constitutive components: civil liberties; freedom of information; access to official information; public culture of transparency; free, plural, and independent media systems; civil society; and associational life.
Assess the legal/regulatory environment	The passage of a national access-to-information law may not be a necessary or sufficient condition for SA to flourish, but it goes a long way in assisting SA advocates in their work.
Build a coalition supporting an access-to-information regime	Access to information undergirds the ability to adopt and deploy SA mechanisms. As a prerequisite for the work of SA, a broad coalition, driven by civil society, should fight for it in places where it does not exist. This should also serve as the basis for a permanent community of practice gravitating around these issues.
Build legal capacity on access-to-information issues	Civil society should be the focus of these capacity-building initiatives, because they serve as permanent checks against corrupt authority.

TECHNIQUES

Deploy the "Critical 8"	The awareness-building phase for SA tools asks the question: Is this tool applicable in a particular context? Making this judgment can be carried out by the "Critical 8" framework. Stakeholders are asked to rate the "Critical 8" and explain how they made score determinations.
Challenge governments in international courts	The system of international courts—and perhaps more important, international norms undergirding international law—can be powerful allies of SA advocates who experience difficulty operating in the domestic context.

Feedback from Participants' Response Cards

Q: What lessons have you learned about how to overcome structural challenges/obstacles in the political context when introducing social accountability mechanisms?

Need to locate SA tools within local sensitivities and sensibilities; need to locate political incentives to transcend the technical nature of SA tools. Capacity building to create political negotiation for a win-win solution.

Awareness building is essential before embarking on any accountability exercise (report cards, etc.); need to bring the government in; need to identify political incentives to build support of elites.

RTI (example of India and Mexico) is an SA mechanism, but needs to be accompanied by political context in which information is not only accessible but can be appropriated into a broad context and to know public opinion and public demand. This requires the complementary right to freedom of opinion and expression and a plural media environment. The citizen report card may not be very distinguishable from a technocratic answer survey unless it is linked to social mobilization around a particular concern or issue. Would the CRC be more effective in the context of a specific service or campaign rather than covering a broad set of services?

Access to information is key to generating genuine demand with SA mechanisms.

Evaluation of the political context in order to implement social accountability; donors need to think long-term; context does matter.

RTI was successful because of the rights-based approach. Better than access to information—RTI gives more legal mechanisms than access to information.

Conditions/features of the political context should be taken into consideration in adopting the social accountability mechanisms that are used in the context/country; the CRC as a diagnostic tool—very good process; political contexts are varied—no blueprint approach to approaching social accountability.

Need to fully understand the complexity of local political context; need for variable approaches, and more importantly defining success in a way that's appropriate to the context. One theme that jumps out is personal/citizen motivation; sometimes anger over injustice isn't the same as motivation to engage productively in accountability. What are multiple sources of motivation (to show up, speak out, etc.) and multiple ways of engaging them?

Government officials may have incentives to support public accountability; they want information about other agencies; they want to know what the public really thinks about their performance.

SA mechanisms would help to overcome contexts such as monopolies or poor government performance, making information public and creating competition among providers. However, SA mechanisms are not applicable as such in every context. They should be adapted to the context and local challenges.

The importance of right to information legislation in reducing corruption—especially in the Indian context.

Understanding the political incentives; building upon indigenous knowledge, rather than "blue prints;" and building partnerships with legislatures, which have the primary function of crafting reform legislation.

Information is critically important not just as a resource for social accountability, and not just as a moral precept, but also as a means and mechanism for changing the expectations of government actors themselves.

Media play very important roles in the institutionalization of SA tools. By correctly presenting the practice and outcomes of SA exercises, they can exert influence on the political context. Political navigation for civil society organizations becomes crucial, especially for democratizing countries. One should be aware of different public interests. Plus, applying one SA tool successfully in one case doesn't mean that it will be successful in other cases with different public interests.

The importance of being patient and thinking about long-term changes; the need to continue working on access to information and right to information in Argentina to contribute to SA mechanisms because this is a key instrument for strengthening democracy all over the world; the political context is really important and the impact is not a right idea to think about in all the times and places; the need to articulate NGOs' and governments' interests, demands, and goals.

The contexts of different tools can vary. Generalizing about all tools should be avoided; the question remains whether a tool should be used even if the context seems hostile; pre-intervention consensus building can help create ideas to overcome obstacles.

There is a need to go beyond the "conventional" political context. One needs to locate social accountability in the "real" political context of the people in which the *cultural* matrix of the stakeholders is fully opened up and accessed. This helps us to understand the concept of social accountability itself as the people have it *naturally*.

Political context is very important and not a universal blueprint that can or should be applied; media are very important in ensuring SA, but maybe rather than looking for objectivity and impartiality (impossible to achieve in reality) we should ask for accuracy and diversity.

What exactly is the impact of SA mechanisms? What are the observable indicators of a developing "public sphere?" I suggest that the WB devote some effort to developing such a database. To be more concrete, indicators of citizen participation (how many people voted in local elections) and citizen awareness would make it possible to evaluate the effectiveness of SA mechanisms.

Public sphere as an arena, with issue and games—a fragmented space, a mosaic; with irrational or semi-rational actor—what triggers demand for accountability can be unexpected, e.g., a film, an actor, and help to overcome structural obstacles.

Not driven by rights but by value of market; FOI [Freedom of Information] laws useless *UNLESS* there are mechanisms to deliver; report cards, etc., not only mechanisms for accountability, etc. Public opinion also is important.

Need to demystify RTI resurfaced in the discussion and I appreciate it. Question lingers: How do we show the political incentives to state actors of RTI? I wrote this because the Philippines has yet to have an RTI law.

Need for enabling legislation and policy; strong partnership between government and state stakeholders; need for champions; culture of openness and transparency.

Is it a matter of good judgment to provide tools/mechanisms of social accountability to people whose lives may be placed in danger by use of these tools/mechanisms?

Incentives matter. One should find out how to *mobilize* these *incentives* in order to bring pressure to bear; any political context can be navigated successfully, focusing on the broad diversity of public officials/legislators, etc., and making use of legal/human resources available; it is important to approach congress/local legislatures due to their relevance for creating checks and balances.

Media and media sector were mentioned and discussed several times as a couple of key areas of change. One way of strengthening media's capability to meet this responsibility would be to contribute to strengthening the media as a sector in its own right; and also to support professional journalism training on the job in areas like health, water, education, land mines.

Session II: Gaining Official Support in Using Social Accountability Tools

The second session discussed approaches in securing official support in SA and presented specific country experiences in implementing SA tools. These experiences illustrate effective approaches and innovations in mobilizing citizen engagement to gain public support.

The session featured a diagnostic framework that enables the user to analyze the spectrum of state support for SA mechanisms (by identifying various modes and sources of state support). This was followed by a presentation of country experiences from Armenia, the Philippines, and Uganda in implementing SA tools. Although the country examples represent different social and political contexts, dialogue with government, social partnerships, mobilization of civil society, and strategic use of the media were common interventions that contributed significantly to the effectiveness of SA mechanisms.

The first speaker, *Harry Blair* from Yale University (Associate Department Chair, Senior Research Scholar and Lecturer in Political Science), presented a framework that maps out the elements that underpin support for SA, particularly the level of state posture, the mode of state response to citizen demand, and the type of SA mechanism that is likely to be adopted. Blair argues that the type of state support spans a spectrum ranging from championship and accommodation to opposition and grudging assent, and each level of support corresponds to a menu of choices for SA mechanisms.

The second speaker, *Varuzhan Hoktanyan* from Transparency International Armenia, highlighted the importance of the political and social dimensions in ensuring effective SA, particularly in the real-world context of Armenia. The indifference of public officials and the growing apathy of civil society were cited as important obstacles to generating genuine demand for change.

The third speaker, *Kenneth Mugambe* from the government of Uganda (Commissioner, Budget Policy and Evaluation Department), presented the government's successful experience in undertaking public expenditure tracking surveys. Mugambe highlighted the positive results in improving transparency and accountability in resource transfers for public services and the institutionalization of public expenditure tracking surveys as a mainstreamed activity in Uganda's budget process.

The fourth speaker, *Redempto Santander Parafina* from the Philippines (Director, Government Watch [G-Watch] of the Ateneo de Manila University School of Government), shared important lessons from their successful ongoing partnership with the government in implementing SA mechanisms to improve governance in the education sector. With the help of committed CSOs and volunteer groups, G-Watch achieved significant results in increasing the overall effectiveness of public service delivery through system reforms aimed at enhancing transparency and accountability.

In the plenary session, the following comments and suggestions were presented on gaining official support in implementing SA tools:

- Keep goals in mind in the process of getting government buy-in. Pursue a two-stage process: first, at the initial stage, when less threatening issues can be raised; second, at the later stage, such as during implementation, when messages can be framed around project accomplishments and gaps that need to be addressed.
- Emphasize that SA tools are complementing and not substituting for government efforts.
- Understand context to effectively persuade government at different levels, including champions and nonchampions.
- Tailor approaches according to specific circumstances, such as where there is no political will, or where political situations are fragile. In such cases, civil society needs to navigate the political landscape to determine areas where they can have most impact. Culture matters. Lack of due consideration to sociocultural factors can weaken citizen demand.
- Discuss SA results with government before undertaking public dissemination. Ensure balanced reporting of both positive and negative findings. This establishes credibility and promotes the value of transparency.
- Timing is important in implementing SA. Typically, governments are more receptive and inclined to support before an election period.
- Framing is important: both overarching broader frames such as service to public interest, and specific, narrow frames involving personal and professional interests.
- Sustainability is the most important measure of what works. Clarity in the larger picture is critical in determining whether small, incremental changes fit in the overall reform process. The preconditions are citizen awareness and knowledge to make action possible. NGOs and donors should consider their roles to make sure that short-term accomplishments add up and are aligned with the larger, broader goals.

Summary of Presentations

Harry Blair of Yale University discussed the spectrum of state posture and support to citizen demand for SA, which provides a means to identify choices of appropriate mechanisms. Blair presented illustrations of the spectrum along a continuum of state response ranging from accommodation to opposition and state support ranging from active to repressive. In cases in which the state takes an active posture, Blair identified four modes of state support—championship, strong backing, encouragement, and statutory endorsement. At the other end of the spectrum at which the state assumes a negative posture, the six levels of support are acceptance, consent, acquiescence, disinterest, forbearance, and grudging assent.

Blair also presented a matrix that mapped out examples of SA initiatives according to the level and mode of state support as well as corresponding sources of authority and required funding. It provides a useful framework for examining the requirements for success and exploring approaches for strengthening state support for SA mechanisms.

Based on an analysis of the patterns along the spectrum of state responses, Blair presented the following observations: (1) the most important mechanisms are not those in which state support is most active, with elections, civil society, and media considered the most fundamental; (2) a majority of mechanisms exist independent of state financing; (3) support for SA mechanisms does not necessarily require state funding to be successful; (4) all authorities for SA mechanisms need continued support from other actors; (5) national and local levels require different SA mechanisms.

Varuzhan Hoktanyan, Vice Chair of Transparency International Armenia, noted the importance of building social partnerships as an optimal strategy for gaining official support and emphasized that in the case of Armenia social and political factors are key determinants of the attitudes of public officials.

Unlike other country examples that have democratic governments or newly democratizing environments, the Armenian political context and SA initiatives operate within a difficult environment. Hoktanyan lamented the negative impact of the country's reversal to an authoritarian regime—as reported by Freedom House and other international organizations—with rising corruption and widespread abuse of political power. The country does have legislation to enhance the application of SA tools, for example, the Law on Self-Governance, which requires the Council of Elders to consult with citizens in budget preparation.

However, Hoktanyan referred to this legislation as "empty formality." The mandates are not used in practice because of the complete indifference of public officials and the apathy of citizens. Donor support is the single most important motivating factor for implementing SA tools. Lack of ownership and political will and an apathetic civil society continue to be problems that jeopardize the sustainability of any reform initiative.

Hoktanyan concluded his presentation with the following suggestions: (1) encourage civil society to be more active by building the capacity of civil society to demand behavior change from public authorities, (2) strengthen civic competence, and (3) use advocacy strategies to promote public pressure from CSOs and international organizations.

Kenneth Mugambe from the government of Uganda (Commissioner, Budget Policy and Evaluation Department), presented Uganda's experience in using SA mechanisms, particularly the use of public expenditure tracking surveys (PETSs) in the education sector. The discrepancy between increased allocations to public education and the poor outcomes in primary school enrollment rates heightened awareness of the need for greater transparency and accountability in budget disbursements. This prompted a closer examination of resource flows from the central government down to the district levels.

The first survey done in 1990–91 found that only 13 percent of per-student, nonwage funds from the central government reached schools, and that public primary education was mostly funded by parents by up to 73 percent of total school spending in 1991. Information on disbursements of capitation grants to schools and recordkeeping were poor at the district level compared with the central level. Local government officials had the informational advantage on the amount of funds received as transfers and benefited in the process by reducing the amount of funds actually used for schools. A follow-up survey in 1995 showed that, on average, less than 30 percent of allocated capitation grants reached schools, and it took about four months for funding to get to the beneficiaries. Weaknesses in monitoring and evaluation and lack of systematic inspections were among the key challenges in the disbursement of funds.

To ensure that resources are allocated to social sectors, the government created a Poverty Action Fund as a ring-fencing mechanism, which also allowed clear tracking of resource flows. Measures to enhance transparency included a government requirement to publish resource transfers at the district level using newspapers and radio. Schools were also required to maintain public notice boards to post information on funds received. Access to budget information triggered debate between civic leaders and politicians and allowed primary schools to demand entitlement from district officials. The 1997 Local Government Act contained provisions for accountability and information dissemination. The government also required districts to deposit all grants to schools in their own accounts and delegated authority for procurement from the center to the schools. By 1999 schools had received more than 90 percent of their capitation grants.

PETS is an institutionalized mechanism in Uganda. The government, as the willing partner, works closely with CSOs and donors. Uganda's long experience shows that the biggest challenge is the weakness of civil society to demand accountability from government.

Redempto Santander Parafina, Director of Government Watch (G-Watch), presented the Philippines' seven-year experience in implementing SA and focused on how partnership for SA can be ensured and sustained. Established in 2000 by an academic institution, the Ateneo de Manila University School of Government, as an anticorruption program, G-Watch is based on a strong partnership between the government and civil society. The program focuses on preventing corruption through active dialogue between the state and the citizens and collaborative efforts in pursuing effective strategies to support reforms to improve governance. Simple and easy-to-use mechanisms were developed and used to monitor delivery of public goods and services, such as textbooks and medicine, as well as in public works and construction of school buildings. The support of government champions who listen and appreciate the benefits of the interventions resulted in positive and proactive response from government.

In the Textbook Program, G-Watch has an active partnership with the Department of Education and a consortium of civil society organizations. Guideposts in establishing partnership include (1) working with a trusted agency official who will listen and act on report recommendations, (2) focusing on system reform, rather than witch hunting or shaming to build rapport and trust, (3) using simple and easy-to-use tools, and (4) comparing the plan with the accomplishment.

Reforms were undertaken in the international competitive bidding process and in the synchronized delivery system. G-Watch was involved in key stages of the process—in the review of bidding documents, the actual bidding, the awarding of contract bid, and in the inspection, delivery, and distribution of the textbooks. Civil society groups, including volunteers among young scouts and church parishioners, played a key role in on-the-ground monitoring of processes and tracking results. The volunteer groups involved increased from eight in the first round to 30 in the fourth round of the program.

Since the inception of the Textbook Program in 2003, about 65 million textbooks have been tracked. The champion within the Department of Education (Undersecretary Luz) ensured that civil society was mobilized effectively in the bidding process and on-the-spot, systematic monitoring of textbook deliveries. The Textbook Count resulted in a 40 percent price reduction and shortened the procurement cycle by half, from 24 months to 12 months. In the next round of Textbook Count, an innovation was introduced that involved the monitoring of textbooks from the district to elementary schools. This innovation was done with the support of a private soft drink company (Coca-Cola), which provided vehicles to transport the goods to remote villages. This addressed the problem of nondelivery of 21 percent of textbooks in elementary schools, particularly in poor districts.

Strong support from middle managers was key to the success of G-Watch. Despite frequent shifts in leadership in the Department of Education—with four successive changes in Department Secretaries within a brief two-year period from 2004 to 2006—the program benefited from the unwavering commitment of midlevel managers. This was crucial in sustaining support for the program from within amid unstable transitions in the institution. Parafina cited other important lessons: (1) adopting a nonconfrontational approach, (2) pursuing innovations and diversified interventions, and (3) mitigating risks of co-optation through constructive engagement and positive response from government.

Approaches and Techniques

Following is a list of approaches and techniques for gaining state support for SA mechanisms.

APPROACHES	
Assessing and improving official support using the spectrum of state posture and state support	This approach provides a systematic framework for examining sources of support and key success factors that each type of SA requires. It is based on the view that levels of state support can vary across a spectrum ranging from intensely active to extremely reluctant support. For development practitioners and CSOs, the approach provides a way of determining the most appropriate SA mechanism and its likelihood for success, as determined by such indicators as the state's mode of support, the source of authority or political mandate required, the financial resources needed, and at what level of government, national or local, it will be operationalized. In cases in which the level of state posture is passive, remedies can be considered to improve the degree of support and move toward the active rung of the scale. For international donor agencies and program specialists, the spectrum provides a menu of choices for development assistance in SA. The rank-ordering technique used in this approach can be applied by developing a matrix and plotting the SA mechanisms according to the degree of state support received.
Mobilizing support from middle managers	As the critical link within the bureaucracy, middle managers can make or break any reform implementation. Many country examples illustrate the importance of marshalling their support to expedite action on the reforms needed. Middle managers committed to support SA become advocates of change within government. Their involvement in the early stages of the SA process helps build their ownership and accountability if they have been part of the overall reform process.
Formalizing partnerships with government agencies	Collaboration and partnering arrangements with government formalized through written agreements, such as Joint Statements or

Memoranda of Agreement, clearly define roles and responsibilities between partners and strengthen commitment in implementing mutually agreed-on objectives and tasks. A public agency that enters into a formal partnership agreement provides a firm expression of its willingness and ability to engage in a collaborative undertaking to support reform initiatives.

Problem-solving sessions among agencies and stakeholders

State-citizen synergies in SA initiatives are strengthened through an atmosphere of productive dialogue and mutual cooperation. Problem-solving sessions provide a positive mechanism of presenting and discussing results of SA. This process fosters a productive exchange of ideas and a shared understanding of the problems that can lead to collaborative action between the government and civil society. A confrontational approach can easily trigger a negative, defensive response from government, particularly when the SA findings presented are perceived as unfavorable or controversial. When this happens, the relationship becomes adversarial and threatens the likelihood of positive action on the part of government.

Identifying champions within government

Champions are catalysts and advocates of change. Successful experiences in SA are often led by reform champions at various levels and stages of the reform process. These actors believe in the benefits of the interventions, are willing to listen, take a proactive stance, and can push for public action.

TECHNIQUES

Analysis of state posture and state support

Mapping out SA mechanisms on a spectrum with designated points corresponding to level of state posture (active, passive, repressive) and level of state response (accommodation, indifference, opposition).

Using a rank-ordering technique, SA mechanisms can also be plotted on a matrix according to state posture and mode of state support, source of legitimizing authority, requirements for success, and state financing and level of operationalization.

This technique provides an instrument to guide the selection of appropriate mechanisms from a menu of choices, as well as a method for strategic positioning in terms of interventions or remedies needed to improve the level of state support, thereby moving up the scale or spectrum.

Establish early engagement

Take government on board at the beginning of the process and adopt a participatory approach. Engage all actors involved to build trust and ownership to create incentives for public officials to support the initiative as partners. Within government, one will find different factions. Work with various actors within government. Less threatening and nonpolitical issues politically can be addressed in the early stages of dialogue.

At the back end, think through how to present and frame accomplishments and gaps that need to be addressed. Make sure that you engage the government as co-owner; it creates incentives for public officials to work with you. If results can be presented in a balanced way, the government may be more receptive. Relationships occur at different levels and should be maintained over time.

Consider the context and focus on the positive

Effective persuasion requires careful consideration of the local, political context. This can help frame issues consistent with the broader development goals and enhance professional incentives to lend support as reform implementers. It is also important to craft clear and consistent messages. Start with what is working and what the gaps are.

Create facts on the ground

In countries where the environment is politically precarious, and where civil society can do the work, providing evidence on the ground boosts the power of information. Find credible people who are influential and respected in government. Use them are spokespersons.

Design simple
and easy-to-use
monitoring tools

Implementation of SA mechanisms depends on and benefits from volunteer efforts in various stages of the design and implementation process. Monitoring of results and performance is one critical area that determines the impact and sustainability of SA. Simple and effective monitoring tools that volunteers with varying skill levels and background can easily use promote inclusive and broader involvement of citizens in tracking gaps between promise and performance.

Feedback from Participants' Response Cards

Q: What approaches and techniques have you found most effective in securing buy-in or support of public officials in using social accountability mechanisms?

The question may be wrongly posed since, as Harry Blair's paper showed, there is a very wide range of SA mechanisms most of which don't require "official" support and some of which may be less effective if they are not seen to be independent, e.g., CRCs. More important is tacit acceptance by public officials; dialogue with public officials and politicians involved in the area of concern; and cooperation in access to information.

Civil society *does not* require the officials' permission to introduce SA mechanisms! These mechanisms arise out of the failure of governments to do their job. Buy-in will occur when government realizes that large numbers of citizens are dissatisfied with this failure. Buy-in is facilitated when contacts are made with officials who are more sympathetic to reforms.

Taking the government on board in the beginning and building confidence/mutual trust; develop a strategy for the dissemination of outcomes of various studies.

When should state buy-in be sought (e.g., citizen report cards) and when is it less important or even antithetical to the functioning of the mechanism (e.g., investigative journalism)? How exactly do we want to define "social accountability?" Many different definitions have emerged implicitly here, though not as yet explicitly.

Leveraging external audiences—either "influence-makers" in other nongovernmental spheres (emirs, politicians' spouses, religious leaders, celebrities) or media watchdogs or NGOs—someone to "look over one's shoulder." Getting early commitments from government actors (*public* if national leaders, no publicity needed if middle-level management).

Focus on changing behaviors of ordinary citizens.

The premise is problematic because sometimes it is not valuable to obtain state support. For instance, we need truly independent journalists.

Political culture matters and you cannot change an obstructive type through awareness creation; public interest lobbying, use credible, powerful people who are influencers of government officials; frame the quest for social accountability as being in the national interest.

Rational, emotional (affective), political loyalty, and other considerations that drive decision-making need to be understood and influenced to secure buy-in.

The citizen report card—but it must be understood that this takes years!

The approach to governments should never be a "permission" approach. You should inform governments of your intention because that helps them to be more receptive, but demanding accountability and implementing monitoring is a right of citizens and civil society organizations so it's not a question of gaining permission.

Highly dependent on nature of accountability mechanisms; some more political than others; see government as partner—show them the *political value* or *market value* of what is being done; rights approach leads to antagonistic relationship with government.

Credibility of CSO; concrete types of intervention and expected results.

Building a mutual partnership with government; credibility and professionalism; avoiding antagonism; complementarity. The support of public officials is gained when there is sustainability. The officials' support can create such sustainability.

NGOs should consider their role and become more professional, and donors more aggressive. Other civil society structures (for example, churches and mosques) should also be considered. Timing is very important; during transformation or revolutionary times, NGOs and other CSOs must actively work with the population.

Procure relationships for the long term; engage public officials with carrots and sticks; seek champions of transparency but also work to *develop* them, and learn to work with those who are not champions; promote co-ownership and co-sponsorship of specific initiatives.

Focus on issues that connect directly with livelihoods (G-Watch and PETS); demonstrate clear incentives; not clear from the presentation (explicitly) but recognized as critical; from the perspective of civil society organizations, the importance of getting research and evidence absolutely right, watertight, and rigorous before presenting it to government officials.

Systems perspective—ecological perspective; using indigenous resources—social, cultural, discursive; finding incentives for governments to cooperate in SA.

Except in the context of dictatorships, dialogue coupled with a collaborative attitude has a better chance of success compared to confrontation. It is useful to understand also that the state is not monolithic, and that there are multiple potential partners within government.

Creating a baseline to compare with results generated by the SA—in order to explicitly show the benefit of engagement; a collaborative approach, so that public officials don't feel threatened by SA mechanisms; institutionalize mechanisms so that they are less vulnerable to changes in leadership.

In order to avoid the mechanism from being appropriated by a single faction of the government or by a political party, the mechanism should be institutionalized. The institutionalization of the mechanism requires building acceptance by all in government/political society (particularly the opposition).

Involving appropriate department/part of government in mainstreaming social accountability into the development process (e.g., M&E [Monitoring and Evaluation] Department in Economic Planning Ministry).

All those in which civil society engages public official beforehand, dialogue being a crucial one.

For a non-practitioner, this strikes me as a "trick" question. Public officials in what type of regime? If the regime is democratic, I would guess that number of votes to be gained would be a key incentive. If non-democratic, perhaps outside donors rather than voters become the key drivers.

Session III: Building Citizen Competence (Informed Citizenry)

The third session focused on building an informed citizenry, and how communication and SA mechanisms can cultivate, enhance, and sustain citizen competence in less-than-ideal real-world political contexts. Building citizen competence implies that we expect citizens to know their rights and be both willing and able to take action so that governments can be held accountable.

The first presenter discussed the importance of speech-based communication and different modes of engagement, as well as lessons learned that are critical to building citizen competence. The second presenter discussed the importance of conceptualizing how SA mechanisms are deployed. Under one dominant conception of democracy, the public itself should define problems and work toward addressing them using SA mechanisms, which enhance information processes and information flows, and promote cross-sectoral partnerships. Moreover, a special focus should be placed on building the competence of young people in ways that take into account developmental processes.

The other speakers presented two real-world case studies that described ways in which an informed citizenry can be cultivated. In the case of the Democratic Republic of Congo, the importance of training journalists to be well informed and independent was stressed. Despite harsh environmental conditions in fragile states such as the Democratic Republic of Congo, radio plays a key role in reaching out to citizens. In Argentina, building capacity of student journalists as intermediaries was shown to be effective, specifically by training students to make access to information requests through school projects.

In the plenary discussion, SA mechanisms were discussed as means to respond to identified problems and to address government failure. However, the challenge is reframing and communicating an issue to convince the public that it deserves serious attention. The different types of journalism—civic, public, citizen, participatory—play an important role in building an informed citizenry, but many obstacles exist in terms of what journalists can report. Also, in some environments, information overload and conflicting messages can stir up fear in people and sometimes create information or transformation deficits. Hence, building an informed citizenry is better stated as building an empowered transformed citizenry.

Getting media attention on SA issues is also a challenge, especially where plurality and competition exist, because a tendency exists to sensationalize. Another concern is that many public officials act deliberately to influence the media agenda. However, the public sphere is about not only media, but also a concept of everyday talk on issues concerning the public that take place everywhere.

Although consultative programming structures and mechanisms are useful in engaging citizens in participatory debate, other strategic communication channels should be considered when trying to influence decision makers. The main focus should shift from educating citizens to building an informed citizenry, because the fundamental task in any political society is to create an effective citizenship where citizens can engage in public argument and listen and participate in public deliberation.

Summary of Presentations

William Keith of the University of Wisconsin–Milwaukee discussed the importance of face-to-face communication and referenced the U.S. Forum Movement, when citizens started talking in public spaces. Study circles, forums, and town halls are forms of getting people together with the goals of mutual learning, education—content and public speaking skills—and deliberation.

Although many types of forums model democratic/civic discourse, lessons are to be learned from the U.S. Forum Movement in particular. For example, the tension between antagonism and cooperation: Is public discourse supposed to be agonistic, or is there a cooperative dimension, and how should these be balanced out? Creating a sense of significance is important, but issues also come up concerning trust and neutrality—hence public forums should not be structurally biased. Good leadership is a crucial aspect in managing people and ideas to keep the process moving. To achieve long-term participation over various topics, other aspects such as entertainment are needed so that people stay continually engaged. One way to do this is to recast arguments into narrative forms that are deemed important and relevant. Finally, teaching public speaking matters and the classroom can be a real place of engagement.

Peter Levine, Director of the Center for Information and Research on Civic Learning and Engagement (CIRCLE), presented two conceptions with which to think about politics, governments, and democracy. Under the first concept, the state governs, makes authoritative decisions, and administers them, while the public has three roles: (1) they know or find out what the government is doing, (2) they discuss among themselves, and (3) they periodically make their own binding decisions or influence decisions that affect governance.

SA is seen as a way of enhancing these three roles by providing ways of making information flow much better (RTI act, disclosure of public budgets, and so on), and providing specific concrete forms of discussion (such as participatory budgeting and getting the public to vote on something). If not a binding decision, the SA process may somehow influence public opinion in terms of voting leaders in and out of office.

Under the second concept, the public, through deliberation and discussion, defines problems and works to address them by creating public goods, facilities, services, cultural products, and norms, among other possibilities. SA, under this conception of democracy, would be accountability to everyone else. Levine ascribes value to both paradigms, but the second concept is more feasible, because it is difficult to imagine consistent and broad public participation in stand-alone deliberative processes created by governments. Deliberation comes most naturally when it is part of everyday work in communities.

Finally, Levine discussed the importance of supporting young people early on to help them become better-informed citizens. Although effective ways of engaging the younger generation may be culturally specific, flexibility could be built in by considering, for example, mixed-aged groups and mentorship arrangements.

Mary Myers, development communication consultant from the United Kingdom, presented her experience in building an informed citizenry in the fragile state of the Democratic Republic of Congo by building a cadre of informed journalists.

The media sector in the Democratic Republic of Congo is disorganized, susceptible to corruption, and lacking in infrastructure. A lack of trust is found among citizens, state, and the media. Furthermore, journalists have no formal training, civil society is weak, citizens are unaware of their basic rights, complexity of the governance is difficult to teach, and tradition does not allow the questioning of authority. Hence, investigative reporting is almost nonexistent, and the watchdog function of the media is limited. Despite many obstacles, radio is still a key source of information for most of the population. Myers states that the most pressing problem in the media sector is economic viability: "you cannot have a press which is editorially independent without it being financially independent."

In the Democratic Republic of Congo, the international community has set up a radio station that is financially independent of interest groups and is therefore able to report in a balanced and unbiased fashion. Also, the Department for International Development's (DFID) training for media managers on business management is important in creating an independent voice. Finally, DFID and other donors have started to think and act strategically about media support and regulation and have linked these explicitly to governance issues. These initiatives should contribute to a better-informed citizenry.

Laura Zommer, Communications Director of the Center for the Implementation of Public Policies Promoting Equity and Growth, presented a case study involving students at the University of Buenos Aires monitoring their access to information rights as part of the Communication Sciences program. Argentina does not have a freedom of information law, but a decree permits citizens to request information from the executive branch. Twelve provincial laws also provide this right.

The objectives of the exercise were to train students/future journalists to formulate requests, understand the importance of access to information and other rights, as well as monitor results of each ministry's performance. At the end of each semester, civil servants, NGOs, and a few journalists are invited to share and discuss the results. Some of the most interesting requests and responses have been covered by the media, which has provided incentive for civil servants to handle requests. Out of the 816 information requests, about 53 percent received responses. In many cases, the students were asking for information already available on official websites, but not easily found.

Approaches and Techniques

Following is a list of approaches and techniques for building an informed citizenry.

APPROACHES	
Broaden journalists' knowledge of SA	Journalists often lack formal training but play a key role in building an informed citizenry. To achieve greater dissemination on SA issues and information on the roles and responsibilities of government, journalists must understand what those roles are and have a protective space to report on these issues and those concerning communities. Furthermore, this approach should provide journalists with an opportunity for innovation and creativity in reporting.
	Some of the techniques include providing journalists with training on governance structures and issues, as well as training on the business side of journalism.
Enhance coordination among development partners to think and act strategically about media support and regulation	As mentioned by Myers and others in the plenary discussion, an independent and plural media system contributes to better-informed citizenry and enforces action to hold governments accountable. However, even in a plural and competitive environment, issues exist such as a tendency to sensationalize and the difficulty of getting media attention on SA issues.
	Techniques to enhance coordination may include better sharing of research and good practice and collaboration with local media to create independent media stations.
Create an inclusive approach that includes young and marginalized groups in building citizen competence	An inclusive approach toward building citizen competence is needed that includes young people and marginalized groups. Young people are often neglected but are the future leaders and need the knowledge and skills to become informed and effective citizens.
	Techniques include establishment of partnerships with schools and universities to incorporate skills to become effective citizens.
Engage citizens in dialogue via different modes of structures and mechanisms	Many ways have been identified to engage citizens in public debate, such as consultative programming (call-ins, listener surveys, and the like). However, strategic communication

channels other than media should be considered in engaging citizens and building competence. Innovative, participatory mechanisms should be deployed using a two-way communication model with new and appropriate technologies, such as blogs and cellular technology (short message service [SMS]).

Techniques can include providing easy access to information and government officials. Content should be developed both in an educational and entertaining way, such as narrative communication formats, and in a language easily understood.

	TECHNIQUES
Promote and develop training for journalists	In addition to investigative reporting, training on governance structures and issues is essential, as well as training on the business side of journalism to create an independent voice.
Establish partnerships with academia to implement interdisciplinary curricula	Partnerships should be established with academia to develop interdisciplinary curricula that reflect the skill sets needed for young people to become effective citizens. Curricula could include public speaking and good leadership skills in the classroom, activities to exercise rights to information and freedoms, knowledge of government structures and understanding of institutions, and engagement of students in developing entertaining content on governance issues. Furthermore, internships and mentor programs could be organized for students to learn directly from their peers.
Engage with marginalized groups	Reach out to marginalized groups and provide training on basic communication skills and exercises on rights to information and freedoms, as well as inform marginalized groups about ways to participate in public debate.
Develop a platform to enhance coordination among development partners	A platform to discuss and share good practice and research on media support and regulation would be useful to better advocate and coordinate efforts toward independent

and plural media systems. Evidence-based research can help influence decision makers to advocate for an independent and plural media system.

Support independent media

The international community should continue to support and collaborate with local media to establish independent media stations. Editorial independence contributes to balanced reporting and a strengthened informed citizenry that is better equipped to enforce actions to hold governments accountable. In addition, an independent press reduces tendency to sensationalize news.

Utilize and raise awareness regarding existing information sources, as well as consultative structures and mechanisms

For building an informed citizenry and engage citizens in public debate, information sources and feedback mechanisms must be promoted and easily accessible. For example, in the case of Argentina, many students were requesting information that was already accessible on the government website, but not easily found. Also, existing consultative programming mechanisms should be promoted, and new information technology should be explored to engage citizens in public debate.

Feedback from Participants' Response Cards

Q: What approaches and techniques have you found most effective in creating an informed citizenry?

The focus should be on how "to form" citizens rather than "to inform" them.

Empowerment/social education workshops at village level and an education that relates to life going on outside the school/college.

Direct, "unmediated" communication between voters and elected officials!

Why may not be needed, waste a lot of time and money. If goal is to resolve a problem then it may be only a political exercise to change the opinion of key decision makers that is needed. Clearly media is important but need to expand the definition to include social media, etc.

Dialogue—Engagement—Managing differences in perspective. These "process" skills are needed so citizens and their government can reach durable agreements on what needs to be done to solve problems. Citizens need to reframe issues; the government won't.

Informed citizenry does not mean active citizenry (ready to be influenced on decision-making). Not always [does] too much information lead to informed citizenry. SA as "public work" will be more effective, than as a stand-alone activity. Direct communication can be very efficient.

Power and influence of the media; importance to enhance citizens' capacity by building their effective citizens' abilities; use of IT [information technology] to get citizens to participate in alternative mechanisms.

Extensive use of the media; plays, dramas where people are illiterate; public forums for discussion; getting people to participate in campaigns, events; exposing children to civic values, behaviors.

Strategic communication, social mobilization, and informed advocacy.

Plan a message/plan how to deliver it. Develop learning networks, not only for the sake of effectiveness, but for their own sake. Take time to develop relationships with other organizations; use carrots and sticks with media and develop capacities.

Need to encourage media plurality and think beyond formal communication channels and rediscover/reinvigorate traditional cultures of orality.

Training journalists and incentivizing them (financially, professionally, through peer mechanisms, and through regulation) to cover governance issues in an informed and interesting way.

Media and education need to work together. We need a model where they complement each other. Skills perspective on citizenship is very important, not just knowledge or attitudes.

Providing *young* people with opportunities for serious civic work.

Empowerment communication strategies; conscientization using Freire's culture circle approach; theatre; PRA/PRCA [Participatory Rural Appraisal/Participatory Rural Communication Appraisal] techniques.

Increasing/supporting young citizens to exercise and learn their civic rights, and therefore, become the next generation of transformative citizens.

Communicative actions that pay attention to the use of frames, narrative, metaphor—ideas and themes and hopes prevalent in every day talk. It is not discrete pieces of information—truth claims false/true—but interpreted bundles of information framed in a compelling narrative that motivates and mobilizes public will.

What was important in the Uganda PETS in education case was the display of information on the budget allocations which made it possible for the beneficiaries to monitor the actual delivery of this money.

I think you have to consider media support in SA, in particular:

- Promotion of *consultative programming structures and mechanisms,* e.g., Internet fora, blogs, news, ombudsmen, listeners call-in, SMS participation with live broadcasts, editorial councils, which includes civil society organizations, viewer surveys, etc.
- *Media literacy* to train NGOs and citizens on how to use media consultative structures
- *Parliamentary* broadcasts
- Build capacity for *investigative journalism and participatory journalism.*

Address both supply side and demand side. Supply side: improve structures and processes to build transparency, explore other venues to reach citizens. Demand side: mobilize civil society, educate messengers and champions, and penetrate informal social networks. Build relationships and trust and agenda even before problem exists.

Despite the cautionary points during discussion, there seems to have been a dominant idea that the media are guardians of democratic and social accountability. But who watches the watch people? Especially when the media have been shown to distort perceived citizen reality on some of the most pressing issues of the day.

Develop autonomous civic sources of information; right to information policies; regulated media pluralism—to limit media concentration/to foment alternative sorts of media.

We didn't really address needs of these constituencies, but instead assumed citizens are a homogenous mass. This produced a rich dialogue, but the missing part of it should be examined in some future setting.

Teaching basic rights, including right to information; create "Justice House" to teach and help citizens how to manage with their violated rights; rural and alternative radio; capacity journalists.

Promoting community communication capacity, including in-person fora, media.

Access to the government-held information.

The media have a key role but one which is not always positive, therefore building a plural media environment, high quality journalism and participatory media, and giving voice to citizens are important. Radio is particularly useful for remote, marginalized, and illiterate groups, and as an oral medium it enables and resonates with the citizen's desire not only to be informed but also to speak. Citizen's communication competence is informed by the media environment but can also be developed in its own right through debate, critical reflection on the media's role, etc.

Session IV: Mobilizing Public Will and Inspiring Citizen Activism

The fourth session discussed issues in promoting public engagement in SA mechanisms and approaches in overcoming obstacles to broad citizen participation.

The session featured a conceptual framework in examining issues that impact the public will and key design elements to inspire civic activism. It also included presentations on case examples of mobilizing citizens, such as the use of unmediated information campaigns in the United States, and the developing-country perspectives from India and Malawi provided insights on the challenges and approaches in getting people to demand and governments to respond.

The first speaker, *Taeku Lee* of the University of California, Berkeley (Professor and Chair of Political Science and Professor of Law), discussed important conceptual issues that underpin approaches to mobilizing public will and presented a framework for identifying what kind of public to be mobilized for a given mechanism and what kind of participatory input and what kind of public influence to be expected. Mapping out the possible types of publics based on these three key dimensions requires a good understanding of power and empowerment.

The second speaker, *Shanto Iyengar* of Stanford University (Harry and Norman Chandler Professor of Communication and Professor of Political Science), presented a brief narrative on why media campaigns fail and discussed the significant opportunities of using information technology and new platforms for unmediated information to engage broad sectors of civil society. The ongoing research on the U.S. experience in using compact disc (CD)–based campaigns provides an illuminating example of its potential in mobilizing citizens in nonelectoral settings.

The third speaker, *Samuel Paul* of Bangalore, India (Public Affairs Centre), focused on the key actors and actions essential in effectively mobilizing public will, namely, the citizens' acceptance of issues based on their felt needs, the government's positive response to address gaps in their performance through active dialogue and discussion with citizens, the support of champions and catalysts, the broad engagement of citizens to promote collective action, and the strategic and extensive use of effective forms of media to widen reach among citizens. As Paul emphasized, "The power of information is critical in creating genuine public demand. Media is a powerful means of reaching people so all forms of available media should be used to ensure people engage in collective action, which is oftentimes difficult."

The fourth speaker, *Christopher Kamlongera* of the University of Malawi (Professor of Drama and Theater Arts and Director, African Center of Communication for Development), highlighted the importance of focusing on the people themselves as the central starting point in designing interventions to mobilize collective public action.

Summary of Presentations

Taeku Lee of UC Berkeley provided a conceptual presentation and discussed important conceptual issues on a broader level, as well as the narrow, practical dimensions in mobilizing public will and inspiring civic activism. At the outset, Lee acknowledged that the meeting's objective of generating genuine citizen demand to ensure the effectiveness of SA was both simple and elusive—simple because of the elegance and attractiveness of the political logic behind SA mechanisms, but not easily translated to mobilized publics and workable institutional mechanisms; elusive because the idea of mobilizing public will where public will does not exist is a nonstarter, especially among those who study people's behavior empirically.

Lee referred to the existing debate in modern political science between Walter Lippmann's elitist view and indictment of public opinion as a "blooming, buzzing confusion" and John Dewey's pragmatist view that goes against an idealized conception of public will, that "one does not need to be fully informed about what shapes people's behavior in order to think about public will." While most political scientists support Lippmann's view, Lee believes that the debate is unfair and clearly one-sided. He further pointed out that "the battle between empirics and normative in modern political science is never fair because it is far too easy to weight 'is over ought,' and to weight 'prediction over possibility.'"

In support of Dewey's view, Lee raised two points: (1) although those with strong beliefs in egalitarianism will find Lippmann's elitist views disconcerting, Lee believes that it should not be totally rejected as long there is recognition that achieving virtuous ends such as egalitarianism, social justice, and SA is a process, and if the goal has not been reached, it does not mean that the process is not worth it; and (2) public will is not an idealized concept, and more thought should be given to how public will can be designed.

Lee concluded his presentation with a brief description of the four key dimensions in thinking about and taking a nuanced view of public demand: (1) What kind of public is it? (2) What is the mode of expression and how do people express themselves politically? (3) What kind of influence are people willing to engage and what are governing elites willing to allow?

(4) What goals/deliverables are at hand to see if things have worked? Lee emphasized that mobilizing public will and inspiring citizen activism involve a process of transformation. It also presents a menu of choices on a range of goals beyond using SA mechanisms—educating the public, empowering the public, changing citizen preferences, changing policy outcomes, or changing the power balance between ruling elites and citizens, a process that requires sustainable participation. In his paper, Lee considered SA to be the benchmark of good governance, providing evidence in achieving three outcomes: (1) transparency in the relationship between principals and agents, (2) answerability of agents and their sense of obligation to justify the choices made on behalf of principals, and (3) power of principals to sanction and punish agents when they fail to meet their obligations.

Shanto Iyengar of Stanford University opened his presentation with a provocative statement that "market-based media do *not* foster accountability." He supported this observation based on the following developments: (1) the rapid spread of market-oriented news has led to a rise in demand for more entertainment or "soft news" rather than more information on politics and public policy in news programming; (2) the economic incentives, especially in competitive markets, prompt media to ignore their civic responsibility resulting in nonsubstantive news coverage and a nonengaged public, particularly notable during national elections; and (3) news coverage is shaped by media management, resulting in a media agenda that reflects the interests of the elite.

Notwithstanding these discouraging trends, however, Iyengar expressed optimism and qualified his observations stating, "But . . . for SA practitioners, all is not lost!" He emphasized that information technology offers many possibilities that have significant potential to effectively inform and engage citizens. He cited promising alternatives through new forms of unmediated information that facilitate revival of direct modes of communication between large groups of citizens and various organizations.

In particular, Iyengar described his current experience with harnessing computer access through the use of CDs. Compared to web-based platforms, which present challenges with speed requirements and further increase the divide in connectivity and web access, CDs have proven to be cost-effective and accessible alternatives that promise a wider audience reach. Other effective tools include electronic newsletters, voter guides, and handbooks—all of which facilitate delivery of information, enhance user control in terms of volume and topics of information accessed, and feature entertainment and interactivity to promote user interest and engagement.

In conclusion, Iyengar briefly described the experience with the CD-based intervention within the U.S. context from 2000 to 2004. Results from empirical studies done in 2000 and 2002, funded through foundation grants, confirm the impact of CD use in building informed citizens and generating a greater sense of citizen engagement. However, the low level of exposure remains the main challenge. As Iyengar noted, this can be boosted by targeting specific constituencies and collaborating with key advocacy groups.

Samuel Paul of the Public Affairs Centre in Bangalore, India, defined the two sides of generating genuine citizen demand. One side is the public acceptance of the issues that demand accountability, and the other is the government response and action on issues presented. Positive response from citizens will happen only if the issues raised are based on citizens' felt needs, on matters deemed personally relevant and significant. Government, on the other hand, needs to view the importance of responding to citizen demand and act responsibly to fill in gaps between what has been promised and what has been achieved.

Paul emphasized three key factors that need to be considered in effective implementation of SA mechanisms. First, information dissemination plays a key role in creating greater citizen demand. To stimulate collective action, the strategic use of various forms of media is essential to broaden reach among citizens. Although civil society works with imperfect institutions and operates within a set of limitations, these constraints should not deter efforts to effectively mobilize the media.

Second, champions and catalysts are needed to lead civic advocacy. To ensure broad citizen engagement, evidence from SA initiatives, such as CRCs, have to be translated in simple and understandable language using street plays and other creative channels of disseminating information.

Third, government response to citizen demands should be facilitated through dialogue with citizens to foster openness and mutual trust. Report findings and recommendations from SA initiatives need to be discussed, understood, and acted on. Building allies within government can stimulate government response on recommended courses of action.

Paul concluded his presentation with an example from India that illustrates the power of information based on a small civil society intervention. Initial demand for greater information and transparency with regard to campaign and elections led another civil society group to seek action from the courts. This experiment reached the attention of the Supreme Court and eventually led to legislation that mandates the collection of information on candidates for dissemination to the voters. Similarly, the CRC initiative in Delhi and other cities has led the head of the National Planning Commission to advise the chief ministers of all the states to adopt this approach. He has also set up a fund that the chief ministers can draw on when they launch their projects.

Christopher Kamlongera of the University of Malawi presented a clear overarching message in implementing SA at the village level: "Start with the people and add value to what they are doing. This will ensure credible, durable, and sustainable activities necessary to improve transparency and accountability."

Kamlongera shared a personal narrative that illustrated how cooperation exists in the village and the opportunities available to allow people to raise issues and build ownership, transparency, and accountability. His experience in providing communication support to the Malawi Social Action Fund made it much more apparent to him that people in the rural villages are being trained in the areas of transparency and SA. Systems should not be transplanted from other contexts without recognizing or taking into account resources that are available locally, and what works on the ground. To neglect local context jeopardizes the sustainability of any development initiative.

In his paper, Kamlongera noted key recommendations in strengthening the effectiveness of SA tools based on his experience in using community score cards: (1) scale up the implementation of SA in Malawi and (2) mainstream SA as an integral part of the social and political agenda in the country.

On communication activities, the following practical approaches were also recommended: (1) adapt the community scorecard process to the local context; (2) sensitize all development service authorities and providers in Malawi about community scorecards; (3) conduct training workshops for development workers and community-based development committees on community scorecard processing; (4) integrate community scorecard process in all core training for development workers in the country; and (5) conduct a nationwide communication campaign introducing the community scorecard process.

The plenary discussion raised other important issues: (1) building political will and public will; (2) understanding and working within the local context, using local leaders and harnessing local creativity; (3) addressing the cost of public participation and use of formal and informal mechanisms of participation; (4) ensuring representation of the poor and addressing a culture of silence; (5) mobilizing the media while at the same time using informal networks and local approaches to effective communication; and (6) recognizing that sustainability is most critical and that it is a long-term process.

Approaches and Techniques

Following is a list of approaches and techniques for mobilizing public will and inspiring citizen activism.

APPROACHES	
Map out types of publics, participatory inputs, and degree of influence	A diverse menu of possibilities for mobilizing public will can be derived using a framework that applies key dimensions that define degrees of public representation, the cost of participatory inputs (cheap to costly), and the extent of influence that ruling elites are

willing to concede. Applying these dimensions on a linear scale provides a more nuanced view of who is the public to be mobilized.

For example, a linear scale that represents participation on a range of inclusive (more representative) to exclusive (more mobilized) and corresponding types of publics can offer a choice of possible publics to be activated depending on the political context and the type of SA mechanism used.

The types of publics that can be mobilized range from inclusive, more representative participation (which includes the general public, random selection, self-selected participants) to more mobilized, exclusive participation (which includes targeted recruits, civic organizations, and professional stakeholders).

Similarly, a scale of participatory inputs, ranging from cheap to costly and corresponding forms of input—passive receptacle and preference expressions (more anonymous) to preference transformation and deliberation and decision making (more informative)—will highlight the obstacles and transaction costs involved in public participation.

Use local, political context and people as the starting points	A people-centered and context-specific approach provides a reliable guide to effectively mobilize public will and inspire civic activism. Start with understanding people's felt needs and aspirations, the obstacles to their participation, as well as their living conditions and external environment (social, political, cultural, media). Recognizing the shifts in people's interest and motivation helps identify other drivers of influence that can be tapped to ensure sustainability of engagement. Use local leaders as key messengers and advocates of citizen activism.
Enlist educational institutions as partners and target the youth as audience	Educational institutions could be tapped as active partners in broadening public access to information using digital media. For example, the impact of CD-based information

campaigns, given their pedagogical value, could be enhanced, and its reach widened by bringing them into classroom discussions. Targeting the technologically savvy youth who represent a significant segment of the population will broaden exposure and visibility.

TECHNIQUES	
Make strategic use of the media, traditional and modern	Media play a central role in building informed and competent citizens capable of demanding accountability from public officials. Results of SA mechanisms should be broadly disseminated and translated in simple, easy-to-understand information.
	Key messages should be clear, consistent, and compelling using effective channels of communication, such as print, radio, and TV, as well as creative platforms such as local plays, street theater, posters, and billboards at strategically located points, to reach as wide an audience as possible.
	The path from awareness creation to citizen activism has several intermediate steps, which include building knowledge, changing attitudes, and empowering citizens. Creativity is a key element of citizen empowerment.
Mobilize formal and informal social networks	Existing social networks, formal and informal, are also effective channels of mobilizing citizen engagement. Strong coalitions could be developed through collaboration of organizations or groups of people with shared objectives but different specialized or issue-based interests.
	Synergies derived from new partnerships can lead to creative approaches in developing context-specific and culture-sensitive means of effectively mobilizing public will and inspiring citizen activism.
Use technology to renew direct communication between groups of organizations and individual citizens	The burgeoning growth of information technology offers numerous and promising alternatives for renewing direct means of communication, while at the same time providing greater user control at reduced cost. This approach brings informed citizenship

back by circumventing the market-driven environment that has reduced news media to shallow, superficial, and entertainment-heavy forms of reporting and journalism.

Various media platforms that incorporate education with entertainment offer interesting and cost-effective options for citizens to escape the barrage of manipulative and non-substantive content in news programming.

Use electronic newsletters, guides, or handbooks

These media platforms provide interactive tools that can deliver significant amounts of data and information on demand. They empower users with greater control in actively seeking out preferred topics of interest and relevant issues of concern. Multimedia CDs and DVDs can be designed to promote engagement and interest using software tools and interactive games to enhance entertainment value.

Feedback from Participants' Response Cards

Q: What approaches and techniques have you found most effective in overcoming obstacles to citizen engagement and mobilization?

The example here can be broken down into two categories: enabling environment and capacity building. *Enabling-environment* approaches include changing the political, legal, regulatory context to ensure freedom of expression, access to information, freedom of association, and media pluralism. *Capacity-building* approaches include establishment of diverse, sustainable, and independent media including community media; building ICT [information and communication technology] infrastructure; education (especially literacy); and building a culture of citizen engagement through political action.

More difficult to specify but very often of crucial importance are the social and political circumstances that raise citizens' desire and readiness to mobilize and that contribute to conscientization and act as catalysts of political upheaval and change.

Start with people's work, with knowing the conditions (political, cultural, media, etc.); base your work on existing formal and informal community systems and networks. Creat[ing] awareness by providing information generated through various technical tools may sometime[s] be enough, but in most cases one would need to support additional mobilization actions to get from awareness creation to public action.

Look for local leaders in the community and recognize that social accountability efforts require long-term support.

Start with understanding obstacles, see how these can be addressed; create supportive environment; find out ways to reach people effectively.

Need to recognize the ebb and flow of conditions that motivate people, so sustainability needs to have multiple sources. In surveying the all-important "local context," a useful framework is the shifting roles and bounds of "inside" and "outside." Typically, government is inside and citizens outside (as people talk about it) but not always. There might be several insides and outsides. Conflict of professionals can lead to passive dependent citizenry.

Start with existing local systems and see how to use or improve them; do your research; understand the socio-political context; environments and situations are highly contextual; realize the context and work with it.

OECD is exploring specific barriers for two groups: (1) willing and unable—many people would share intent but face education, discrimination, self-confidence barriers; (2) able but unwilling—large numbers of people can participate (face no external barriers) but choose not to. Why? How can they be enticed and encouraged?

Start with the people; knowing them culturally and all!

From existing social capital, facilitate small but visible changes; continuously engage indigenous knowledge with technical expertise to surpass localized obstacles.

Participation in creating the activities and media for mobilization; creating awareness does not guarantee action; other interventions might be needed.

Engage local leaders and pay attention to local context and the mechanisms of social accountability that each community has. The media (traditional and new ones) are essential to increase mobilization.

Willingness to stay on course, irrespective of initial cynicism (e.g., CRCs); need to transcend the technicality of SA mechanisms and link them with political structures and processes; need to recognize traditional spaces of public debates (non-formal media).

How to institutionalize and sustain participation; this would probably enable citizen engagement and mobilization; the most effective approach seems to be at a local level where the results are more concrete and service providers closer.

Using existing social networks; examining existing institutional framework; using various media to disseminate information but using social networks to obtain feedback.

There are many existing models that attempt to capture behavior/attitude change processes. This work should draw on these models.

Building strong civil society, working on coalitions between organizations with civil society, crafting frames and narratives that interpret in an empowering way; emphasize the "we" and not the "me" as a way of lowering the costs and diversifying the risks of participation.

No time in this session to raise the question of what might be called "selective engagement." When some societal group gets engaged at the cost of other groups, e.g., Hindus engaged in the Indian community while Muslims are left out. Countless examples here. Accountability in this kind of context could be very destructive. Challenge is how to ensure some kind of pluralistic accountability.

Identify clearly the players. Allow communities to explore creatively ways to use SA tools; start from "felt need"; and start from work of the community.

Lowering costs of collective action by creating an enabling public space.

Media interventions. Dissemination of information gathered through the implementation of various SA tools will help in mobilization of public will. Using traditional ways to ensure accountability in formulation of public will.

It depends on political situation. One should first understand very well the political context. Leadership matters strongly. People will be mobilized and active if leadership will trust people. Media shall be more balanced and market-based approaches can impede the mobilization issues.

Creating space for expression is important to bring people together. Develop media access where possible, if commercial media is accessible, even better. If not, alternatives can be used successfully. Leadership and mediation by civil society organizations matters. Know the conditions/environment you work in.

Can IT and educational technology be used to help developing countries overcome cultural values that prevent people from demanding accountability from government? Example: Uganda PETS—PTA [parent and teacher association] members not too willing to question teachers re: where funds for schools have not been used. Example: culture of silence.

Media, whether commercial or not, can often foster and inspire citizen engagement but it all depends on country and context.

On a gigantic scale, people engage voluntarily to create public goods. For example, restoring the graveyard in Malawi (Chris K.'s story). Can we strengthen public accountability by tying citizens' review of their government to ordinary, daily voluntary public work?

Session V: Achieving Behavior Change in Public Officials through Mobilized Public Opinion

This session explored approaches and techniques used in mobilizing public opinion to ensure behavior change among public officials, which would thereby lead to more accountable government.

The first speaker stressed that accountability is necessary for the proper functioning of any rights regime. An access-to-information regime, responsive government, and an active part of civil society that specializes in this type of politics are all preconditions for the successful adoption of SA mechanisms. Moreover, SA works best within the cultural and institutional context of a representative democracy. Corollary contextual requirements include cultural, social, and institutional conditions conducive to accountability and access.

The second speaker related experiences in deploying CRCs in India and Kenya. The process included the following key components: locating institutional anchors, building awareness and creating consensus, deploying dissemination strategies through media coverage and sponsored campaigns, taking stock of internal champions and external triggers, and codifying good practices.

The third speaker talked about the need to couple public scrutiny with open and inclusive policymaking. A cross-nationally comparative analysis of 40 SA projects was carried out using an approach measuring the following: scrutiny of government, proximity of citizens and government, and citizen engagement.

Additional ideas that arose during the open forum include the following:

- The need for an active journalism profession free from fear and able to mediate the supply and demand sides of governance.
- The need to take stock of conditions for systemic change (for example, leadership for progressive change within the government apparatus to overcome strongholds of resistance).
- Garnering support of international financial institutions.
- Depending on the nature of behavior change, time frames can range from immediate to as long as three generations; one must match length of time given for behavior sought to theory of behavior change. Sometimes people have good reasons for not changing, such as cultural norms.

- Translators are essential to attaining wide buy-in.
- Observatories/networks/third sectors are good for documenting, housing, disseminating, and monitoring changes.
- Continual learning should be institutionalized and incorporated in governance processes.
- SA mechanisms can provide a potential win-win situation for all major stakeholders.

Summary of Presentations

Enrique Peruzzotti of Torcuato Di Tella University in Argentina stressed that accountability is necessarily based on a rights regime. Access to information coupled with a responsive government is a crucial precondition to the exercise of accountability. Another precondition is an active segment of civil society that specializes in this type of politics and has autonomous sources of information. Society needs a social infrastructure for the exercise of SA (such as professionalized NGOs and social movements). Agencies of control should be shared among and bolstered by wide networks of societal actors. This type of network includes international regimes and organizations.

The gap between politicians and citizens is reduced by accountability mechanisms. Accountability must be exercised primarily by actors who are external to government. Negotiated interaction between actors assumes asymmetry of power—that is, one party has the authority or right to improve sanctions. Although some institutional arrangements are formal (such as voting), others are informal (such as civil society action). SA works best within the cultural and institutional context of a representative democracy.

The corollary contextual requirements include the following: (1) *cultural*—politics of accountability and a culture of rights; citizens should remain cognizant of the right to demand better services; (2) *social*—acceptance of political processes; for this, professional NGOs are crucial and need to be supported; (3) *institutional preconditions*—access to information regime; this type of regime provides entry points within government agencies that exercise control.

Gopakumar Thampi of the Public Affairs Foundation and the Public Affairs Centre in Bangalore related experiences in deploying CRCs in India and Kenya. The process included the following key components: (1) locating institutional anchors, national and local consortia: as a result, visibility increased in India; (2) awareness building and consensus creation on what tools and approaches are used to assess the "Critical 8" (see session 1 for elaboration on this point); (3) dissemination strategies through media coverage and sponsored campaigns—this is how findings were internalized in the Kenyan experience; (4) the locus of reforms necessarily seen as residing in internal and external factors; (5) learning-from-experience needing to be codified in good practices.

The power of the SA mechanism is derived from moving from anecdotal to factual, and the ability to differentiate "noise" from "voice." Effective context setting and consensus creation require sponsors of SA tools to be open and honest about what each tool is designed to do (and not do). It should also be noted that neutrality and objectivity create buy-in among various stakeholders.

Successful SA initiatives have external triggers and internal champions—that is, the clamor of public opinion is a trigger, but the critical processes of adopting and using the tool effectively depend on key internal actors. Strategic communication should advance knowledge and understanding of incentives and disincentives ("pats and slaps").

Joanne Caddy, policy analyst at the Organisation for Economic Co-operation and Development's (OECD's) Directorate for Public Governance and Territorial Development, underscored the importance of going beyond public scrutiny into the realm of policy. SA processes should include open and inclusive policy making. Civic engagement is a prerequisite for the work of reform around the world. The OECD focuses on the functions of information, consultation, and participation, in contrast to organizations such as the World Bank, which focus heavily on the development of tools.

Informed by these principles, a comparative analysis was carried out on 40 SA projects/programs. A novel comparative approach was adopted with the following key components: (1) scrutiny—initiatives that aim to enhance assessment, analysis, and review of government actions, (2) proximity—initiatives that aim to reduce distance between citizens and government by identifying citizen needs and preferences, and (3) engagement—initiatives that aim to incorporate citizens into decision-making processes.

The study found that the main barriers to the success of SA can be summarized in a duality: Some actors are willing but unable to support and carry out reform, whereas others are able but unwilling. Inability is usually linked to various types of political constraints. Unwillingness often arises from negative past experiences (that is, people develop distrust in using their voice). Some considerations for moving forward are summarized through the following questions: How can reforms harness multiplier effects? Does support for and the effective use of SA tools conserve resources? What are the rights and responsibilities undergirding SA? How much does context matter?

According to University of Kentucky Professor *Chike Anyaegbunam,* understanding the determinants of behavior change that support SA is a transdisciplinary issue. As such, it is well served by adopting a social ecology model, which spans individual, interpersonal, organizational, community, and public policy levels of intervention and analysis. Furthermore, publics and their opinions can be described in various ways: latent, aware, and/or active. The largest challenge is moving public opinion from latent to active. This can be achieved by adopting a three-dimensional conception of communication: top-down (from the government to local stakeholders), bottom-up (from local stakeholders to the government), and horizontal (through social networks).

Obstacles to successful SA implementation include (1) noninvolvement of local stakeholders in planning and program formulation, (2) a low sense of power and political efficacy on the part of reformers, (3) ineffective capacity-building methods, and (4) inadequate promotion of SA efforts.

Approaches and Techniques

The following is a list of approaches and techniques for achieving behavior change in public officials through mobilized public opinion.

APPROACHES	
Take stock of horizontal and vertical accountability mechanisms	This approach provides a systematic way of thinking about accountability: in terms of horizontal mechanisms (workings and interactions of the complex machinery of internal controls established by representative democracy) and vertical mechanisms (electoral and social actions of nonstate actors, including the intermediate place of civil society).
Create comprehensive five-pronged framework	This broad analytical approach comprises the following five components: cultural, social, institutional conditions, quality of the public sphere, and international regimes.
Establish initiatives from below and initiatives from above	The building of SA mechanisms can follow two different roads: It can be the product of autonomous initiatives from below by actors who view themselves as carriers of rights, or, alternatively, it can be promoted by more powerful actors from above interested in building a social and institutional environment conducive to the exercise of accountability.
Cultivate collaboration	Collaborative approaches negotiated between civil society and government have led to successful adoption of SA mechanisms.
Cultivate an evaluative culture	Evaluation must become an essential rather than an optional component of SA initiatives if their full impacts are to be asserted and current practice improved.
Ensure feedback and follow-up	SA initiators must demonstrate how participants' contributions and input are being used to maintain public interest and involvement.

Adopt a three-dimensional communication paradigm	The three dimensions are top-down (from the government to local stakeholders), bottom-up (from local stakeholders to government), and horizontal (through social networks).
Adopt a systems perspective through a social ecological model of analysis	The five levels of the social ecological model are the following: social structure, policy, and systems, community, institutional/organizational, interpersonal, and individual.
Assess the type of public being engaged	Different types of publics require different interventions. For example, a latent public needs to be moved to an awareness stage before any sort of action is expected of them.

TECHNIQUES

Identify an organizational anchor	Working with an institutional anchor (such as a government official and/or agency) provides legitimacy to the exercise of SA mechanisms and brings in clear ownership within the government.
Find institutional champions	Make repeated presentations of the SA tool to potential institutional champions and stress its neutrality and diagnostic power.
Hold brainstorming sessions with stakeholders	Design highly interactive and focused brainstorming sessions with a small team of staff from each relevant department. Make sure that the group is representative of all levels within the organization. Create consensus on the diagnosis of problems and generate specific reform measures. Discuss these widely to create broad ownership.
Present alternative tools to stakeholders	Present multiple tools and allow participants to discuss the utility, replicability, and contextual fit of the tools, and select the tool they deem best for the evaluative task.
Hold multistakeholder workshops on the tools	Consult with stakeholders on the following issues: concept, methodology, outcomes, and applications. This provides a space to understand, discuss, and critique the tool. Collectively evaluate the merit and contextual fit of the tool.
Select local drivers carefully	The civil society field is extremely competitive; the selection of a "lead organization" needs to be managed in an open and transparent manner.

Circulate draft findings	Draft reports should be circulated to each relevant service/ministry to provide them with the opportunity to pose questions and clarifications.
Form stakeholder alliances at the national and local levels	Facilitate a balance between national-level dialogue and local responsiveness.
Institutionalize findings through government response and action	Include a government response step in the process, sometime after the tool's findings are made public.
Prepare media in advance and educate them on the details of the tools	Preparatory sessions for the media before press conferences ensure that key messages are understood, reported, and articulated in a positive and constructive manner. Also, a holistic understanding on the part of journalists will allow them to report on positive and negative findings, be sensitive to shades of gray, and convey findings in a value-neutral manner.
Deploy mobile digital schools toward public opinion mobilization	These schools consist of the following: mobile teacher (MT4 player), a place where people already gather, course content in the form of an oral library (A/V based), trained mentors, collective learning process, and cascade effect through community sharing.

Feedback from Participants' Response Cards

Q: Is mobilized public opinion a sufficient condition for achieving behavior change in public officials? What else may be necessary?

It is a necessary but not sufficient condition [that] among other factors necessary for achieving change are: correct choice of the target (what should be changed and who among officials can change things); taking into account the interests of public officials and institutions they represent; system of incentives and sanctions public officials can face; times and timing; culture, especially political culture.

Mobilized public opinion is important but not sufficient for behavior change in public officials. Need also incentives/sanctions, international pressure, use of judiciary, or other institutionalized systems.

Public opinion alone is not enough. The public official has to want to change and has to be in conditions in which change is possible. From a behavioral perspective this requires incentives and/or sanctions. However, it also requires cognitive change if it is to be sustained. The education and culture of public servants need to have a change orientation or a focus on learning and continued improvement. In addition, government has a responsibility, if not a *raison d'être,* to consider competing proposals for change and argument for the "do nothing" option in order to take policy decisions in the public interest. This requires responding to public opinion(s) and to pressure from other interest groups with a fair and transparent assessment of the options, and published reasons for decisions. These processes need to be reinforced by internal checks and balances (the legislator, opposition parties, ombudsman, judicial review) and by external watchdogs (the media, civil society monitoring).

Recognition of diversity and unequal demands among publics; incentives, sanctions, and enforcement of existing regulations; present win-win solutions, institutionalize the mechanisms that lead to behavior change.

No. Strong sanctions—penalties which directly affect the pockets of public officials, changes behavior immediately. In the context of macro-level issues like economic liberalization, etc., good governance is a precondition for attracting capital/investment etc. So *public* officials are forced to make changes in their behavior.

Necessary, indeed crucial, but not sufficient. Need to invest in systemic public administration change so that traditional accountability systems (e.g., internal audit, external audit, parliamentary oversight) are strengthened, and not undermined, by attention to external social accountability pressures. Need to understand how to change formal structures/processes to open up spaces for citizens but also how to ensure "win-win" scenarios that can enable public officials to see that public engagement can help them to do their jobs better.

No, public opinion is necessary but not sufficient. There are the necessary conditions, such as a strong judiciary system, an enabling environment, etc. There's also a methodological consideration: to go from individual change to cultural/societal change. We need to plan *long* term, so that change sticks in the structure of society.

Need structures of support for long-term change; legal conditions should include transparency and access to information; effective sanctions;

incentives (institutional, formal, and informal) are useful. We should acknowledge a difference between distinct types (and levels) of public officials.

Embedding public opinion in institutional structures and processes (e.g., social audit, performance appraisal).

Session VI: Brainstorming and Action Steps

The final session focused on highlighting key insights from participants on two specific points:

1. The main issues arising from each of the discussion topics.
2. Recommended areas for action, as well as effective approaches and techniques for overcoming challenges.

Following is a summary of the group presentations made during the plenary session.

Session One: Analyzing the Public Sphere and Political Context

Participants emphasized the importance of understanding the public sphere, the political conditions that impinge on democratic processes, and participatory spaces that allow citizens to freely express and demand government accountability and action in delivering meaningful change. The two most important messages that came out of the discussions are (1) the power of information will empower the people and (2) context matters, but can any political context be navigated?

Although the final measure of success in SA can be clearly defined as holding authority accountable, access to information, political plurality, inclusive participation, and democratic spaces for citizen engagement were identified as critical levers in creating conditions that foster accountability and sustained participation.

A conducive environment warrants interventions to improve the policy and regulatory framework, as well as citizen capacity to demand accountability. On the policy/supply side, critical elements are the following:

1. Access to information, as a rights-based legal framework accompanied by whistleblower protection
2. Media support and active engagement of professional media on SA and the need to diagnose practical problems confronting media professionals
3. Support for legal activism, as a means for civil society organizations to legally challenge acts of authority.

On the demand side, the important mechanisms are the following:

1. Development of networks, both formal and informal, to enable effective and strategic information-sharing mechanisms that boost civil society capacity to generate evidence-based research.
2. Strategic use of the media, as well as creative, interactive, visually based content to promote citizen interest and activism. In India, a film on Gandhi revived strong, deeply held values and raised awareness and inspired civic activism, especially among the youth. Context and translation are important. Without translation, it is hard to encourage civic engagement.

Session Two: Gaining Official Support in Using Social Accountability Tools

While some participants emphasized that not all SA mechanisms require official support (or permission), broad recognition was seen of the importance of the state's positive posture toward SA objectives. It opens up avenues for the state to listen, to acknowledge their public responsibilities, and to respond to citizens' demand for action. The ability to gain official support places the burden on civil society, on their willingness and capacity to engage with government, to negotiate change, and to manage conflict under adversarial conditions.

The participants highlighted two key elements that can bolster civil society efforts in gaining official support for SA. First is the importance of strategic positioning. This involves an examination of the posture and attitude of CSOs, as well as the manner in which they choose to engage along a continuum ranging from an adversarial to a cooperative role. What position or posture will result in a favorable outcome?

In addition, the willingness and capacity of CSOs to form broader coalitions with other organizations (religious, trade unions, and the like) can help amplify their voice and strengthen collective efforts in demanding response from the government. Taking on a collaborative approach should also include seeking allies and champions within government, recognizing that it is not a monolithic institution. CSOs also need to gain a better understanding of the role of oversight institutions (such as ombudsmen and the judiciary) in SA. They can identify ways to mobilize support of the political, legal, and judicial systems, particularly in implementing and enforcing sanctions needed to strengthen the impact of SA mechanisms. Strong advocacy efforts and strategic use of the media should underpin SA initiatives to keep issues alive, maintain citizen interest, and sustain reform momentum.

The second important ingredient is the credibility of CSOs. Credibility builds trust and confidence and is central to developing strong partnerships. It establishes the foundation for openness and willingness on the part of government to listen and respond to civil society initiatives needing state support. Collaboration between the state and civil society is a two-way street that demands accountability and transparency from both parties. In mobilizing civil society to gain official support, participants identified the challenge of adapting approaches relevant to country-specific contexts. This underscores the importance of developing a methodology that can guide effective priority setting, which participants believe is a challenge that CommGAP is uniquely placed to support.

Session Three: Building Citizen Competence

In discussing the issues of citizen competence, the focus was on both the "how" and the "what." Participants highlighted the importance of strategic interventions at three levels: (1) institutional, (2) individual, and (3) social. At the institutional level, partnerships with educational institutions (schools and universities) are essential to establish the linkages that reinforce values and capacities that enhance citizen knowledge and build confidence. At the individual level, developing personal skills and competencies should build on core strengths and roles of specific groups and segments of the population (for example, youth, women, unorganized groups). At the social level, building a strong network of coalitions through competent and capable social networks, both formal and informal, bolsters the impact of collective action.

Specific recommendations presented include the following:

1. Get youth involved. Be inclusive, include marginalized groups, minority, women, and others.
2. Teach students, minority groups, and other groups about government issues and how to create entertaining radio programs about government.
3. Develop skills in knowing how to ask the right questions, demand answers, gain access to information (comprehensible information), hold officials to account, assert one's rights in the face of oppression, repression, and fear, and require reliability standards.
4. Master tools for creating and using spaces for civic discourse.
5. Declare an SA Day to bring heightened citizen awareness on the successes of SA efforts and challenges that need to be addressed.
6. Make people self-efficacious; educate them in effective engagement and in the exercise of citizen voice.
7. Build skills in public speaking, discussion, and debate.
8. Develop an understanding of how institutions work, their roles and responsibilities, and where to seek assistance when they fail to perform.
9. Mobilize the media, train *animateurs* (community media).
10. Introduce creative ways of teaching and developing citizen competence, combining education and entertainment in various tools, such as introducing civic processes in board/video games, comic books, radio, and TV, as well as using narrative formats, soap opera, and theater to build citizen knowledge and skills.

Key messages about citizen competence can be summarized under three headings: (1) competence in information seeking (rights, process, and methods) through formal institutions at all levels of education (primary, secondary, and postsecondary); (2) competence of independent and professional media infrastructure, which precedes governance literacy; and (3) "citizen-ness" as a set of key communication skills.

Session Four: Mobilizing Public Will and Inspiring Civic Activism

Discussions on mobilizing public will and overcoming obstacles to engagement crystallized four important issues and relevant recommendations for CommGAP to support SA objectives.

First, media play a central role, but they can also hinder rather than help the process and outcomes of SA. The question is, "How do we get media to adopt and operate as a public service model, responsibly serving the public interest, and help create a conducive environment that promotes the objectives of SA?" The recommendation is to "find the right mix of regulation and incentives to create and sustain an enabling environment."

Second, improve horizontal forms of communication and explore the use of new communication technologies. The recommendation is to strike the right balance between creating a favorable political and regulatory environment and the right set of incentives to infrastructure that can facilitate access to information technology.

Third, although CSOs are critical partners of government in SA, the risk of co-optation exists, where CSOs operate as an arm of government. The recommendation is to find ways to encourage formation of a new breed of NGOs, develop creative measures to reduce barriers to their formation, and guarantee their credibility and commitment to uphold the principles of integrity, transparency, and accountability.

Fourth, build as a movement something sustainable to keep the focus on SA. On the development community side, the World Bank and international donors should continue to keep the spotlight on accountability and governance and the contributions that communication can provide in the process. In addition, the World Bank should push SA, media training, and strategic communication as integral parts of a core curriculum for its training programs.

Session Five: Achieving Behavior Change among Public Officials

Although behavior change was clearly recognized as a long-term process, effective means to address it can involve both short- and long-term measures. Participants identified two levels of critical interventions: one requires focusing on systemic/institutional change and the second is influencing change at the individual level.

Specific recommendations for CommGAP include the following:

1. Focus on activities that support both supply and demand side of governance and accountability and in areas where the most impact can be

gained. Establishing criteria for choosing activities that affect both demand and supply sides can help in focusing on priority areas.

2. Conduct comparative analysis of similar tools and the results achieved in various contexts.
3. Focus on the normal practice, and not just good or best practice, in looking at practical experiences in SA. How well and how easily can these be applied in different settings? What are the negative impacts of efforts that were not anticipated in the early stages of design or implementation?
4. Recognize the critical role of state and grassroots intermediaries. Know when it is best to let the local people take over their own development. Investigate the magic of communities at work without the influence of external interventions.
5. Develop simple and participatory evaluation tools and frameworks that effectively measure our performance relative to what are we trying to achieve.
6. Develop new media and the promise of local communities generating the content themselves. Use powerful audiovisual formats.
7. Target capacity-building efforts at public officials and civil society groups. For public officials, capacity building could consider the following: conducting in-service training and not just induction training; tracking alumni and finding out if and how the training influenced changes in the way they conduct their work; establishing an award system to celebrate what is achieved, enhancing incentives for better performance; creating arrangements to facilitate development of tacit knowledge; mentoring and peer-to-peer learning to create opportunities for knowledge sharing and provide real-time answers to operational problems; and mapping available competencies and expertise to be developed as a useful roster of resource people that can be tapped to support SA initiatives.

Glossary

- *Citizen Report Cards (CRCs)* are participatory surveys that solicit user feedback on the performance of public services. CRCs can significantly enhance public accountability through the extensive media coverage and civil society advocacy that accompanies the process.
- *Community Score Cards (CSCs)* combine the participatory quantitative surveys used in the CRC with village meetings whereby citizens are empowered to provide immediate feedback to service providers in face-to-face meetings.
- *Public Expenditure Tracking Surveys (PETS)* are a quantitative survey that tracks the flow of public funds to determine the extent to which resources actually reach the target groups. The unit of observation is typically a service

facility rather than a household or an enterprise. The survey collects information on transfer procedures, amounts, and timing of released resources.

- *Participatory budgeting (PB)* is a process through which citizens participate directly in the different phases of the budget formulation, decision making, and monitoring of budget execution. PB can be instrumental in increasing public expenditure transparency and in improving budget targeting.
- *Social auditing* is a process that collects information on the resources of an organization, and this information then is analyzed in terms of how resources are used for social objectives and shared publicly in a participatory process.

Notes

1. Douglass, Frederick. 1985 [1857]. "The Significance of Emancipation in the West Indies." Speech, Canandaigua, New York, August 3, 1857; collected in a pamphlet by the author. In *The Frederick Douglass Papers. Series One: Speeches, Debates, and Interviews. Volume 3: 1855–63*, p. 204. Ed. John W. Blassingame. New Haven, CT: Yale University Press.
2. This learning event is the basis for this book, with several participants contributing case studies and reflections. In addition to this report, knowledge gaps will be identified that can be filled through further research conducted by CommGAP. Participants will continue to help shape this research agenda.
3. Citizen report cards (CRCs) are participatory surveys that solicit user feedback on the performance of public services. CRCs can significantly enhance public accountability through the extensive media coverage and civil society advocacy that accompany the process.
4. The "Critical 8" are as follows: *Political Context*—How would the political institutions in the country support or hinder methodologies such as CRCs? *Decentralization*—Do local bodies have a reasonably high degree of financial and policy-making power? *Ability to Seek Feedback from Citizens*—Would organizations feel safe conducting public feedback exercises such as CRCs? *Citizens' Ability to Voice Experience*—Do citizens feel free to give honest feedback about government services? *Presence and Activism of Civil Society Organizations*—Are there active CSOs in the country? Are they independent and nonpartisan? *Survey and Analysis Competency*—Are there demonstrated local skills for survey and analysis? *Quality of Media*—Are the media independent? Do they cover issues related to public services? Will they cover CRC findings and present them in an unbiased manner? *Responsiveness of Service Providers*—Do service providers seek consumer/user feedback? How open would they be to independent assessments of their performance?

Appendix B

The World Bank's Communication for Governance and Accountability Program presented the following speakers at its workshop titled "Generating Genuine Demand with Social Accountability Mechanisms" in Paris in November 2007.

Presenters

Chike Anyaegbunam is Associate Professor at the University of Kentucky with joint appointments in the Colleges of Communications and Public Health, where he teaches Integrated Strategic Communication, Marketing Research, Communication Theory, and Participatory Communication. He specializes in designing strategic communication programs for projects related to empowerment and civic engagement, health, the environment, agricultural safety and health, and economic development. He is currently the director of the CDC/NIOSH-funded social marketing program to promote tractor safety in the United States. Anyaegbunam earned his Ph.D. in Journalism and Mass Communication from the University of Iowa in 1994, with Development Support Communication as a special focus, and has worked for a variety of national and international projects sponsored by the World Bank, FAO, UNICEF, USAID, the Pfizer and Robert Wood Johnson Foundations, and the National Cancer Institute through the Appalachian Cancer Network. He was the 1992–93 editor of the *Journal of Communication Inquiry* and is the lead author of a widely used book on participatory rural communication appraisal (http://www.fao.org/docrep/008/y5793e/y5793e00.htm). He has also coauthored articles published in several academic journals and book chapters on participatory rural communication research, including a chapter in the *First Mile of Connectivity* (http://www.fao.org/docrep/X0295E/X0295E00.htm). Since 1975, Anyaegbunam has lived and/or worked in several countries, including Italy, Liberia, Namibia, Nigeria, Mozambique, South Africa, the United States, Zambia, and Zimbabwe.

Harry Blair, Associate Department Chair, Senior Research Scholar and Lecturer in Political Science at Yale University, has focused his research and applied work over the last 15 years on democratization issues, primarily civil society and decentralization. Earlier he had concentrated on South Asian politics and rural development, mainly in India and Bangladesh. On democratization, he has worked in Eastern Europe (principally Balkan countries), Latin America, and Southeast Asia, as well as South Asia. As a consultant, he has served with DFID, FAO, the Ford Foundation, SIDA, UNDESA, UNDP, USAID, and the World Bank. Before coming to Yale, he held academic positions at Bucknell, Colgate, Columbia, Cornell, and Rutgers universities. He holds a Ph.D. from Duke University. His most current publications deal with gauging civil society advocacy, postconflict state building, participatory local governance, and Bangladesh political parties. These publications and other recent writing can be found at http://pantheon.yale.edu/~hb94.

Joanne Caddy is a Policy Analyst at the OECD's Directorate for Public Governance and Territorial Development. She is currently responsible for leading work on "Open and Inclusive Policy Making," which examines OECD country experience in fostering public engagement. In 2006 she was seconded to the New Zealand State Services Commission for a year, where she served as a Senior Adviser and helped draft the SSC "Guide to Online Participation." This guide was written on a wiki, with inputs from a broad community of practice, and was published online in 2007. Her contributions to the field of public participation include the following OECD reports: *Citizens as Partners: Information, Consultation and Public Participation in Policy-making* (2001) (and accompanying handbook of the same title), *Open Government: Fostering Dialogue with Civil Society* (2003), *Promises and Problems of E-democracy: Challenges of Online Citizen Engagement* (2004), and *Evaluating Public Participation in Policy Making* (2005). From 1998 to 2000, she worked for SIGMA, a joint program providing support to public administration reform in Central and Eastern European countries, based at the OECD and financed mainly by EU-Phare. She earned a B.A. in Natural Sciences at Cambridge University, an M.A. in Political Science at the Johns Hopkins University, and a doctorate in Political Science at the European University Institute.

George Cheriyan is the Associate Director of CUTS International, India, an NGO pursuing social justice and economic equity within and across borders. He heads one of the program centers, CUTS Center for Consumer Action, Research & Training, based in Jaipur. He has more than 20 years of experience in working in the development/NGO sector. Good governance and social accountability (SA) are his areas of interest, and he is presently managing the implementation of two SA projects in partnership with the World Bank and the Partnership for Transparency Fund, along with various other projects. Cheriyan has been a member of the United Nations Roster of Consultants on Sustainable Development since 1995 and a member of International Resource Team of the World Bank Institute on Sustainable Development since January 2007. In this capacity, he oversees the training programs on SA tools in various South Asian countries. He has also been a Member of the State Advisory Committee of the Rajasthan Electricity Regulatory Commission since March 2007. He has written and published numerous articles in leading national news dailies, news magazines, journals, periodicals, and edited books. His publications includes the research paper "Enforcing Right to Food in India: Bottlenecks in Delivering the Expected Outcomes" as part of the International Project on "Hunger & Food Security" of the United Nations University–World Institute of Development Economics and Research, November 2006.

Varuzhan Hoktanyan is Vice-Chair of Transparency International (TI) Armenia (Armenian chapter of Transparency International), which promotes effective public policy and good governance to prevent corruption, strengthen democracy, and contribute to the development and stability in the region. At the time of the workshop, he was involved as a Political Party Expert in a project that aims to advocate changes in the Armenian electoral legislation on the threshold of February 2008 presidential elections in Armenia. He is also involved in the development of CSOs' recommendations to the new anticorruption strategy of Armenia the drafting of which now is in process. He is the coauthor of a number of TI Armenia's publications, such as "Monitoring of the Parties' Campaign Finances during the 2003 Parliamentary Elections" (2003), "National Integrity Systems Transparency International Country Study Report: Armenia 2003" (2004), and "Anti-Corruption Policy in Armenia" (2006). From 2003 to 2007, he directed several projects his organization implemented in the general secondary education area of Shirak province, Armenia. Methodologies used in these projects were based on the application of a number of SA tools, such as community scorecard, public budget tracking, and participatory and transparent monitoring. Since 2002 he has taught Political Science to undergraduate students at the State Engineering University of Armenia.

Shanto Iyengar holds the Chandler Chair in Communication at Stanford University, where he is also Professor of Political Science. His areas of expertise include the role of mass media in democratic societies, public opinion, and political participation. He is currently a Visiting Postdoctoral Fellow at the Sage Center for the Study of the Mind, University of California–Santa Barbara. Iyengar received his Ph.D. in Political Science from the University of Iowa and completed postdoctoral training in Psychology at Yale University through the support of the National Institute of Mental Health. Before joining the Stanford faculty, he taught at the University of California–Los Angeles and the State University of New York–Stony Brook. Iyengar is the author of several books, including *News That Matters: Is Anyone Responsible?* and *Media Politics: A Citizen's Guide.* Since 2006, Iyengar has contributed a research column for Washingtonpost.com.

Christopher F. Kamlongera is Professor of Drama and Theatre Arts at the University of Malawi and Director of the SADC Centre of Communication for Development (previously in Harare, Zimbabwe, but now relocated and registered as the African Centre of Communication for Development in Malawi). He received his Ph.D. from the School of English, University of Leeds, in 1984 and has lectured at the University of Malawi, from which he took a leave of absence to work for the SADC Centre of Communication for Development (1997–2007). He has edited and published several books and articles on theater for development, English language, and communication for development. He has served on the Steering Committee of the first World Bank Congress on Communication for Development and has served as consultant for FAO, CTA, OXFAM, the Swedish Cooperative Centre, and the World Bank, among several other development agencies.

William Keith is Professor of Communication at the University of Wisconsin–Milwaukee. He received his Ph.D. from the University of Texas at Austin. His work focuses on the role of argumentation in multiple contexts, including science and public discourse, and the history of the speech field and speech pedagogy. Keith has taught at Oregon State University, Northwestern University, and the University of Oslo. He has also lectured frequently on democracy and speech pedagogy at Duke University, Indiana University, Kansas State University, and the University of Washington. He has published widely in the rhetoric of science, argumentation, and deliberative democracy. He coedited *Rhetorical Hermeneutics* with Alan Gross (SUNY Press, 1998) and most recently *Discussion as Democracy* (Lexington Books, 2007), which won the National Communication Association Diamond Anniversary Award 2008 and the Daniel Rohrer Award from the American Forensic Association for Best Book of 2007.

Taeku Lee is Professor and Chair of Political Science and Professor of Law at the University of California, Berkeley. He is the author of *Mobilizing Public Opinion* (University of Chicago Press, 2002), which received the J. David Greenstone and the V. O. Key book awards; coauthor of *Why Americans Don't Join the Party* (Princeton University Press, forthcoming); and coauthor of *Asian American Political Participation* (Russell Sage Foundation Press, under contract). He has also coedited *Transforming Politics, Transforming America* (University of Virginia Press, 2006), coedited *Accountability through Public Opinion* (World Bank Press, 2010), and is completing the *Oxford Handbook* *of Racial and Ethnic Politics in the United States* (Oxford University Press, under contract). Lee has served in administrative and leadership positions at UC-Berkeley and in advisory and consultative capacities for academic presses and journals, research projects, nongovernmental organizations, think tanks, and private corporations. Before coming to Berkeley, he was Assistant Professor of Public Policy at Harvard's Kennedy School of Government. Lee was born in South Korea, grew up in rural Malaysia, Manhattan, and suburban Detroit, and is a proud graduate of K-12 public schools, the University of Michigan (A.B.), Harvard University (M.P.P.), and the University of Chicago (Ph.D.).

Peter Levine (www.peterlevine.ws) is Director of CIRCLE, the Center for Information and Research on Civic Learning and Engagement, in Tufts University's Jonathan M. Tisch College of Citizenship and Public Service. Levine graduated from Yale in 1989 with a degree in Philosophy. He studied Philosophy at Oxford on a Rhodes Scholarship, receiving his doctorate in 1992. From 1991 until 1993, he was a research associate at Common Cause. In September 1993 he joined the faculty of the University of Maryland. In the late 1990s, he was Deputy Director of the National Commission on Civic Renewal, chaired by Senator Sam Nunn and William Bennett. He is a member of the Deliberative Democracy Consortium's steering committee (www .deliberative-democracy.net), a cofounder of the National Alliance for Civic Education (www.cived.org), and former Chair of the Executive Committee of the Campaign for the Civic Mission of Schools (www.civicmissionofschools. org). Levine is the author of *The Future of Democracy: Developing the Next Generation of American Citizens* (University Press of New England, 2007), three other scholarly books on philosophy and politics, and a novel. He also coedited *The Deliberative Democracy Handbook* (2006) with John Gastil and co-organized the writing of *The Civic Mission of Schools,* a report released by Carnegie Corporation of New York and CIRCLE in 2003 (www.civicmissionof schools.org).

Kenneth Mugambe is the Commissioner for Budget in the Ministry of Finance, Planning, and Economic Development in Uganda.

Mary Myers is a freelance consultant specializing in radio in Africa. She works from home near Salisbury, in the heart of the English countryside. Myers holds a Ph.D. from Reading University, where her thesis subject was educational radio for rural women in Eritrea. She has worked with the United Kingdom's Department for International Development on many projects, papers, and publications since going freelance in 1996. From 2002 to 2003 she was an adviser on communications and media within DFID's Social Development Division. Currently Myers has a long-term contract as Media Adviser to DFID and to France's Coopération Internationale in the Democratic Republic of Congo. She has written DFID's guidelines *Monitoring and Evaluating Information and Communication for Development Programmes,* and she authored the background paper on communications in development for Tony Blair's Commission for Africa. Myers has traveled and worked in more than 20 countries in Africa, but most recently she has carried out trainings, evaluations, feasibility studies, desk studies, and monitoring missions in Chad, Democratic Republic of Congo, Madagascar, Malawi, Sierra Leone, and Uganda. Myers works not only for DFID, but also for other NGOs and bilateral and multilateral agencies, including the World Bank. Her current interests include the use of "edu-tainment," using radio for better governance, media regulation, and evaluating the impact of media interventions in developing countries.

Redempto Santander Parafina (a.k.a. DonDon) has made significant accomplishments as a youth leader in his advocacy for participatory governance. As Director of Government Watch (G-Watch), a corruption-prevention project of the Ateneo School of Government, he has engaged various public and nongovernment institutions and coordinated the participation of volunteer citizens in monitoring government programs, such as textbook delivery and school-building construction programs. His effort to involve youth, especially the Boy Scouts and the Girl Scouts, in the monitoring initiatives is considered a notable contribution. The impact of his work is well recognized, and his continuing engagements are considered a model of effective partnership for good governance. Among the governance networks in the Philippines in which DonDon plays important roles are the Transparency and Accountability Network and the Coalition against Corruption. He is also an associate of the Partnership for Transparency Fund, an international civil society organization advocating good governance. DonDon is involved in various civic and academic groups. He is currently the chairman of the Ten Outstanding Boy Scouts of the Philippines Association and Auditor of the Medieval Studies Society of the Philippines. In 2006 he was included in the list of Rotary Youth Leadership Awardees. He studied Philosophy at the University of the Philippines.

Samuel Paul is the founder and first chairperson of the Board of Public Affairs Centre (PAC) in Bangalore, which pioneered the use of citizen report cards. He was for many years Professor of Economics and later Director of the Indian Institute of Management in Ahmedabad. He has been a special adviser to the ILO, United Nations Commission on Transnational Corporations, World Bank, and other international agencies. Paul is the author of several books and has taught at the Harvard Business School, Kennedy School of Government, and Princeton's Woodrow Wilson School of Public Affairs. He is a recipient of both national and international awards. Paul's latest book (coauthor) is *Who Benefits from India's Public Services?* (Academic Foundation, New Delhi, 2006). Paul was a member of the Committee on the Indian Prime Minister's Awards for Excellence in Government, Karnataka Government's high-powered Committee on "Greater Bangalore," and the World Bank's Advisory Council for South Asia. He established the Public Affairs Foundation as a sister organization of PAC to provide advisory services within India and abroad.

Enrique Peruzzotti (Ph.D. in Sociology, New School for Social Research) is Associate Professor at the Department of Political Science and International Studies of the Torcuato Di Tella University in Buenos Aires. He has recently coedited the volume *Enforcing the Rule of Law: Social Accountability in the New Latin American Democracies* (Pittsburgh University Press, 2006). Peruzzotti has published articles on social accountability, democratic theory, and democratization in *Global Governance, Citizenship Studies, Journal of Democracy, Constellations, Thesis Eleven, Revista Mexicana de Sociología, Journal of Latin American Studies, Política y Gobierno, Journal of Human Development,* and *Metapolítica,* as well as numerous articles on edited volumes. In 2003–4 he was a Visiting Fellow at the Woodrow Wilson Center for International Studies. He has also been a Visiting Fellow at the Rockefeller Foundation Center in Bellagio, Fulbright Fellow at the University of Columbia, and Visiting Fellow at Cornell University, the University of New Mexico, and the Latin American Institute of the University of London. Peruzzotti is a recurring Visiting Professor at the Doctorate program in Social Science of FLACSO Ecuador. In 2008, he was a Visiting Fellow at the ESRC Non-Governmental Public Action Programme, London School of Economics. Peruzzotti has worked as a consultant for the IDB, UNDP, and the Ford Foundation.

Jorge Romero León has been Executive Director of Fundar, Centre for Analysis and Research, since January 2007. He holds an M.A. in Political Science from the New School for Social Research, in New York, where he is also a Ph.D. candidate. His areas of specialization include democratic theory, identity politics, sovereignty, and accountability. His professional expertise extends to the areas of public policy, budget practices, and SA mechanisms. He has worked in Fundar since 2000 on projects related to budget and policy analysis, monitoring the legislative branch, and the dynamics of legislative committees and budget negotiations. He also worked as adviser and information coordinator in the Senate for the minority Partido Acción Nacional in 1998 and as an adviser and project coordinator in the Ministry of the Interior and the Mexican Institute of Social Security in 1999 and 2001.

Gopakumar Thampi heads the Public Affairs Foundation, a nonprofit company, and the Public Affairs Centre, a nonprofit CSO, both based in Bangalore. Thampi holds a doctorate in Entrepreneurial Studies and postgraduate qualifications in Economics, Journalism, and Mass Communication. He is also an alumnus of the European Center for Peace and Conflict Resolution based in Austria, having completed an Advanced Diploma Course on Peace and Conflict Resolution. Developing concepts and approaches to strengthen accountability of institutions in the governance and development sector constitute the core of Thampi's current professional experience. A large part of this work has been carried through applications of participatory monitoring systems and public advocacy tools in South Asia, Africa, and East and Central Asia. Thampi was a former Head of the Asia Desk at the Transparency International Secretariat in Berlin.

Laura Zommer graduated in Communications Sciences and as an Attorney-at-Law from Universidad de Buenos Aires (UBA). Presently she is Communications Director of the Center for the Implementation of Public Policies Promoting Equity and Growth, Professor of Rights to Information at UBA's Social Sciences Faculty, and a contributor to *Enfoques,* the Sunday supplement of *La Nación* newspaper. Previously she was Cabinet Chief at the Secretariat for Interior Security of the Ministry of Justice and Human Rights (2003–04) and a writer specializing in General Information and Politics at *La Nación* (1997–2003). For her work as a journalist, she obtained a grant to the El País of Madrid and received the "Argentine Attorney Award" from the Asociación de Entidades Periodísticas Argentinas in 2005, the "Italian Young Journalist Prize" in 2002, the "In Depth Journalist Award" from Inter-American Press Association, Houston, 1999, and the "Public Good" award from ADEPA [Asociacíon de Entidades Periodísticas Argentinas (Argentine Media Owners Association)]. 1998.

Index

Figures, notes, and tables are indicated with f, n, and t following the page number. Arabic surnames beginning with "al" or "al-" are alphabetized by the following part of the name.

ECO-AUDIT
Environmental Benefits Statement

The World Bank is committed to preserving endangered forests and natural resources. The Office of the Publisher has chosen to print *Accountability through Public Opinion: From Inertia to Public Action* on recycled paper with 50 percent post-consumer waste, in accordance with the recommended standards for paper usage set by the Green Press Initiative, a nonprofit program supporting publishers in using fiber that is not sourced from endangered forests. For more information, visit www.greenpressinitiative.org.

Saved:
- 17 trees
- 5 million British thermal units of total energy
- 1,647 pounds of net greenhouse gases (CO_2 equivalent)
- 1,816 gallons of waste water
- 482 pounds of solid waste

green press
INITIATIVE